THE PRIDE ATLAS

First published in the United States of America in 2023
by Chronicle Books LLC.

Conceived, designed, and produced by The Bright Press,
an imprint of The Quarto Group.

1 Triptych Place, London,
SE1 9SH, United Kingdom
T (0) 20 7700 6700
www.Quarto.com

Printed and bound in Singapore.

MIX
Paper from responsible sources
FSC™ C007207

Publisher: James Evans
Editorial Director: Isheeta Mustafi
Art Director: James Lawrence
Senior Designer: Katherine Radcliffe
Managing Editor: Jacqui Sayers
Development Editor: Abbie Sharman
Project Editor: Kath Stathers
Layout and Design: Anna Gatt
Picture Research: Anna Gatt
Cover Design: Angie Kang
Sensitivity Reader: Veronica Vega,
Salt and Sage Books

10 9 8 7 6 5 4 3 2 1

Library of Congress Cataloging-in-Publication Data available.

Chronicle Books LLC
680 Second Street
San Francisco, California 94107
www.chroniclebooks.com

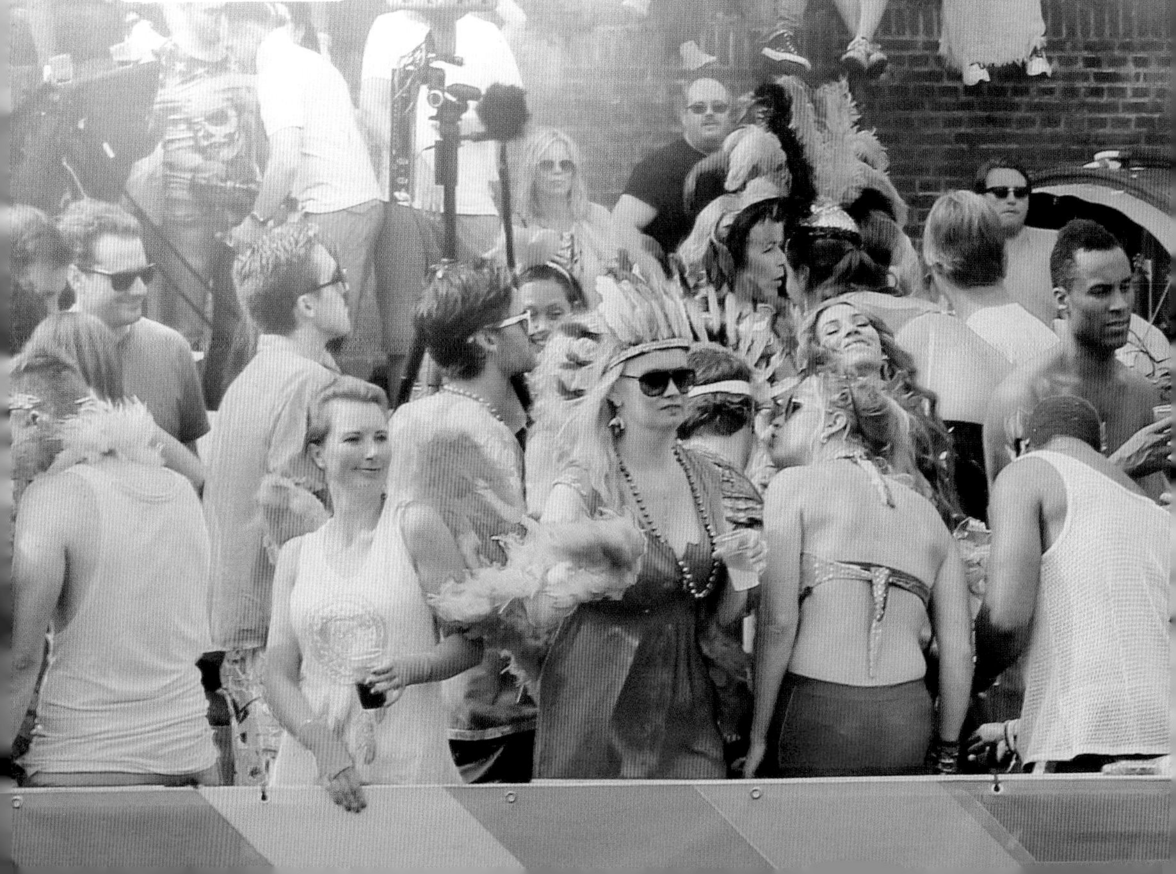

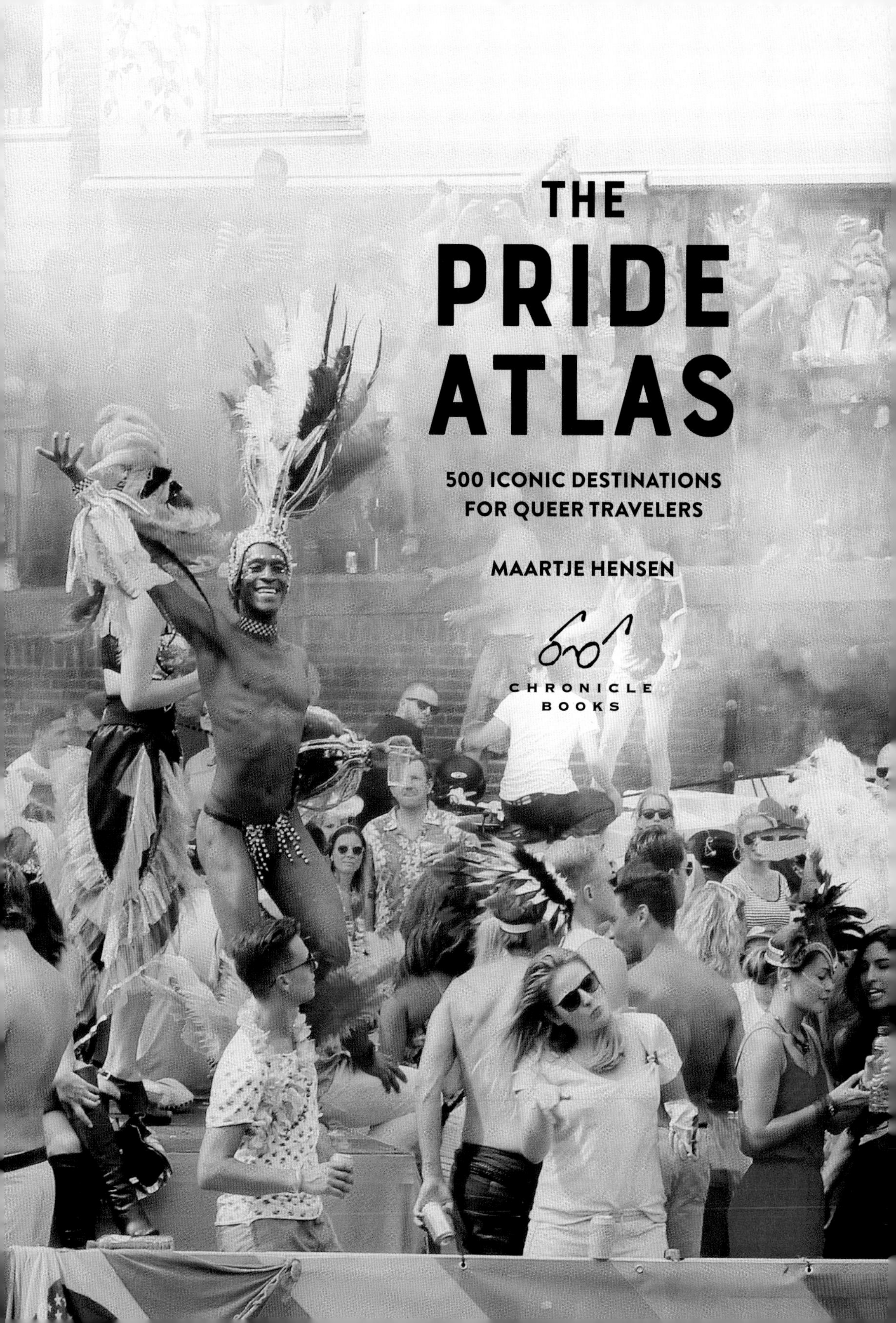

THE PRIDE ATLAS

500 ICONIC DESTINATIONS FOR QUEER TRAVELERS

MAARTJE HENSEN

CHRONICLE BOOKS

CONTRIBUTORS

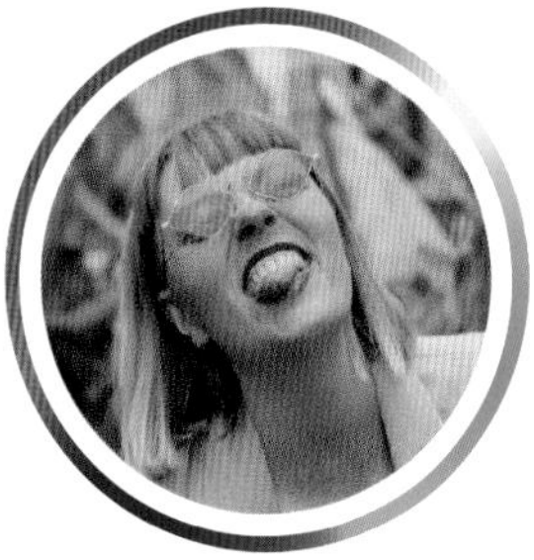

Maartje Hensen

Maartje (she/they) is a queer traveler, photographer, and writer from the Netherlands. She founded a queer travel and lifestyle brand, *Once Upon a Journey*, with her significant other, Roxanne Weijer (she/her). After being fully nomadic for three years, they are Amsterdam-based again. Maartje has also founded a photography business specializing in LGBTQ+ stories. Follow her on Instagram at **@onceuponajourney** or online at **onceuponajrny.com** and **maartjehensen.com**.

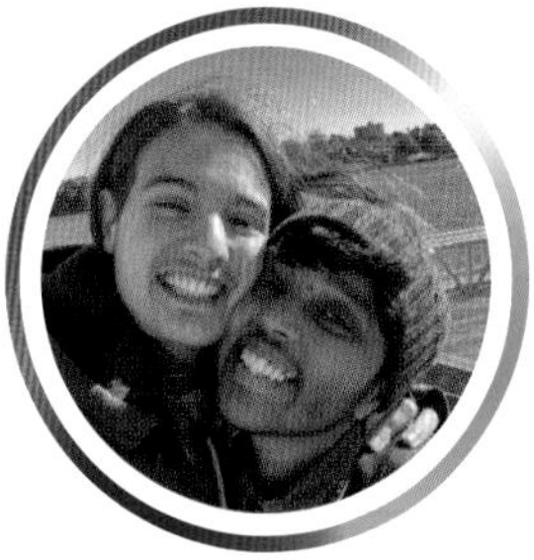

Sujay Abhilash and Erick Jackaman

Sujay (he/him) and Erick (he/they) are a trans couple currently living in Sydney, Australia. Originally from Singapore and London respectively, they have lived and traveled together across Europe and Asia-Pacific and have featured in publications including *Gay Times*, *Gay Cities*, and *Tripadvisor*. Between them, they have worked with My Genderation, TransM London, the Museum of Transology, and the Mardi Gras Film Festival in Sydney. Follow them on Instagram at **@twotransnomads**.

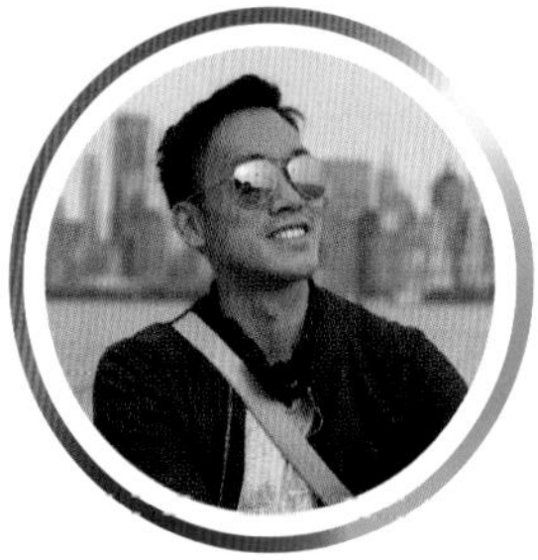

Barry Hoy

Barry (he/him) is a travel and lifestyle writer who showcases local experiences and great destinations around the world. He is a contributing writer for *Passport Magazine*, *Out Traveler*, *Passion Passport*, and other publications and blogs. If he's not on the road, he's most likely planning his next trip from his home in New York City. He shares his adventures with boyfriend Teraj via Instagram **@asianmapleleaf** and on his travel blog at **asianmapleleaf.com**.

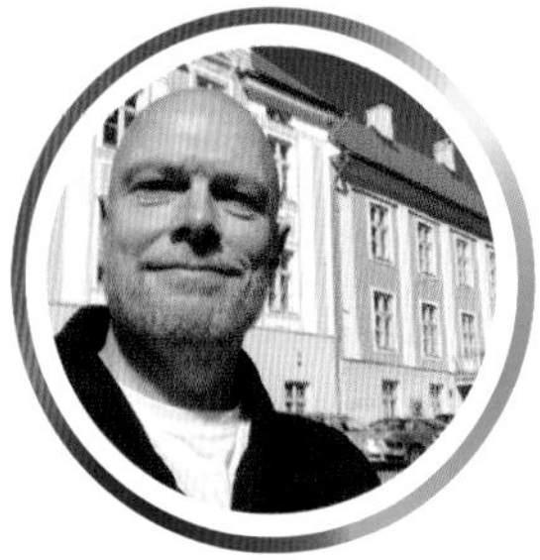

David Hudson

David (he/him) is an award-winning journalist who has written extensively in the LGBTQ+ media over the past three decades. His work has appeared in *Attitude*, *Out In The City*, *Metro*, and the websites *Gay Star News*, *Vacationer*, *Queerty*, and *Gay Cities*, among others. He has enjoyed Pride festivals from Toronto to Reykjavik, but also loves exploring his home city of London, England, which constantly throws up new discoveries and delights.

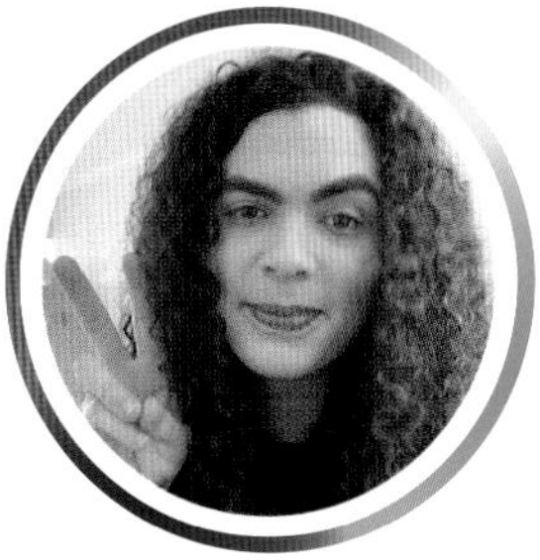

Abeni Jones

Abeni (she/her) is a writer and editor whose work has appeared in *Autostraddle*, *Fast Company*, *Travel + Leisure*, *Travel Weekly*, *them.*, *The Washington Post*, and other online publications. She primarily focuses on LGBTQ+ issues, especially literature and travel, and has a particular interest in exploring the nuances of how trans women show up in and move through the world. She is based in Portland, Oregon.

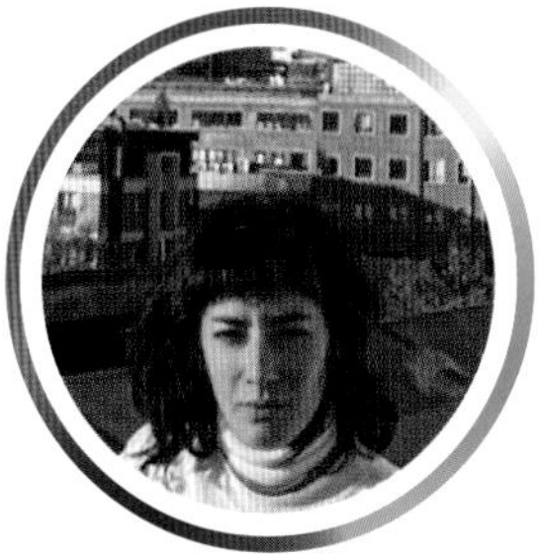

Charis McGowan

Charis (she/her) is a queer British-Caribbean journalist who reports on human rights in South America. She has lived in Chile since 2012; it is where she came out and consequently she grew close to the local LGBTQ+ community, joining the fight for marriage equality and adoption rights—which were achieved in 2021—and working to tell the stories of under-represented voices in the media. She has written for the BBC, *The Guardian*, *The Telegraph*, *Foreign Policy* and more.

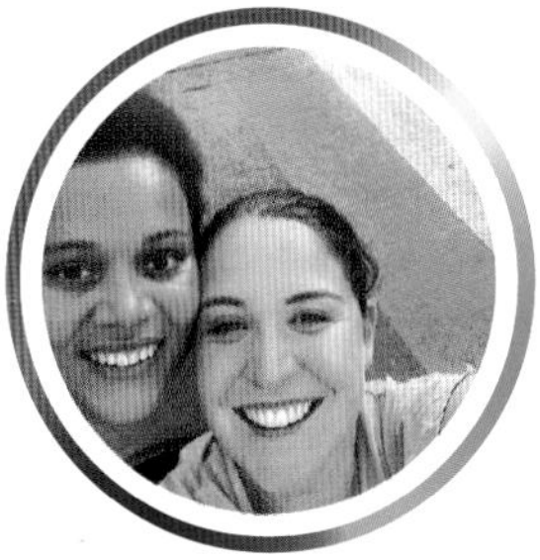

Marlie Regis and Sarah Laine

Shortly after meeting in their hometown of London, England, Marlie (she/her) and Sarah (she/her) set out on a six-month trip to South America, which has turned into five years of traveling the world, through Asia and on to Australia. They run an Instagram account and blog which showcase different cultures and adventures, and give LGBTQ+ representation in a space where it is lacking. Find them on Instagram at **@cloud_walks** or online at **cloudwalks.co.uk**.

Aisha and Lexie Shaibu-Lenoir

The Queer Nomads, Aisha (she/her) and Lexie (she/her), are a proud married couple living in London, UK. Avid travelers and activists, their work championing the representation of queer women of color within the travel industry, for UK Black Pride, and on intersectional community projects has led to their inclusion in *Attitude*'s "Top 100 LGBTQ+ trailblazers" and in *DIVA*'s "Pride 2022 Power List." Follow them on Instagram at **@thequeernomads** or online at **thequeernomads.co.uk**.

CONTENTS

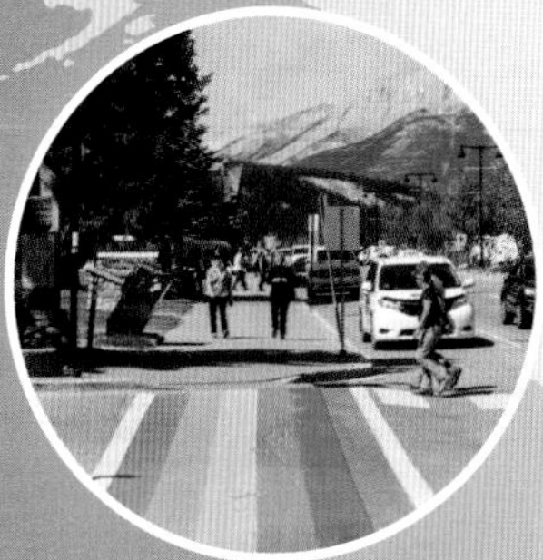

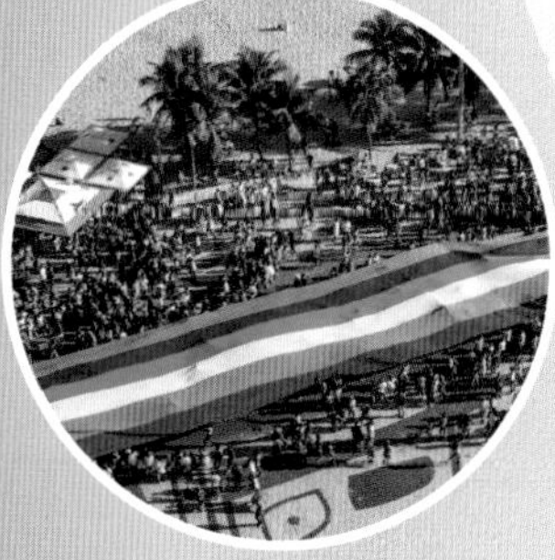

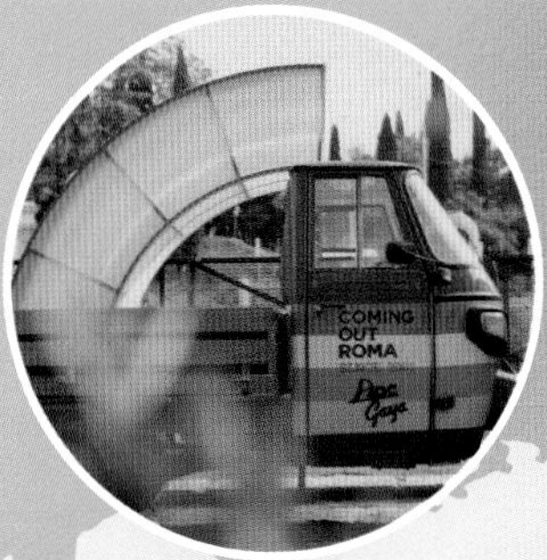

The entries in this book are arranged geographically by continent. Each entry number is color coded:

- Pride events and festivals
- Club, bar, café, or restaurant
- Cultural activity
- Great escape
- Neighborhood
- Memorials and murals

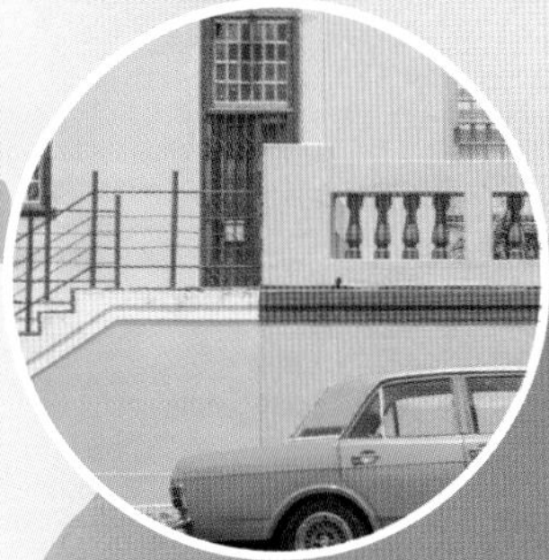

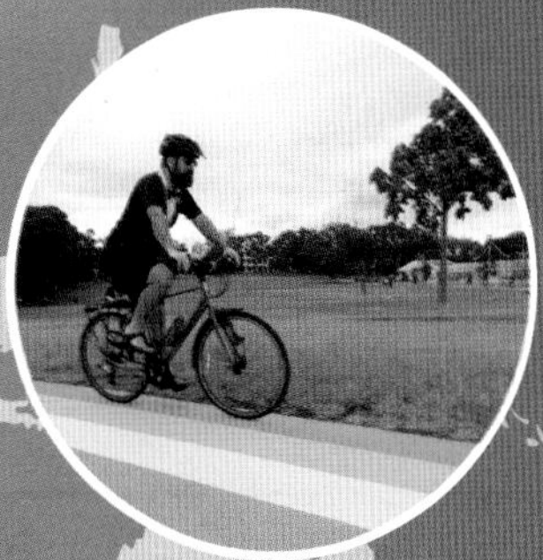

INTRODUCTION

For as long as I can remember, I wanted to see the world, immerse myself in other cultures, and learn from others. When I met the love of my life—an avid traveler—a world trip was inevitable. Our subsequent nomadic years opened my eyes, mind, and heart. As a queer couple, our travels required more preparation, adaption, and concealment than the travels of our cisgender/heterosexual counterparts.

The world is imperfect; the simple act of waving a rainbow flag can be life-threatening in some countries. At the time of writing, about 70 countries criminalize homosexuality, and more than 30 countries *de facto* criminalize gender identity and free expression for transgender people.

But there is increasingly more to celebrate. More than 30 countries have marriage equality, and 15 recognize a neutral gender-marker on passports. The world is also more connected, bringing communities together and allowing us to hear from reclaimed, once-silenced voices. Decolonization movements worldwide are revitalizing queer cultural heritage and increasing awareness about intersectionality.

Because queer people have always been around, we're no monolith; we come in all shapes and sizes. As LGBTQ+ travelers, we have the opportunity to connect with queer people globally, support their businesses, and gain new perspectives on LGBTQ+ culture.

Travel is for everyone because—contrary to popular belief—it doesn't have one look. Travel is for everyone because—contrary to popular belief—it doesn't have one look. Not all destinations can be everything to everyone, but there is something for everyone in this book. You deserve to go on the trip of your dreams; to experience radiant queer joy; to be celebrated.

LGBTQ+ travel is much more than Pride events and queer nightlife. There are also monuments, solidarity co-ops, museums, bookstores, restaurants, camping, and honeymoon-perfect destinations. We get to share five hundred of these places with you in this book, divided into five region-themed chapters. A big challenge was finding a balance between a queer traveler's well-being and geographical diversity. Queer culture is more visible and safer in certain regions, which is why some regions are particularly well represented. But don't let this fool you into thinking this is all there is. LGBTQ+ people are everywhere, and sometimes you must dig deeper to find an underground scene!

Hopefully, *The Pride Atlas* expands your horizons and inspires you to go *out* into the world, to (un)learn from others—as I have from my fellow contributors—and to keep an open mind and heart. Because, like gender, the world doesn't fit into a binary. Travel is not black and white, good or bad, right or wrong. It's beautifully fluid, challenging, and colorful.

Maartje Hensen (she/they)
Lead Author

@onceuponajourney
onceuponajrny.com

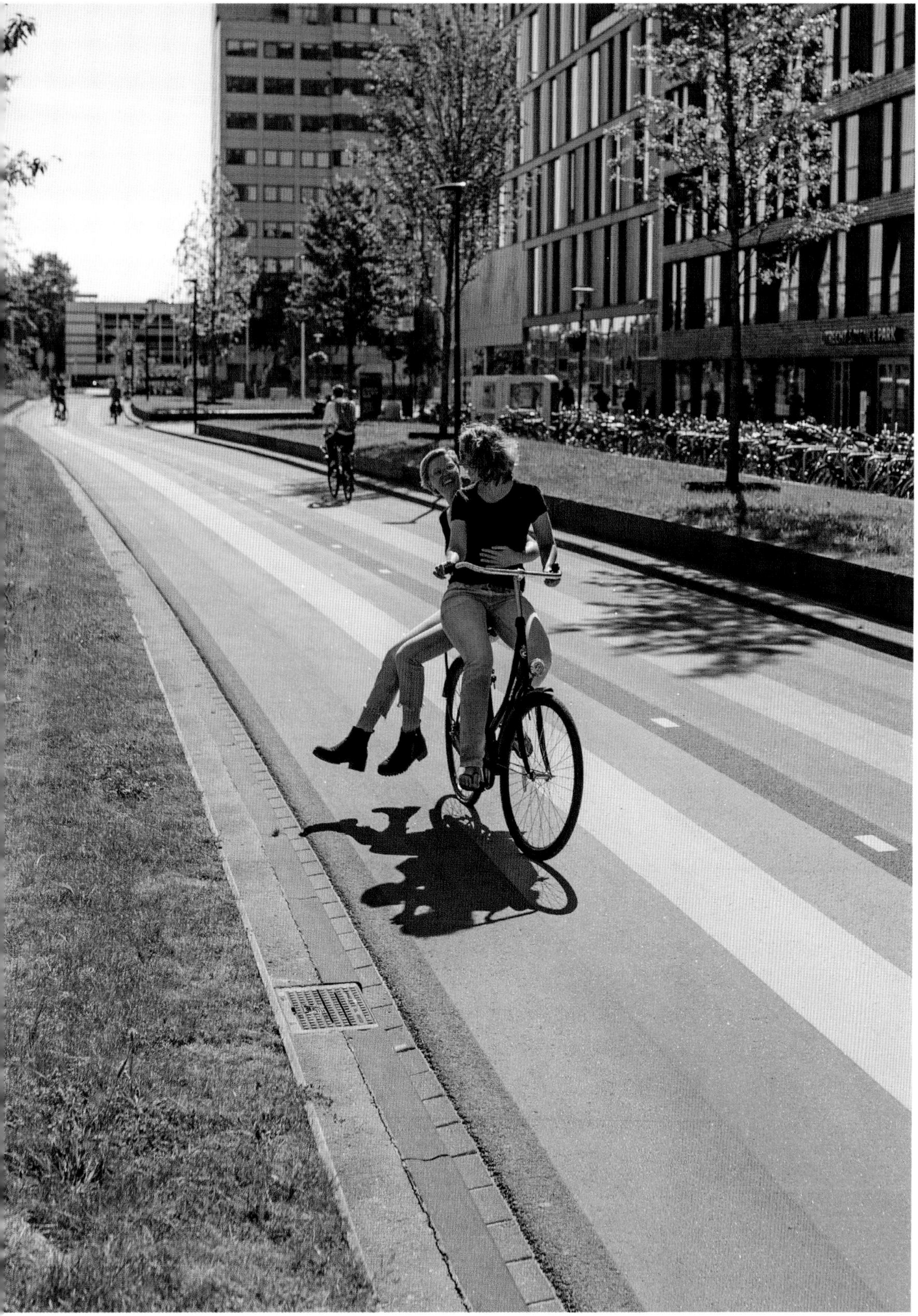

TRAVEL TIPS

Learning how to travel as an LGBTQ+ traveler can be daunting. The five hundred places and events in this book give a good idea of where to go, but there's much more to travel than a destination. A trip requires planning, packing, and a journey to get there. And as the world is ever-changing, so is the travel landscape. We no longer rely on compasses, the experiences of one person, or paper maps; we can now access nearly everything we need with a few clicks, allowing us to travel more safely and be more connected.

Great travel experiences start with research, including safety research. Legislation alone doesn't determine a destination's social climate, but it does indicate whether laws protect you and in what ways. Check a destination's LGBTQ+ rights—remember that about 70 countries still criminalize homosexuality and more than 30 countries criminalize trans people. Equaldex.com is a great, crowdsourced knowledge base of LGBTQ+ rights, and the annual Spartacus Gay Travel Index (GTI) is also useful. That's not to say you can't travel wherever you want, as long as you're aware of the risks. Travel, after all, is a personal choice: your trip, your rules, your comfort zone.

Beyond gender and sexuality laws, consider laws regarding medication and sex toys. Sex toys and prosthetics (or packers) are illegal in some countries, including Thailand and the Maldives. If you travel with medication, or travel documents with a different gender marker, make sure you carry the required documentation and doctor's letters. And make sure your travel documents are all in order: i.e. in the same name/gender, your passport is valid, you follow the visa rules, and you have travel insurance. Beyond laws, consider the social climate. In some countries, public displays of affection such as kissing are regarded as indecent behavior for all couples, and gender expectations can vary.

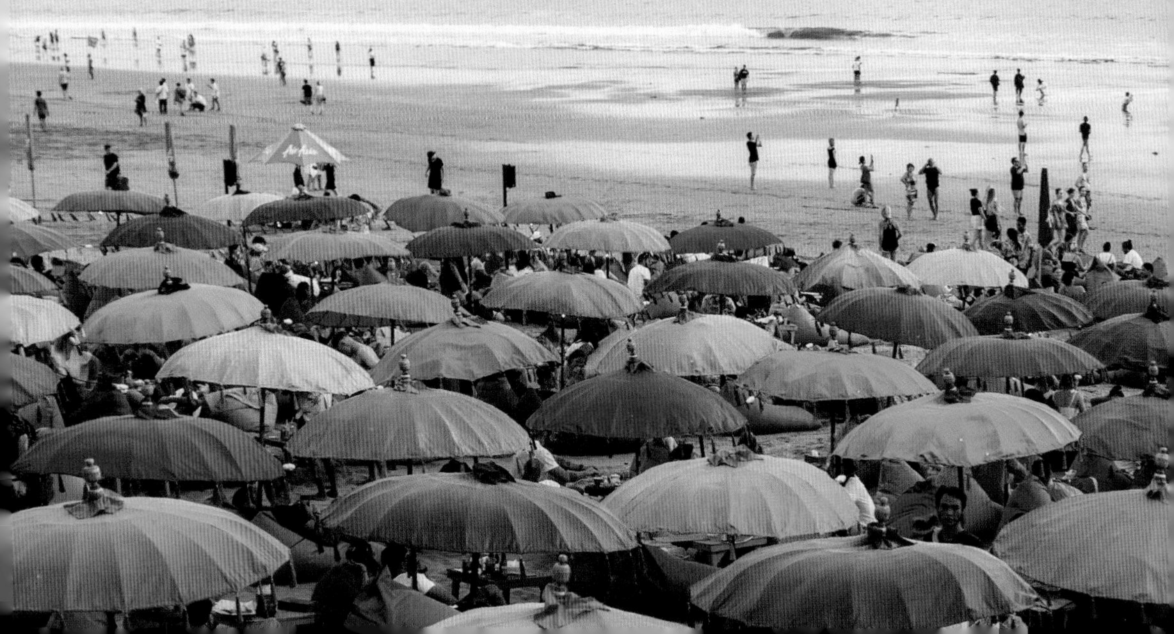

Take advantage of the online community and find LGBTQ+ folks at your destination or travelers who have visited before. They know best what it's like to be there as a queer person. Queer locals know what spaces, events, and areas are best to visit and have a unique, in-depth understanding of the local LGBTQ+ scene. Travelers may have a better understanding of what it's like when you're just visiting—that can be a different experience. Many Facebook groups can help you connect with LGBTQ+ travelers, ex-pats, and locals, as can apps such as Meetup, Couchsurfing, or dating apps (but be careful!). You could even join a group trip; there's safety in numbers. Getting a global phone plan or a local SIM card for your trip is a smart way to stay connected.

Quoting Audre Lorde: "There is no such thing as a single-issue struggle because we do not live single-issue lives." LGBTQ+ travel is not a monolith. Intersectionality is key when traveling; your whole identity influences your experience. Skin color, ethnicity, body size, gender, religion, nationality, class, disabilities, and whether you're traveling solo, as a couple, or with kids will all change your experience and how you plan and travel. Find travel resources that fit your identity. Prominent travel publications such as *AFAR*, *Matador*, and *Travel + Leisure* offer insightful, intersectional articles and guides. Find blogs that you can relate to, and social media posts via hashtags such as #accessibletravel, #blacktravel, #familytravel, and #solofemaletravel.

+ A wealth of resources is available to help you plan your trip and have a good time. For LGBTQ+ travelers, the International LGBTQ+ Travel Association (IGLTA) remains one of the biggest information hubs, recommending welcoming partners globally and offering travel guides. The *Everywhere is Queer* map is an excellent resource for finding LGBTQ-owned businesses worldwide, and the app Blapp can help find Black-owned businesses to support globally. Lastly, have fun and enjoy yourself! Keep an open mind. Although you should always be aware of safety, and consider the possibility of bad situations and people, the truth is when traveling, you usually meet a larger number of warmhearted, welcoming people than bad ones.
Go OUT there and see how beautiful the world can be!

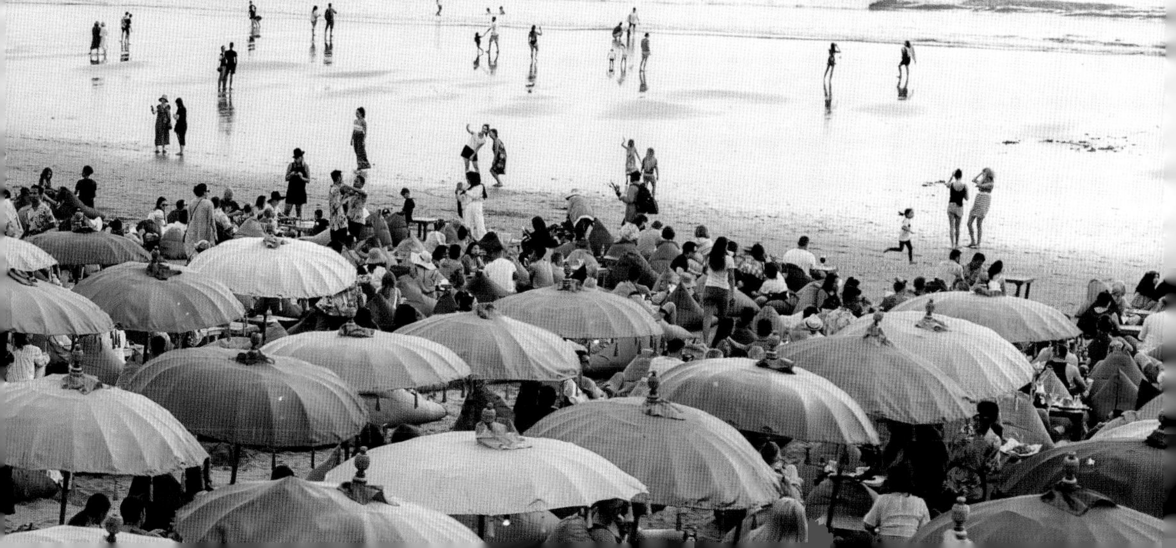

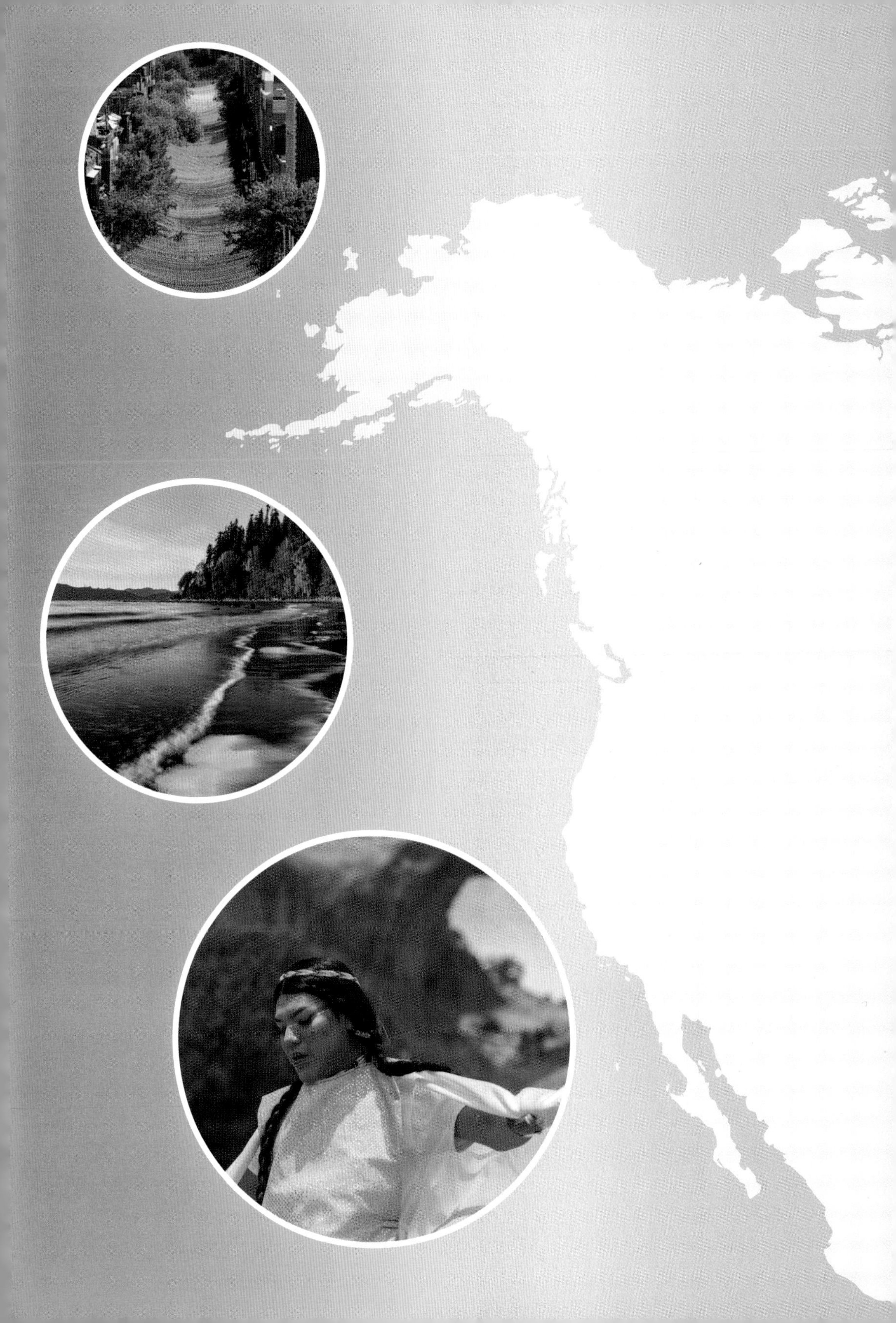

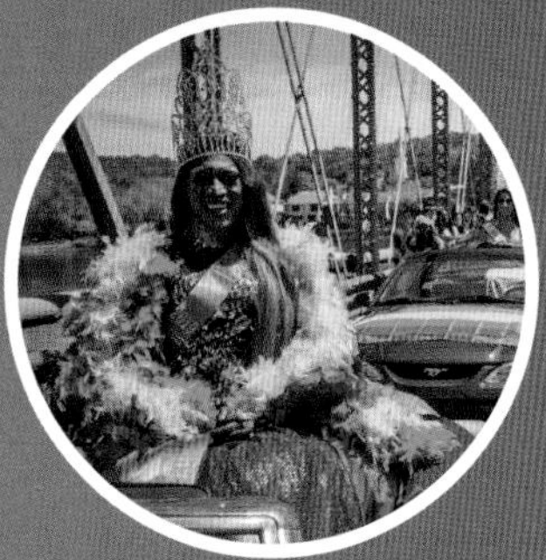

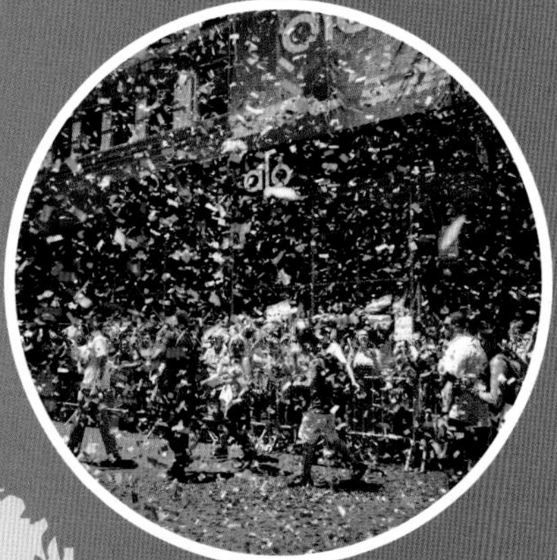

CHAPTER ONE

NORTH AMERICA

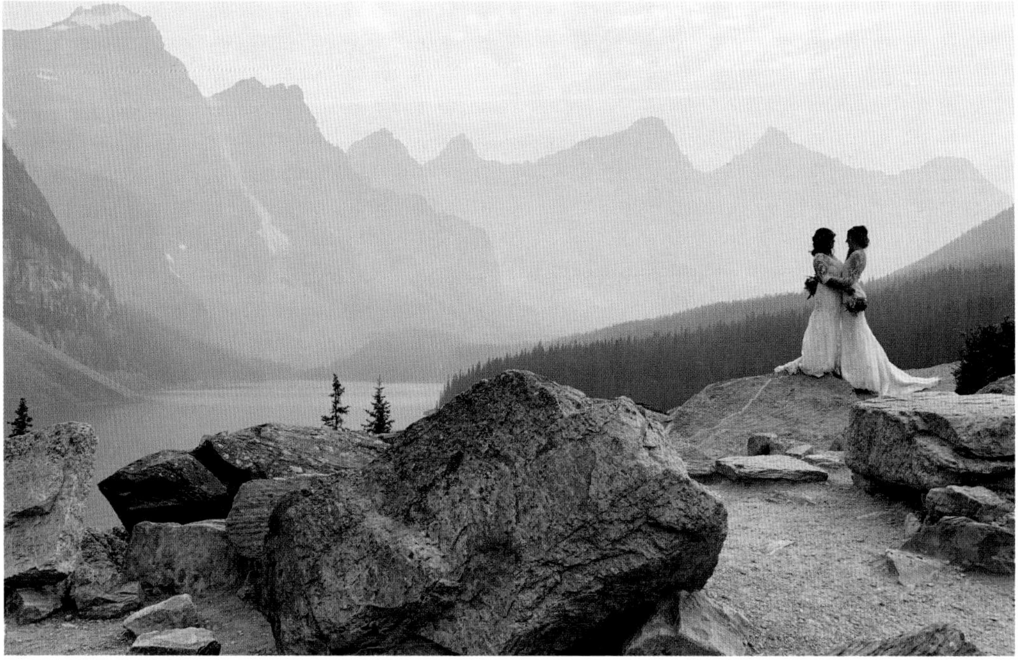

1 Take pride in the Rockies

▲ Banff, Alberta, Canada

When to go: Fall
Best for: Escaping into nature

Banff is a picturesque town in the Canadian Rockies and home to the awe-inspiring Banff National Park. The contrasting seasons offer adventures to suit every taste. All year round, visitors can relax in natural hot springs, enjoy the stunning views from a gondola, and soak up culture at local museums, galleries and shops. In the winter, there are ski slopes to enjoy, frozen-lake ice-skating, and dog-sledding. The warmer months bring out the wild flowers and the autumnal hues—and Banff Pride in the fall. It's a fabulous week of Pride marches, drag brunches, queer shows, and more, all surrounded by snow-peaked mountains.

2 Keep track of transgender history

Transgender Archives, University of Victoria, British Columbia, Canada

When to go: All year
Best for: Transgender print material

Containing over 120 years of trans history, from 23 countries (on six continents), the Transgender Archives are home to some of the most significant trans-created publications in the world. Featuring nineteenth-century sexological publications, oral histories, "cross-dressing" magazines, 1970s transgender scrapbooks and erotica—you won't find these in your local library!

3 Make rainbows on ski slopes

Jasper, Alberta, Canada

When to go: April
Best for: Outdoor activities

Located in the beautiful Canadian Rockies, Jasper National Park is a famed destination for world-class skiing in the winter and scenic hiking trails in the summer. In the middle of the national park is Jasper, a quaint town that is home to an inclusive community of five thousand residents. Jasper hosts the Rockies' only gay ski week, held every spring, complete with a rainbow-flag parade down the mountain.

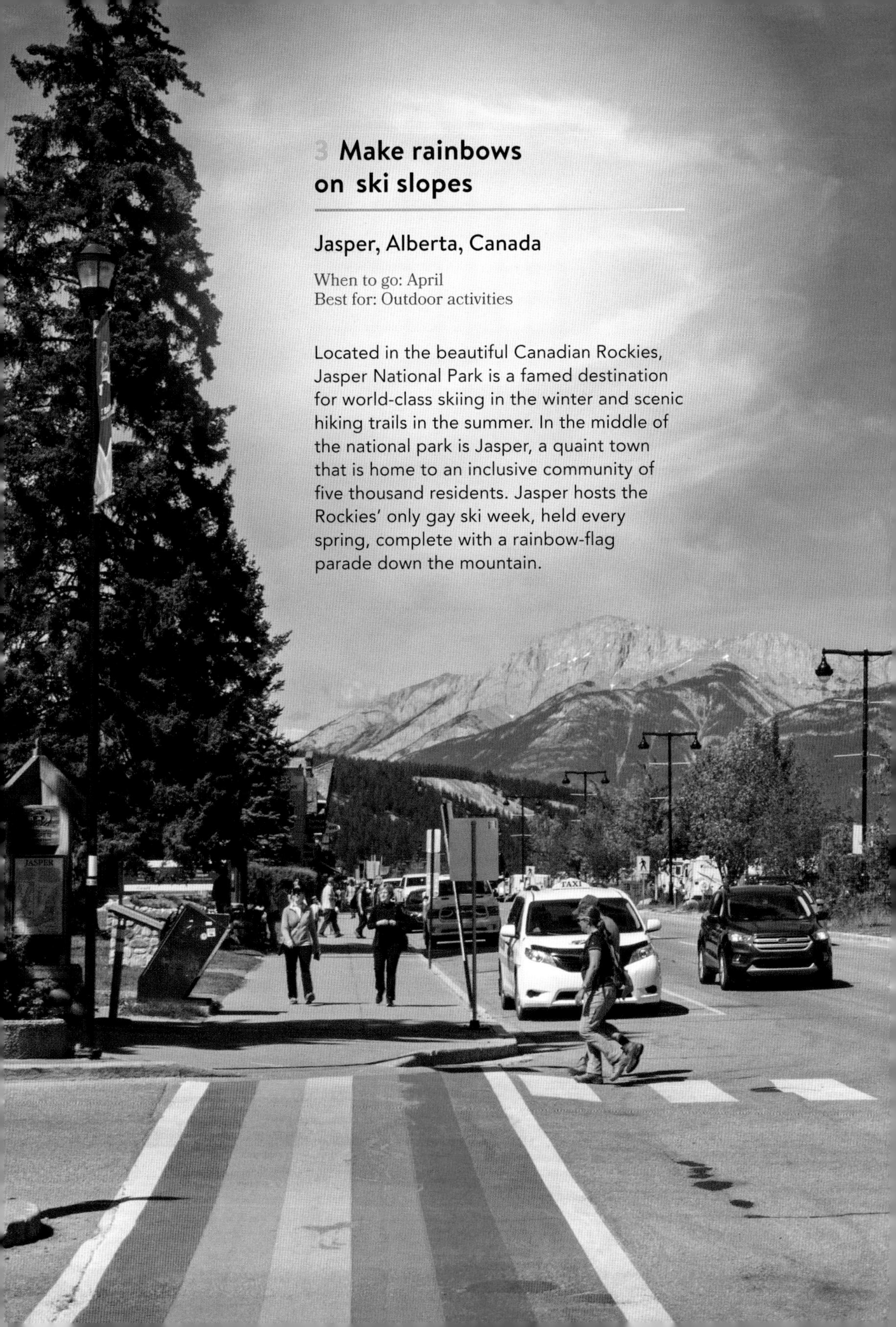

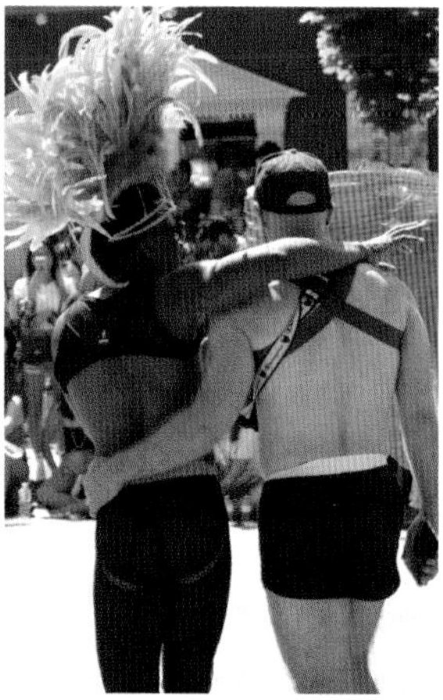

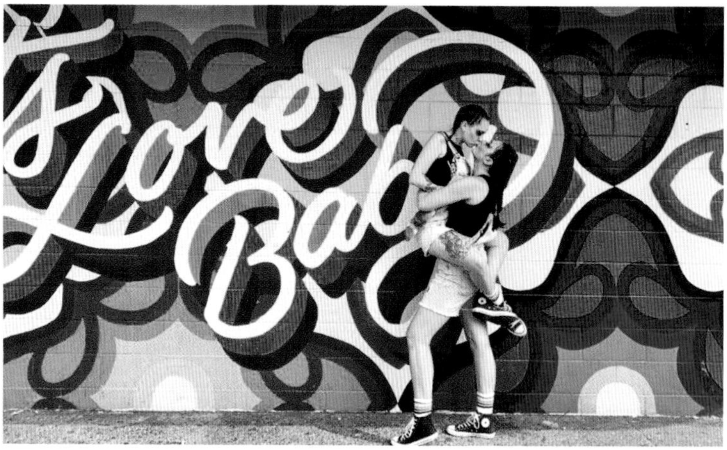

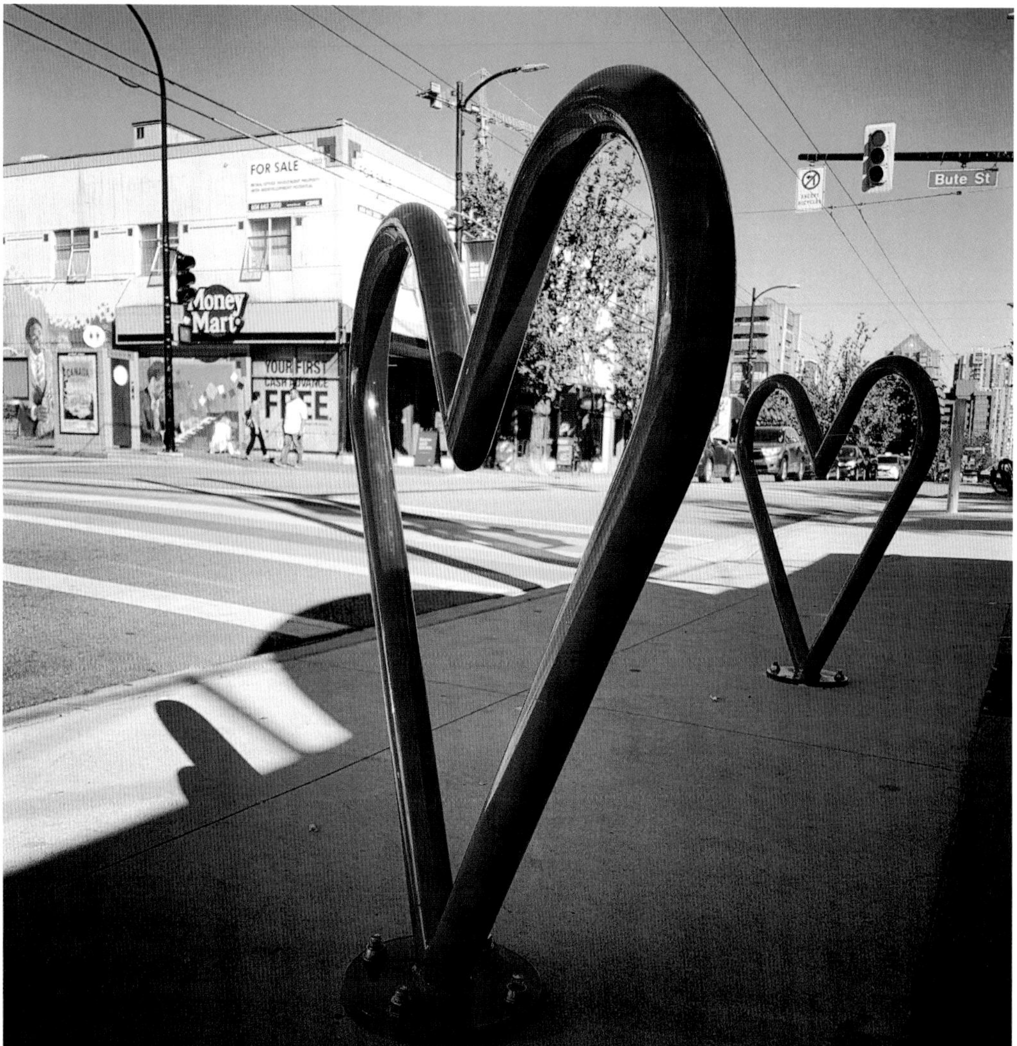
FOR SALE
Money Mart
YOUR FIRST
Bute St

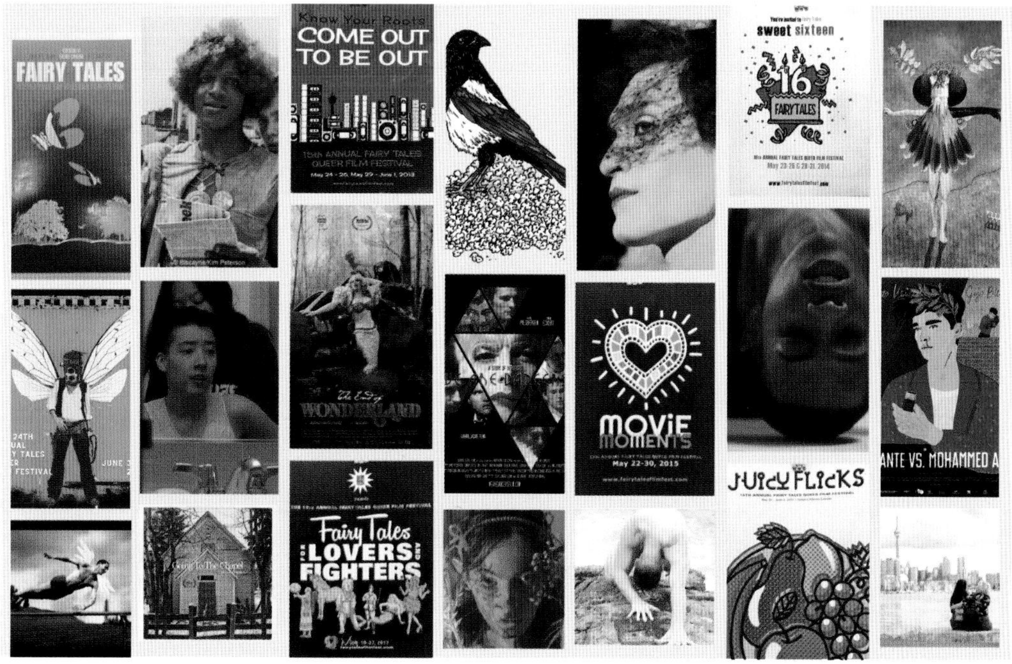

4 Feel the love in the heart of Vancouver

◀ Davie Street, Vancouver, Canada

When to go: July to August
Best for: Friendly faces

Davie Street, in the West End of Vancouver, is home to one of Canada's largest LGBTQ+ communities. Visitors and locals alike enjoy nearby LGBTQ-friendly beaches and vibrant nightlife. Davie Street is also home to Vancouver Pride, bringing the biggest celebration of the year to the area in late July. Davie Street's local businesses are warm and welcoming, and there are many organizations committed to bringing together members of the LGBTQ+ communities.

5 Little queer culture on the prairie

▲ Fairy Tales Queer Film Festival, Calgary, Canada

When to go: June
Best for: Celebrating LGBTQ+ arts

This LGBTQ+ film festival in Calgary faced many setbacks when it started out, including picket lines from conservative groups, serious threats directed at the organizers, and a lack of financial support. But, fueled by passion and a sense of duty, the festival—by and for LGBTQ+ people—is still standing and thriving a quarter of a century later. Every year, dozens of inspiring, compelling, and thought-provoking films bring together the LGBTQ+ community.

6 Whistle in the (chilly) wind

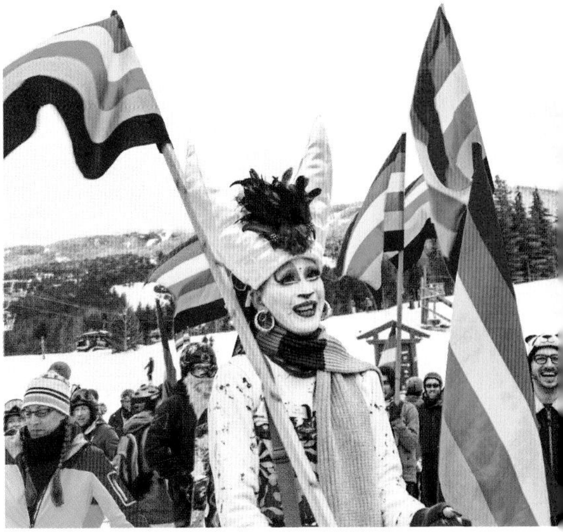

Whistler Pride and Ski Festival, British Columbia, Canada

When to go: January and February
Best for: A snowy, winter Pride

One of the most prominent LGBTQ+ ski weeks in North America happens in the charming town of Whistler, north of Vancouver. Whistler Pride and Ski Festival has been running for three decades and is still going strong. The first event was a small-scale, gay ski weekend; now, it's a week-long festival attracting thousands of visitors. There's a slope for everyone, with two hundred marked trails between two mountains. The festival's biggest highlights are the Pride Ski + March and the closing party. The parade happens partly on the slopes; skiers and riders swoosh down the slopes with a giant Pride flag, before handing the flag over to the marchers of the parade. The entire town joins in, making it a fun mix of locals and visitors, LGBTQ+ people, and allies. You'll experience Canadian hospitality at its finest, and both Whistler and its people will steal your heart. Fair warning: you'll want to return.

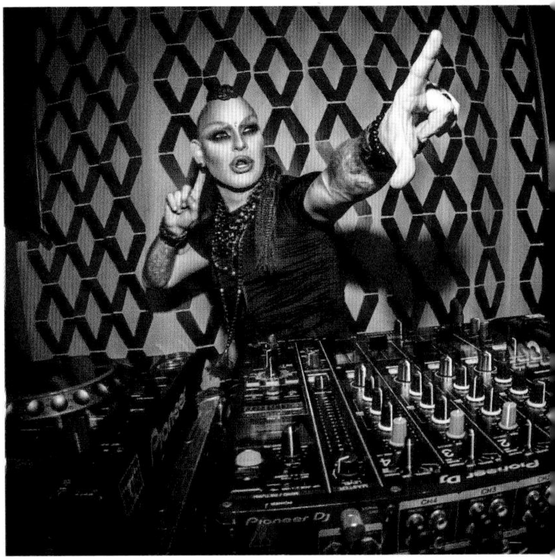

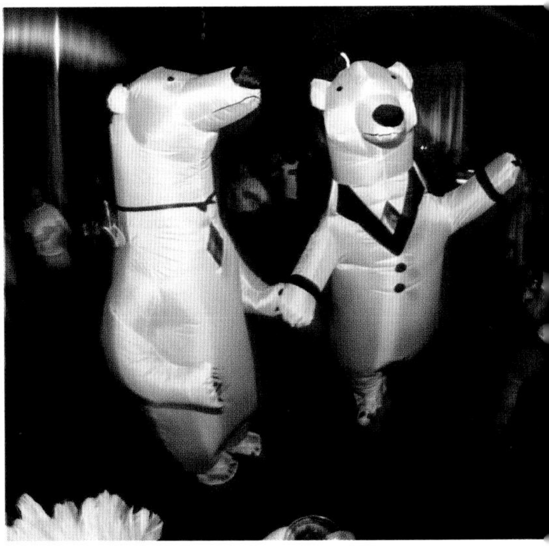

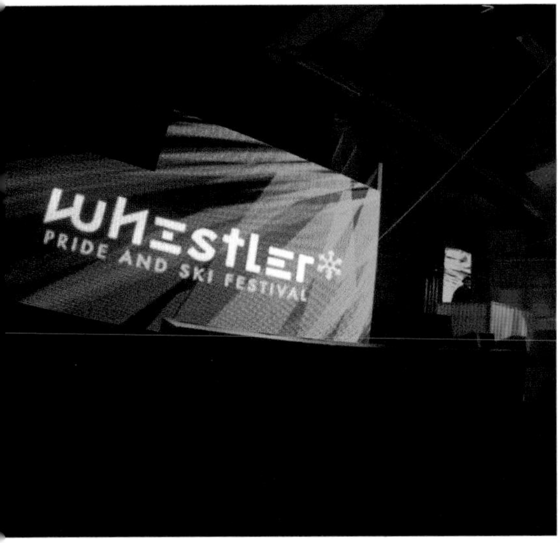
whistler
PRIDE AND SKI FESTIVAL

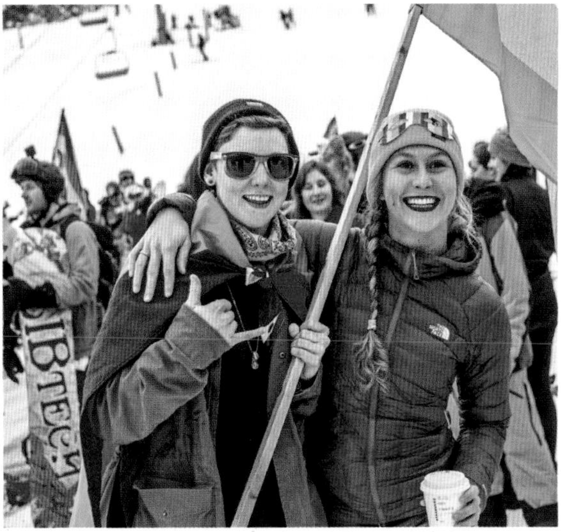

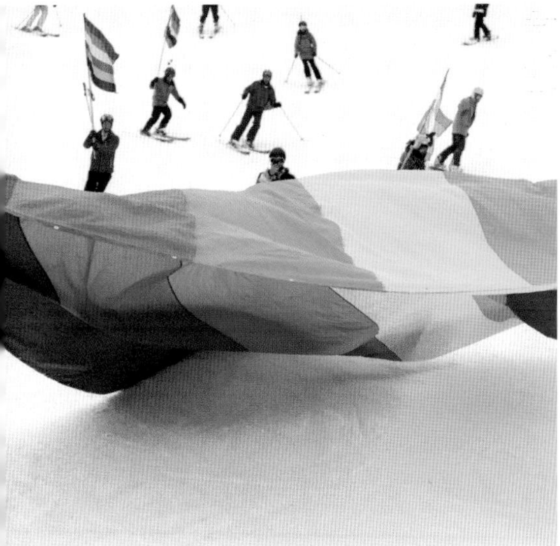

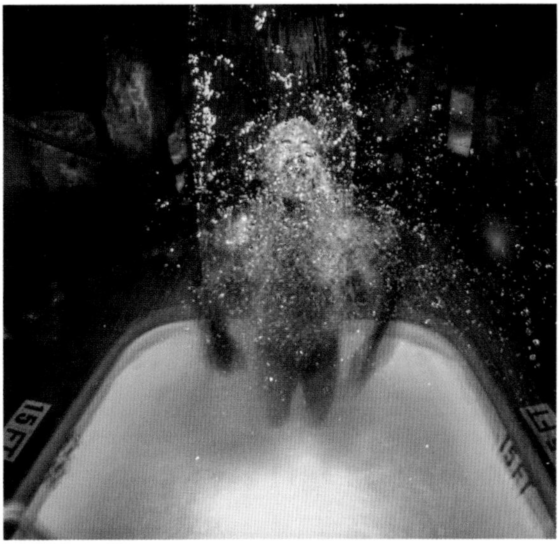
15 FT
15 FT

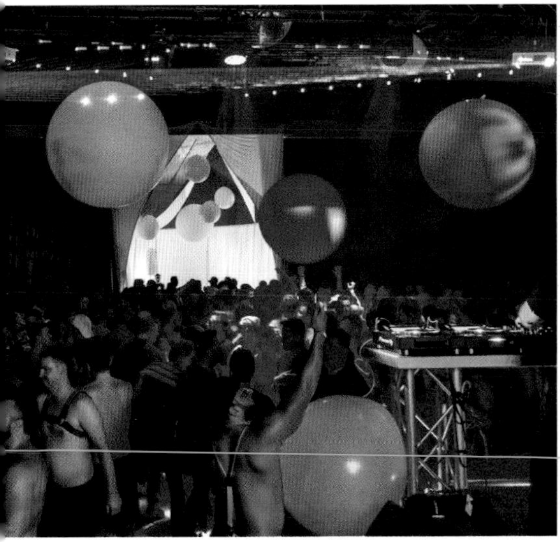

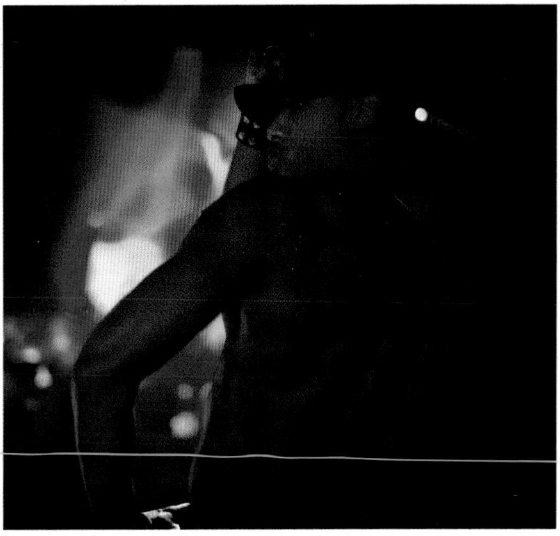

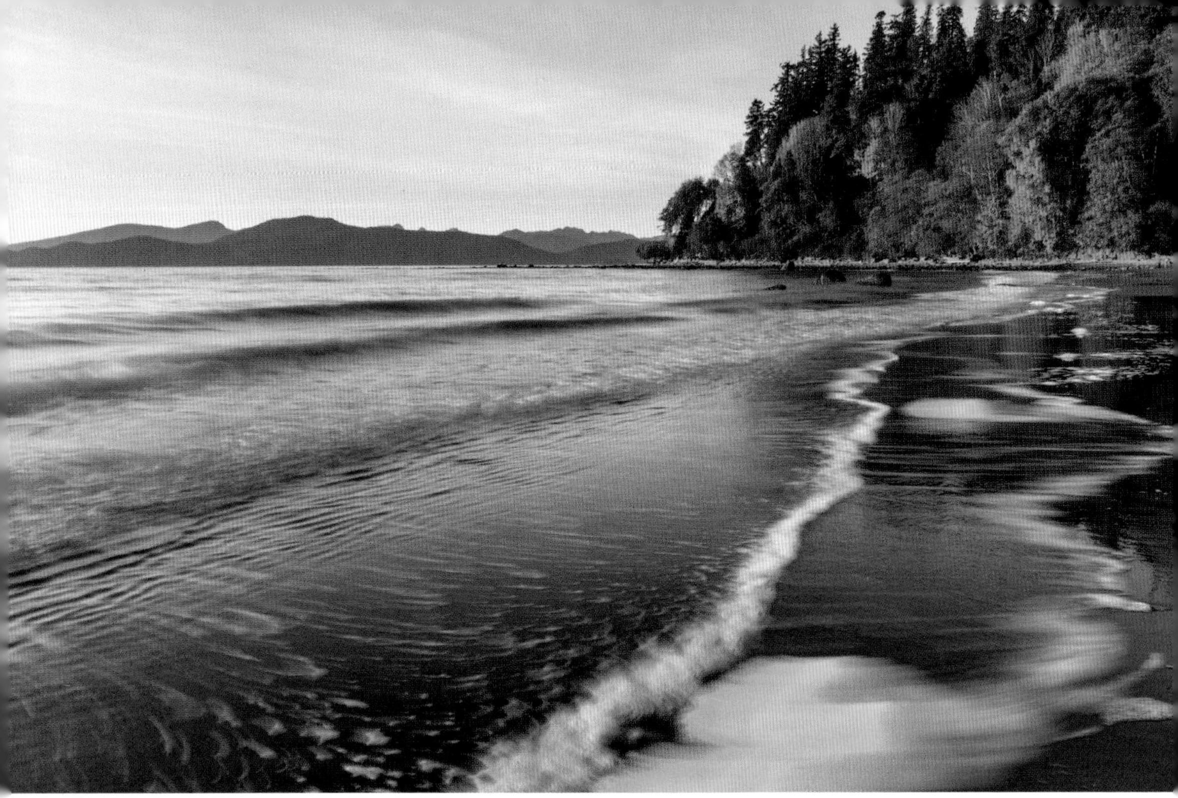

7 Undress to impress

▲ ▶ Wreck Beach, Vancouver, Canada

When to go: May to September
Best for: Nude sunbathing

North America's largest clothing-optional beach comes with a challenge: a steep, five-hundred-step staircase down the side of a cliff. Considering nude beaches are historically secret and secluded, this isn't surprising. But it does mean that Wreck Beach is not accessible to everyone. You'll find a fabulous 4.8-mi/7.8-km stretch of sand if you can make the trip down the steep, lush trail. Respect and privacy make this a welcoming place for LGBTQ+ people. Beach-goers include students from the nearby UBC and visitors looking for relaxed, naked sunbathing.

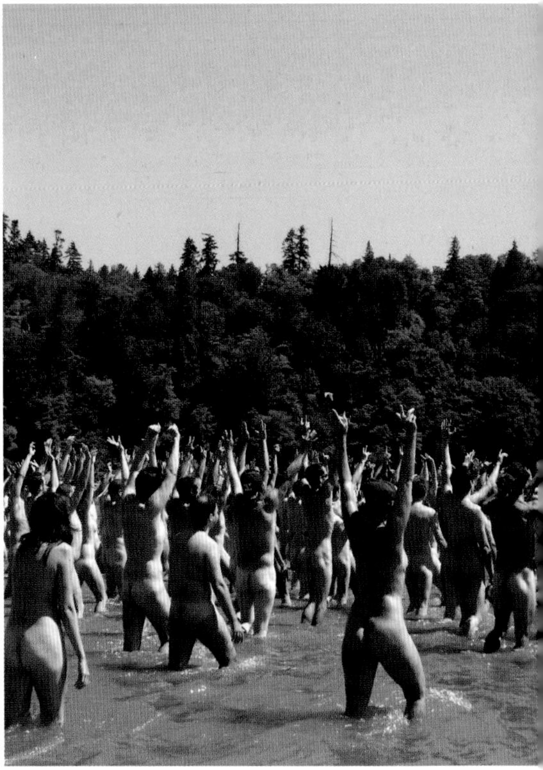

8 Feel the amour

▼ Fierte Montreal, Canada

When to go: August
Best for: Rainbows, love, community

Fierte Montreal is one of the largest gatherings of the LGBTQ+ community in the Francophone world. Held every year at the end of August, visitors are invited to enjoy free entertainment, participate in community projects, and be amazed by the annual Pride Parade, where participants adorn themselves with colorful costumes and messages of hope and love.

9 Scissor magic

Haircuts for Anyone, Montreal, Canada

When to go: April to October
Best for: Affirmative queer haircut

As the name "Haircuts for Anyone" suggests, this is Montreal's most inclusive and affirmative hair salon. Nothing beats a fresh haircut by queer scissor magicians, paid on a sliding scale. Queer person of color (QPOC) barber Miwa—aka Scissor Daddy—and trans hairdresser J. J. Levine cut all hair types in J. J.'s cozy, small salon.

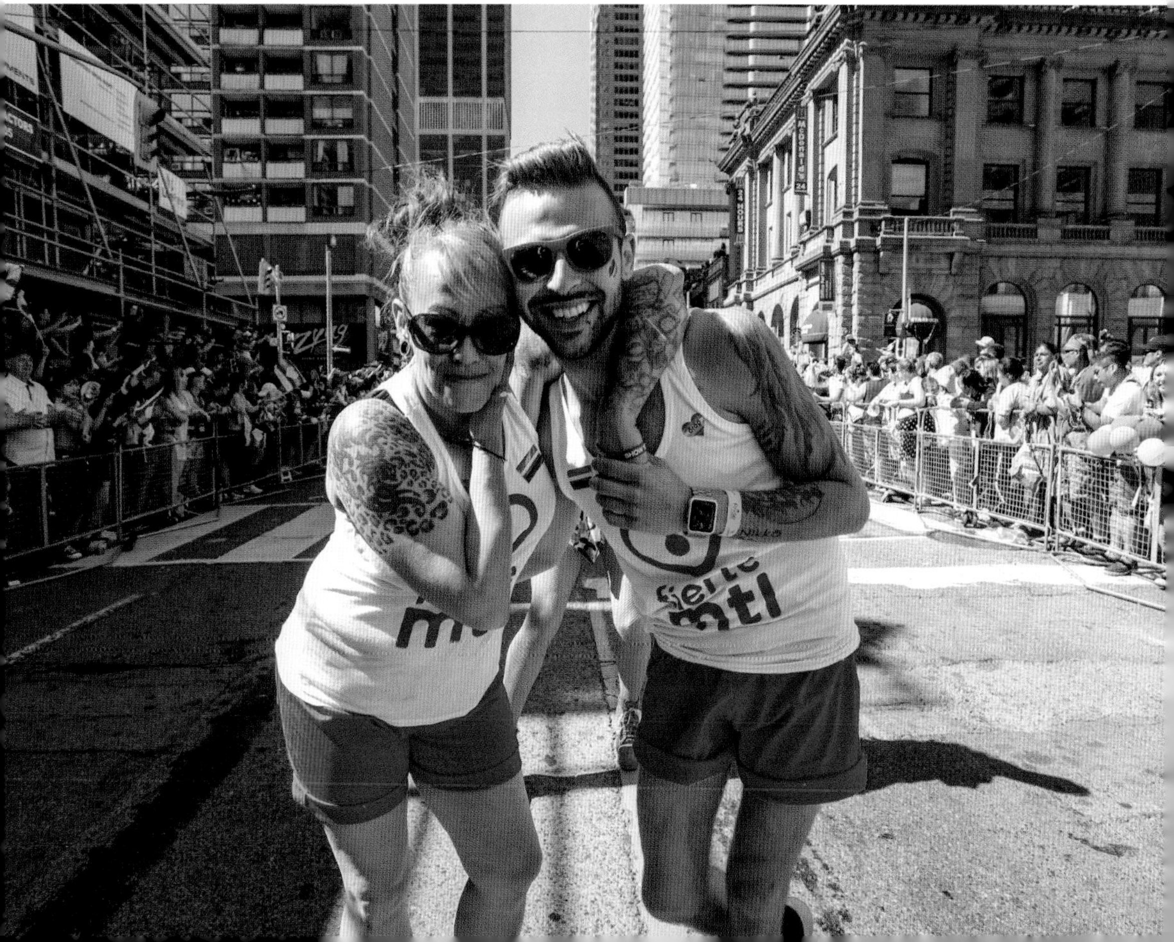

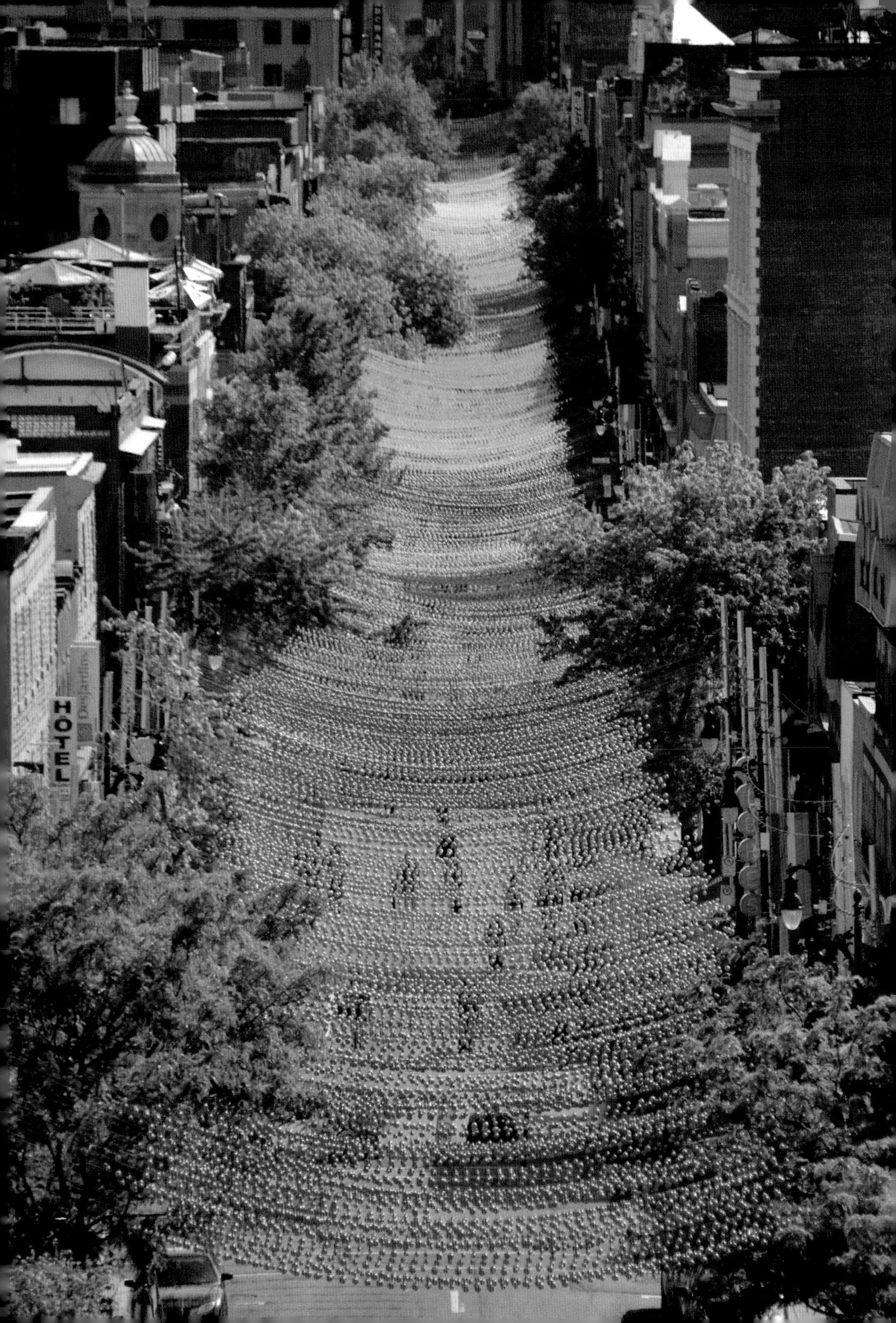
HOTEL

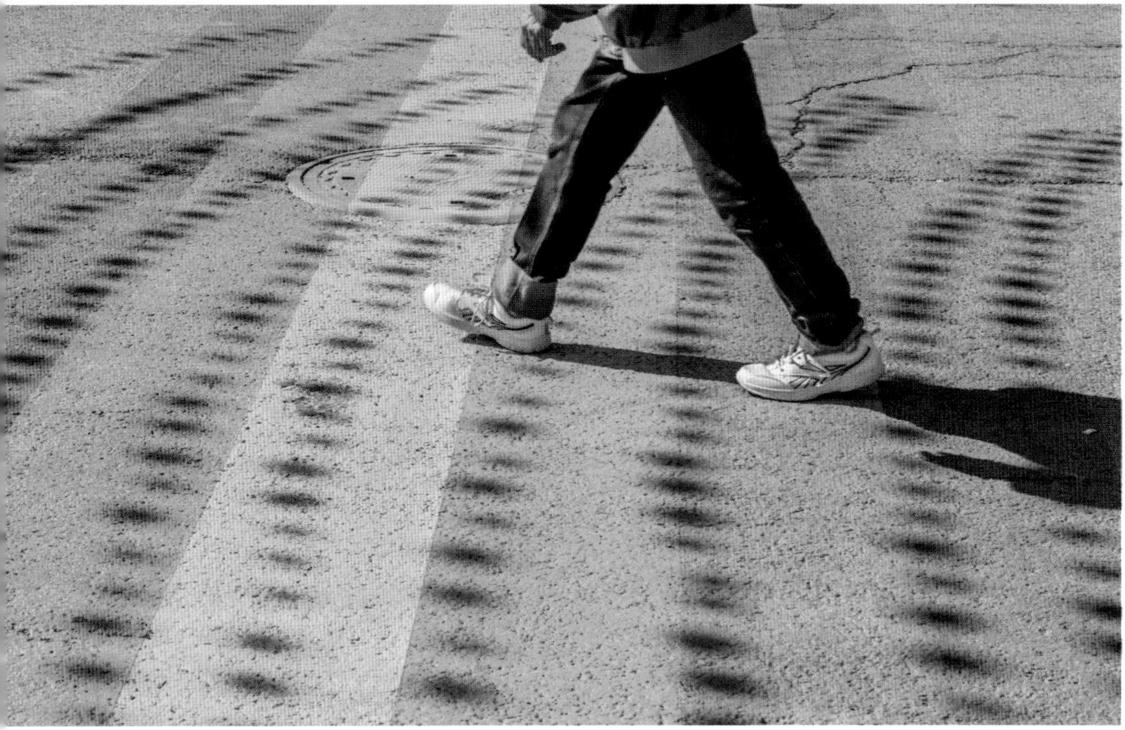

10 Parlez-vous queer culture?

◀ ▲ Sainte-Catherine Street, Montreal, Canada

When to go: All year
Best for: French-speaking North American charm

Montreal is a unique, culture-clash destination. Although visually it might look like many other North American cities, it harbors a distinctly European flavor due to the fact that everyone speaks French. The city's queer village is the biggest LGBTQ+ neighborhood in North America, with plenty of bars, cafés and stores to explore. It's situated along Sainte-Catherine Street, with the Beaudry metro station complete with distinctive rainbow pillars at the center of the action.

11 Party with benefits

Black & Blue Festival, Montreal, Canada

When to go: Canadian Thanksgiving weekend
Best for: Money-raising fun

There are not many LGBTQ+ events that can rock an Olympic stadium, but the headline party of Montreal's Black & Blue Festival is one such gathering. As well as the main event, which welcomes all regardless of identity, associated benefit events run across the extended Canadian Thanksgiving weekend in October. Dating back to 1991, funds raised go to HIV-related causes.

12 Sample some queer beer

Brasserie Harricana, Montreal, Canada

When to go: All year
Best for: Artisanal beers

Queer women and lifelong friends Marie-Pier and Cynthia run micro-brewpub Brasserie Harricana. Since opening in 2014, it has become a staple for the local community. The place is famous for the great variety of beers brewed on site. The warm, modern, salmon-colored decor hints at the brewpub's history. In the 1970s and 1980s, Marie-Pier's parents ran Brasserie Harricana in Amos, Quebec. The chairs and tables are from the original brasserie, and you can find iconic family recipes on the menu.

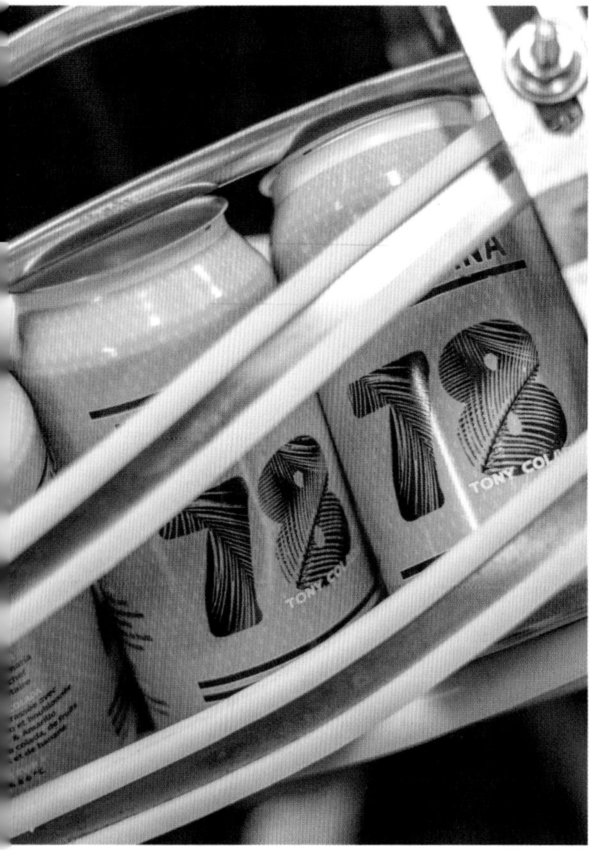

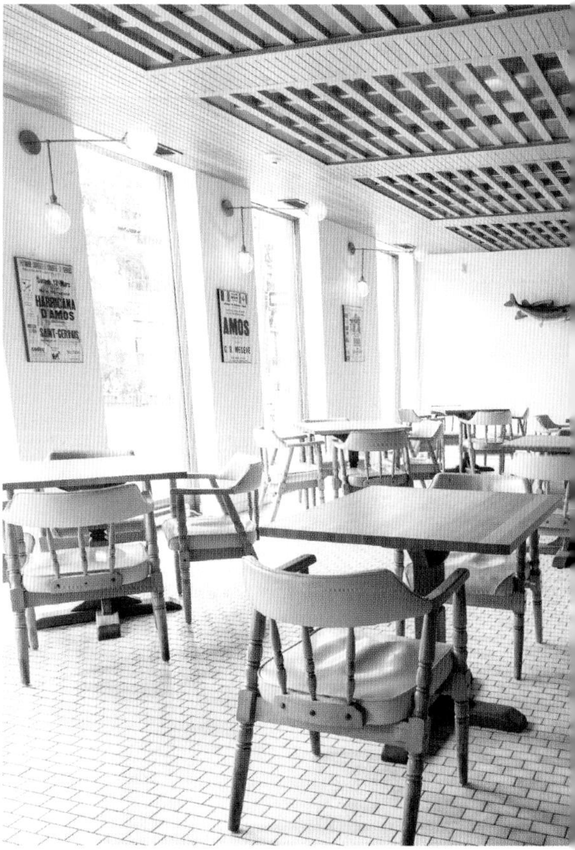

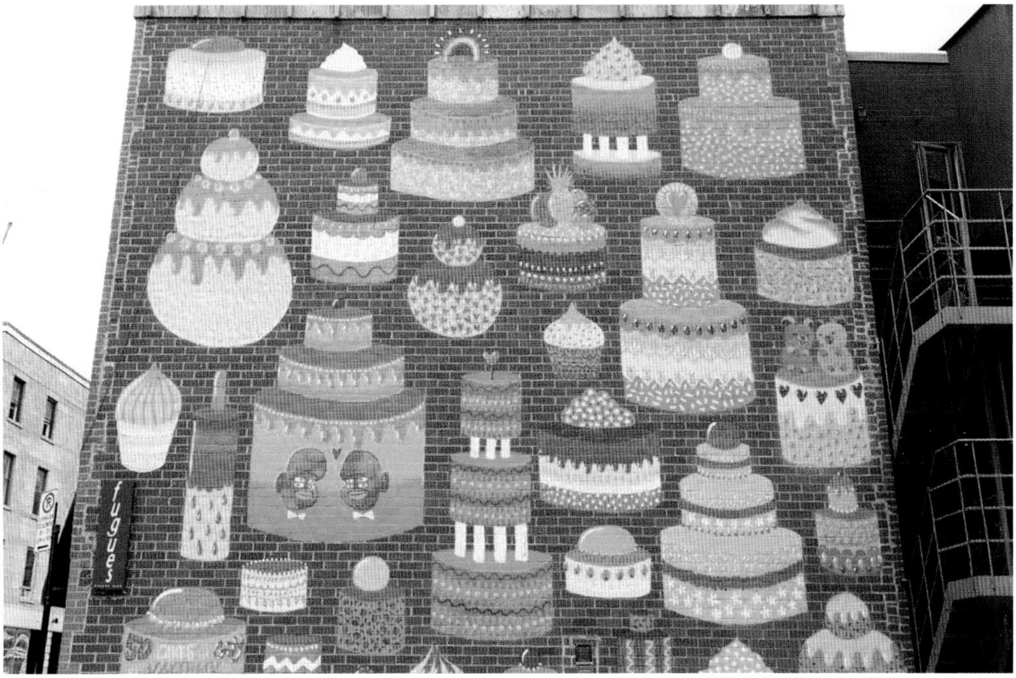

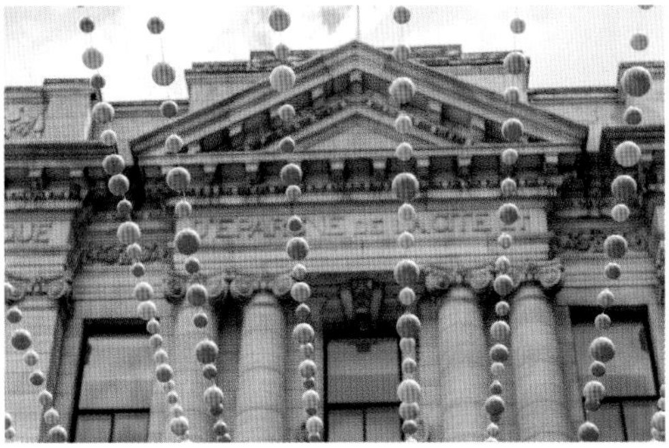

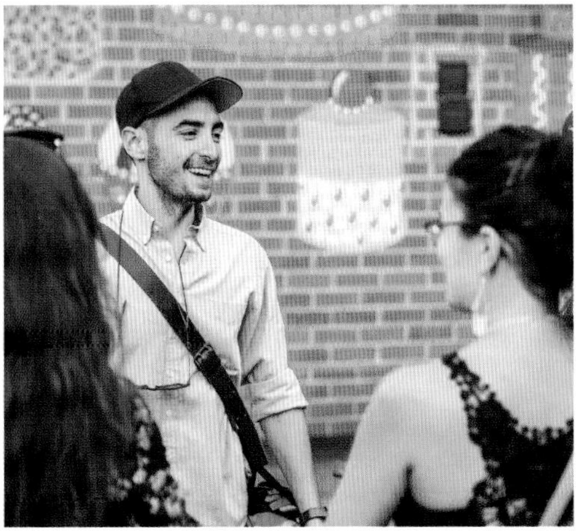

13 Let's get local

Spade & Palacio, Montreal, Canada

When to go: May to October
Best for: Non-touristy tours

Spade & Palacio is the brainchild of queer friends Danny and Anne-Marie. Sitting at LGBTQ-staple Brasserie Harricana, the two Montrealers came up with the concept of supplying non-touristy tours for visitors, led by authentic and passionate guides who invite you into their local Montreal lives. The first tour was "Beyond the Market," a food tour to promote local, young, and female entrepreneurs. This has since expanded to offer street-art tours, and bike tours on locally built, hot-pink bikes. What a way to see the city!

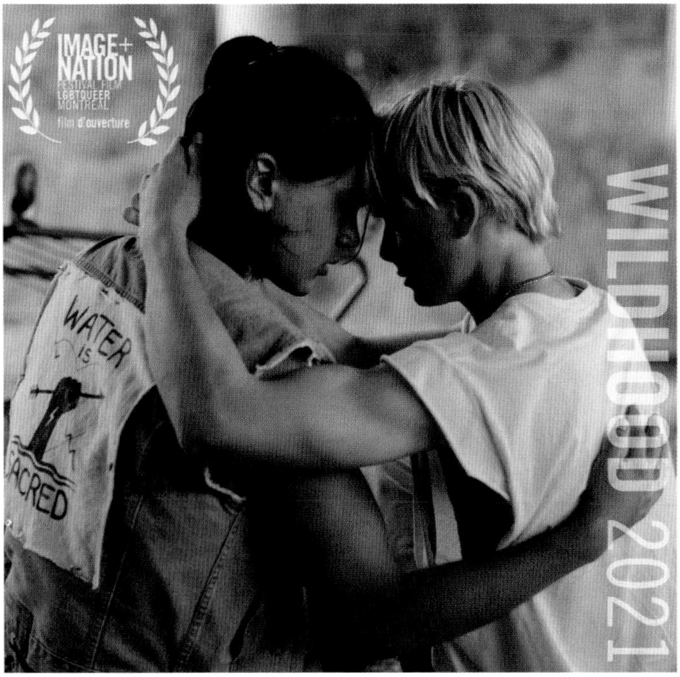

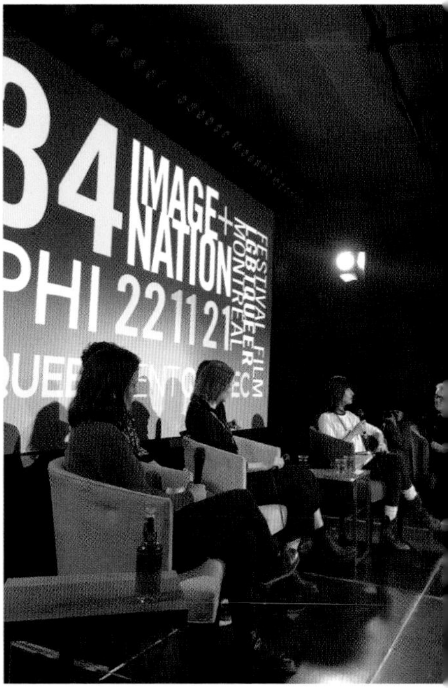

14 Let your imagination roll

▲ image+nation, Montreal, Canada

When to go: November
Best for: Inclusive film screenings

Canada's oldest LGBTQ+ film festival, image+nation, has featured films of stories and experiences of LGBTQ+ people for close to four decades. Besides the annual eleven-day festival in Montreal, the festival has a virtual home to share new, queer storytelling year-round and a space for queer creators to explore, present, and discuss their work. From big hits to unknown gems, local and international films bring the authentic, diverse, queer community to life on screen. As a queer person, seeing yourself represented on screen can be life-changing and, in some cases, life-saving.

15 Shop til your eyes pop

Venus Envy, Halifax, Canada

When to go: All year
Best for: Getting your sexy on

Get your sexy on at Venus Envy, an independent, education-based sex shop and bookstore located on Barrington Street in Downtown Halifax. Since its foundation over two decades ago, Venus Envy has been women-led, welcoming, affirmative, and informative. Besides genderless toys, they sell gender-affirming products, inclusive sex-education books, and sexual health professionals host shame-free workshops.

16 Hello sailor

▶ Woody's and Sailor, Toronto, Canada

When to go: July to August
Best for: People-watching

These one-of-a-kind sister bars are two of the oldest bars in Toronto, located in the heart of Toronto's gay village on Church Street. Famous for being the filming locations for the American version of the TV series, *Queer as Folk*, Woody's and Sailor are among the hottest bars in the area and a must-see for everyone visiting Toronto. They also host a raft of special events, such as drag shows, and contests for best chest, ass, and legs, and have received numerous awards.

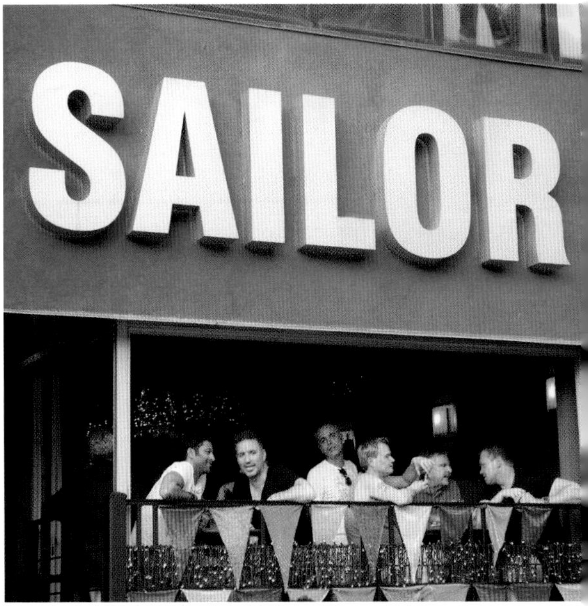

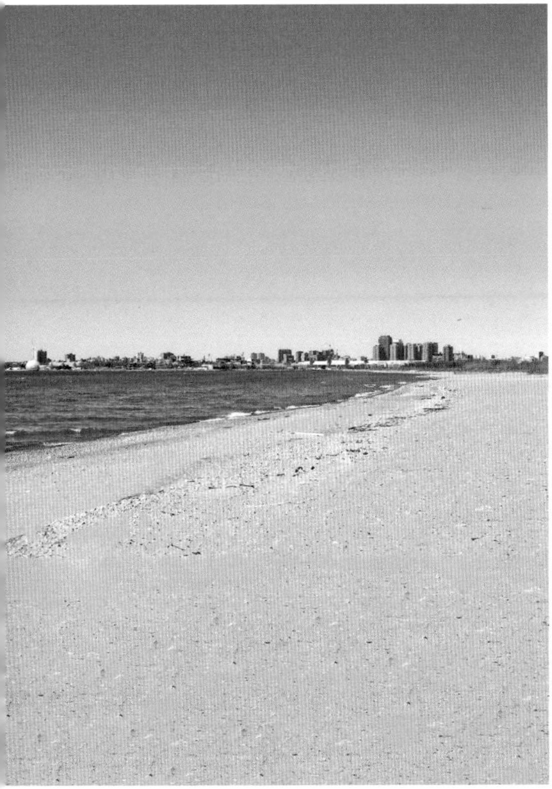

17 Free your body

◀ Hanlan's Point, Toronto, Canada

When to go: July to August
Best for: Feeling free

Just a short, scenic ferry ride from Toronto, on the shore of Lake Ontario, nude-beach enthusiasts can find Hanlan's Point. Since the 1950s, Hanlan's Point has been a popular meeting spot for the local, queer community away from the hustle and bustle of the city. Clothing remains optional at the city's popular, unofficial "gay beach," but no photos please.

18 Get ready for a mega-Pride

Toronto, Canada

When to go: Late June/early July
Best for: Canuck Pride with a political edge

Pride Toronto is so much more than a one-off parade. The Ontario capital's Pride festivities take place across a whole month, including a rainbow myriad of inclusive cultural activities, discussions and other events. There's a separate Trans March (on Friday evening) and Dyke March (on Saturday evening), before the main Pride parade (on Sunday). Justin Trudeau attended the event in 2016: the first serving Canadian prime minister to march in one of the country's Pride parades. The bulk of the parade runs down Yonge Street, where crowds line rooftops and other elevated vantage points to get the best view. Afterward, entertainment is provided at stages in Dundas Square, and the Church and Wellesley district: the city's gay neighborhood. The carnival atmosphere and partying always runs late into the night.

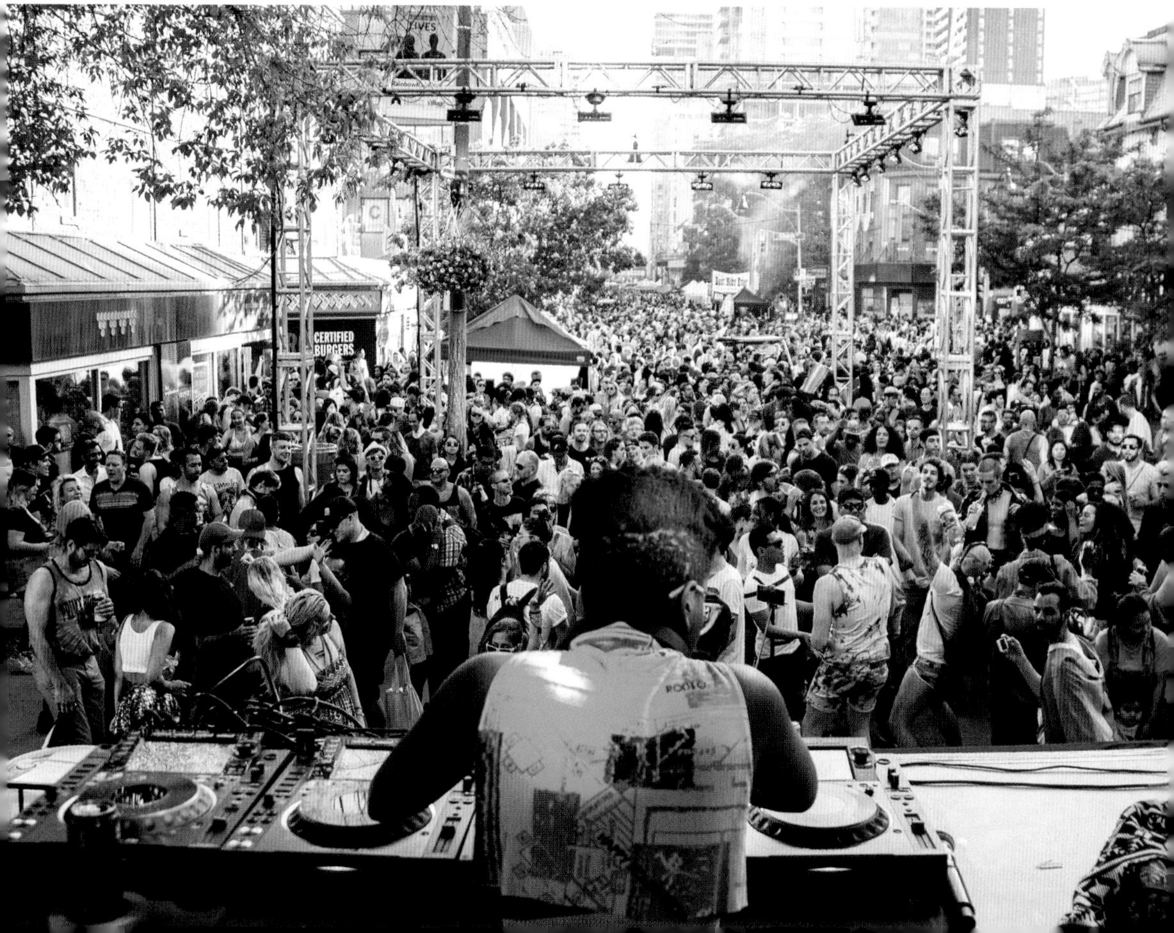

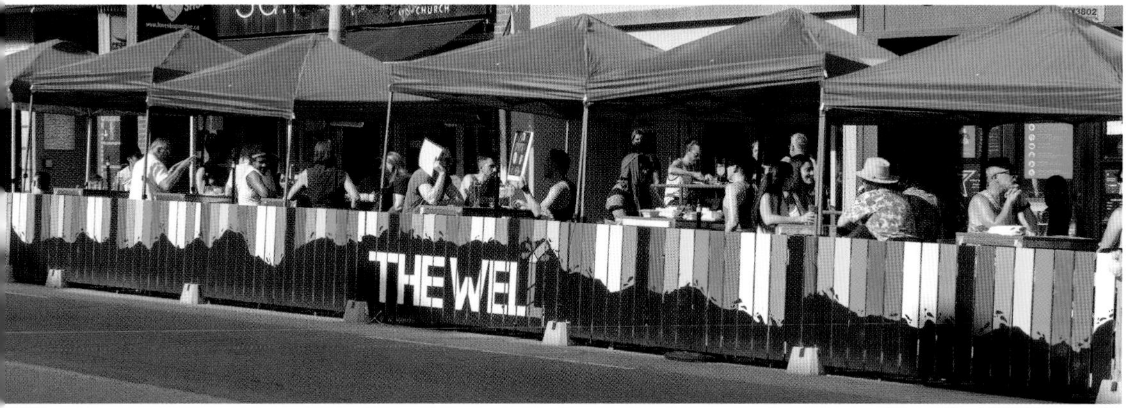

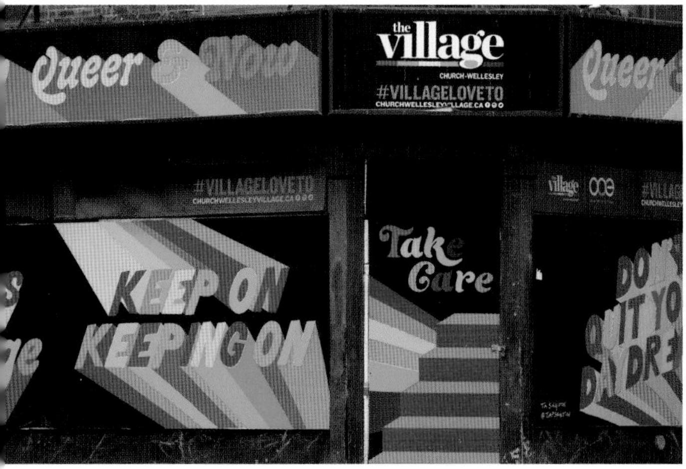

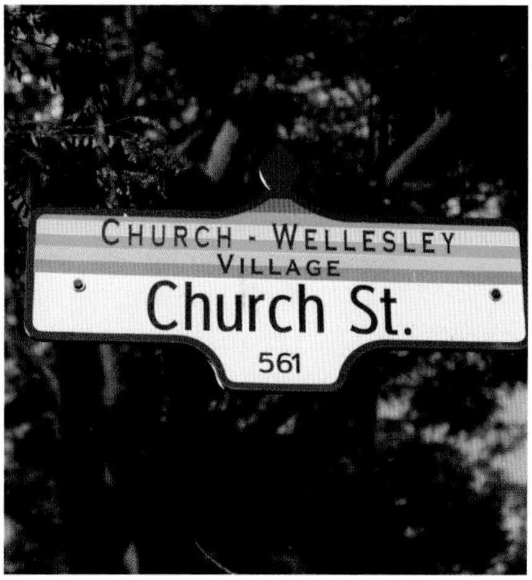

19 Find what you're looking for—at church

Church and Wellesley Village, Toronto, Canada

When to go: All year
Best for: Being at the epicenter of queer Toronto

Toronto's gay village lies in the blocks within Church, Wellesley, and Carlton streets—look out for the rainbows which adorn the street signs and the crossings at the district's borders. Sidestreets, with Victorian-era houses and apartments, add a dash of historic charm. Church and Wellesley offers a laid-back, village-within-a-city vibe, with plenty of restaurants, bistros, galleries, bars and—for those wanting steamier fun—bathhouses. Daytime cafés provide plenty of curbside people-watching opportunities. Evening venues to explore include The Garage and O'Grady's. The 519 is the city's LGBTQ+ community center, offering everything from indigenous storytelling and legal advice to art workshops and activities for older folk. George Hislop Park, dedicated to one of the city's most influential gay activists, offers space for a few moments of quieter contemplation.

20 Dorothy wears Prada, too

Yorkville, Toronto, Canada

When to go: July to August
Best for: Shopping, shopping, and more shopping

Welcome to the "Mink Mile," a glamorous shopping district steps away from the gay village. Designer shopping, fancy art galleries and high-end restaurants adorn the strip, but there are options for those looking for a more rugged experience. Anyone up for a beer and some rugby at Hemingway's? Or if you are looking to see some stars, visit during the Toronto International Film Festival, held each year in the fall.

21 Black-affirming block party bliss

▶ Blockorama, Toronto, Canada

When to go: June
Best for: Celebrating ABC LGBTQ+ culture

At many of the whitewashed, commercialized Pride events, it can be easy to forget the debt owed to trans women of color in the birth of Pride. With this in mind, in 1998, community collective Blackness Yes! acted on the necessity to reclaim space at Pride Toronto and Blockorama was born, celebrating African, Black, and Caribbean (ABC) LGBTQ+ history, resistance, and liberation. At Blockorama, beats from the African diaspora fill the air, performances bless your eyes, and food from the community marketplace treats your taste buds.

22 Screen idols

LGBTQ+ film festivals, Toronto, Canada

When to go: Late March to late April and late May to early June
Best for: Culture vultures

Grab some popcorn and make yourself comfortable; Toronto is blessed with not one but two LGBTQ+ film festivals. Inside Out (May to June) has been running since 1991 and is the biggest queer film festival in Canada. The more recent Toronto Queer Film Festival (March to April) began life in 2016 and is known for the diversity of its screenings.

23 Putting the queer into archives

The ArQuives, Toronto, Canada

When to go: All year
Best for: Canadian LGBTQ+ history

While many libraries have systemically erased the histories of trans and queer Black, Indigenous, and people of color, the ArQuives strives to recover and preserve Canada's LGBTQ+ history. This is no stuffy archive, but more of an interactive museum with photographs, films, artworks, audio recordings, and artifacts. Exhibitions of clothes and banners from historical protests bring Canadian LGBTQ+ history to life.

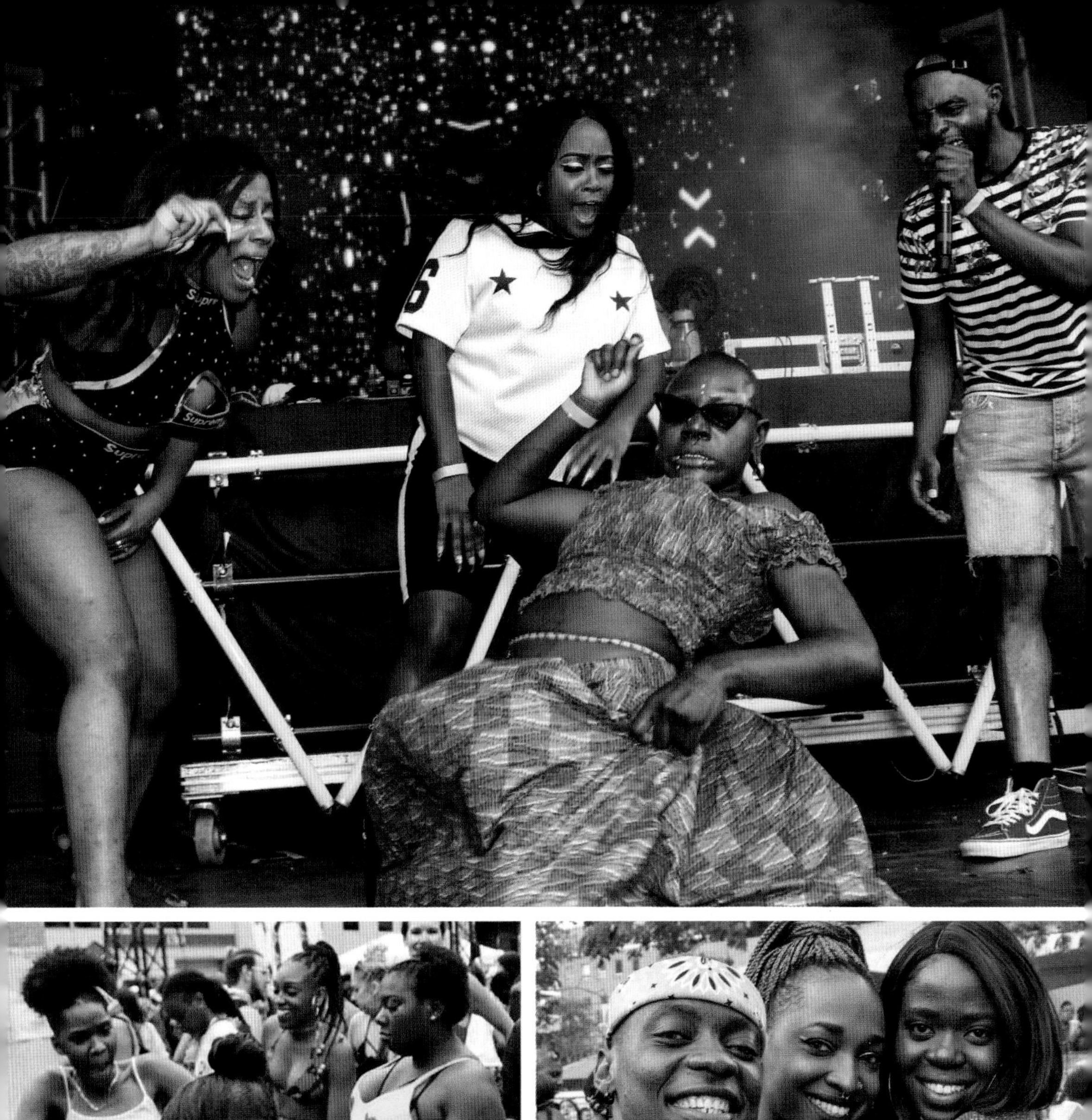

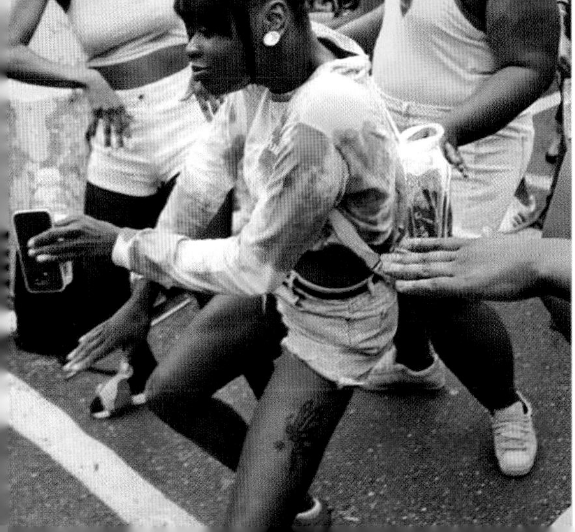

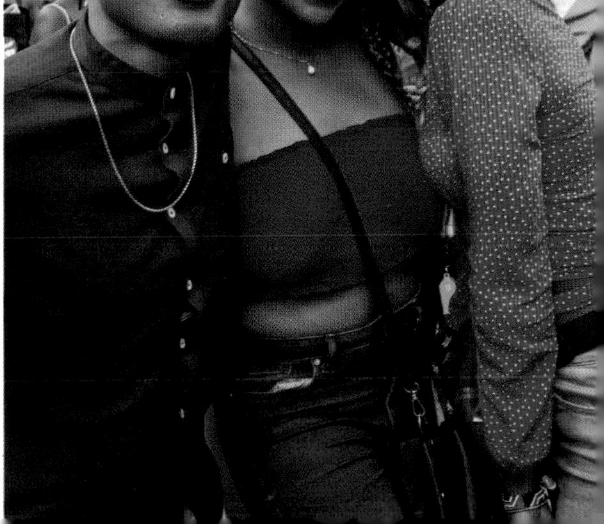

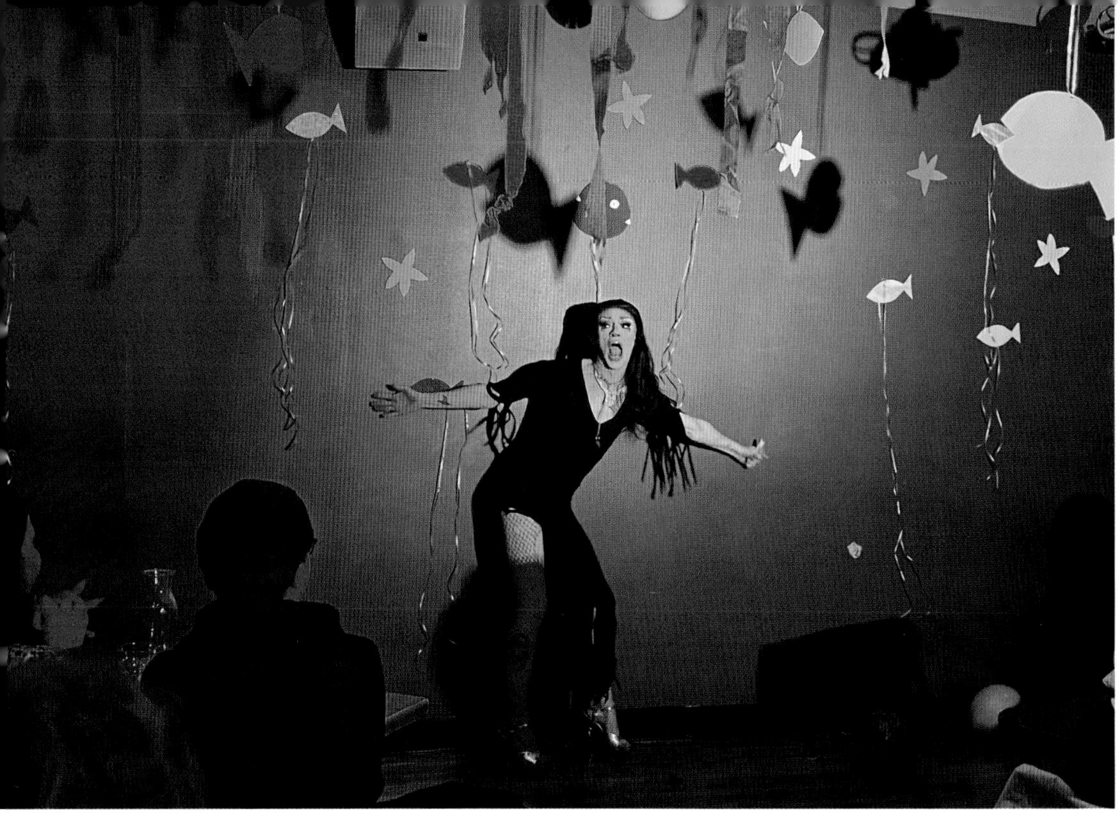

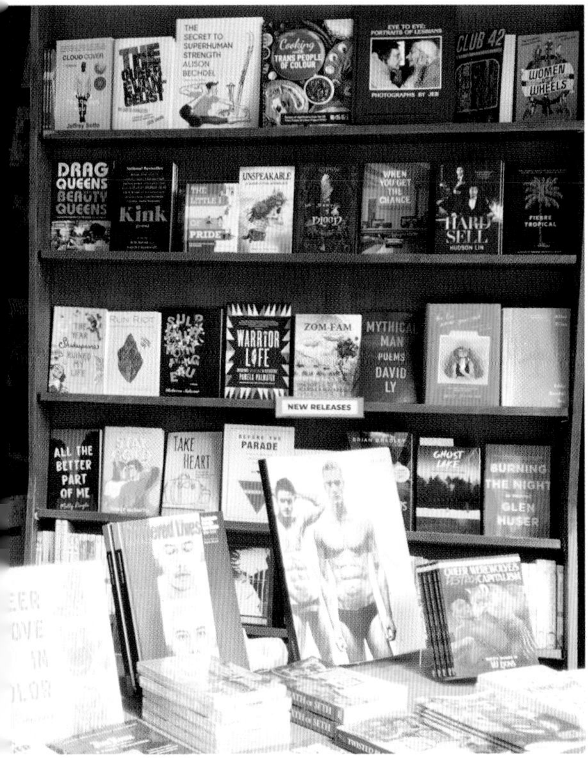

24 The oldest gay bookstore in the world

◀ ▲ Glad Day, Toronto, Canada

When to go: All year
Best for: Drag brunches and bookworms

Glad Day's history dates back to 1970, when activist Jearld Moldenhauer began hauling LGBTQ+ books in a backpack to community meetings. This mobile set-up later transferred to a small, second-story room on Yonge Street. When it outgrew this, and under the guidance of new owners, Glad Day relocated to its current home in 2016. The larger premises allows space for a much-needed café, which hosts popular drag brunches. Glad Day also runs "Naked Heart—The LGBTQ Festival of Words," one of the biggest queer festivals in the world.

25 Reclaim the activism

▶ Anchorage Pride, Alaska, USA

When to go: June
Best for: Keeping the fight alive

Anchorage, which boasts nearly half of the remote, icy US state's population, started out small Pride-wise. In the early years as few as 50 marchers took part, sometimes with bags over their heads to evade persecution. While the event has grown to a week-long celebration, it hasn't lost its activist character. Recent years have featured screenings of films about Stonewall, interactive storytelling, and skill-sharing workshops as well as parties and parades.

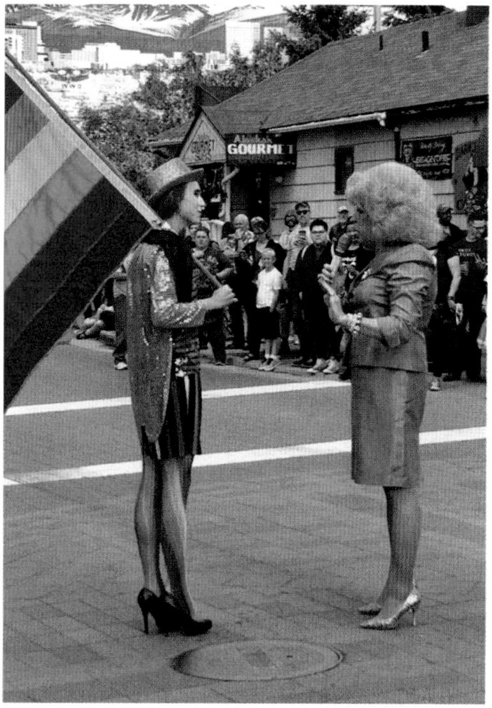

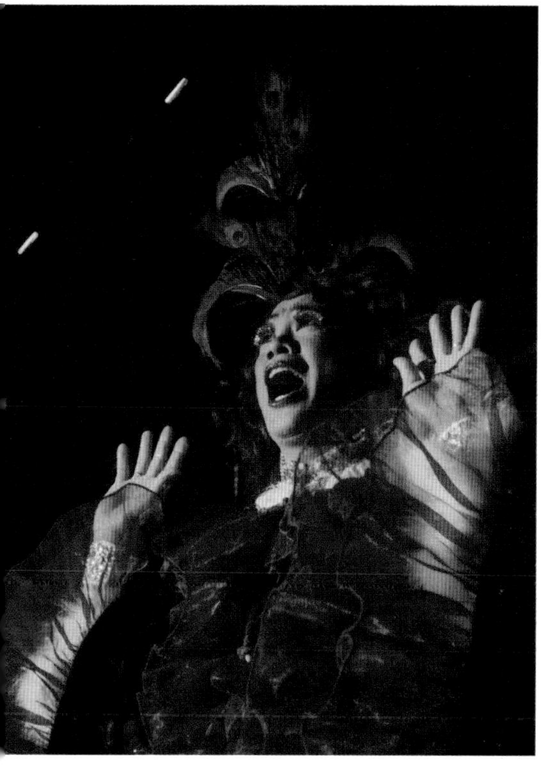

26 Life is a cabaret

◀ Mad Myrna's, Anchorage, Alaska, USA

When to go: All year
Best for: Fabulousness

Mad Myrna's is celebrating over two decades of fabulousness as Anchorage's premiere gay bar and nightclub. There's an event every night of the week, from comedy shows to karaoke, and a popular Diva Variety Show every weekend.

27 Camp at night, camp by day

Some Are Camp, Guerneville, California, USA

When to go: August
Best for: Summer camp "she-nanigans"

Just a couple of hours drive north of San Francisco, at queer-favorite swimming destination the Russian River, Some Are Camp is a three-night, outdoor camping party like no other. Generally, in the summer months Guerneville is a go-to for lazy relaxation, in the river, on an inflatable. For the Some Are Camp weekend, however, that lazy vibe is replaced with an intoxicatingly queer party atmosphere. Expect daytime dancing, swimming, food, and more dancing, with drag queens galore and multiple DJs spinning chill beats in the morning and jams throughout the day. For those less inclined to dance for three days straight, there are costume contests, live music, slip-n-slides, food-eating contests, and semi-quiet nights around multiple campfires—a great way to make new friends.

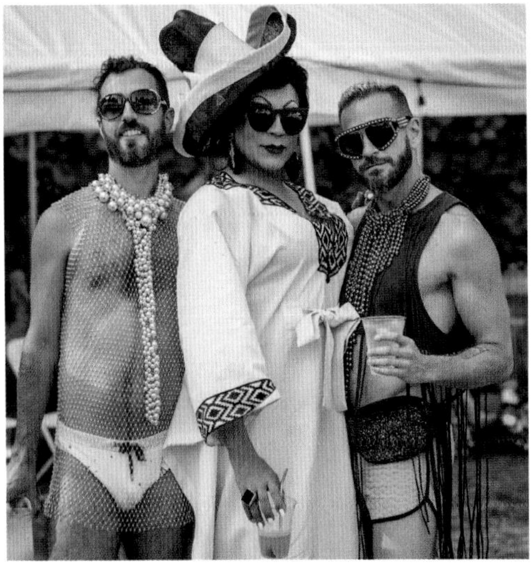

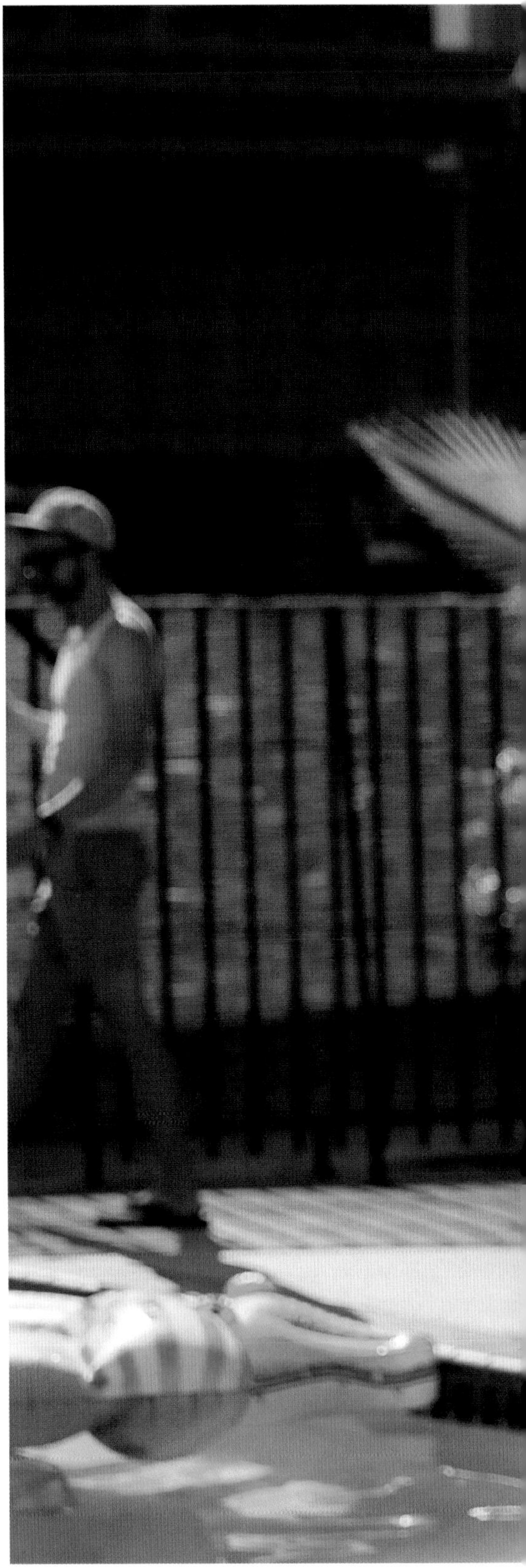

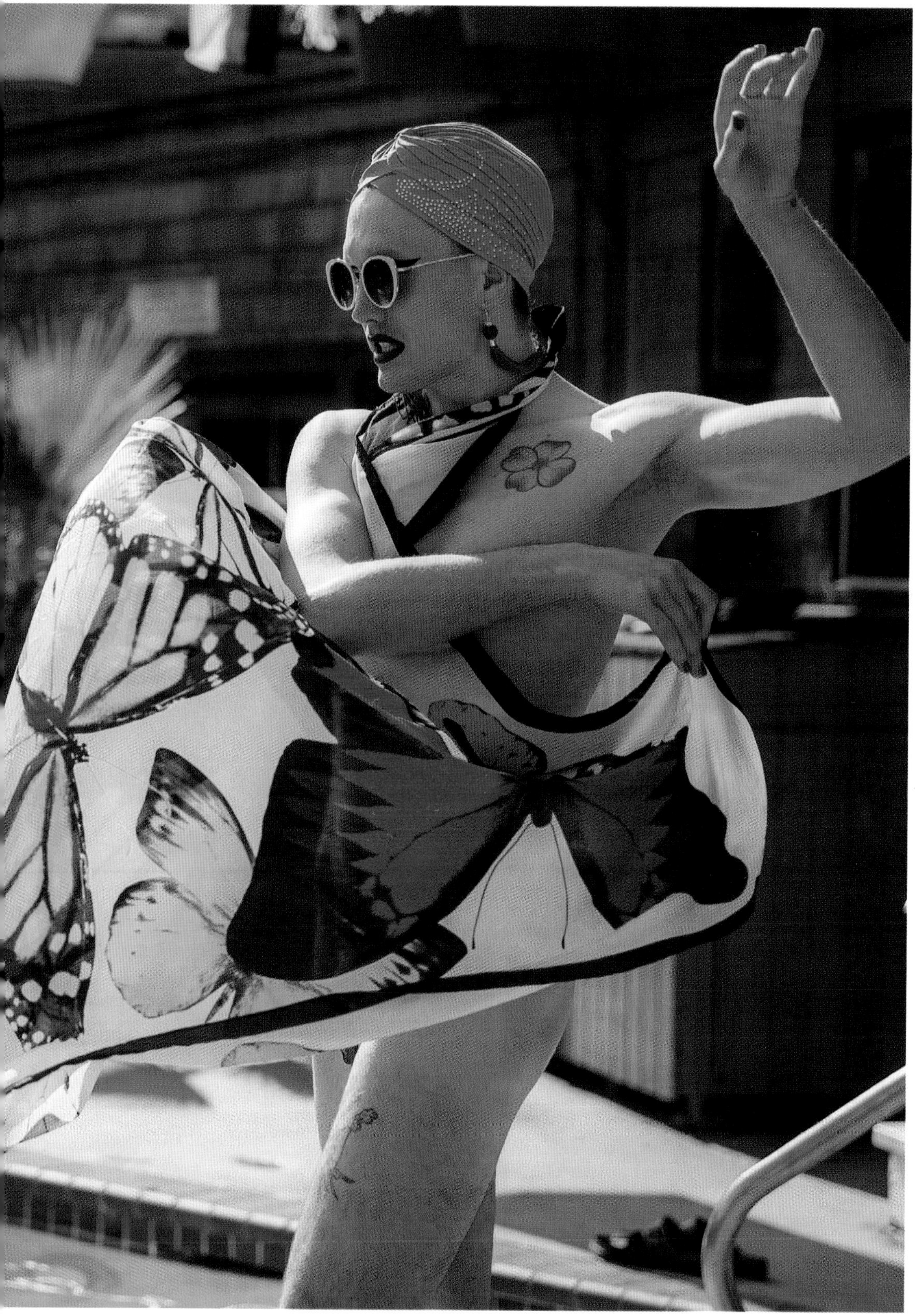

28 From riots to rights

The Transgender District, San Francisco, USA

When to go: All year
Best for: Trans rights in action

San Francisco is well-known for its LGBTQ+ heritage, but its importance to transgender history is often overlooked. In 1966—years before Stonewall—the Compton's Cafeteria riot broke out in the Tenderloin neighborhood, which has been a hub for trans people as far back as the 1920s. An aggressive response to violent police harassment, particularly against trans women, the Compton's riot marked a turning point in the history of trans-activism in San Francisco. The Transgender District, founded in 2017 by three Black trans women, is the first legally recognized trans district in the world, and encompasses six blocks of the Tenderloin. It focuses on tenant protections and economic support for residents of the area, arts, cultural competency, and preserving trans history, and hosts numerous events throughout the year.

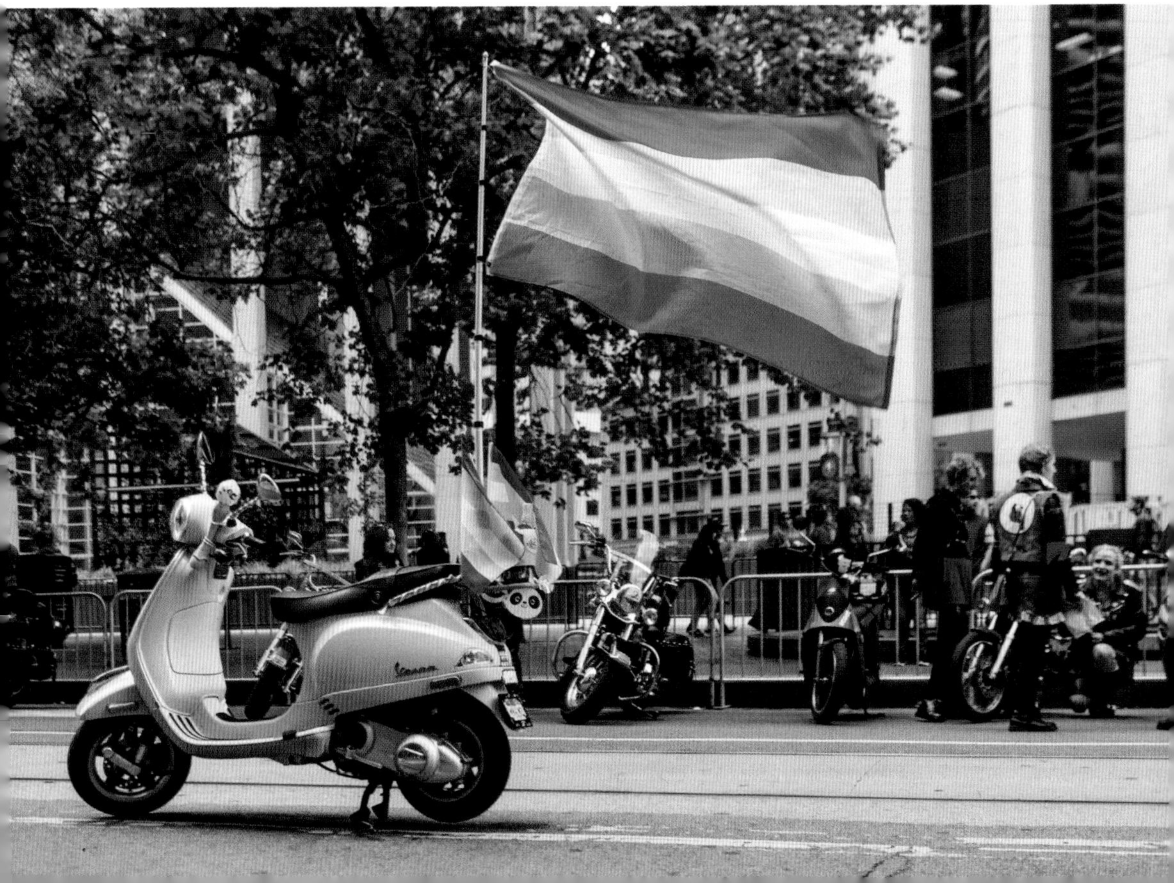

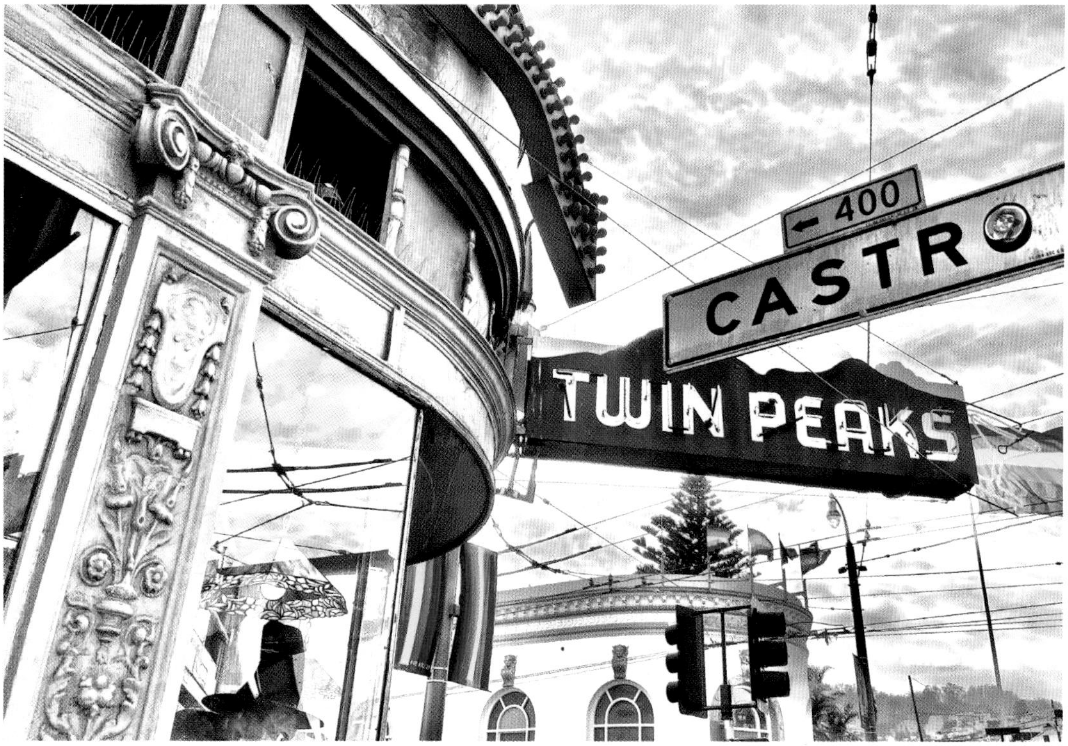

29 Window on a queer world

Twin Peaks, San Francisco, USA

When to go: All year
Best for: Window seats

The Twin Peaks bar is often the first thing people notice when they arrive in the Castro neighborhood. It's directly across from the Castro Muni Station and has an iconic neon sign jutting out from its corner. When the bar turned queer in 1972, its new lesbian owners did something radical: they kept the venue's large windows uncovered. Before this, queer venues had blacked-out windows or hid behind discreet doors. Twin Peaks broke the mold, earning it historic landmark status by the city's Board of Supervisors in 2013.

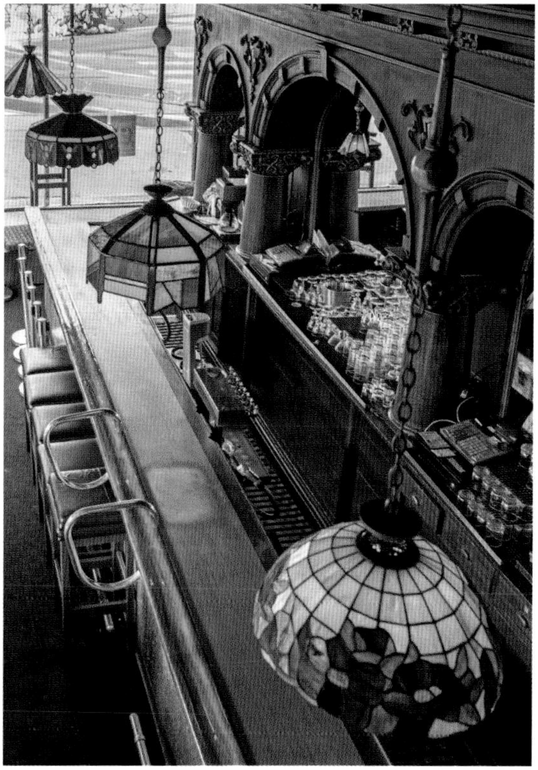

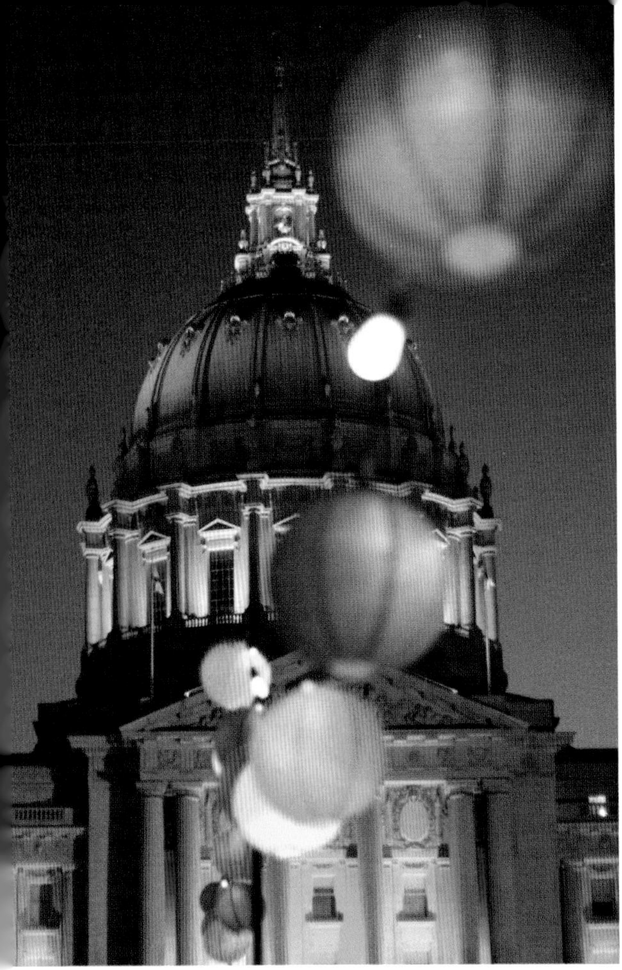

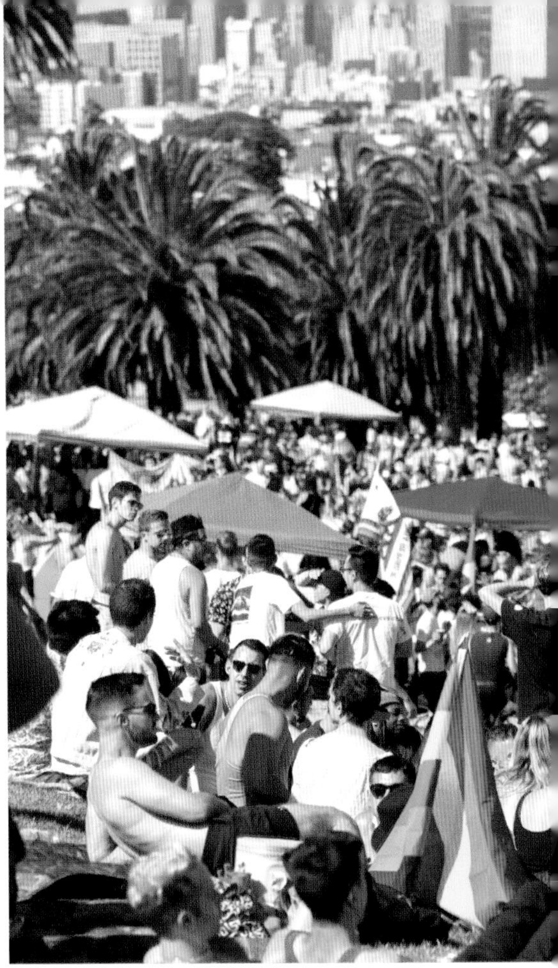

30 Pride for the people

▲ ▶ San Francisco Pride, San Francisco, USA

When to go: June
Best for: City-wide celebrations

With a massive parade, world-class live entertainment, and celebrations across San Francisco for the month of June and beyond, there's a reason SF Pride is legendary. It includes the alternative "People's March," which is critical of the corporate and police influence on the main celebration, and intended to better align with the historical activist spirit of Pride.

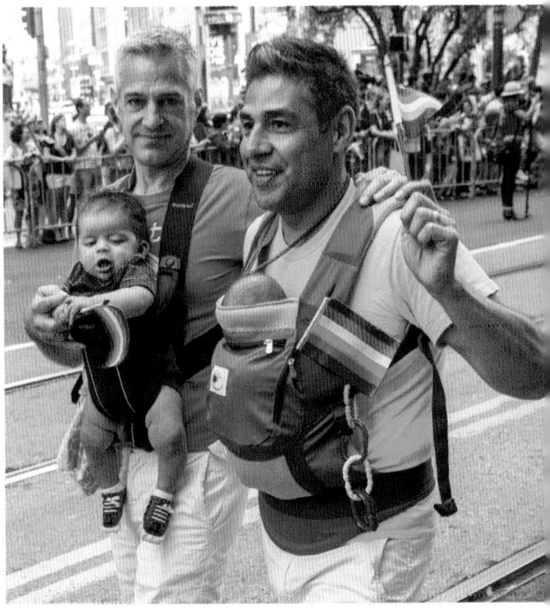

31 Power to the Powwow

▶ Bay Area American Indian Two Spirit (BAAITS) Powwow, San Francisco, USA

When to go: February
Best for: Celebrating US Indigenous heritage

From 1969 to 1971, Native American activists occupied San Francisco Bay's Alcatraz Island, an action that galvanized the country's Indian Rights movement. Four decades later, activists gather on the island for the BAAITS Powwow, now the largest Native LGBTQ+ gathering in the USA, an annual cultural celebration focused on celebrating all LGBTQ+ people by putting Two Spirit communities at the heart and center.

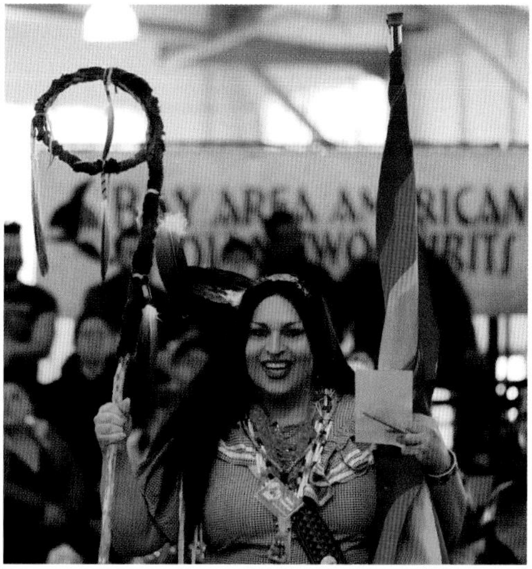

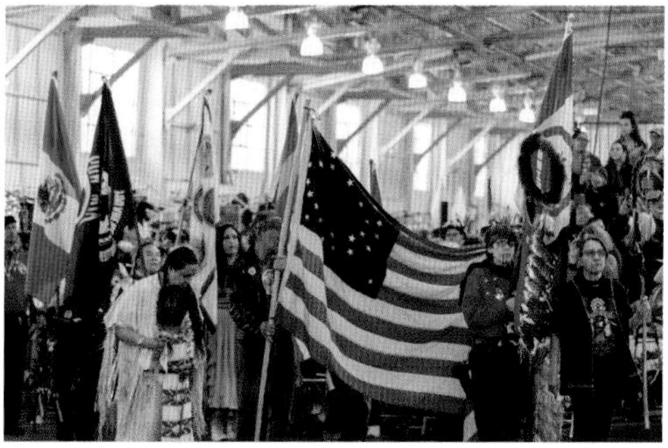

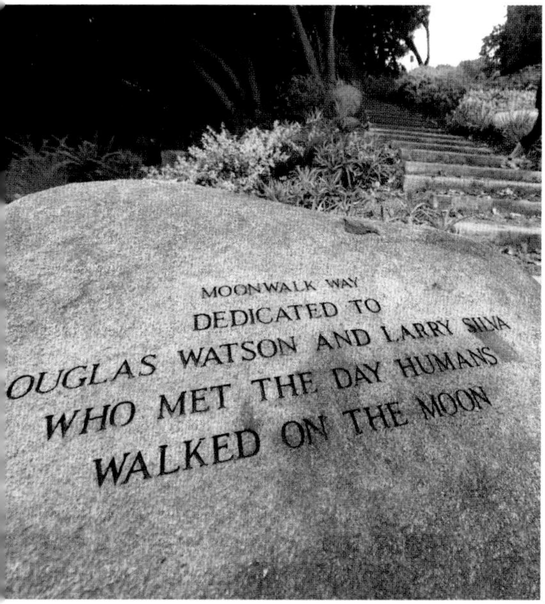

32 Rocks of remembrance

◀ National AIDS Memorial Grove, Golden Gate Park, San Francisco, USA

When to go: All year
Best for: Remembering those gone too soon

Conceived in 1989, when San Francisco was in the grip of the AIDS pandemic, the National AIDS Memorial Grove is a place of remembrance and catharsis for those who have been affected by HIV or who have lost loved ones. This beautifully maintained woodland grotto has rocks which bear the names of those no longer with us.

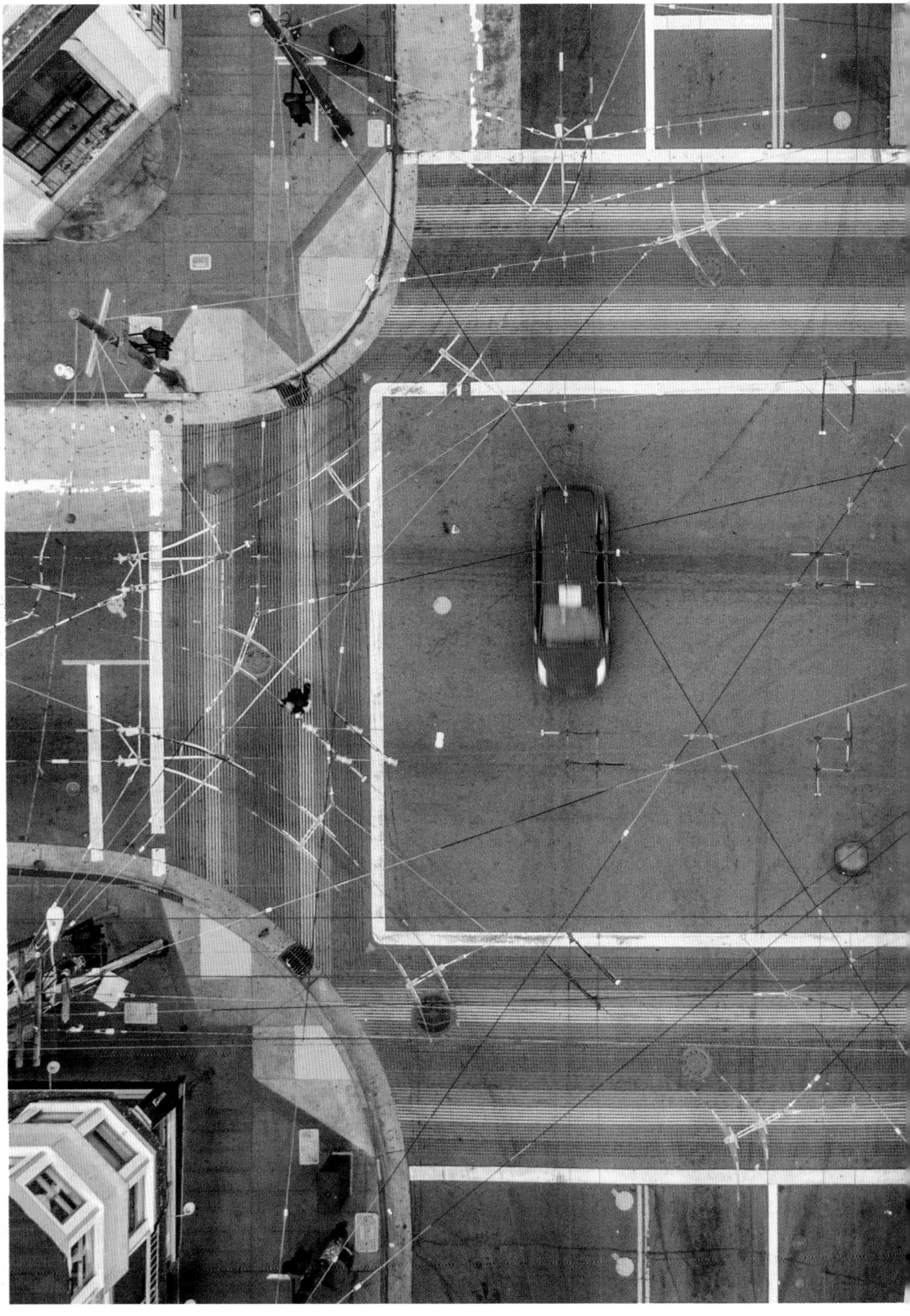

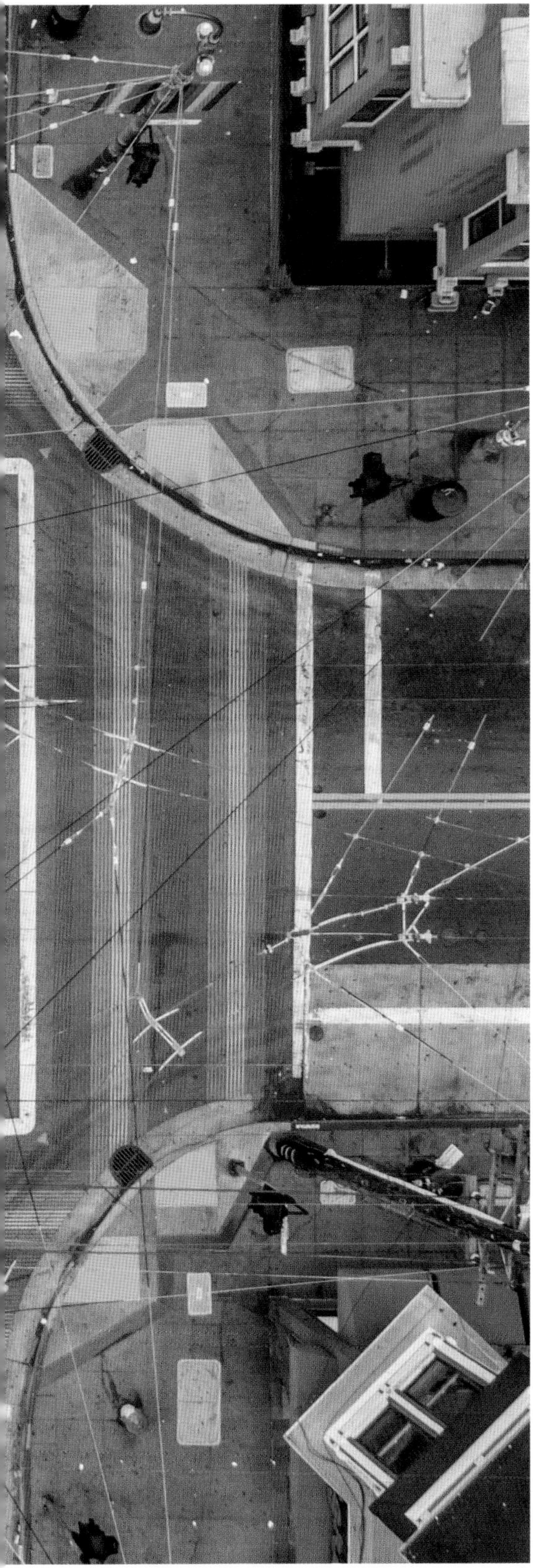

33 Colorful Castro

The Castro District, San Francisco, USA

When to go: All year
Best for: Feeling surrounded by queer history

Castro District is unmissable: rainbow streetwalks, banners on the streetlights, and rainbow murals greet you. At the rainbow-colored 18th Street and Castro Street intersection, you're standing at the heart of one of the oldest gayborhoods in the USA. Castro's rich LGBTQ+ history—starting in the 1960s—surrounds you. If you look down Castro Street, you can see where Harvey Milk opened his Old Camera Shop. Back then, the gay bar Harvey's—on the corner—was called Elephant Walk, which was targeted and damaged by the police after the White Night Riots. Learn more about San Francisco's world-changing queer history at the GLBT Historical Society Museum. Walk the Rainbow Honor Walk to celebrate LGBTQ+ trailblazers, or join a walking tour to hear from a queer local.

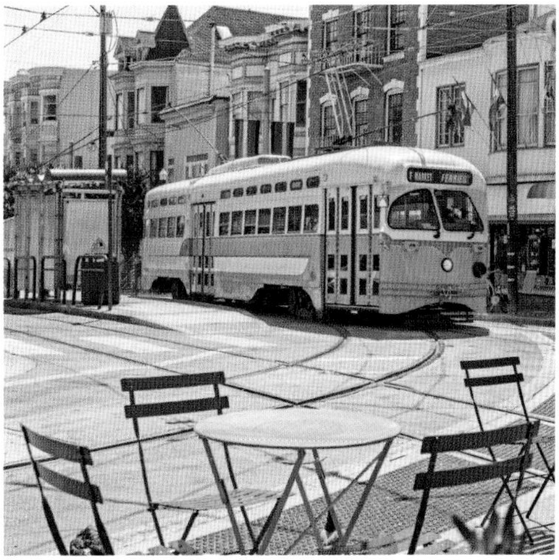

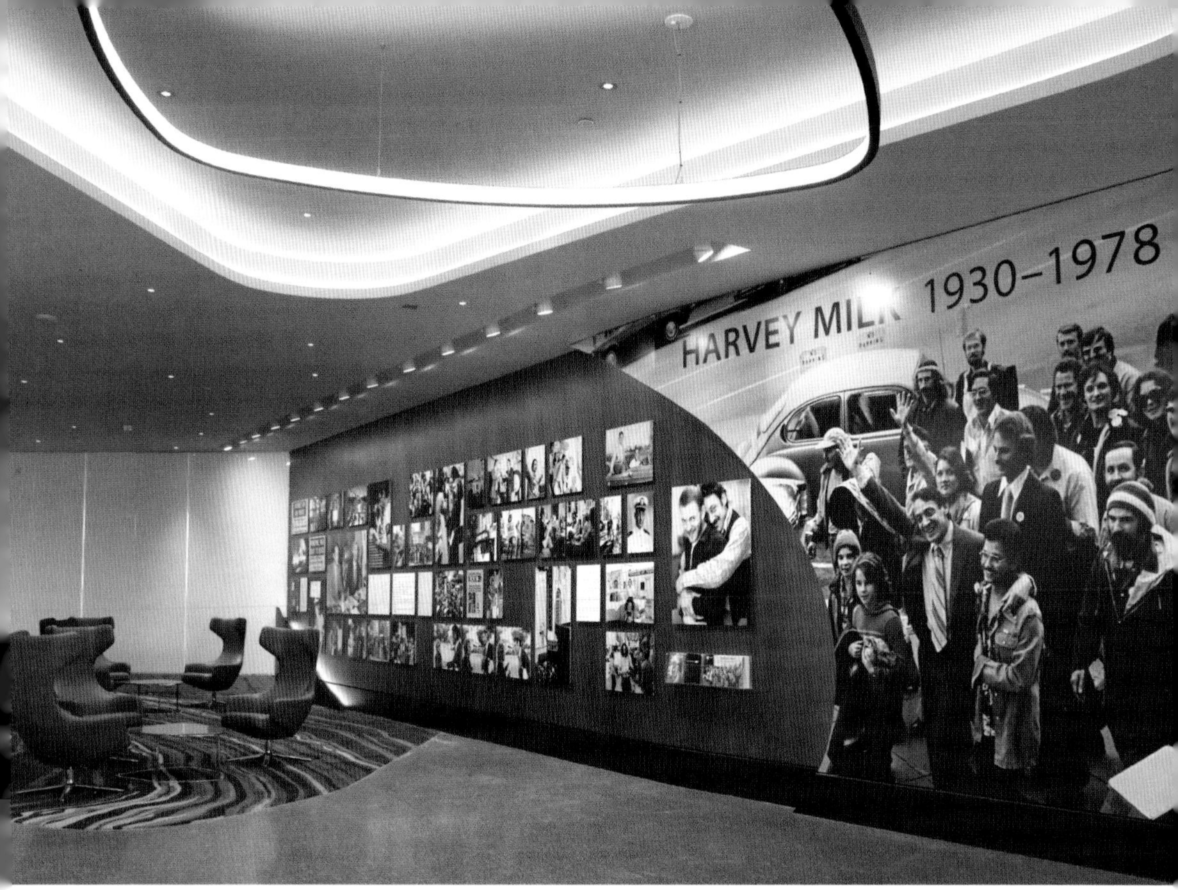

34 San Francisco's big, gay welcome

▲ Harvey Milk Terminal One, San Francisco International Airport, San Francisco, USA

When to go: All year
Best for: Remembering a hero

Harvey Milk was assassinated in 1978, a year after becoming the first out, gay-elected official in California. In his memory, San Francisco International Airport named its revamped terminal "Harvey Milk Terminal 1" in 2019, complete with a permanent display about Milk's life. It's often lit up in rainbow colors during Pride season.

35 Short ones are more juicy

San Francisco Transgender Film Festival, San Francisco, USA

When to go: November
Best for: Cutting-edge trans films

Founded in 1997, San Francisco Transgender Film Festival has a legacy of punk aesthetic and community activism. The festival, one of the first trangender film festivals in the world, screens almost exclusively short films, actively carves out a space for subversive trans-made work, and may be the only trans film festival to hold an evening of purely 18+ films.

36 Drink up, get down

▼ ▶ Gay Wine Week(end), Sonoma, California, USA

When to go: July
Best for: World-class wine

Sonoma County in California is known to produce some of the best wines in the world—and for being a lovely relaxation destination with its gorgeous rolling hills, pleasant weather, and excellent restaurants. It's a high-end, LGBTQ+ vacation spot, especially during Gay Wine Weekend. Visitors from around the world flock to the area for wine tastings and tours, relaxing pool parties, drag brunches, and classy soireés at fancy hotels.

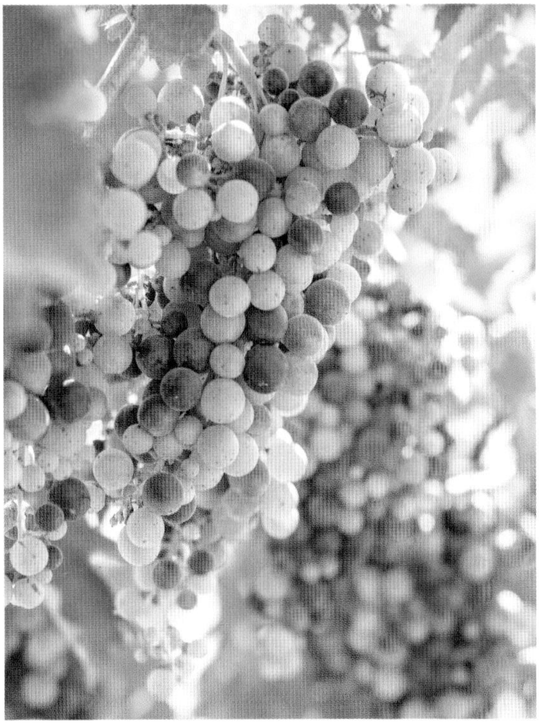

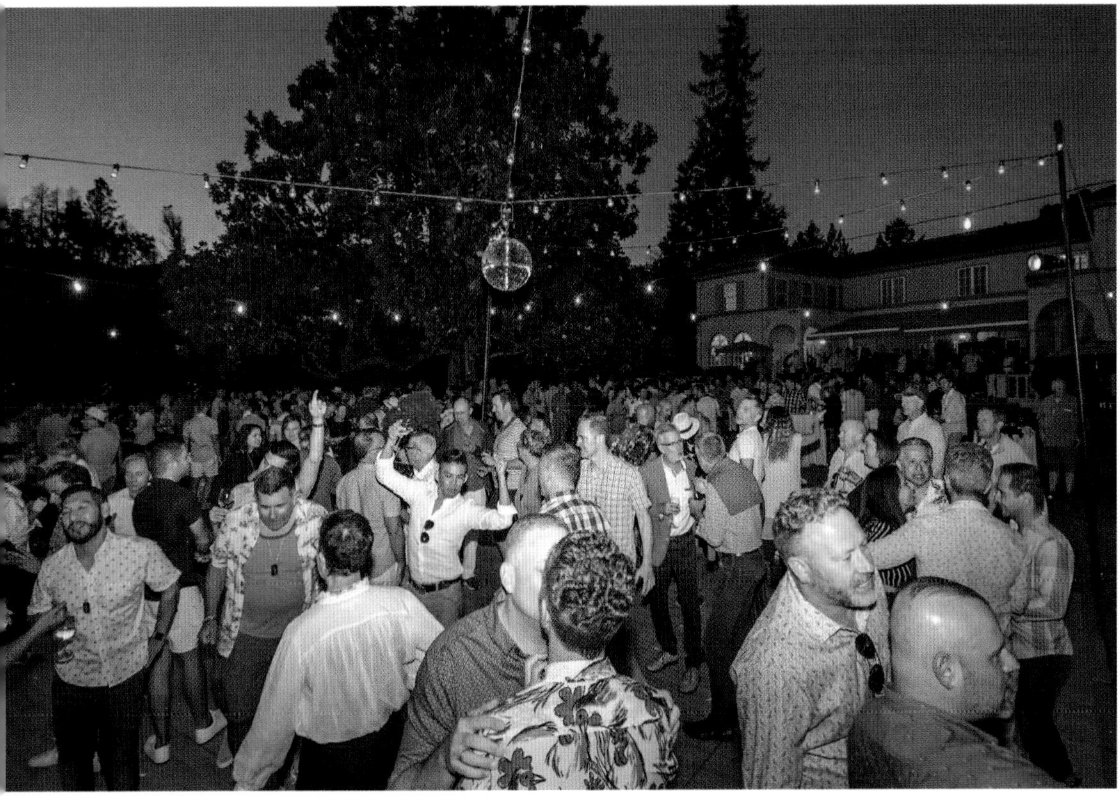

37 Paradise by a beach bar at night

Hula's Bar and Lei Stand, Honolulu, Hawaii, USA

When to go: All year
Best for: Sunset Mai Tais

This legendary Honolulu gay bar does the basics, but extremely well: excellent food and drinks, quality live music, a perfect beachfront location, and proud promotion of the "aloha" spirit.

38 True lesbian royalty

▼ Iolani Palace, Honolulu, Hawaii, USA

When to go: All year
Best for: History lessons

In 1893, an American sugar planter, with the support of the US government, organized a coup in Hawaii and overthrew Queen Liliuokalani, the reigning monarch. Liliuokalani's great-grand niece, Abigail Kawananakoa, is a lesbian and the current heir to the last line of Hawaiian royals if a restoration of the monarchy ever occurs. Iolani Palace—which was the home of the Hawaiian monarchy—is the only official royal residence in the United States and it's now considered the "spiritual and physical multicultural epicenter of Hawaii."

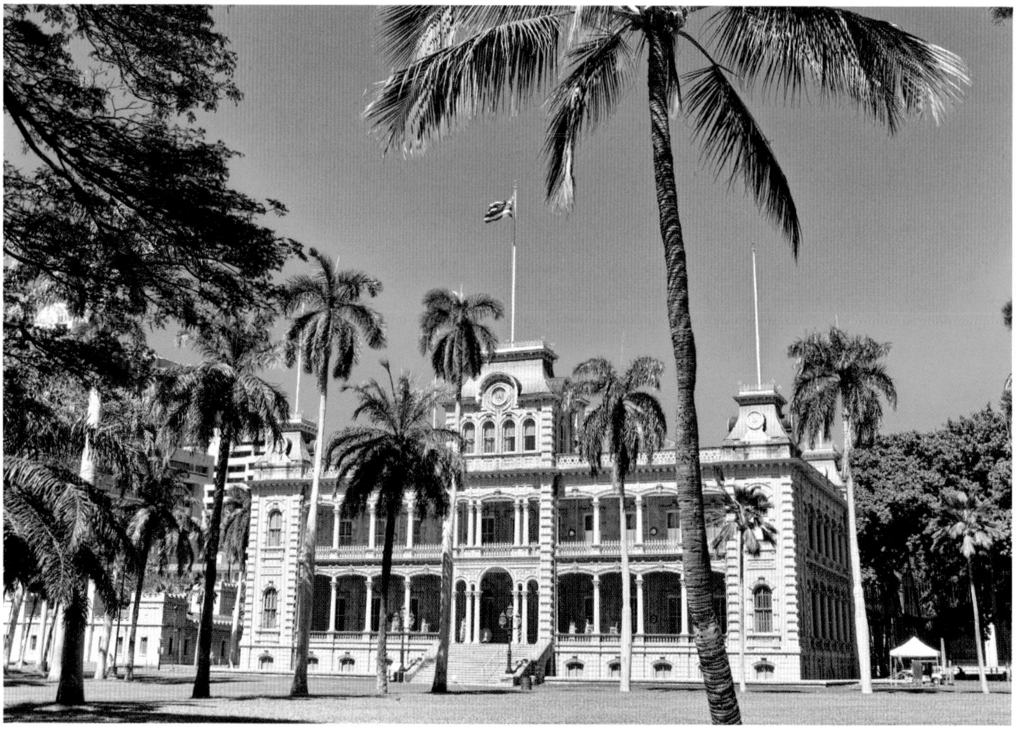

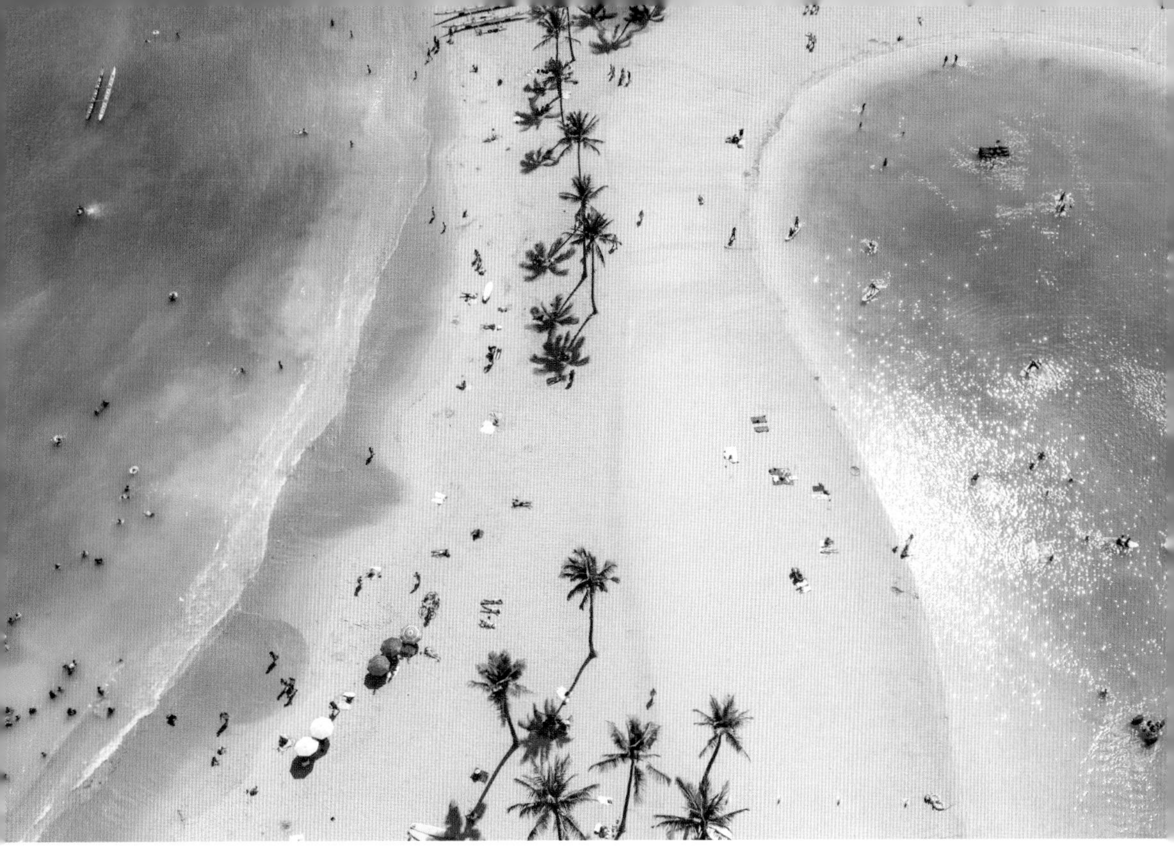

39 Soak up the sun

▲ ▶ Waikiki, Hawaii, USA

When to go: All year
Best for: Being gay in paradise

Hawaii is lovely to visit year-round, but late spring or late fall have fewer crowds and lower prices. The epicenter of LGBTQ-Hawaii is Waikiki, home to queer-friendly hotels, bars, and nightclubs, including Hula's, as well as "gay beach" Queen Surf. It's pretty close to downtown, so no nudity or cruising is allowed—if you're looking for that, Diamond Head beach below the lighthouse is slightly more secluded and permissive.

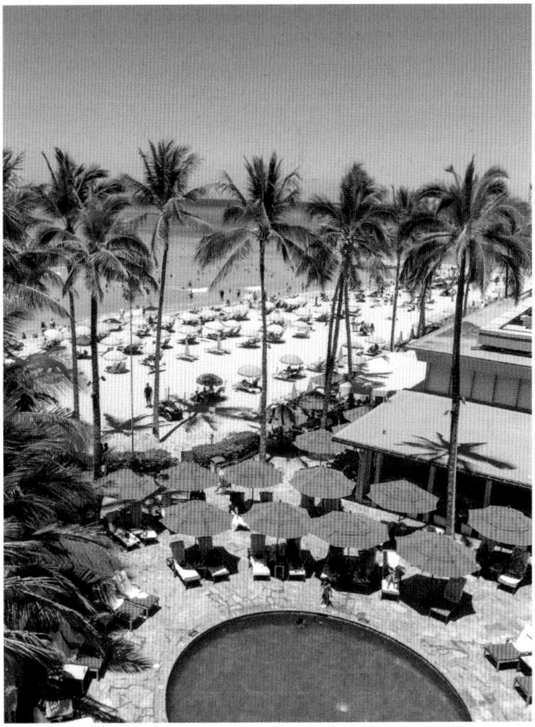

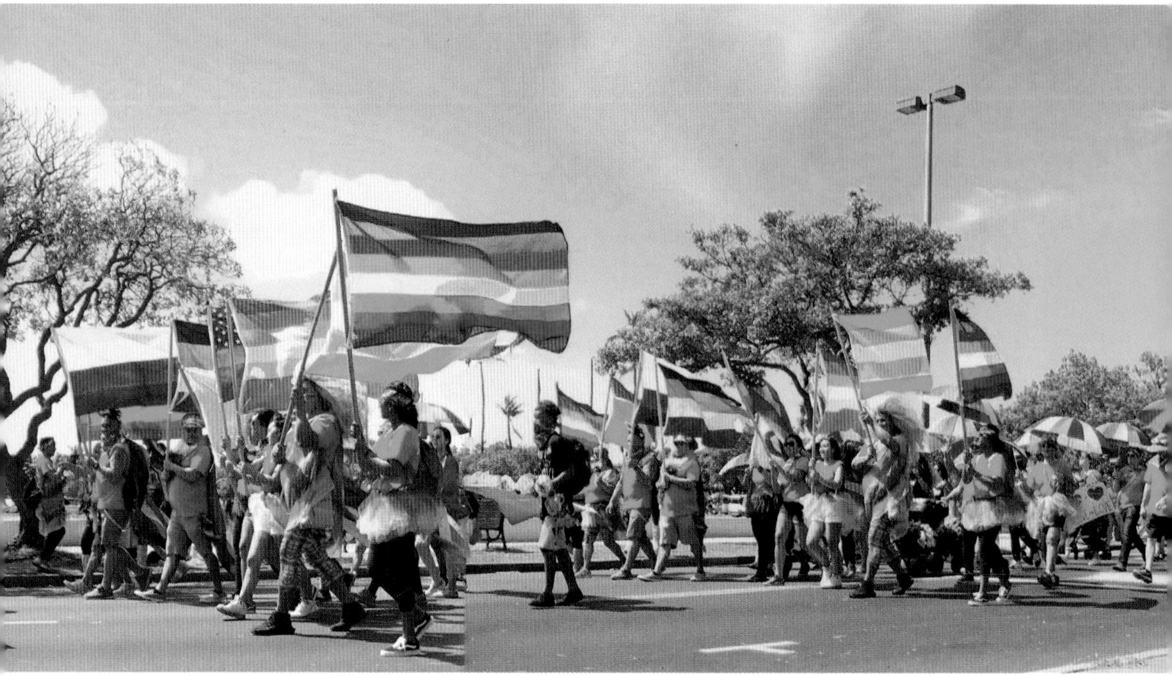

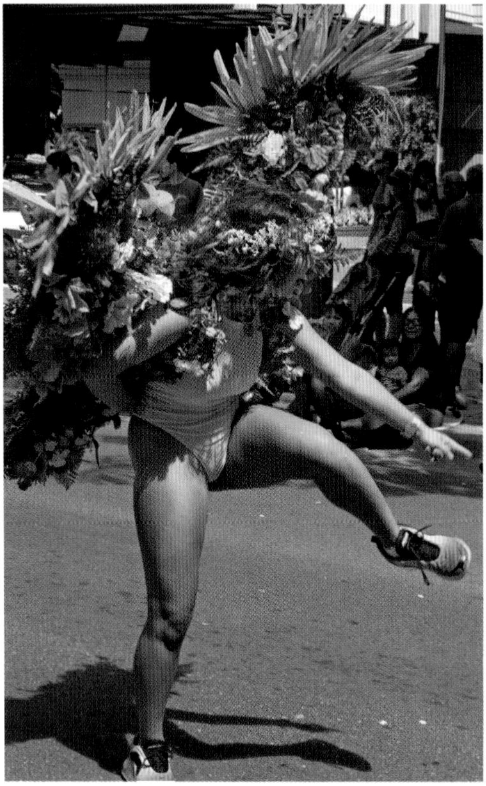

40 Hawaii Pride-O

◀ ▲ Honolulu Pride, Hawaii, USA

When to go: October
Best for: Gays and leis

Like many other Pride celebrations, Honolulu's features educational events, dance parties, and bar specials day and night, as well as a major parade and festival. Unlike many others, it occurs in October—it's essentially summer year-round in Hawaii—and has a strong emphasis on celebrating Hawaii's Indigenous culture. Film screenings, celebrations of diversity, and cultural events throughout the month complement the big parade and festival on October 15.

41 Keep it weird

▼ Portland Pride, Portland, Oregon, USA

When to go: June
Best for: A very slightly weirder Pride experience

The "Keep Portland Weird" ethos is in full effect, especially during Pride. Portland banned police from the parade, for example, and it frequently features a drag race—a high-heels-encouraged running race!

42 Move to the groove

Portland Gay Skate, Portland, Oregon, USA

When to go: First and third Mondays of the month
Best for: Showing out on the go

Roller skating has always been a little queer—roller derby, anyone?—and Portland's Gay Skate is more popular than ever thanks to TikTok. Gay Skate is a blast for both long-term skaters and new enthusiasts for the sport.

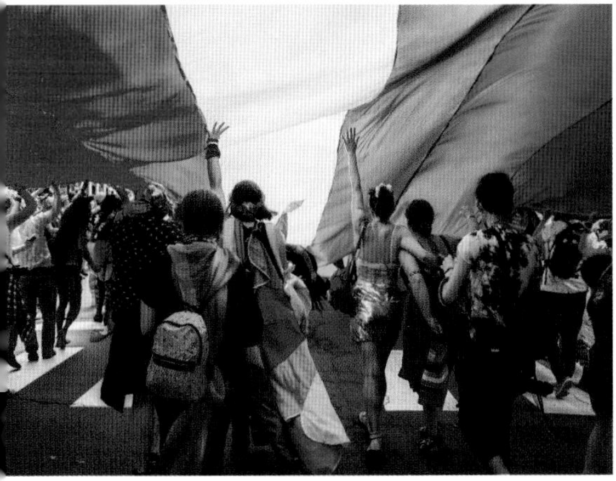

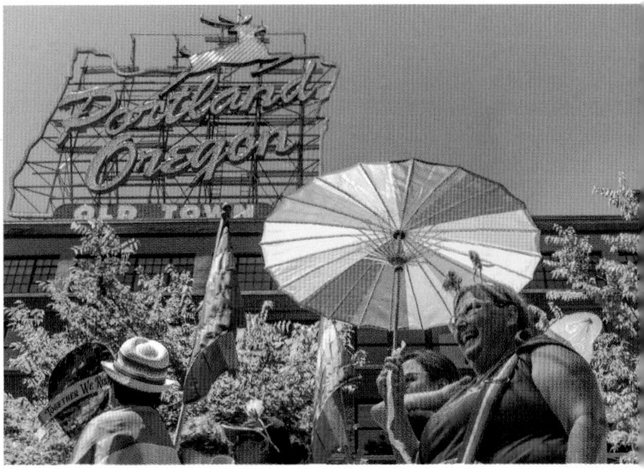

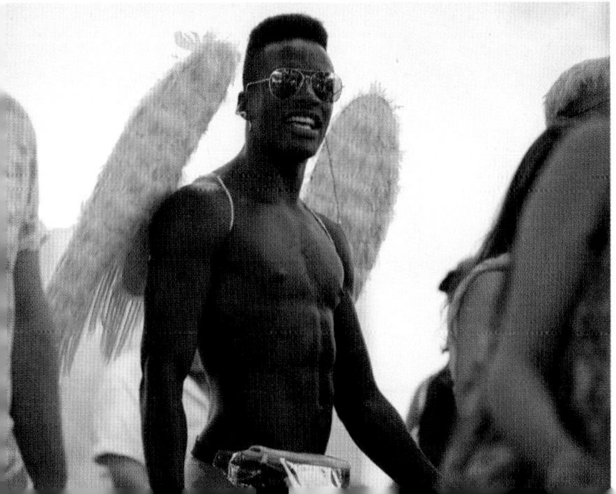

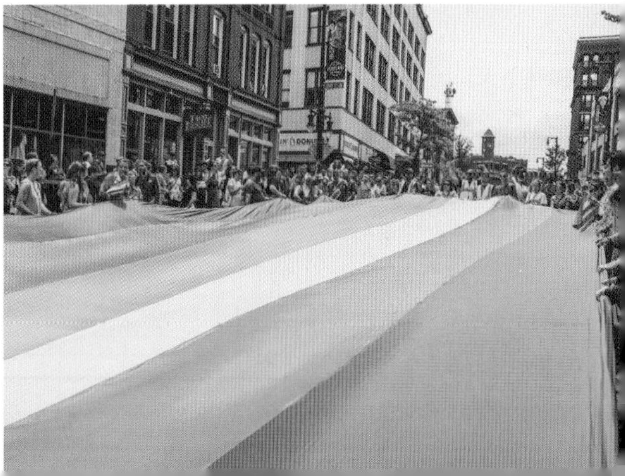

43 Hello cowboy

Copper Cactus Ranch, Arizona, USA

When to go: Anytime but August (when it's closed)
Best for: Chilling in the desert

Copper Cactus is a men's retreat in the foothills of the Superstition Mountains, next to Tonto National Forest. Explore the local, cactus-lined trails including the Peralta Trails, chill in the pool, gaze at the cosmos in the brilliantly clear night sky, or take part in a clothing-optional drum circle around the fire pit.

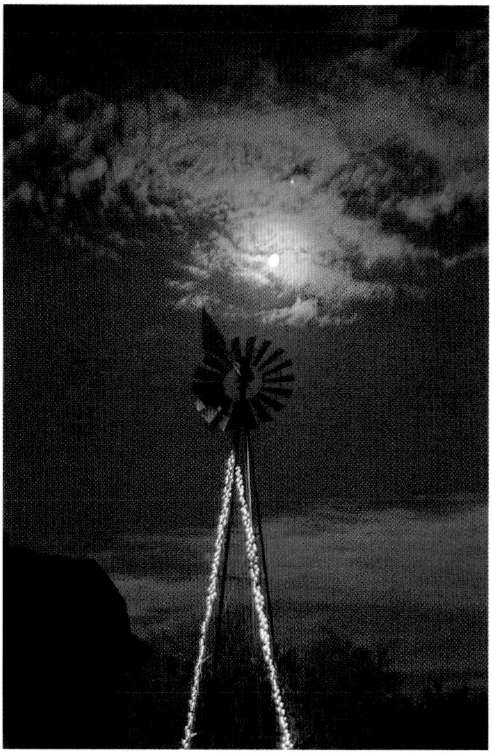

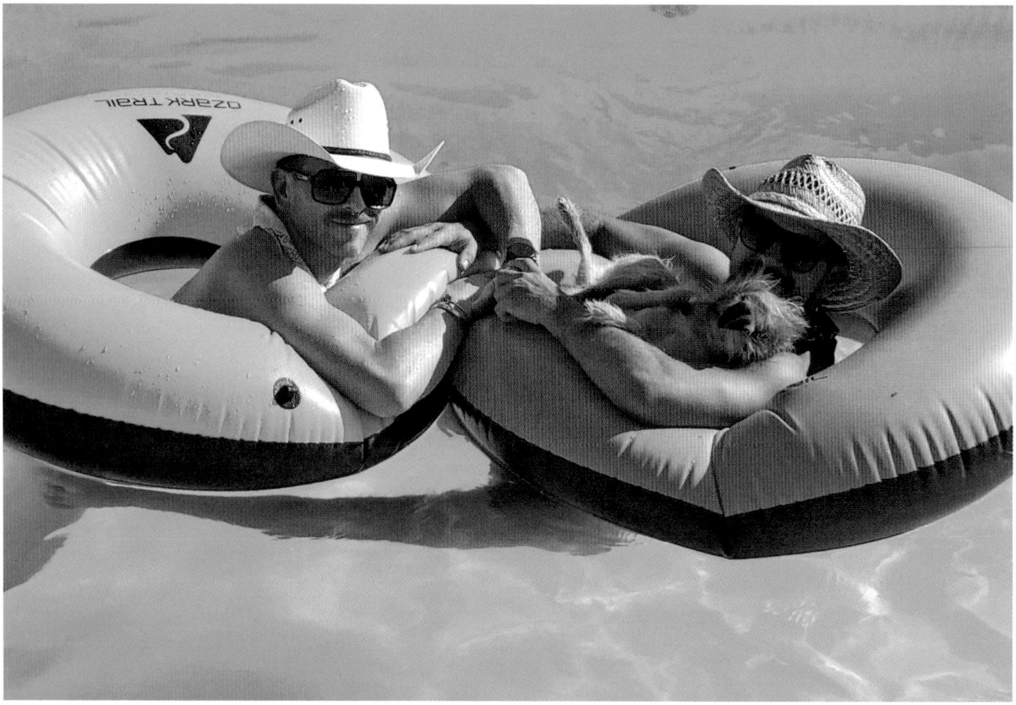

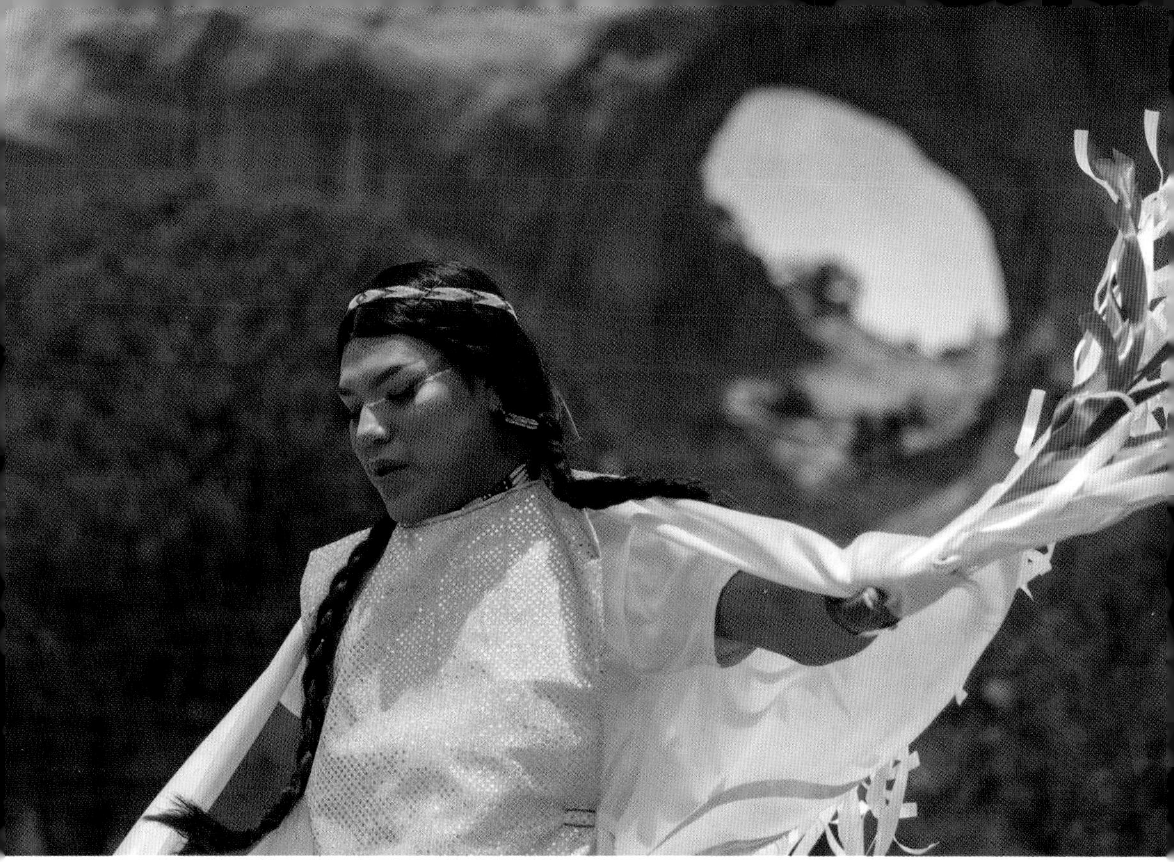

44 Reclaim the nation

Navajo Nation Pride, Window Rock, Arizona, USA

When to go: June
Best for: Celebration through decolonization

The Navajo community asserts that, prior to colonization, forced relocation, and compulsory boarding-school attendance, its culture affirmed and even revered LGBTQ+ community members and especially transgender women. This reclamation of history is one of the primary goals of Navajo Nation Pride, the largest Indigenous Pride celebration in the USA. In addition to music and a parade, Indigenous perspectives are foregrounded via a number of storytelling events.

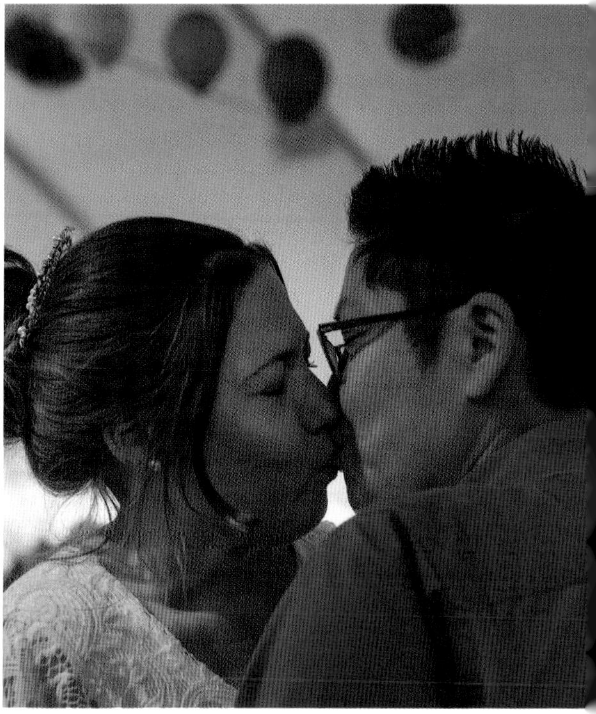

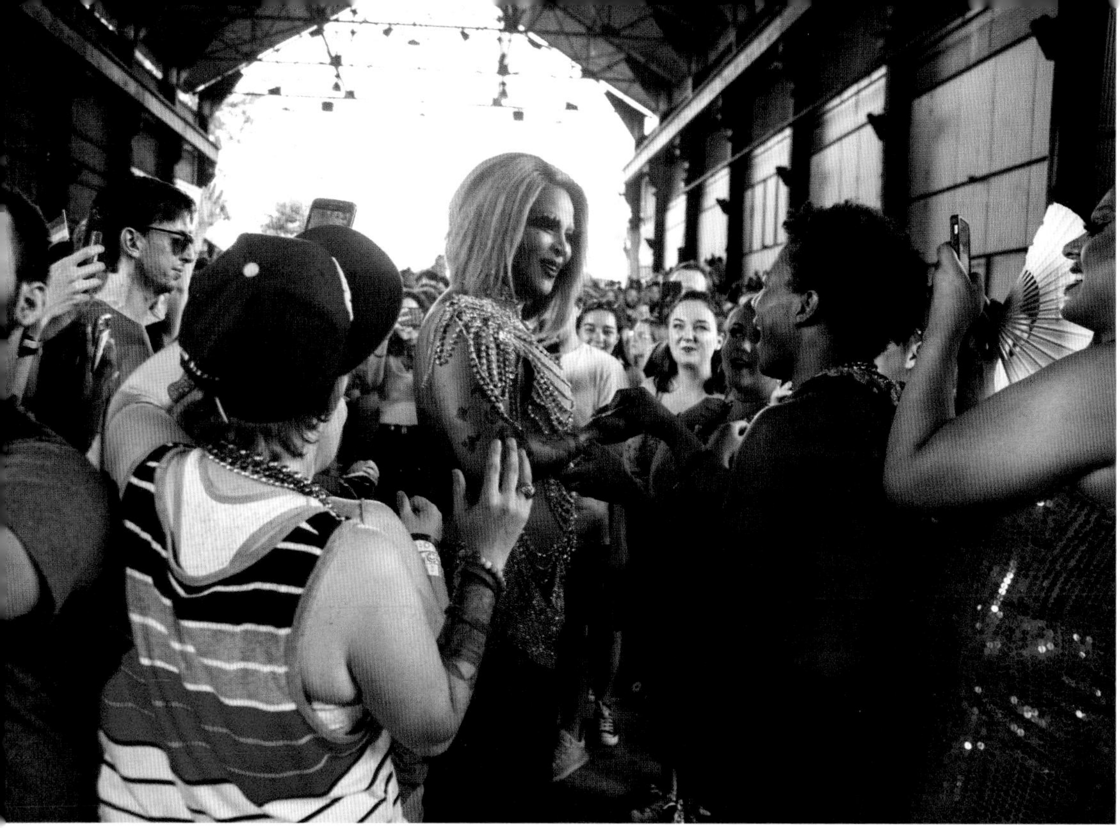

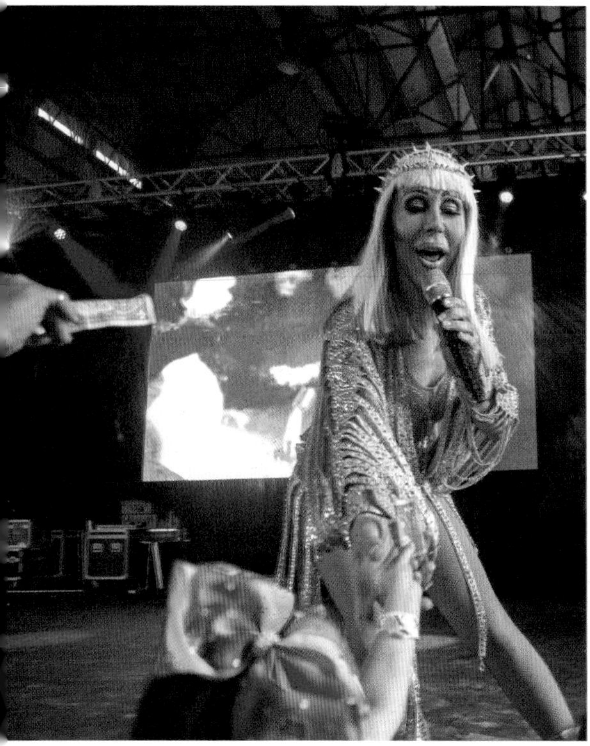

45 Southern-fried Pride

◀ ▲ Central Alabama Pride, Birmingham, USA

When to go: April or June
Best for: Eschewing stereotypes

Despite sharing a reputation with the rest of the American South as conservative and largely anti-LGBTQ+, Birmingham is a diverse major city with a burgeoning queer scene and a Pride festival to make it visible. Central Alabama Pride features pageants in which queer, trans, non-binary, and drag performers compete to secure the titles of Mister, Ms, Miss, MR, and Mx Central Alabama Pride.

46 Don't drink at the rink

▼ Rainbow Skate Night, Glendale, California, USA

When to go: Wednesday nights
Best for: Sober fun on wheels

Bringing queer people and allies from all over the Los Angeles area, Rainbow Skate Night at Moonlight Rollerway is a purposely sober event that gives LGBTQ+ communities a fun social alternative to the bar scene.

47 Sing your heart out

White Horse Bar, Oakland, California, USA

When to go: Monday or Tuesday nights
Best for: Belting an off-beat tune to an off-beat crowd

Possibly the oldest continuously operating gay bar in the United States, the White Horse is an institution that has seen it all. Today, it's one of the East Bay Area's best queer hangouts with its relaxed, divey feel. It's especially popular among lesbians. Don't miss its epic karaoke nights.

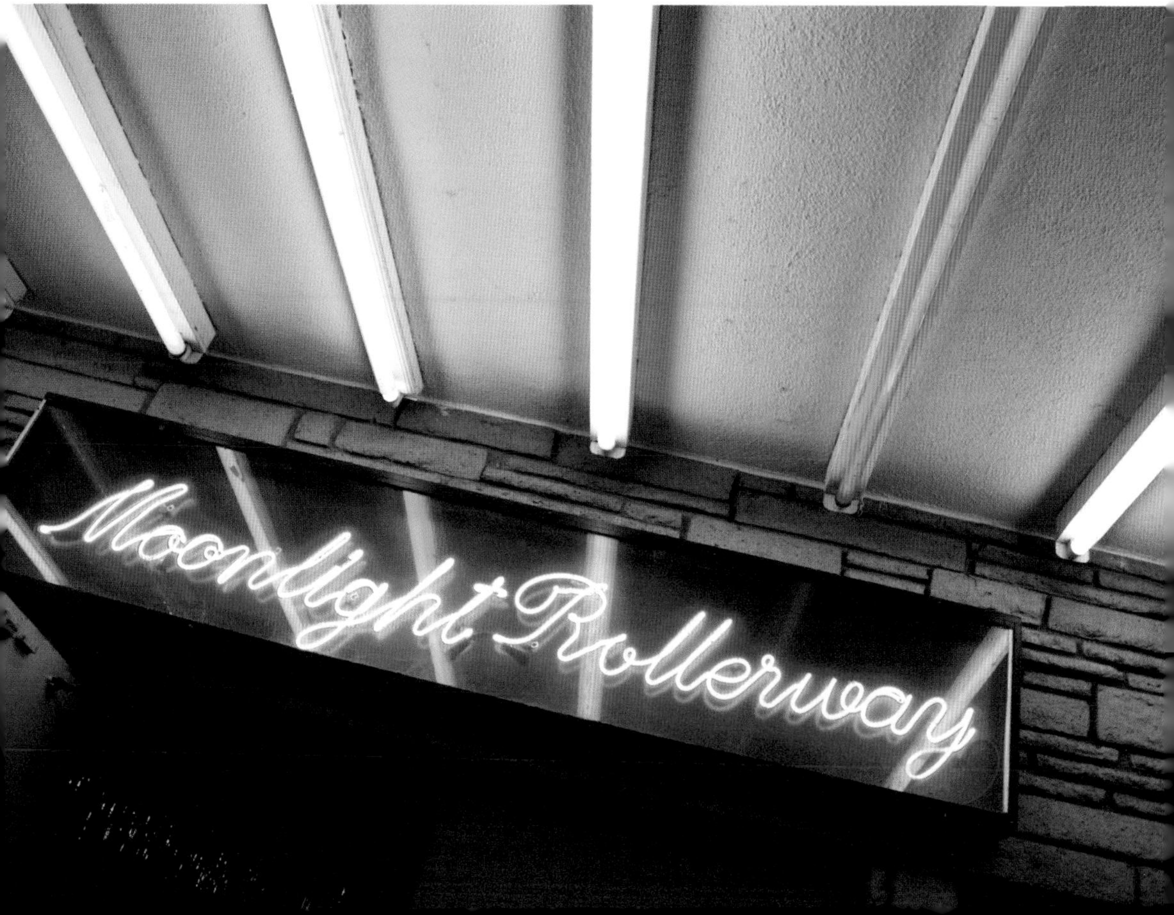

48 Street talking

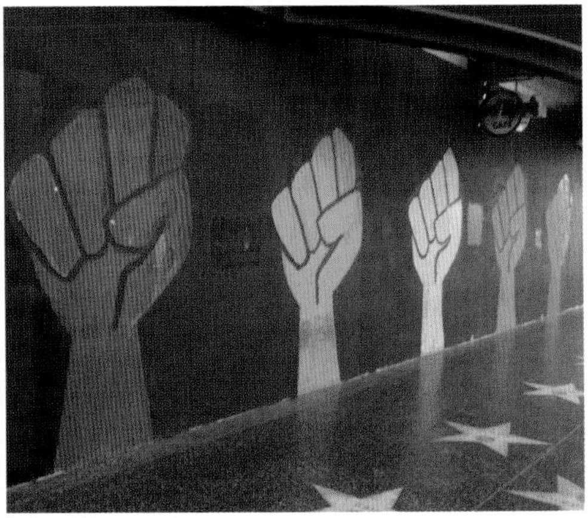

▼▶ All Black Lives Matter Mural, Los Angeles, USA

When to go: All year
Best for: Black queer modern history

What started out as a temporary art piece, painted by hundreds of volunteers on June 13, 2020, is now memorialized on the streets of Hollywood Boulevard following a push for a more permanent tribute. Honoring the Black Lives Matter movement, this mural features colors from the non-binary, transgender, and rainbow Pride flags.
As you walk down this street, you just might be able to imagine what it must have been like to take part in the All Black Lives Matter protest in 2020, which saw 40,000 people marching down this very road to amplify Black queer voices. This recreation of the original mural is undoubtedly an important part of our queer history.

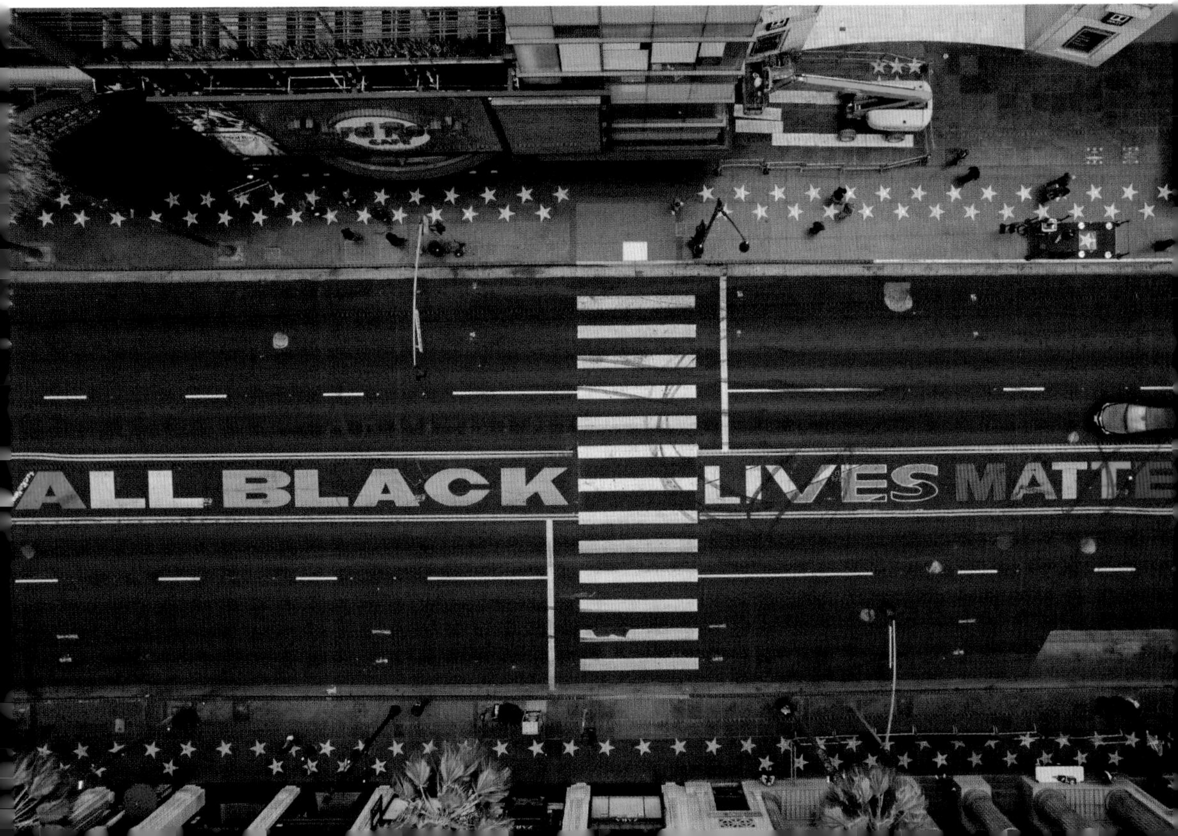

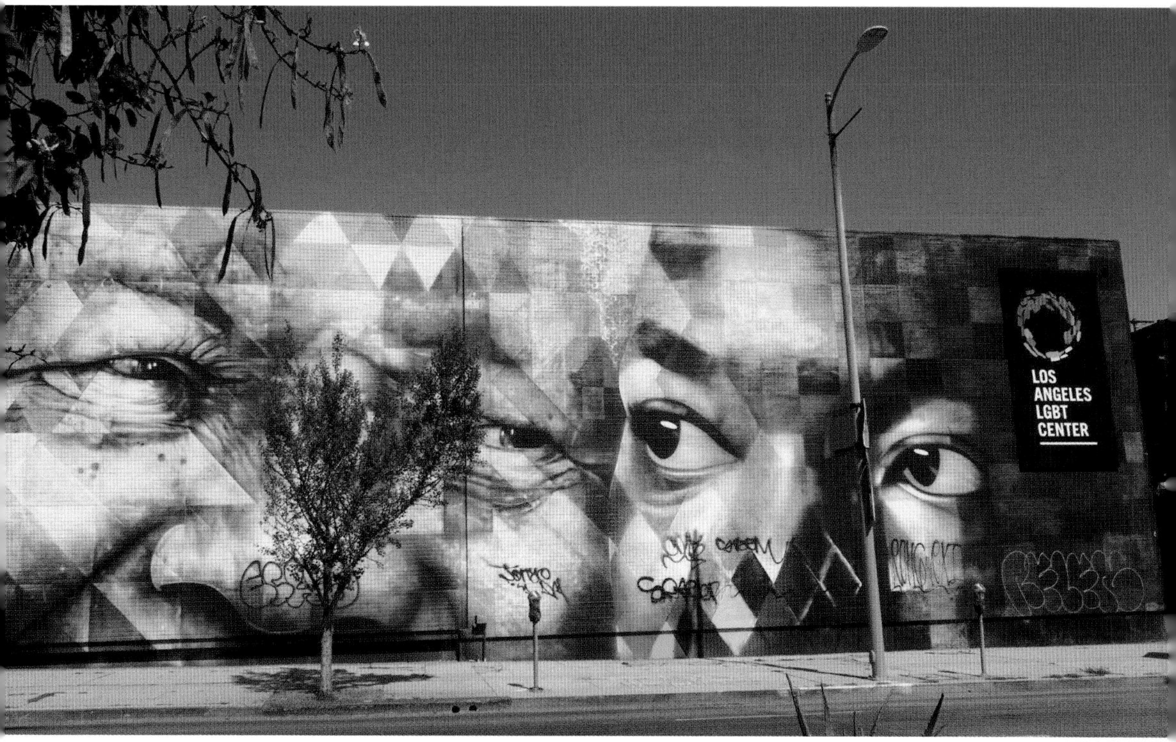

49 You can't be it if you can't see it

Outfest Film Festival, Los Angeles, USA

When to go: April or August
Best for: Film buffs

Outfest is more than just a film festival; it's also a nonprofit organization that empowers LGBTQ+ filmmakers by not just screening their films, but supporting their careers, too. The film festival takes place in August, while Outfest Fusion, a festival focused specifically on LGBTQ+ filmmakers of color, takes place in April. Both are a must for any queer film-lover, and are accessible both in-person and through online streaming.

50 The heart of the matter

▲ The Los Angeles LGBT Center, Los Angeles, USA

When to go: All year
Best for: Looking after yourself, body and soul

The Los Angeles LGBT Center is one of the biggest LGBT centers in the world, with over eight hundred employees. It's also one of the most respected. Beginning life back in 1969, it has grown to cover multiple venues, with its headquarters now located at its Anita May Rosenstein Campus. It provides many support services for L.A. residents, and also boasts the award-winning Liberation Café, regular exhibitions, and acclaimed theater productions at its Lily Tomlin/Jane Wagner Cultural Arts Center.

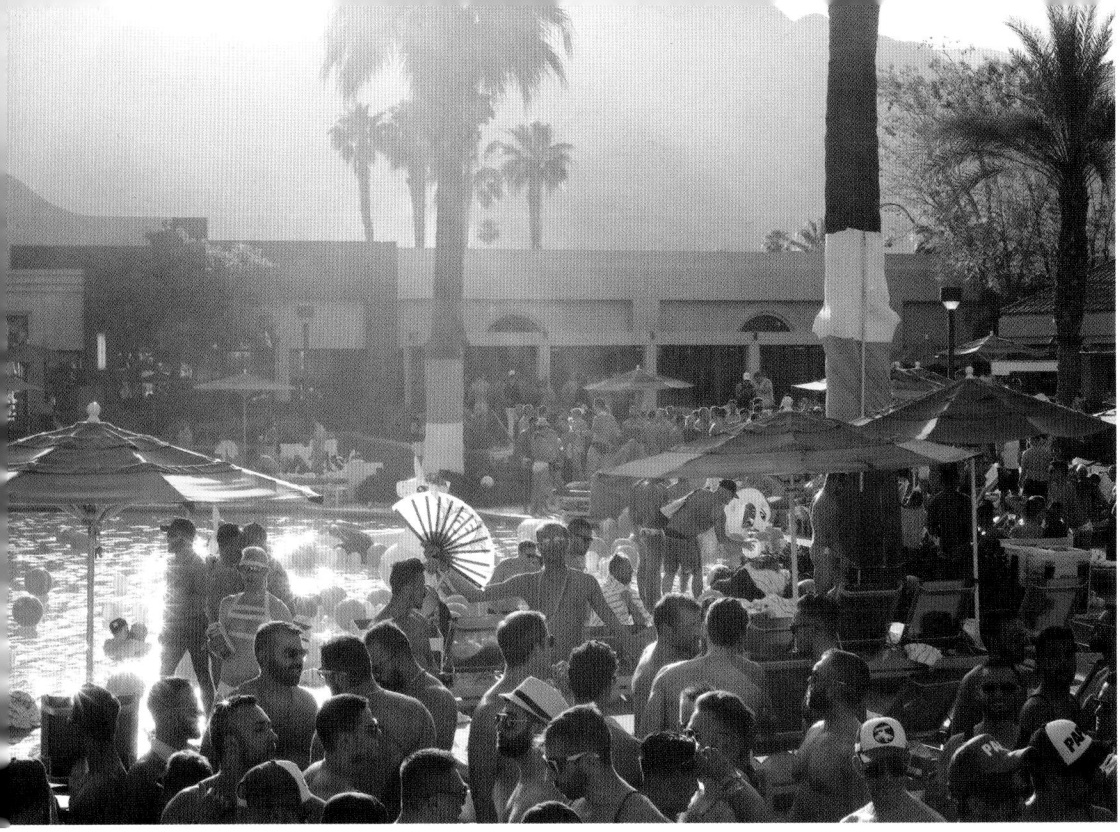

51 Summer camp, grown-up style

A-Camp, Ojai, California, USA

When to go: Summer
Best for: Queer nostalgia

This inclusive, queer-women's summer camp features classics, but with a queer twist: arts and crafts, for example, might mean making your own dildo. The dance parties are legendary, cruising is encouraged, and the panels and workshops are always enlightening.

52 Nose-to-nipple dancing in the desert

▲ White Party Palm Springs, California, USA

When to go: Late April
Best for: Shirt-free raving

Dating back to the early 1990s, White Party Palm Springs has become the biggest gay circuit party in the USA. The festival takes place over a long weekend and attracts around 30,000 muscled-up guys who can't wait to get their shirts off. It's also famed for its big-name performers, with the likes of Ariana Grande, Jennifer Lopez, Kylie Minogue, and Lady Gaga entertaining the crowds. This is one for those who like to party hard. However, be warned: you'll likely need a separate vacation just to recover.

53 Let it all hang out

Clothing-optional resorts, Palm Springs, California, USA

When to go: Spring or fall
Best for: Evening out your tan

The summer weather frequently hits over 100 degrees Fahrenheit (38 degrees Celsius) here, but queer culture is always hot in the LGBTQ+ magnet that is Palm Springs. If you want to cool down by stripping down, you have plenty of options. One of the best "swimsuit-optional" resorts for gay men is the Santiago Resort, with the area's largest pool, an outdoor spa, two-man showers, two-man hammocks, and incredible views of the mountains.

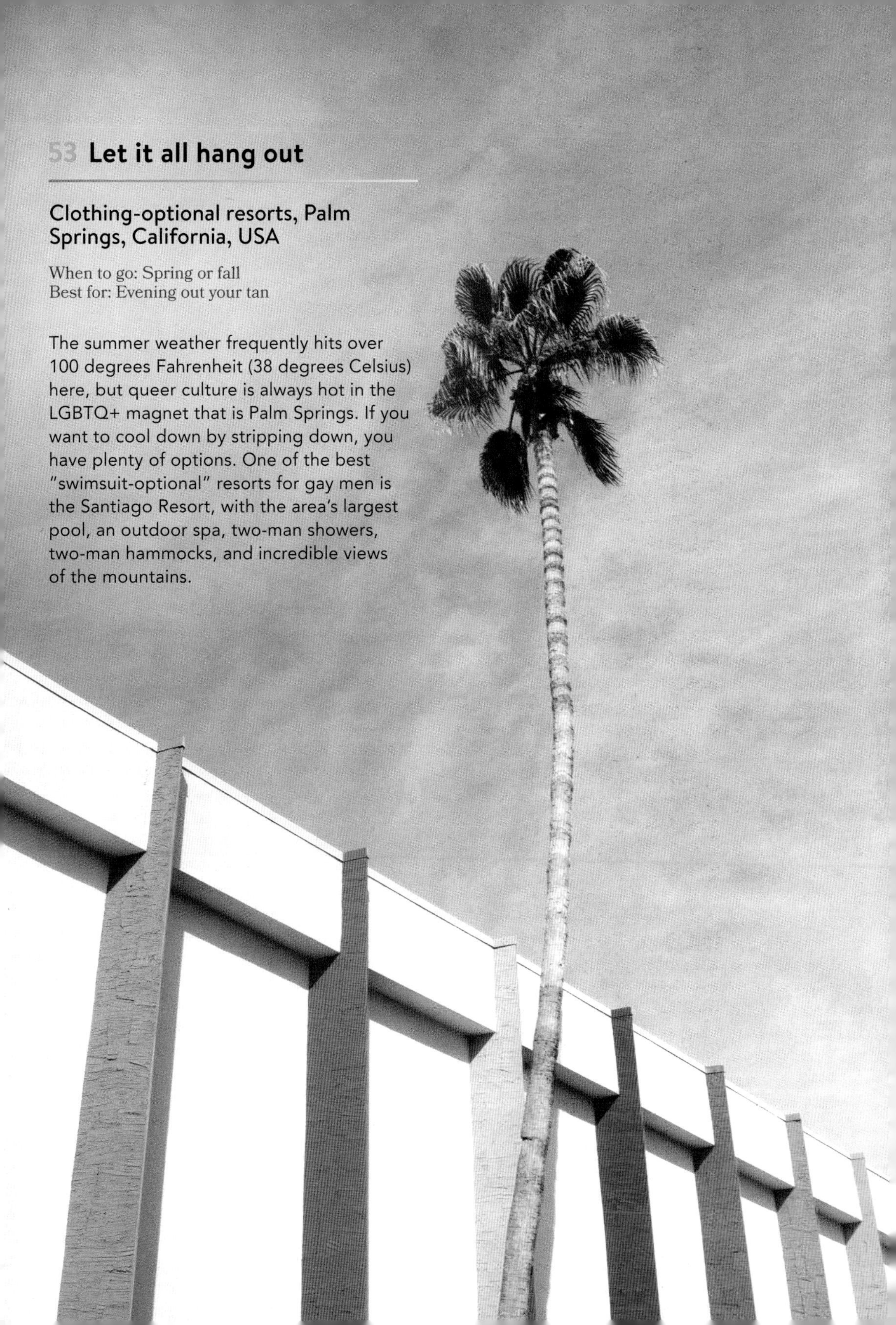

54 Girls just want to have fun

Dinah Shore Lesbian Weekend, Palm Springs, California, USA

When to go: September
Best for: Lesbian bacchanalia

Many longtime attendees of Dinah Shore liken it to a temporary nirvana—thousands of lesbians, queer women, and non-binary cuties (and a few men accompanying them) swarm here for boozing, cruising, pool parties, countless dance parties, and general revelry. It was already popular, but TV show *The L Word* catapulted Dinah Shore into the largest annual party destination for queer women in the world. World-class concerts—past headliners have included Salt N' Pepa, Lady Gaga, Lizzo, Pat Benatar, and Katy Perry—a Black and White Ball, pre- and after-parties galore, and seemingly limitless club nights are infused with a powerfully sexy lesbian vibe that only seems possible when women outnumber men 10-to-1, and nearly everyone is queer. While bikinis or electrical tape over one's nipples are common outfit choices, women of all ages (over 21), body types, and levels of comfort with showing off their bodies attend in numbers. Often referred to as the "lesbian spring break," Dinah Shore is a monumental event in lesbian history that's still going strong after 20 years.

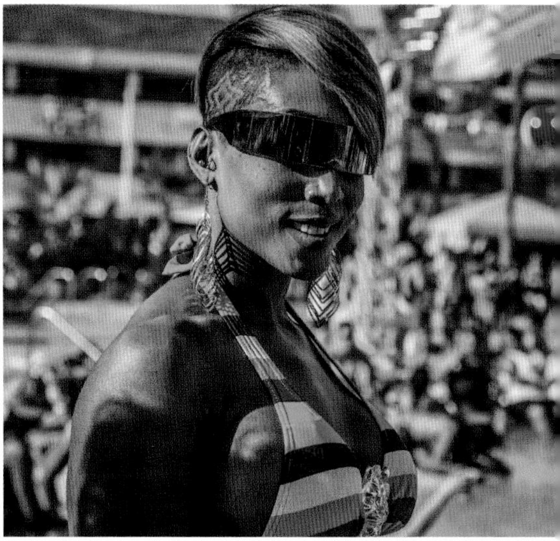

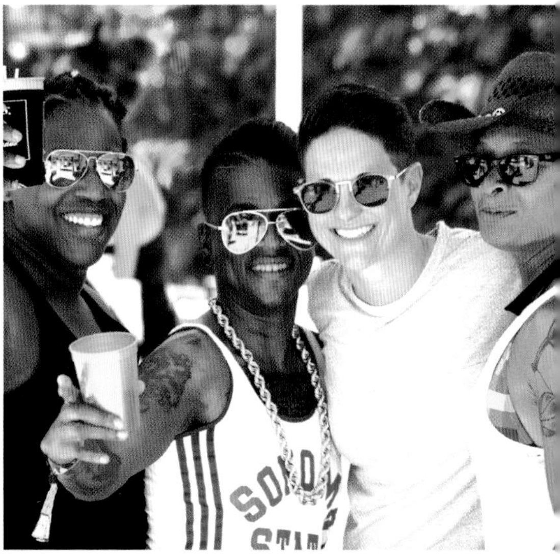

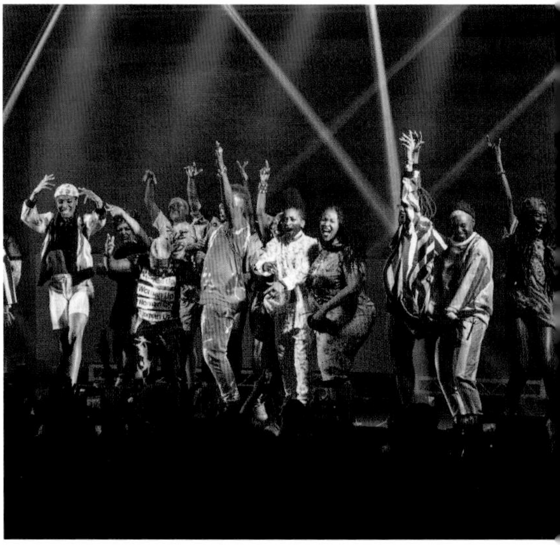

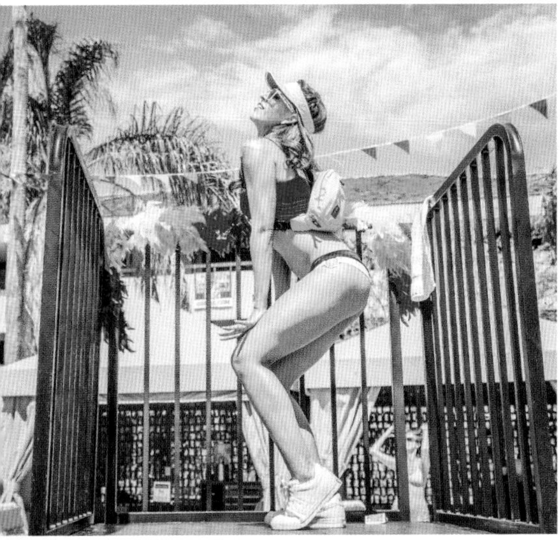

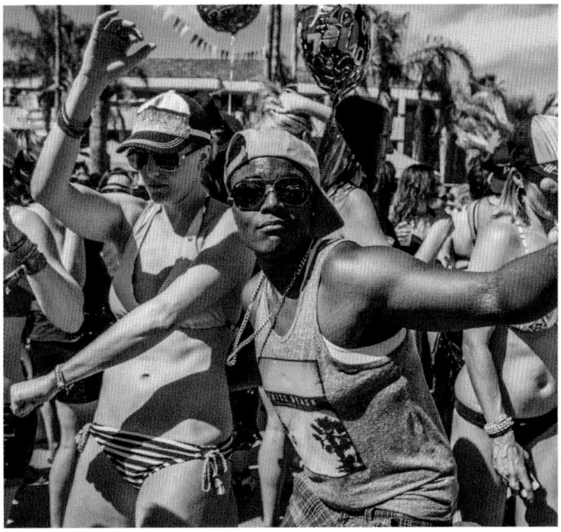

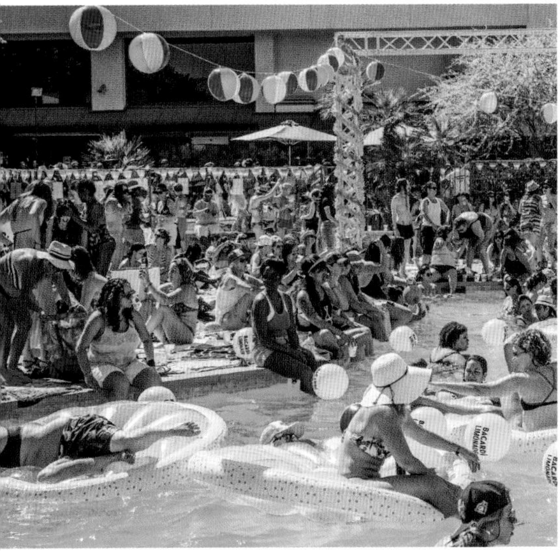
BACARDI

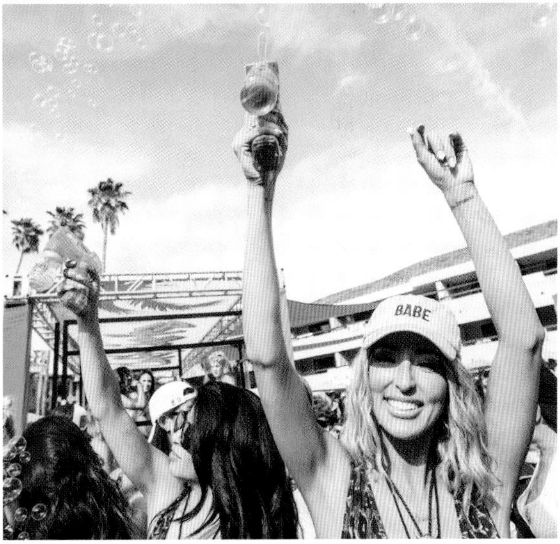
BABE

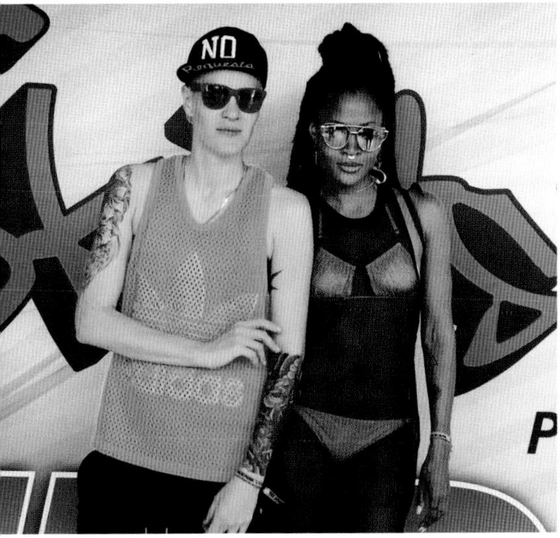
NO

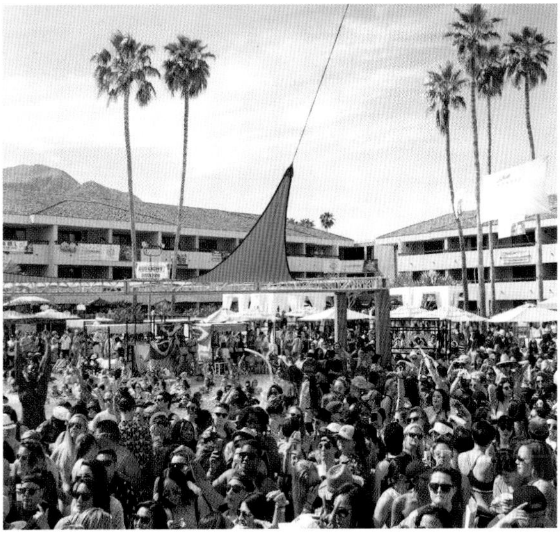

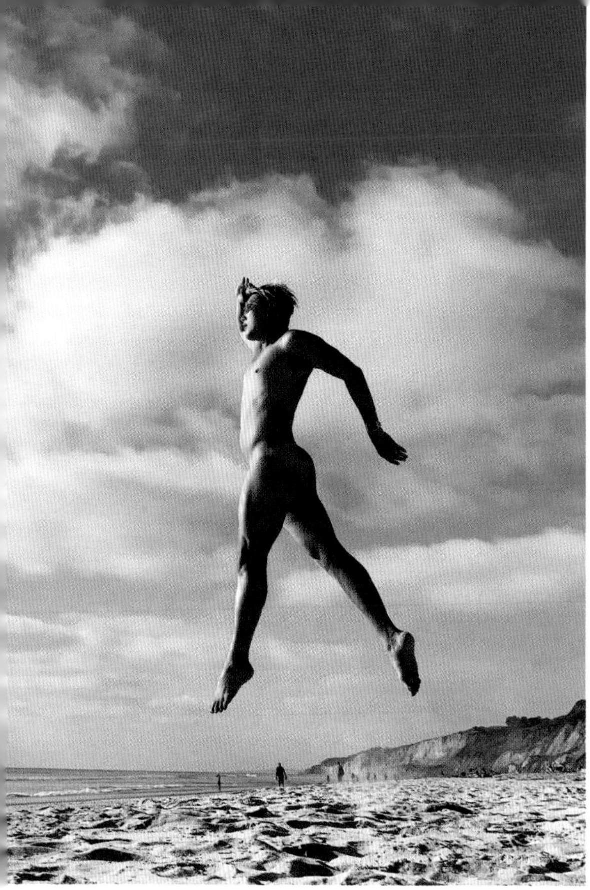

55 Sun that bum

◀ Black's Beach, La Jolla, California, USA

When to go: Summer
Best for: An all-over suntan

Like many clothing-optional gay beaches (though it must be said nudity is not strictly legal here), men are the primary denizens of Black's, although everyone is welcome. This beach isn't easy to get to—it's at least a 20-minute hike—but its beauty is epic. There are other gorgeous beaches in the area, as well as LGBTQ-friendly bars, clubs, restaurants, and hotels, so rounding out your trip won't be difficult to do.

56 Dine out and dive into diversity

▶ Hillcrest, San Diego, USA

When to go: All year
Best for: Supporting LGBTQ-owned businesses

In the 1970s, when LGBTQ+ people started to move in and set up businesses here, Hillcrest was a hippie area. Nowadays, trendy boutiques and restaurants with international cuisines line the streets. The LGBTQ+ scene is still vibrant. Hillcrest is home to—allegedly—the world's first gay brewery and one of only 21 bars for queer women in the USA: Gossip Grill. On Sundays, don't forget to visit the fresh and fabulous Hillcrest Farmers Market.

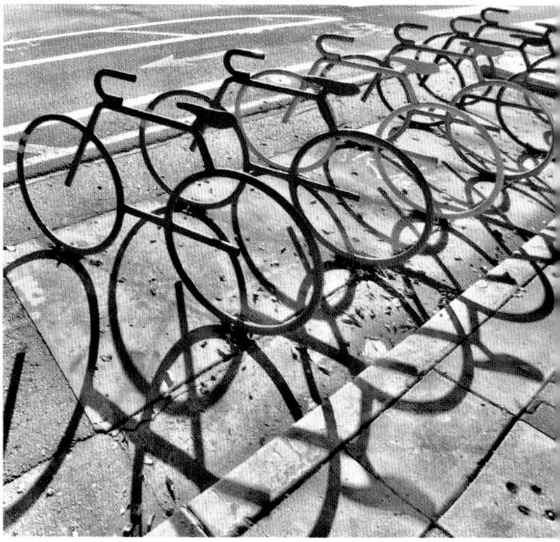

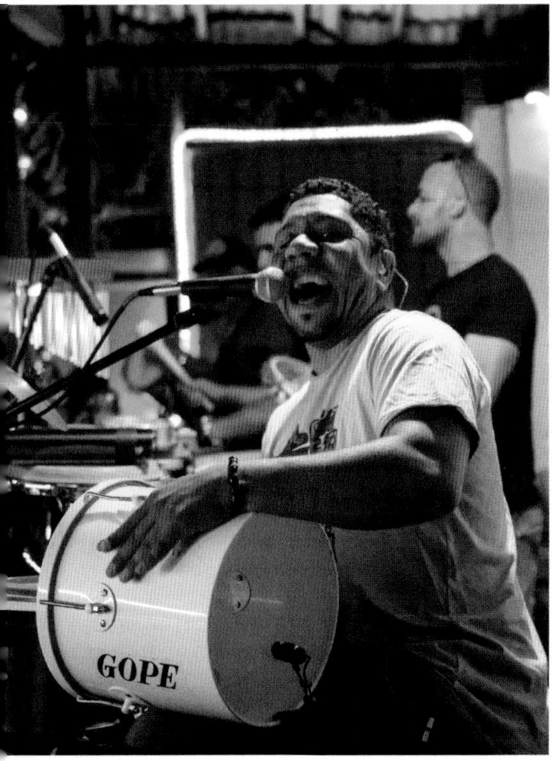

57 Discover the hole full of history

◀ ▼ The Hole In The Wall, San Diego, USA

When to go: All year
Best for: Outdoor drinking

If you like gay bars with a little bit of history, San Diego's Hole In The Wall punches well above its weight. It sits in a depression dug in the early 1900s to access an aqueduct that ran between Mission Bay and San Diego Bay. It became an illegal speakeasy during the Prohibition era, before establishing a reputation as a safe space for the city's local LGBTQ+ community in the 1940s. Hidden behind an unremarkable entrance, the interior opens up onto a tropical, courtyard oasis.

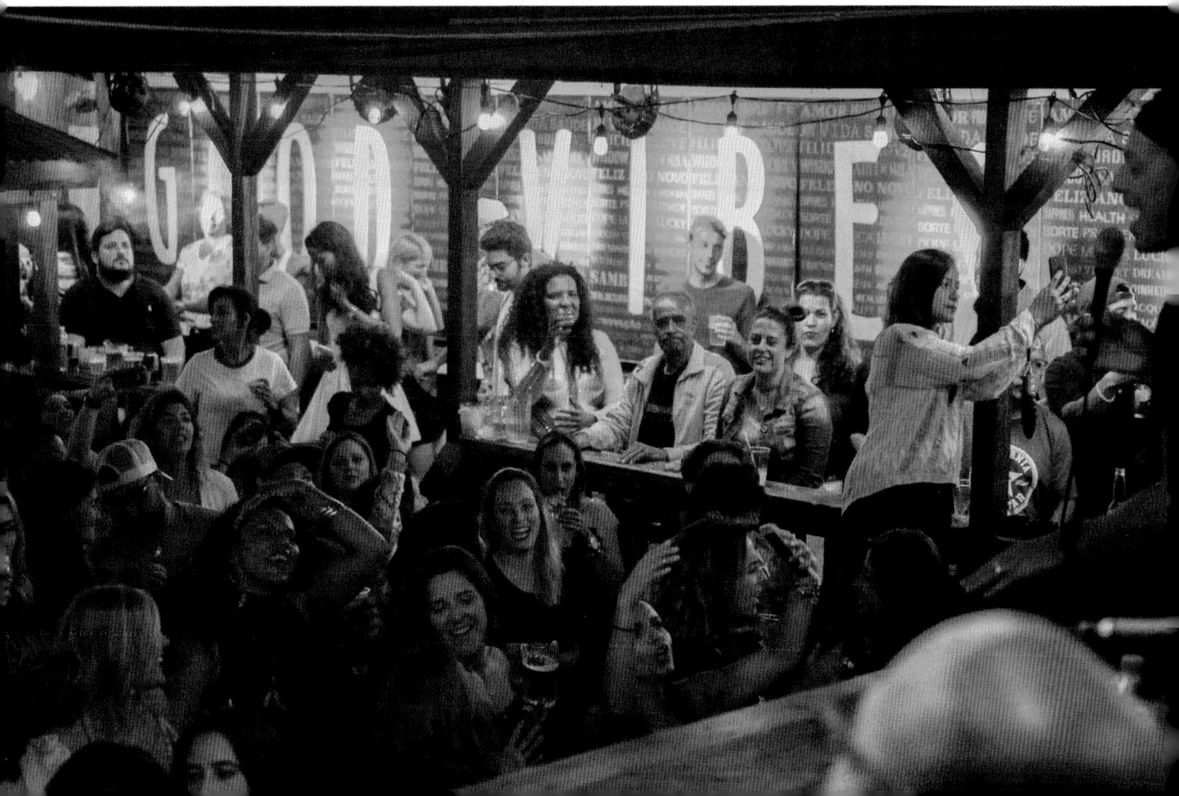

58 Move over, WeHo

Silver Lake, Los Angeles, USA

When to go: All year
Best for: Escaping L.A. excess

Though West Hollywood has a reputation as L.A.'s "gayborhood," Silver Lake is a more diverse, inclusive, family-friendly neighborhood that has been an LGBTQ+ haven for decades. A riot against police violence here, at the Black Cat Tavern in 1967, launched *The Advocate* magazine into existence and galvanized gay rights in California. The neighborhood celebrates this history—a monument on Cove Avenue has been officially renamed the Mattachine Steps to honor the first major gay rights organization in the USA—while also feeling utterly modern. The Black Cat still exists, though it's no longer explicitly gay. This is true generally; while Silver Lake is very LGBTQ-friendly, it has more of a hip, liberal vibe these days rather than an explicitly gay one. "Mixed-crowd" bars like Akbar and Los Globos are LGBTQ-friendly, and host recurring queer nights and fetish parties. Explicitly gay culture does still exist here though: the Eagle is home to leather, fetish, and/or biker subcultures, all-male bathhouses like FLEX remain, and the Off Sunset Festival occurs every March.

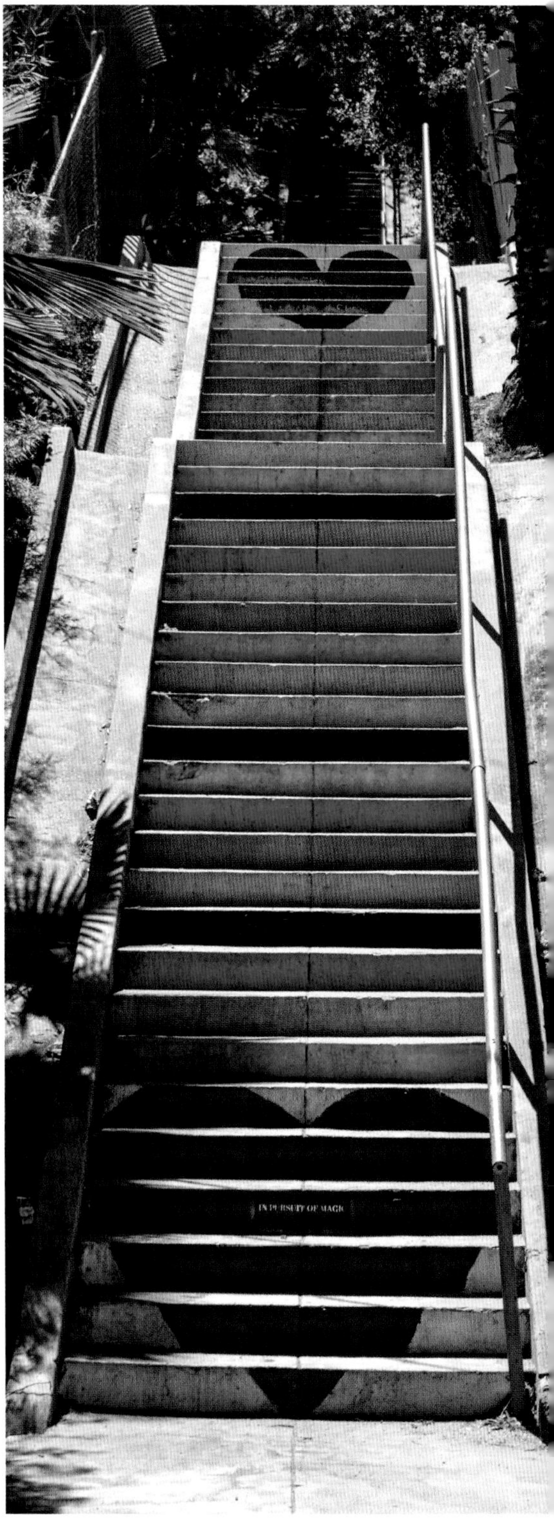

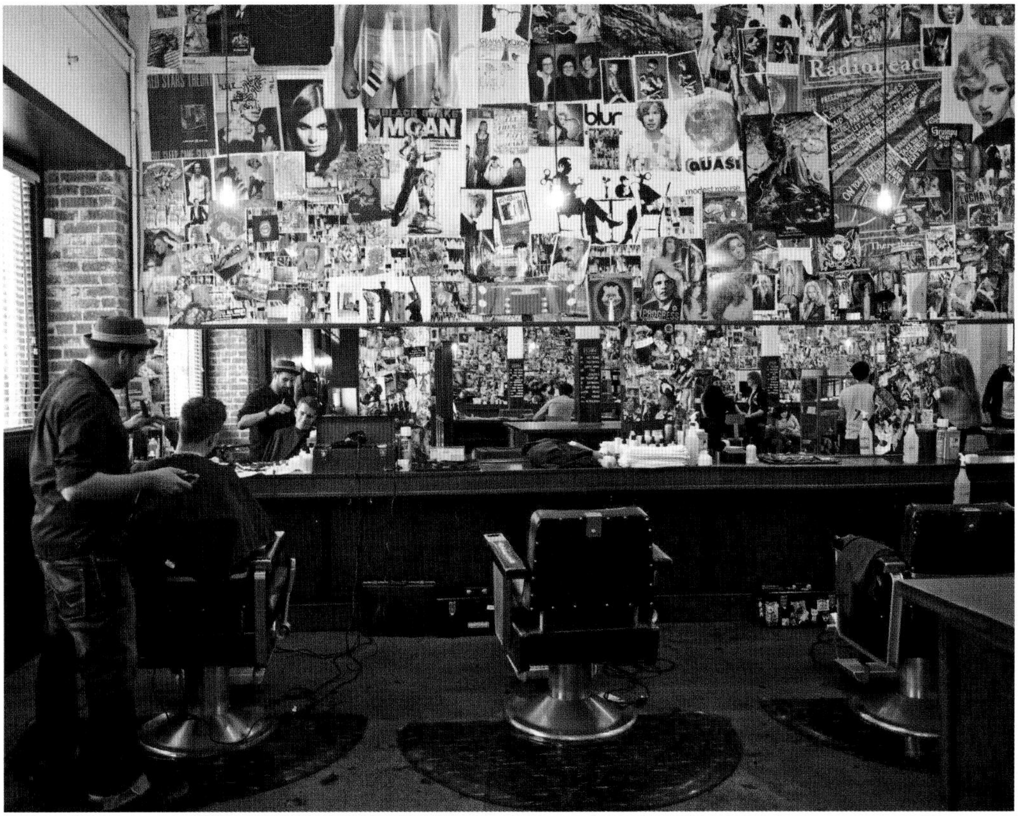
blur
QUASI

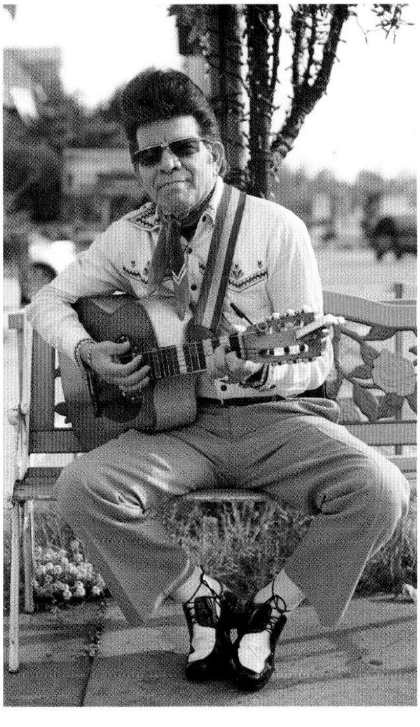

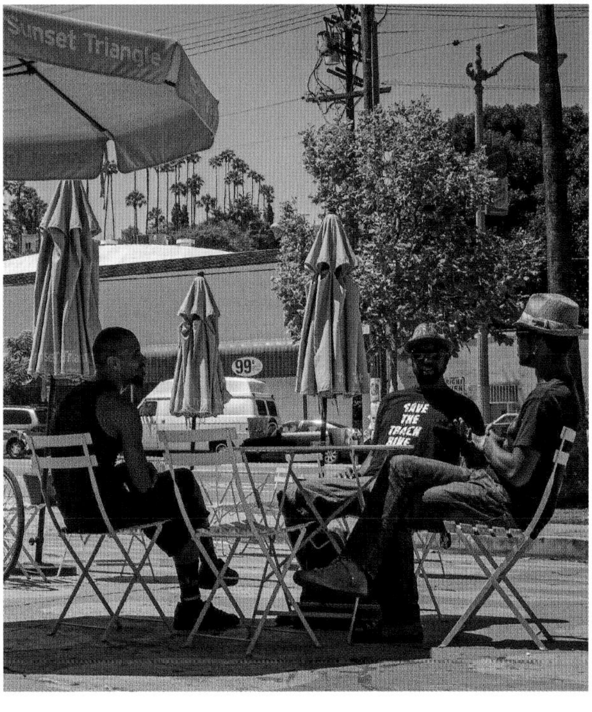
SAVE THE TRACK BIKE

59 Hit the slopes smiling

▼ Aspen Gay Ski Week, Aspen, Colorado, USA

When to go: January
Best for: Snow-sport enthusiasts

The oldest gay-skiing event in the United States, Aspen Gay Ski Week brings LGBTQ+ visitors from around the world to enjoy one of the premier snow-sport destinations there is. In addition to skiing and snowboarding, there are featured meals, happy hours, dance parties, film events, comedy shows, and indoor pool parties. Even better, the entire event is a fundraiser for AspenOUT, a local nonprofit serving Aspen's LGBTQ+ residents.

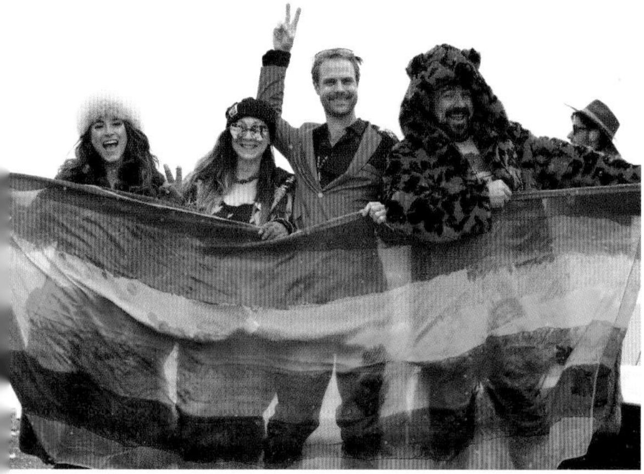

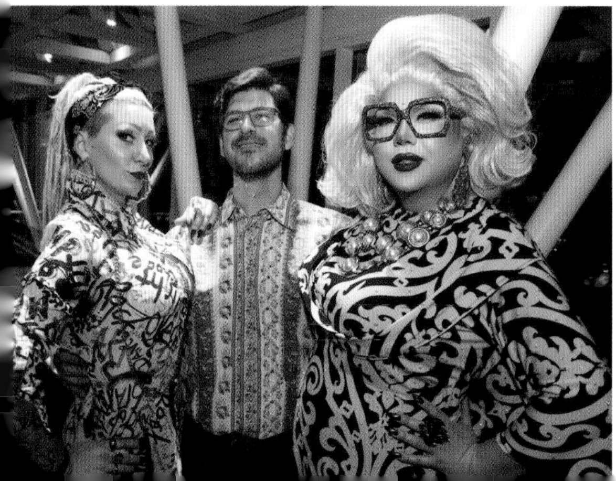

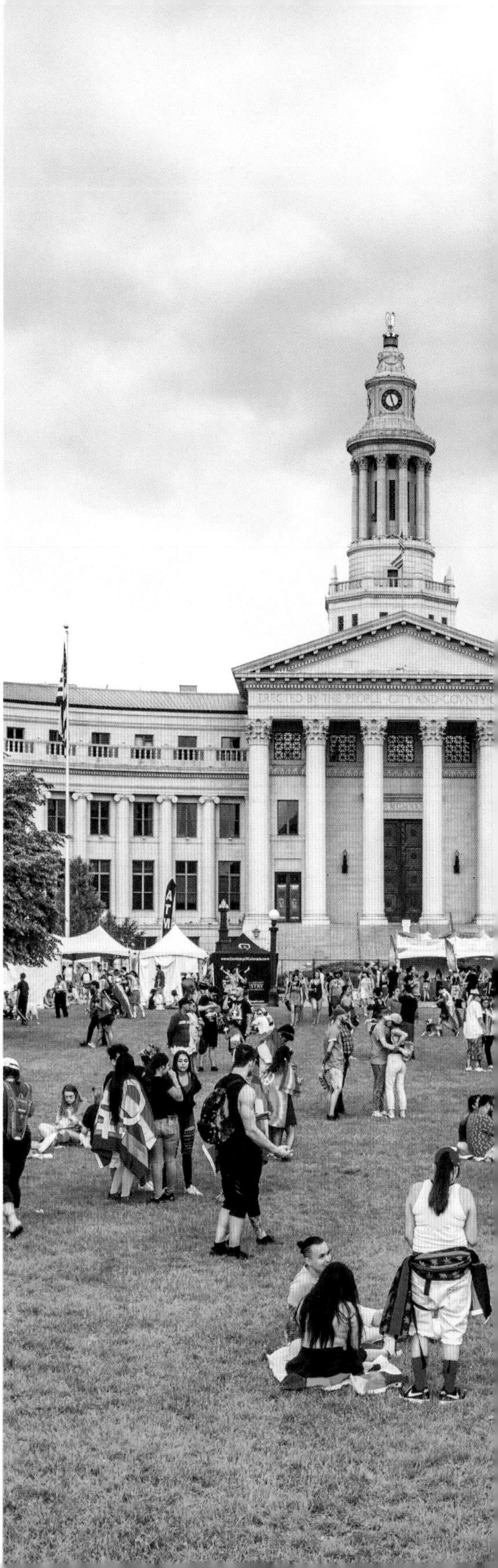

60 Join the mile high club

Capitol Hill, Denver, Colorado, USA

When to go: All year
Best for: Visiting one of the last lesbian bars around

Capitol Hill is the Mile High City's "gayborhood," with all manner of bars to choose from: Charlie's has rotating theme nights; R&R is very laid-back and divey; recent addition Denver Sweet is "bear-inspired" and features a rooftop bar; X Bar, formerly Her Bar, has rebranded as a more general LGBTQ+ establishment; but one of the few remaining lesbian bars in the United States, Blush & Blu, is still going strong here.

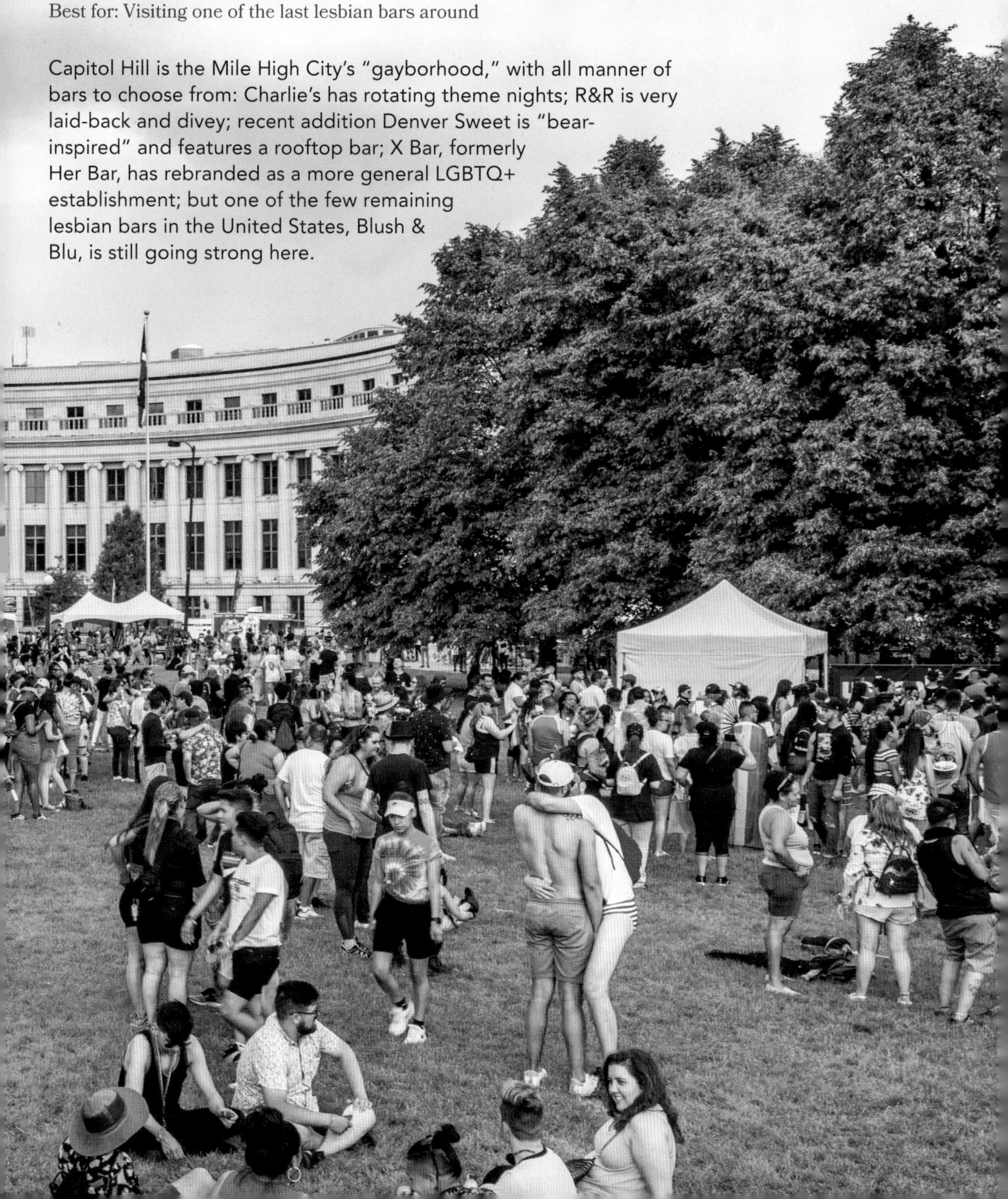

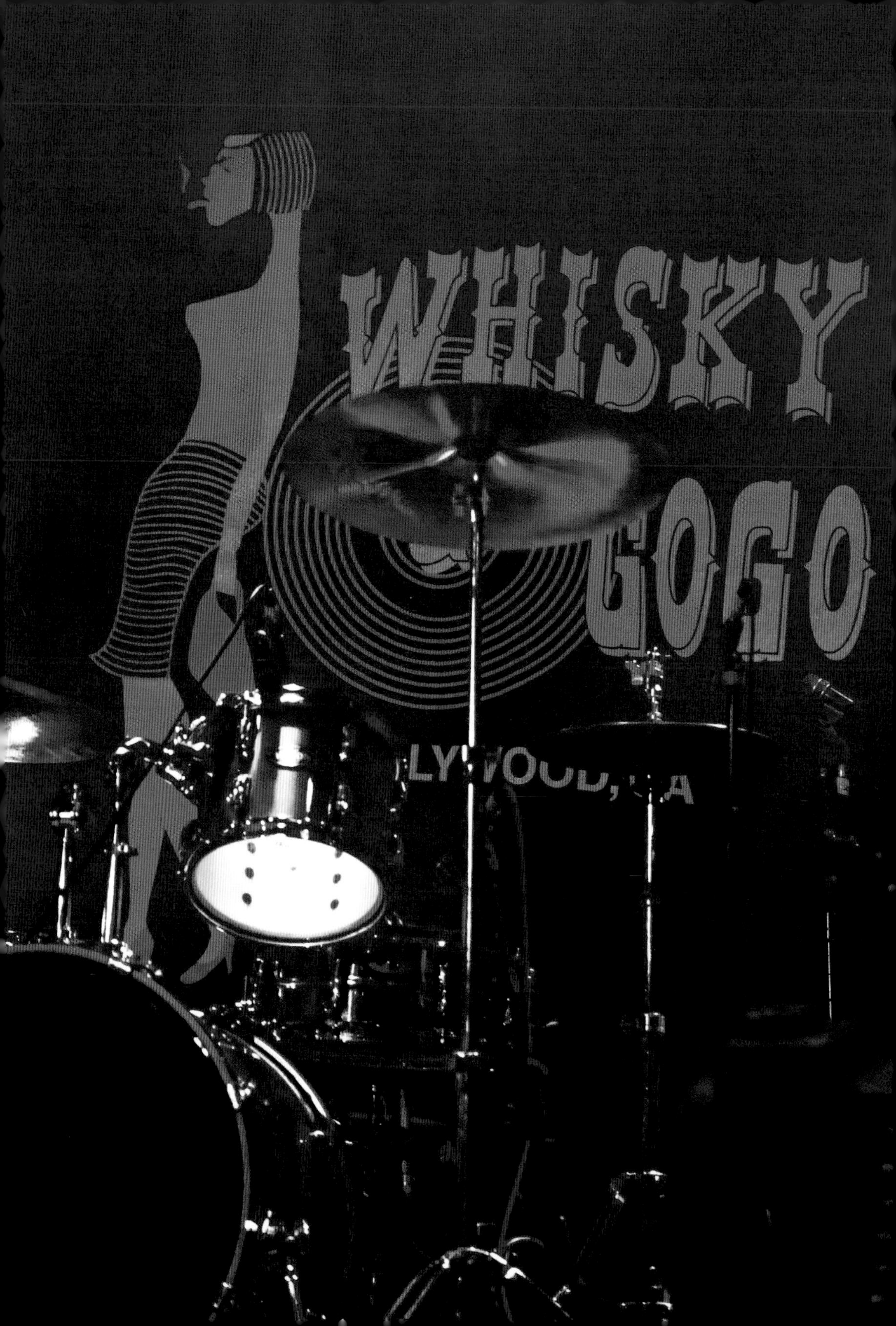
WHISKY
GOGO

61 Discover the city that's queer to its roots

◀ West Hollywood (WeHo), California, USA

When to go: All year
Best for: Everything LGBTQ+

From its origin, the city of West Hollywood (WeHo for short) has been queer. It gained city status in 1984 with a majority LGBTQ+ city council and the USA's first out lesbian mayor, Valerie Terrigno. And it's a vibe. For many queer women, a visit to WeHo means reliving scenes from *The L Word*. For other gays and theys, WeHo is famous for its bustling, queer nightlife, concentrated on and around Santa Monica Boulevard. The Chapel At The Abbey is the most famous LGBTQ+ spot; although the crowd is predominantly queer men, there are special nights and events for other members of the LGBTQ+ community. If you're not into clubbing: don't skip WeHo. Make a visit to WeHo's Design District for art, fashion, design, culture, and more. If you're here in June, it's L.A. Pride, and on October 31 there's a fabulous Halloween Carnival.

62 It's camping, but not as you know it

Sawmill Camping Resort, Dade City, Florida, USA

When to go: All year
Best for: Nightlife under the stars

Though Sawmill is called a "camping" resort, it's unlikely you'll be pitching a tent in the wilderness around a campfire. You will be surrounded by nature, but also: a heated, clothing-optional pool, a zip line, beach volleyball, a cigar bar, a nightclub, a live music stage, and four bars. Comedy shows, dance parties, lube wrestling, and much more attract primarily gay men. Talk about "glamping..."

63 Black is the new Black

South Florida Afro Pride, Fort Lauderdale, Florida, USA

When to go: October
Best for: Social justice

South Florida Afro Pride was only founded in 2020, but it is already filling a major niche. The Miami metro area is more than 25% Black, and includes people from the Americas, Africa, and the Caribbean. Because this Pride celebration caters to these communities, it has an overt focus on social justice alongside dance parties, cultural celebrations, and a parade.

64 No shame in coming second

Wilton Manors, Fort Lauderdale, Florida, USA

When to go: All year
Best for: Beachfront life

Wilton Manors is considered the second-gayest small city in the United States—in terms of its per capita LGBTQ+ demographics—and by the same metric, nearby Fort Lauderdale is the gayest midsize city. That means gay-owned businesses and nightlife abound here, and there's a major LGBTQ+ community center, plenty of queer-friendly bed and breakfasts and hotels, and even the Stonewall National Museum and Archives if you'd like to brush up on your LGBTQ+ history. Start out with a walk up and down internationally known Wilton Drive, have a burger at Rosie's, and perhaps make your way to Sebastian Street Beach, considered one of the best gay beaches in the United States.

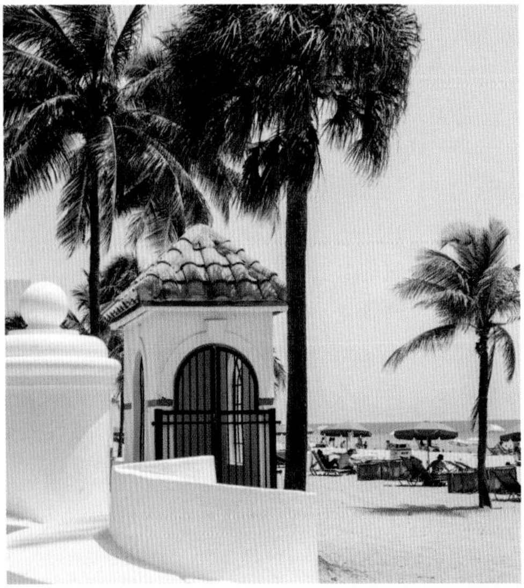

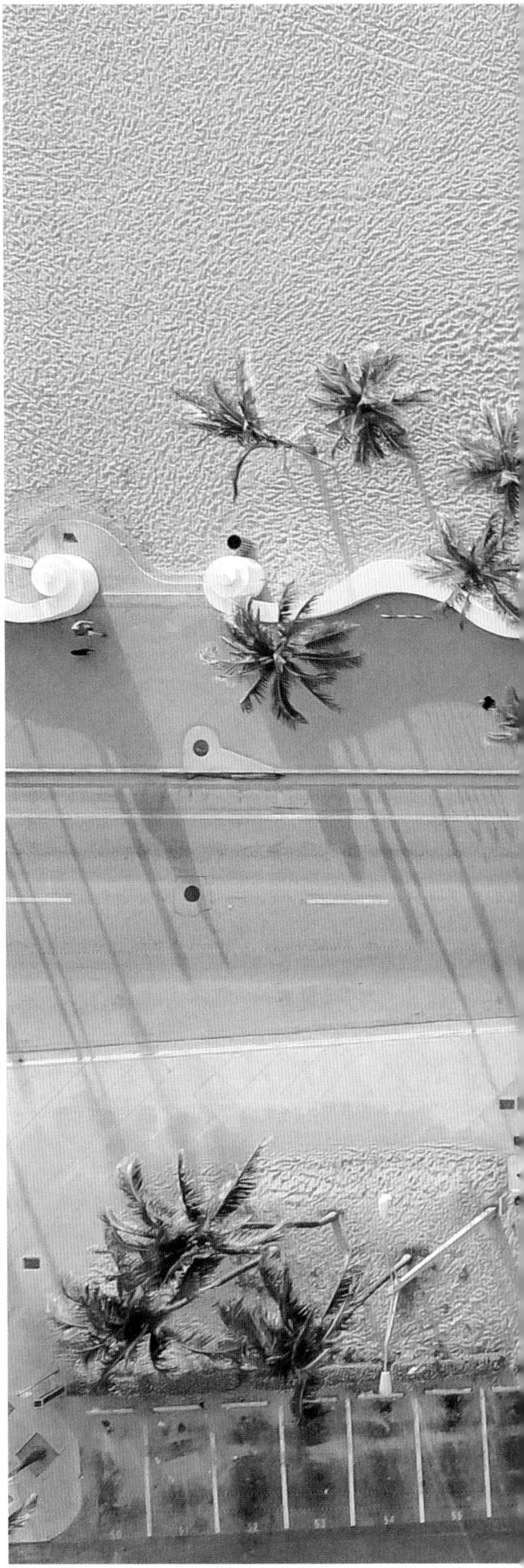

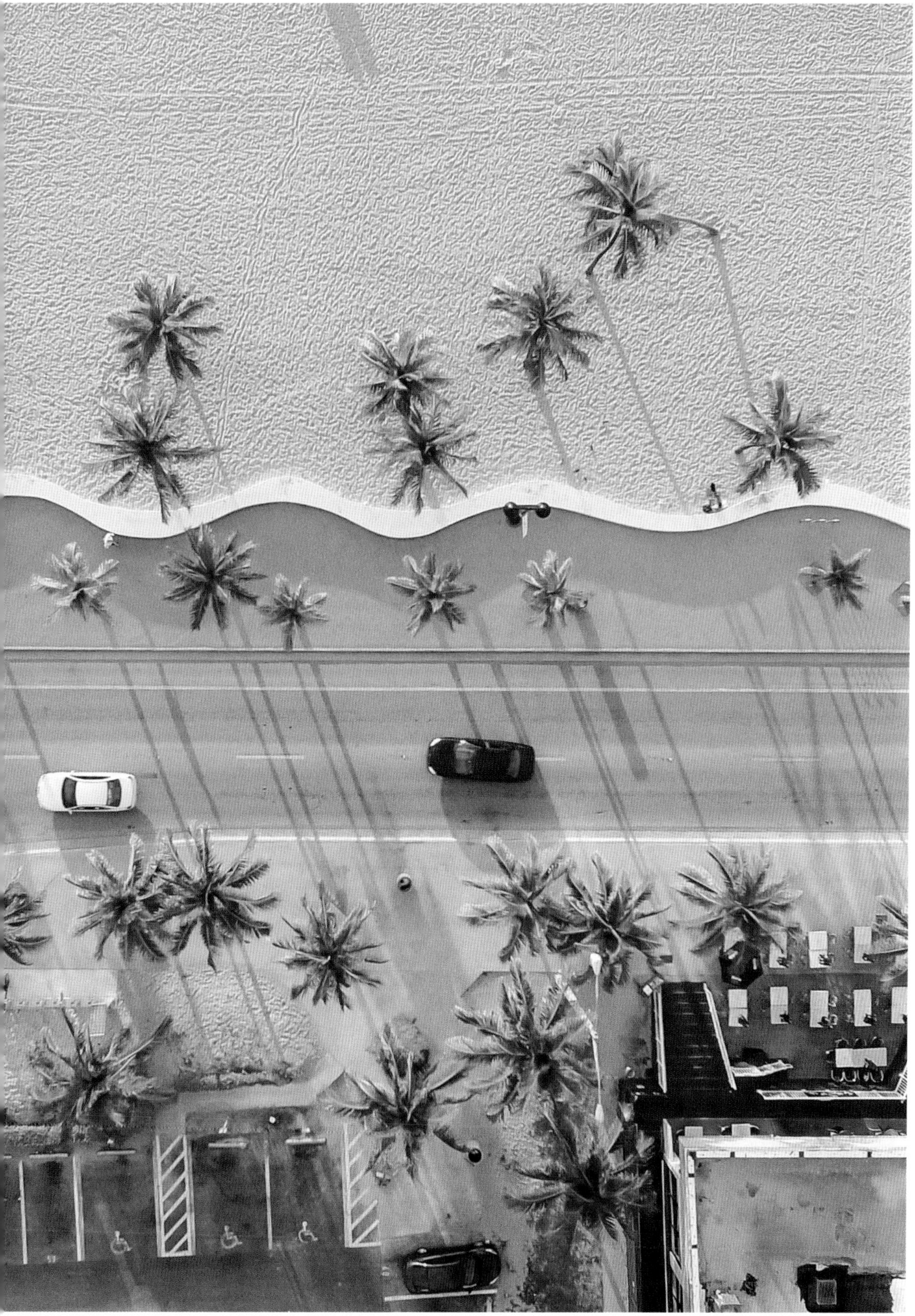

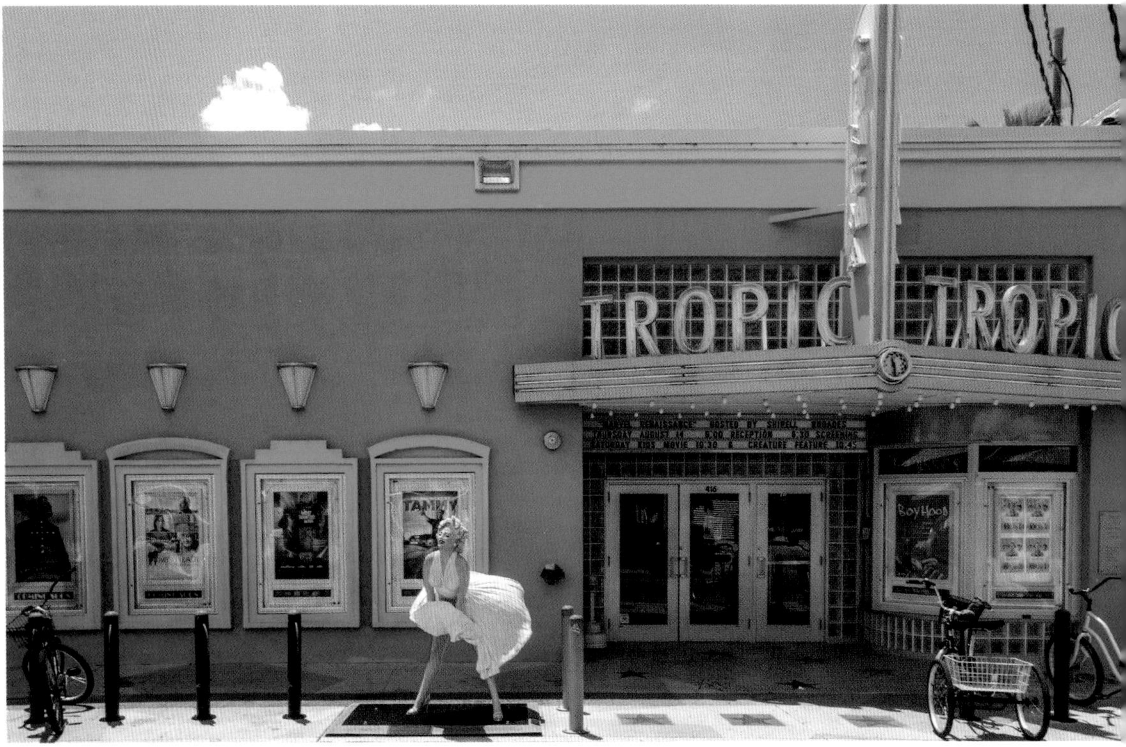

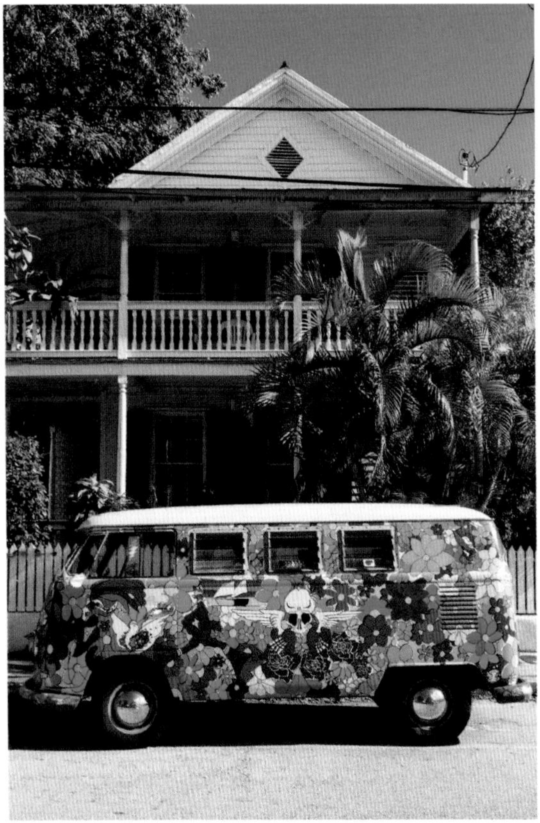

65 The keys to happiness

Key West, Florida, USA

When to go: All year
Best for: Cuban coffee and Key Lime pie

Ever wanted to see a rainbow flag stretched between oceans? At Pride each year, the locals of Key West stretch a giant rainbow flag from one side of the island to the other, uniting the Atlantic and Pacific oceans. Key West began to tempt gay travelers in the early half of the twentieth century and it still offers a very gay-friendly welcome. Playwright Tennessee Williams was one of its most famous LGBTQ+ inhabitants, and his former home can still be visited. The gay neighborhood can be found near the Old Town's historic Duval Street. Enjoy a cocktail by your guesthouse pool, or a Cuban coffee on Mallory Square to take in the stunning sunsets.

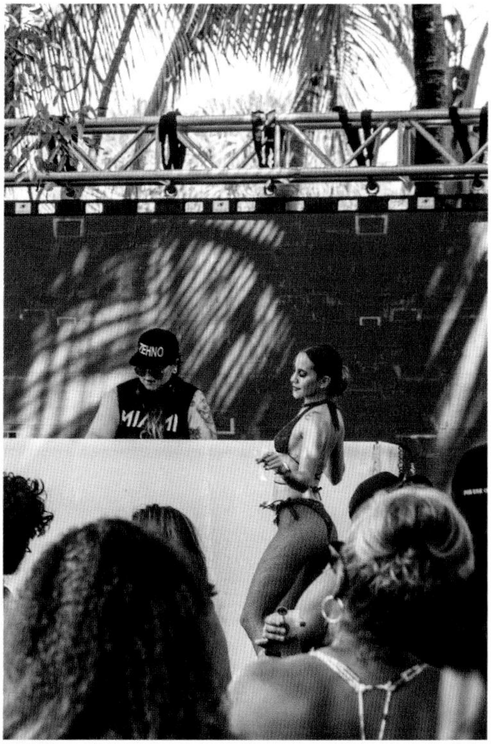

66 Who says pool parties are for kids?

Aqua Girl, Miami, USA

When to go: October
Best for: Keeping it sexy by the beach

Aqua Girl is a queer-women-centric pool party extravaganza that takes place over a long weekend—five days—in South Beach. It isn't as large as Dinah Shore, but it's just as fun and just as sexy. It's also a fundraiser for the Aqua Foundation for women, a local charity supporting LGBTQ+ women in South Florida, and donations can get you VIP access to some of the parties.

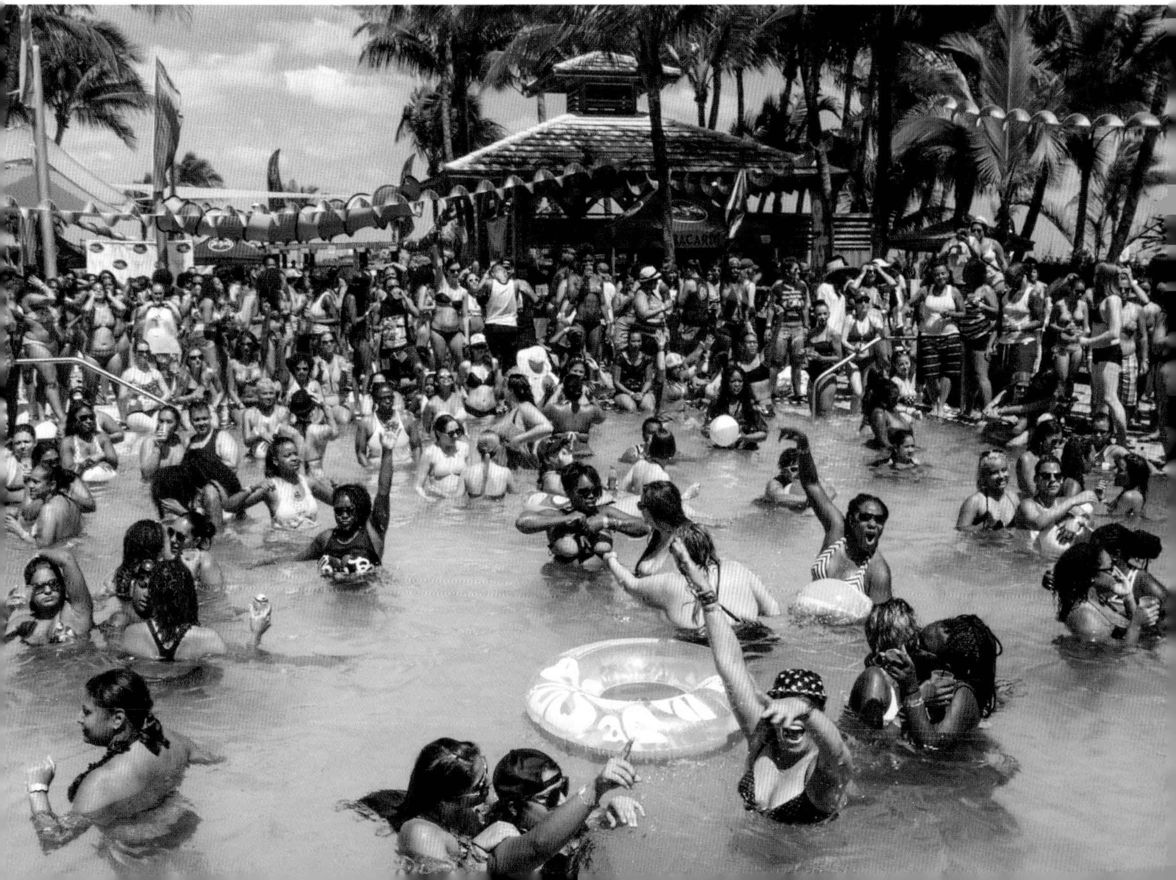

67 Live it up to the eighth degree

Gay 8 Festival, Miami, USA

When to go: February
Best for: Pride with Latin flavor

Occurring up and down 8th Street in Little Havana, Miami, Gay Ocho is one of the largest queer, Latin celebrations in the United States. A celebration of diversity, inclusion, dance, music, art, and culture, this three-day event features live entertainment, cultural programming, community engagement, and lots of delicious food to celebrate Miami's Latin LGBTQ+ communities.

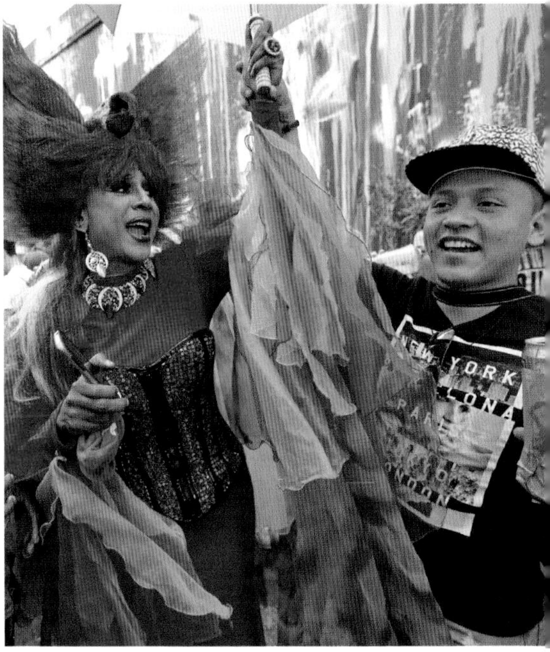

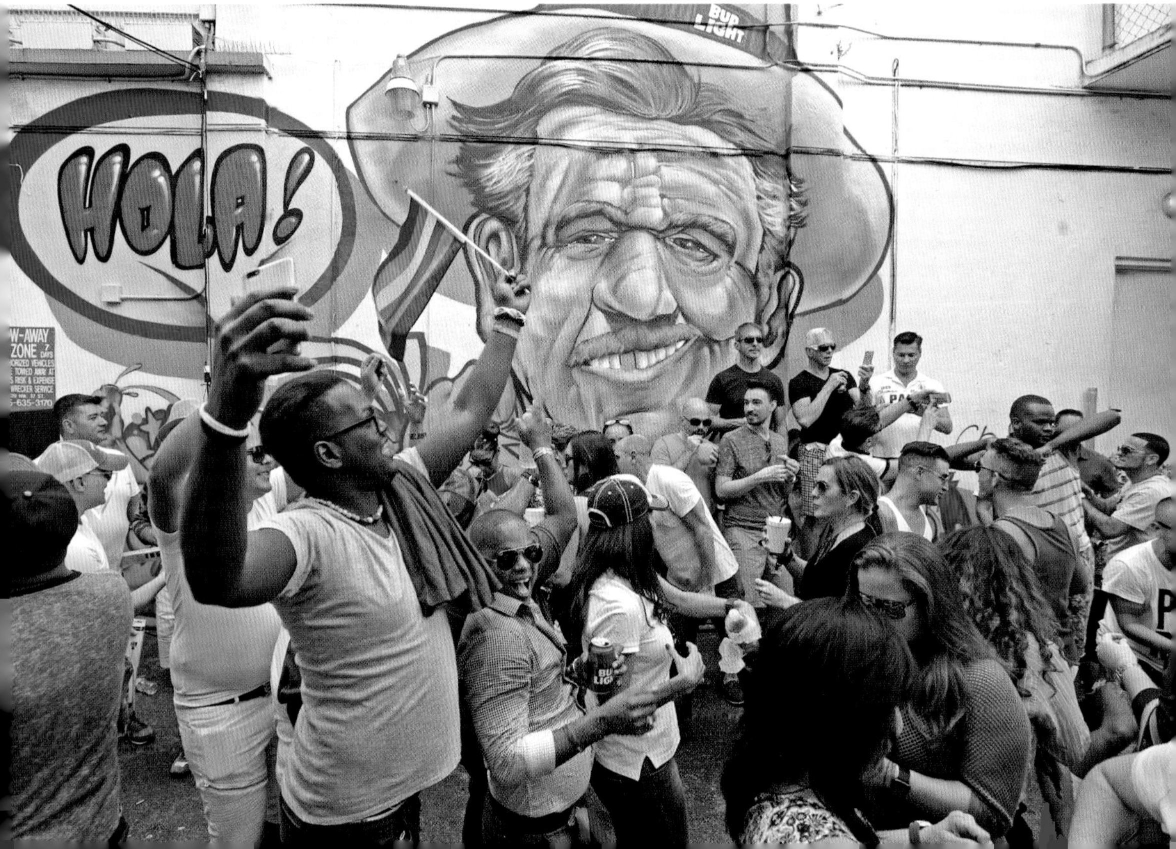

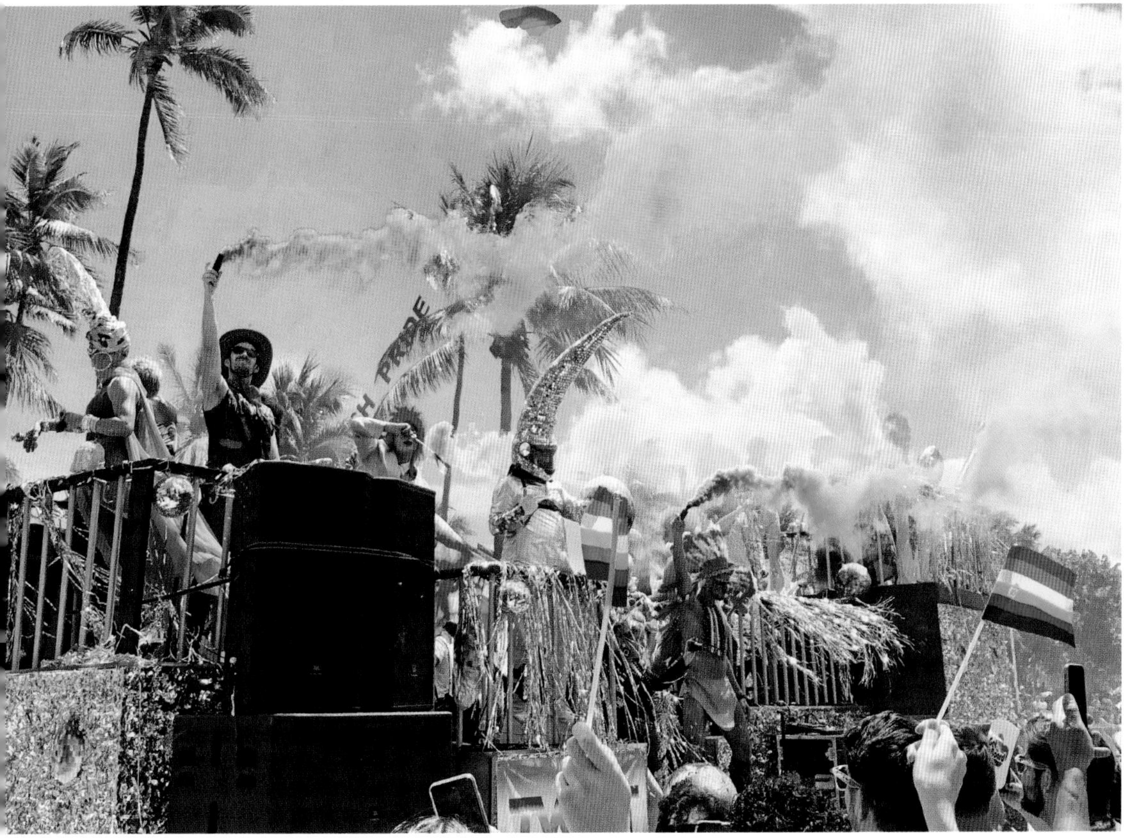

68 Party in the city where the heat is on

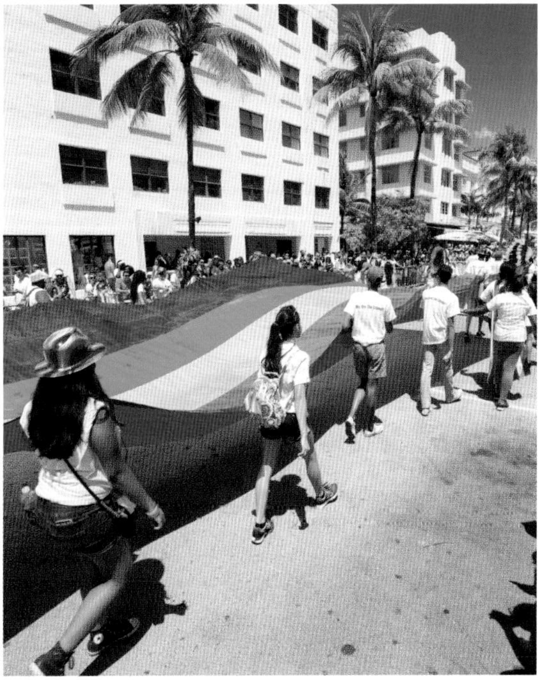

Miami Beach Pride, Miami, USA

When to go: April
Best for: Sun, muscle men, and a great time

Everyone loves a party in the sun and on a beach, and Miami Beach Pride ticks off all the boxes for the perfect Pride celebration. This giant party takes place every spring and features beachfront stages full of hit performances from pop to Latin music, celebrating Miami's unique LGBTQ+ community. If the beach is not enough to entice partygoers, rooftop pool parties with stunning views of Miami Beach may do the trick.

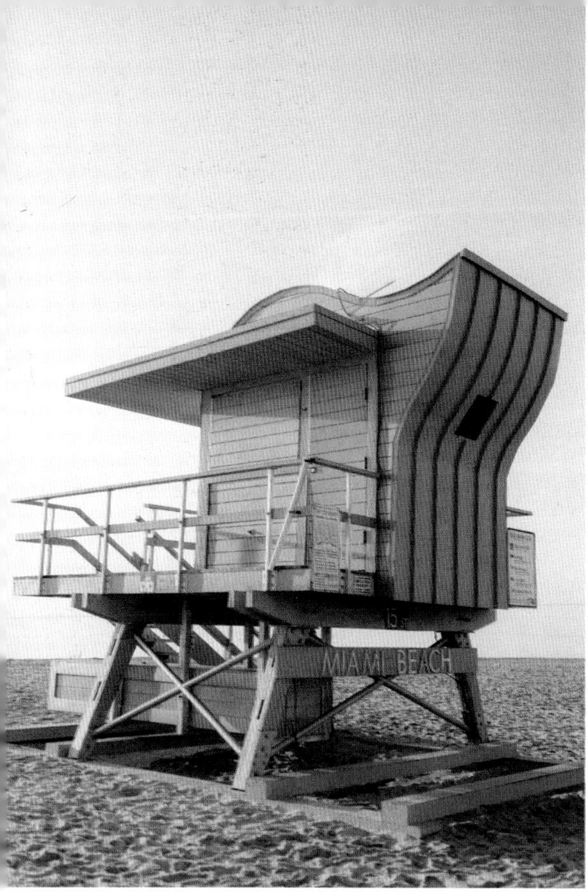

69 Soulmates, sun, sea, and sand

South Beach, Miami, USA

When to go: March to May
Best for: A queer beach holiday

Miami's South Beach (SoBe) is famous for its colorful lifeguard towers on the beach, Ocean Drive's pastel Art Deco buildings, and its lively queer scene. The intersection of 12th Street and Ocean Drive is the best place to start queering around; it marks the LGBTQ+ heart of Miami. Drink mimosas at Palace's iconic drag brunch in true gay fashion, boost your endorphins at SoBe's rainbow volleyball field, or sunbathe at rainbow-marked 12th Street Beach.

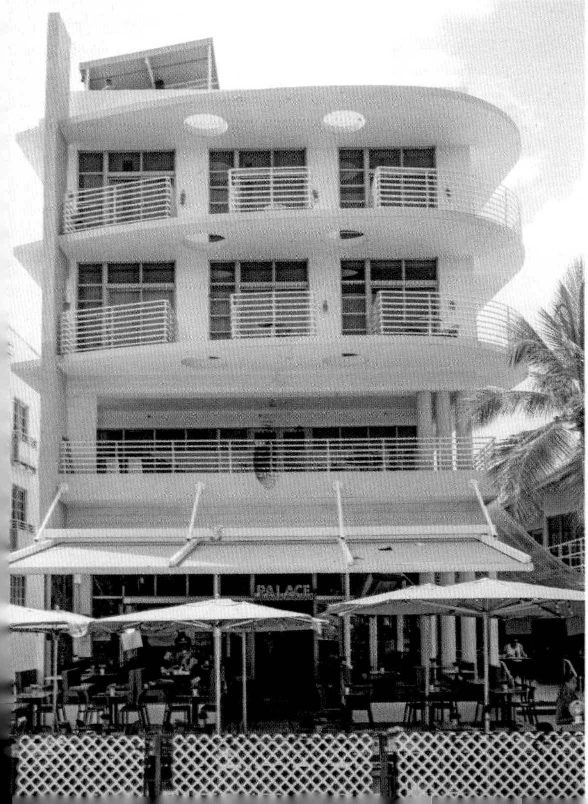

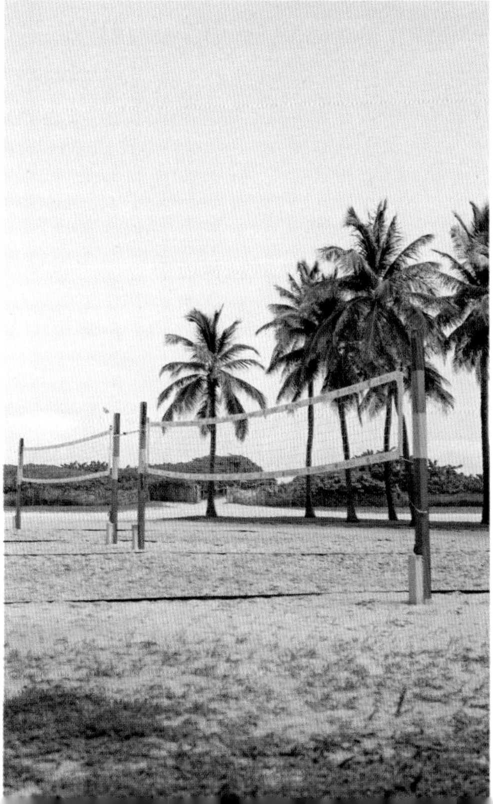

70 From warehouse to winner

Wynwood, Miami, USA

When to go: All year
Best for: Street art

Miami isn't just for beach and party lovers. In Wynwood, art lovers can marvel at art-covered buildings and visit over 70 galleries. Stop by the outdoor museum Wynwood Walls to see work by the most significant street artists. Wynwood was a collection of warehouses not long ago; now, it's Miami's cultural creative hub and hippest hangout.

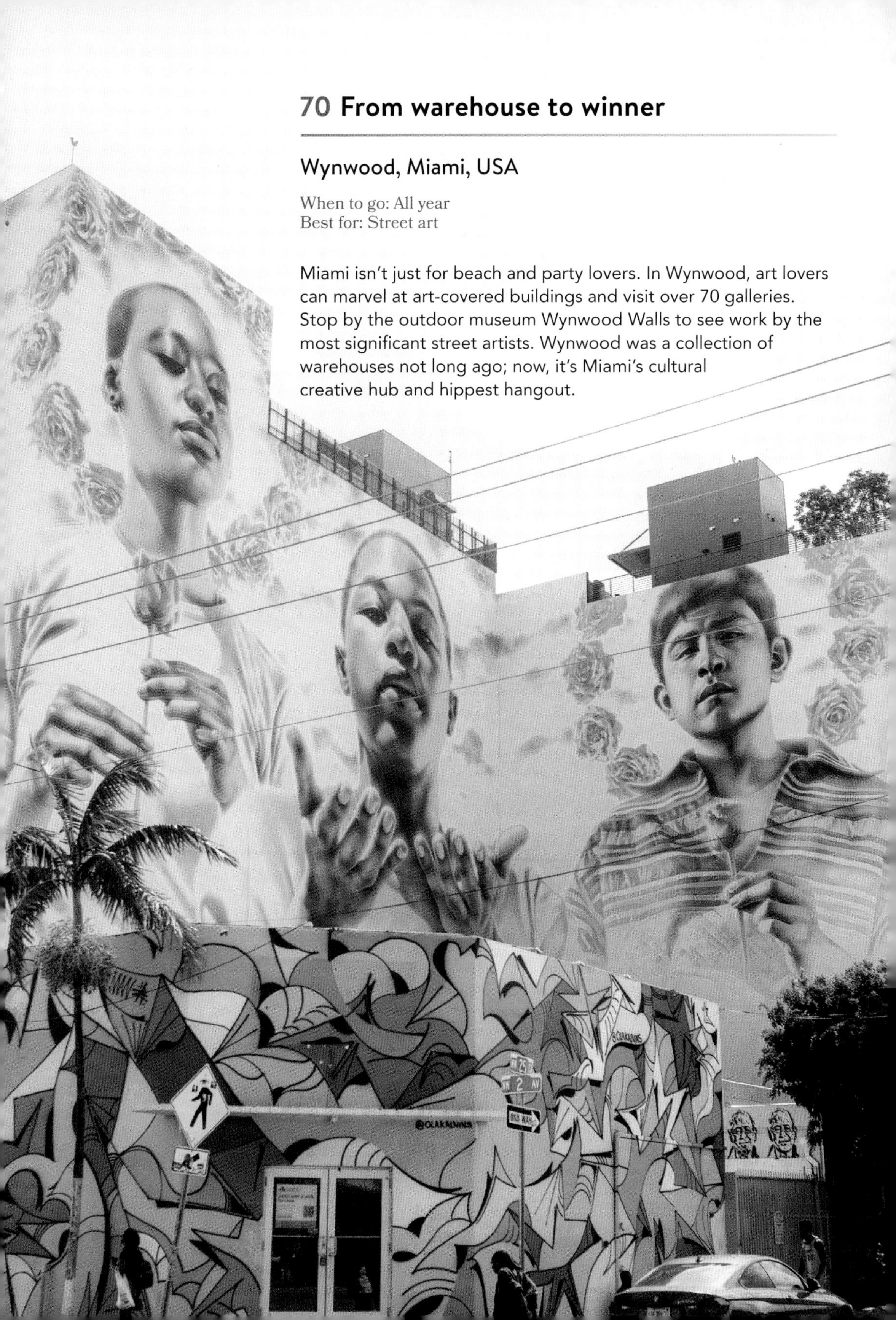

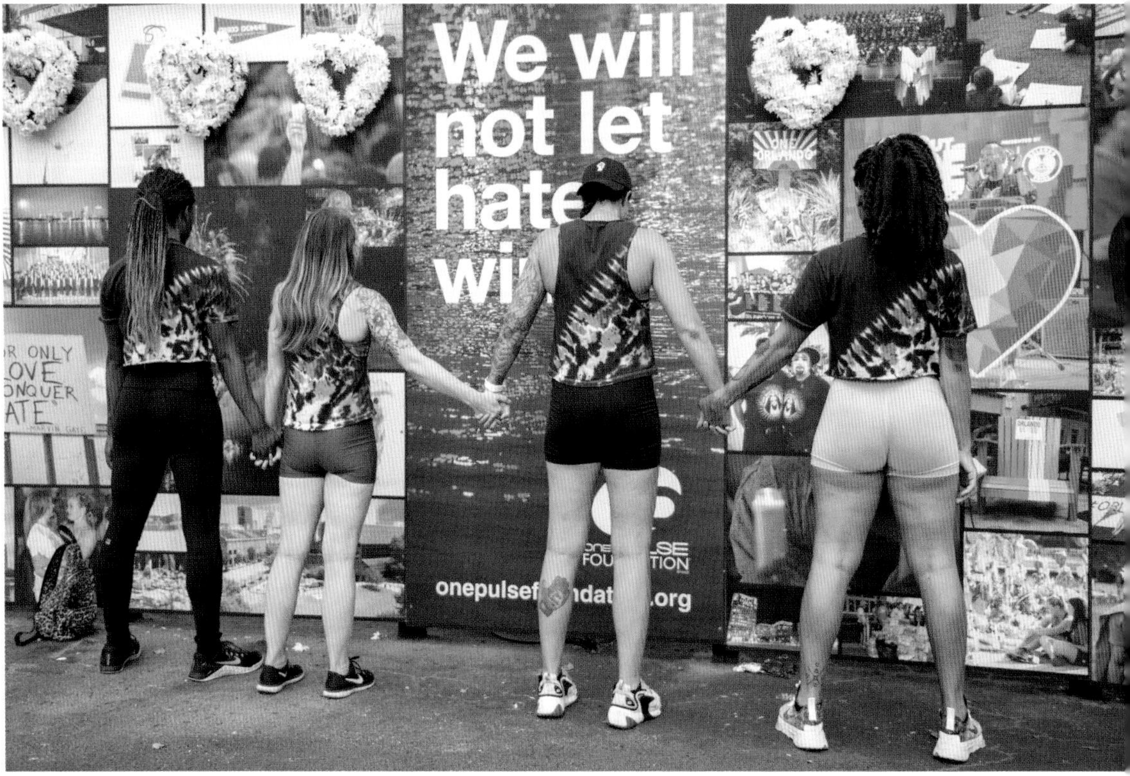

71 Fight hate with resilience

Pulse Memorial, Orlando, Florida, USA

When to go: All year
Best for: Somber reflection

In 2016, 49 people—primarily LGBTQ+ Latinos—were gunned down in a tragic mass-shooting at the Pulse nightclub in Orlando. The interim memorial is a testament to resilience, and an opportunity to reflect and honor those whose lives were lost. The location will eventually be home to a museum intended to transform the grief of that day into a center for history, education, and resilience.

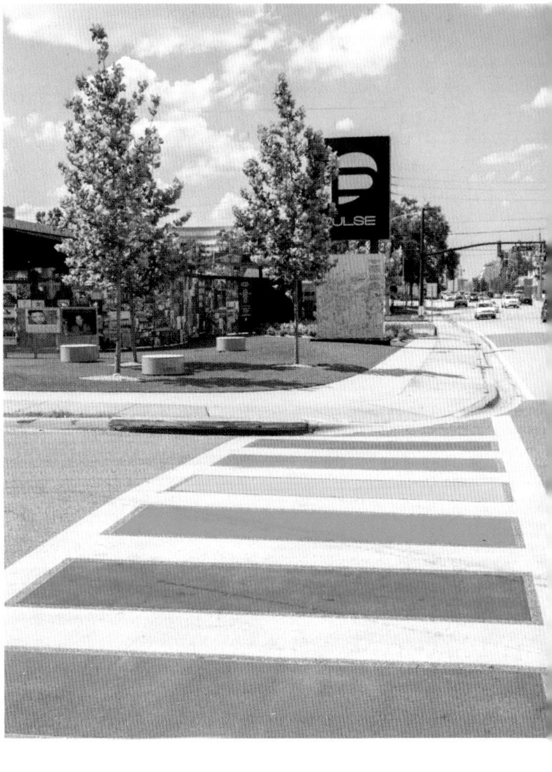

72 Turn Disney World all shades of pink

One Magical Weekend, Orlando, Florida, USA

When to go: June
Best for: Family fun, rides, and tiaras

Every June at Walt Disney World Resort® in Orlando, attendees can enjoy America's most magical LGBTQ+ weekend with four days of gay pool parties, extended theme-park hours, and the best queer company. Riptide is the weekend's not-to-be-missed signature event held in the Typhoon Lagoon Waterpark, with late-night water rides and DJs spinning tracks until dawn.

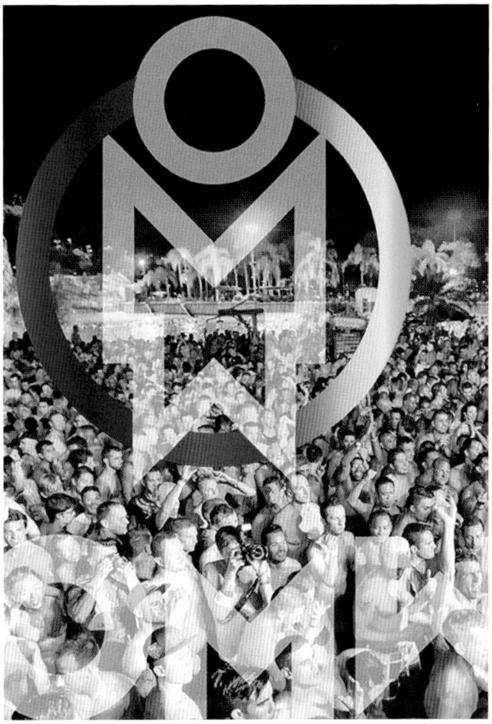

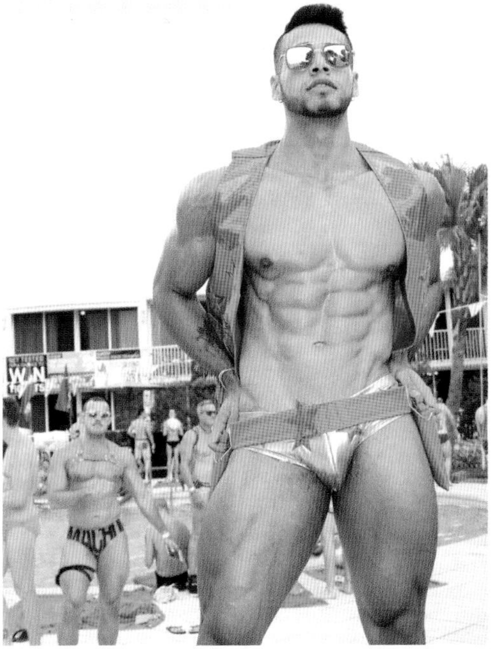

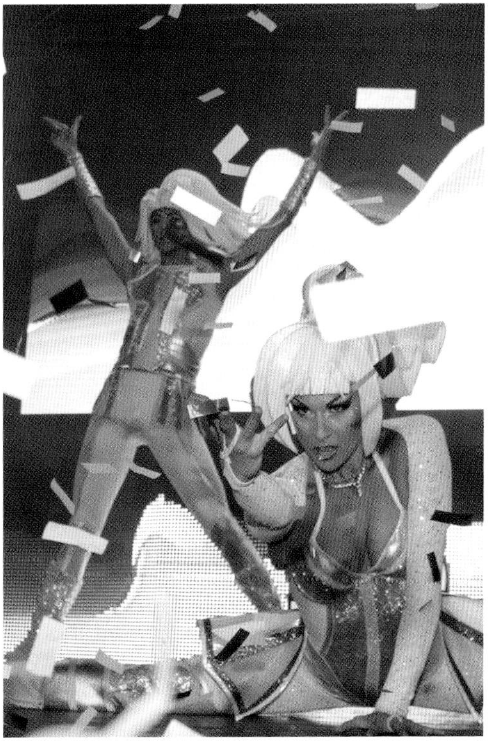

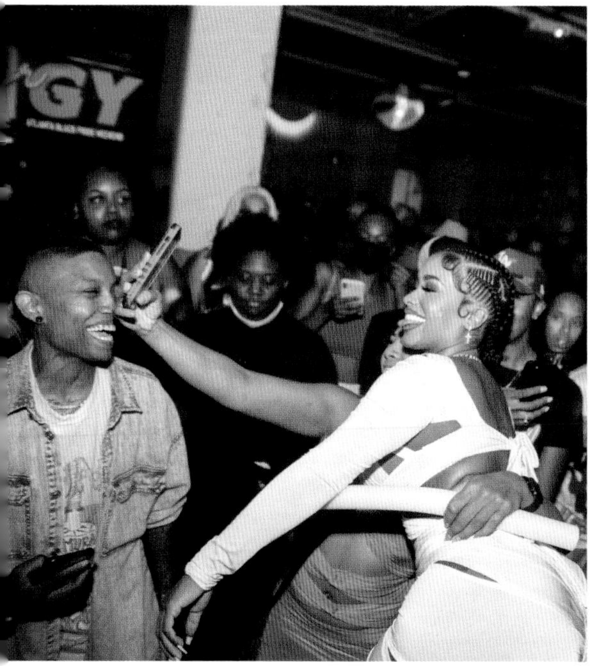

73 Pick your party

◀ ▼ Atlanta Black Pride, Atlanta, Georgia, USA

When to go: August to September
Best for: No-holds-barred partying

The largest Black Pride event in the United States, Atlanta Black Pride is a nearly week-long celebration, with more parties than anyone could hope to attend. Fully inclusive, there are women-centric events—including Naked Hustle at iconic strip club Magic City—and trans-centric events, such as the Trans Life Awards.

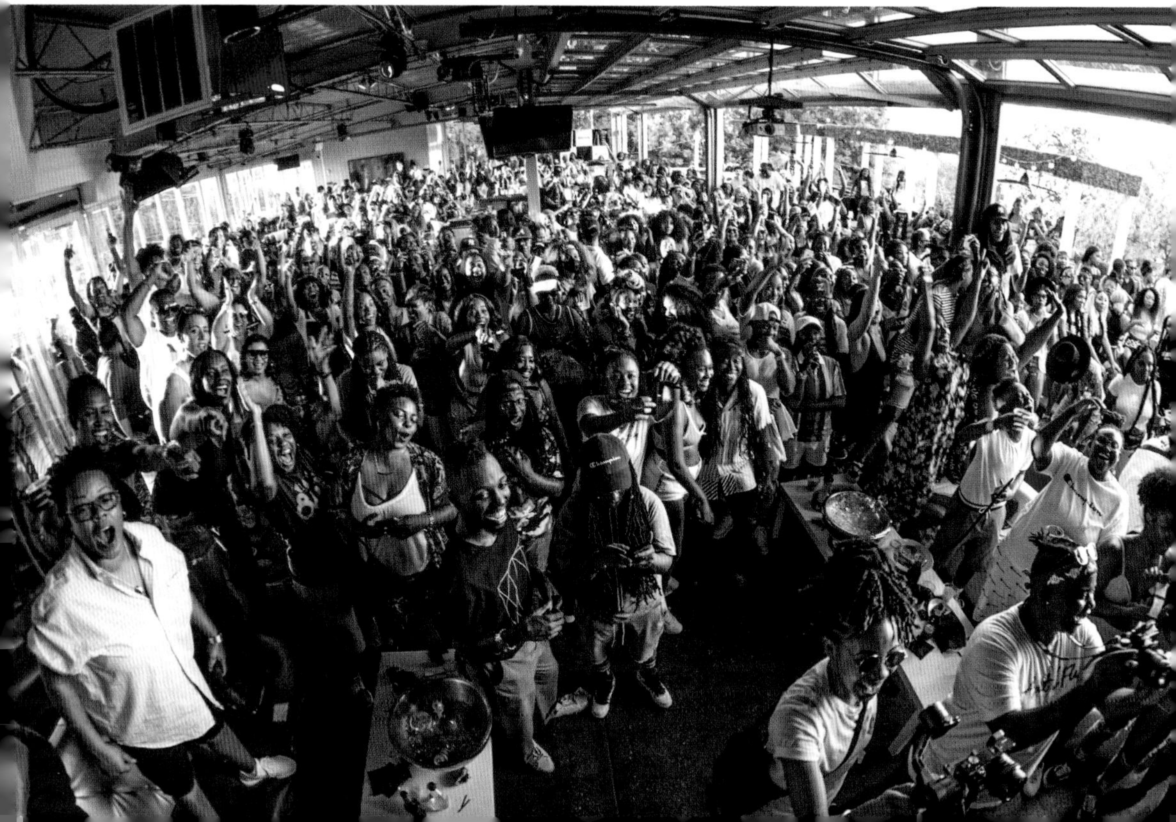

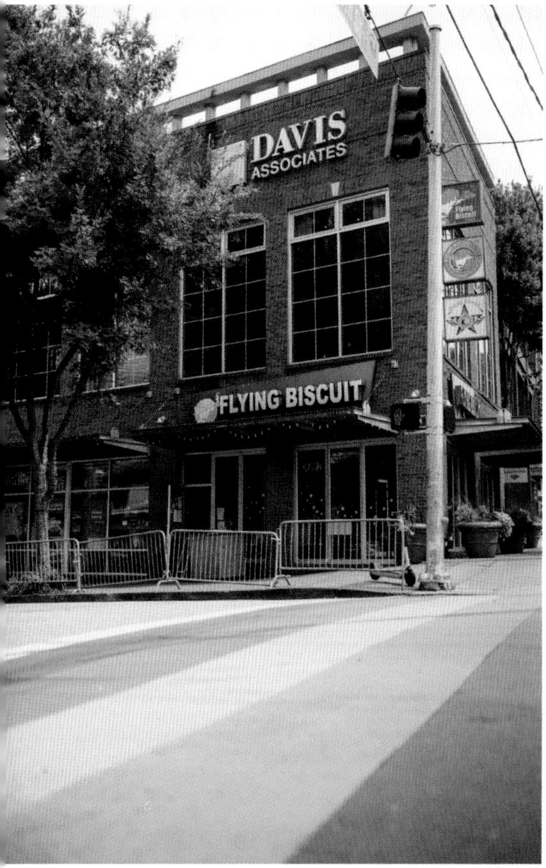

74 Barhop uptown, downtown and Midtown

◀ Midtown, Atlanta, Georgia, USA

When to go: March to May and September to November
Best for: The Southern queer experience

A square of vivid rainbow stripes at 10th and Piedmont Streets mark the epicenter of Atlanta's most LGBTQ+ neighborhood, Midtown. On the corner, you'll find a lesbian-founded Flying Biscuit Café, well-known for its all-day Southern breakfast. From here it's only 70 steps to Atlanta's iconic gay bar, Blake's. You'll find the South's only lesbian bar a 10-minute walk away: My Sister's Room (MSR). On the edge of Midtown, Atlanta BeltLine and queer bar Friends on Ponce are well worth a visit.

75 Read all about it

Women and Children First Bookstore, Chicago, USA

When to go: All year
Best for: Opening your mind

This iconic, trans-inclusive, feminist bookstore, one of the USA's largest and open since 1979, features readings year-round, stocks hard-to-find women authors and feminist works both classic and contemporary, and hosts a number of reading groups so you can sharpen your critical analysis with like-minded folk.

76 Meet the sportspeople out in front

National Gay & Lesbian Sports Hall of Fame, Chicago, USA

When to go: All year
Best for: The sports-loving queer

Though women's sports have historically been much more accepting of queer athletes than men's, the National Gay and Lesbian Sports Hall of Fame was established shortly after Jason Collins came out to become the first out gay NBA player. Athletes from a wide variety of sports are represented, including basketball, baseball, athletics, martial arts, and many others.

77 Drop by, if you're in the neighborhood

▼ ▶ Northalsted and Andersonville, Chicago, USA

When to go: August
Best for: A gay, family-friendly outing

Northalsted was formerly known as "boystown" and Andersonville as "girlstown." Northalsted is one of the oldest officially recognized gay neighborhoods in the United States, while Andersonville retains much of its lesbian identity—Women & Children First bookstore is still a landmark. Vintage stores, boutiques, and casual, funky eateries abound. Also check out Market Days, featuring live music, art, and parties every August.

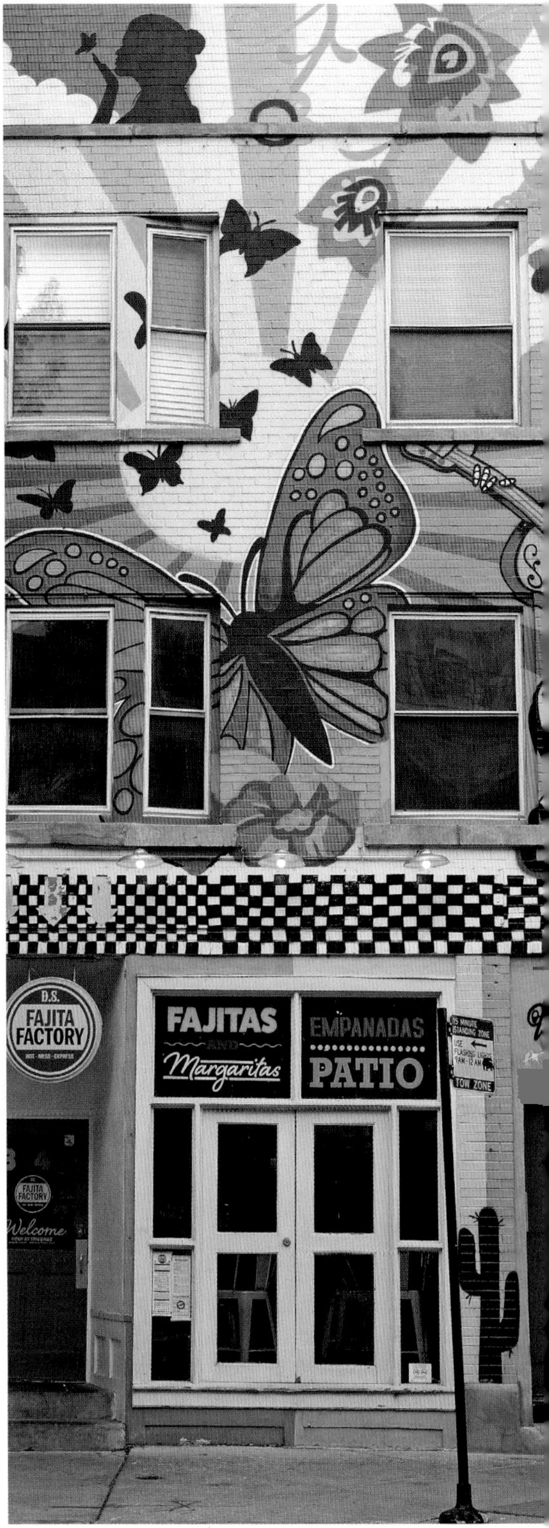

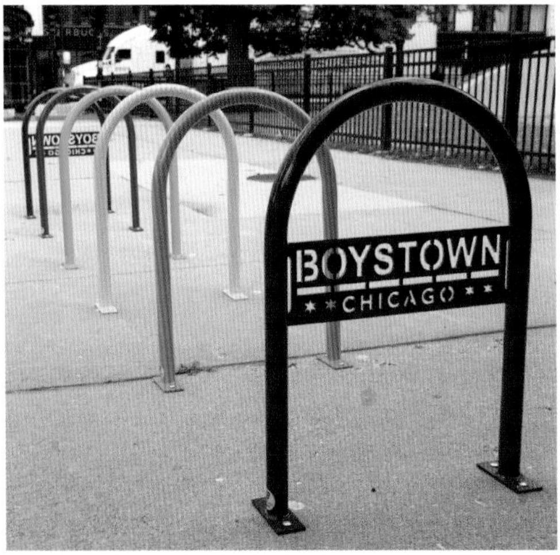

78 Walk among giants

▶ The Legacy Walk, North Halsted Street, Chicago, USA

When to go: All year
Best for: Paying homage

The Legacy Walk is a unique stopping point in Chicago's Lakeview "gayborhood." A series of 25-ft/8-m tall rainbow pylons run along North Halsted Street. Each bears brass plaques commemorating notable activists and LGBTQ+ figures: people such as Keith Haring, Walt Whitman, James Baldwin, Frida Kahlo, Bayard Rustin and Audre Lorde. The Legacy Walk's first 18 pylons were dedicated on National Coming Out Day, October 11, 2012, with more memorials added each year. In 2019, the Legacy Walk was granted historic landmark status.

79 Slap on those chaps

International Mr. Leather, Chicago, USA

When to go: May
Best for: Leather enthusiasts

Going strong for decades, Chicago's International Mr. Leather is the largest leather conference and competition in the world. It's a cross between a trade show, a beauty pageant, and a Pride festival, but centered entirely around the Leather and Bootblack communities. Leather enthusiasts, vendors, and fans gather here to build community, buy and sell, and, of course, compete for the title of International Mr. Leather.

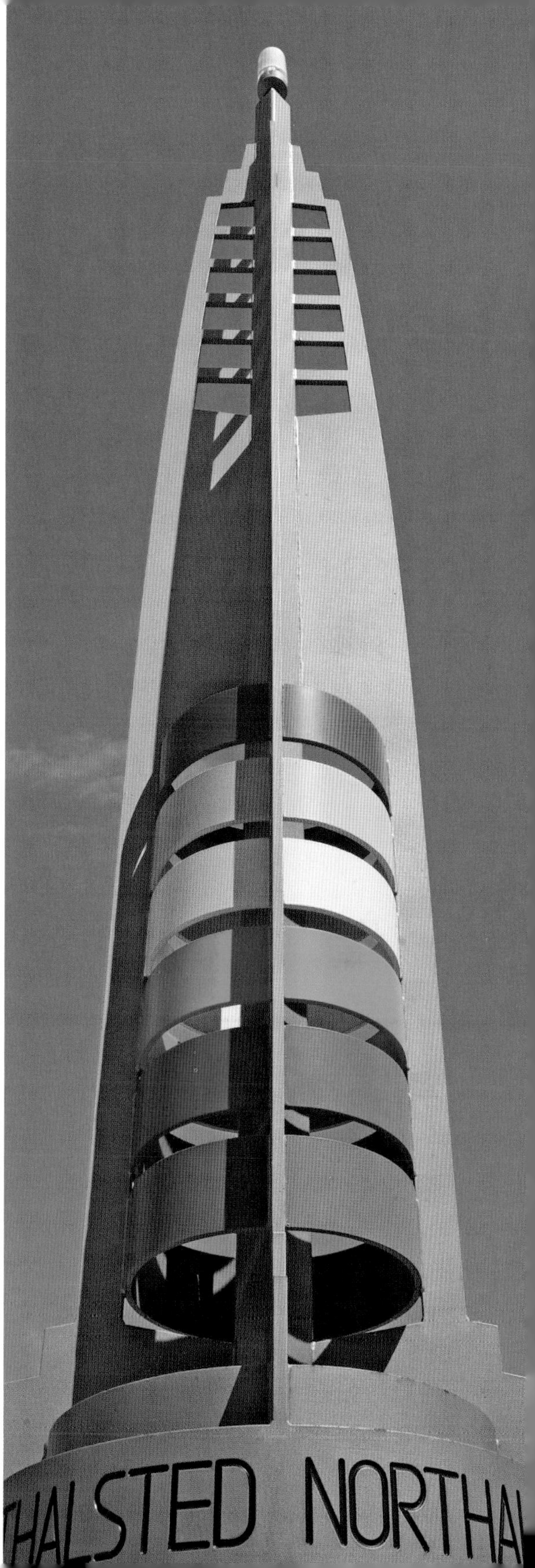

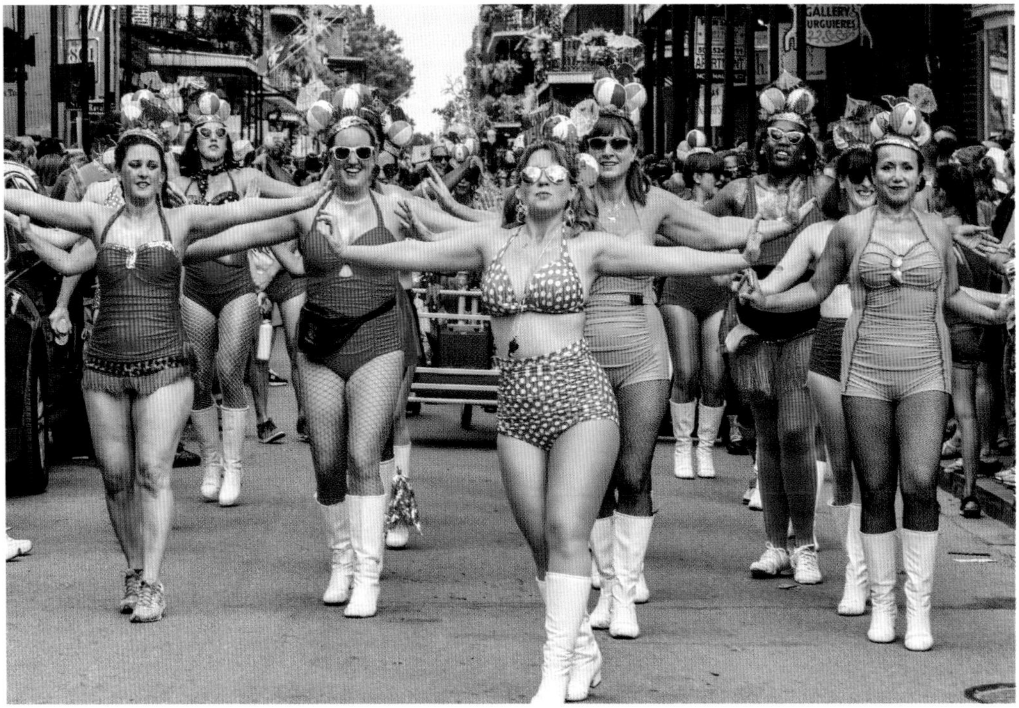

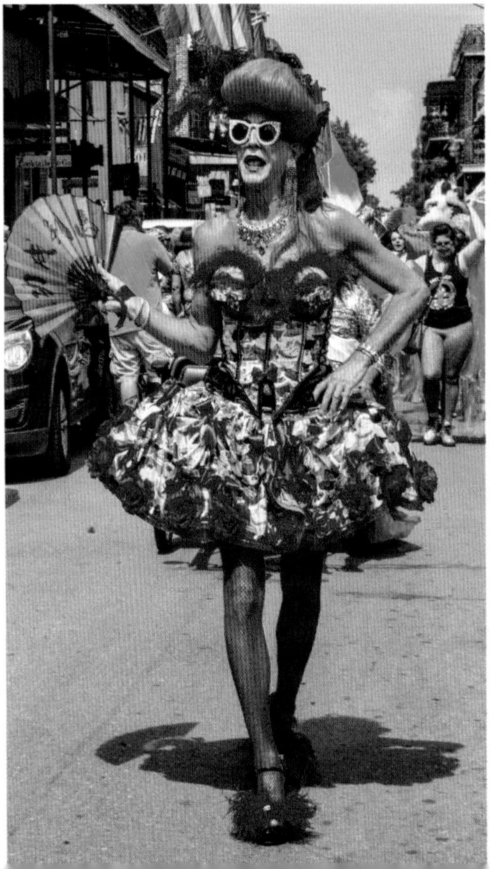

80 Mardi Gras who?

◀ ▲ Southern Decadence, New Orleans, Louisiana, USA

When to go: September
Best for: Debauchery

New Orleans is known for hosting a parade or street party nearly every week of the year, but Southern Decadence is, true to its name, one of the rowdiest. The festival is similar to Mardi Gras, with parades and bead-tossing, though it's much sexier and LGBTQ-centric—and often larger in both scope and attendance.

81 Step up while you dress up

LGBT Halloween, New Orleans, Louisiana, USA

When to go: October
Best for: Putting the fun in fundraising

Halloween is, to many, "gay Christmas," and New Orleans does it like no other. While costume contests and dance parties are *de rigueur* for any Halloween celebration, New Orleans' LGBTQ festival has always been a fundraiser for the Lazarus Project, a home for people living with AIDS. Over the years, the annual celebration has raised nearly $5 million for the cause.

82 Escape to the woods

▼ Campit Resort, Fennville, Michigan, USA

When to go: Mid-April to mid-October
Best for: Log-cabin realness and getting back to nature

If your idea of vacation heaven is a log cabin in the woods, then this rural Michigan camping ground ticks all the right boxes. Campit can be found 10 minutes from the towns of Saugatuck and Douglas. Aimed at the whole LGBTQ+ community, it offers 33 acres/0.1 km^2 to explore or just kick back and relax. The Lake Michigan beaches are not far away, and there's a busy calendar of theme weekends.

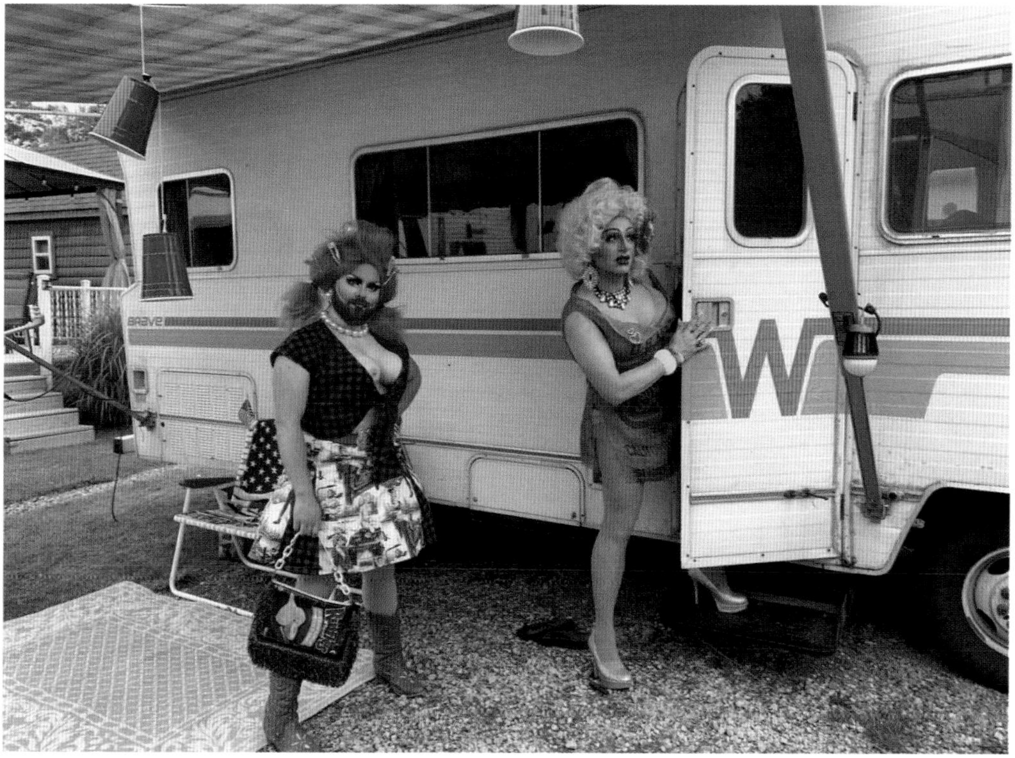

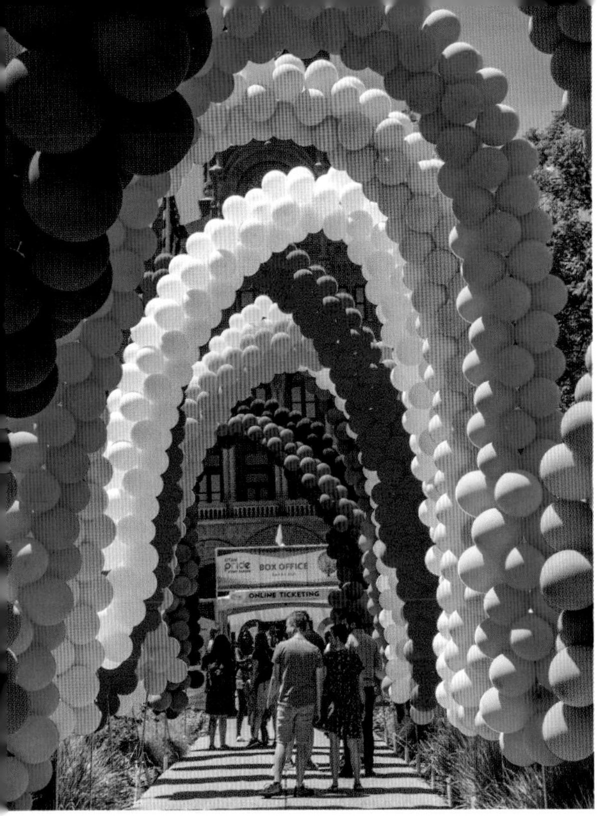

83 Gayer than L.A.

◀ Salt Lake City, Utah, USA

When to go: June
Best for: Unexpected Pride

Salt Lake and Mormonism are inseparable—so many are surprised to find that Salt Lake City is extremely LGBTQ-friendly. Statistically it has more LGBTQ+ couples than Los Angeles, and in 2019 the city elected a lesbian mayor. Salt Lake City Pride is huge, but also the Marmalade "gayborhood" has plenty of LGBTQ-centered establishments, and the bars and nightlife are a whole scene.

84 See yourself on the big screen

Connecticut LGBTQ Film Festival, Hartford, Connecticut, USA

When to go: June
Best for: Excellent films

The longest-running film festival in Connecticut, Out Film CT runs through the early weeks of June as a lead-in to Pride. The overall quality of films is high due to its rigorous screening process.

85 Camp it up

Camp Camp, near Portland, Maine, USA

When to go: Late August
Best for: The summer camp vibe

This beloved and welcoming week-long summer camp aimed at all LGBTQ+ adults has been running since 1977. It offers many of the things you associate with camp—hiking, lake swimming, canoeing, softball, plus arts and crafts such as pottery and figure drawing—as well as some activities more queer-oriented, such as Broadway dance. It's all set in the beautiful, pine-filled countryside of southwestern Maine. It's said around 75 percent of those who attend each year are repeat visitors: a testimony to a supportive, empowering, and unique escape.

86 What happens on Naples Drive...

▼ The Fruit Loop, Las Vegas, Nevada, USA

When to go: All year
Best for: Debauchery in the desert

Las Vegas is known for its permissive culture and hedonism, so LGBTQ+ folks are welcomed throughout the city. If you're looking for queer-specific fun, though, the Fruit Loop is the tongue-in-cheek name for a "gayborhood" of LGBTQ-centric nightclubs and businesses on East Naples Drive.

87 "They didn't know we were seeds"

Transgender Memorial Garden, St. Louis, Missouri, USA

When to go: Transgender Day of Remembrance
Best for: Paying respect to trans lives lost

Set up by volunteers, the Transgender Memorial Garden in St. Louis, Missouri, reminds the world of just some of the people lost to violent discrimination and hate. It was dedicated on November 20, 2015: Transgender Day of Remembrance. A sign at the entrance features a quote from Greek poet Dinos Christianopoulos: "They tried to bury us. They didn't know we were seeds." Besides hackberry and redbud trees, some plants were chosen specifically to attract butterflies. The insects represent transformation for many in the trans community.

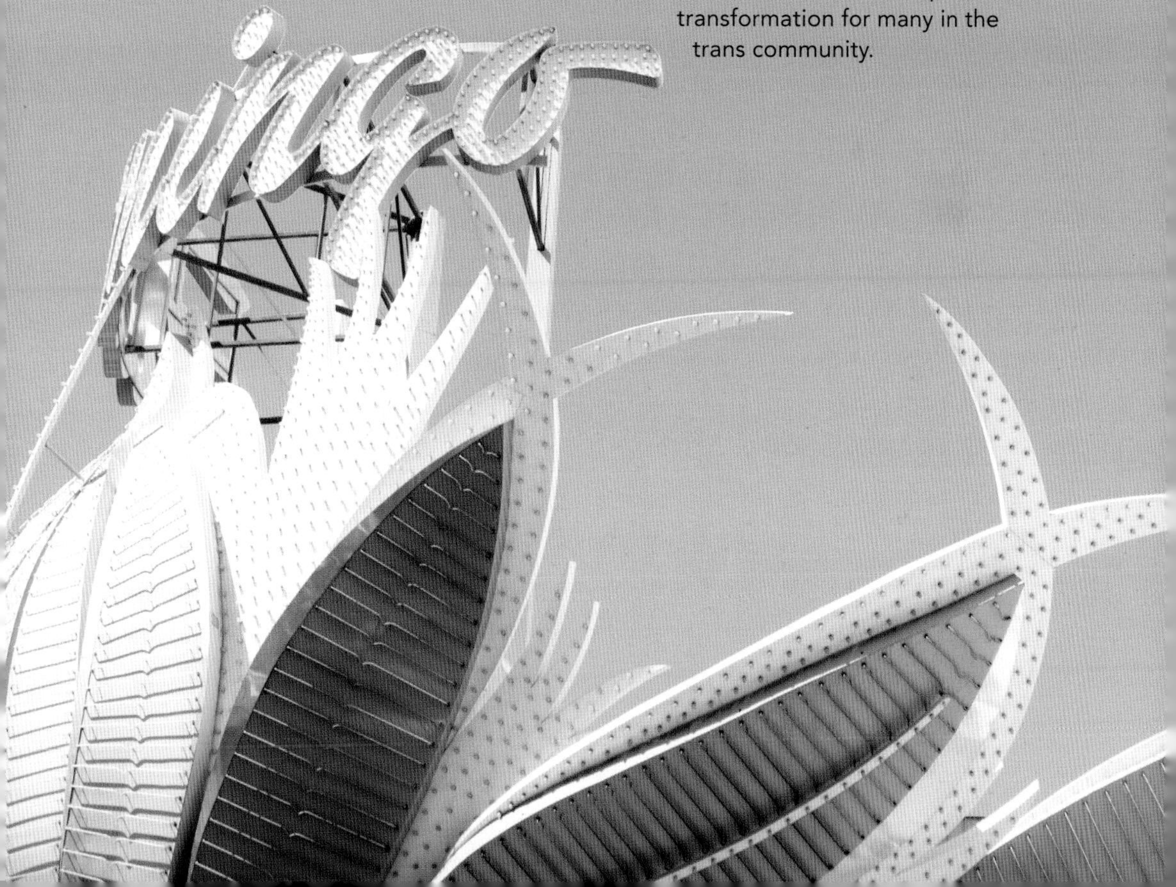

88 Not so lone star

Austin Pride, Texas, USA

When to go: August
Best for: Finding friends

Austin has a reputation as a counter-cultural oasis in the middle of a largely conservative state. It's a welcome pocket of LGBTQ-friendliness in the US South, and its massive Pride celebration reflects this.

89 Keep it country

▼ Nashville Pride, Tennessee, USA

When to go: June
Best for: Queer music lovers

Known as an epicenter of American music, Nashville Pride features over 250 concerts; big-name queer headliners of the past have included Salt N' Pepa, Kim Petras, Orville Peck, Lizzo, and Big Freedia. This massive Pride features installation art, as well as adult, family, and youth sections to the high-energy festival.

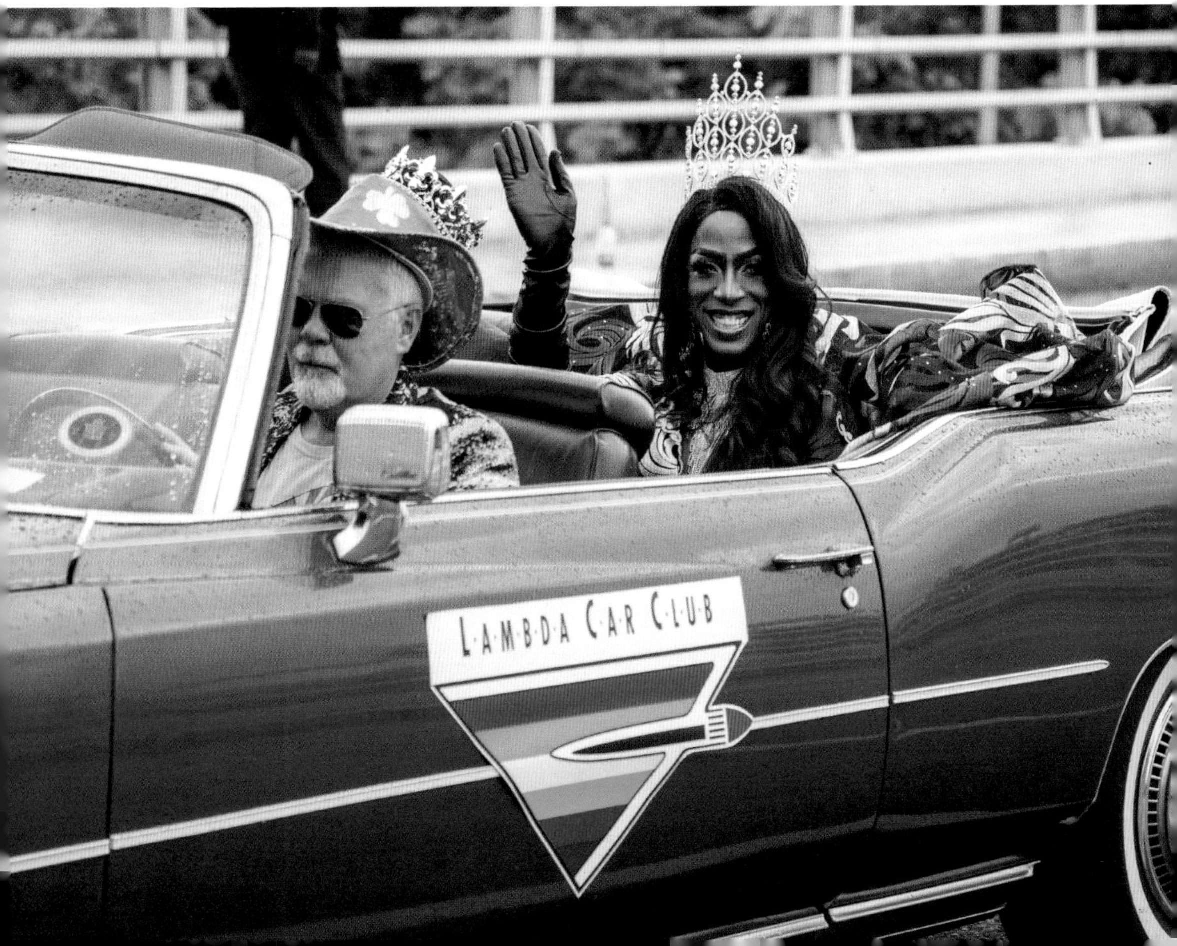

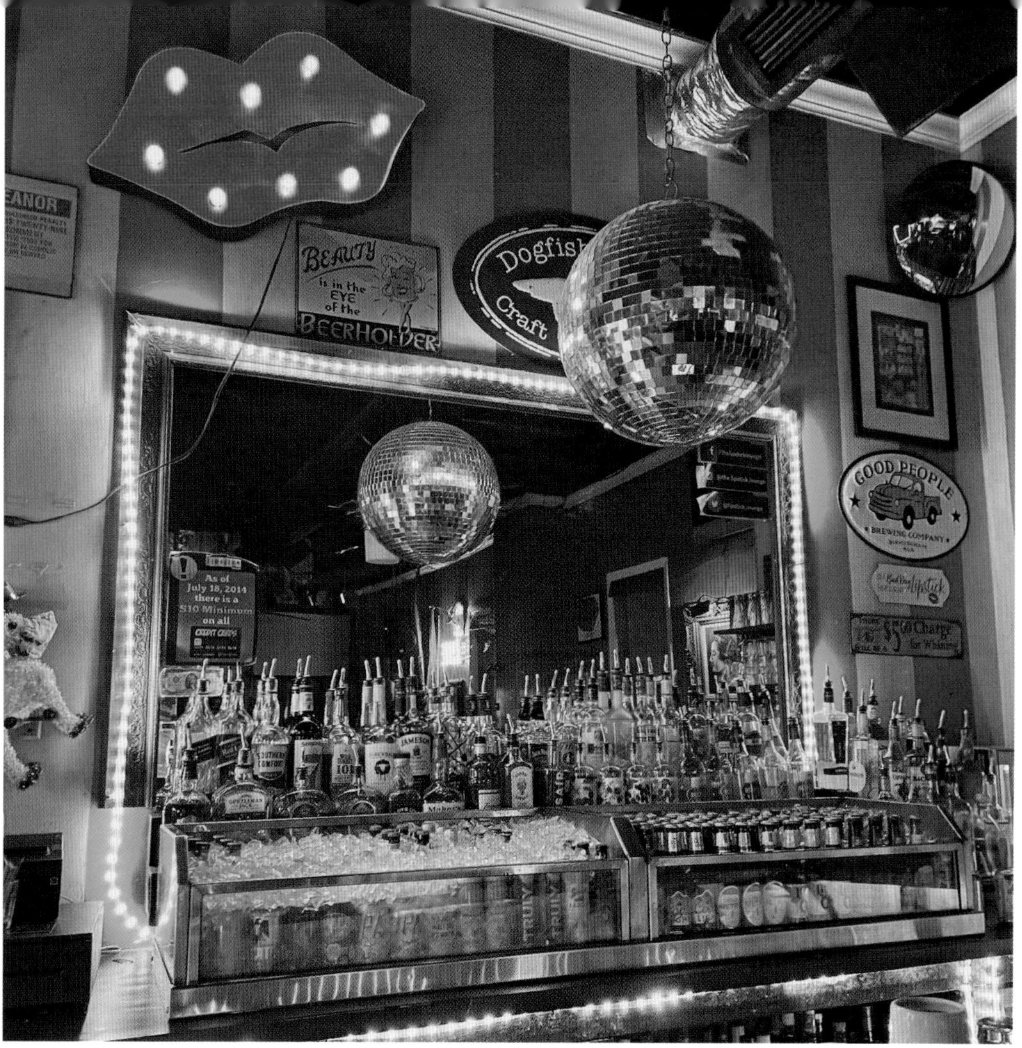

90 Sing your heart out

▲ Lipstick Lounge, Nashville, Tennessee, USA

When to go: All year
Best for: Tracy Chapman impressions

The Lipstick Lounge, a beloved lesbian-owned-but-inclusive-of-all bar that some Nashville residents consider "church," has been making the case that karaoke is gay for 20 years.

91 Southern comfort

Tri-State Black Pride, Memphis, Tennessee, USA

When to go: June
Best for: Celebrating being Black and queer

Memphis sits nearly at the intersection between Arkansas, Mississippi, and Tennessee, so this Pride festival brings Black queer and trans folks from a wide geographical area to celebrate together.

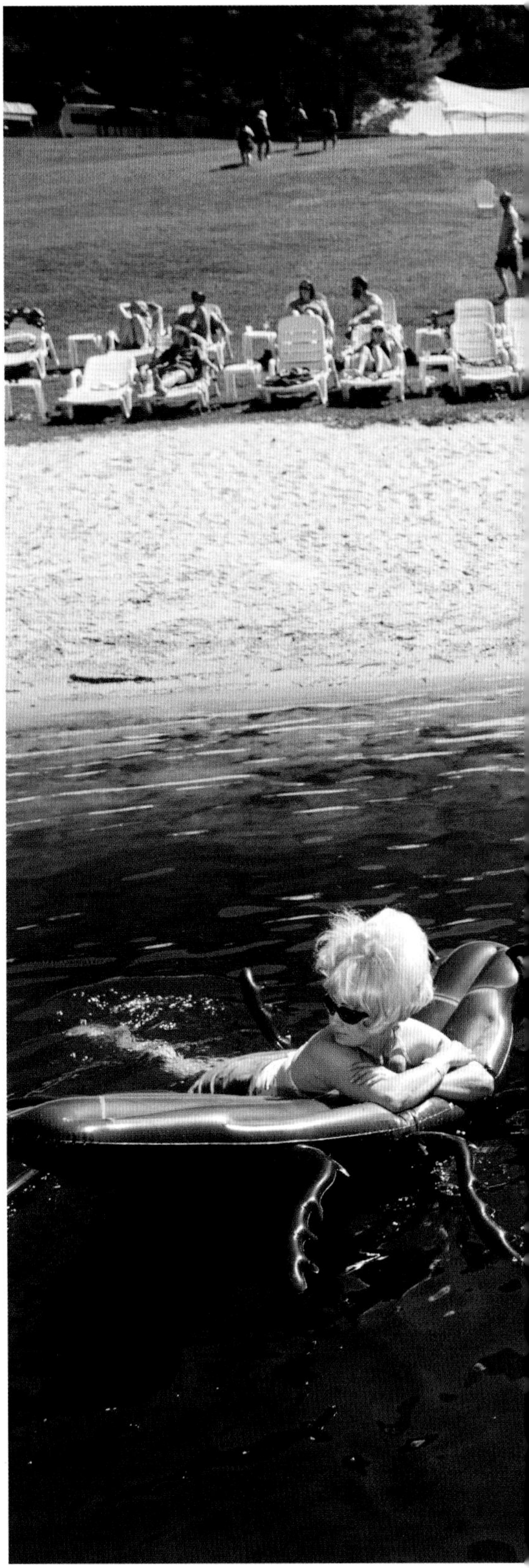

92 An alternative way to take the Waters

Camp John Waters, Kent, Connecticut, USA

When to go: September
Best for: Filthy film lovers

Pioneering filmmaker John Waters is known for campy, controversial, cult-movie classics starring drag queen Divine, such as *Pink Flamingos* and *A Dirty Shame*, as well as mainstream hits like *Hairspray*. He has expressed equal joy in the high and the lowbrow, and Camp John Waters channels his boundlessly creative spirit into this all-inclusive, adult "sleep-away camp." The weekend features the requisite outdoor activities, such as campfires and swimming in the lake, as well as costume contests, themed dance parties, film marathons, karaoke, and—drumroll please—a one-man show from Waters himself. Guest celebrity "camp counselors" such as Debbie Harry, Ricki Lake, and Kathleen Turner have also been part of the fun in the past.

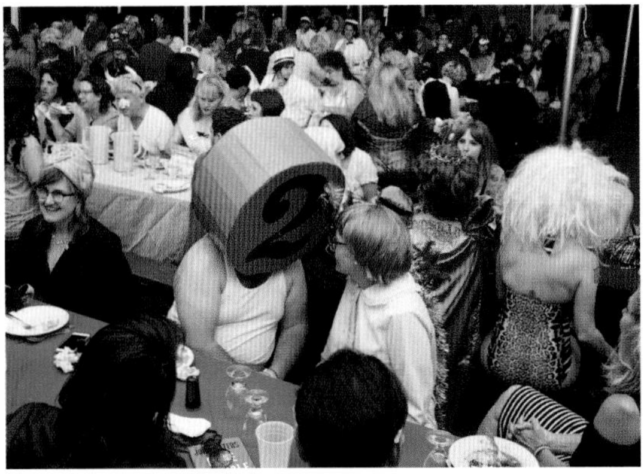

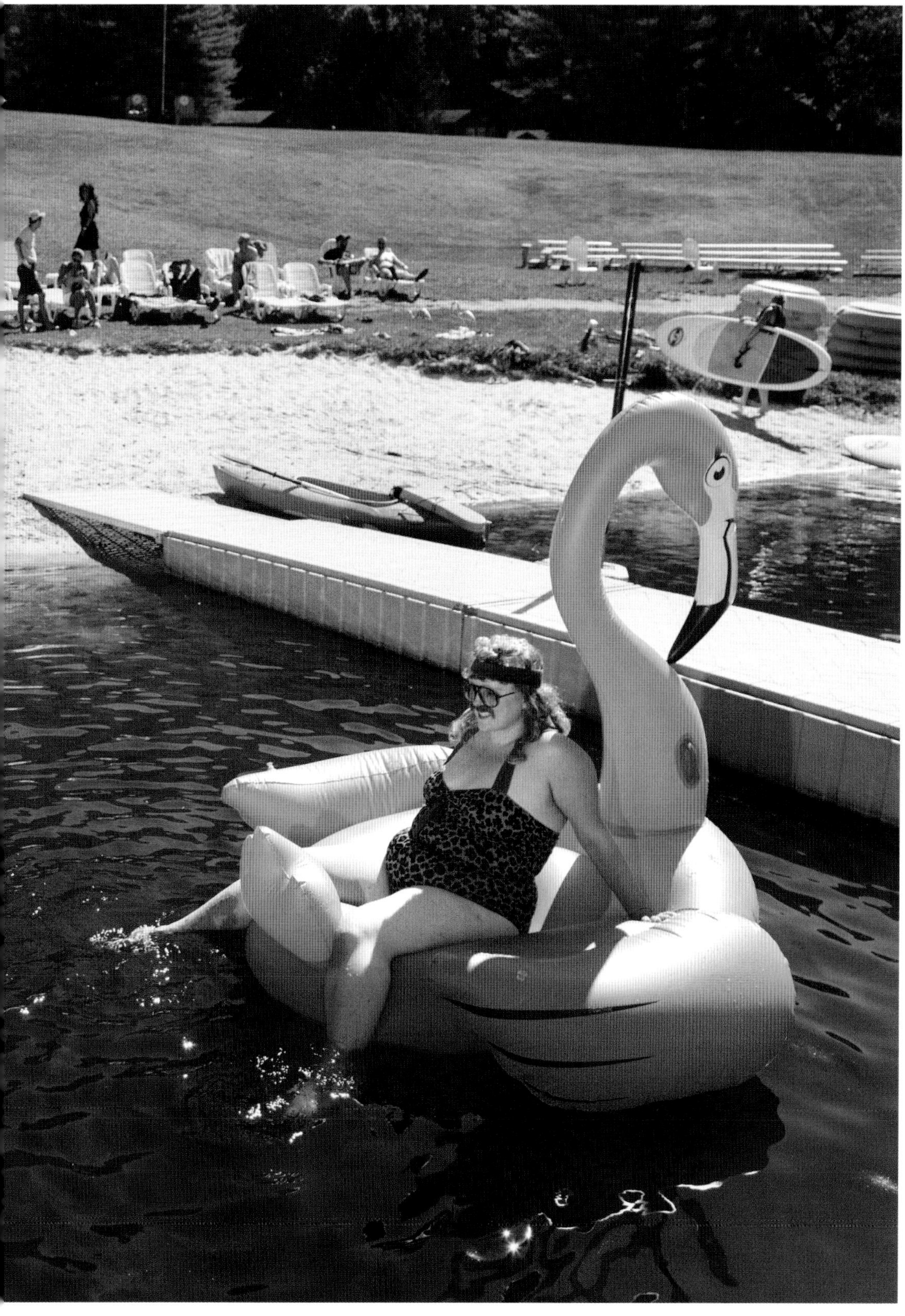

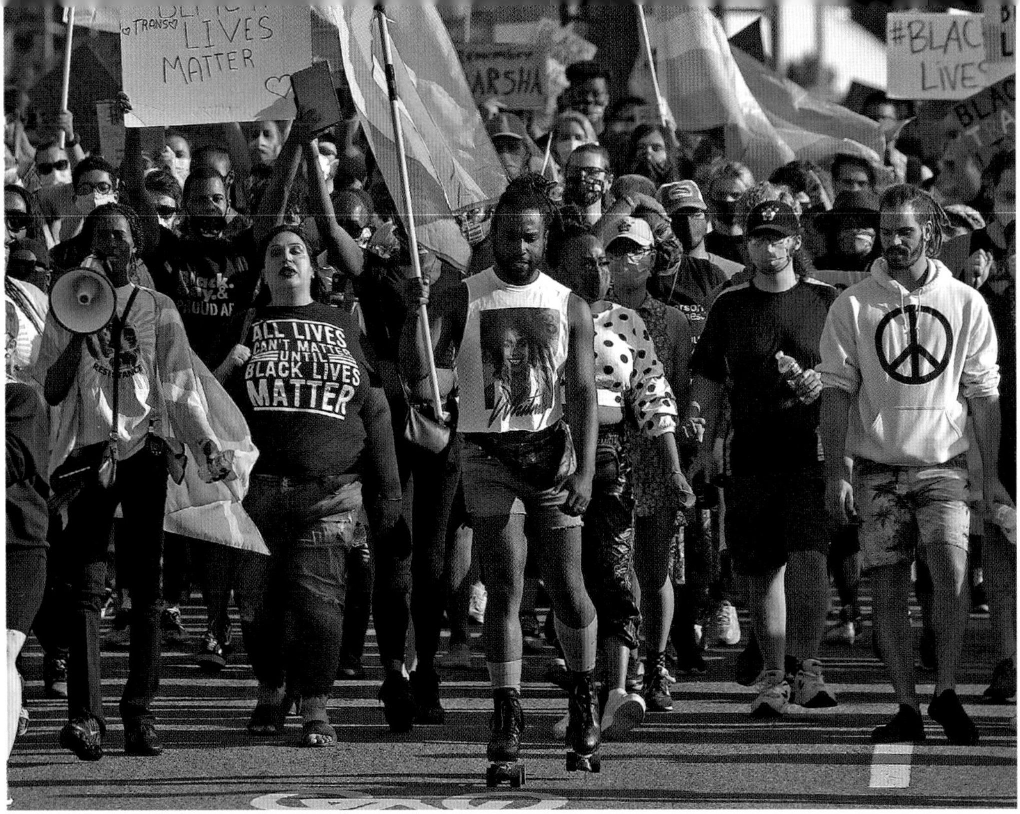

93 Simply divine

Divine mural, Baltimore, Maryland, USA

When to go: All year
Best for: Paying tribute to a drag icon

One of Baltimore's most famous sons was Harris Glenn Milstead, better known as the drag queen Divine. He rose to fame in the cult movies of gay director John Waters, and also enjoyed success as a singer of hi-NRG hits in the 1980s. He sadly died of a heart attack in 1988, aged 42. Milstead is honored in Baltimore's gay neighborhood of Mount Vernon with a mural by the street artist Gaia. Emblazoned with the title of one of Divine's dance hits, "I'm So Beautiful," it sits on the side of a house at 106 E. Preston Street.

94 No lives matter 'til all lives matter

▲ Trans Resistance March and Vigil, Boston, Massachusetts, USA

When to go: May
Best for: Showing support for Black trans lives

Mainstream LGBTQ+ Pride celebrations frequently focus on the L and the G, and rarely the rest, and have historically prioritized white voices over everyone else's. This march and festival for Black trans lives is an effort to take Pride back to its activist roots as a Black and trans-led protest against police harassment, and features performances, food, local vendors, and community resource sharing.

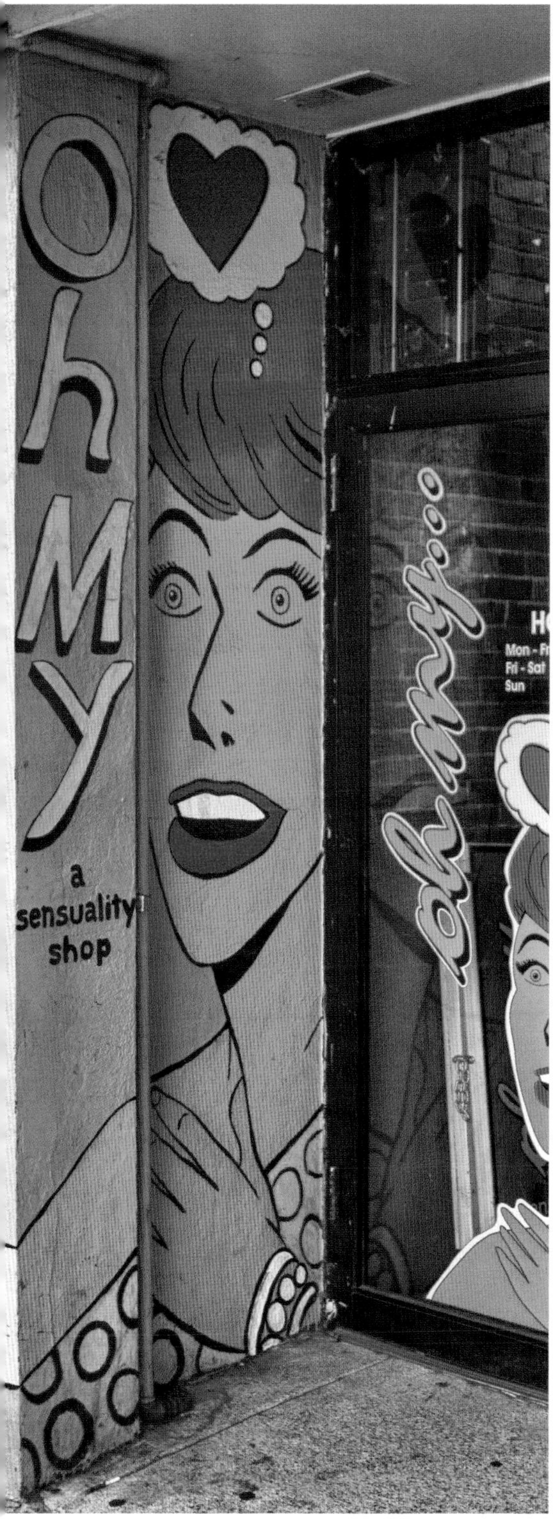

95 Lesbian learners

◀ Northampton, Massachusetts, USA

When to go: May to September
Best for: Queer women

Sometimes called "lesbianville," Northampton is home to Smith College, a small, women's, liberal arts school firmly associated with lesbianism in the public consciousness—and the vibe of the town doesn't dispel the notion. It is a very LGBTQ-friendly place with free-spirited "granola" vibes: hiking, veganism, and craft beer. The town itself is so inclusive of the whole queer community that very few venues—even if they're queer-owned, like Familiar's—feel the need to designate themselves as LGBTQ-specific. As such, FitzWilly's and The Dirty Truth aren't specifically "lesbian bars," but they are some of the most popular hangouts. Nearby Amherst is also a beloved small, LGBTQ-friendly town.

96 Just don't wear orange

▼ The Club, Provincetown, Massachusetts, USA

When to go: All year
Best for: Eating seafood and watching waves

This waterfront bar and restaurant in Provincetown had been a lesbian hangout for decades before Lea Delaria of TV-show *Orange Is The New Black*–fame took it over in 2019 and renamed it The Club. It features live entertainment every night and gorgeous views of the harbor through full-length windows across the restaurant.

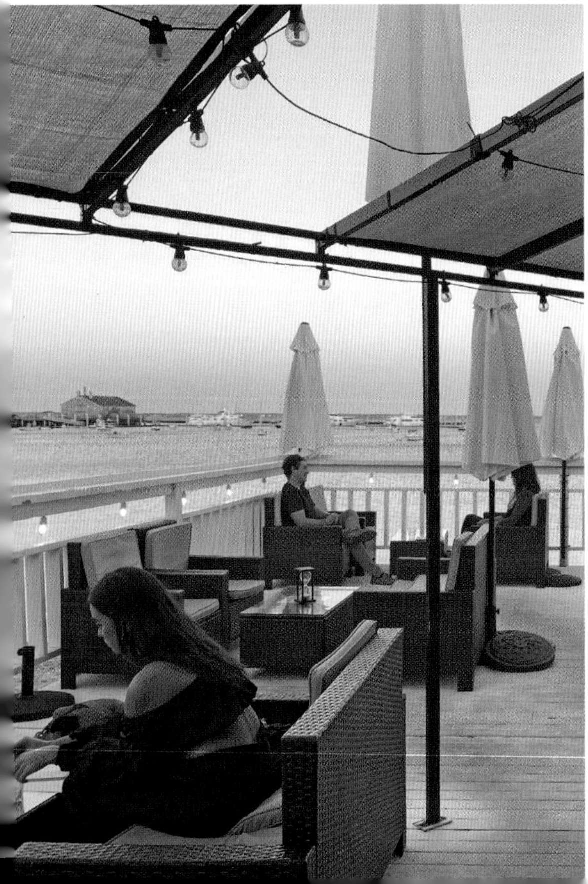

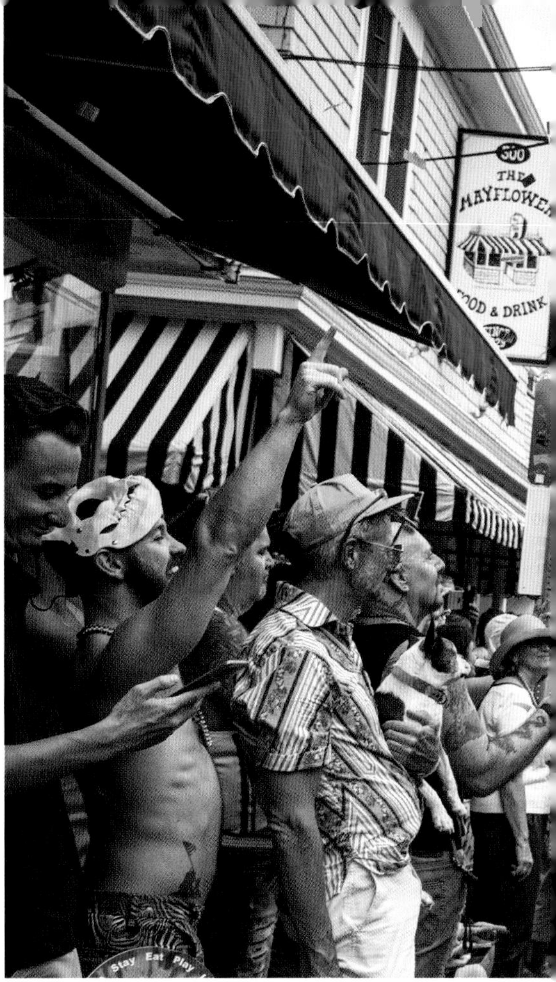

97 Dance back in time

Atlantic House, Provincetown, Massachusetts, USA

When to go: All year
Best for: Merging history and the present

Arguably the oldest gay bar in the United States, Atlantic House (or A-House) has been around for two hundred years. The Little Bar is the original tavern and features a jukebox and fireplace, while upstairs is the Macho Bar, catering to bears and leather enthusiasts. There's also an outdoor patio and, centuries later, still a lively dance floor throughout the summer.

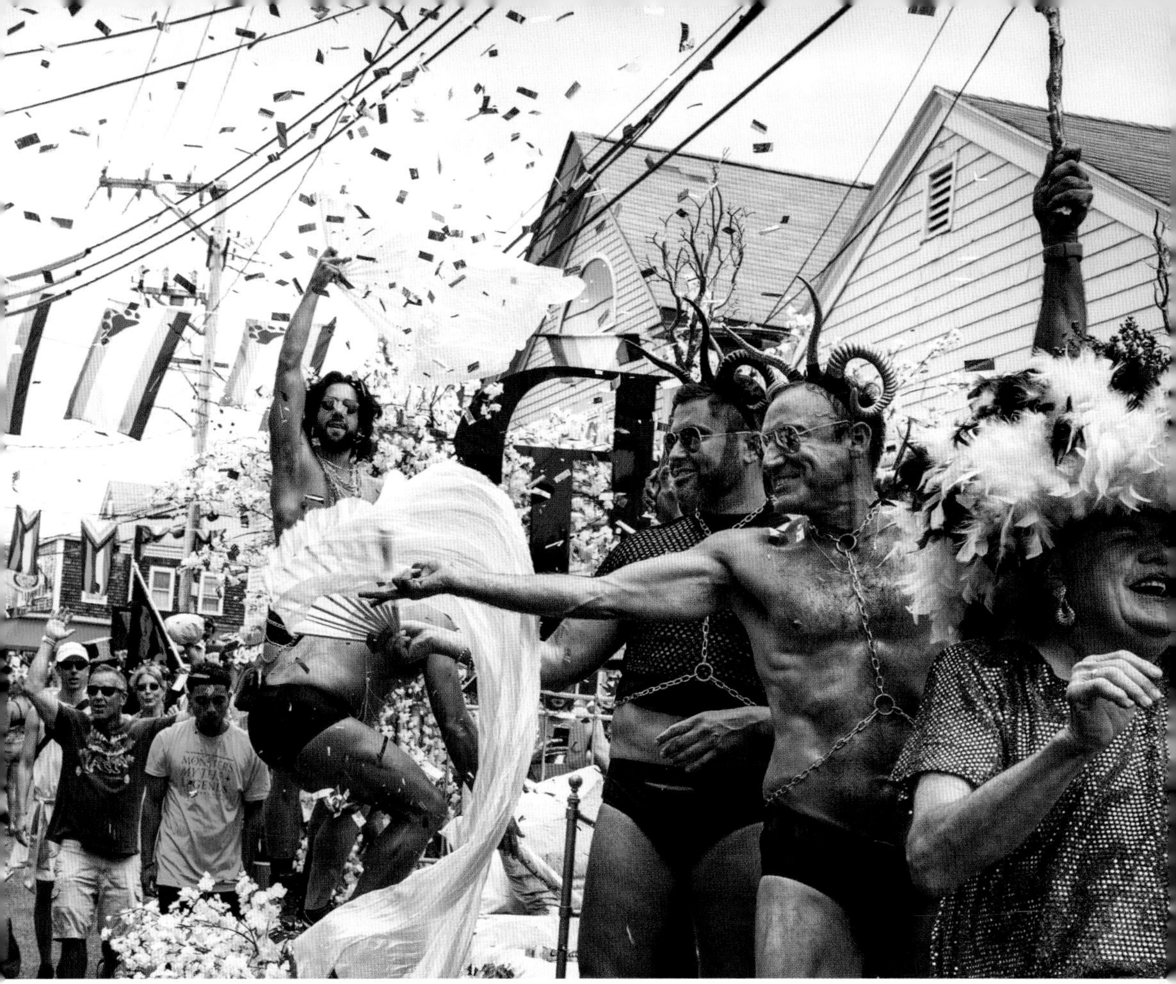

98 Cape Cod cool

▲ Provincetown, Massachusetts, USA

When to go: All year
Best for: Beautiful homes and hot homos

Provincetown has attracted LGBTQ+ visitors since the early twentieth century. They don't just come for the lobster roll and salt-water taffy: it's one of the queerest places in the USA. The summer season comes alive with a heavy calendar of festivals. Family Week, Bears Week, and Provincetown Carnival are just three of the busiest.

99 Where it's good to be a gay girl

Provincetown for Women, Massachusetts, USA

When to go: All year
Best for: Mingling

Provincetown For Women hosts lesbian-centric events year round, including Single Women's Weekend and Women's Week in October, Womxn of Color Weekend in June, and Girl Splash in July.

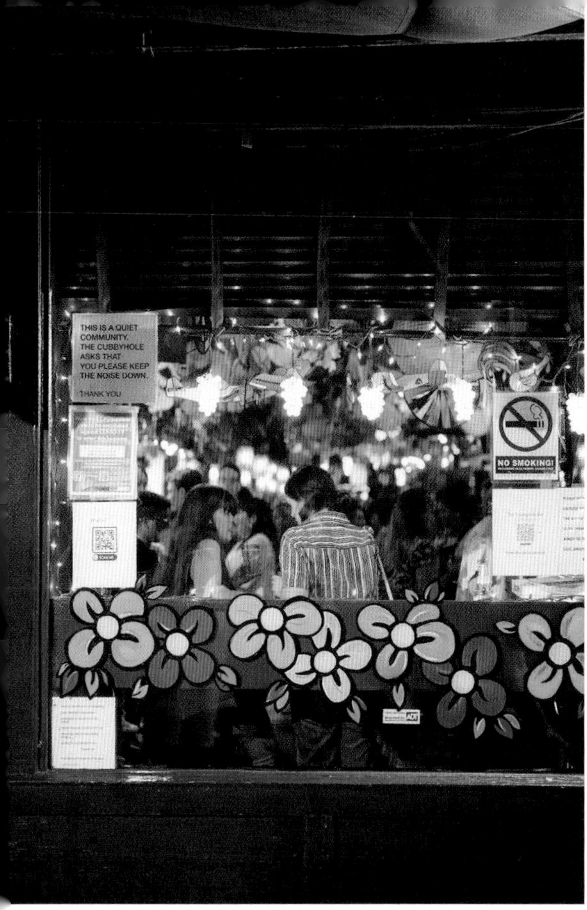

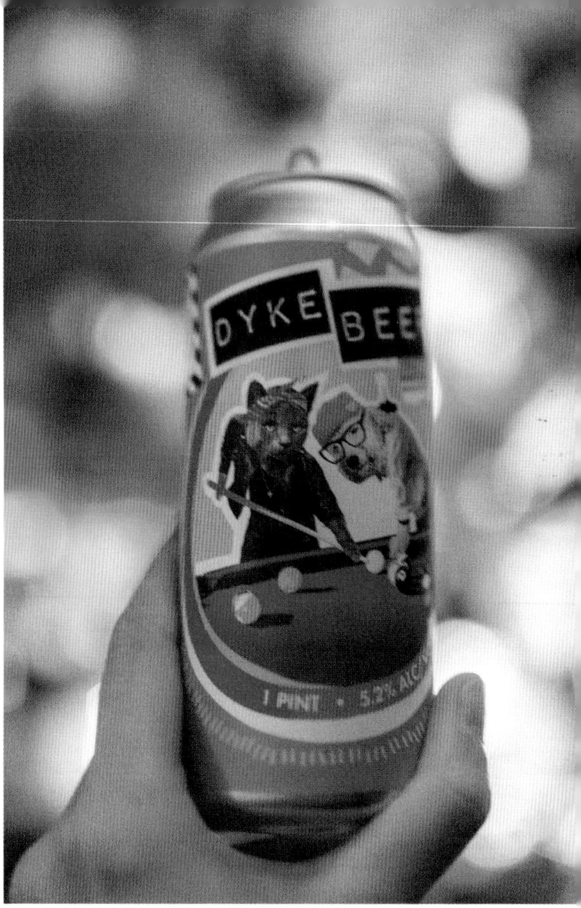

100 Find your cozy place

▲ Cubbyhole, New York, USA

When to go: All year
Best for: Being in the thick of it

Visiting this lesbian and queer women's bar is an experience. As the name suggests, it's a small space—360 ft^2/33.5 m^2. It gets packed and muggy quickly, but that is part of Cubbyhole's charm. Eclectic ornaments—usually seasonally themed—of all shapes and sizes decorate the ceiling. If you manage to squeeze through the crowd, you can find a funky retro jukebox in the back. Complete the experience by drinking the locally founded Dyke Beer when you're here.

101 Even clubs can grow old gracefully

▶ Henrietta Hudson, New York, USA

When to go: All year
Best for: Cocktails

Henrietta Hudson started as a thriving LGBTQ+ nightclub in New York, founded by two lesbians and donated boom boxes. Since turning 30, the venue has matured from the longest-running women's queer bar in the United States into a more mature and calmer safe space. Visit the charcuterie bar, or enjoy a cocktail in one of the many comfy nooks.

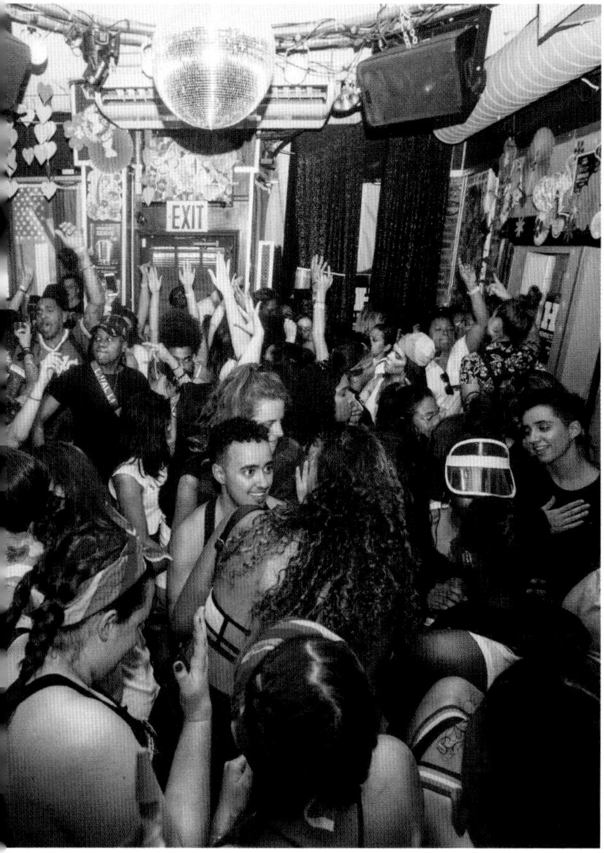
EXIT

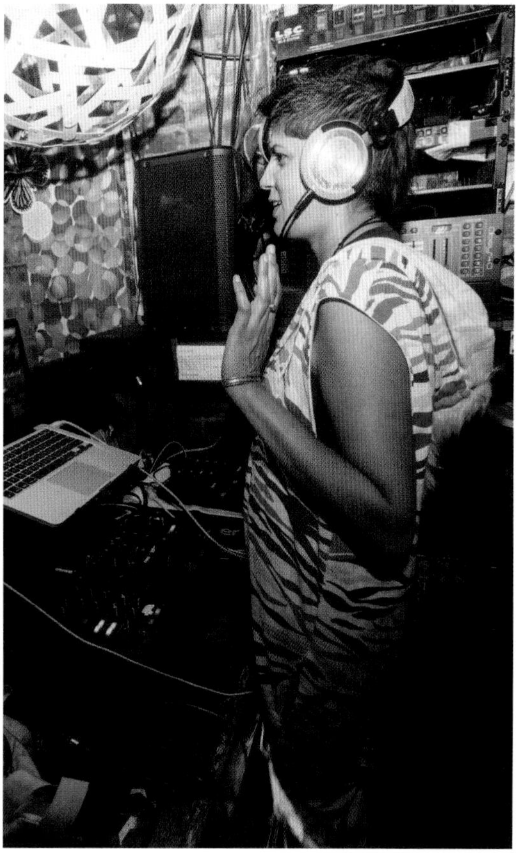

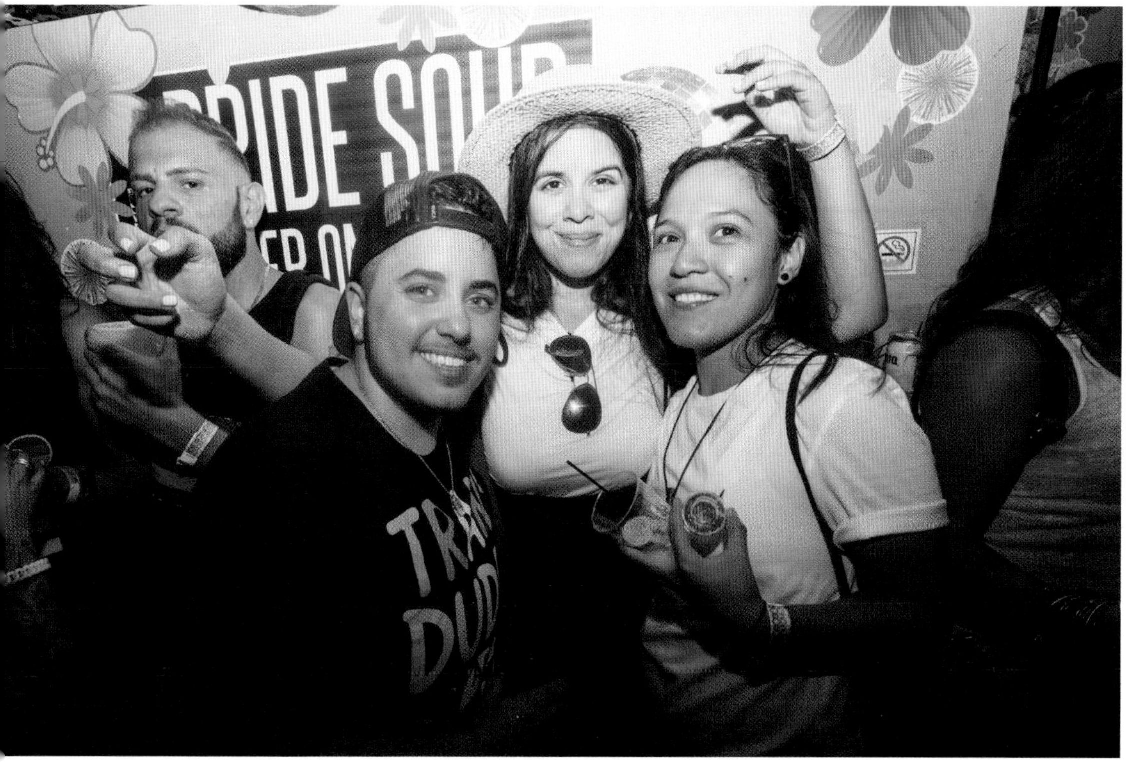
PRIDE

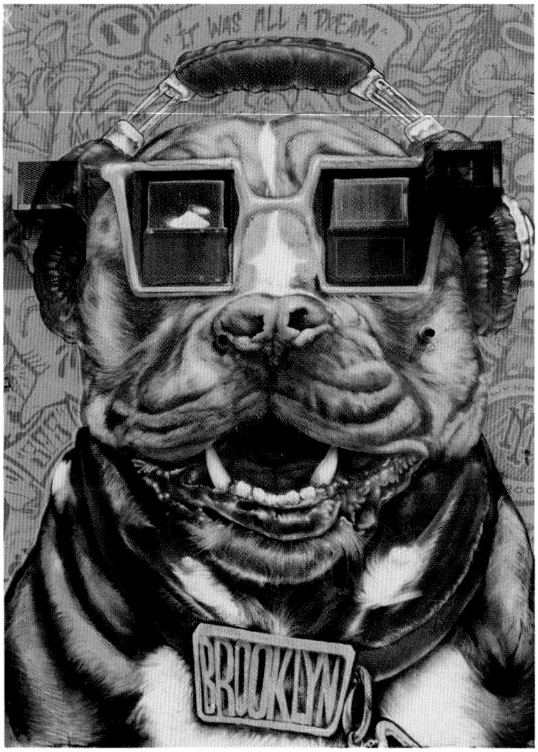

102 Art for all to see

Bushwick, New York, USA

When to go: All year
Best for: Marveling around NYC's artsiest neighborhood

Bushwick, in Brooklyn, has transformed over recent years into an edgy, artsy, inclusive neighborhood, full of vibrant murals. The murals began in 2011 when Bushwick local Joe Ficalora began using the medium of street art to transform what was a gritty and rundown area. The Bushwick Collective is an ever-growing collection of nearly a hundred blocks of murals that have transformed the area into an open-air art gallery. The Collective's annual Block Party brings the neighborhood together with street art, music, food trucks, and local vendors.

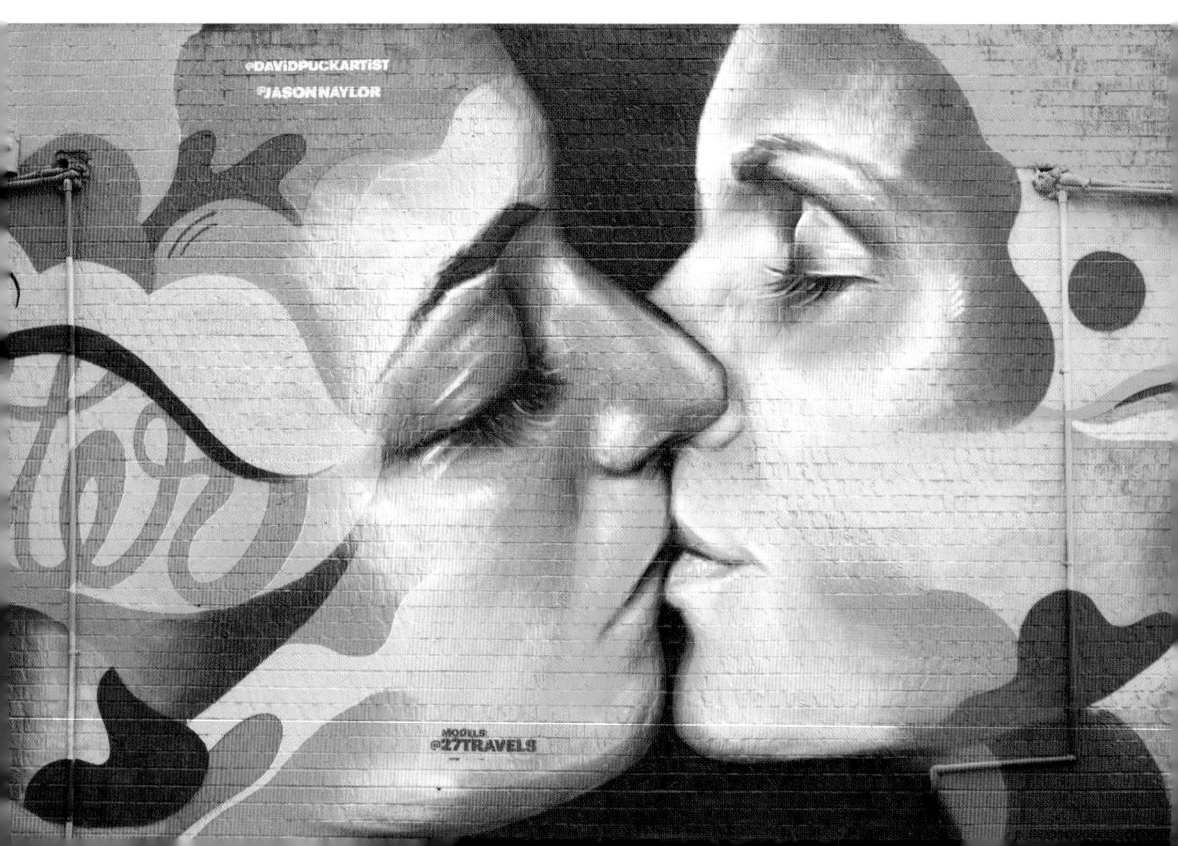

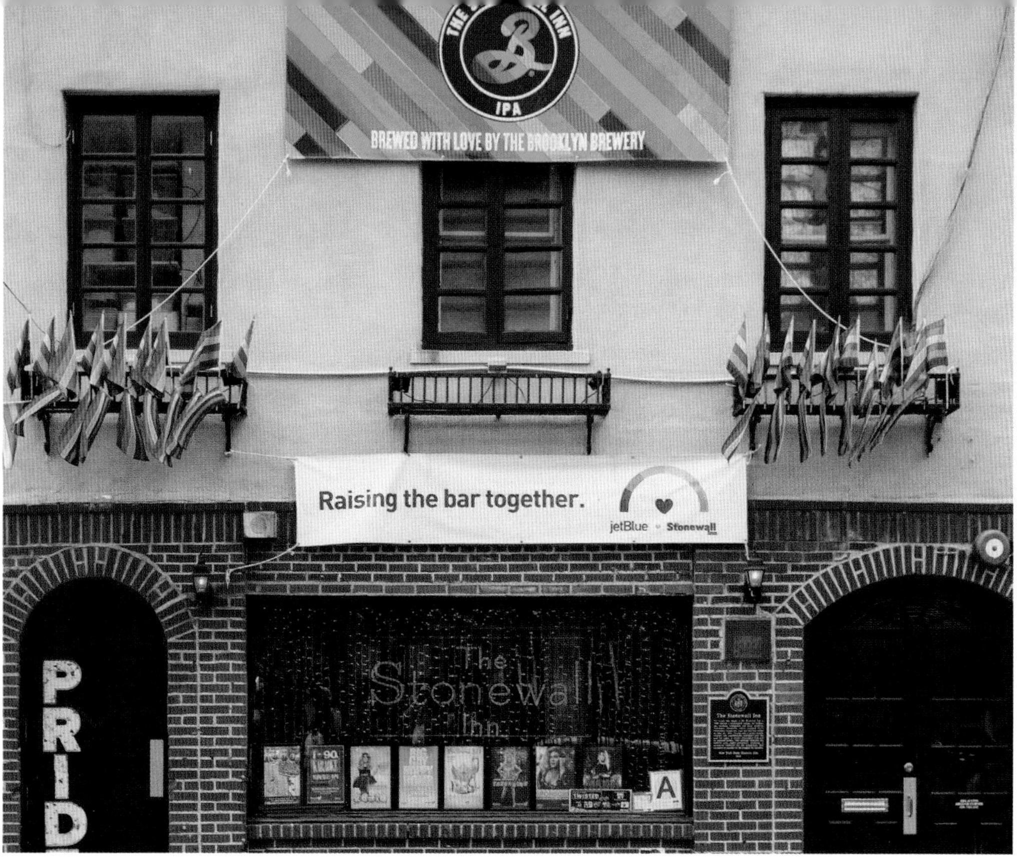

103 In the beginning there was Stonewall

The Stonewall Inn, New York, USA

When to go: All year
Best for: Honoring queer history

New York City's Stonewall Inn is probably one of the most famous gay bars in the world. This is because the original inn (located a couple of doors away) was the site of the Stonewall Uprising—six nights of LGBTQ+ people, including key figures Marsha Johnston and Sylvia Rivera, angrily protesting against police brutality following a police raid on the inn. At the time, the Stonewall was one of the biggest gay bars in the United States. The raid that took place on June 28, 1969, was not the first. In fact, police had conducted a similar shakedown earlier that same week. This time, patrons decided they'd had enough. They did something that customers at queer bars rarely ever did: they fought back. A year later, a march took place to commemorate the event. That became New York City's first Pride march: a movement that quickly spread worldwide. President Barack Obama recognized the area outside the Stonewall Inn, including the small, adjacent Christopher Park, as the Stonewall National Monument in 2016, making it the first LGBTQ-monument in the US National Park system.

104 Counterculture

▼ Reclaim Pride, New York, USA

When to go: June
Best for: An antidote to mainstream Pride

Like many alternative Pride events around the United States, Reclaim Pride NYC hosts a Queer Liberation March every year to counter New York's mainstream Pride Festival, due to the latter's affiliation with corporations, moneyed interests, police departments, and family friendliness. It hopes to reclaim Pride's historically progressive, radical, activist character.

105 Art is for lovers

Leslie Lohman Museum, New York, USA

When to go: All year
Best for: Gay erotic art historians

One of the premier museums dedicated to LGBTQ+ art, the Leslie Lohman's year-round exhibitions feature tens of thousands of pieces, including by luminaries such as Andy Warhol, Tom of Finland, and Robert Mapplethorpe. As with many LGBTQ+ institutions, its original mission focused on gay men and the "outsider art" they created amidst a violently repressive, heteronormative culture, but the vision has since expanded to include artists across the spectra of queer identity.

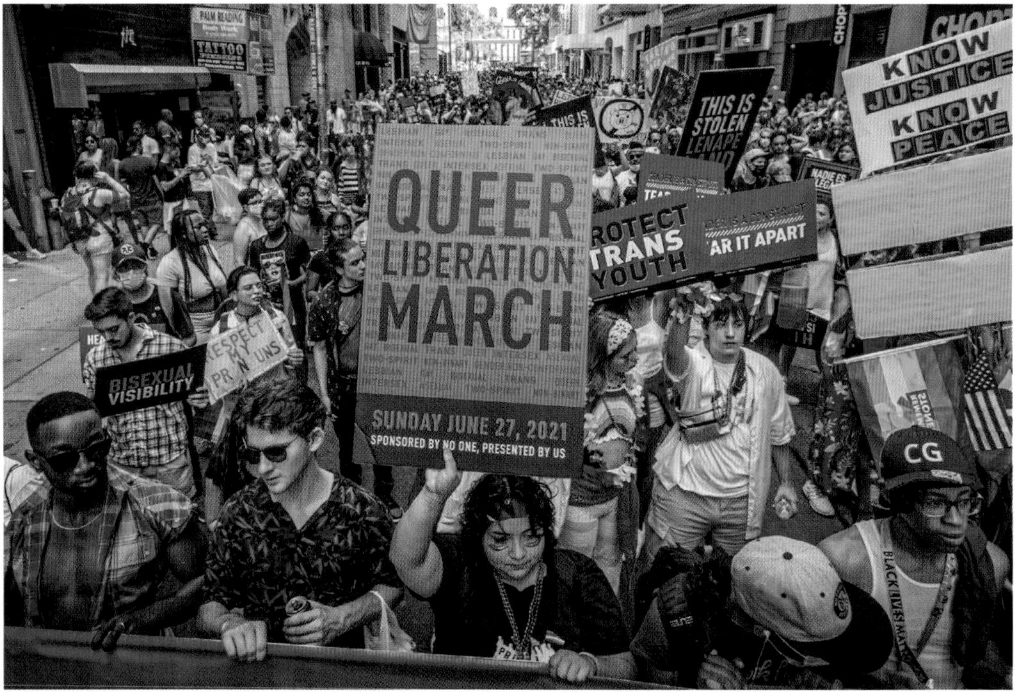

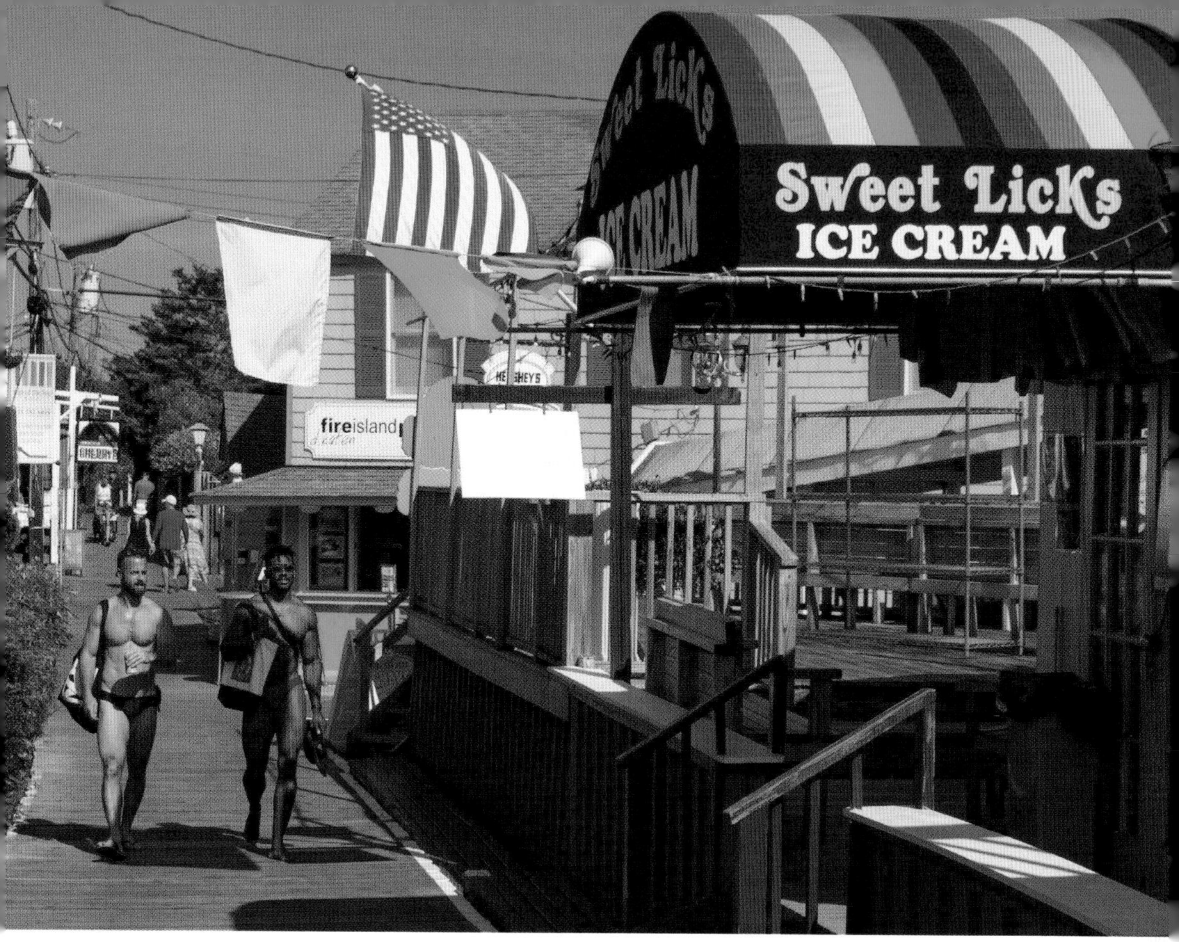

106 Feel the heat

▲ Fire Island, New York, USA

When to go: June to August
Best for: Wild pool parties

Fire Island has long been a home to and haven for LGBTQ+ visitors and residents alike, and today remains a very popular location for groups to rent large house shares for weekend stays. The island, reachable only by ferry, has two main LGBTQ sections: Pines and Cherry Grove. Pines is popular with gay men, while Cherry Grove boasts a more diverse scene, and is also frequented by lesbians and queer women. Widely known for wild pool, underwear and beach parties, Fire Island even has its own reality show. Once a year in July, the island also hosts a large weekend event, the Pines Party. Crowned the "jewel of New York's queer nightlife calendar," Pines Party brings thousands of gay men to the island, while raising money for the Stonewall Community Foundation and local charities impacting the LGBTQ+ communities on the island and in New York City.

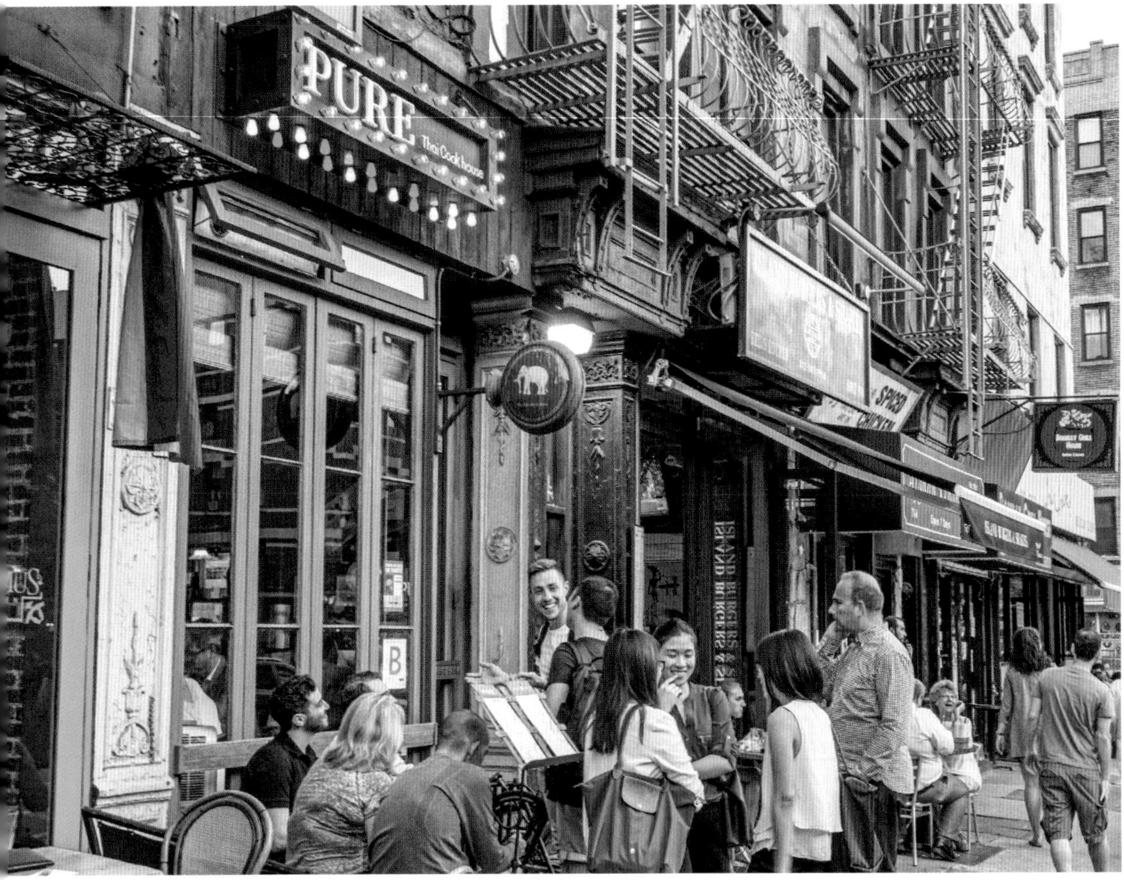

107 Gordon isn't here, but the party is

Hell's Kitchen, New York, USA

When to go: All year
Best for: Thai food, Broadway shows, and endless gay bars

No, this Hell's Kitchen is not Gordon Ramsay's famous cooking competition; it's one of the largest gay neighborhoods in NYC, located just west of Times Square in midtown Manhattan. This area has so many gay-owned shops, restaurants, bars, and nightclubs that it would be impossible for any visitor to stop by them all in one trip. Some local favorites include The Q, a four-floor dance palace where you can party the night away; Rise Bar, where you go to be seen; Flaming Saddles, for some country fun; and, Hardware, a—you guessed it—former hardware-store-turned-drag-queen watering hole.

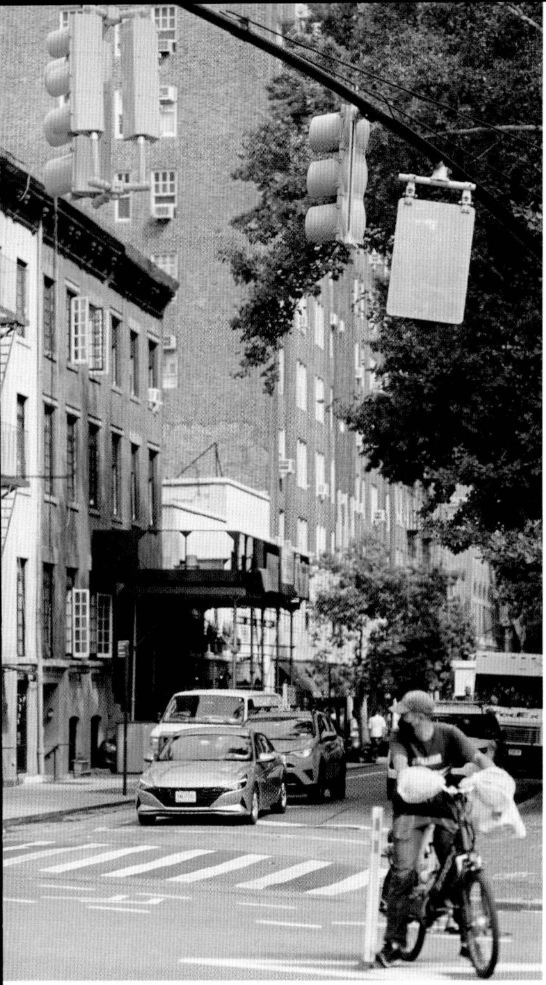

108 Roots of Pride

Greenwich Village, New York, USA

When to go: All year
Best for: LGBTQ+ history

Home to the location of the Stonewall Uprising and thus the unofficial birthplace of the gay rights movement, Greenwich Village holds an important place in history for the LGBTQ+ community in NYC and around the world. The area attracts creatives of all types—artists, musicians, designers—but continues to be an inclusive neighborhood for the community.

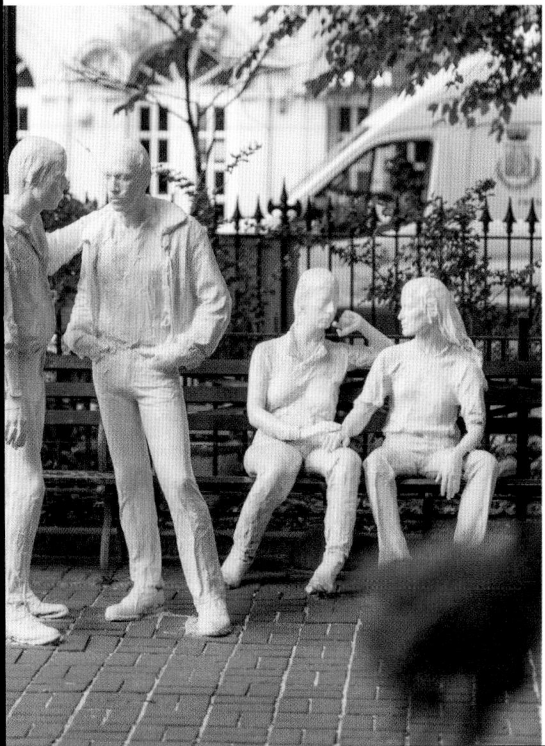

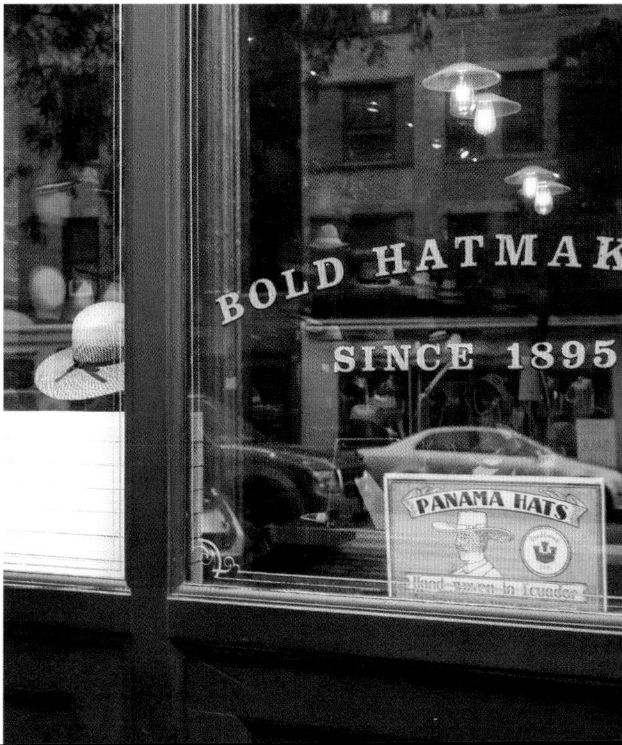

109 Concrete jungle where dreams are made of...

New York Pride, New York, USA

When to go: June
Best for: Celebrating love

Possibly the biggest Pride celebration in the USA, NYC Pride is the ultimate destination for members of the LGBTQ+ community and their allies to celebrate, educate, and inspire alongside each other. Pride events takes place during the entire month of June, with parties, performances, street fairs, and family events spanning across all five boroughs of the city. The entire city comes together to celebrate, and even Broadway Playbills adorn rainbow banners across their front covers, replacing the iconic bright yellow. The highlight of NYC Pride is the annual Pride March, which started back in 1970 and has now become one of the largest Pride marches in the world. The March goes down the famed Fifth Avenue, through Greenwich Village, passing Stonewall Inn and the Stonewall National Monument. If you are looking for something more unique, head over to Coney Island in Brooklyn for the annual Mermaid Parade, which celebrates the city's creative spirit and crowns a new King Neptune and Queen Mermaid every year.

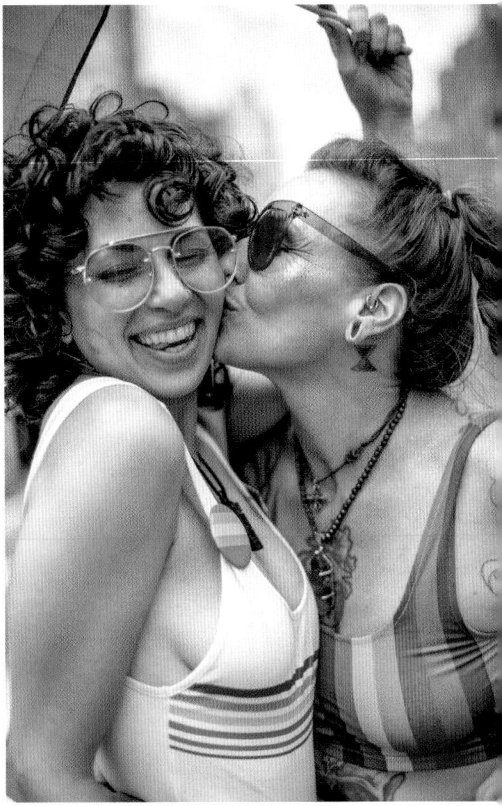

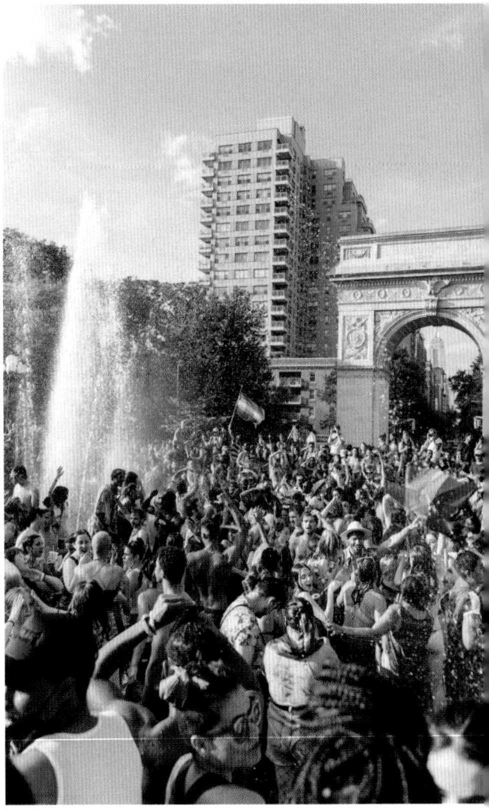

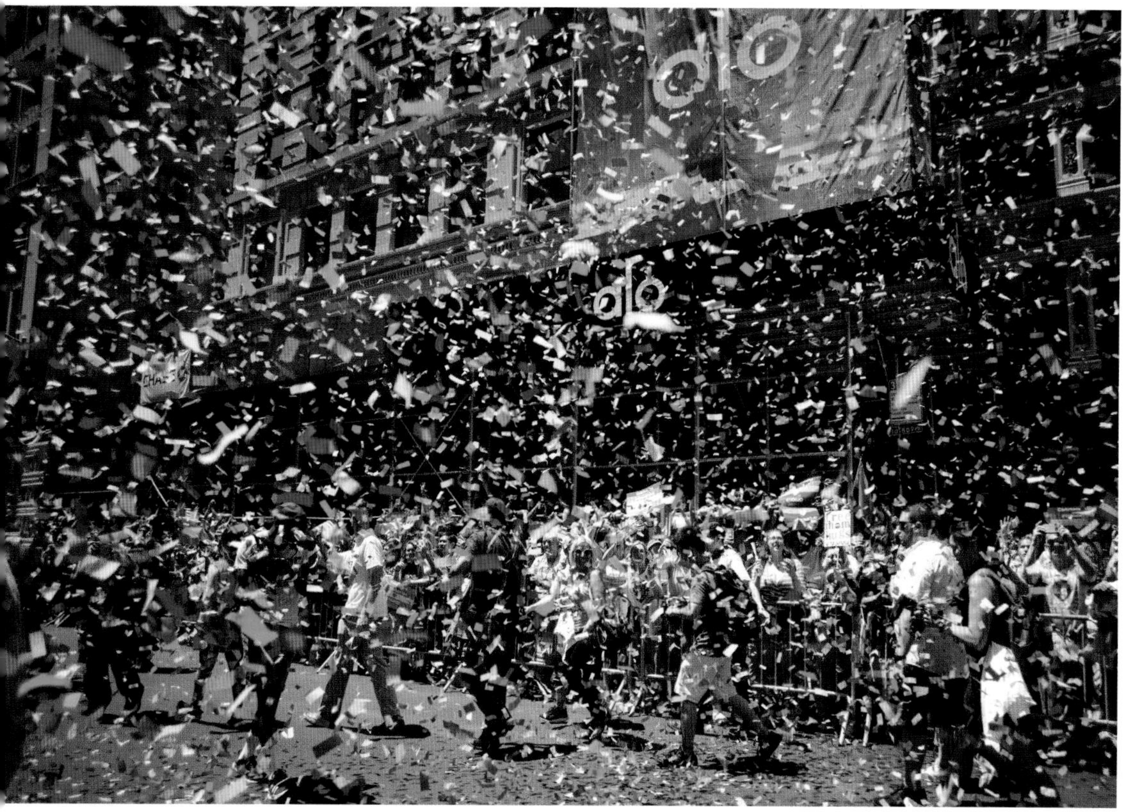
alo

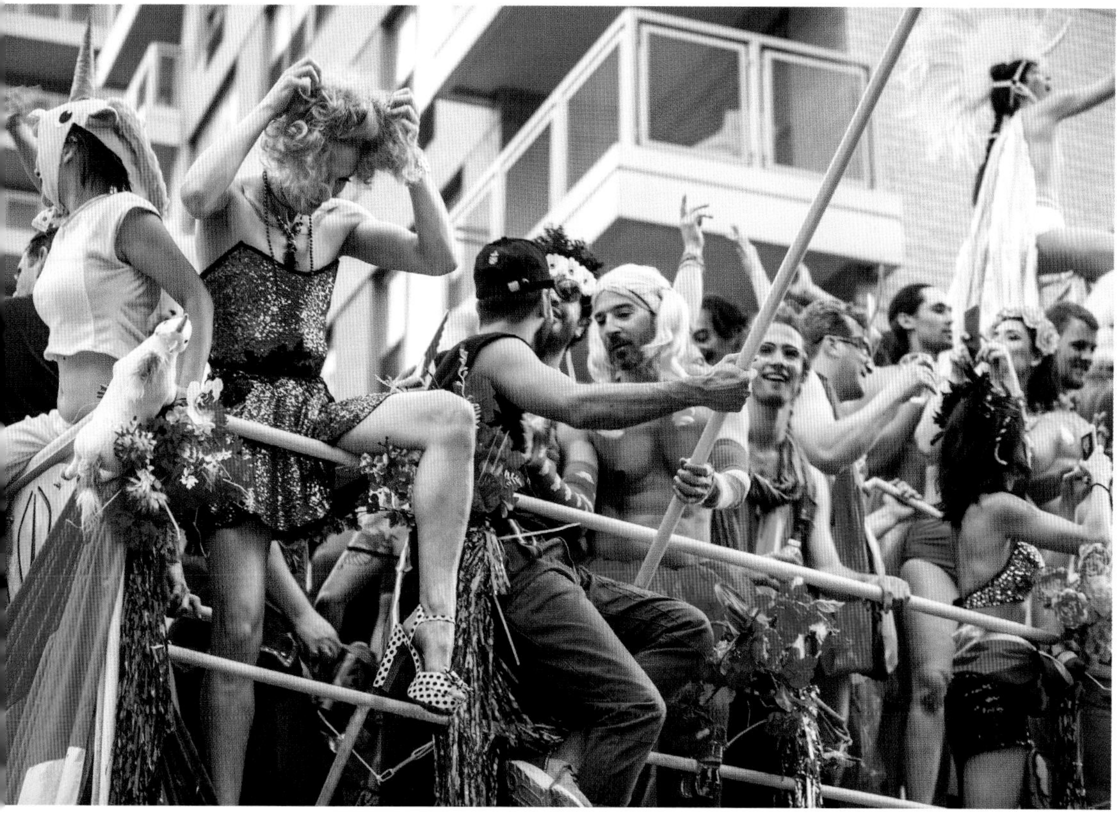

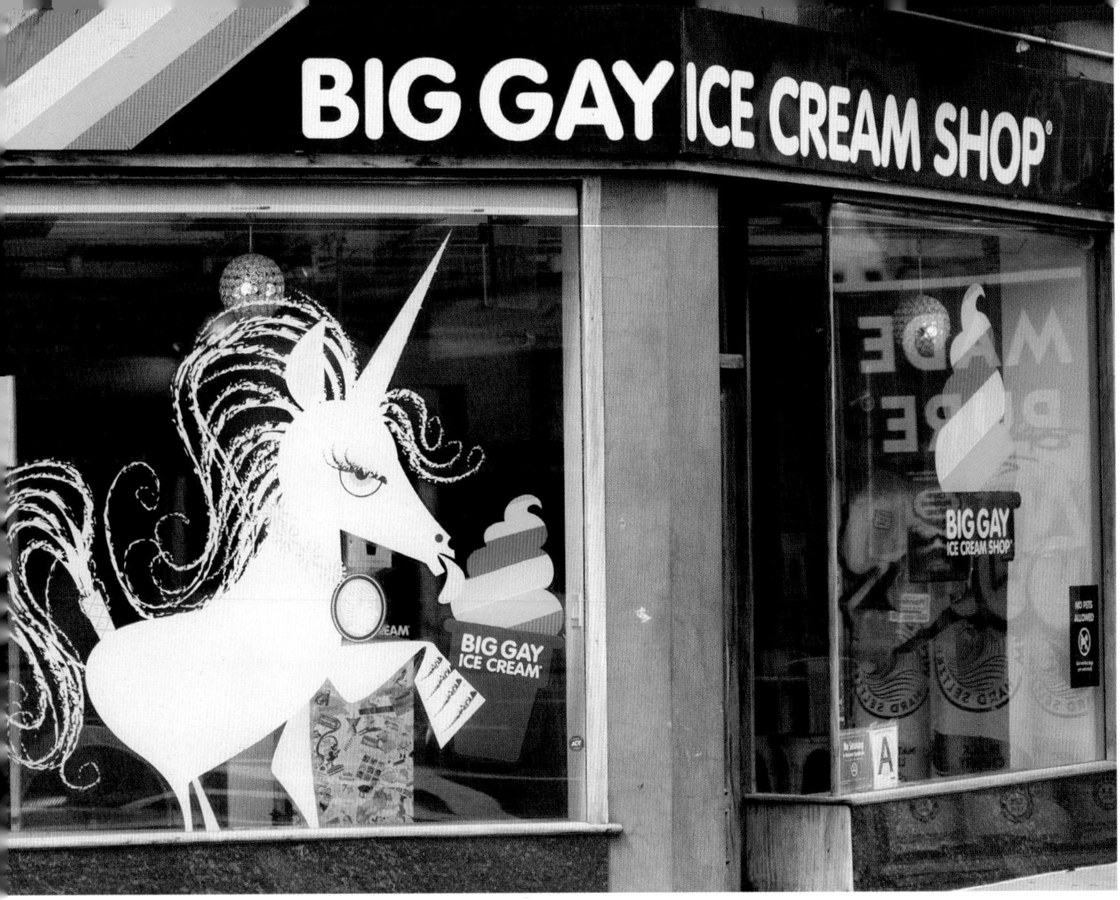

110 Chill out with all the toppings

▲ Big Gay Ice Cream, New York, USA

When to go: All year
Best for: Legendary ice cream

Humid NYC summers ask for it: ice cream. Not just any ice cream. Big Gay Ice Cream (BGIC). Gay couple Douglas Quint and Bryan Petroff started BGIC with an ice-cream truck in 2009. Nowadays, BGIC has multiple brick-and-mortar locations, a theme song, and a cookbook. Besides the founders' sexuality, "gay" also refers to its original definition, "happy." Douglas and Bryan's mission is to keep the fun in ice cream.

111 When a community center has it all

The Center, New York, USA

When to go: All year
Best for: All things queer

For over 30 years, The Center has been the heart and home of the NYC's LGBTQ+ community. Beside hosting more than 15,000 cultural events annually, it also offers support with health and wellness programs. Walk in to see what events are on their calendar, get a coffee in the lobby, view artwork by LGBTQ+ artists, visit the comprehensive LGBTQ+ archive or bookstore, and regain energy in the cozy and lush courtyard.

112 The little bar that made history

▶ Julius', New York, USA

When to go: All year
Best for: Raising a toast to activists of yore

Julius' in Greenwich Village began to attract queer custom in the 1950s. At the time, it was illegal for bars to knowingly serve gay customers. One evening in April 1966, three men from the gay-rights group the Mattachine Society walked in, told the bartender they were homosexual, and ordered a drink. They took along a photographer to capture the moment staff refused them. Local media outlets widely reported on this "Sip-in Protest." As a result of their actions, authorities subsequently dropped the discriminatory liquor law.

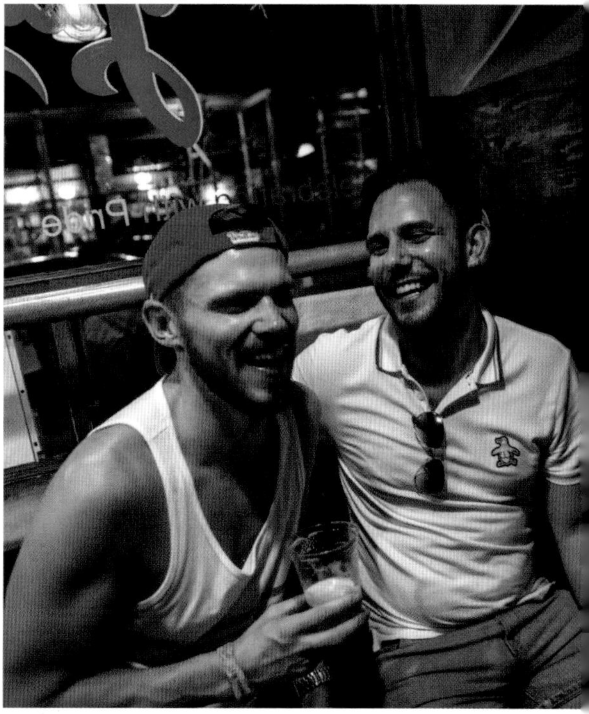

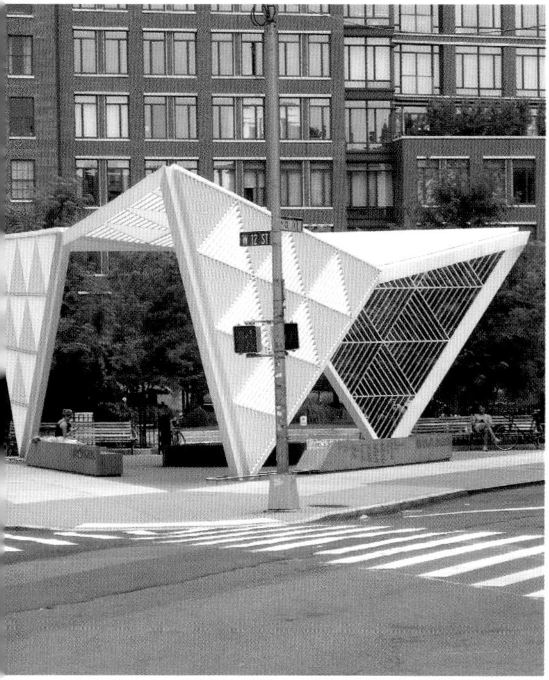

113 Never forget

◀ New York City AIDS Memorial, New York, USA

When to go: All year
Best for: Paying tribute

The New York City AIDS Memorial, dedicated in 2016, honors the New Yorkers who have died of AIDS and the contributions of doctors, caregivers, and activists who have battled to change the outcome of the epidemic. Located in Greenwich Village at St. Vincent's Triangle public park, this symbolic monument is the perfect place to visit and pay homage to all those who have fought against inequality and discrimination during the AIDS pandemic.

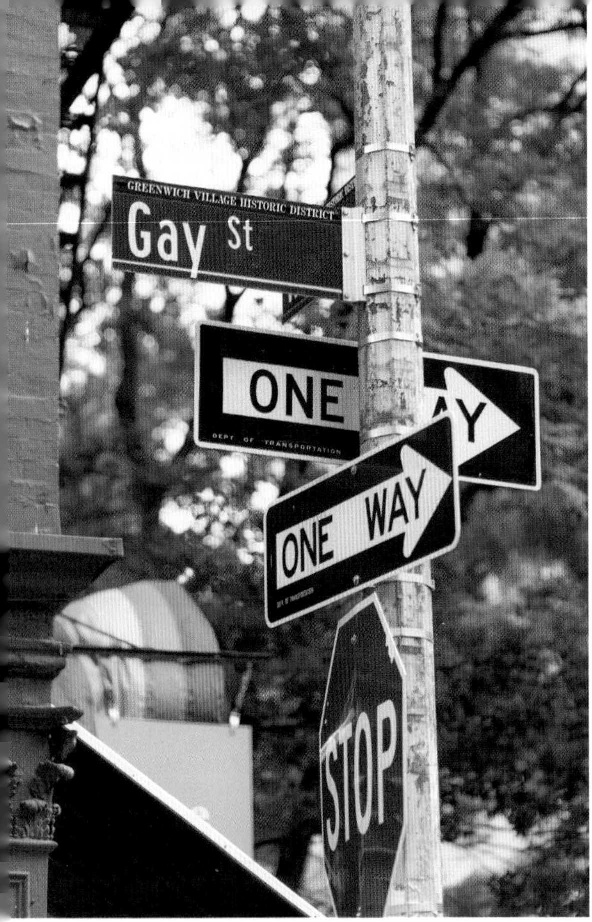

114 Acceptance is a choose-your-own-way street

◀ Gay Street, New York, USA

When to go: All year
Best for: Fun photoshoot

Although Gay Street is very much in the gay part of town, its name dates back to at least 1827 and wasn't inspired by the LGBTQ+ community at all. For World Pride 2019 and to commemorate the fiftieth anniversary of the Stonewall riots, the street was temporarily named Acceptance Street, with a street sign that honored the full spectrum of the LGBTQ+ community, including extra signs such as "Lesbian St." and "Bisexual St."

115 Reflect on an activist's actions

▶ Marsha P. Johnson State Park, Brooklyn, New York, USA

When to go: All year
Best for: A relaxing picnic

Renamed in 2020 after Marsha P. Johnson—legendary activist and Stonewall catalyst—this park features a lovely view of the Manhattan skyline over the East River.

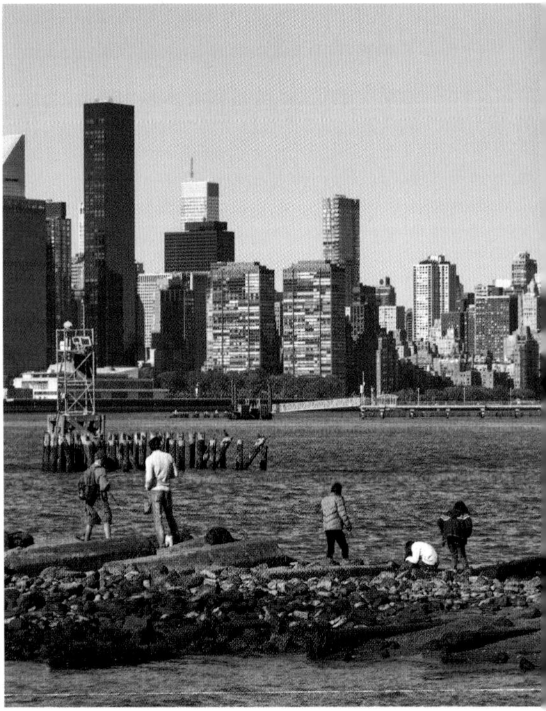

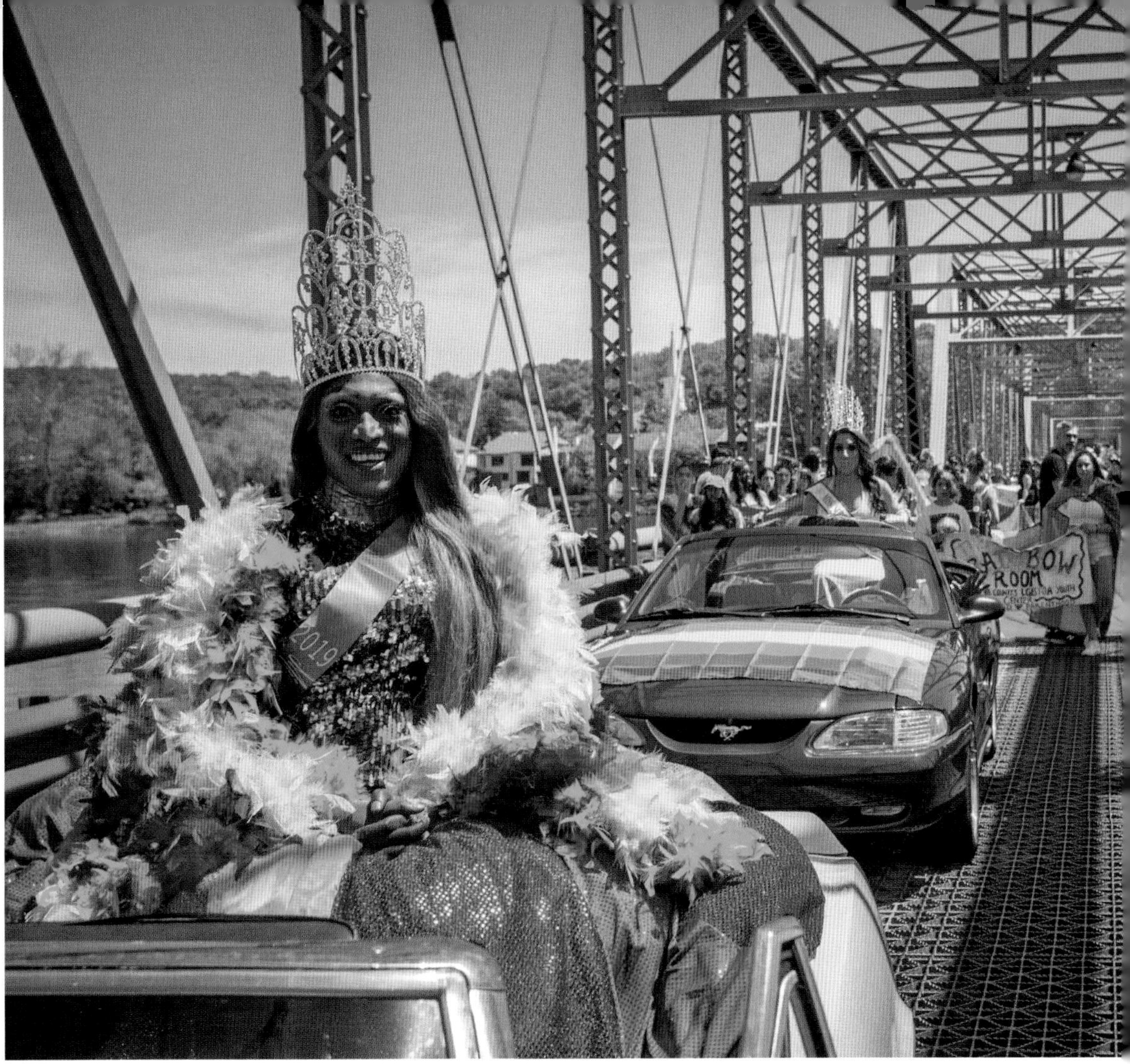

116 Give me hope

▲ New Hope Celebrates, Pennsylvania, USA

When to go: May
Best for: Refined celebrations

Since the early 1900s, artists looking to escape big-city life have flocked to New Hope. Its location is perfect for a quick retreat—just an hour from Philadelphia and two hours from NYC. New Hope Celebrates is an annual Pride event in May—the signature event is the Annual Pride Parade that spans over two states, celebrating the inclusive communities of Lambertville, New Jersey, and New Hope, Pennsylvania.

117 The great outdoors

Woods Camping Resort, Lehighton, Pennsylvania, USA

When to go: May to October
Best for: Digital detox

The Woods Camping Resort in Pennsylvania is one of the most well-respected LGBTQ+ camping grounds in the United States. Nestled in the Pocono Mountains, it's entwined by 4 mi/6.4 km of hiking trails, forested peaks, lakes, valleys and riverside beaches. You can take time for yourself, or join in activities such as lakeside yoga or volleyball, and if you don't have a tent or RV, rent a cabin or resort home instead. Open since 2004, the resort's ethos is simple: "Less digital interaction and more real-life interaction." So, ditch the dating apps and say "howdy" to your neighbors instead.

118 Lose yourself in a gay book

▶ Giovanni's Room, Philadelphia, Pennyslvania, USA

When to go: All year
Best for: Queer literature

Named after a heartbreaking James Baldwin novel, Giovanni's Room is the oldest gay bookstore in the United States and is considered the "center of gay Philly." In 2014 it almost closed, though it is now run by Philly AIDS Thrift. Bookstores have suffered a lot in recent years as online shopping has grown, but these spaces, which often serve as community centers as much as bookstores, are more important than ever.

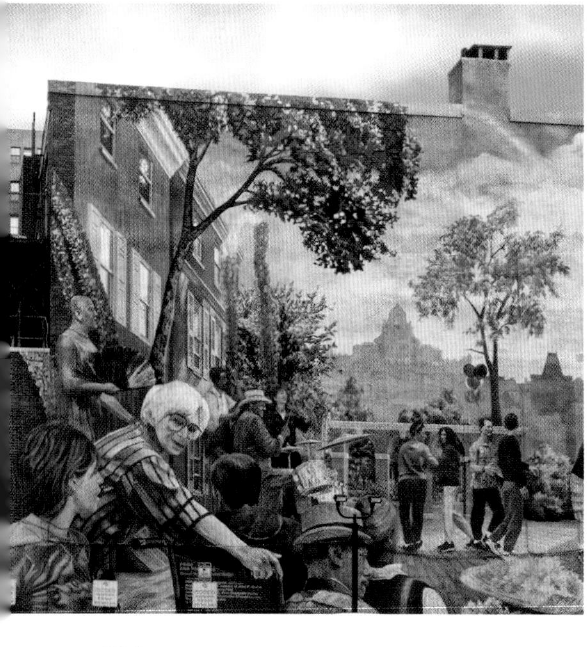

119 Forget prejudice, it's Pride and Progress now

◀ Pride And Progress Mural, Philadelphia, Pennyslvania, USA

When to go: All year
Best for: Public art aficionados

The William Way LGBT Center offers an array of services, but whether you need them or not, the gigantic mural that graces the building, called *Pride and Progress*, is a cultural landmark.

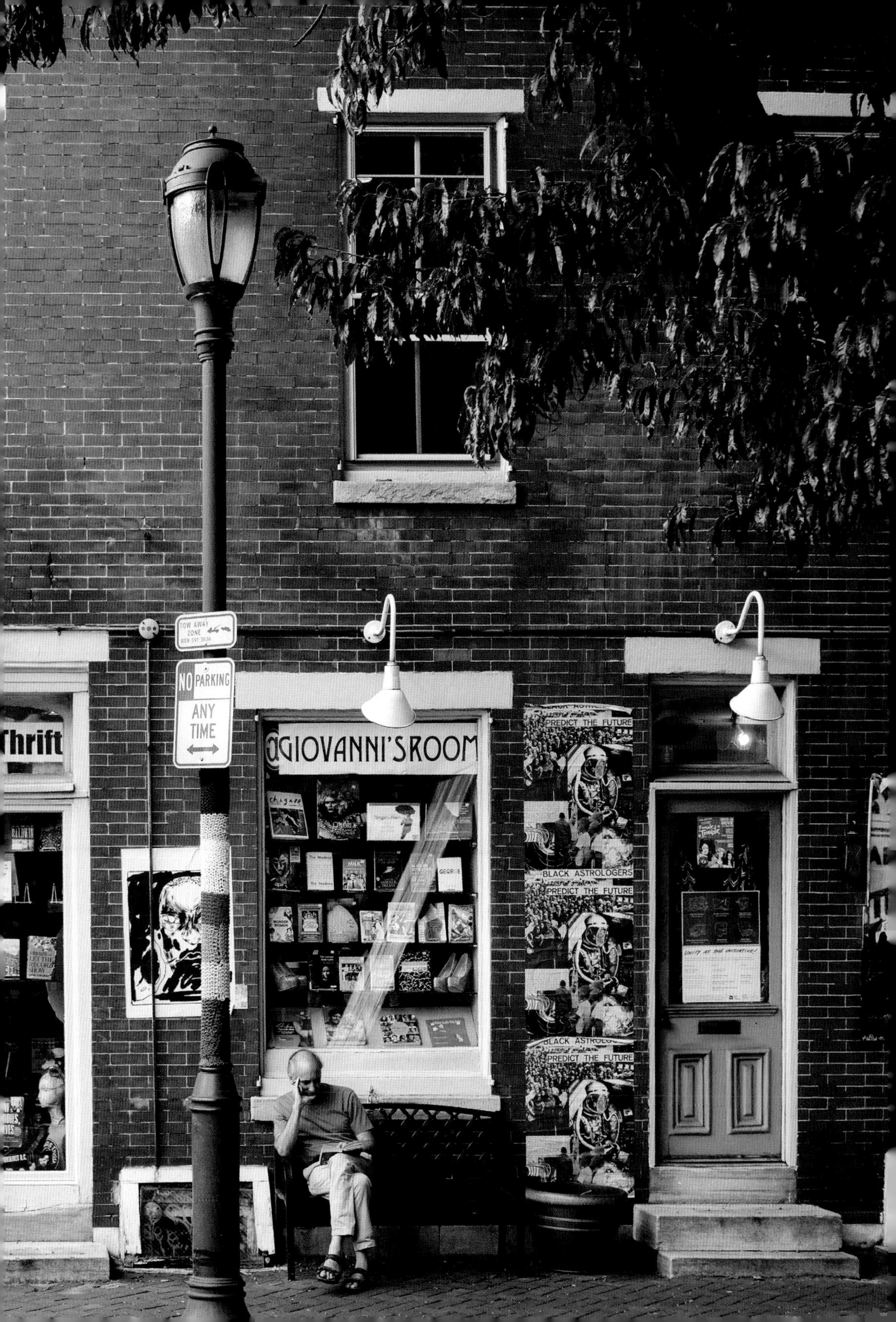
TOW AWAY ZONE
NO PARKING
ANY TIME
Thrift
GIOVANNI'S ROOM
PREDICT THE FUTURE
BLACK ASTROLOGERS
PREDICT THE FUTURE
PREDICT THE FUTURE

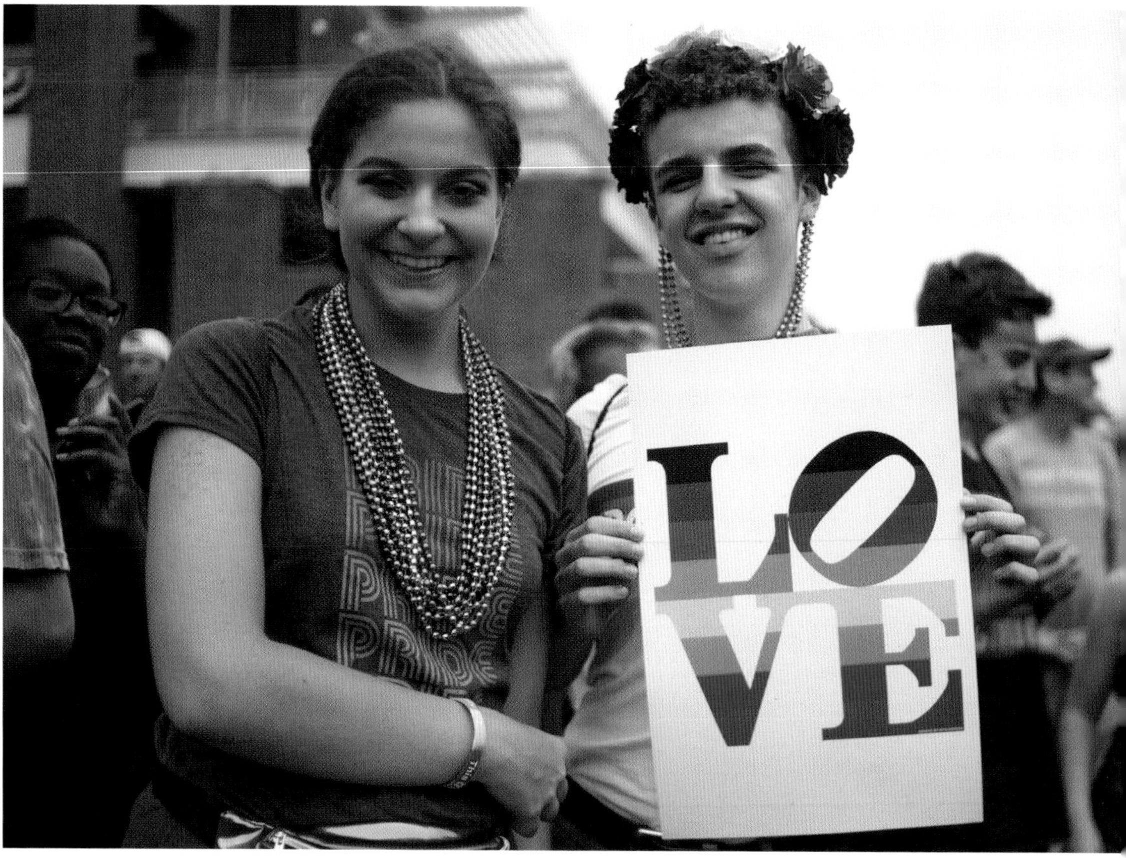

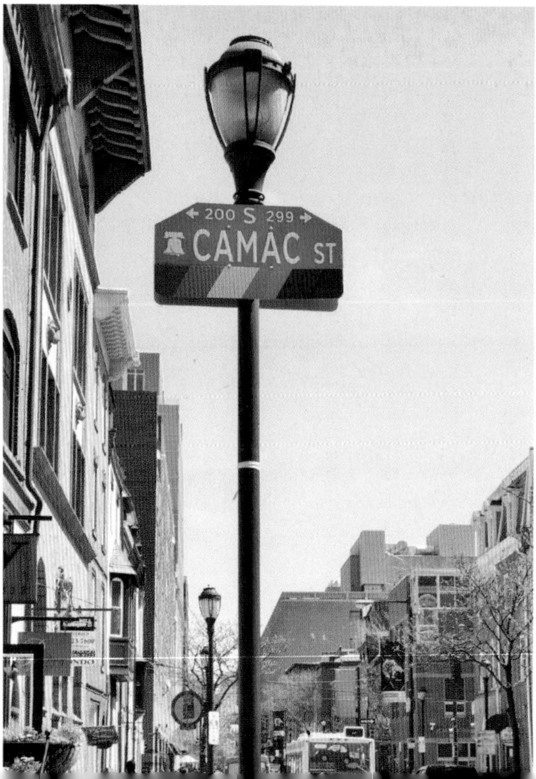

120 The city of brotherly love

◀ ▲ Washington Square, Philadelphia, Pennyslvania, USA

When to go: October
Best for: Loving that love is love

Washington Square West is home to the William Way LGBT Community Center, a number of LGBTQ+ bars and clubs within walking distance of each other, as well as gay bathhouses like Club Philly and Sansom Street Gym. Washington Square Park itself is also a lively, lovely urban park perfect for queer couples and families to take a stroll. The city's name comes from the Greek for brotherly love.

121 Love is love

Outfest, Philadelphia, Pennsylvania, USA

When to go: October
Best for: Coming out

This annual festival comes to the gay village in midtown Philadelphia every fall. Philly was the first city in the United States to host an annual National Coming Out Day event, which had a calmer, more family-friendly vibe compared to the large parties of New York City. Now, Outfest is a large, outdoor block party with lots of drinks, drag shows, and music.

122 Light up the night

▼ Rhode Island Pridefest, Providence, Rhode Island, USA

When to go: Late June
Best for: Glow sticks

Rhode Island Pridefest stands out from other Pride parades across the United States as it's one of only a handful that takes place after dark. As the sun sets, the festivities begin. Light-decked trucks trundle through the gay district and past the downtown area's popular street art, while rainbow illuminations light up the Rhode Island State House. In 2018, *National Geographic* rated Providence as one of the world's top seven destinations with Pride celebrations.

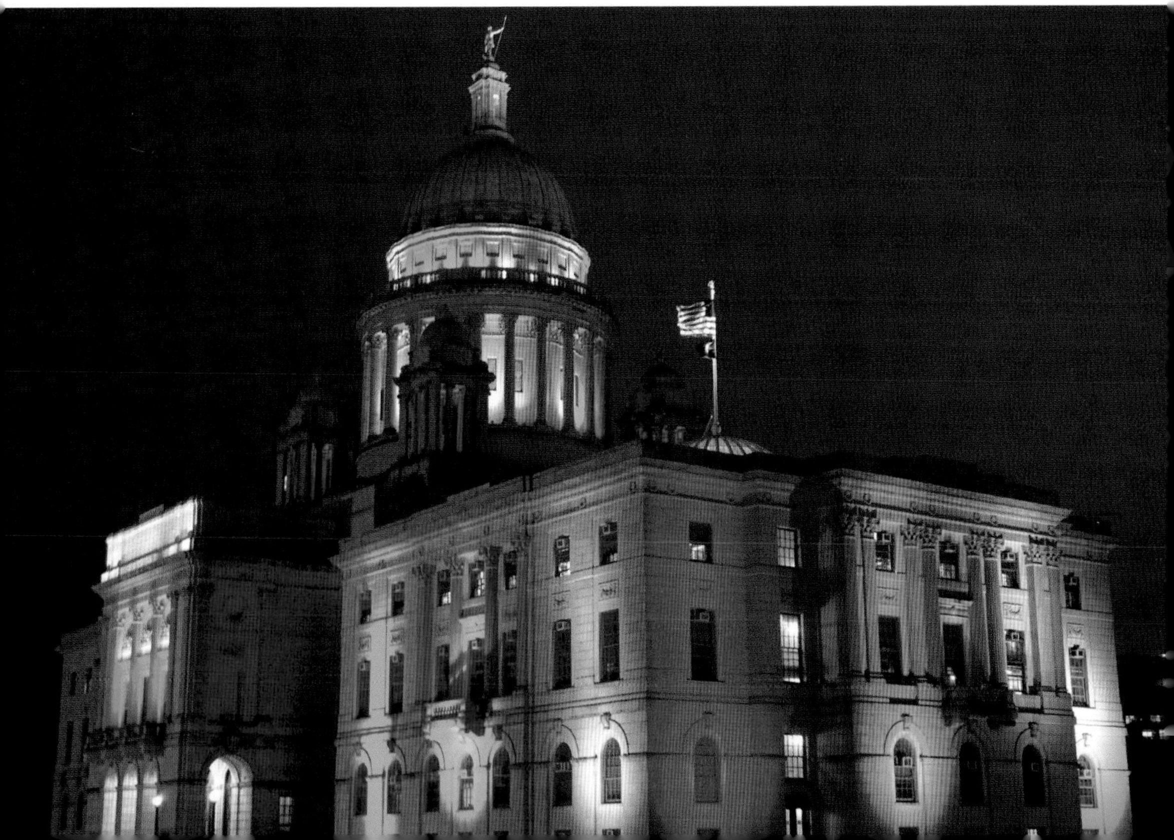

123 Ladies of the lake

Burlington, Vermont, USA

When to go: August or January
Best for: Cozy cuddles after outdoorsy days

Beautiful Burlington is so lesbian-friendly that residents joke about "coming out as straight." LGBTQ+ folks of all stripes are welcome to the largest city in Vermont, the first US state both to legalize civil unions in 2000, and gay marriage in 2009. People come all year to enjoy the beautiful scenery around Lake Champlain, and snow sports are also popular, with nearby Stowe hosting a Winter Pride Festival and Gay Ski Week in January.

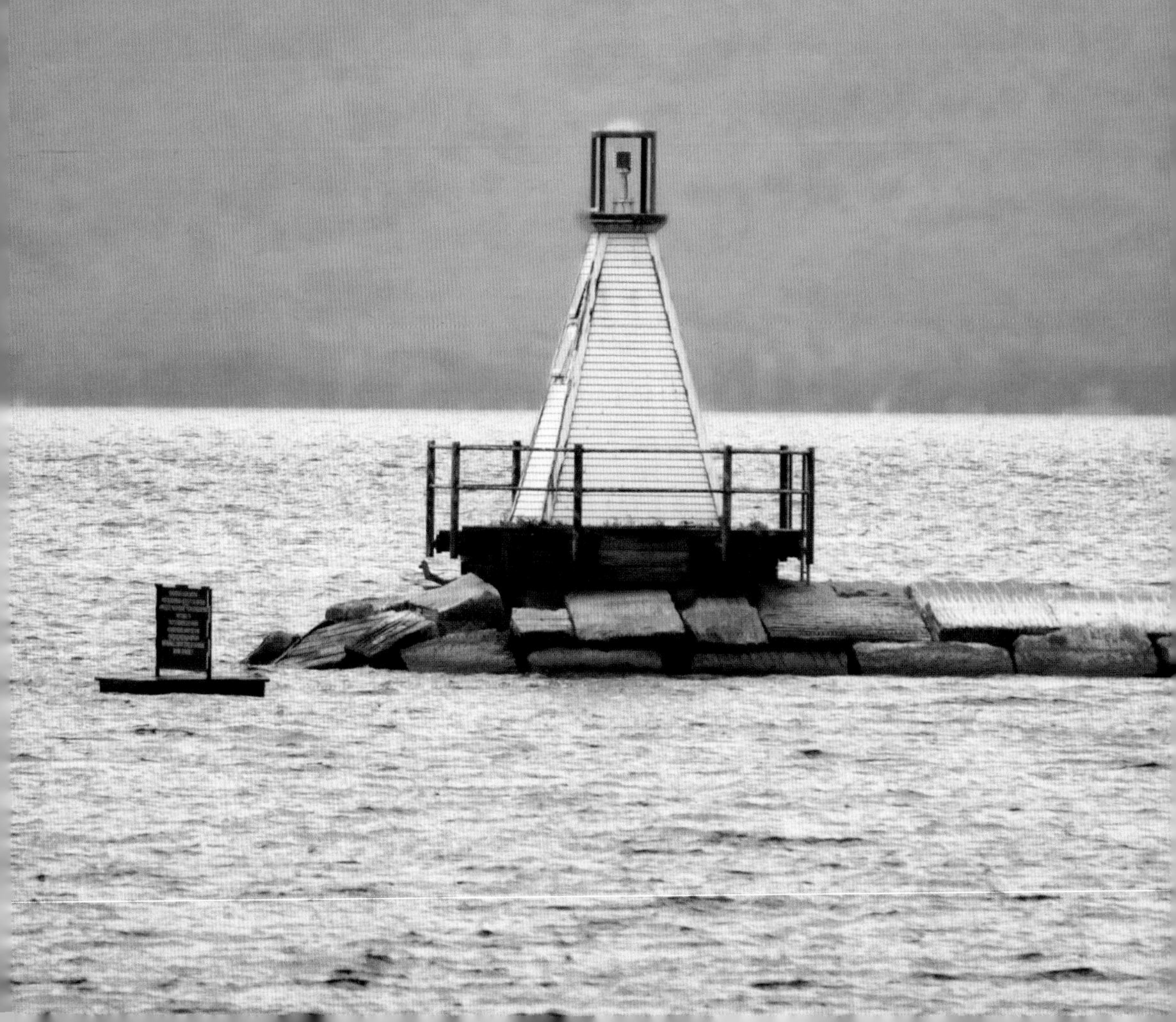

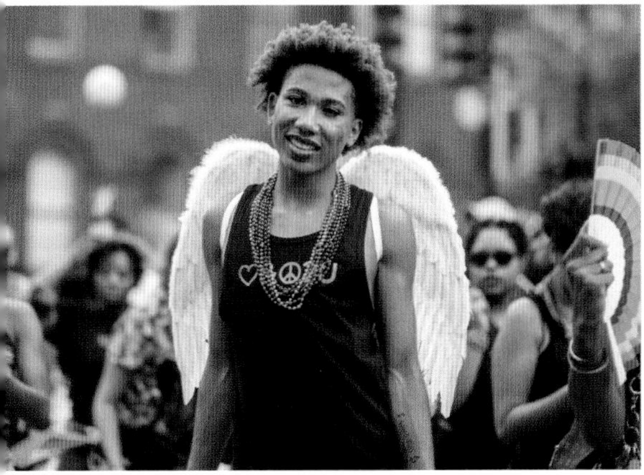

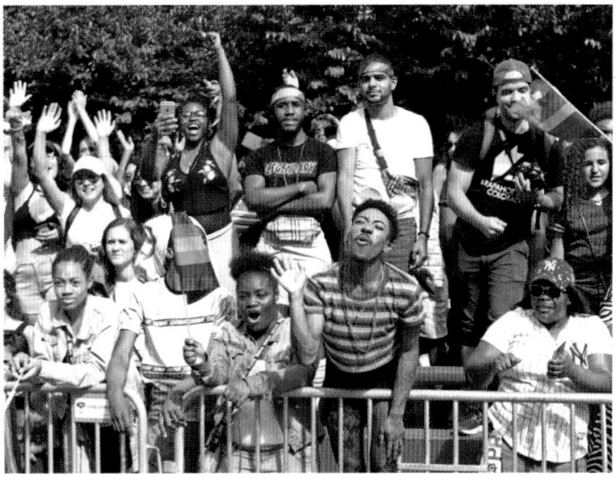

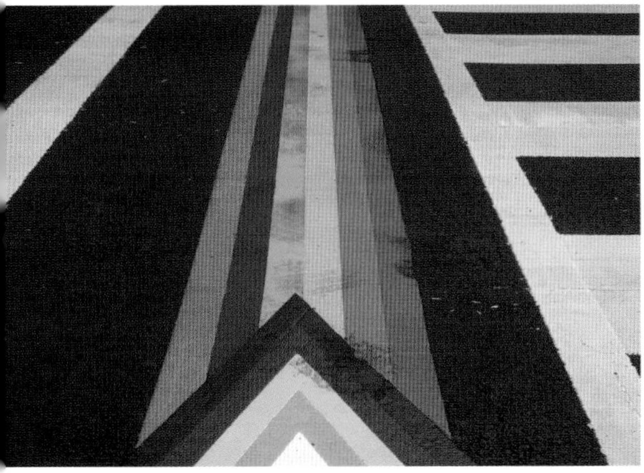

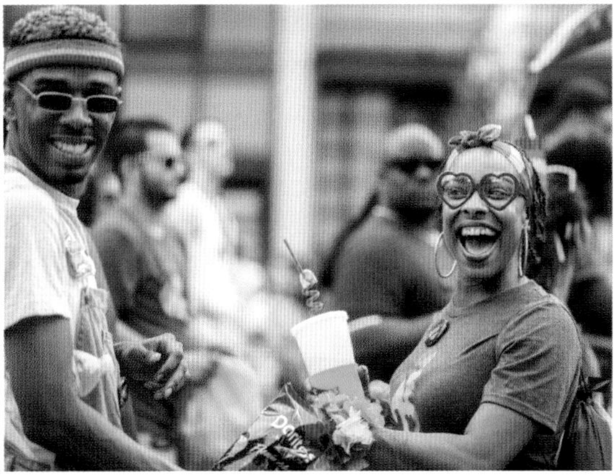

124 Serious stuff

▲ DC Black Pride, Washington, D.C., USA

When to go: May
Best for: A political approach

Rather than being distributed across the city, DC Black Pride is more like a conference—it's centered in a single hotel, with a ball, vendor fair, town halls and panels, film screenings, poetry slam, and even a Praise party on Sunday. That being said, you can still find the requisite dance parties and bar celebrations across town.

125 Rest in LGBTQ+ peace

LGBT Section, Congressional Cemetery, Washington, D.C., USA

When to go: All year
Best for: Quiet reflection

The LGBT section in Washington's Congressional Cemetery started when Vietnam-veteran Leonard Matlovich used his grave to critique homophobia, with its iconic inscription: "When I was in the military they gave me a medal for killing two men—and a discharge for loving one." Other LGBTQ+ veterans purchased plots near his, including some, who because they were HIV-positive, were excluded from other cemeteries.

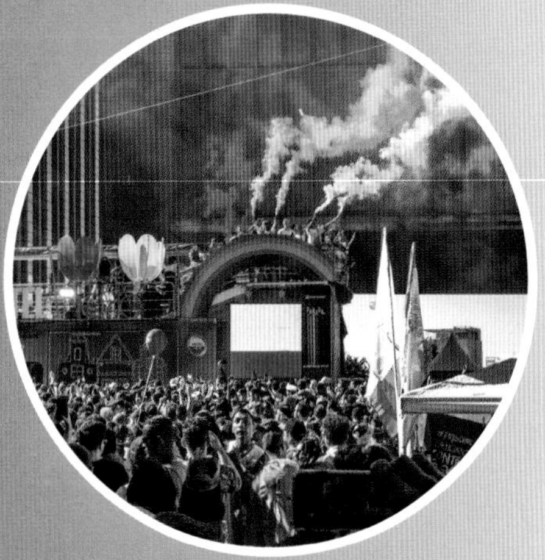

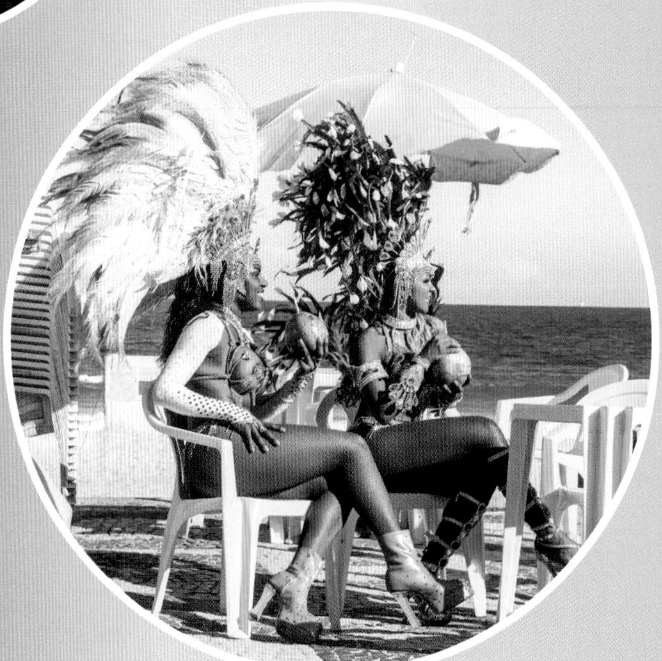

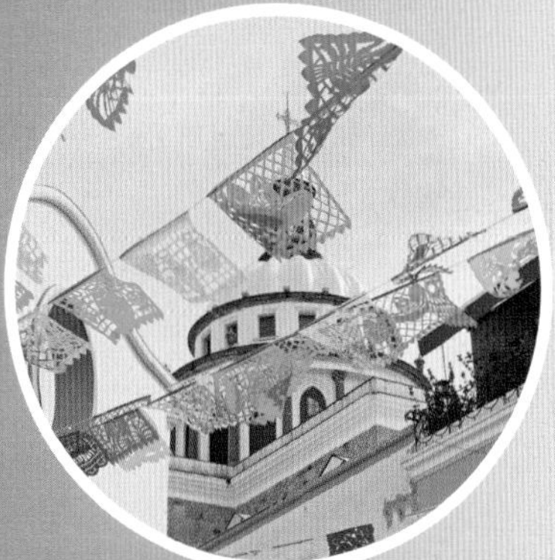

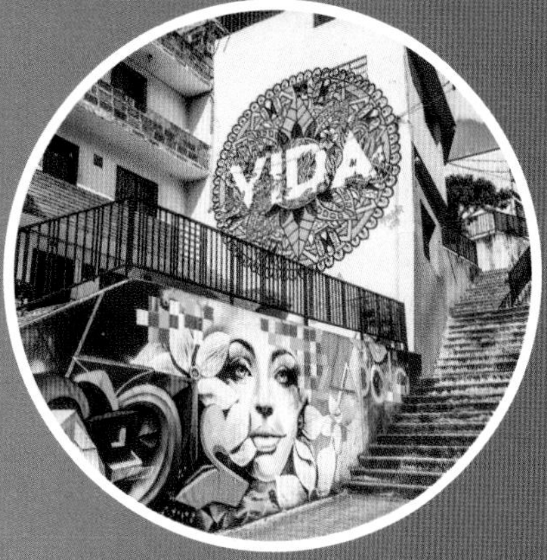

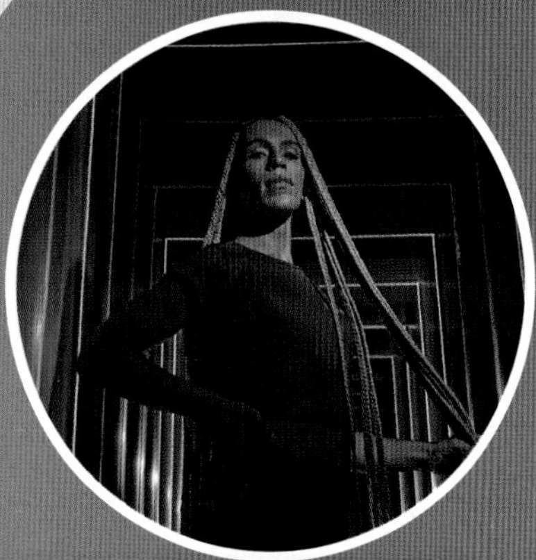

CHAPTER TWO

LATIN AMERICA AND THE CARIBBEAN

126 Find your El Local community

Santurce, San Juan, Puerto Rico

When to go: All year
Best for: Community

While the number of out-and-proud gay spaces in Puerto Rico is quickly rising, places that cater to queer women, transgender, and non-binary people (especially of color) are harder to find. Local and international LGBTQ+ sub-communities connect in alternative venues such as El Local, La Respuesta, El Hangar, and Club 77. If you're looking to explore Puerto Rico's underground scene, these are the best starting points.

127 Food made with love

▶ Jungle BaoBao at Jungle Bird, San Juan, Puerto Rico

When to go: All year
Best for: Inclusive eating

Trans, queer chef Paxx Caraballo runs the kitchen at San Juan's Jungle Bird bar, called Jungle BaoBao. Caraballo is passionate about Asian-Rican fusion food, and running a kitchen with inclusivity and love at its core. That's something you taste in their food. While the menu is ever-changing, a must-eat is the Crack Eggplant—the only permanent dish.

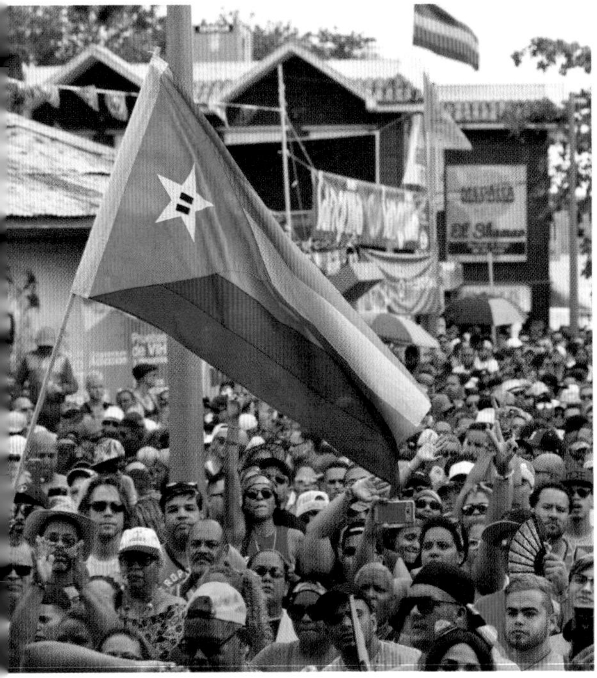

128 Party because a fairy godmother said so

◀ Orgullo Boquerón, Puerto Rico

When to go: June
Best for: Weekend party

Known as the "LGBTQ+ capital of the Caribbean," Puerto Rico celebrates at least four Pride events in June. Beach-town Boquerón—in Cabo Rojo—hosts the second-biggest Pride parade and street party, initiated by the late Rosalina "Talin" Ramos Padró, pioneering Puerto Rican LGBTQ+ activist and *madrina honoraria* (honorary godmother) to the community.

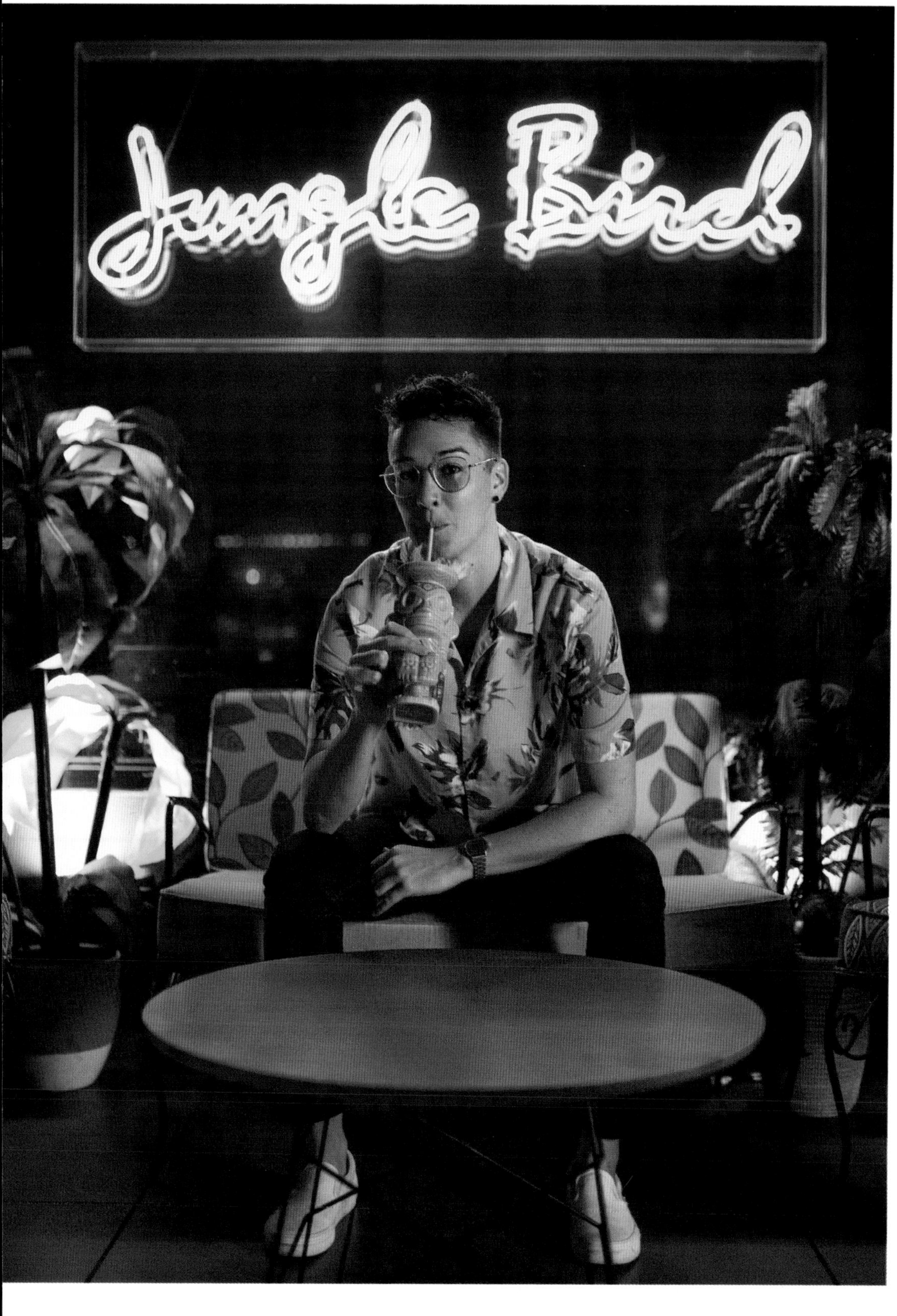
Jungle Bird

129 The calm after the storm

El Hangar en Santurce, San Juan, Puerto Rico

When to go: All year
Best for: Cultural-political events

Community center El Hangar is a landmark of the queer-led, cultural-political movement in Puerto Rico, built on a *parcela* (a piece of land) with an abandoned hangar. After Hurricane Maria in 2017, it became a refuge for the marginalized: poor people, immigrants, trans and queer people, and sex workers. El Hangar now holds regular queer events like queer markets, healing spaces, and parties.

130 Ride the waves

Condado Beach, San Juan, Puerto Rico

When to go: All year
Best for: All things salty and sandy

See the sun emerge from the Atlantic Ocean, feel the fresh breeze of the ocean, and listen to the sounds of the waves—which can be big at Condado Beach. And that's exactly why it's perfect for watersports. From late morning, the beach gets busier—especially on Sundays—and chairs and umbrellas pop up from the beach hotels and resorts. If you're looking for a queer crowd, head to the gay area in front of The Tryst Beachfront Hotel.

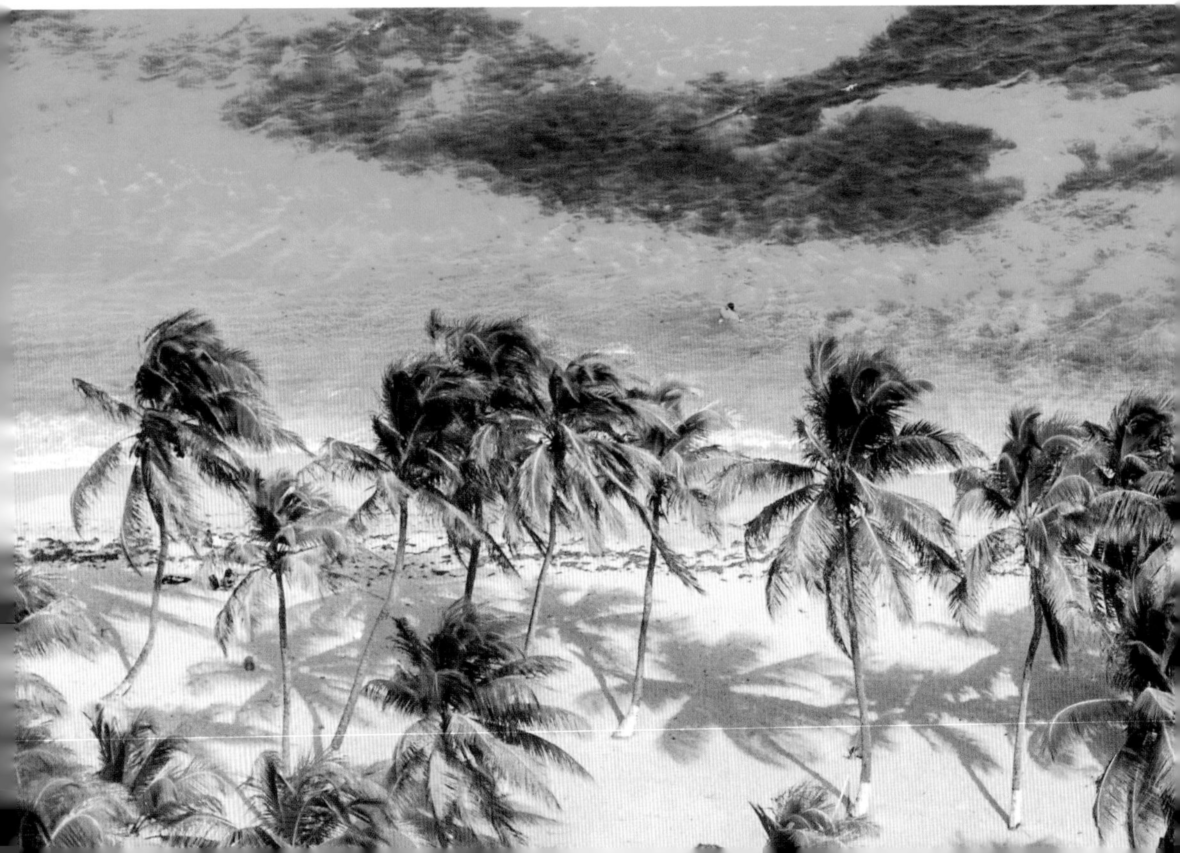

131 On the wings of love

▼ Guadeloupe

When to go: January to June
Best for: Holidays in nature

Not every LGBTQ+ traveler is looking for a vibrant urban queer scene when traveling. Guadeloupe—locally known as *Gwada*—is perfect if you're a queer traveler just looking for natural beauty. The archipelago's main islands are in the shape of the wings of an emerald butterfly which, surrounded by the Caribbean Sea and the North Atlantic Ocean, looks like it's flying through a blue sky. The tropical rainforest of Guadeloupe National Park—on Basse-Terre Island—is home to stunning hiking trails, an active volcano to climb, innumerable, refreshing waterfalls, and a diver's paradise. Use Guadeloupe's efficient ferry system to go on day trips to other islands. And if you're looking for something romantic, visit the popular honeymoon-island of Les Saintes. Guadeloupe is one of the more LGBTQ-friendly regions in the Caribbean; civil unions have been legal since 1991, so booking a honeymoon suite as LGBTQ travelers shouldn't be an issue.

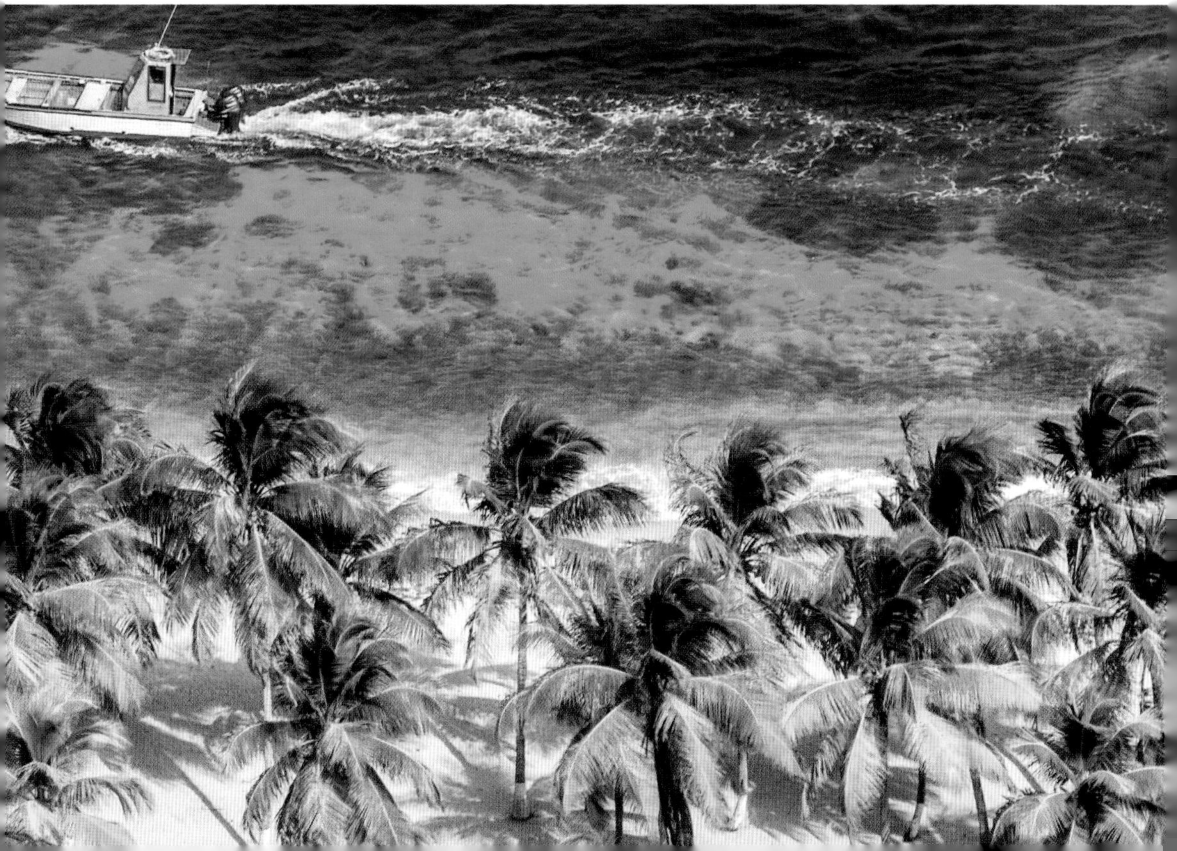

132 Live and let live

▼ Curaçao Pride, Curaçao

When to go: September
Best for: Week-long Pride festivities

The vibe of the Dutch Caribbean island Curaçao (*Kòrsou* in Papiamento) is *Biba i laga biba*: live and let live. There are gay bars and hotels in Curaçao, and queer visitors feel welcome everywhere on the colorful island. But there is still a need for more equality elsewhere in the Caribbean, which is why Dutchman Frank Holstag initiated Curaçao Pride in 2013. Inspired by the week-long Amsterdam Pride, highlights are the Pride walk, Pride happy hours, and the fabulous White Party.

133 Carnival for one and all

Curaçao Carnival, Curaçao

When to go: January to April
Best for: A cultural, uniting folk festival

Curaçao holds one of the Caribbean's most colorful carnivals. Its motto is *karnaval pa un i tur, i pa uni tur* (carnival for one and all, and uniting one and all), and the celebration lasts multiple weeks. Three meaningful events are Festival Di Tumba, Gran Marcha, and Marcha di Despedida. Festival Di Tumba is a hallmark of the island's culture, celebrating traditional ABC-islands music rooted in African culture. It's a four-day competition where artists compete to make their Tumba song the anthem of the carnival parades.

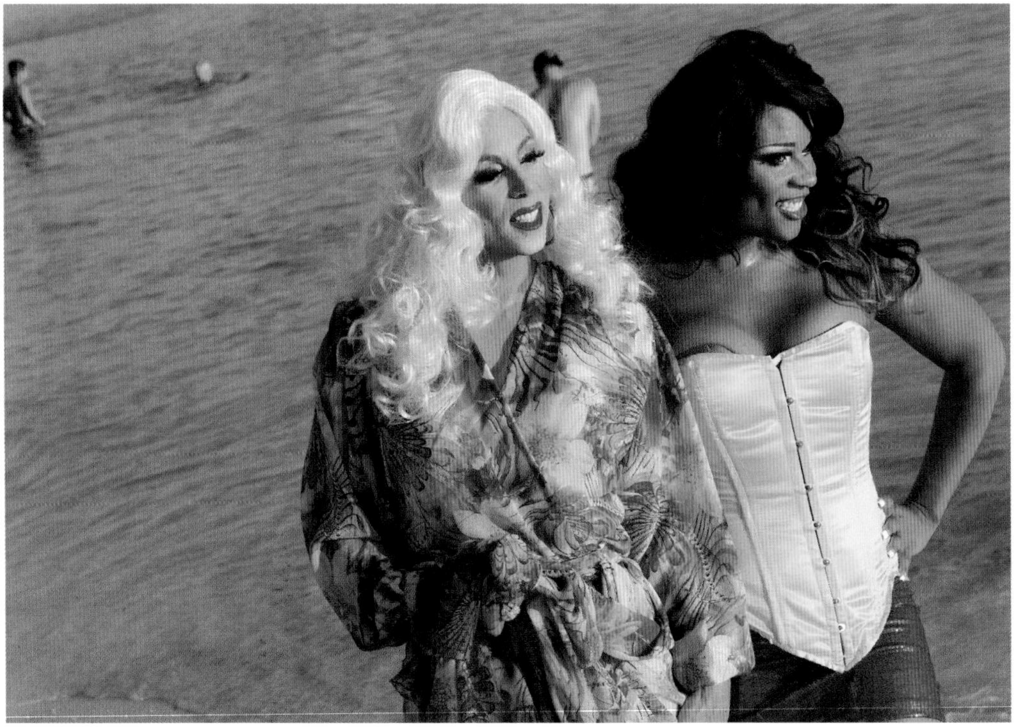

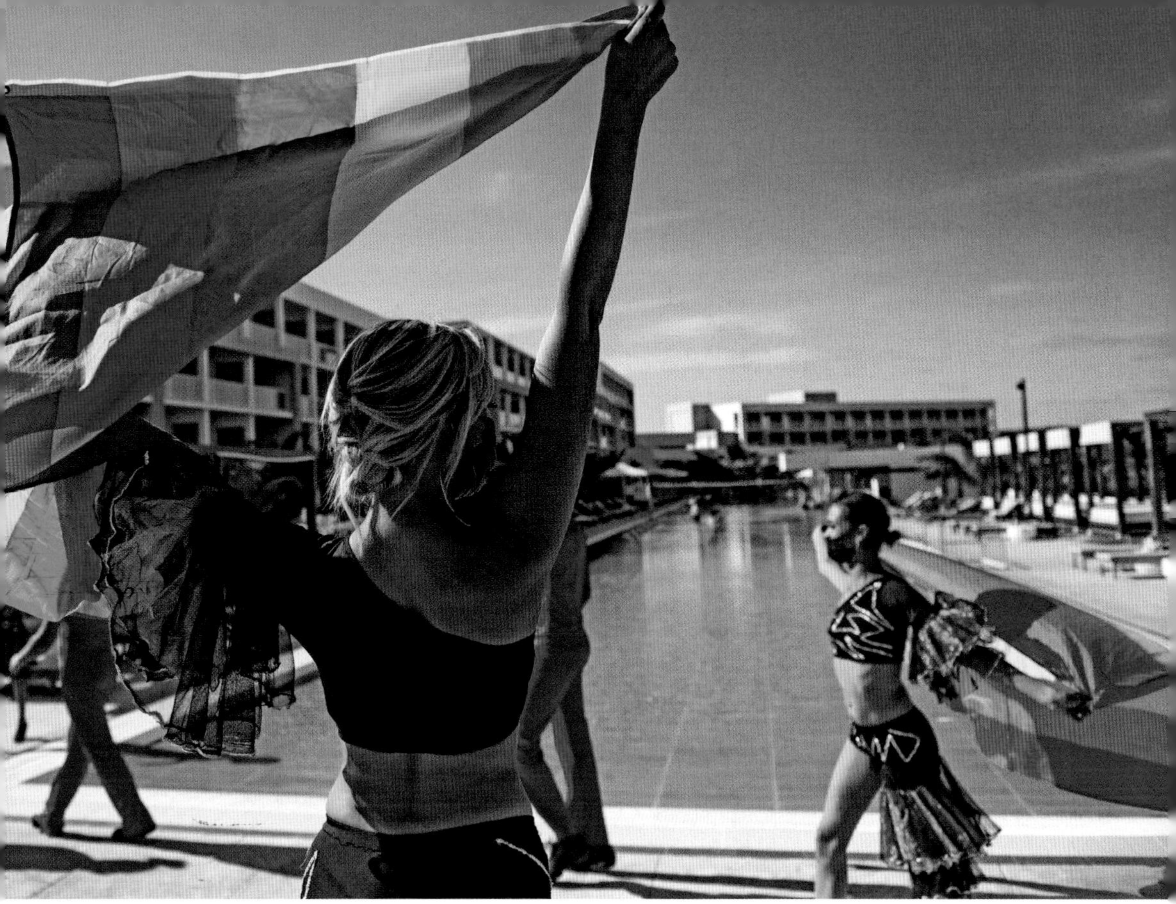

134 An inclusive all-inclusive

▲ Gran Muthu Rainbow Hotel, Cuba

When to go: November to April
Best for: All-inclusive vacationing

The Gran Muthu Rainbow Hotel is Cuba's first LGBTQ+ hotel. Found on Cayo Guillermo, a small island off the north coast of Cuba, it has everything an all-inclusive beach resort needs—sun-kissed, white powdery beaches; calm, shallow, crystal-clear waters; plus five-star catering and an extensive entertainment program—including queer shows.

135 Find your quiet space

Magens Bay, St. Thomas, US Virgin Islands

When to go: April to June
Best for: Caribbean beach dreams

In the lush, emerald-green Magens Bay Park is one of the world's finest beaches—perfectly complemented by the sea's many shades of blue. The 1-mile/1.6-km-long fine, white-sand beach is well-visited and family-friendly. At one end of the main beach you'll find Little Magens Bay Beach, separated by rocks. Nudity isn't legal, but you'll find it unofficially tolerated on this predominantly gay beach.

136 Lose the tan lines

▼ Cupecoy Beach, Sint Maarten

When to go: November to May
Best for: Clothing-optional beach chilling

Secluded Cupecoy Beach in Sint Maarten is the ultimate chill-beach, located at the island's southwestern tip. Sandstone cliffs make a stunning backdrop for this LGBTQ-friendly, clothing-optional beach. During sunset the cliffs turn golden, and the dramatic views of Saba in the distance make it an unforgettable experience. Depending on the tides and the preceding hurricane season, the beach can vary in size. When it's low tide, check out the beach coves to get the ultimate sun-baking experience, shielded from the wind.

137 Love on the beach

Sandcastle on the Beach, Frederiksted, St. Croix, US Virgin Islands

When to go: April to June
Best for: Romance

Gay couple Ted and Chris had stayed at the hotel Sandcastle on the Beach, in the US Virgin Islands, many times and dreamed of owning it and sharing it with the world. Their dream became a reality in 2017 and now the boutique hotel on one of Frederiksted's best beaches promotes love and kindness to all. The owners also sponsor local LGBTQ+ events to bring the community together.

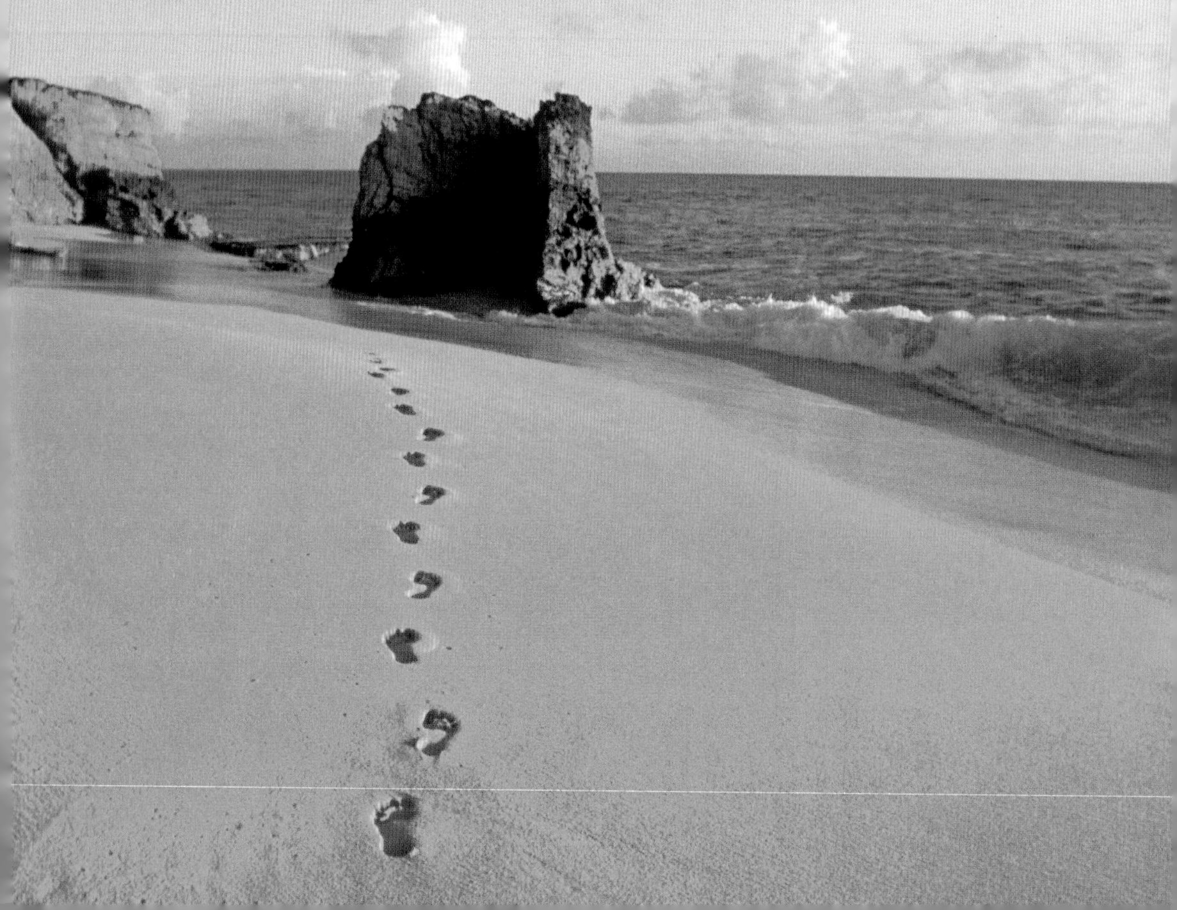

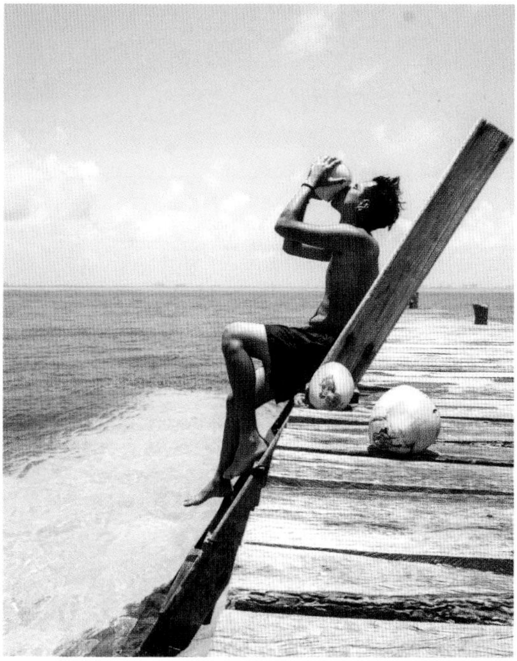

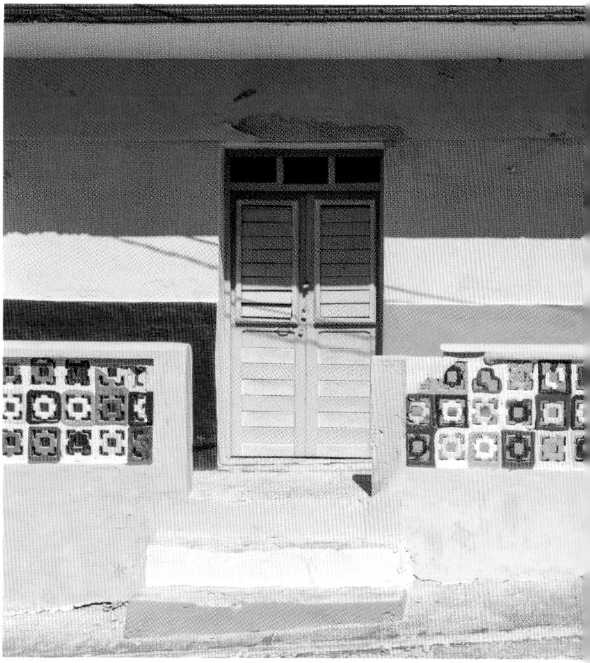

138 Women by name...

▲ Isla Mujeres, Quintana Roo, Mexico

When to go: January to April
Best for: Peace

Isla Mujeres (which translates as "women's island") owes its name to the discovery of many small figurines of women found on the island when it was colonized by the Spanish. The figurines were offerings to the Maya goddess of love, fertility, water, and the moon, Ixchel. The ruins of a temple to Ixchel are found on the rocky coastal cliffs at Punta Sur, the most southern tip of the island. Isla Mujeres is a peaceful sanctuary where you can relax at Playa Norte, rent a golf cart to see all the street art, or try out a watersports activity—there's a fascinating underwater sculpture park to dive or snorkel around.

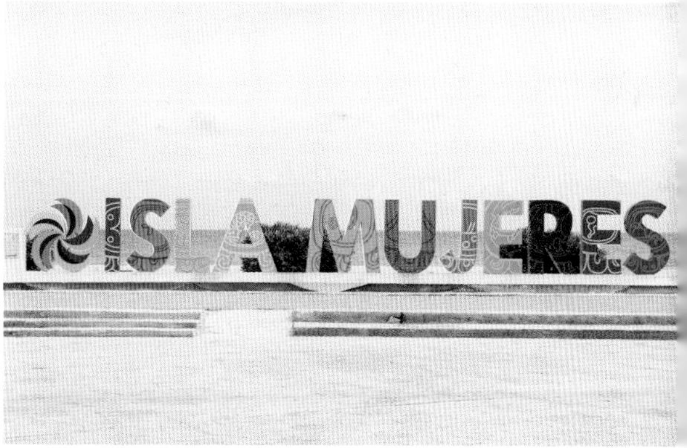

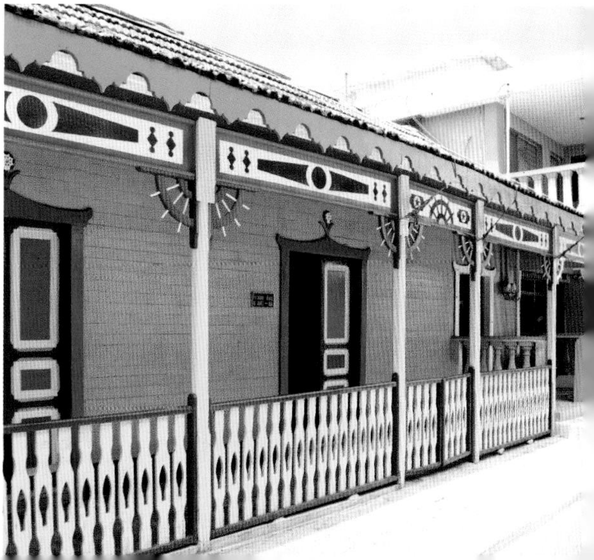

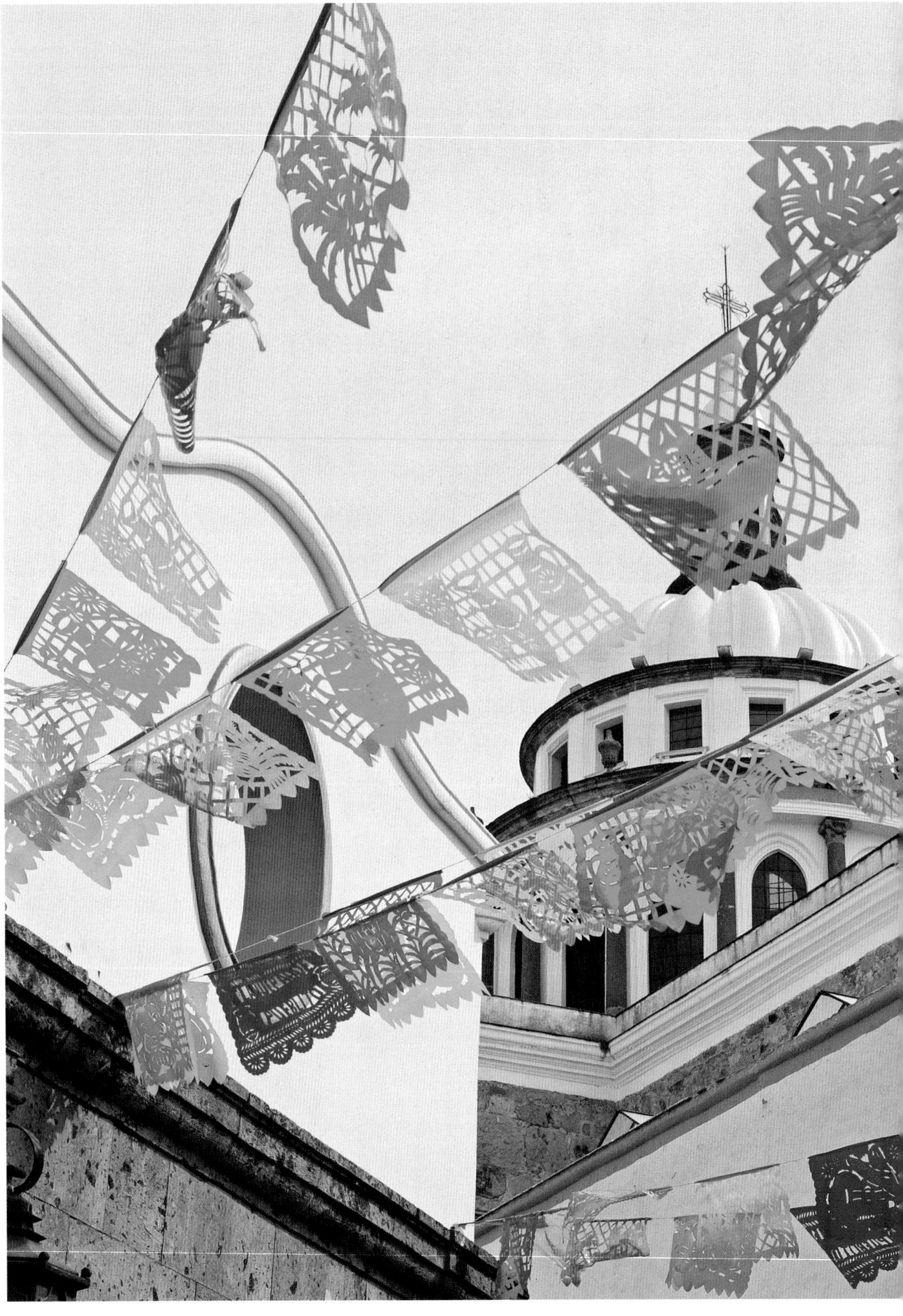

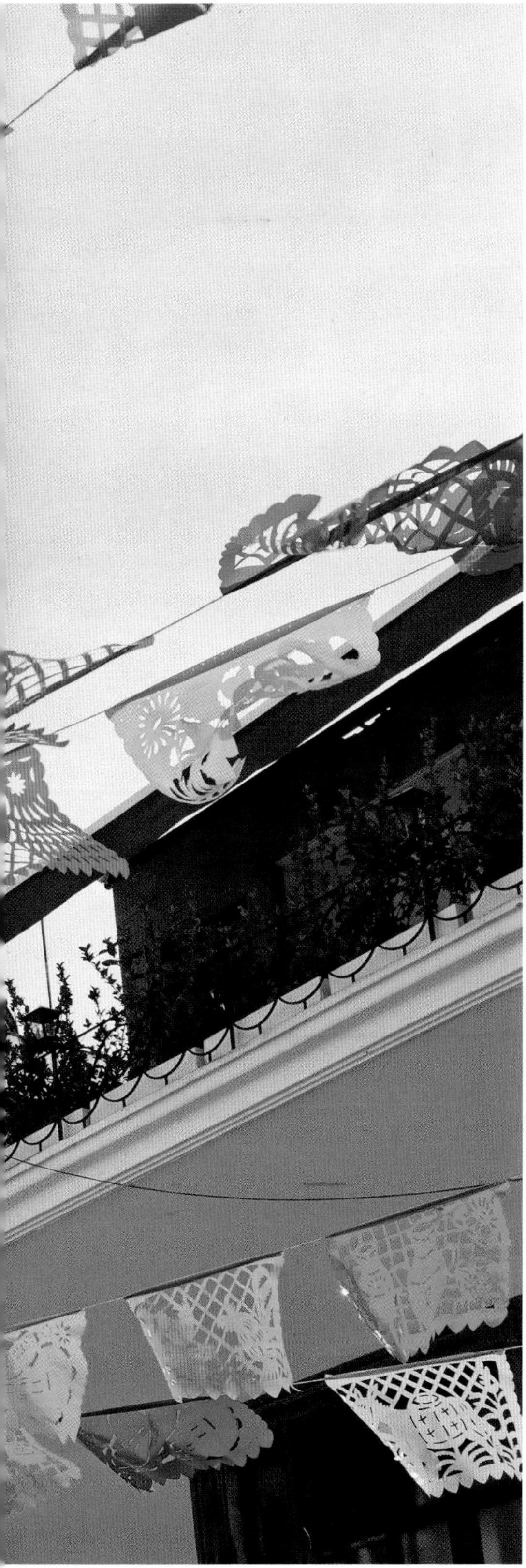

139 My big gay taco

Guadalajara, Mexico

When to go: All year
Best for: A queer city break

Although many queer travelers to Mexico visit Mexico City and the wildly popular Puerto Vallarta, fewer discover Guadalajara which, as well as a beautiful, old city center, has a thriving LGBTQ+ scene and a reputation for being one of Latin America's most queer-friendly cities. Guadalajara's LGBTQ scene is focused around *Zona Centro*, the historic center. At its heart is Tacos Gay—a late-night taco shop operated by LGBTQ+ people, just beware of how hot their spicy sauce can get. All around this area there are LGBTQ-owned and operated places, from accommodation to restaurants and coffee shops. At night, there is an abundance of welcoming bars and clubs. Caudillos Disco Bar is a riot in an old colonial mansion, and La Gozadera and Green Light are other popular LGBTQ clubs. The slightly more upmarket Chapultepec Avenue is another popular area for LGBTQ hangouts, especially for the younger, student crowd. Away from Guadalajara, you can enjoy day trips to the artsy, colorful, and vibrant city of Tlaquepaque, and the town of Tequila—yes, the very place where the agave-based drink is from.

140 Maya magic in Mérida

Mérida, Mexico

When to go: December to March
Best for: A culturally enriching city break

Mérida is a pedestrian-friendly and compact city that is built on the old Maya settlement of T'Hó—which translates as "City of Five Hills," referencing the city's pyramids. It's perfectly positioned to visit many other Maya archeological sites such as Chichén-Itzá and Uxmal. The city's Gran Museo del Mundo Maya Mérida is great for a better understanding of the city's history as well as Maya culture. As with many Indigenous cultures, gender and sexuality weren't as binary and boxed-in as they are now, LGBTQ phobias came with the Spaniards and the Catholic religion. *Centro Historico* is the best place to start exploring the city, and there are many welcoming and inclusive venues, including cantinas Casa Chica, La Negrita, and Cadadía Bar-Café. From Mérida, you can also visit the particularly camp pink lake, Las Coloradas, as well as see flamingos in Celestun, and the yellow town of Izamal.

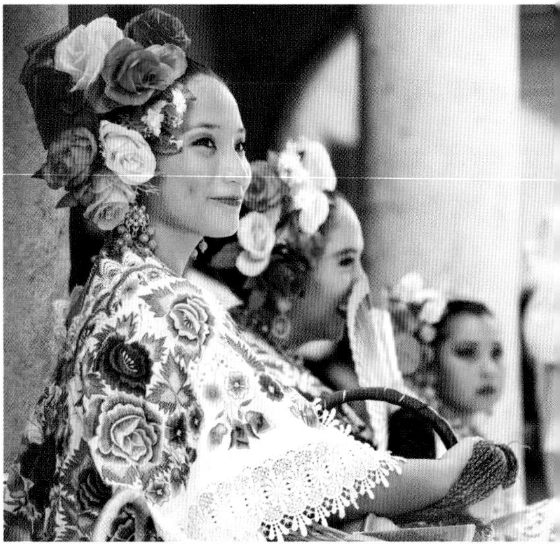

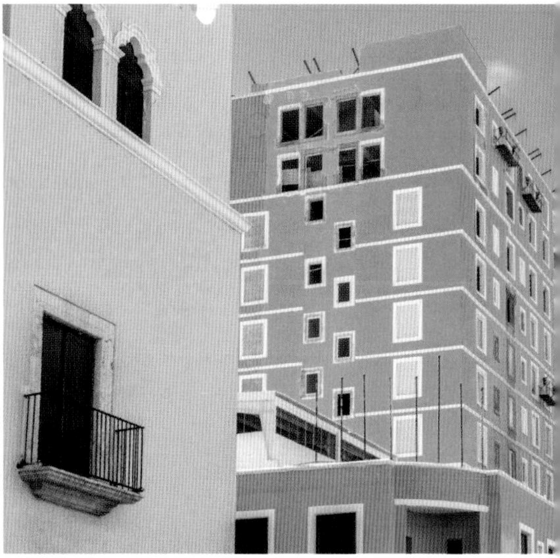

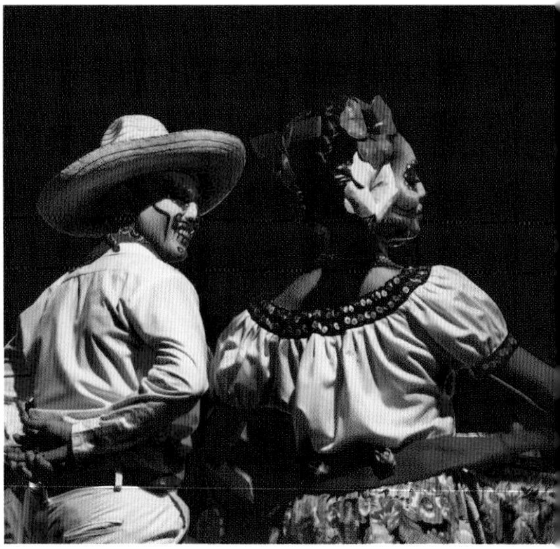

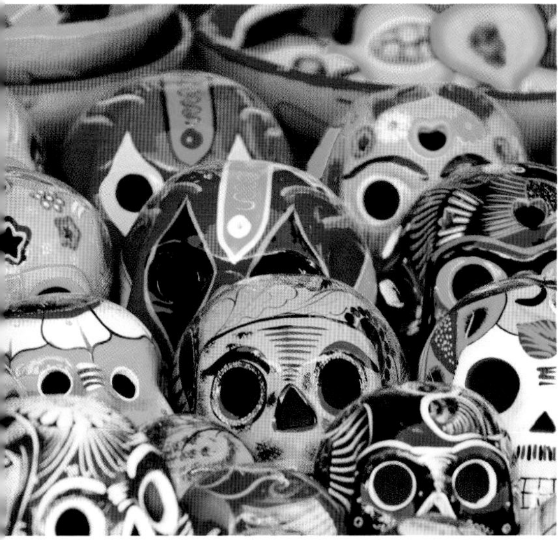

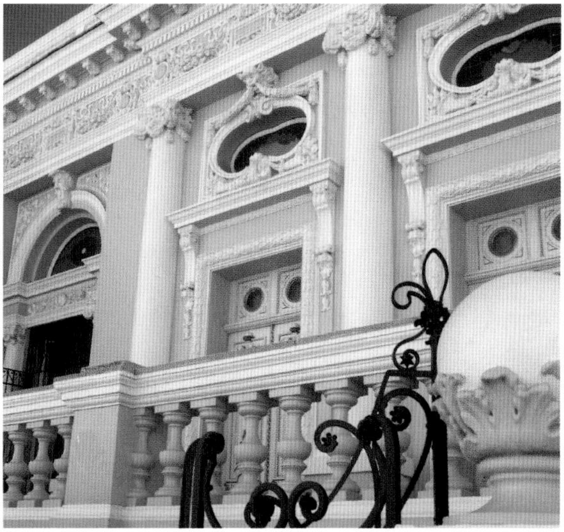

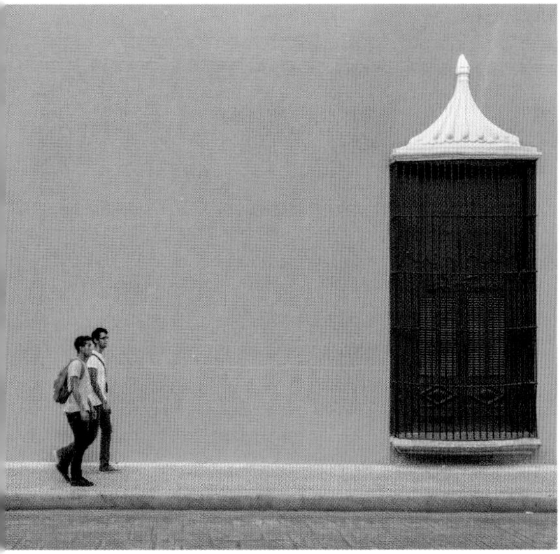

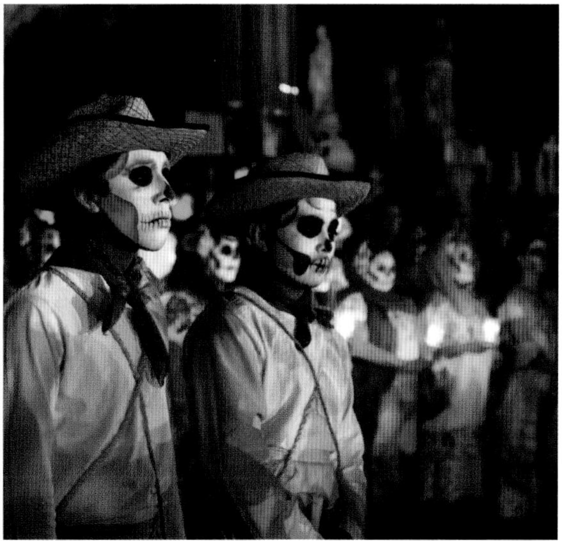

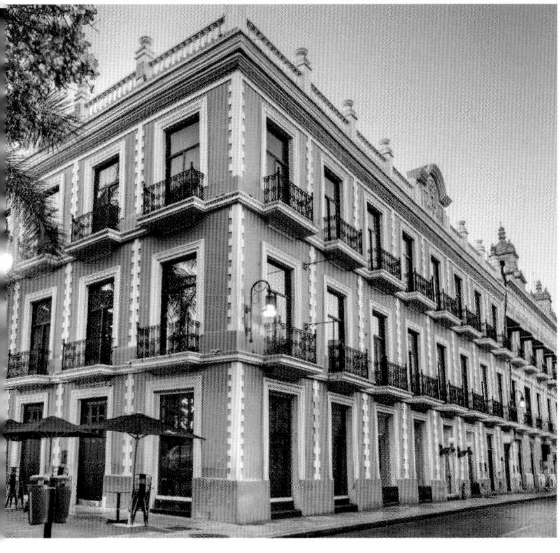

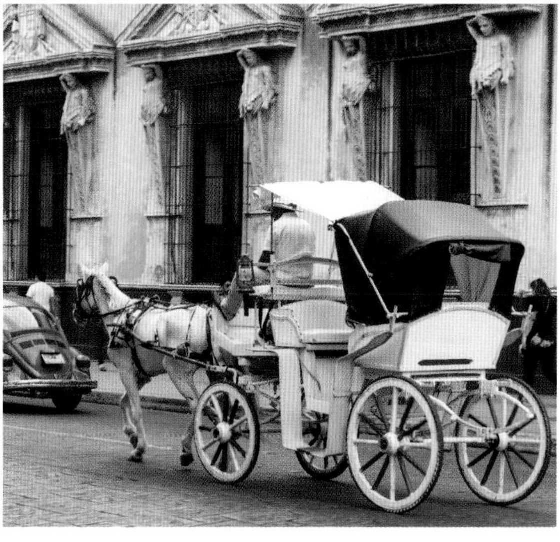

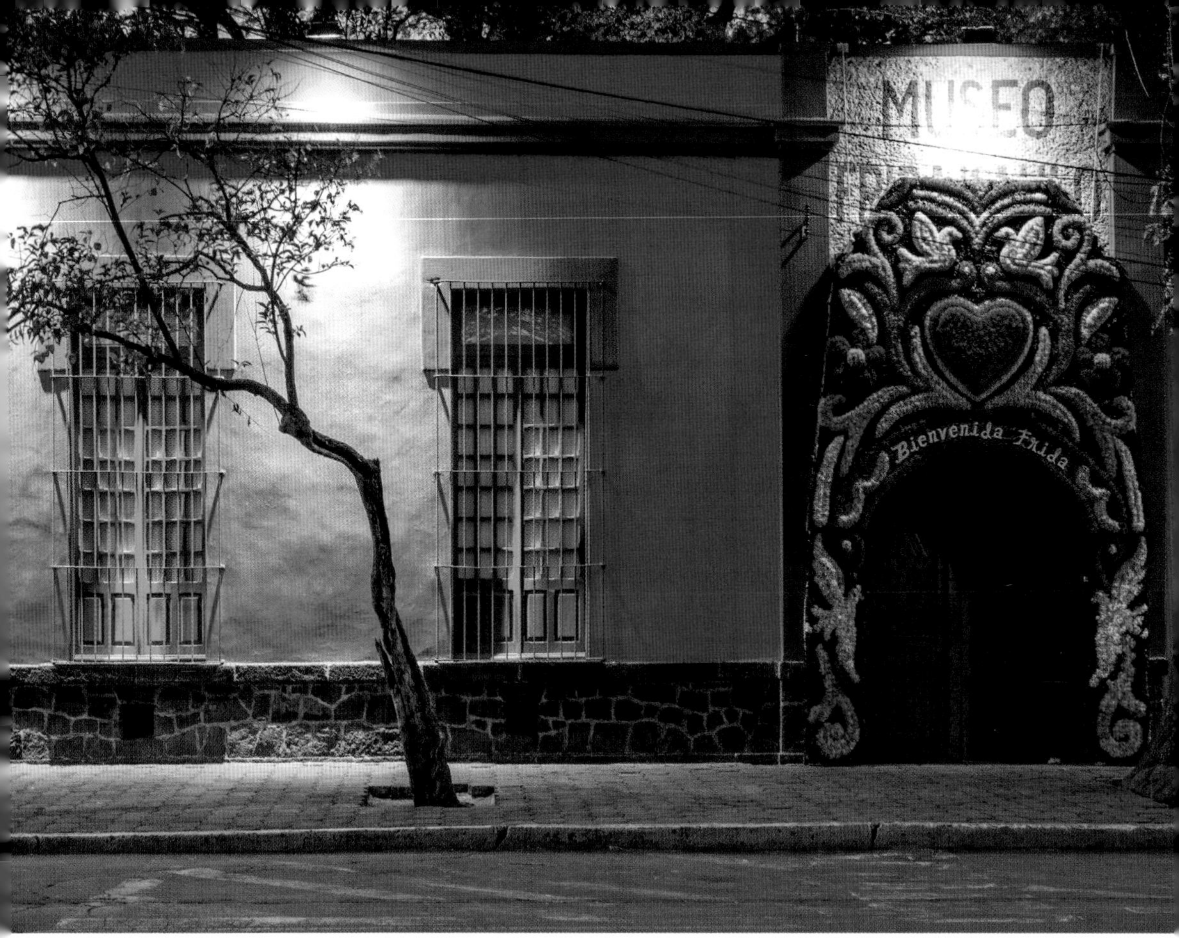
MUSEO
Bienvenida Frida

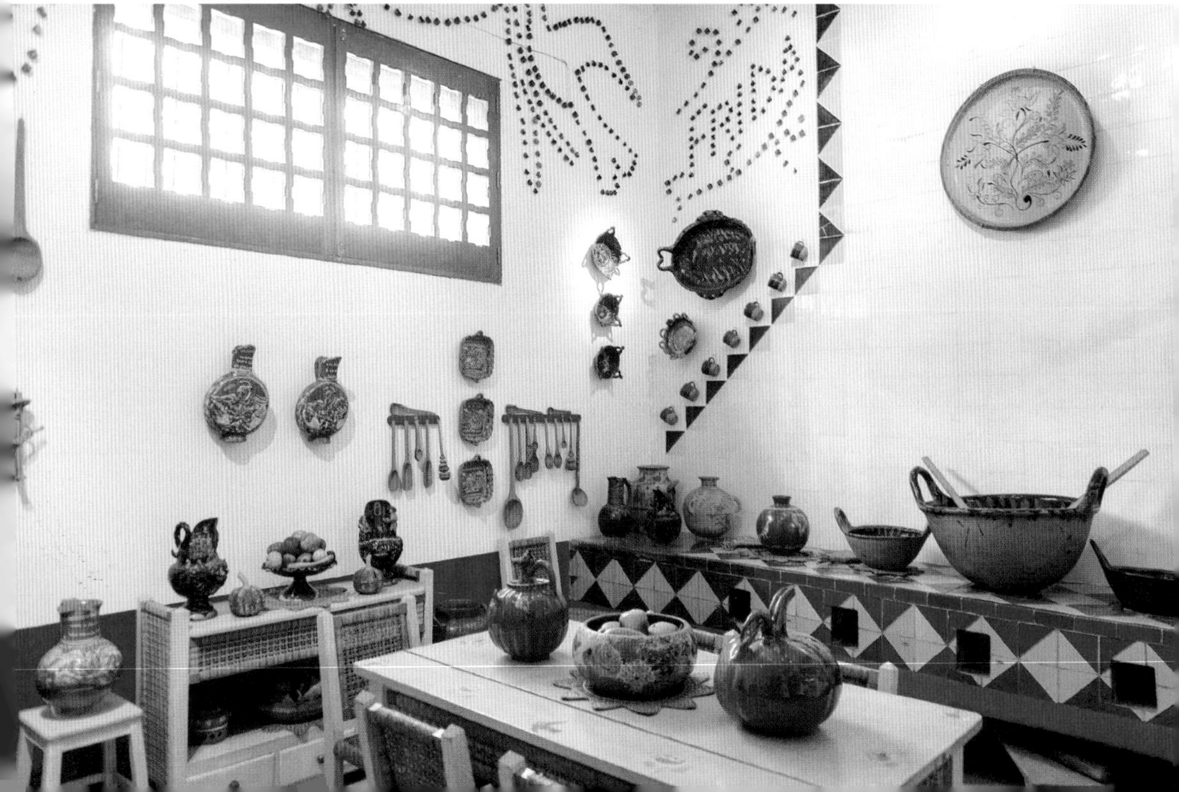

141 Free your inner Frida

◀ Frida Kahlo Museum, Mexico City, Mexico

When to go: All year
Best for: Art lovers

Pay homage to LGBTQ+ icon Frida Kahlo by visiting the *Casa Azul* (Blue House), where she spent a significant amount of her life. She lived here with her family and, later, with her husband, Diego Rivera. Her bisexuality was no secret, and her queer and disabled identity are an integral part of her art and legacy. Although there isn't much of her artwork on display, instead you get to look inside the everyday life of Frida Kahlo.

142 In the pink

▼ Zona Rosa, Mexico City, Mexico

When to go: All year
Best for: Nights out

Zona Rosa is home to Mexico City's most famous LGBTQ+ scene. In the 1990s, LGBTQ+ people moved in because of the area's accepting and safe environment. Nowadays, it's also known for its large Korean community. Zona Rosa is a popular shopping and nightclub area, and Calle Amberes is at its heart. You can find sex shops, bookstores, movie theaters, hotels, bars, and nightclubs. The scene is very club-focused and mainly caters to men, as with many "gayborhoods." Places that are particularly LGBTQ-welcoming are Kinky Bar, Lollipop, and Cabaretito.

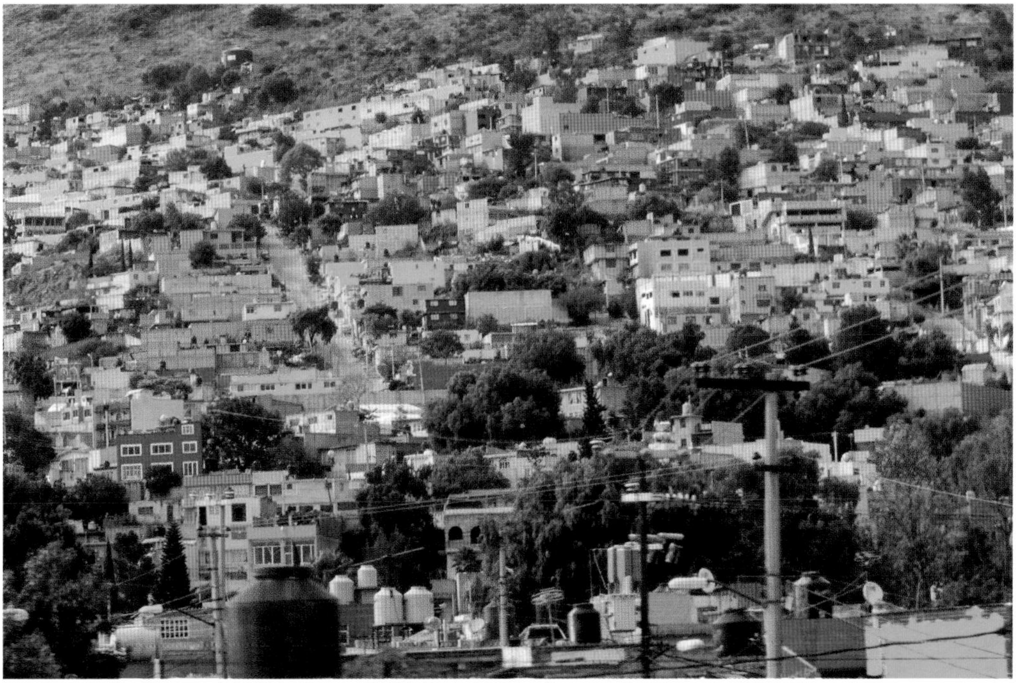

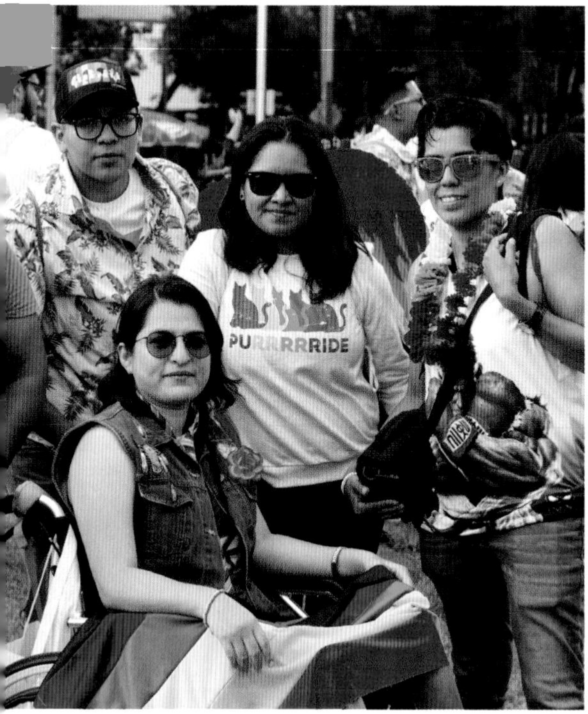

143 Shout it from the *zócalo*

◀ ▼ Mexico City LGBT Pride Parade, Mexico

When to go: June
Best for: Amplifying Mexican LGBTQ+ voices

Mexico City is the most populous city in North America, and for its Pride parade, LGBTQ+ people from all over visit the city, making it one of the biggest Pride parades in Latin America. While the city offers relatively progressive LGBTQ+ rights, violent crime and homophobia still exist. The *Marcha del Orgullo LGBT* (LGBT Pride parade) has a solid celebratory and political character, and traditionally starts at the Angel of Independence in Zona Rosa and ends at the city's *zócalo* (main square).

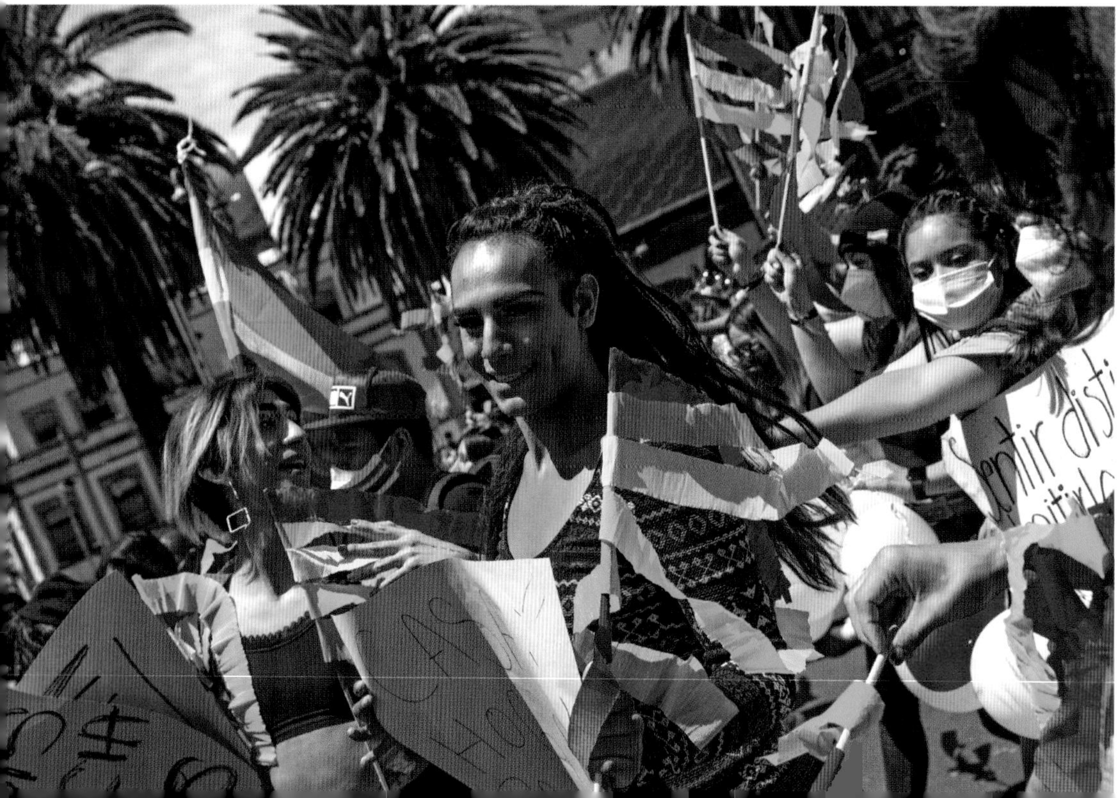

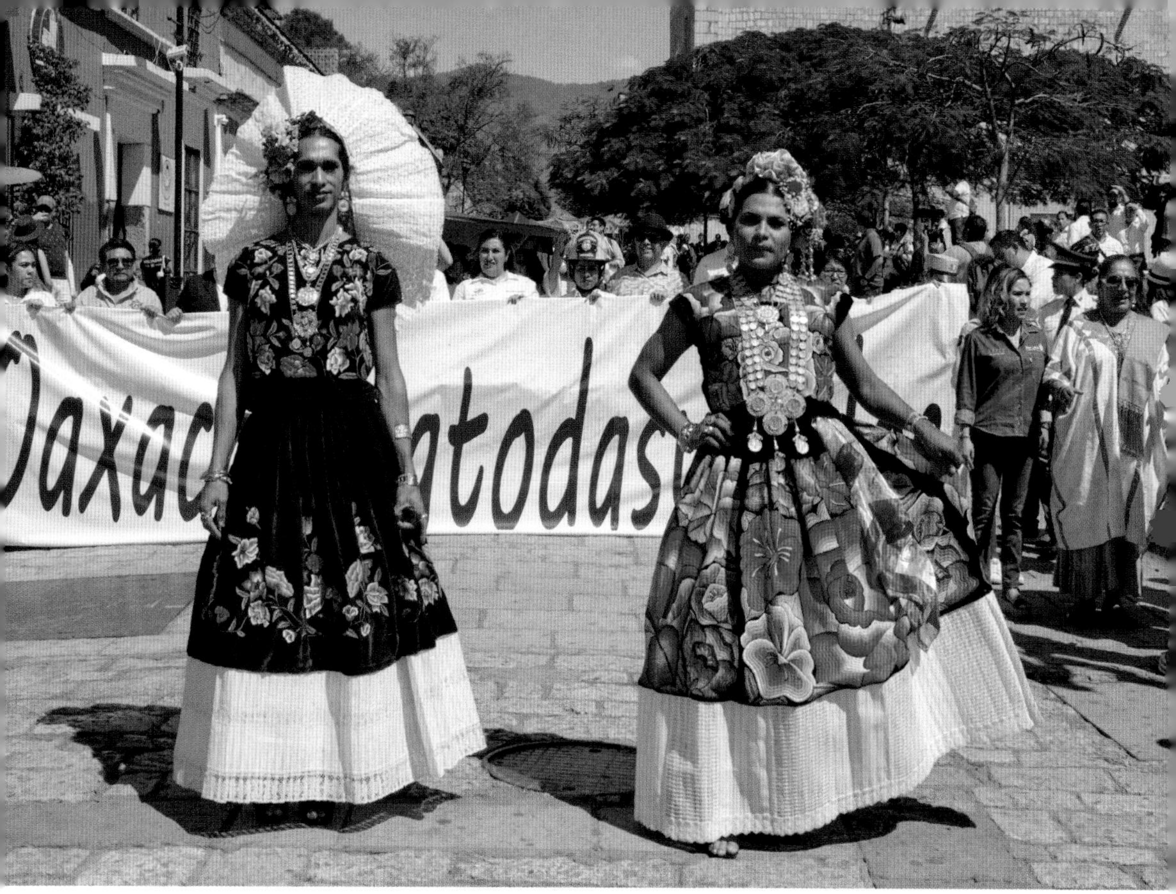

144 Women in the spotlight

Museo de la Mujer, Mexico City, Mexico

When to go: All year
Best for: Mexican gender history

Learn about women's history in Mexico, from pre-Hispanic times to the present, at the Museo de la Mujer,. Gender-based violence still exists, and the fight for gender equality isn't over yet. Every last Wednesday of the month there are special events at the museum.

145 Putting the muxe in Mexico

▲ Oaxaca state, Mexico

When to go: All year
Best for: Going beyond the gender binary

Mexico's Oaxaca state has a rich history of gender diversity. In the town of Juchitán de Zaragoza, there is a significant presence of *muxe*—people who would be considered a "third gender" in a Western framework. Indigenous Zapotec cultures celebrate sexual and gender diversity. Muxe are a part of these cultures and traditions, not separate from them. Connect with the queer community at Club 502 in Oaxaca City.

146 Perfection by the Pacific

Puerto Vallarta, Jalisco, Mexico

When to go: November to May
Best for: Gay bears and whale watching

On the edge of Banderas Bay in the state of Jalisco, Puerto Vallarta (PV to those in the know) is one of the most popular sunshine destinations for queer travelers. Many tend to make for the Blue Chair Beach Club, with its blue and green sun loungers overlooking the Pacific, or the Mantamar Beach Club; both are in the town's Zona Romántica. Here you'll find plenty of LGBTQ+ businesses, from jewelry and clothing shops to bars, clubs and cafés. The district is next to Puerto Vallarta's "old town," although old is—of course—relative. Puerto Vallarta was little more than a fishing port one hundred years ago. The bulk of its tourism has sprung up since the 1950s. In recent years, themed festivals such as the bear-oriented "Beef Dip," have further boosted PV's international profile, while nature-lovers flock here for the opportunity to spot whales and sea turtles.

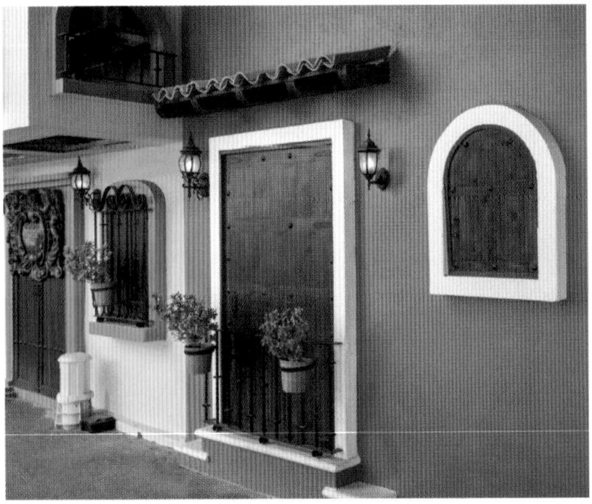

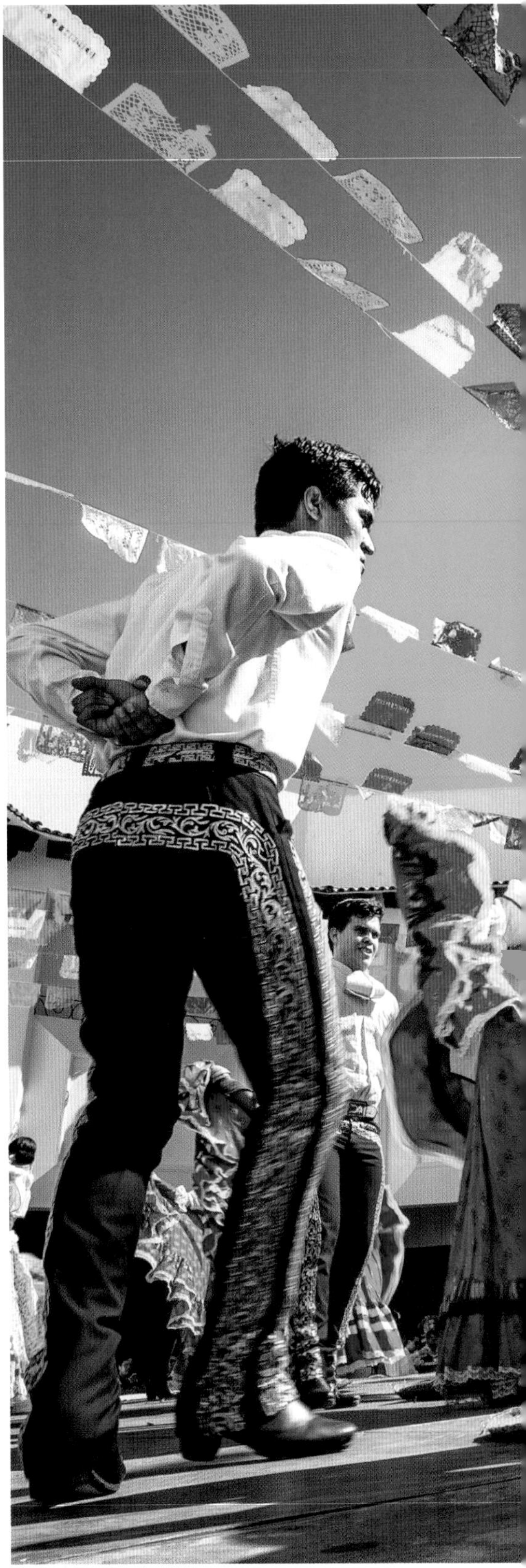

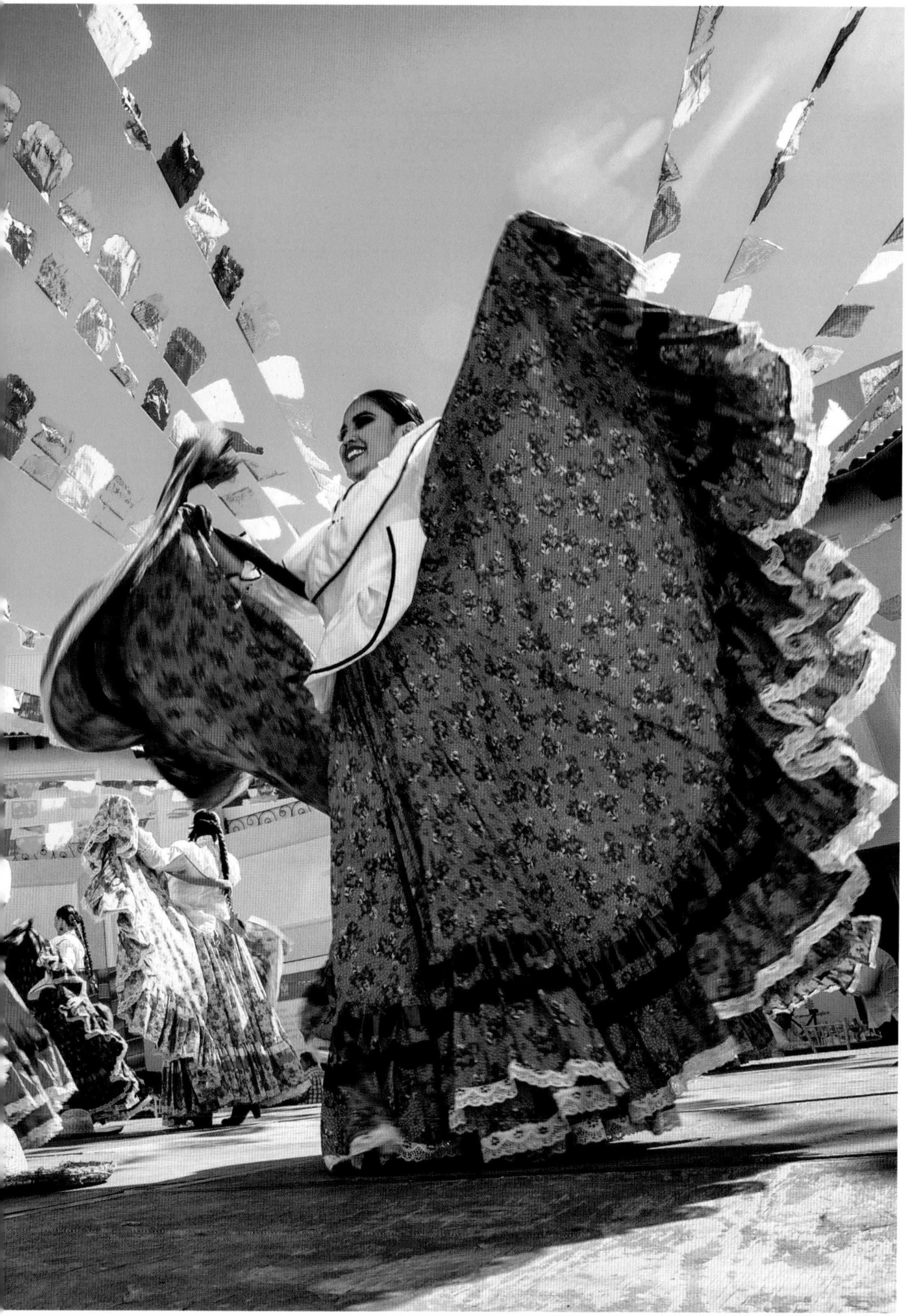

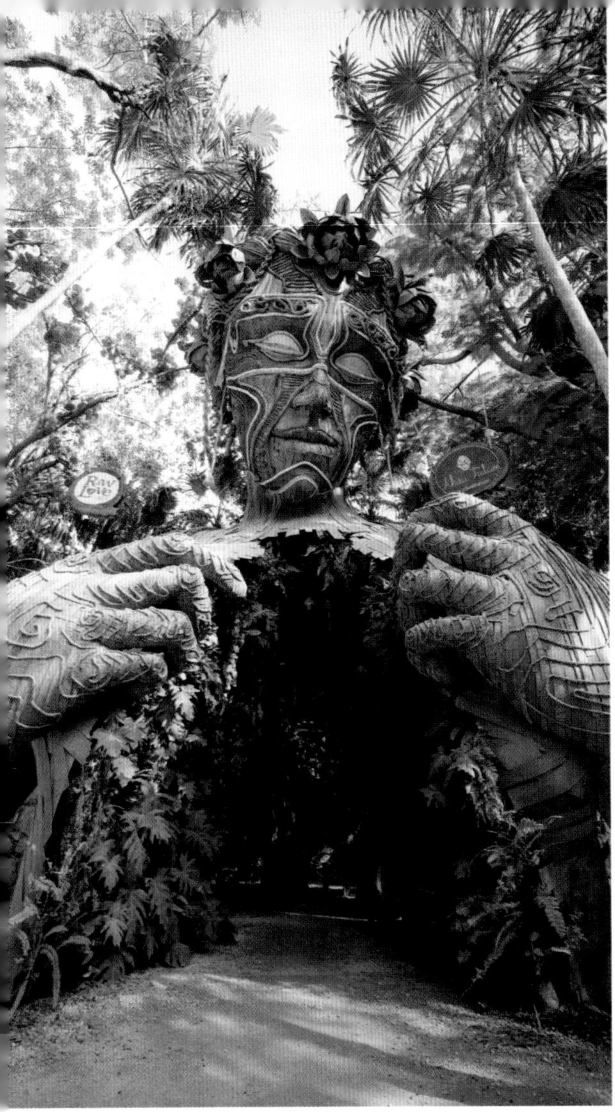
Raw Love
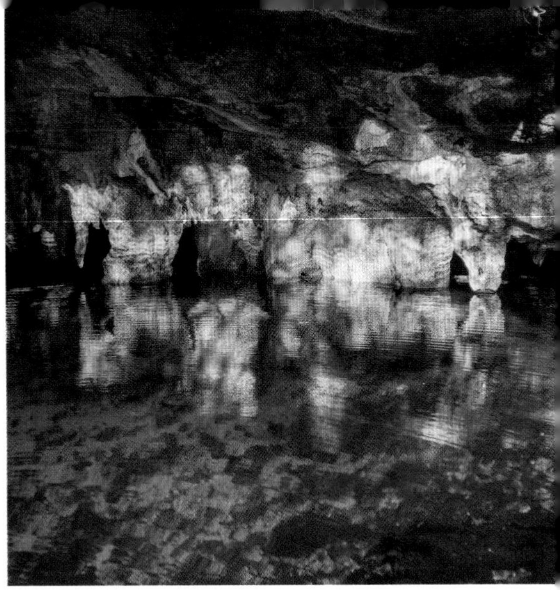
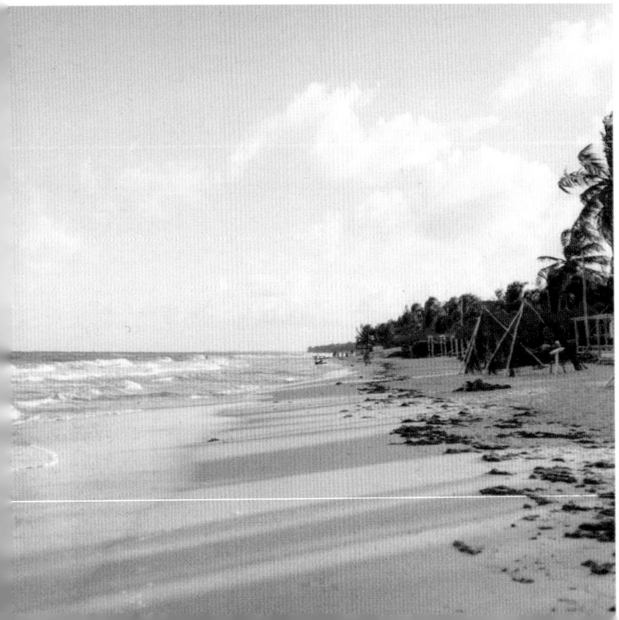
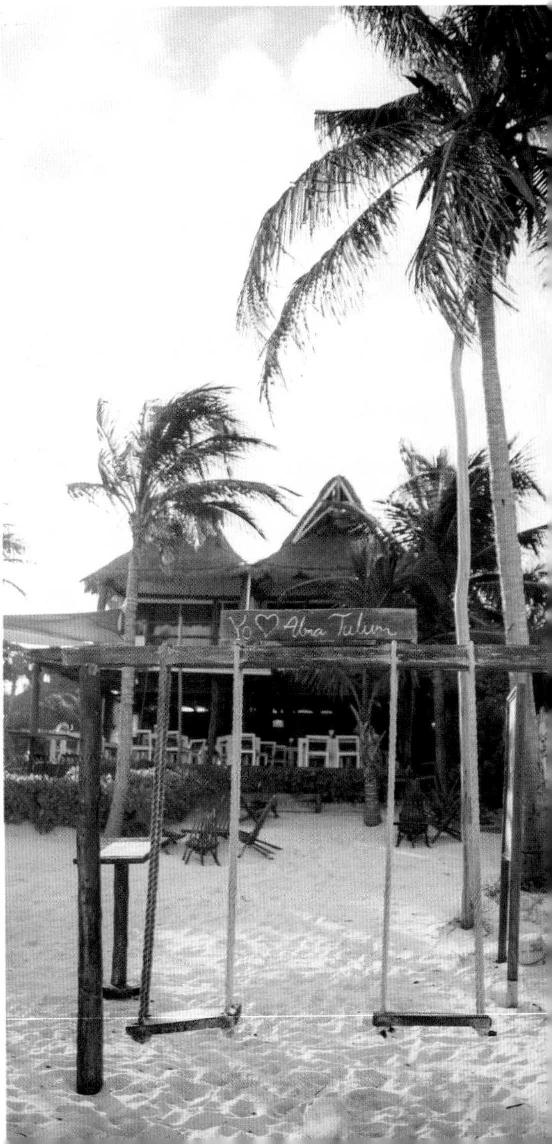
Yo ♥ Abra Tulum

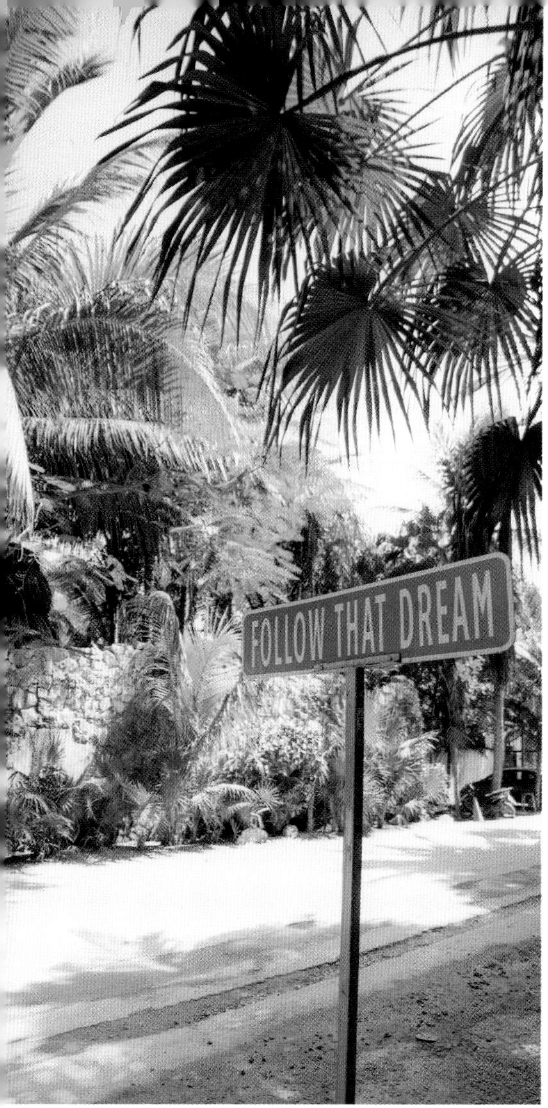

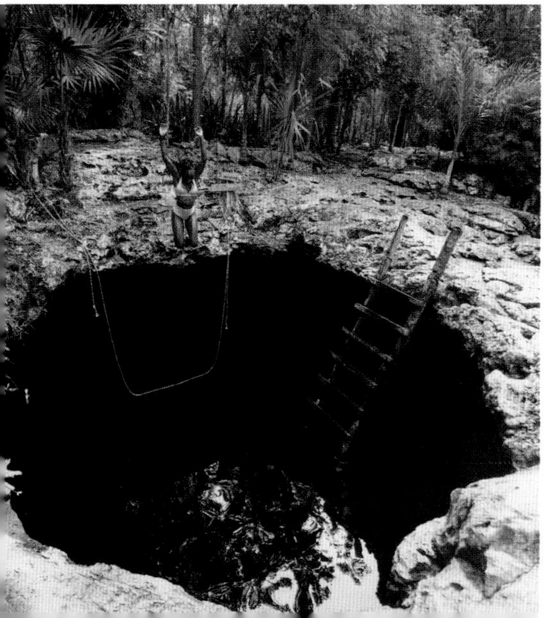

147 Too good Tulum

Tulum, Mexico

When to go: October to December
Best for: Boho beach holidays

Tulum is famous for its relaxed beach vibe, magical cenotes (water-filled sinkholes), and well-preserved Maya ruins. While the town neatly divides into Tulum archaeological zone Tulum pueblo, and Tulum beach—each with its own unique character—overall, the town has a distinct boho vibe. Tulum was built on the site of the pre-Columbian Maya city Zamá—one of the last cities built and inhabited by the Maya—and there are well-preserved sites in the Tulum archaeological zone. In Tulum pueblo (the downtown area), you can find artisanal shops and restaurants with both local and international cuisines. And while Tulum only has one LGBTQ+ party—Fruity—the atmosphere in its nightlife is open and welcoming to all. The Tulum beach area has probably changed most over recent years. Where it was once a quiet beach town that attracted slow travelers and artists, it has now developed into a tourism hot spot with a strip of high-end hotels, resorts, and beach clubs. One thing not to miss while you're here is swimming in a cenote—you can even go scuba diving in some of them.

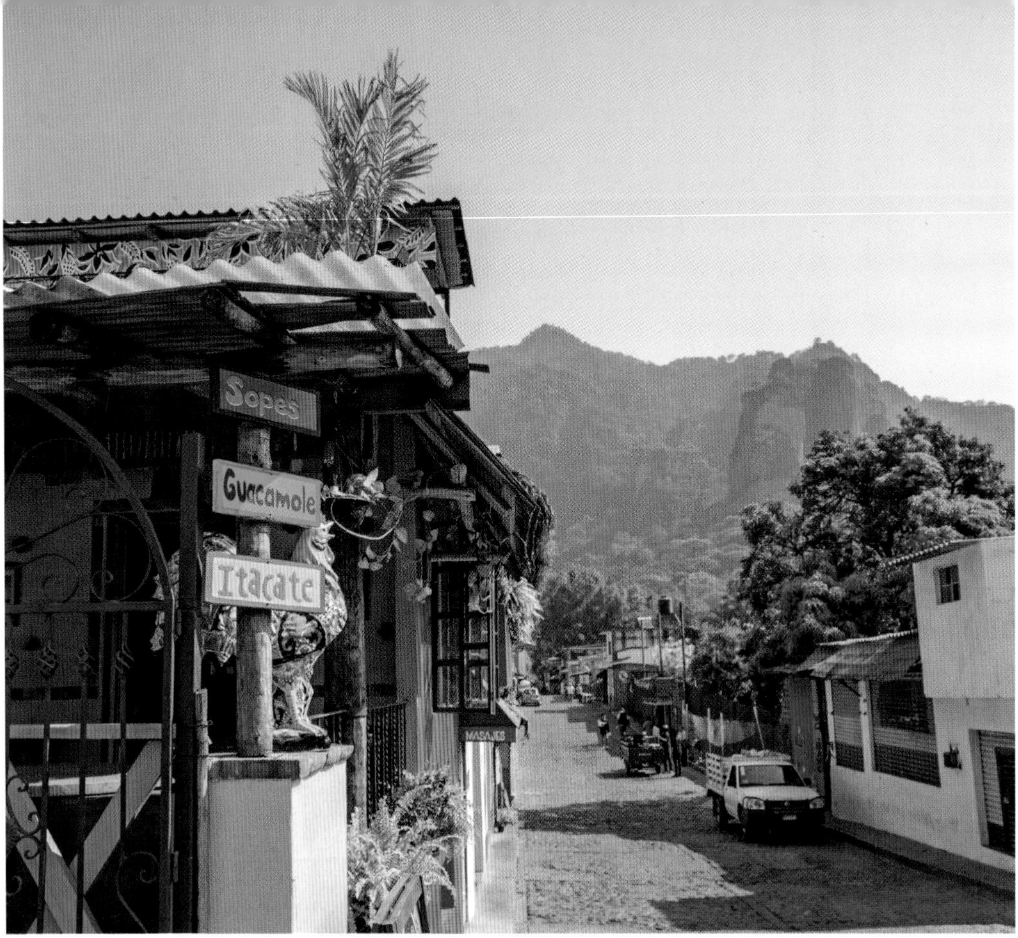

148 Queer as folk

▲ Tepoztlán, Mexico

When to go: All year
Best for: Immersive queer history

One of Mexico's most famous folk singers, Chavela Vargas, moved audiences with sweeping love songs and her intense singing style. Born in 1919, Vargas had a string of high-profile lovers, including Frida Kahlo. Tepoztlán is a hub of bohemian culture that the singer called her home. Here she'd invite punters to endless rounds of tequila in the local bars. Walk through the somnambulant streets while listening to her songs for a sonically queer Mexican experience.

149 Passport, guidebook, glitter

Guacherna Gay, Barranquilla, Colombia

When to go: February
Best for: Dressing up

Glittering, queer, carnival-queens with fabulously feathered wings—Guacherna Gay is South American carnival at its campest. Proudly calling itself the "party for everyone," Guacherna Gay is now on Barranquilla's cherished Cultural Heritage list.

150 Show your pride *pura vida* style

▶ Marcha de la Diversidad, San José, Costa Rica

When to go: June
Best for: Optimistic, happy vibes

Costa Rica is the happiest country in the world according to the Happy Planet Index. It's the country of *pura vida*, an expression of happiness, optimism, and living life to the fullest. It's a vibe *Ticos* (Costa Ricans) annually bring to the Marcha de la Diversidad, a lively parade that attracts tens of thousands of people. After the parade, continue the party at one of the LGBTQ+ bars, La Avispa, Club El Teatro, or Puchos. And if you're staying long enough, join Pride on the Beach in Manuel Antonio in July.

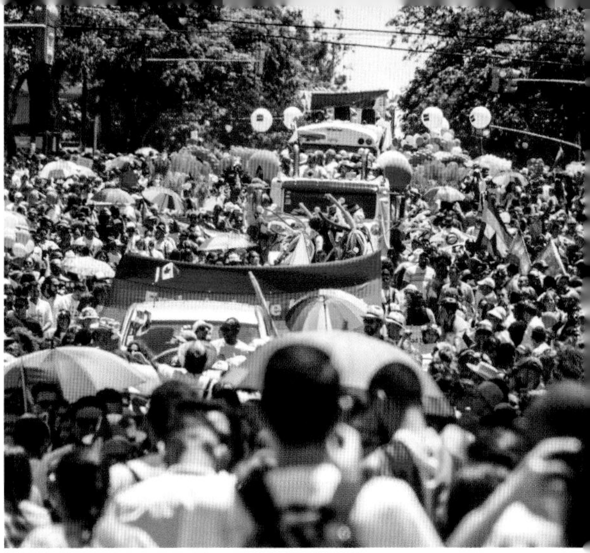

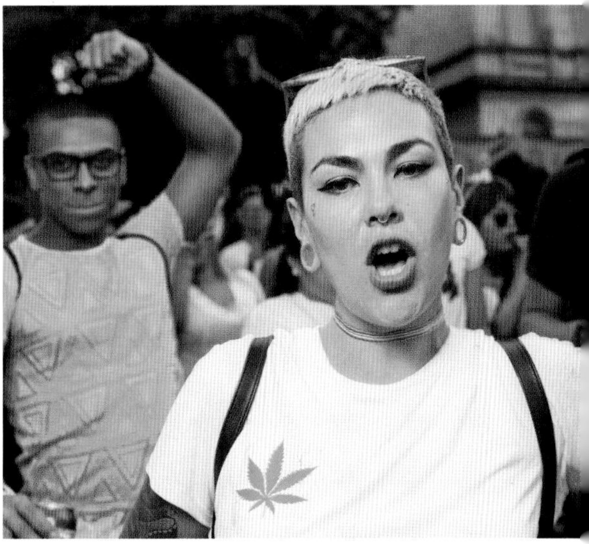

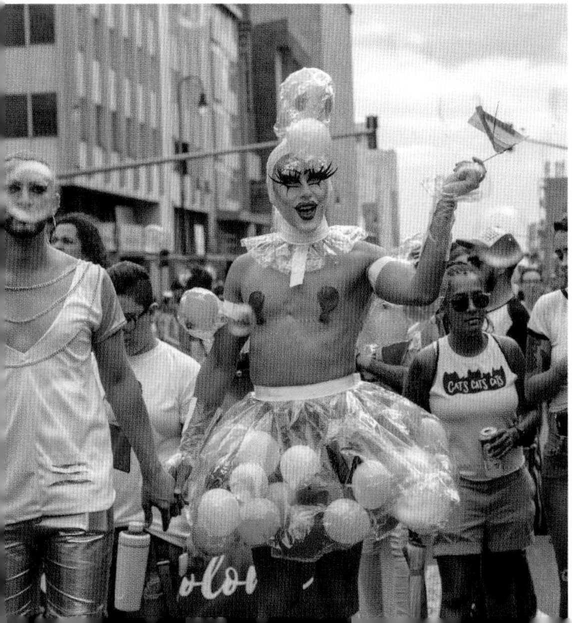

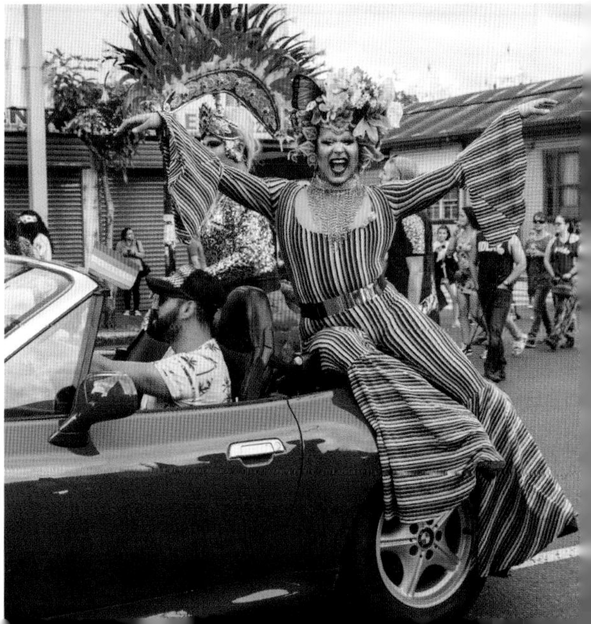

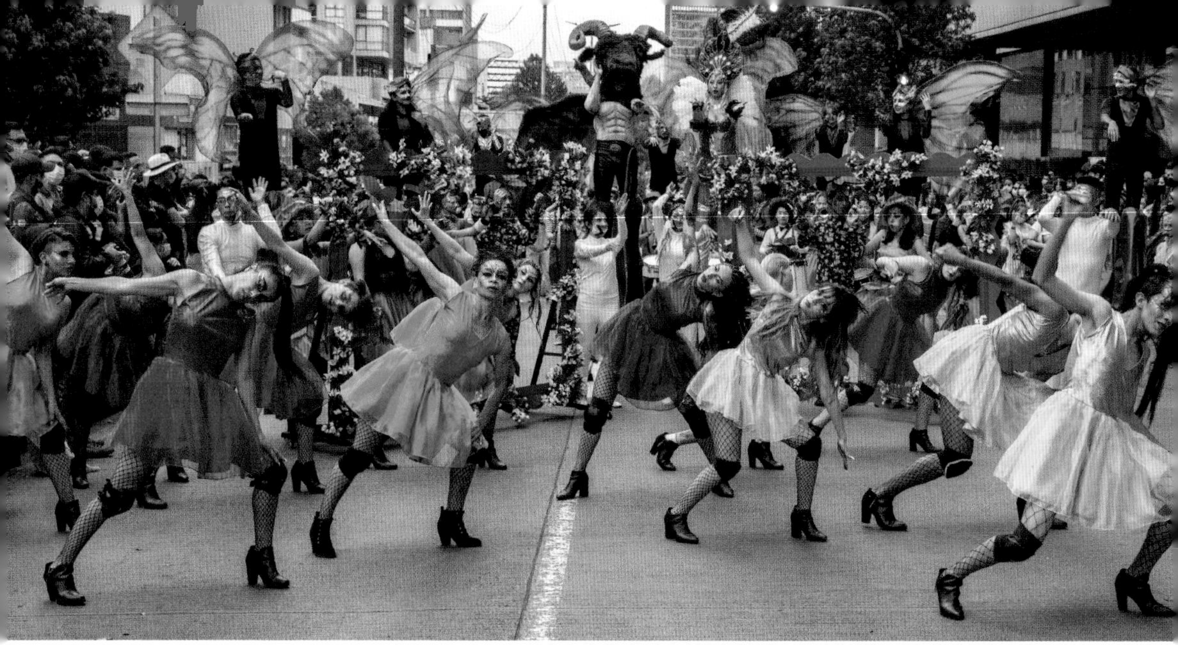

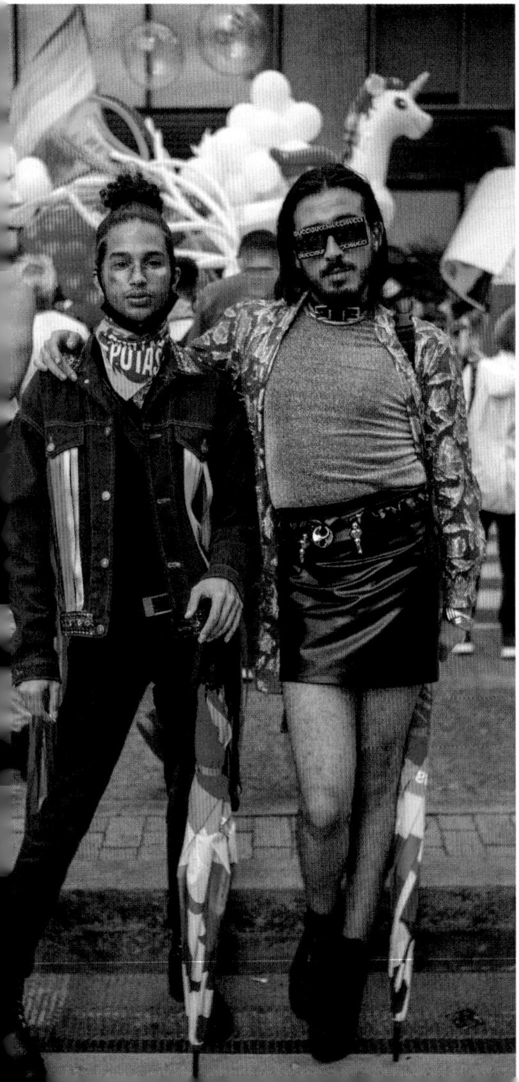

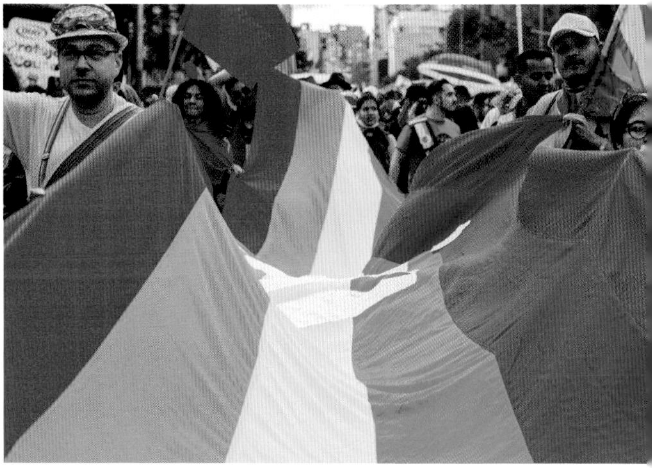

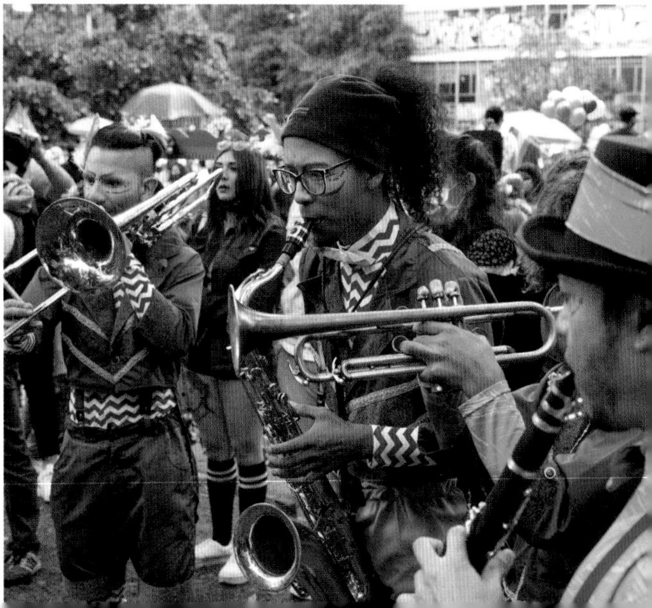

151 Chip chip Chapinero

◀ Chapinero, Bogotá, Colombia

When to go: All year
Best for: Clubbing and bar-hopping

Largely known as the party hub of Bogotá, Chapinero is also the queer heart of the city. The district is filled with LGBTQ-friendly venues, from gastronomy, to bars, and even saunas. If you're visiting in July, Bogotá's Pride is known to have one of the world's wildest LGBTQ+ parades, followed by fabulous parties in the Chapinero district.

152 One club, 13 dance floors

Theatron, Bogotá, Colombia

When to go: All year
Best for: Party, party, party

Located in Chapinero, Bogotá boasts the largest LGBTQ+ club in Latin America: Theatron. Situated in an old movie theater, Theatron is almost more of a small town than a nightclub. Inside there are 13 different dance floors, several restaurants, and even a sex shop. To top it all off, the inexpensive entry price includes bottomless drinks until 2:00 a.m. on Saturdays.

153 Shake it like a superstar

Bogotá Salsa Tour, Bogotá, Colombia

When to go: All year
Best for: Moving those hips

There's no better way to experience Colombia than dancing salsa. If you're keen to learn some moves from the country's top queer salsa dancers, then head to Bogotá Salsa Tour. Book a private class or join one of their LGBTQ-friendly group sessions. Whether you want to lead or follow, we're all equals on the dance floor.

154 Popcorn and chill

Ciclo Rosa, Bogotá, Colombia

When to go: September
Best for: Queer films

Founded in 2001, Ciclo Rosa is Cinemateca de Bogotá's LGBTQ+ film season; and it's one of Latin America's longest-running events for queer audiovisual work. Explore your choice of shorts, video essays, documentaries, and feature-length films.

155 Beauty and the beach

Cartagena Pride, Colombia

When to go: July to August
Best for: All round Pride brilliance

Cartagena is a spectacular, historical city in northern Colombia that looks out onto the azure waters of the Caribbean Sea. Pride is an explosive occasion here, where international visitors mingle with welcoming locals to create a thriving atmosphere. With beach-volleyball tournaments, drag shows, and outdoor parties, it's more of a festival than a single march. Experience Pride in Colombia's most picturesque city.

156 Bloom in Medellín

▼ Medellín Flower Festival, Medellín, Colombia

When to go: August
Best for: Fabulous flowers

With over-the-top floral displays and a Latin pop soundtrack, it's hard to believe that it took until 2021 for there to be a dedicated LGBTQ+ event at Medellín's fantastic Feria de las Flores. The week-long flower festival sees the town transformed by flower installations and the highlight is the flower parade—a flotilla of stunning floral floats that are judged for their elaboration and creativity. It's a magical, colorful vibe—and it's Colombia, so there's always a party.

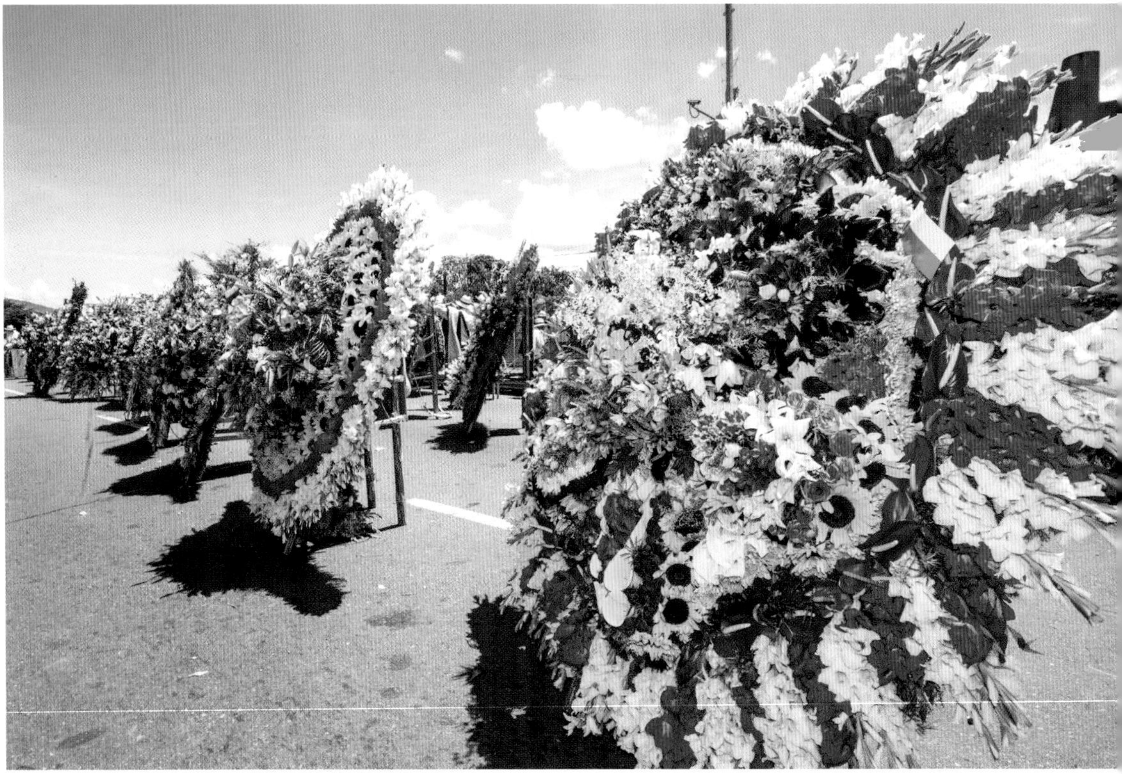

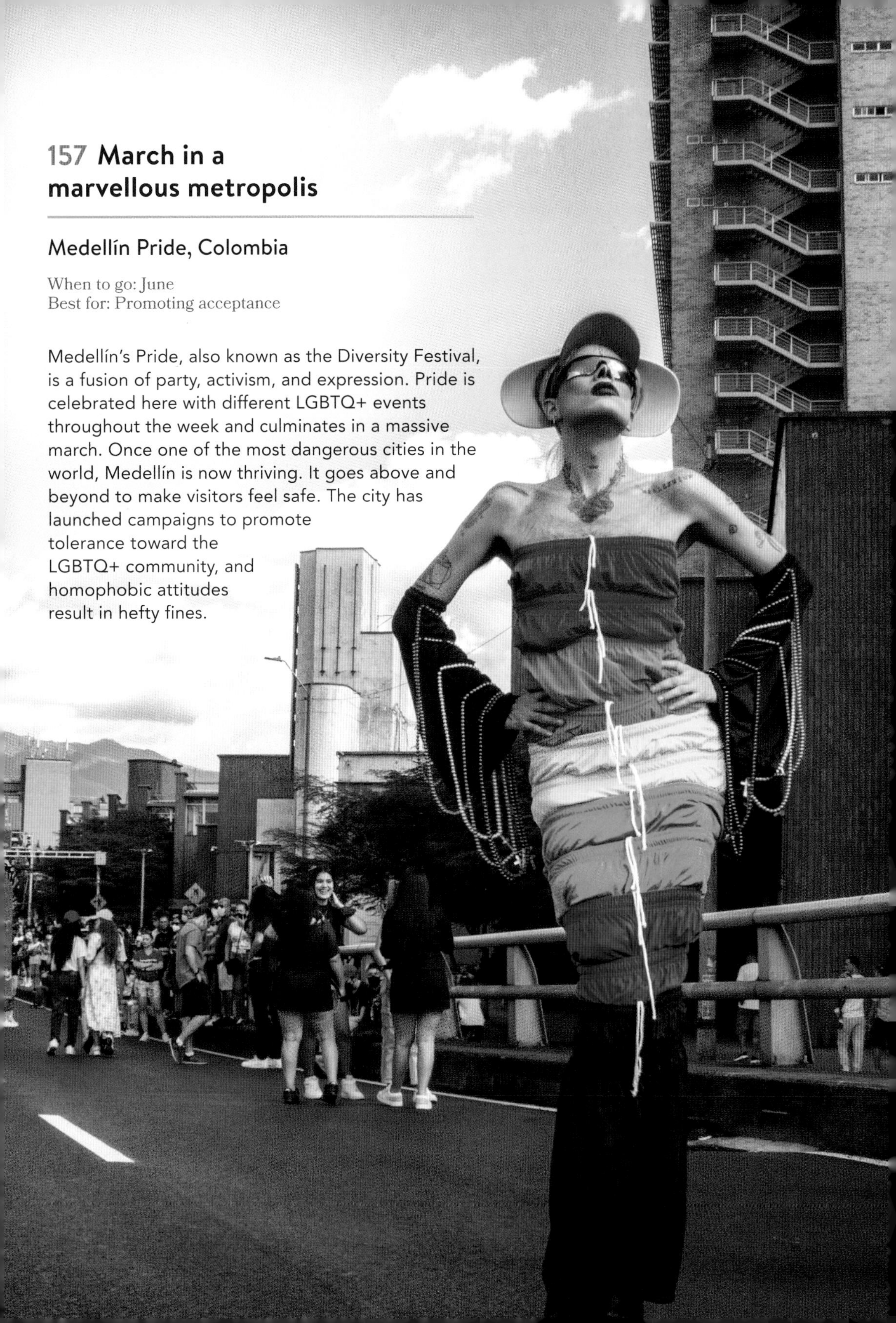

157 March in a marvellous metropolis

Medellín Pride, Colombia

When to go: June
Best for: Promoting acceptance

Medellín's Pride, also known as the Diversity Festival, is a fusion of party, activism, and expression. Pride is celebrated here with different LGBTQ+ events throughout the week and culminates in a massive march. Once one of the most dangerous cities in the world, Medellín is now thriving. It goes above and beyond to make visitors feel safe. The city has launched campaigns to promote tolerance toward the LGBTQ+ community, and homophobic attitudes result in hefty fines.

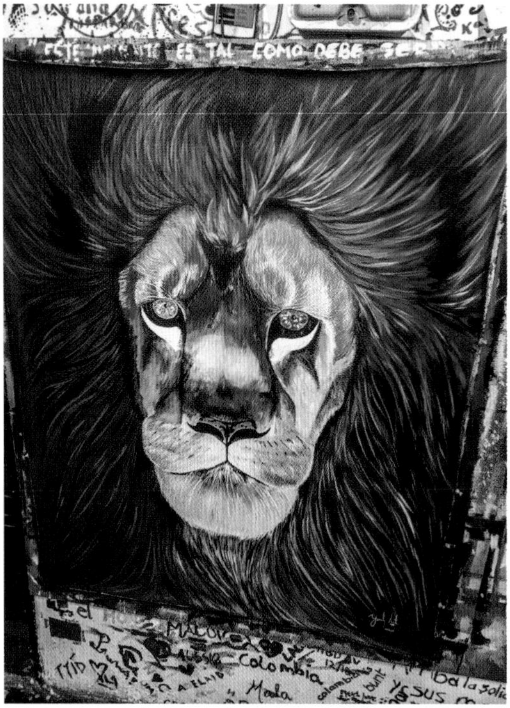
ES TAL COMO DEBE SER
Colombia

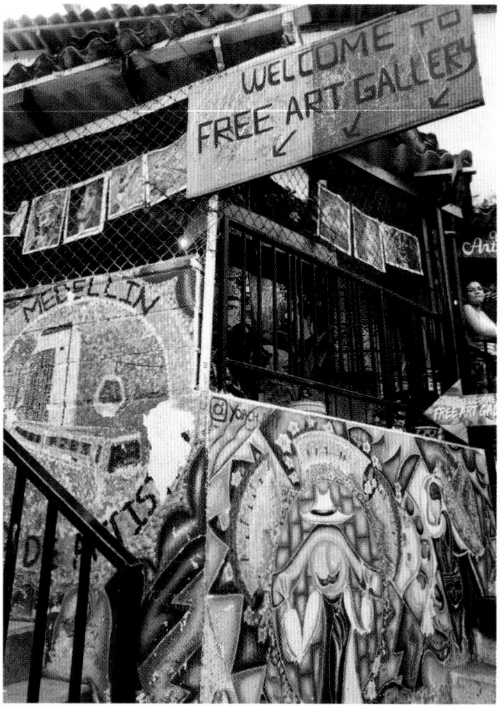
WELCOME TO
FREE ART GALLERY
MEDELLIN

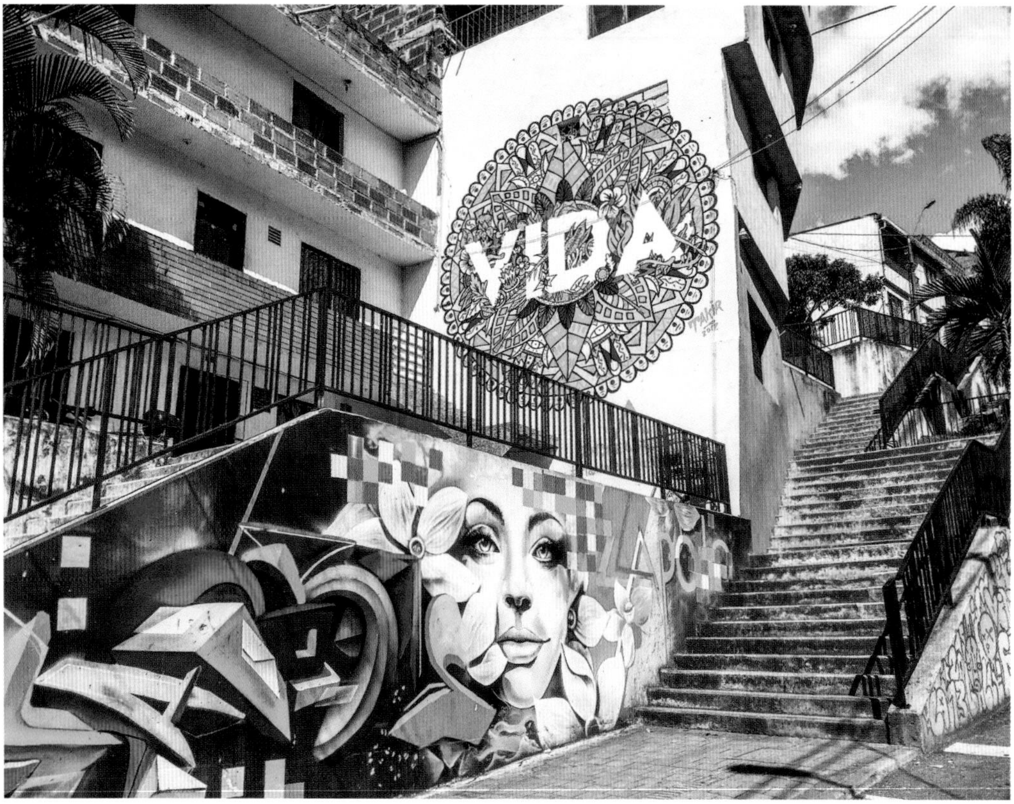
VIDA

158 Community of color

◀ Comuna 13, Medellín, Colombia

When to go: All year
Best for: Inspirational positive change

The Comuna 13 neighborhood has had the most awe-inspiring transformation since Medillín's dark days of the 1990s. Now, it is a stunning, open-air art gallery filled with beautiful rainbow colors and smiling faces. Join a tip-based walking-tour to hear stories from locals and to learn about the transformation of the area. Additionally, there are buskers, cafés, galleries, and bars adding vibrancy to the streets.

159 Join the resistance

SinVergüenza, Quito, Ecuador

When to go: All year
Best for: Refuge

SinVergüenza, which translates as "No Shame," is an activist collective formed to resist oppression. The collective throws thriving, intersectional parties that rally for rights soundtracked by the thumping beats of *perreo*, a "freaky" style of reggaeton.

160 Comradeship on the cobbles

Orguio, Quito, Ecuador

When to go: June
Best for: Supporting Ecuador's queer community

Quito's annual Pride march is an important day to make visible LGBTQ+ demands and bring voices together to be heard. March through the sloping, cobbled streets of Quito and join the rallying cry for rights in a country where homophobic attitudes are still, sadly, commonplace.

161 Want a good time? Foch yeah!

Mariscal, Quito, Ecuador

When to go: All year
Best for: Feeling welcome

The district of Mariscal is the LGBTQ+ hub of Quito. Go to the area around Plaza Foch, which is affectionately known as the LGBTQ+ friendly Pink Zone, to find all the main bars, clubs, and restaurants. There is always a buzz in the air and crowds of like-minded people.

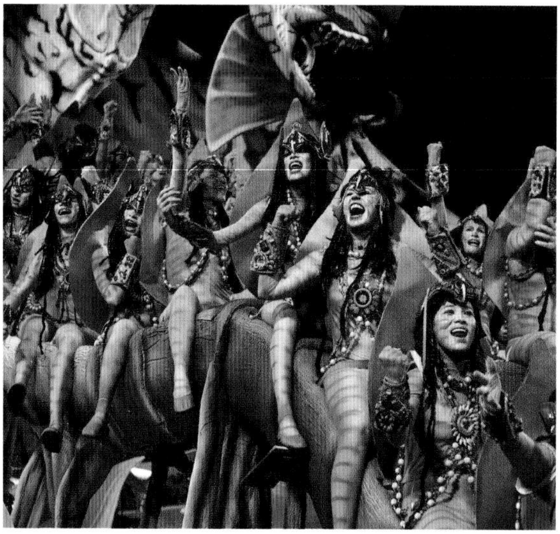
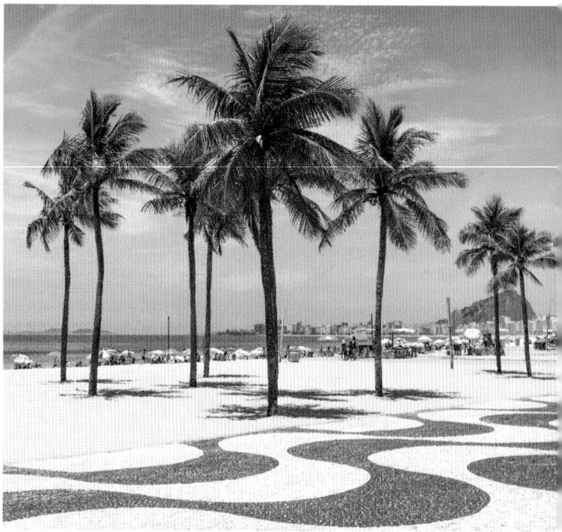
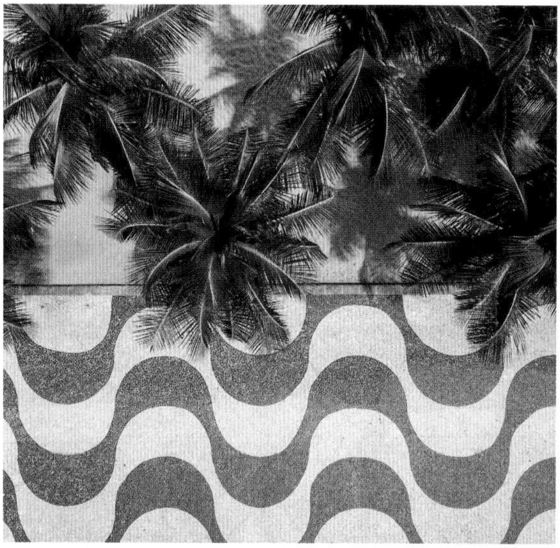
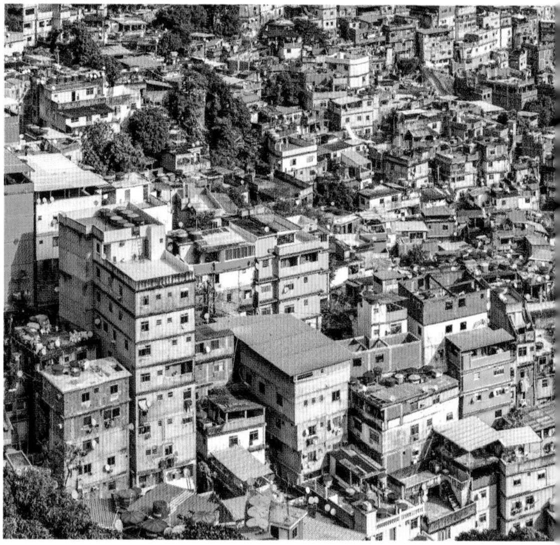
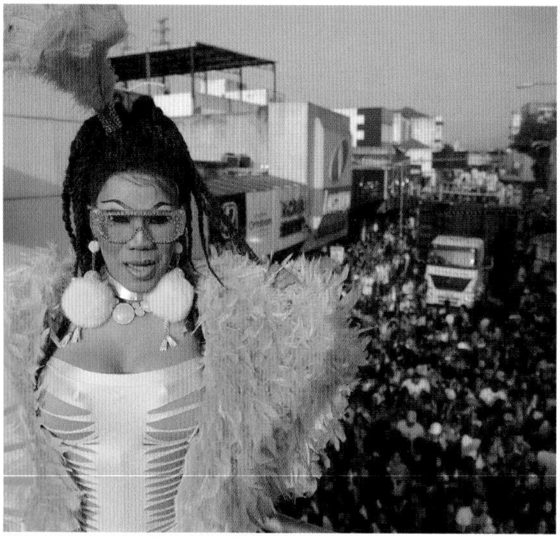
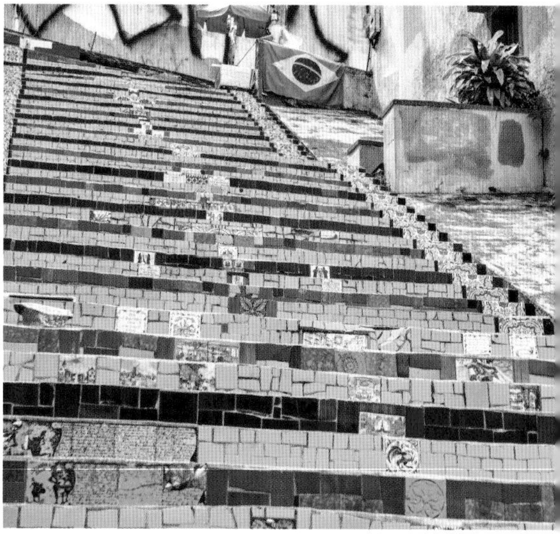

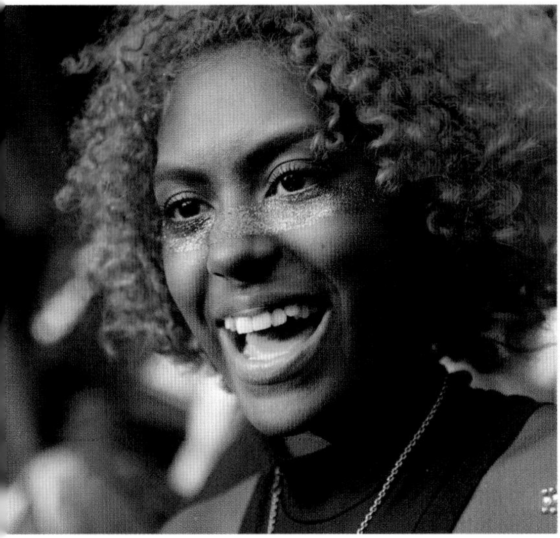

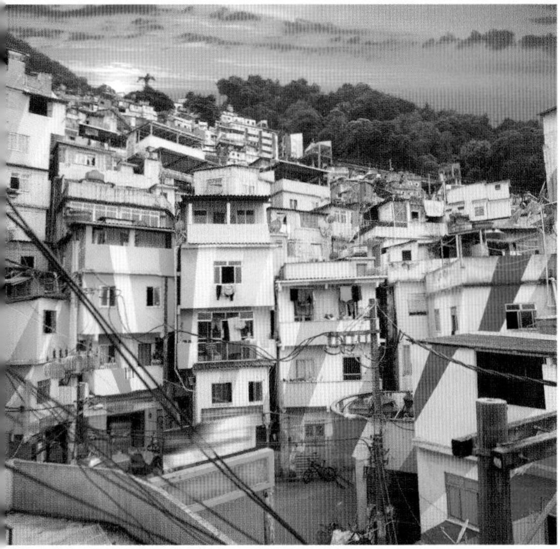

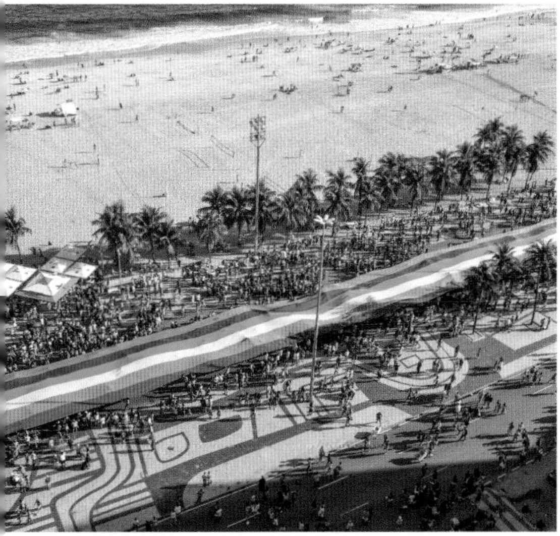

162 Sexy sauntering in sunny Rio

Rio de Janeiro, Brazil

When to go: All year
Best for: Gorgeously gay beaches

Rio de Janeiro is South America's premier tourist destination, where sweeping stretches of white, sandy beaches meet warm, turquoise waters. Rio de Janeiro is charming, beautiful, and also really gay. The city's inherent beach culture is campy and fabulous, where flexing, muscular men and toned women flock to the gay section of Ipanema's beach to flaunt their bronzed bodies, and the numerous nighttime queer parties are sweaty, sexy affairs. Learn some samba steps and work it on the dance floors in gay-friendly areas by the Copacabana and Praia do Leblon. If you are visiting in the Pride months, Rio's annual march attracts over one million people, where carnival traditions are infused with gay flair for spectacular, extravagant performances. Be streetwise as crime is common, and make sure to stick to gay-friendly neighborhoods for the safest experience. In the meantime, put on your beachwear, grab a caipirinha, and head to the beach!

163 Beach beauty

Ipanema Beach, Rio de Janeiro, Brazil

When to go: All year
Best for: Sightseeing

World-famous for its namesake role in the 1960s Bossa Nova hit "Girl from Ipanema," this iconic beachside area is a must-visit on any trip to Rio de Janeiro. Ipanema has plenty of LGBTQ+ clubs, bars, and saunas to enjoy—but the star attraction is the world's most-famous LGBTQ+ beach. All you have to do is look out for the rainbow flags amid the stretch of sandy white, and get yourself set up! Frolic in the sand with some beach volleyball, or treat yourself to an ice-cold cocktail from one of the many beach bars. You can also be perfectly entertained doing nothing at all: stretch out and enjoy the sun, the sea, and the sights...

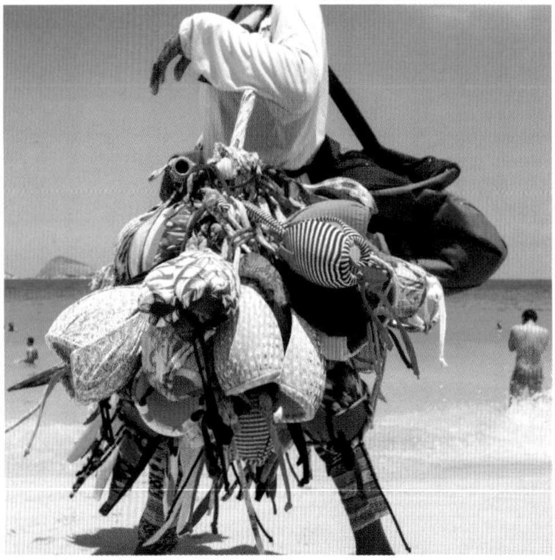

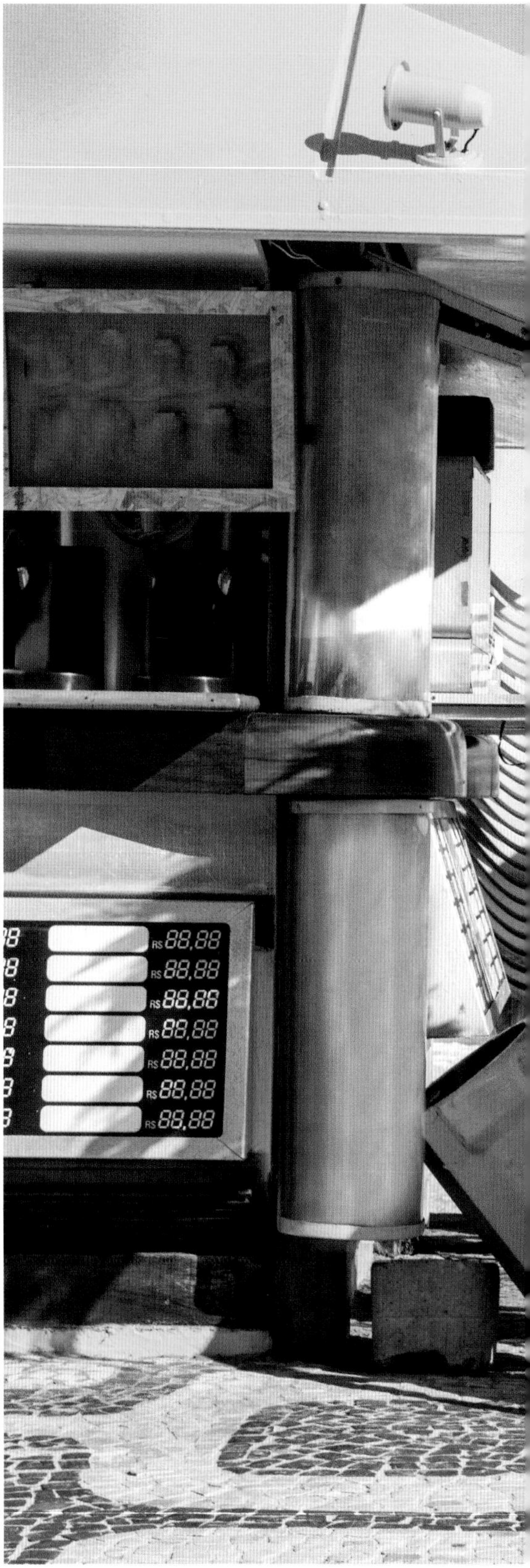

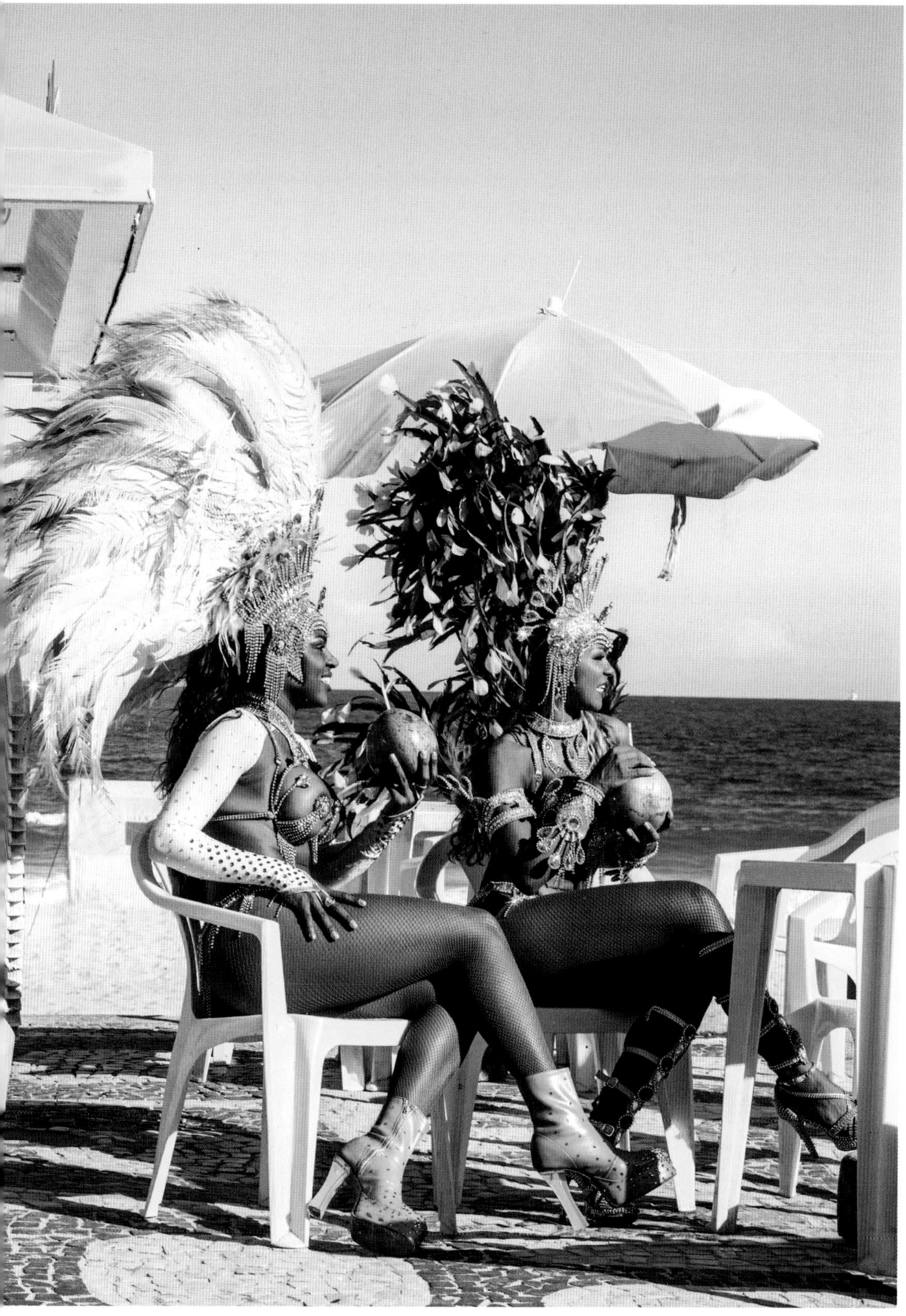

164 Putting the queero in Rio de Janeiro

▼ Farme de Amoedo, Rio de Janeiro, Brazil

When to go: All year
Best for: Stylish eats and drinks

Also known just as "Farme," this is one of Rio de Janeiro's most-famed LGBTQ+ streets and the perfect place to cool down once you've finished bronzing your bod at Ipanema beach. Arrive at dusk to delight in cocktails and hip eateries. There are also plenty of LGBTQ-friendly accommodation options, so you'll be close to everything you need in the fashionable beachside zone.

165 Honor a rights hero

▶ Marielle Franco Mural, São Paulo, Brazil

When to go: All year
Best for: Paying respects

Marielle Franco was a lesbian activist and councilwoman who fought for equality in her home city, Rio de Janeiro. A Black woman from a favela slum, her political ambition was to eradicate corruption while advocating for Black, women's, and gay rights. She was shot and killed in 2018, and her killers have still not been identified. This mural in the district of Pinheiros pays tribute to her.

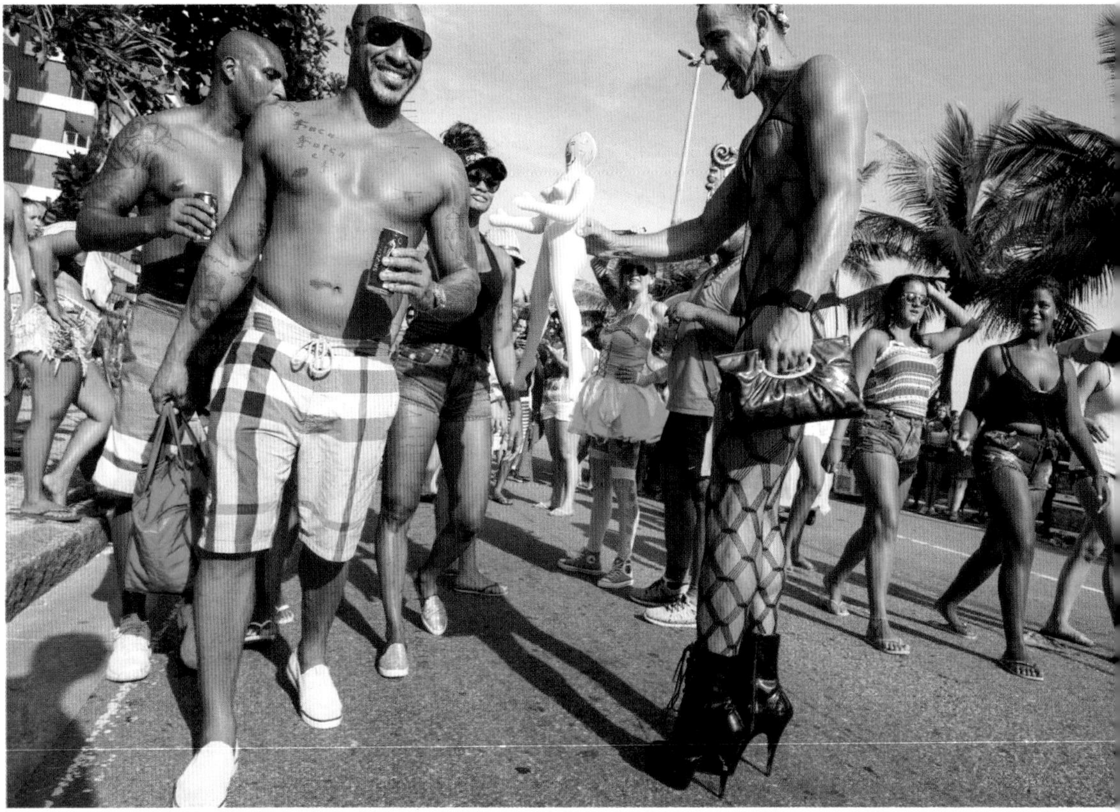

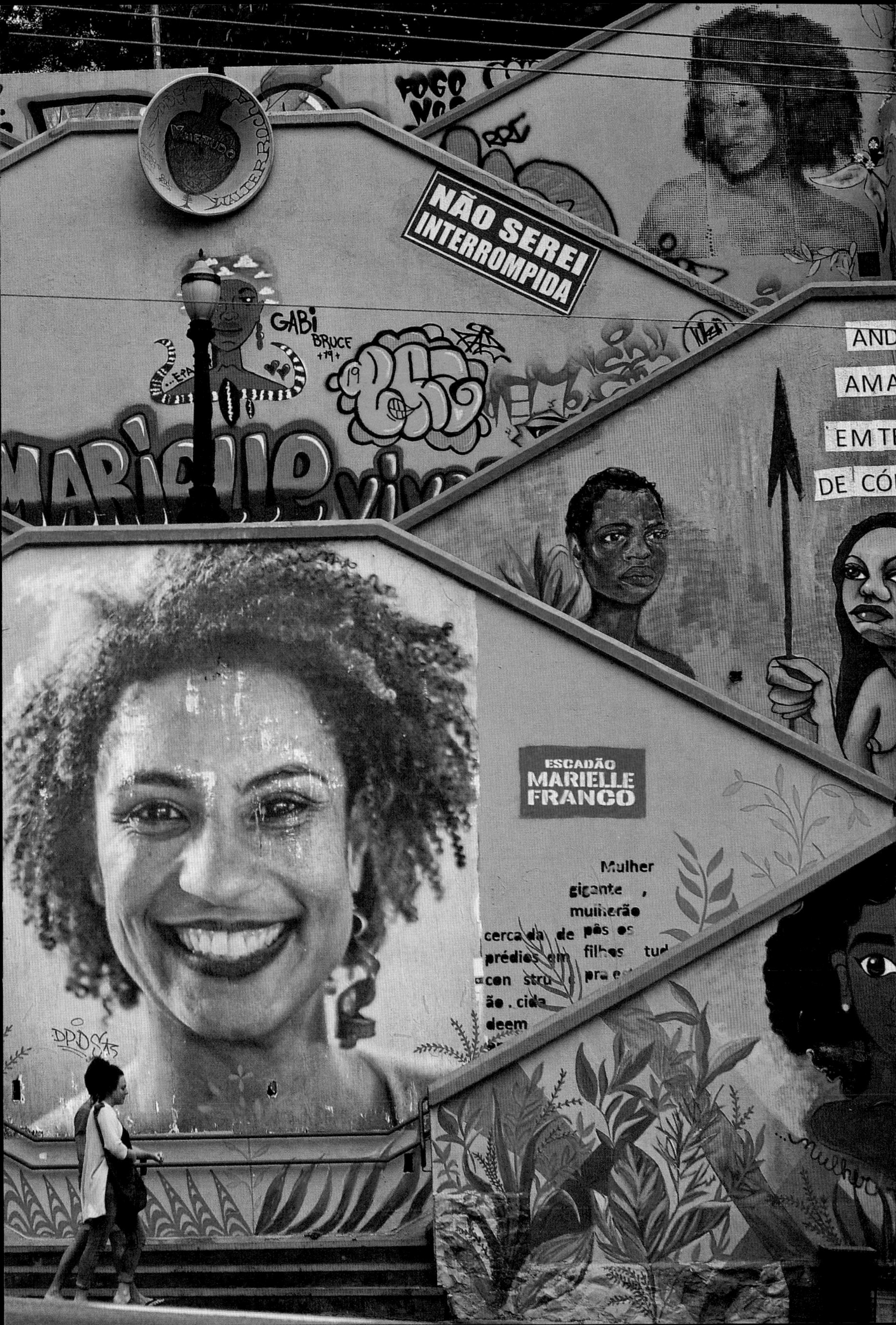
NÃO SEREI INTERROMPIDA
GABI
BRUCE
ESCADÃO MARIELLE FRANCO
Mulher
gigante ,
mulherão

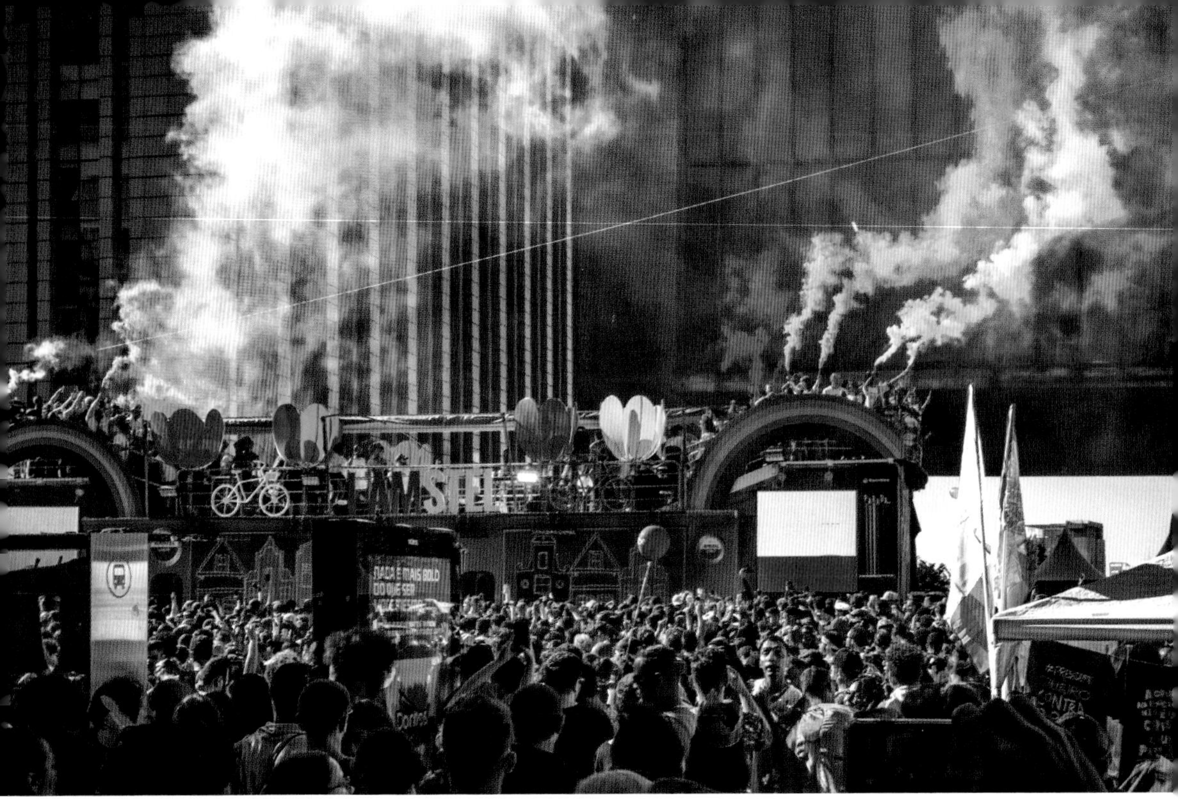

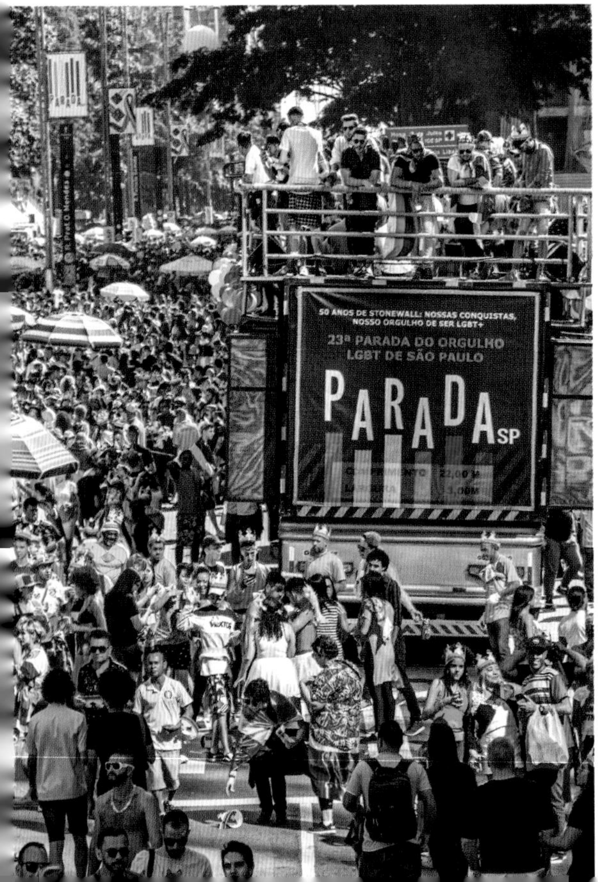

166 Millions march

São Paulo Pride, Brazil

When to go: June to July
Best for: Feeling the force of the community

São Paulo's Pride is a mega-festival in Brazil's most populous city, attracting up to five million attendees. One of the largest Pride parades in the world, the day-long event includes carnival floats, dance troupes, and pop-star performances. Homophobia, however, is rampant in Brazil, where violent acts of hatred toward the LGBTQ+ community continue to be shockingly present. That's why São Paulo's Pride is much more than a party—it is still very much an act of resistance and solidarity. Join in and march with purpose and pride, put on your most colorful clothes and be as fabulous as you can.

167 Stay where it's gay

▼ Rua Augusta, São Paulo, Brazil

When to go: All year
Best for: Heart of the action

If you're in São Paulo to soak up its revered gay nightlife, you need to head to Rua Augusta, just next to Frei Caneca. The street is full of plenty of LGBTQ-friendly bars, restaurants and hotels.

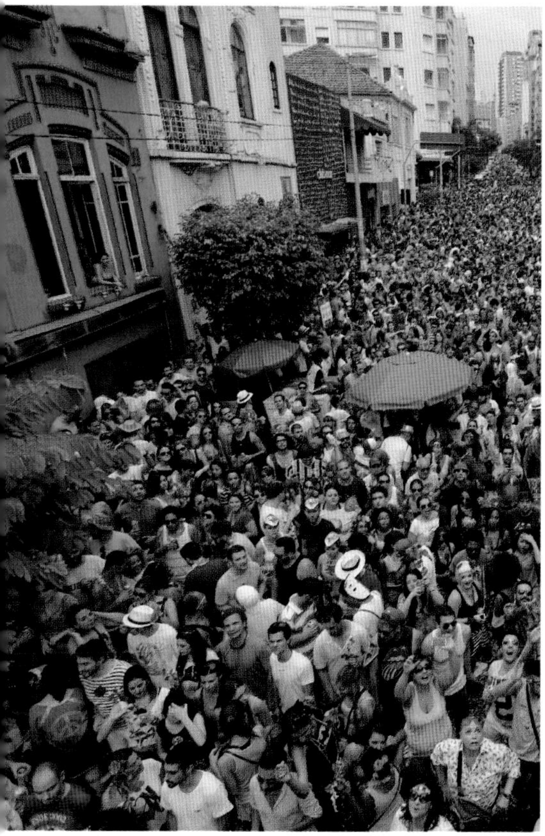

168 A street for your desires

Frei Caneca Street, São Paulo, Brazil

When to go: All year
Best for: Concentrated fun

The heart of São Paulo's queer neighbourhood, Frei Caneca (nicknamed 'Gay Caneca') could be the gayest street in South America. It has something for everyone – whether it's teens and young 20-somethings new to exploring LGBTQ+ nightlife, or seasoned travellers looking for a safe space to sit and chill. Make this street your first destination in São Paulo and have fun exploring every inch of it. Start with lunch at an open-air restaurant, then head to the delightfully queer mall, which offers a range of shops, eateries, a cinema and an LGBTQ+ library. By evening, you'll be in need of a drink: pub crawl down the street's abundant LGBTQ+ bars before ending the night on the dance floor.

169 Mix it up

MixBrasil Festival, São Paulo, Brazil

When to go: All year
Best for: Innovative queer films

MixBrasil is an annual cultural festival focused on sexuality in all forms of expression. Entries include film, dance, and performance, and works are judged for innovation and transgressive appeal.

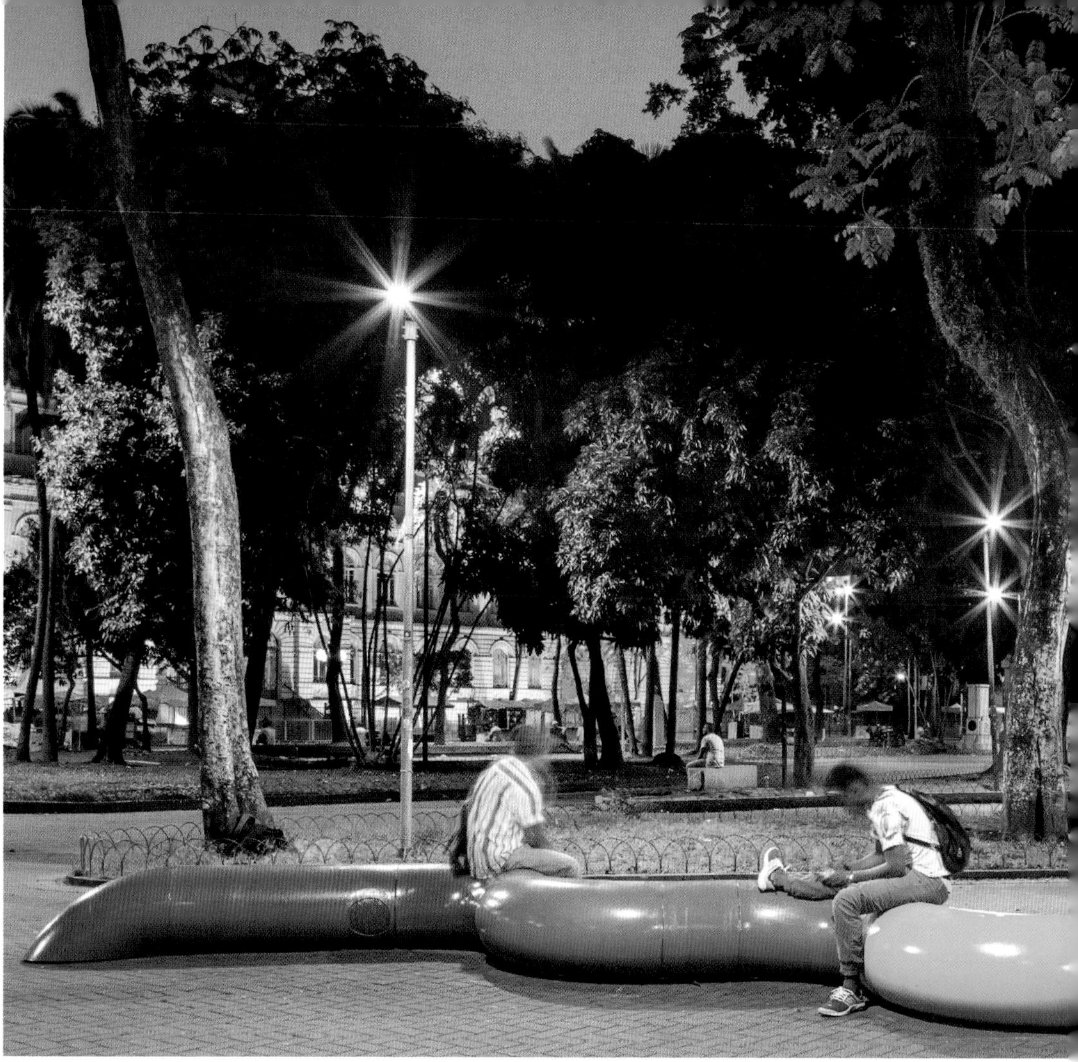

170 Sounds of solidarity

▲ My Heart Beats Like Yours Memorial, São Paulo, Brazil

When to go: All year
Best for: Never forgetting

Brazil is statistically the most dangerous country in the world for trans people and violence toward the LGBTQ+ community is far too common. This interactive sculpture commemorates the LGBTQ+ lives lost, while honoring the bravery of Brazil's activists. Designed by architectural firm Estúdio Guto Requena, it transmits audio recordings of the LGBTQ+ community including their heartbeats, whose rhythms inform the movement of a light display. It is located in Praça da República, where the city's first LGBTQ+ activist meeting took place in the 1970s.

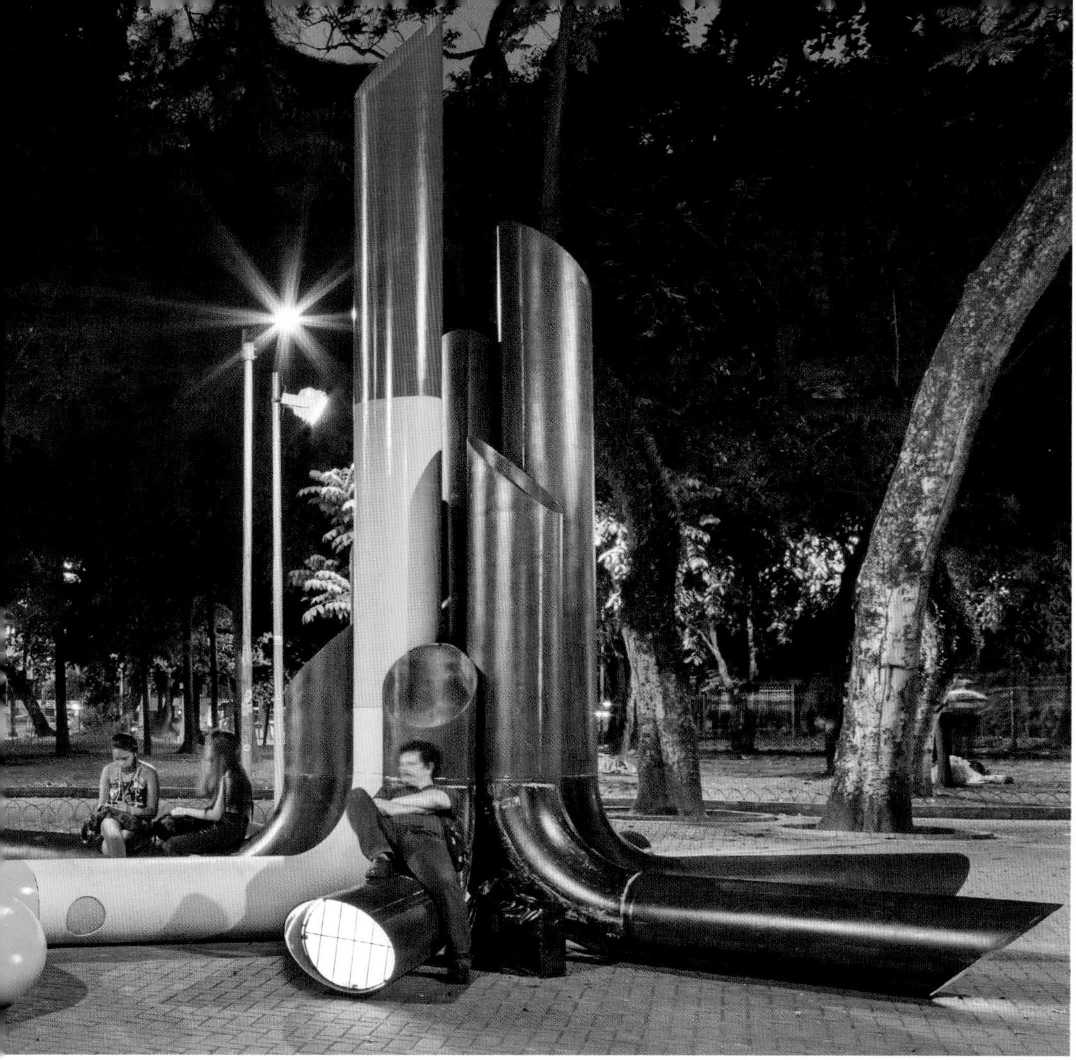

171 Feel the fame

Aloka Club, São Paulo, Brazil

When to go: All year
Best for: Clubbing with São Paulo's coolest

Situated on Frei Caneca Street, Aloka is a trendy nighttime establishment where it seems all of Brazil's queer icons have hung out before they reached celebrity status. If you're feeling famous, Aloka is where you'll want to be seen.

172 Strike a pose

Blue Space Drag Club, São Paulo, Brazil

When to go: All year
Best for: Cool clubbing

Nicknamed "mini Broadway," Blue Space hosts full-on theatrical drag-queen performances. The events bring together Brazil's best costume designers, makeup artists, and legendary queens, who join forces to put on truly out-there shows.

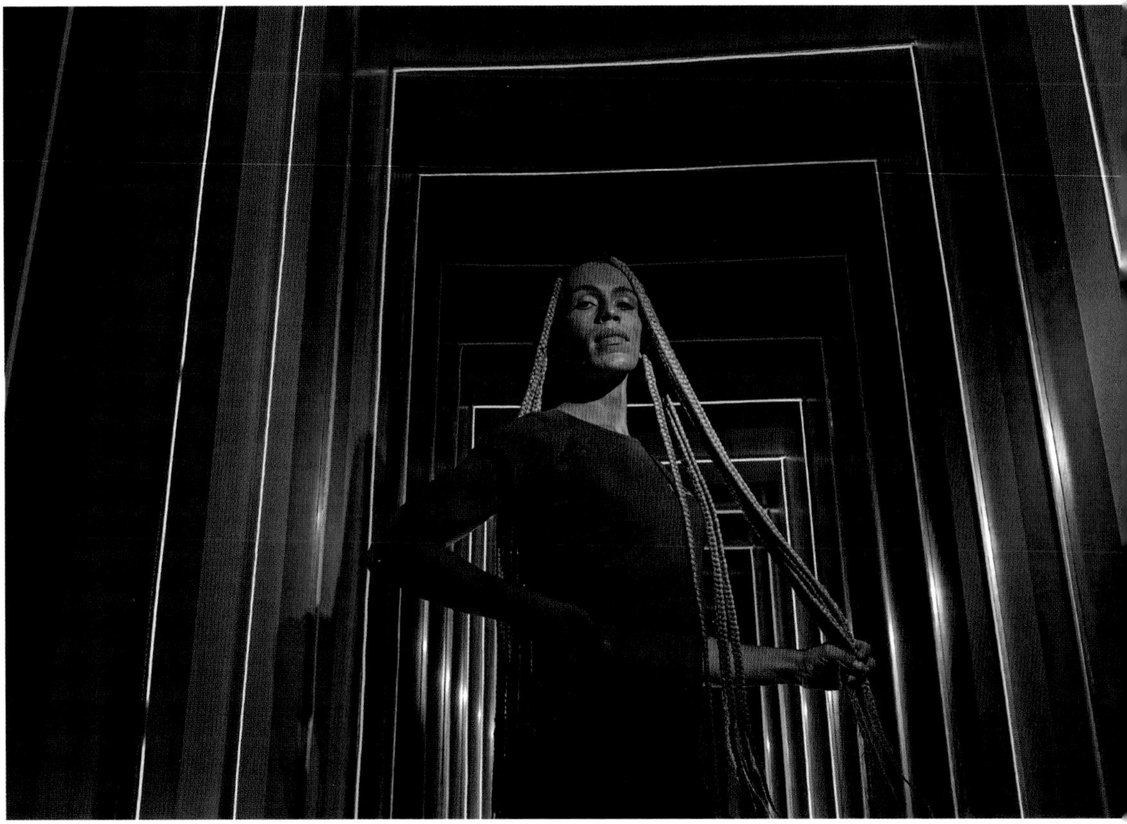

173 #nofilter

▲ Boleia Bar, São Paulo, Brazil

When to go: All year
Best for: Girls and 'gramming

You'll feel like you are walking into a real-life Instagram filter when you enter Boleia Bar's rainbow-lit hallway. Inside, enjoy mingling in this thriving hot spot of trans and cis lesbian ladies, and sip quirky gummy-bear cocktails. Flaunt, flirt, and dance to the hottest beats laid down by sexy queer DJs.

174 Dress to impress

▶ Isaac Silva Store, São Paulo, Brazil

When to go: All year
Best for: Threads with meaning

Trans designer Isaac Silva creates beautiful, tropical garments inspired by the vibrant Afro-culture of Brazil's northeast region, where Silva was born and raised. A form of fashion activism, his clothes are inspired by Brazil's Black and Indigenous cultures, and boldly embrace body diversity, with genderless clothes to fit all shapes and sizes. Silva's swanky flagship store in São Paulo is definitely worth a visit.

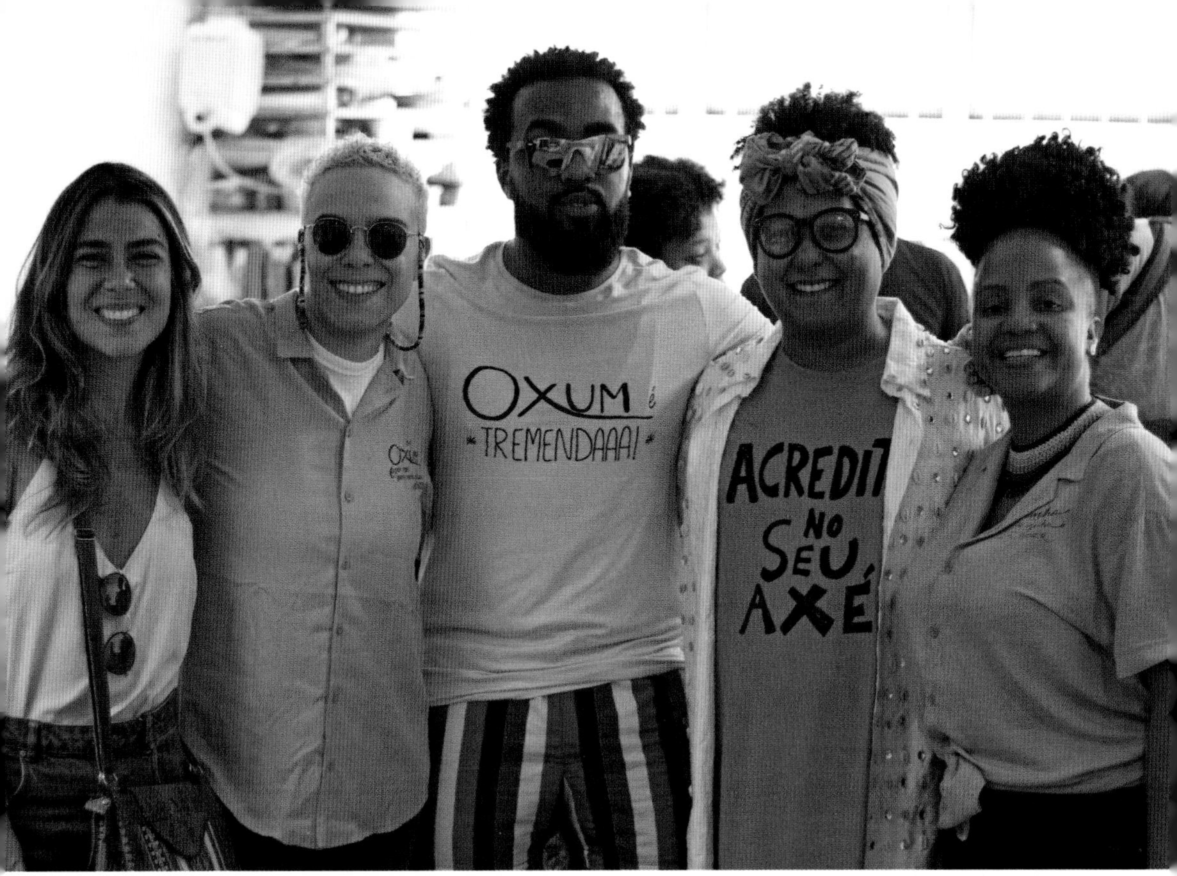
OXUM é
TREMENDAAA!
ACREDIT
NO
SEU
AXÉ

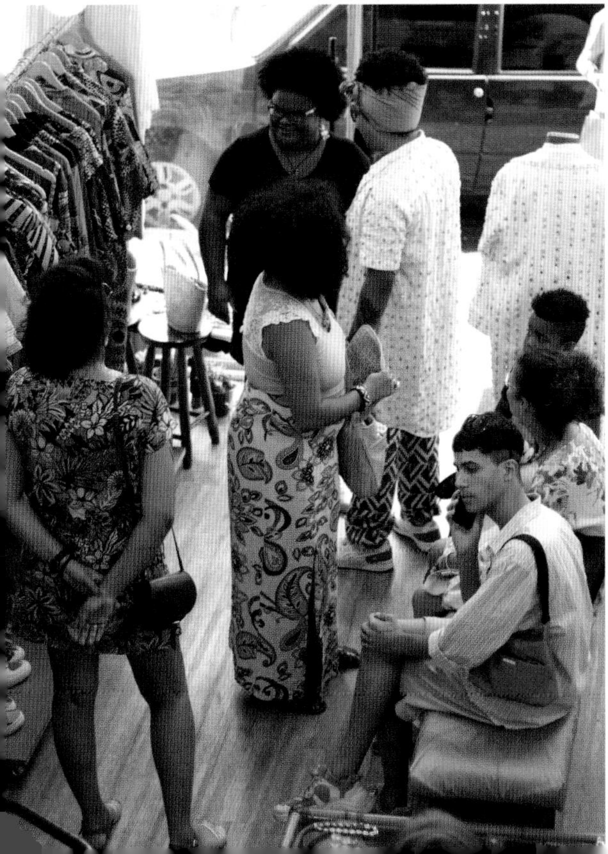

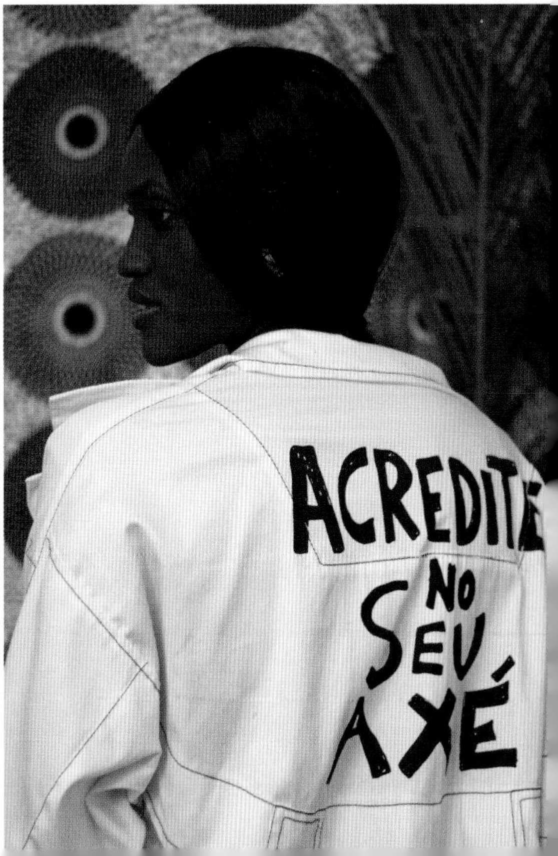
ACREDIT
NO
SEU
AXÉ

175 Glam time

Punta Pride, Punta del Este, Uruguay

When to go: March
Best for: Partying with celebs

Punta del Este is playfully known as Uruguay's Miami, full of glam apartments and beautiful beaches. It is a paradise for all to enjoy, especially during Punta Pride. Visitors can expect luxury LGBTQ+ boat and sunset parties, and club nights to keep you up 'til dawn—and then some. For gay men, the Undarius Hotel is a male-only hotel based at Chihuahua Beach—the only nudist beach in Uruguay.

176 Out in front

▼ Montevideo Pride, Montevideo, Uruguay

When to go: September
Best for: Feeling empowered

Uruguay has a reputation for being South America's most progressive country and is *way* ahead on the LGBTQ-equality front. With inclusive social policies and zero-tolerance for homophobic attitudes, Uruguay ranks as one of the best places for LGBTQ+ happiness in the world. The Pride march, locally known as the Diversity March, takes place each year on the last Friday of September and is held to fight for equality on all levels.

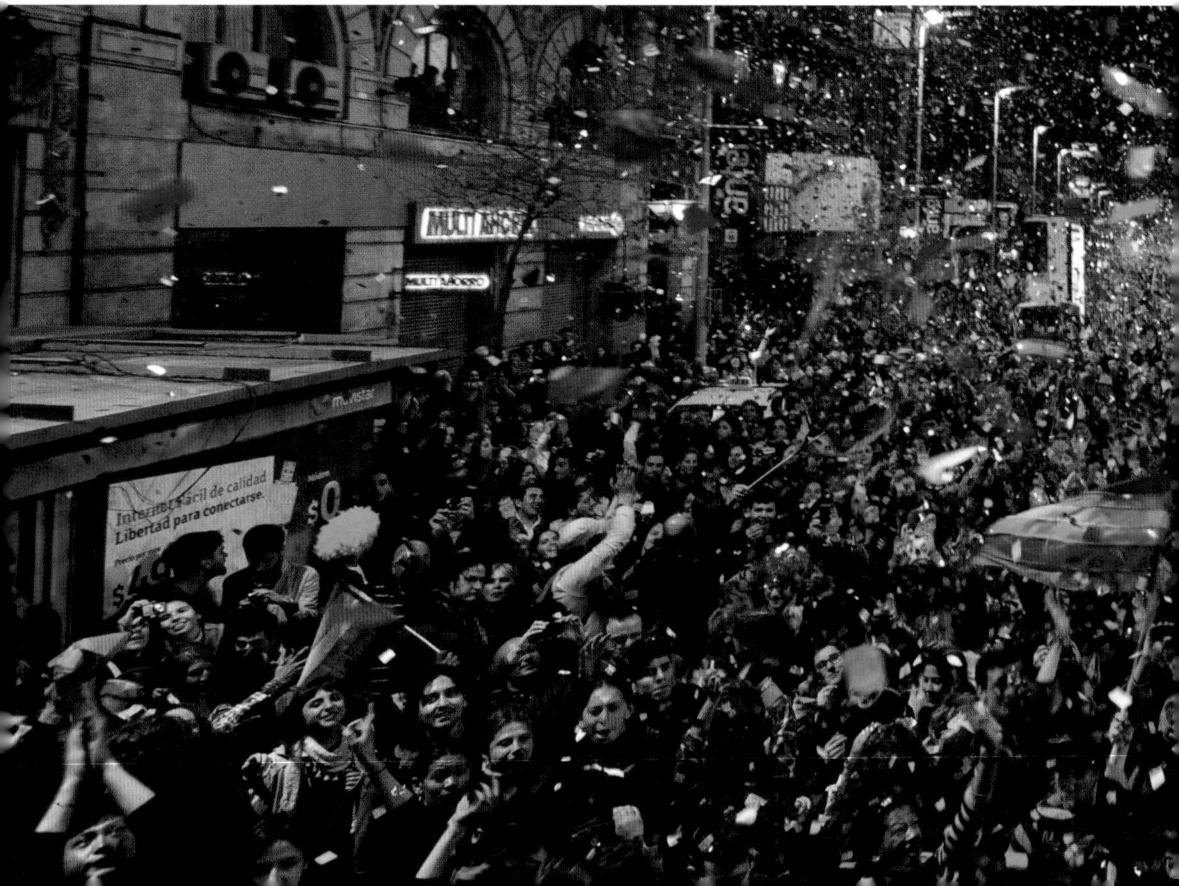

177 Break the chains

Chains Bar, Montevideo, Uruguay

When to go: All year
Best for: Bears and boys

Chains is an iconic establishment that attracts an older gay crowd on weekdays and a slightly younger one at weekends. If you're a lover of boys and bears, this Montevideo hangout is for you.

178 Have the time of your life

I Tiempo, Montevideo, Urugay

When to go: All year
Best for: Montevideo at its campest

This Uruguayan establishment declares itself *the* gay club of Montevideo, so it's a must-go for any LGBTQ+ visitor. Come for karaoke nights, pop anthems, and Friday drag shows to live the ultimate Uruguayan queer experience. Open Thursday to Sunday, it's the perfect spot for an unforgettable night out full of revelry. Make friends, meet lovers, and have fun.

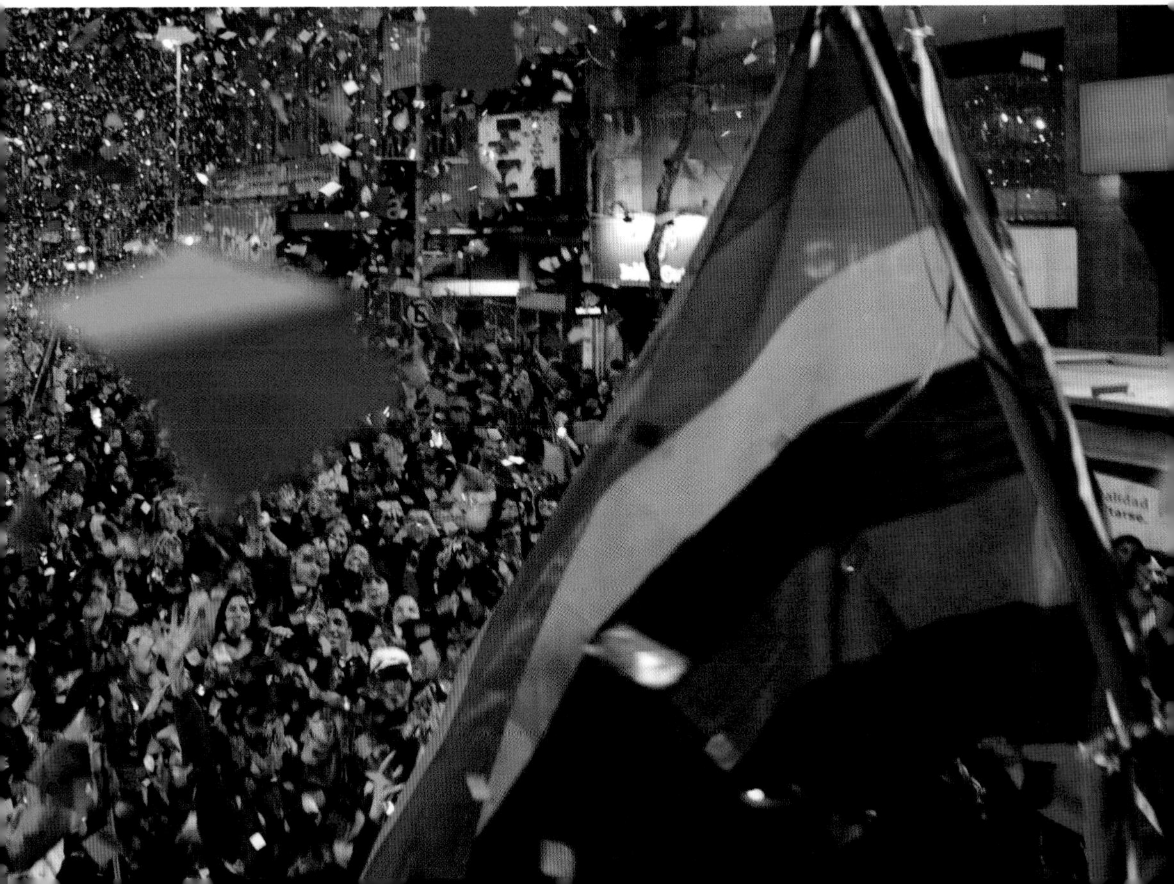

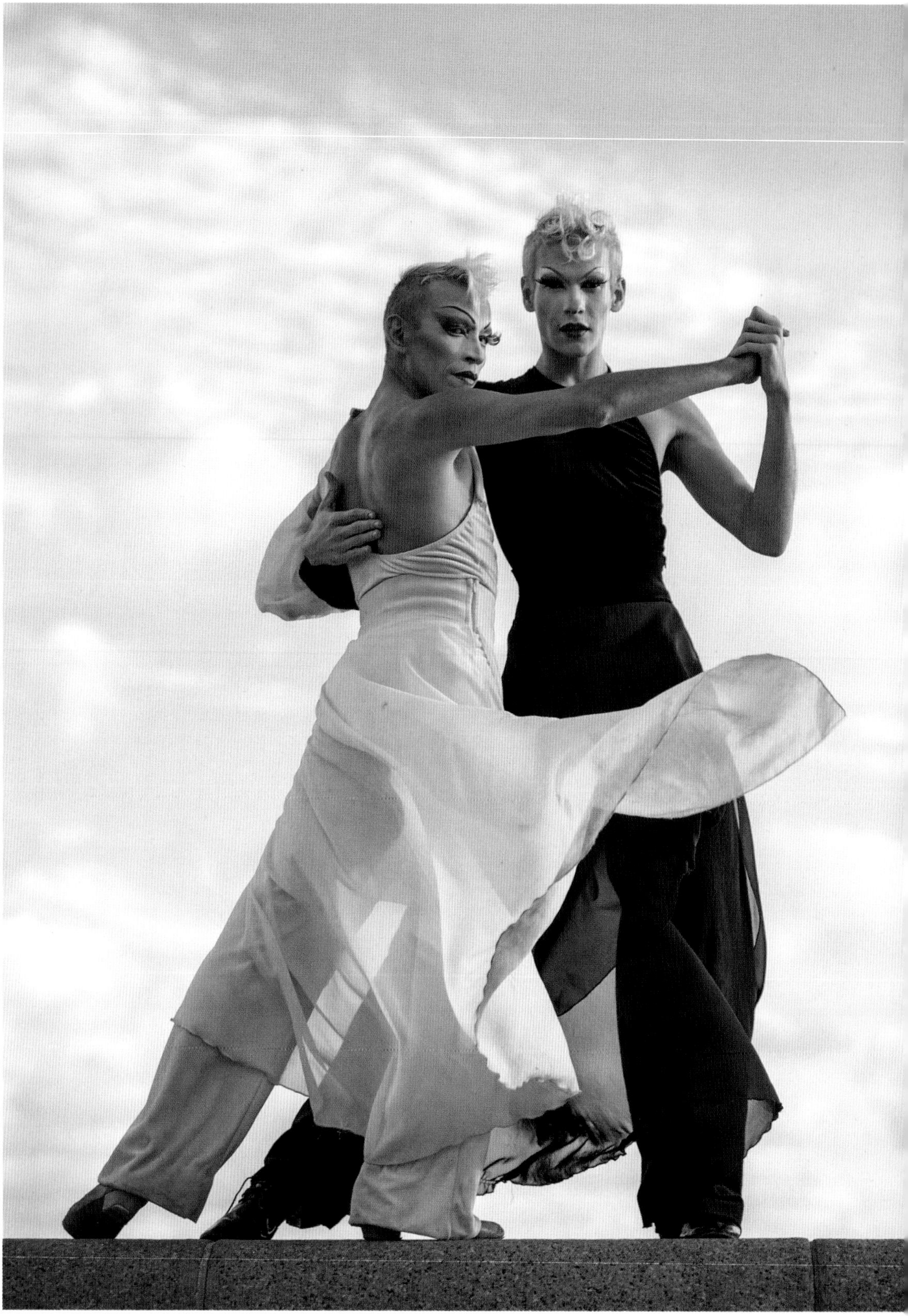

179 Get tango-ed

Queer Tango, Montevideo, Uruguay

When to go: All year
Best for: Foot-stomping passion

Tango originated in the late nineteenth century from the bustling trade ports along La Plata River, which separates Uruguay from Argentina. That means that this world-famous dance of passion is just as much Uruguayan as it is Argentinian. In recent years, Montevideo has been fighting hard to demonstrate its credentials as a tango capital and take some of the limelight back from its Argentinian neighbor. Being one of the most open-minded countries in Latin America, Uruguay's capital offers queer and inclusive opportunities to dance a tango that's free from the hetero norm. Check out the Tango Queer Uruguay collective, which runs classes throughout the year. They also host an annual Queer Tango festival around October and November, which includes performances and workshops—a perfect place for you to learn the steps and release your emotion on the dance floor.

180 Proudly served pasta

La Fonda Restaurant, Montevideo, Uruguay

When to go: All year
Best for: Lovingly made dishes

Look out for the rainbow flag proudly flying outside this revered Montevideo restaurant. La Fonda is LGBTQ-friendly *and* one of the best restaurants in town, especially if you're a lover of pasta.

181 A space for us

▶ Plaza de la Diversidad Sexual, Montevideo, Uruguay

When to go: All year
Best for: Feeling the love

This very special plaza in Montevideo's Old Town is a collaborative community project. In the early 2000s, neighbors and activists worked alongside the government to transform an abandoned plaza into an LGBTQ space, which today is used for exhibitions, murals, performances, and community events. The plaza is defined by a slanted triangular deck, which references the pink triangles gay men were forced to wear under the Nazi regime.

182 Let's go girls

Realidad Paralela, Santiago, Chile

When to go: All year
Best for: Dancing with the girls

Famous lesbian party Realidad Paralela is a weekly club night that rotates across different Santiago clubs. It features electro, pop, and reggaeton dance floors, with lesbian DJs on the decks.

183 Chillin' in Chile

Chueca Bar, Santiago, Chile

When to go: All year
Best for: Everything lesbian

Chueca Bar is a trendy, lesbian hot spot, packed with women who travel across the city to come to this special place. The bar also hosts one-off nights including intimate queer concerts and activist workshops.

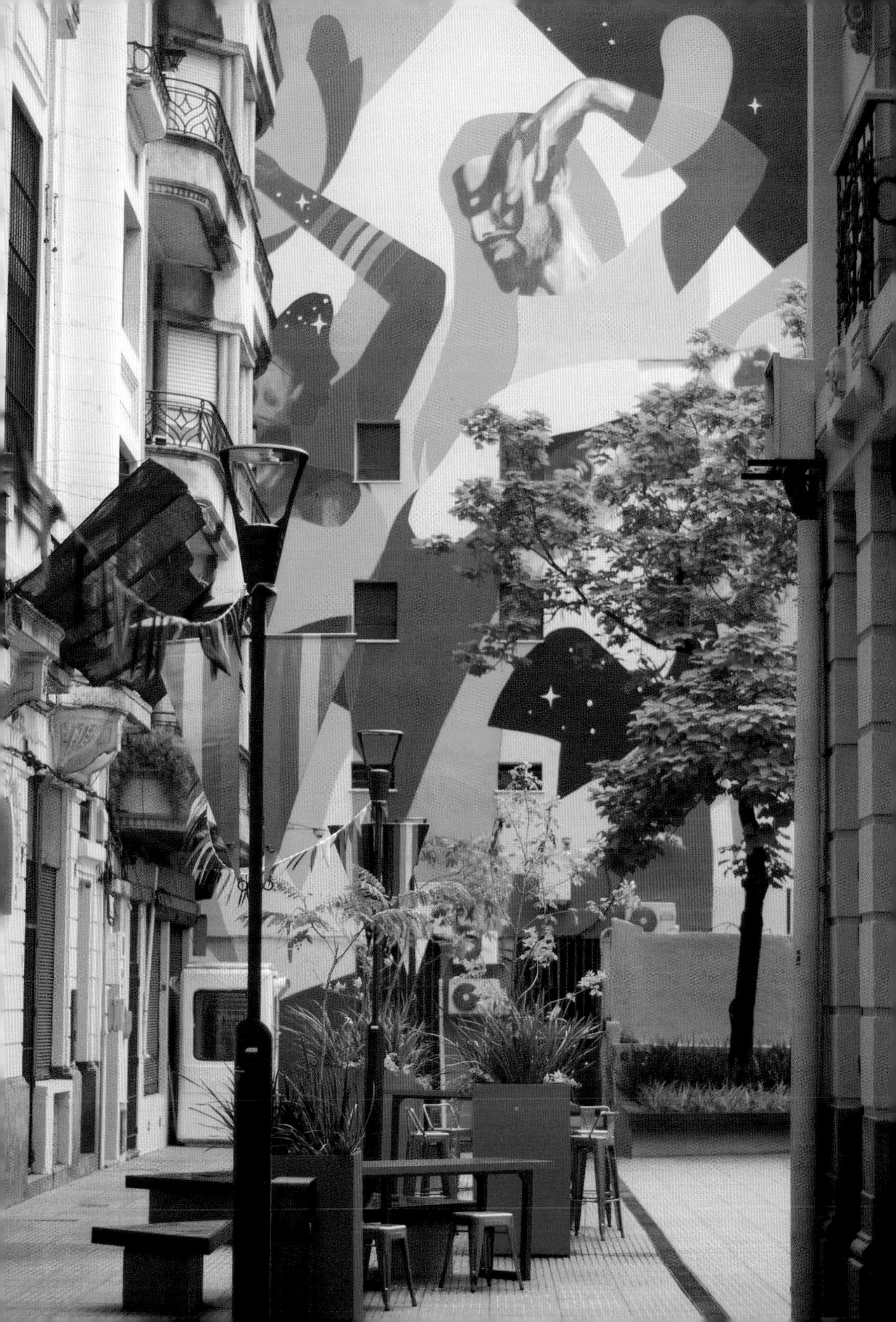

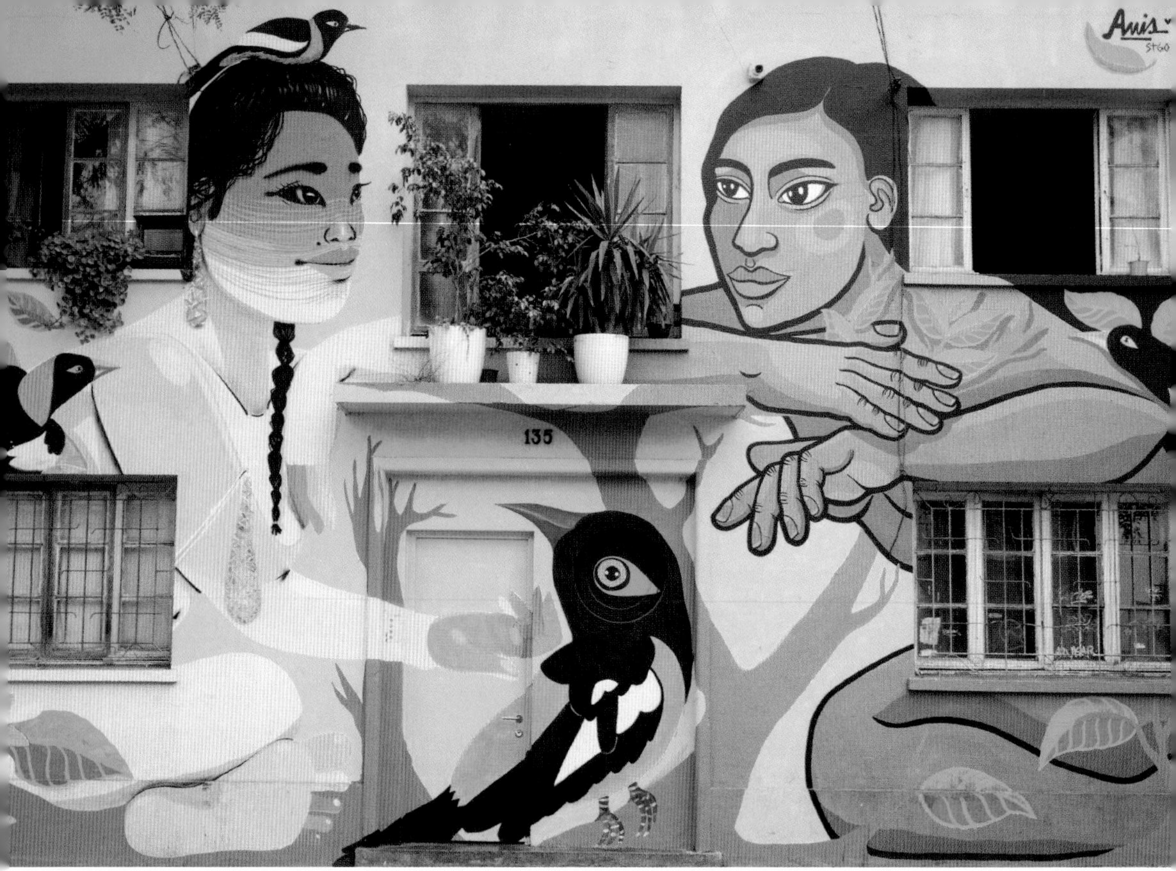

184 Paint the town rainbow

▲ Bellavista, Santiago, Chile

When to go: All year
Best for: Bar crawls

Bellavista is Santiago's leafy central district that's packed full of bars. If you're looking for a party, you have to come here. During the day, you can sip cocktails and enjoy the city's best restaurants, but at night the area really comes alive. Head to the streets of Bombero Nuñez and Antonia López de Bello to find LGBTQ+ bars and discos blasting music and packed full of gay, lesbian, and queer people! From pop-bangers to K-pop specials or reggaeton beats, you'll definitely find a dance floor to your liking.

185 A cult classic

Blondie, Santiago, Chile

When to go: All year
Best for: Unexpected nights out

Traveling with a large group and can't decide where to go? Blondie. On a date? Blondie. Want to take your mom out for a dance? Blondie. An epic, underground palace, the club has four dance floors and caters to a mixed and LGBTQ+ crowd. Dance with the hipsters, punks, goths, grandmas, teens, and everyone in between. For fans of Depeche Mode, the Spice Girls, and fetish nights.

186 Pride, protest and party

▼ ▶ Santiago Pride, Santiago, Chile

When to go: All year
Best for: Finding your community

Unfortunately, Santiago's Pride is not alone in being pink-washed by supermarket and telecom floats, but join the back of the parade if you're looking for the authentic queer folk. Here you'll find the real Pride—LGBTQ+ people wave flags of Chile's icons and activists, marching to demand justice and equality. At the end of the march, Bellavista's clubs host massive parties, so be sure to make plans for the nighttime.

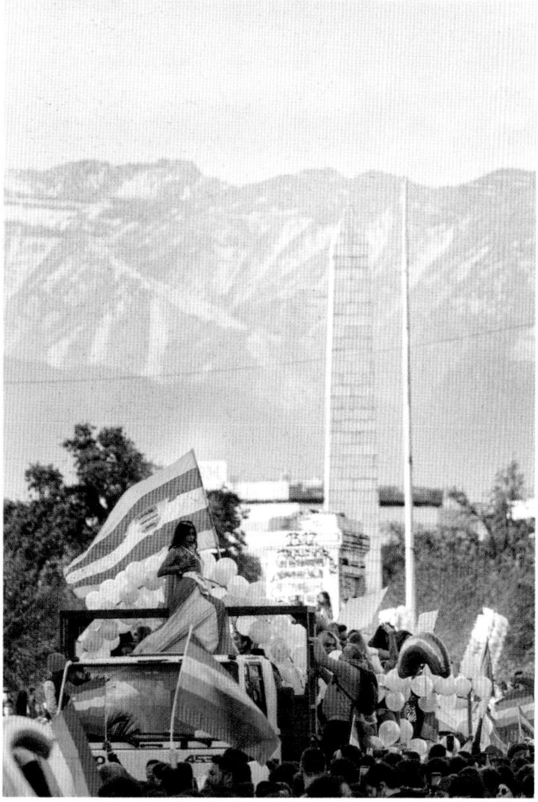

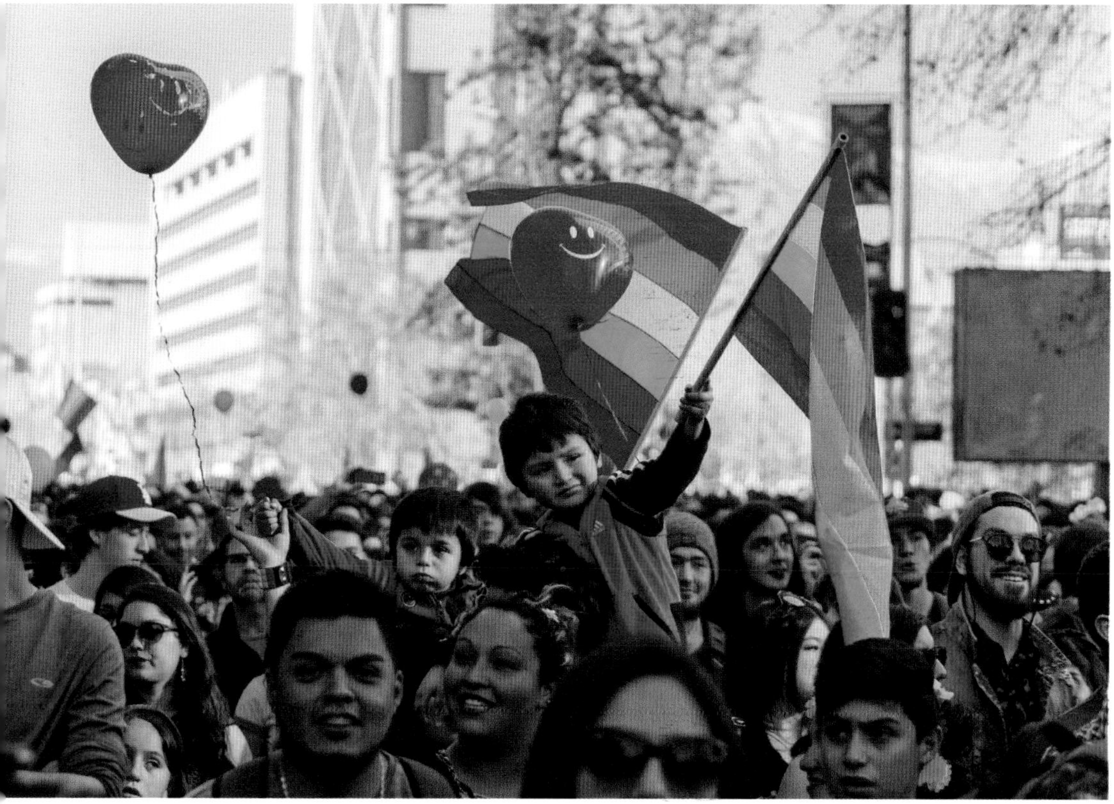

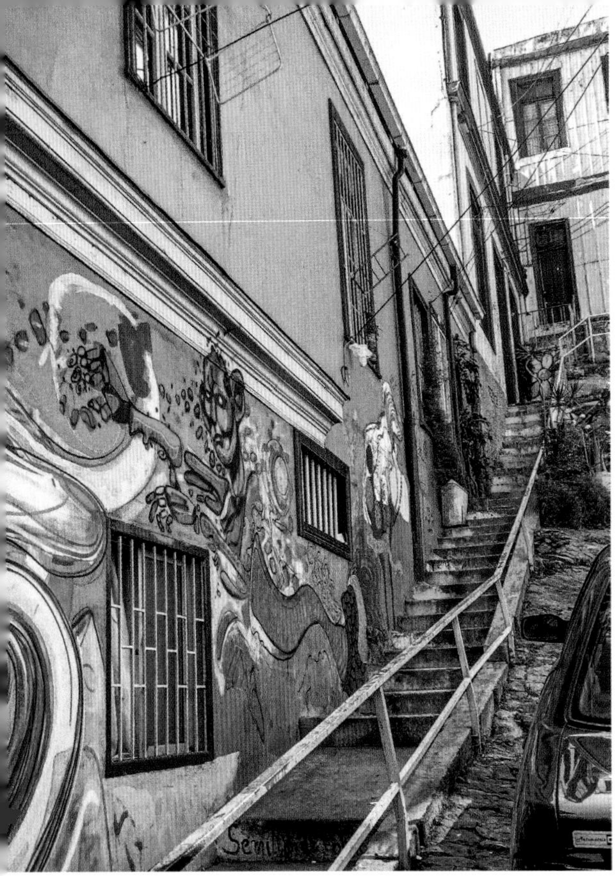

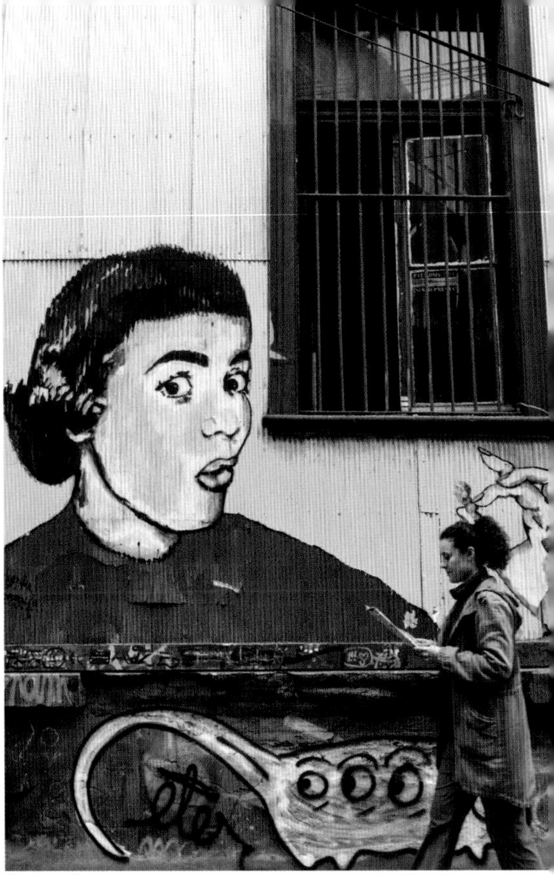

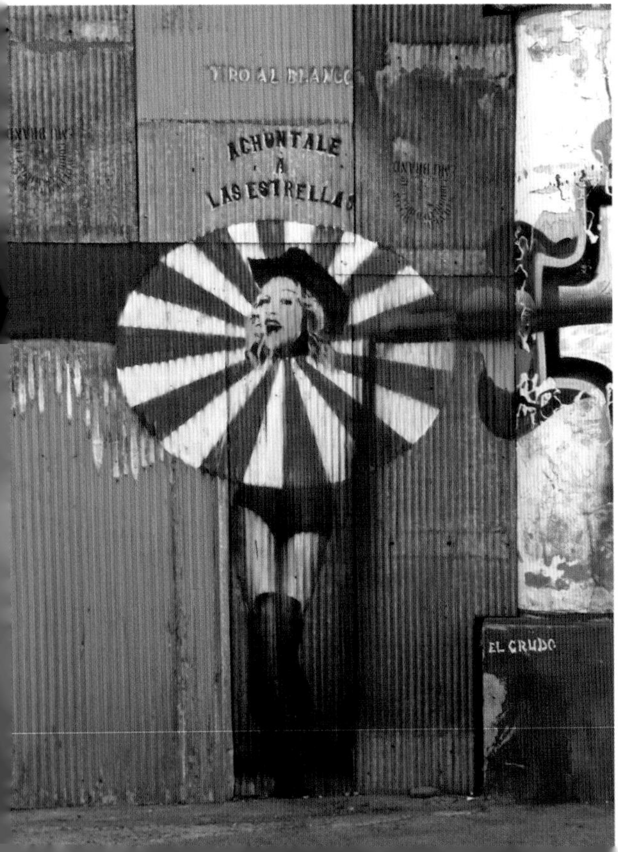
TIRO AL BLANCO
ACHUNTALE
A
LAS ESTRELLAS
EL CRUDO

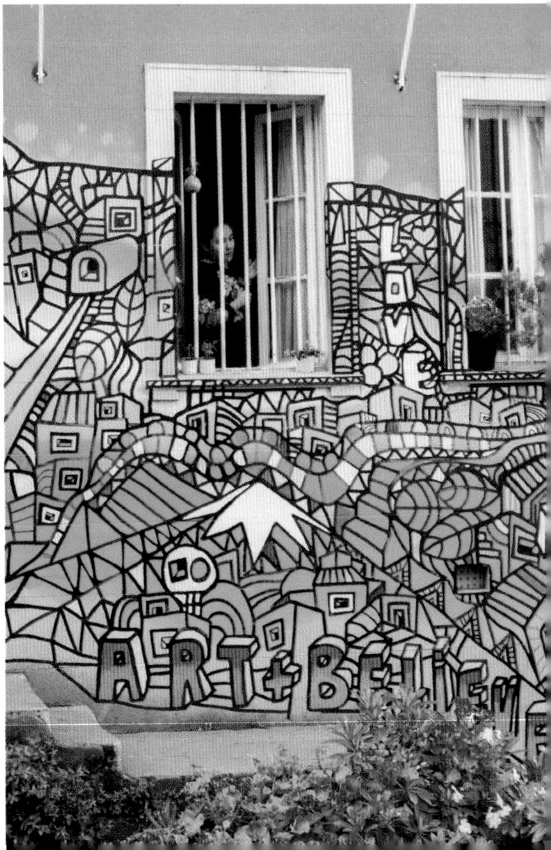

187 Putting the kitsch in kitchen

Sarita Colonia, Santiago, Chile

When to go: All year
Best for: Kinky ceviche

Santiago's tastiest Peruvian restaurant, Sarita Colonia is a proudly queer establishment. The trans kitchen celebrates the kitsch and advocates diversity while serving the city's best pisco sour cocktails and ceviche.

188 Party by the port

Pagano, Valparaíso, Chile

When to go: All year
Best for: Nonstop dancing

Pagano is a legendary LGBTQ+ bar in Chile's wildest city: Valparaíso. Dance like no one is watching and let loose. There's no pretentiousness or formalities here; just do your thing on the dance floor.

189 Walls of protest

◀ Valparaíso, Chile

When to go: All year
Best for: Street art

Valparaíso, locally known as Valpo, is a city of vibrant, artistic energy. Here, the streets are full of colorful murals and some of the world's greatest street artists have made their mark on the scene. Valparaiso's graffiti tradition started as a creative form of protest against the Pinochet dictatorship in the 1970s, and today the artistic soul of the time remains. Hop on a century-old funicular tram up to the colorful hillside barrios, or find your way through twisting, rainbow-painted staircases.

190 Be captivated by historical, lesbian love

Gabriela Mistral Museum, Elqui Valley, Chile

When to go: All year
Best for: Heart-wrenching love letters

Gabriela Mistral (1889–1957) is a Nobel poet laureate from northern Chile known for writing poetry that celebrates women and childhood. It was only after her death that love letters between Mistral and her longtime partner, Doris Dana, confirmed her queerness and assured Mistral's place as a present-day lesbian icon. Her house in the somnambulant Elqui Valley is a beautiful place to learn more about her poetry. Sadly, many of Chile's conservative institutions refuse to acknowledge Mistral's lesbianism.

191 Turn Thursday into Thursgay

▼ Club 69 at Niceto, Buenos Aires, Argentina

When to go: All year
Best for: Wild dancing

Club 69 is a special event hosted every Thursday at Niceto Club. It is a variety show featuring a fantastic array of drag queens, break-dancers, and strippers, all performing to a background of house and electro beats. It is widely (and wildly) regarded as one of the best queer parties in Buenos Aires.

192 Get gay in Guemes

Barrio Guemes, Córdoba, Argentina

When to go: All year
Best for: Expressive expression

Argentinians love to dance *all* night and there's no better place to do so than Barrio Guemes. Córdoba is a young student city and you can feel that youthful energy here, especially in the bouncing nightlife.

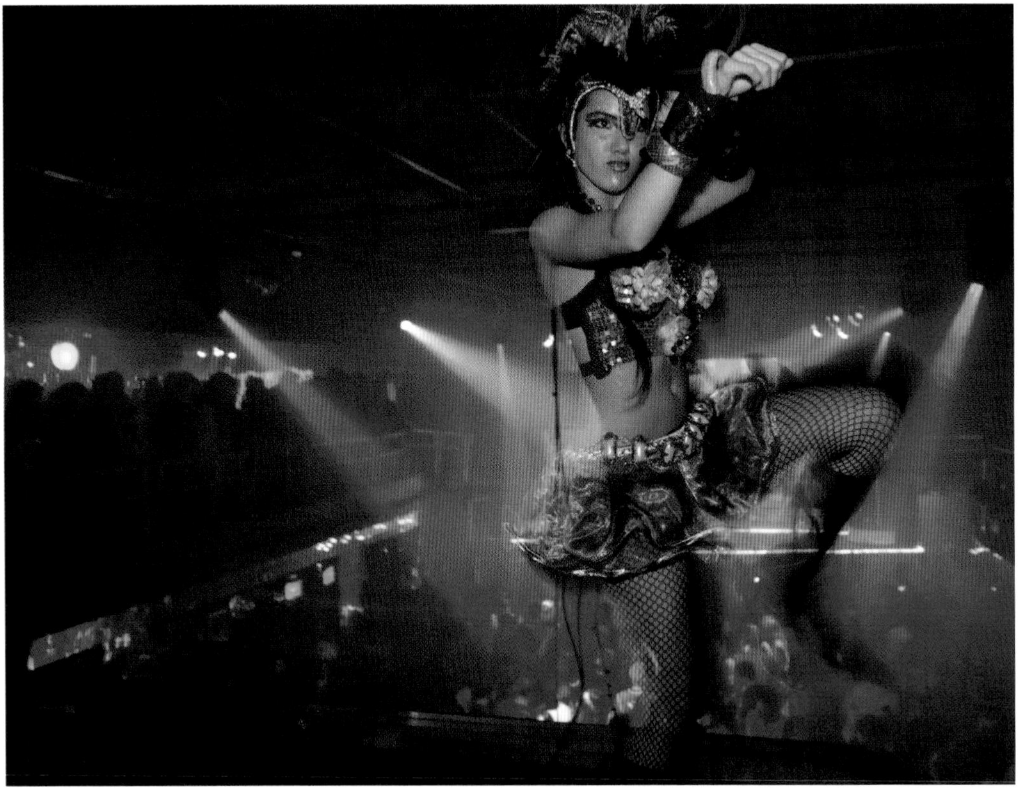

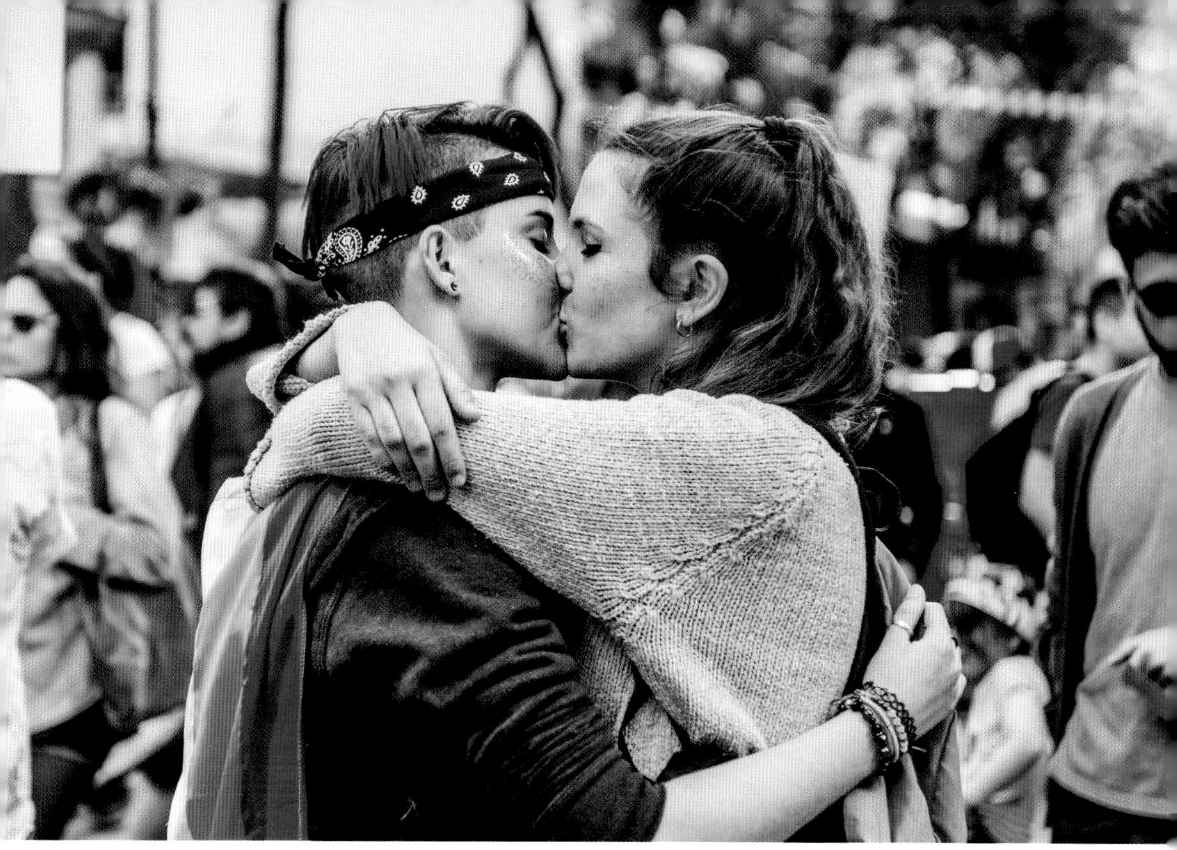

193 Pride and passion

▲ ▶ Buenos Aires Pride, Argentina

When to go: November
Best for: Pride with intensity

Argentinians are known for their passion, and the Buenos Aires Pride march is the LGBTQ+ community at its fiercest, where the city's queer community converges to demand justice and rights. Join your community as they march through rainbow sculptures, from the iconic Plaza de Mayo to the National Congress building. Don't forget to snap a selfie next to Buenos Aires' national monument the Obelisco, which supports the occasion by sporting rainbow-colored lights.

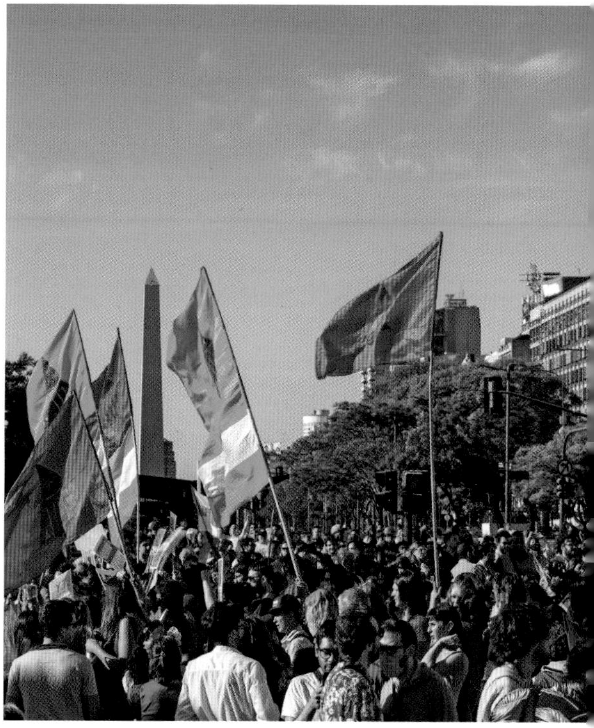

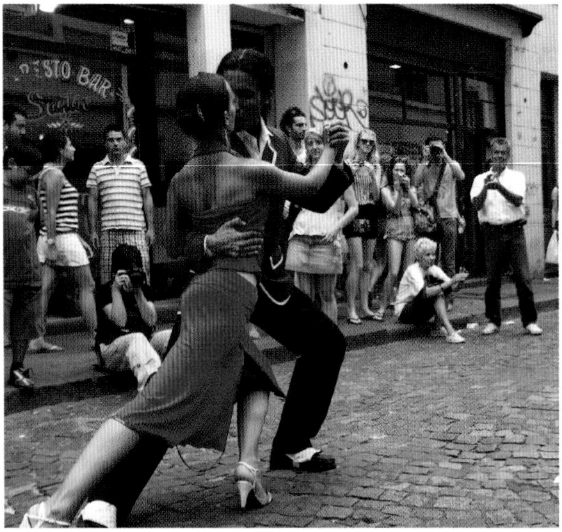

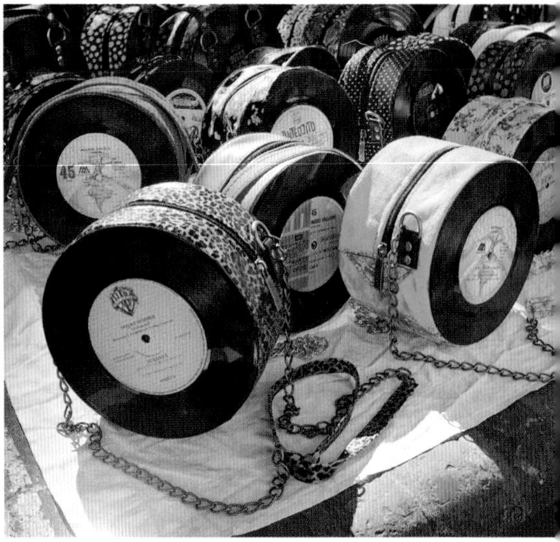

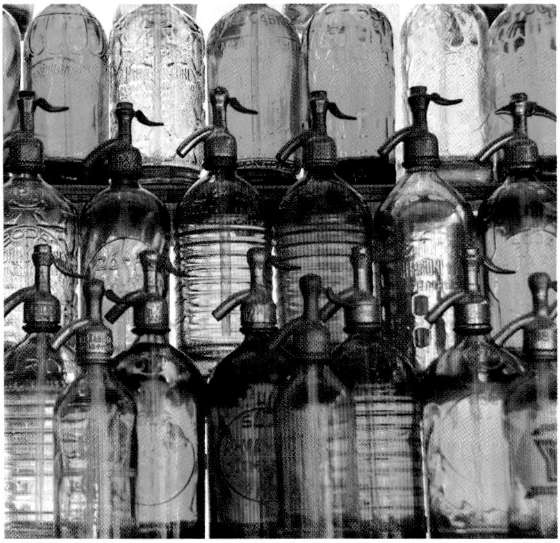

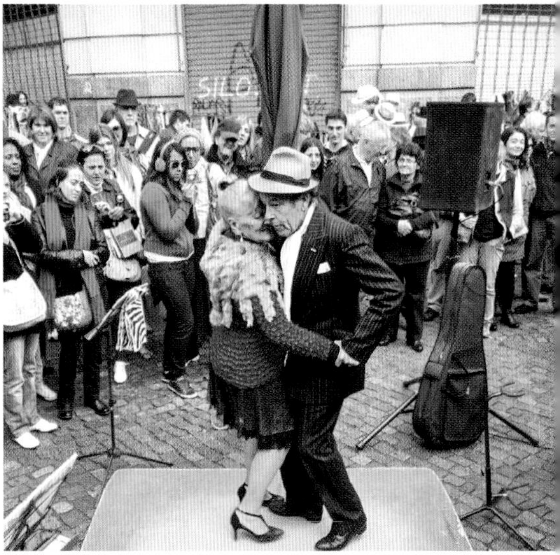

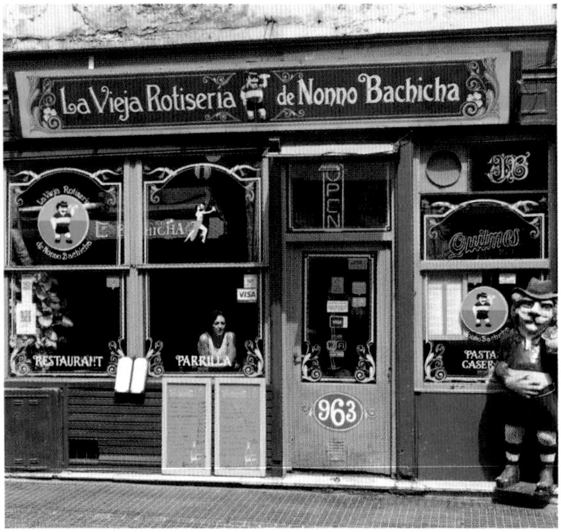
La Vieja Rotiseria de Nonno Bachicha
OPEN
Quilmes
VISA
RESTAURANT
PARRILLA
963

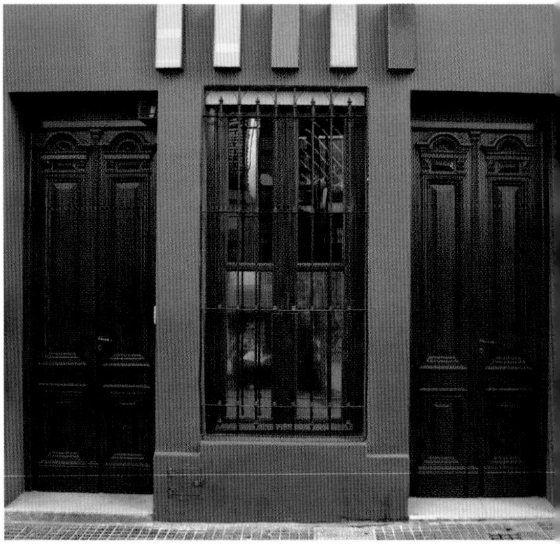

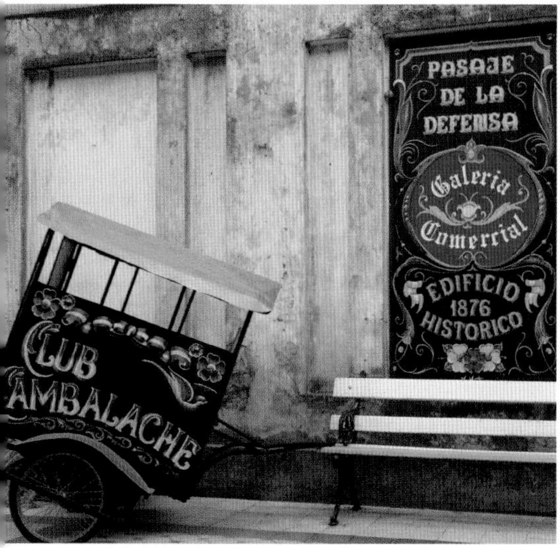

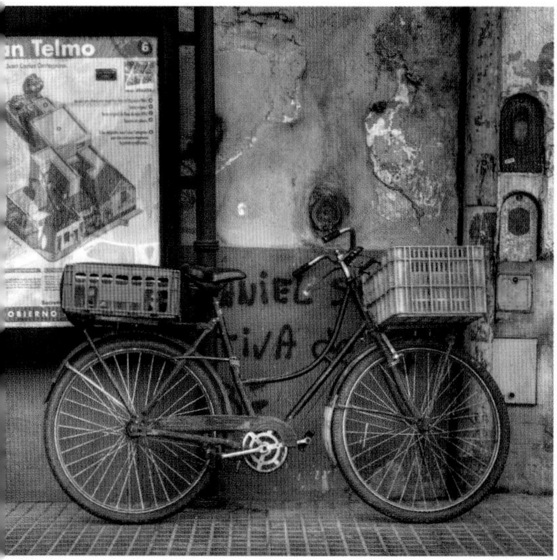

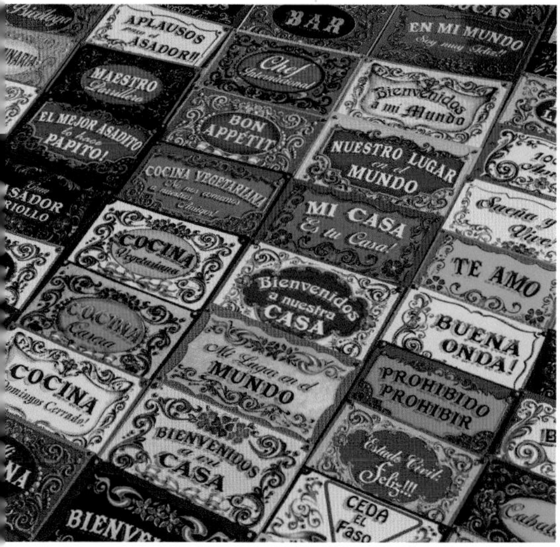

194 Channel your inner boho in San Telmo

San Telmo, Buenos Aires, Argentina

When to go: All year
Best for: Trinkets and vibes

One of the most popular districts or *barrios* in Buenos Aires is San Telmo. It is the oldest barrio in the city and its bohemian vibe brings a vibrant atmosphere to the area. Wander around the cobblestone streets admiring all the fantastic street art and grab a rare find at one of the many antique or craft stores, or at the weekly street market. Plus there's an array of delicious food available from the area's funky eateries. Conveniently located by the Sunday market is one of Buenos Aires' most beloved LGBTQ+ spots, Pride Café. Fuel yourself up before the market with *dulce de leche* waffles, or celebrate your purchases after with a delicious cocktail. For queer men, the local men-only guesthouse, Lugar Gay Bed & Breakfast, has a rooftop terrace and hot tub.

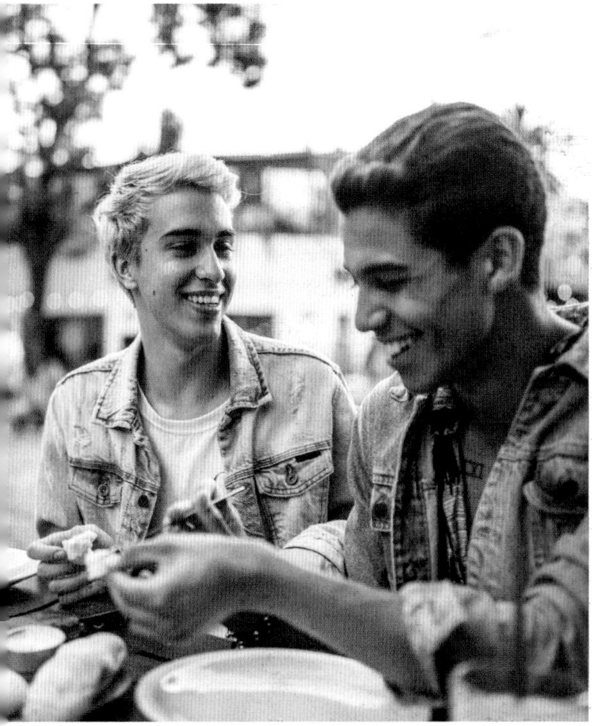

195 RuPaul on the big screen

◀ ▼ Palermo Soho, Buenos Aires, Argentina

When to go: All year
Best for: Cocktails with a side order of culture

Buenos Aires combines faded European majesty with South American pizazz. Palermo Soho is one of its more genteel, affluent, and trendy neighborhoods. Typically, some of that hipness comes from its popularity with the local LGBTQ+ community. There are a handful of venues and queer-friendly businesses here, such as the camp and glittery video bar Peutou, or the atmospheric Work. The former attracts a young crowd with screenings of the latest episode of *RuPaul's Drag Race*, while the latter draws weekend hedonists with its throbbing, electro beats.

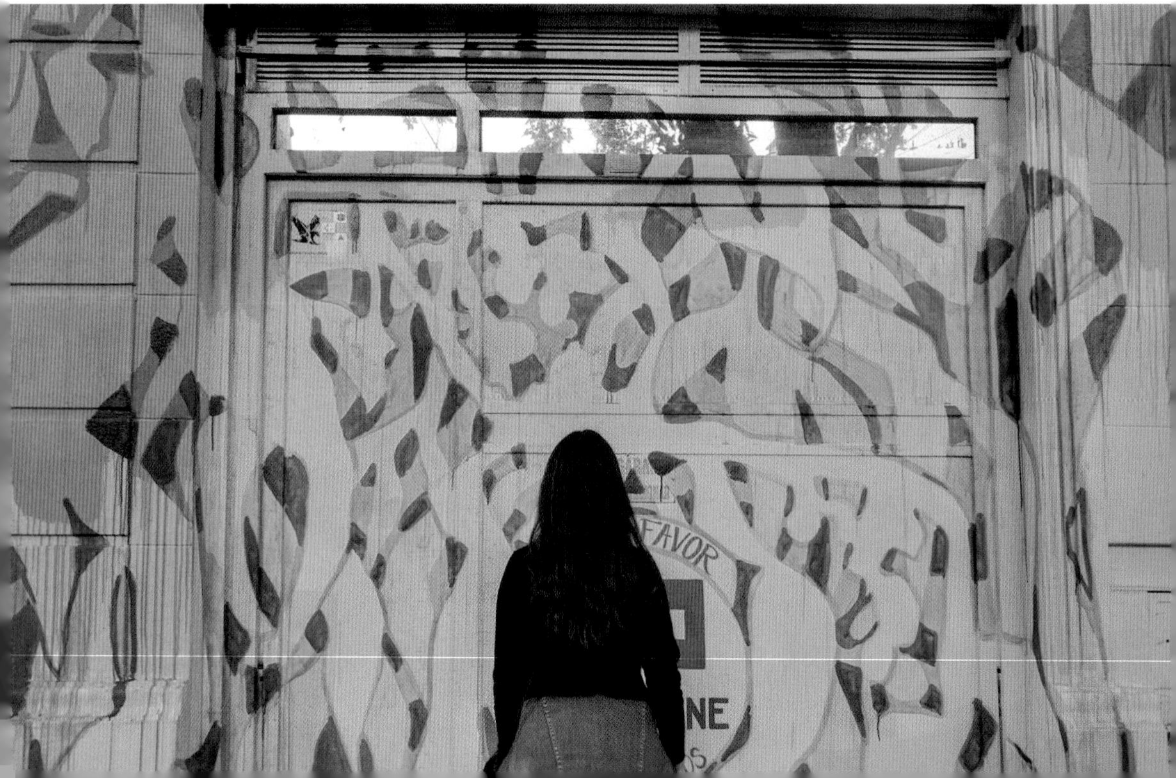

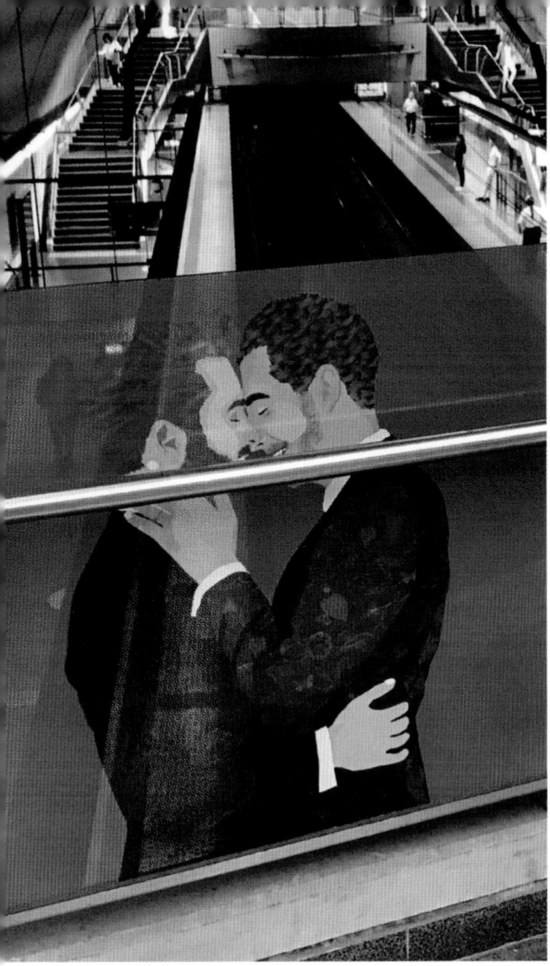

196 Traveling in the name of

◀ Santa Fe–Carlos Jáuregui station, Buenos Aires, Argentina

When to go: All year
Best for: Political selfie

Buenos Aires' centrally located Santa Fe–Carlos Jáuregui subway station was renamed in 2017 in honor of the LGBTQ+ activist Carlos Jáuregui. Born in 1957, Jáuregui co-founded the Comunidad Homosexual Argentina (Argentine Homosexual Community) and led the first Pride march through the streets of Buenos Aires in 1992. He died of AIDS-related complications in 1996. The subway has staircases decorated in rainbow colors, and there's artwork depicting Jáuregui and LGBTQ+ couples by queer artist Daniel Arzola.

197 Cakes and poems

Maricafé, Buenos Aires, Argentina

When to go: All year
Best for: Rainbow cake

Offering cakes, books, and poetry readings, Maricafé is something of an institution in Palermo Soho. Its signature rainbow cake might draw you in, but you can lose hours in here browsing the bookshelves full of queer history.

198 It takes two

Juernes Dance School, Buenos Aires, Argentina

When to go: Thursday evenings
Best for: Tango

The tango is one of South America's most beloved, and sensual, dances. It originated on the borders of Argentina and Uruguay in the late 1800s, but it's not just for straight couples. There are festivals dedicated to queer tango around the world, which jettison the set "male" and "female" roles. In Buenos Aires, there are LGBTQ-friendly tango lessons every Thursday night at Juernes dance school.

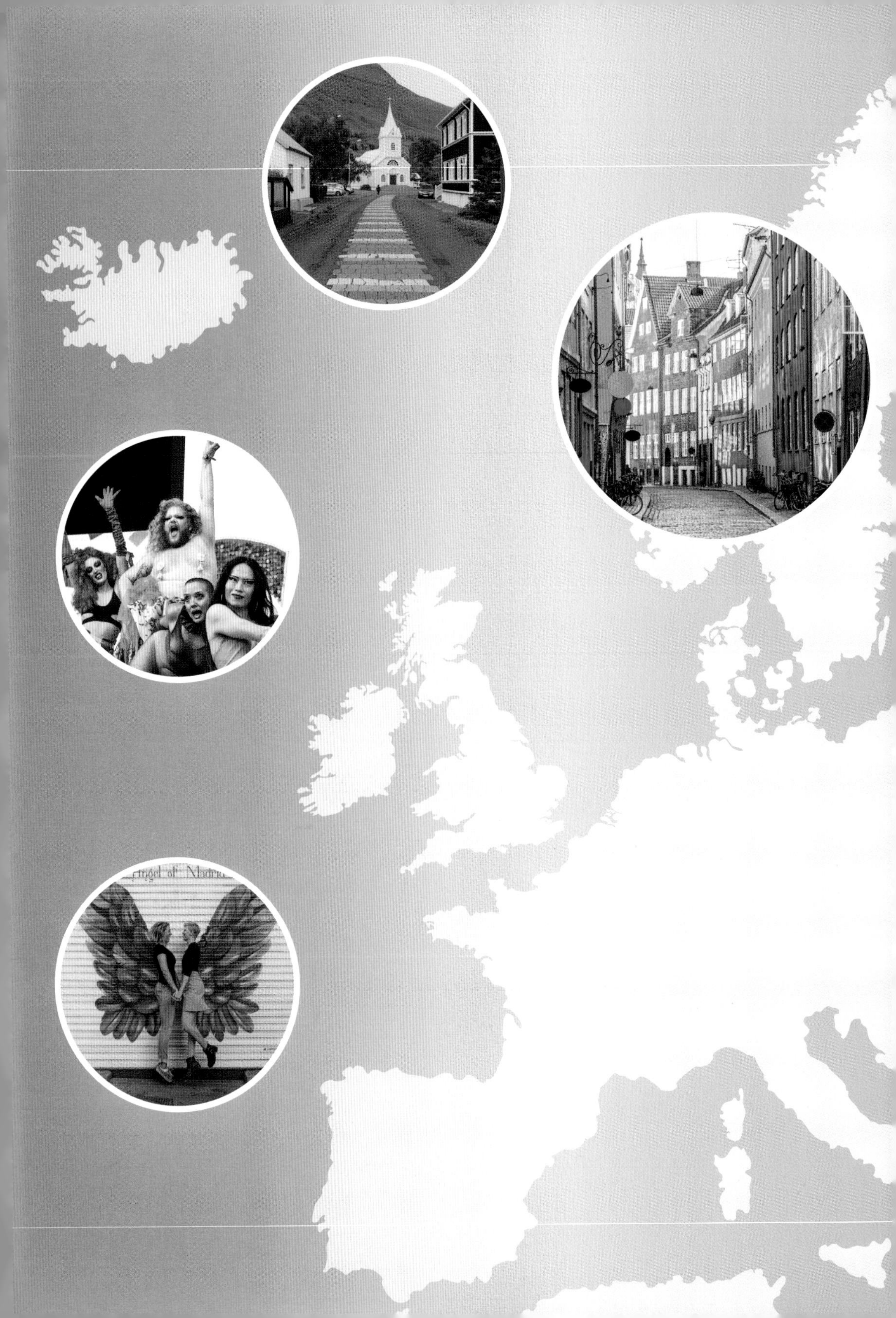

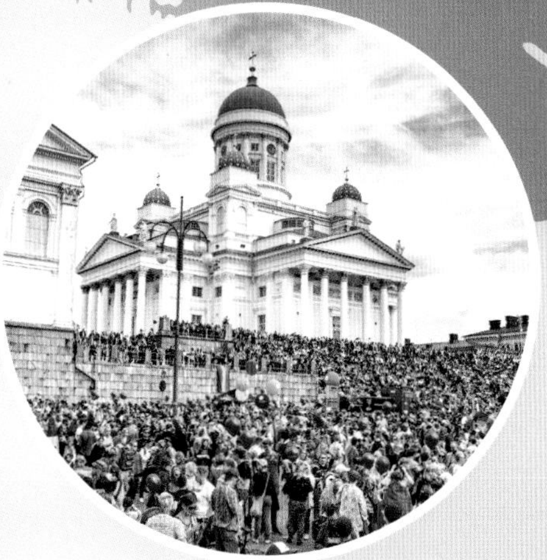

CHAPTER THREE

EUROPE

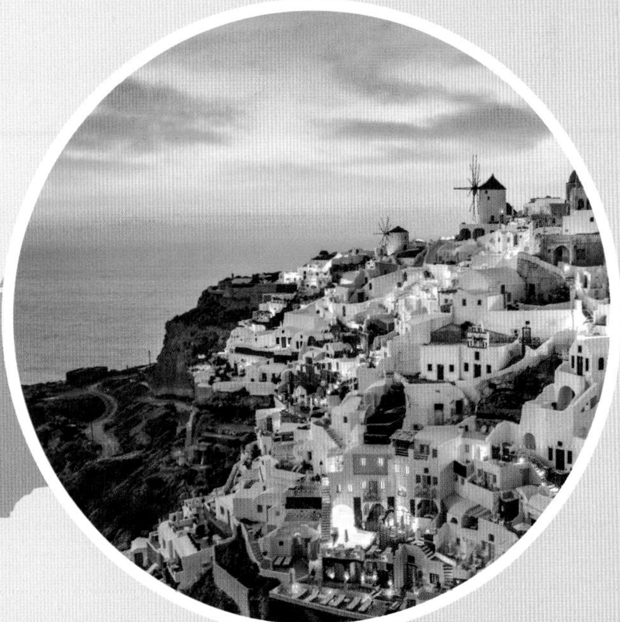

199 Modest and meaningful

Nuuk Pride, Greenland

When to go: June
Best for: Pride in a far-north place

Greenland (or Kalaallit Nunaat) is about the size of Mexico but has a population of 56,000 people, making it the least densely populated country in the world. While the laws and social climate are progressive (in a low-key way), there are not enough LGBTQ+ locals to create and maintain a lively LGBTQ+ scene. But in 2010, LGBTQ+ Inuit woman Nuka Bisgaard organized Nuuk's first Pride. The colorful, musical, yet modest parade drew over one thousand participants, making it one of the country's largest demonstrations ever.

200 Let's have a kiki

▼ Kíkí Queer Bar, Reykjavík, Iceland

When to go: All year
Best for: Connecting

The best place to connect with LGBTQ+ locals and visitors is at Kíkí Queer Bar, Iceland's only LGBTQ+ bar and club. A brightly painted rainbow covers the façade of Kíkí Queer Bar, so you can't miss it. The party gets most fun on the weekends around midnight. The dance floor quickly fills up, and it's a friendly and mixed crowd. If you're looking for a more low-key place, visit the LGBTQ-friendly Bravó, located just below Kíkí Queer Bar.

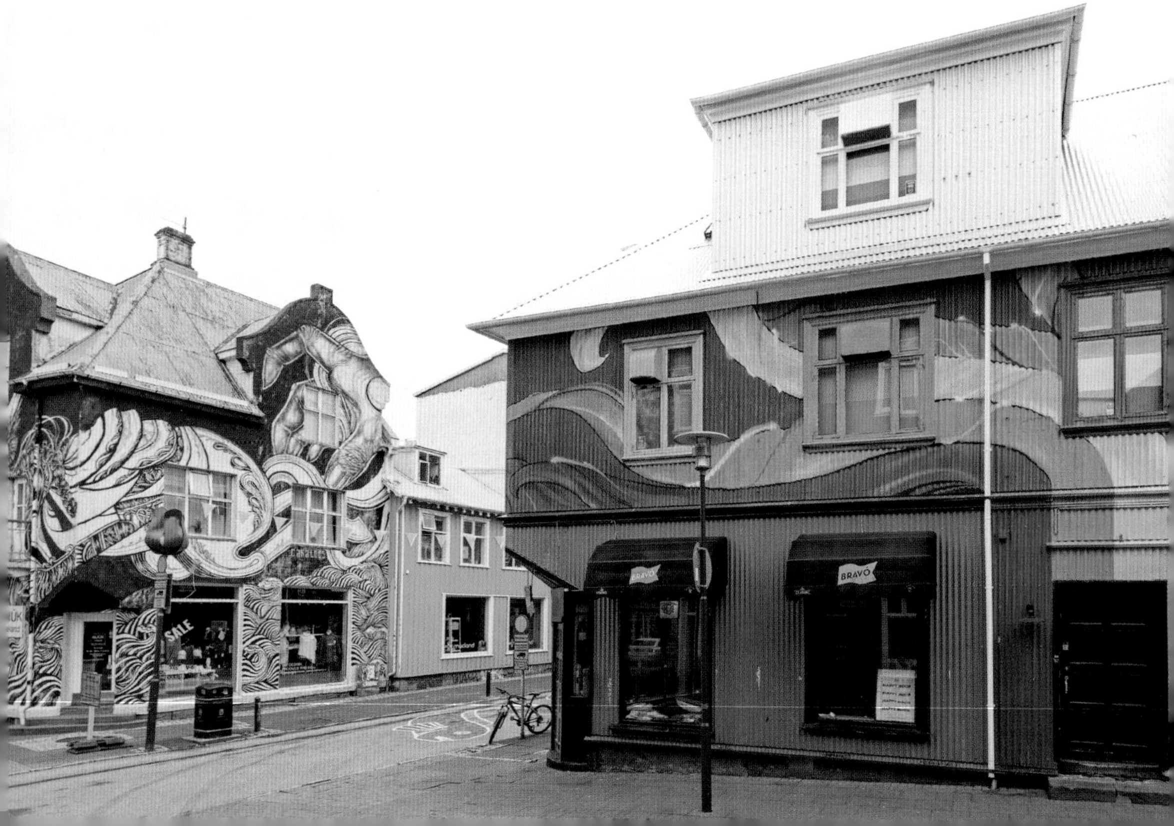

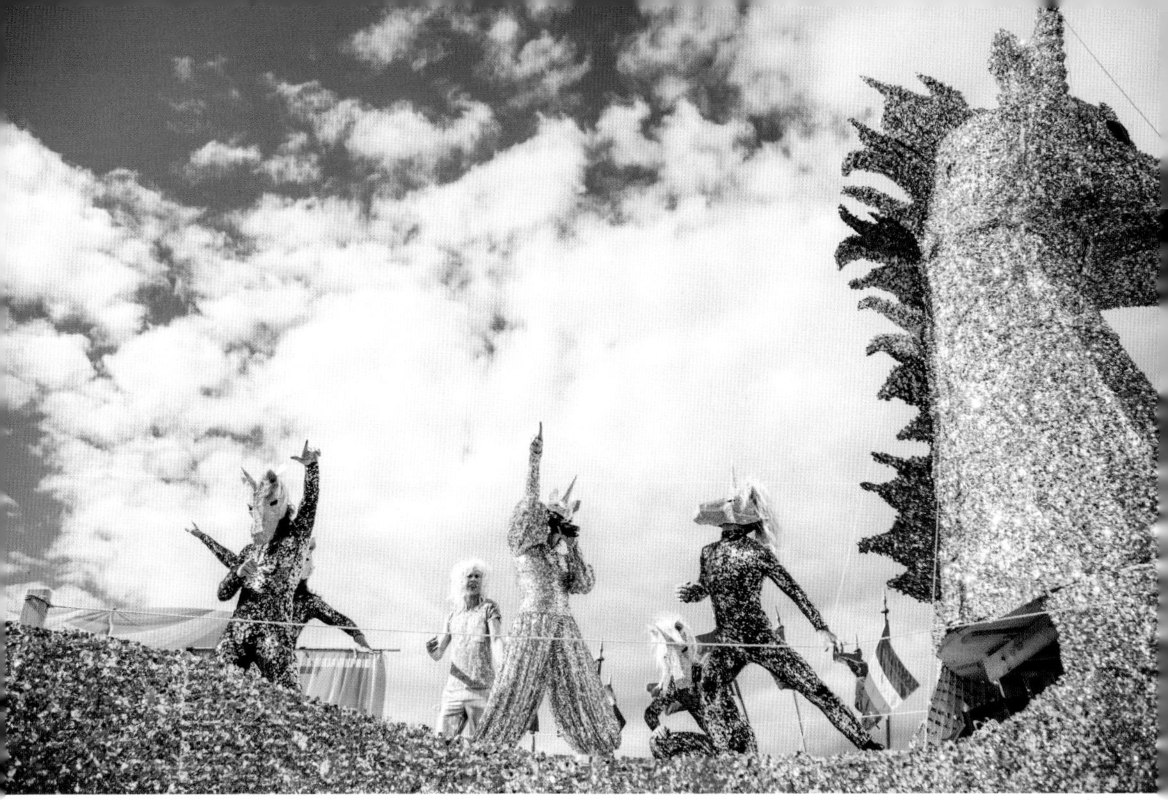

201 Ice magic

▲▶ Reykjavík Pride, Iceland

When to go: August
Best for: Discovering the land of fire and ice

Iceland is unlike anywhere else on earth, famed for its volcanic activity, glaciers, geysers, and rugged wilderness. It's also one of the most LGBTQ-friendly places in the northern hemisphere and was the first country in the world to elect an out gay head of government, Prime Minister Jóhanna Sigurðardóttir, in 2009. Around one-in-three of all Reykjavík's residents come out to support the parade, making it one of the most welcoming Pride events in the world. The city throws its support behind the event and paints rainbow colors onto different landmarks each year.

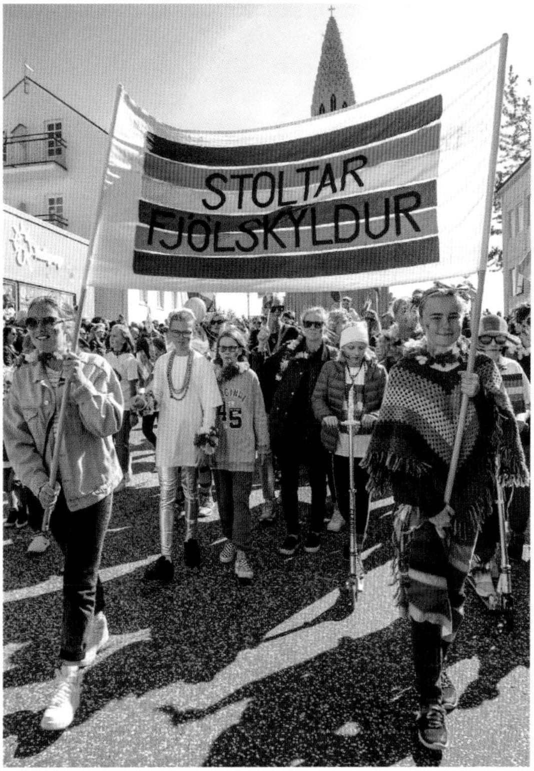

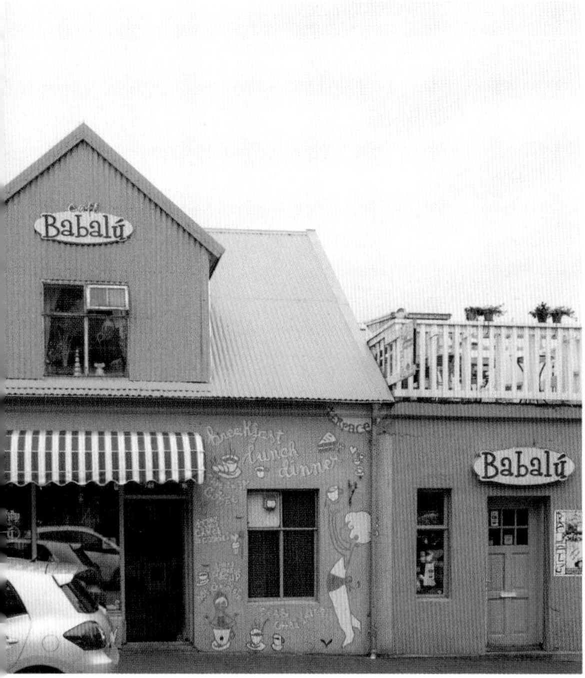

202 Feel the force... of cheesecake

◀ Café Babalú, Reykjavík, Iceland

When to go: All year
Best for: Unique bathrooms

The atmosphere at gay-owned Café Babalú is cozy and eclectic, with comfortable furniture, board games, a café cat, and intriguing decor that is different in every corner. The café is known for its great coffee and famous cheesecake made with Icelandic *skyr* (a yogurt-like dairy product found throughout Iceland). The bathroom here is unforgettable too: it's floor to ceiling Star Wars, including speakers playing the theme tune on repeat.

203 Snuggle up

▶ Iða Zimsen, Reykjavík, Iceland

When to go: All year
Best for: Book and coffee lovers

Not everyone is into big and fabulous events, and it's places like Iða Zimsen that offer a warm, friendly, and queer safe space that makes everyone feel welcome—it's even dog-friendly. Iða Zimsen is a lesbian-owned café, bookstore, and gift shop, loved by locals and tourists for over a decade. The comfy chairs by the window are the best spot to snuggle up and read a book while nursing a warming drink.

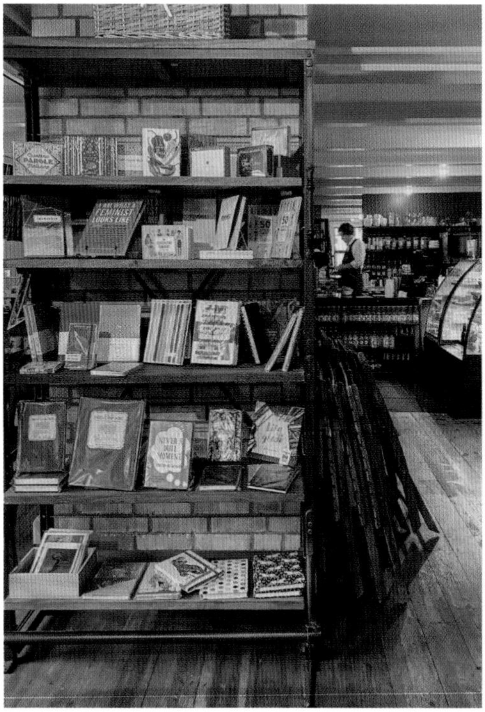

204 Follow the rainbow brick road

Regnbogastræti, Seyðisfjörður, Iceland

When to go: April to October
Best for: A rainbow detour from Iceland's ring road

One of Iceland's most picturesque towns lies in the East Fjords: Seyðisfjörður, with just seven hundred residents. In 2014, resident Snorri Emilsson couldn't travel to Reykjavík Pride (it's an eight-hour drive away). So, instead, Emilsson went to the main street—Norðurgata—and started a Pride event with just six friends. In 2016, over two hundred people joined Seyðisfjörður Pride, and the locals got together to paint rainbow stripes on Norðurgata. The street is now known as Regnbogastræti (Rainbow Street), and walking along it you'll see a few of the best-preserved wooden buildings of Iceland and the iconic blue church.

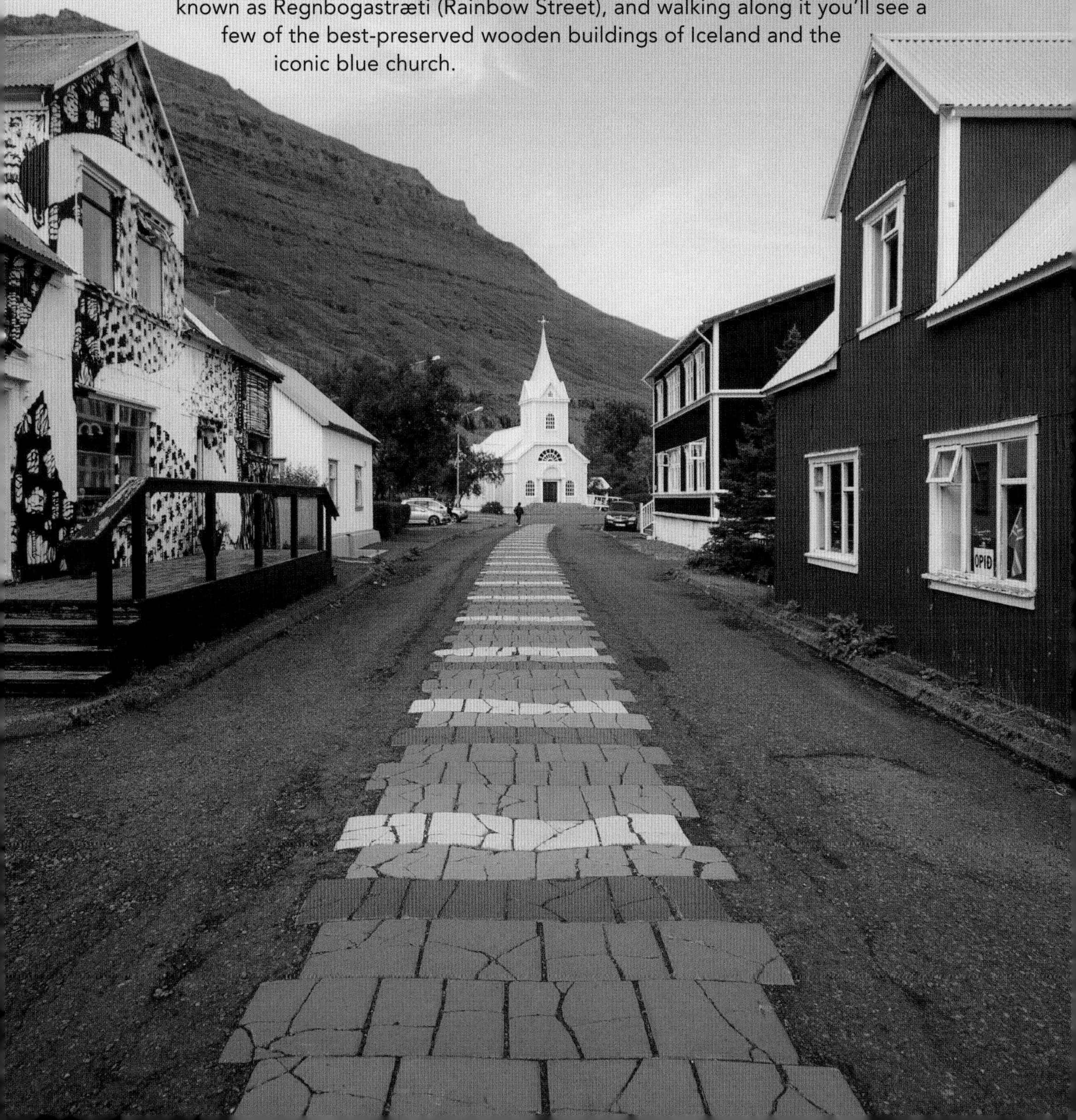

205 Forget apps, matchmake IRL style

The Outing Festival, County Clare, Ireland

When to go: February
Best for: Music and matchmaking

What better way to find the love of your life, than a real-life meet-cute festival? In 2013, the Lisdoonvarna Matchmaking Festival (which has been running for more than 170 years) decided to throw an LGBTQ+ spin-off, and The Outing Festival was born. It's now a fantastic LGBTQ+ weekend, with a fun fusion of (folk) music, comedy, queer arts, performances, and dating events. It's a lot, and it's fabulous. And you might just find "the one."

206 St. Patrick's rival

▼ ▶ Dublin Pride, Ireland

When to go: June
Best for: Great vibes in an iconic city

In 2015, the legislation for marriage equality alongside its progressive gender recognition laws helped Dublin to be recognized as a very inclusive destination. Dublin Pride started off as just a small, one-day event, but is now celebrated over ten fabulous days and rivals the St. Patrick's Day Festival for size and popularity.

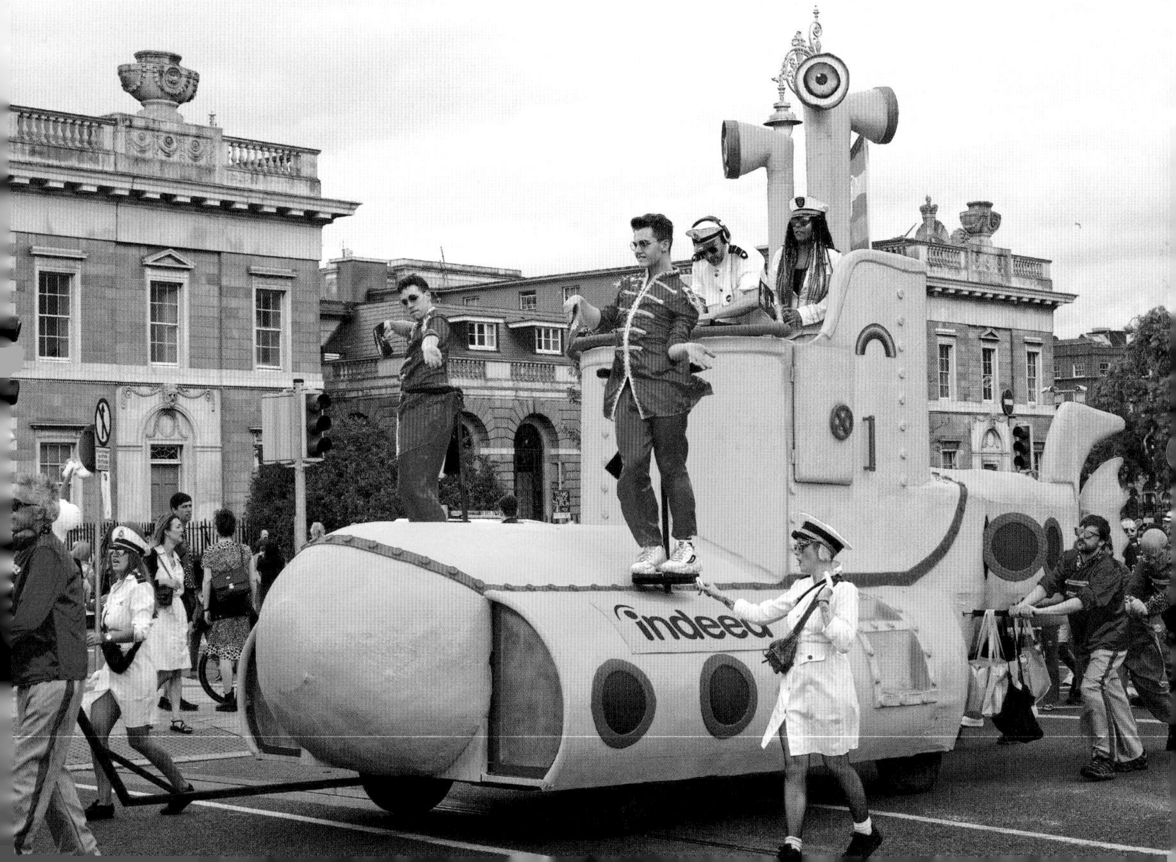

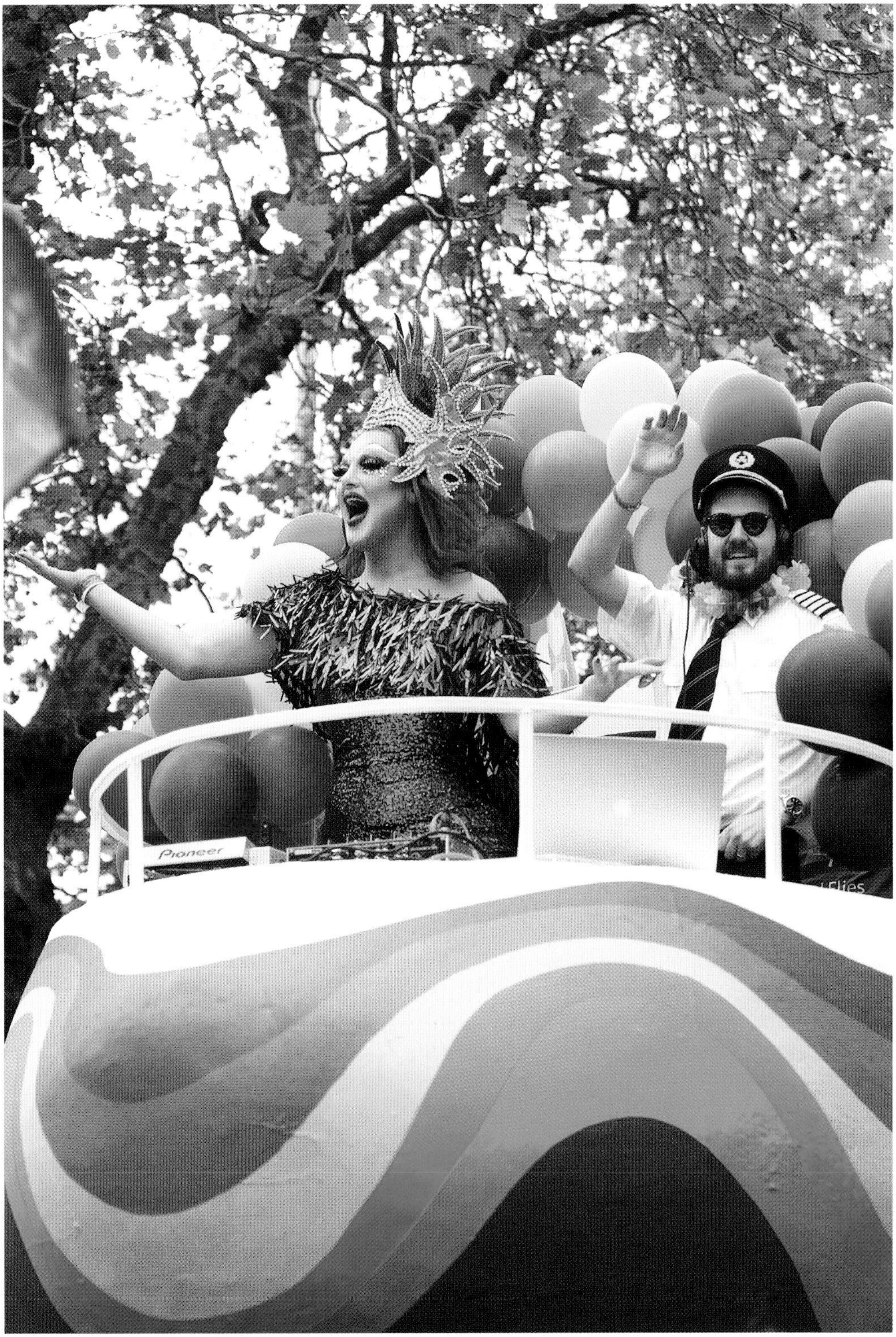
Pioneer

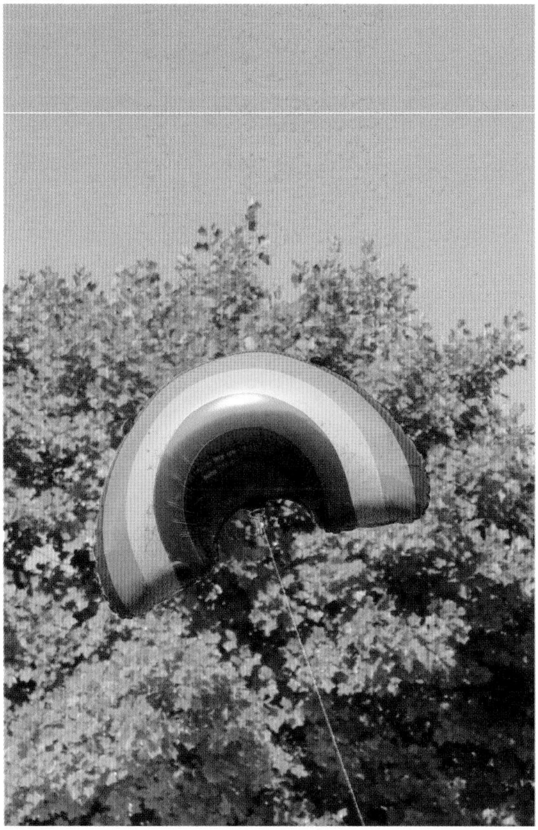

207 Go west country

Bristol Pride, England

When to go: July
Best for: Marching through historical streets

Bristol Pride is one of the fastest-growing Pride festivals in the UK; it centers on the community, features international acts, and hosts a variety of lively events leading up to Pride day. Filled with friendly locals, why not join the fun and get involved by starting the Pride day with a march down the city's historical streets, then, after taking over the town with a rainbow, witness an array of famous headline acts. The Spice Girls' Melanie C, Alexandra Burke, and Sophie-Ellis Bextor have all graced the stage for Bristol Pride. Bristol is two hours from London and boasts an eclectic street-art and music scene.

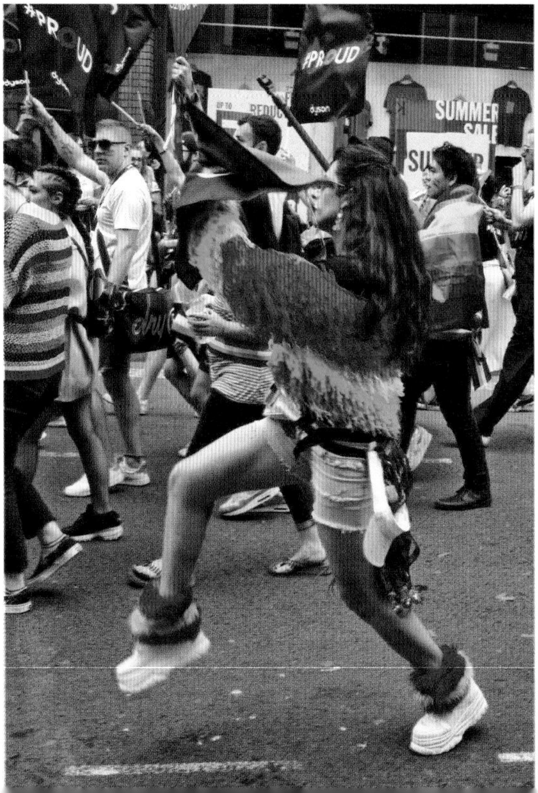

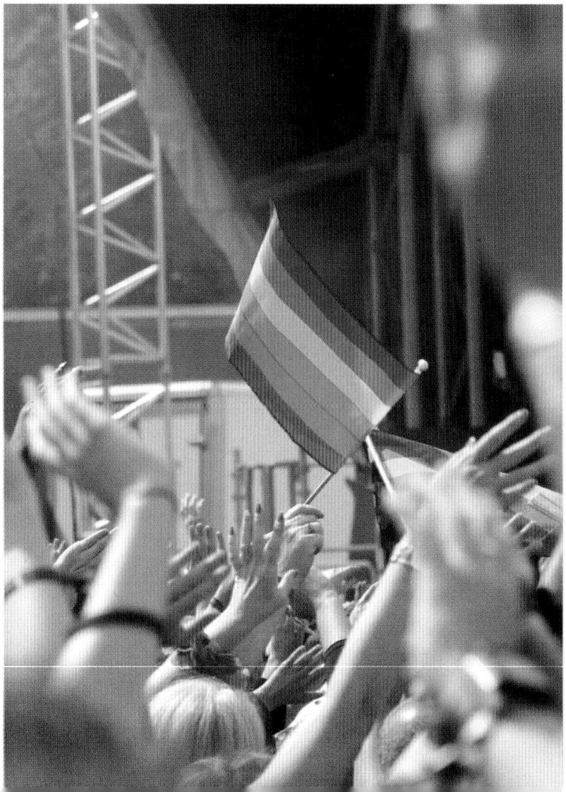

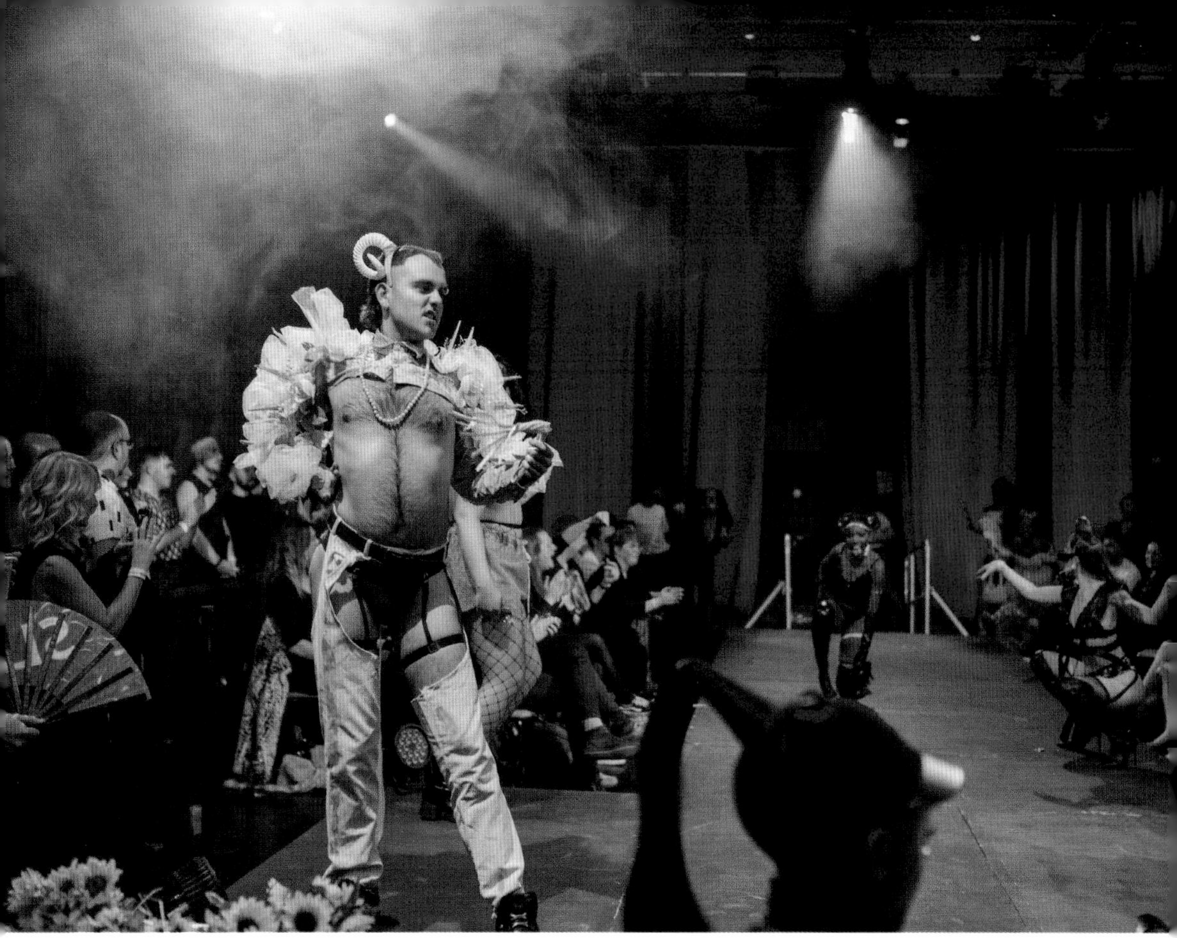

208 Let it all out

SHOUT Arts Festival, Birmingham, England

When to go: November
Best for: Arty queerness

The premier LGBTQ+ arts festival in the West Midlands, SHOUT has been running since 2009. It now encompasses film, theater, music, dance, exhibitions, and amazing vogue balls. Cult movie director John Waters is just one of the well-known speakers who has participated in this annual celebration of all things queer and arty.

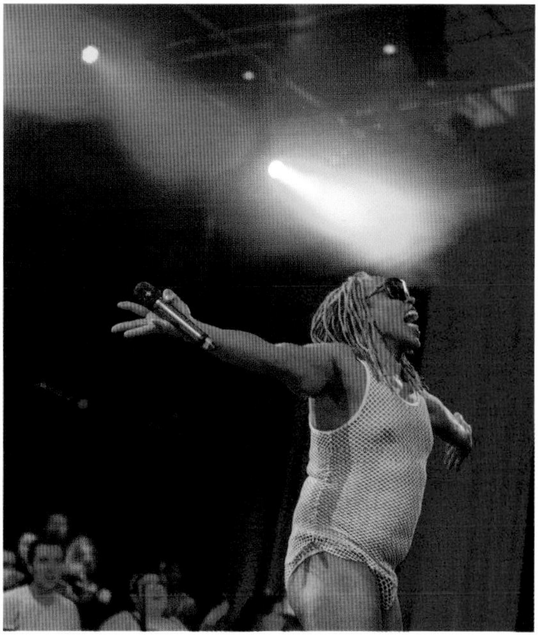

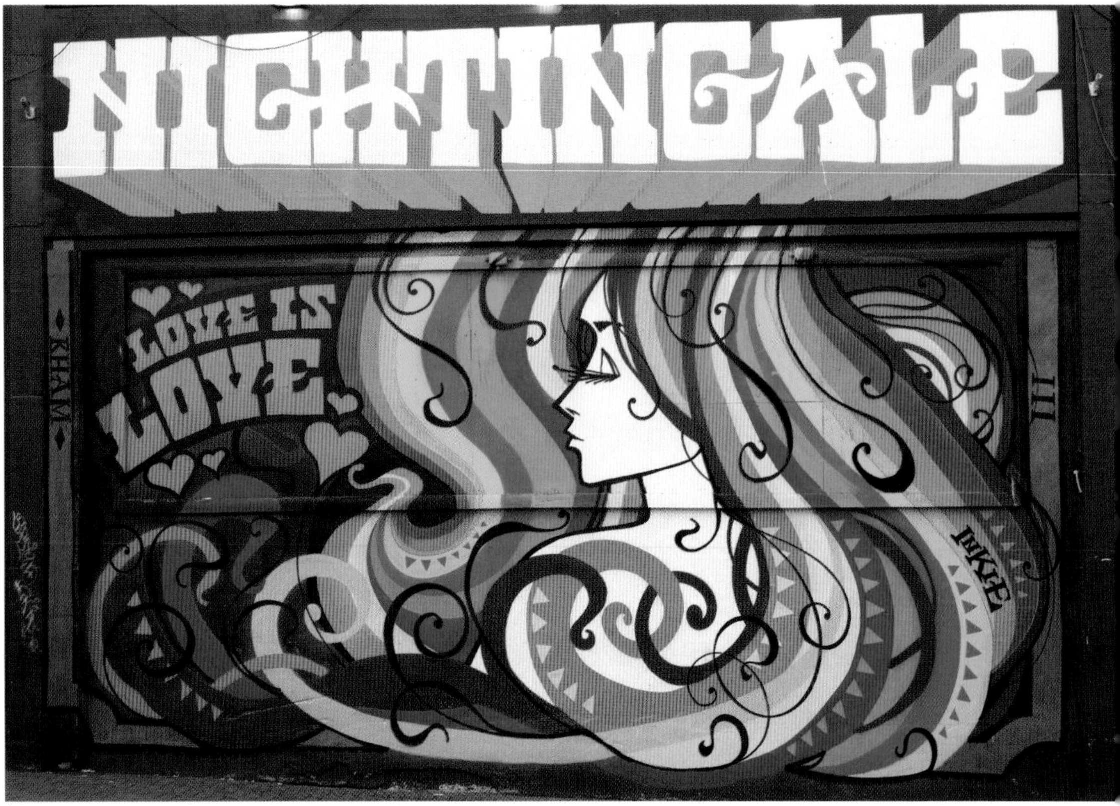

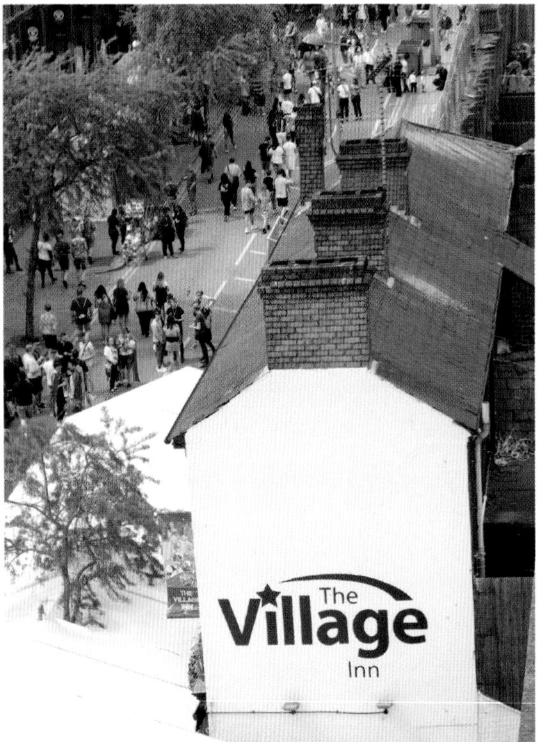

209 Brimful of Brum

Hurst Street, Birmingham, England

When to go: All year
Best for: Late night parties and clubs

Located on the edge of Birmingham's Chinese Quarter, "Brum's" Gay Village extends from Hurst Street to Inge Street to form a gayborhood that is bursting with gay clubs, iconic bars, and pubs. Stroll through some of the venues for a casual social, or party until sunrise. Head over to The Fox, a lesbian bar that welcomes everyone, to watch the city's talented drag performers, enjoy karaoke on Fridays, and DJ nights every Saturday. Birmingham Pride also takes place on Hurst Street every year, when the area brims over with Brum pride.

210 Not the only lesbians in the village

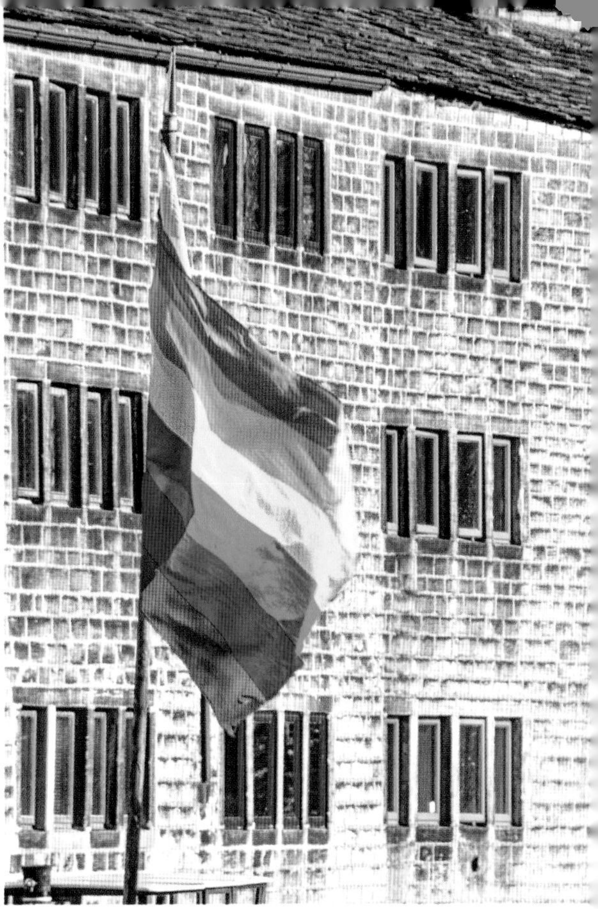

Hebden Bridge, England

When to go: All year
Best for: Local walks and queer culture

Hebden Bridge is known as the lesbian-capital of the UK, with more queer women per square foot than London or Brighton, despite only having a population of four thousand people. It's a quaint, family-friendly market town nestled in the stunning hills of West Yorkshire. During the 1970s a group of lesbians settled here and, over time, the town earned the reputation of having a higher proportion of lesbians. There is a high concentration of LGBTQ+ residents, queer businesses, and safe spaces for the community.

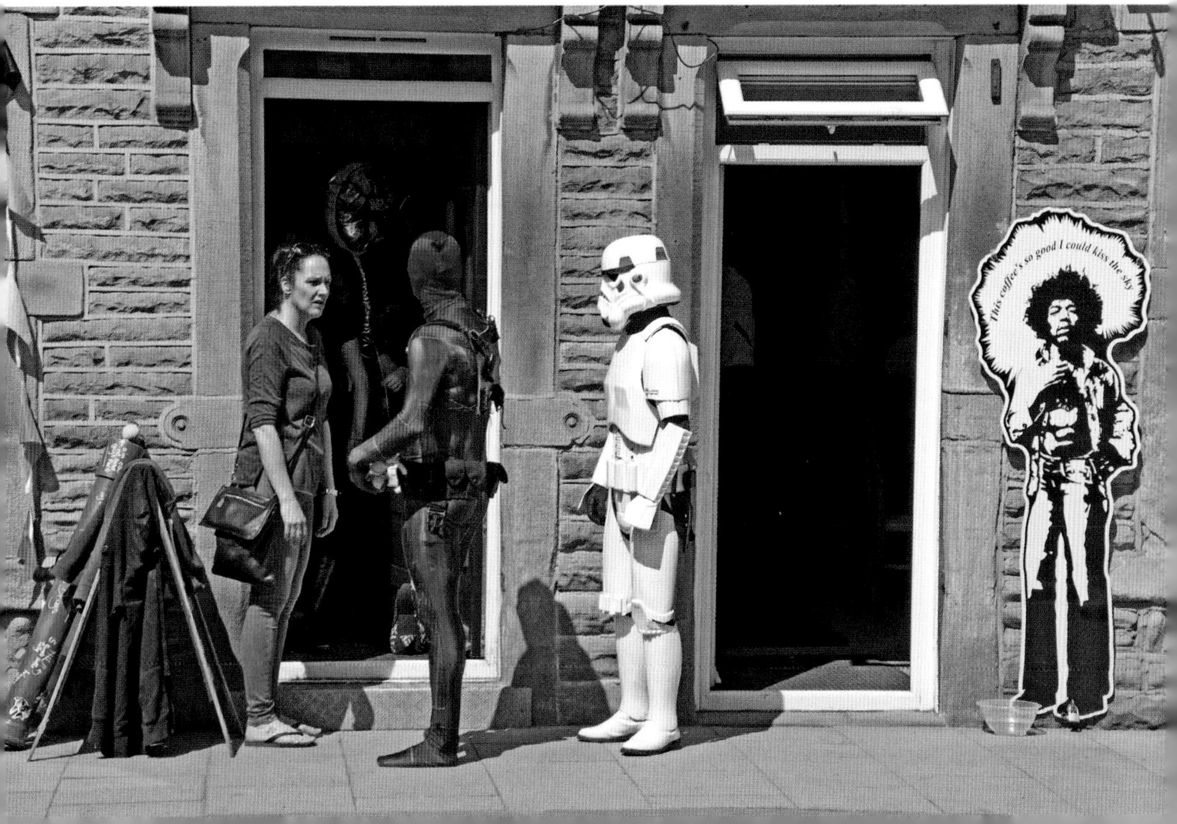

211 Two for the price of one

Brighton and Hove Pride, Brighton, England

When to go: August
Best for: Visiting the UK's queer capital

The Pride Parade kicks off the weekend, traveling along the busy seafront to London Road (where the locals go). The weekend full of Pride antics offers two main events; the low-cost "Village Party," which fills each street in Kemptown with varying music genres and drag acts, and "Fabuloso in The Park," which promises a lineup of huge megastars to keep you entertained all day.

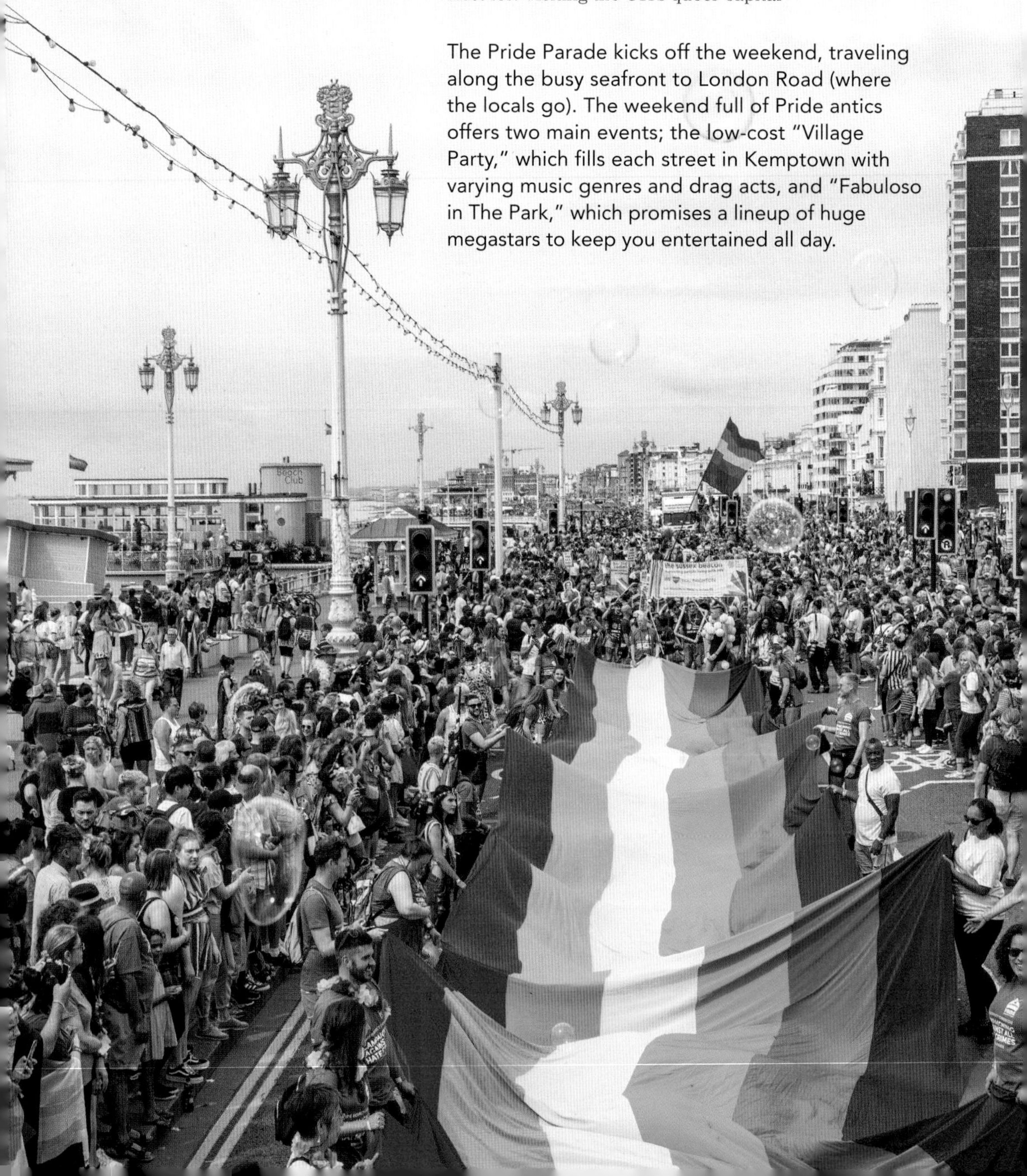

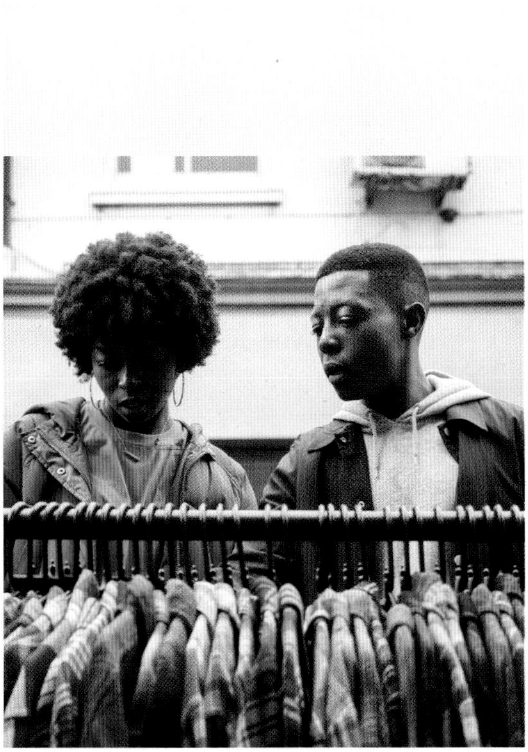

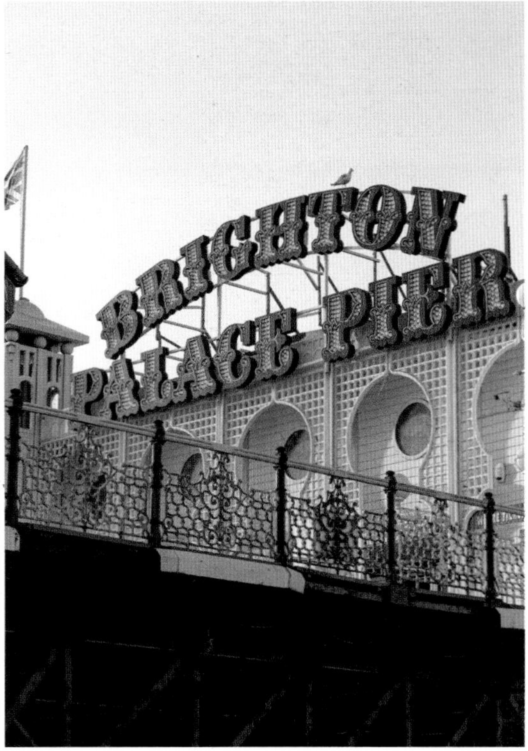

BRIGHTON
PALACE PIER

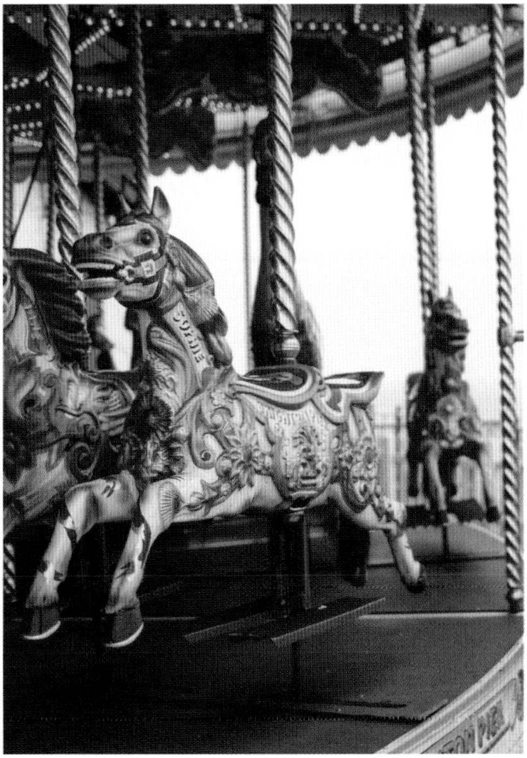

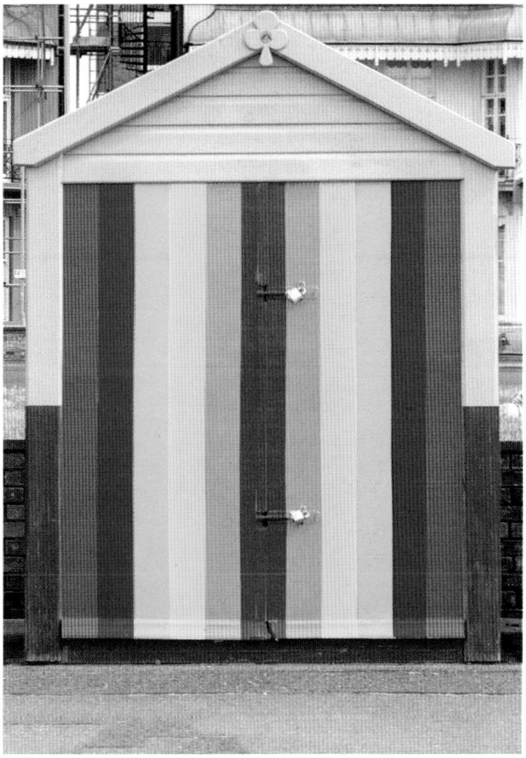

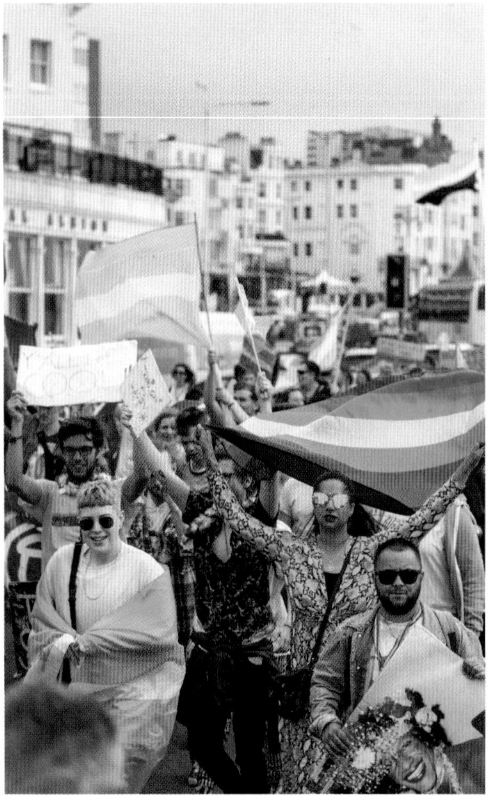

212 Putting the T first

Trans Pride Brighton and Hove, Brighton, England

When to go: July
Best for: Trans joy

Join thousands of trans people as they march along the Brighton seafront in the largest annual protest for trans-liberation in Europe. The procession leads to a family-friendly park filled with live music, community stalls, and sports workshops—one year this even included sword fighting. After spending the day reveling in trans joy and spotting local trans celebs (these could include Munroe Bergdorf, Travis Alabanza or Fox Fisher), hit up the afterparty for live drag performances.

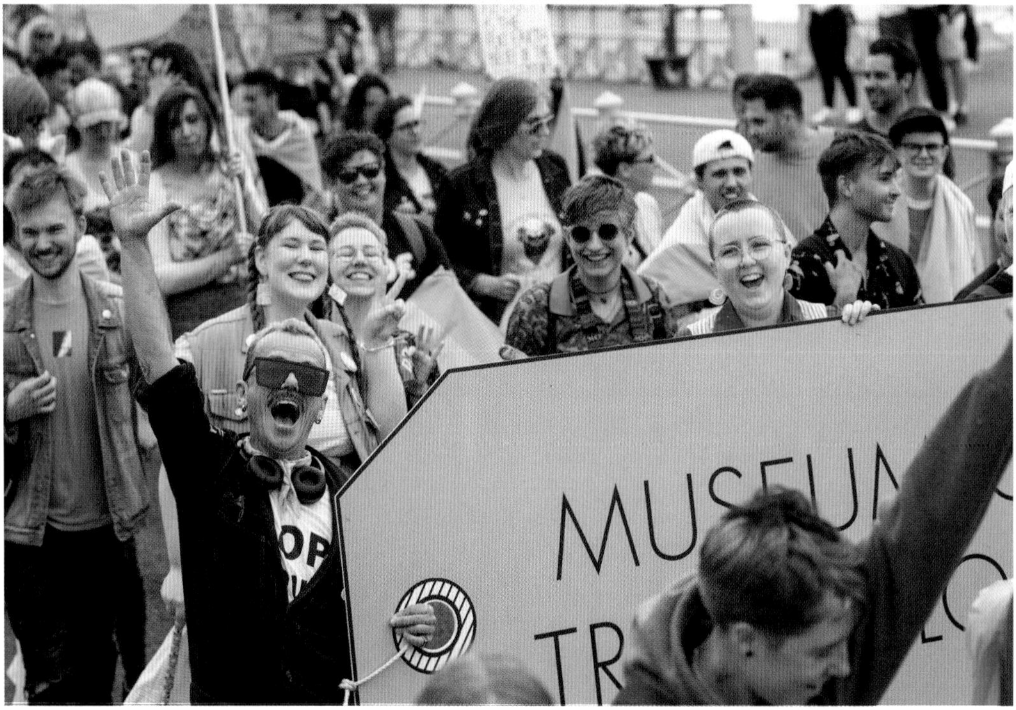

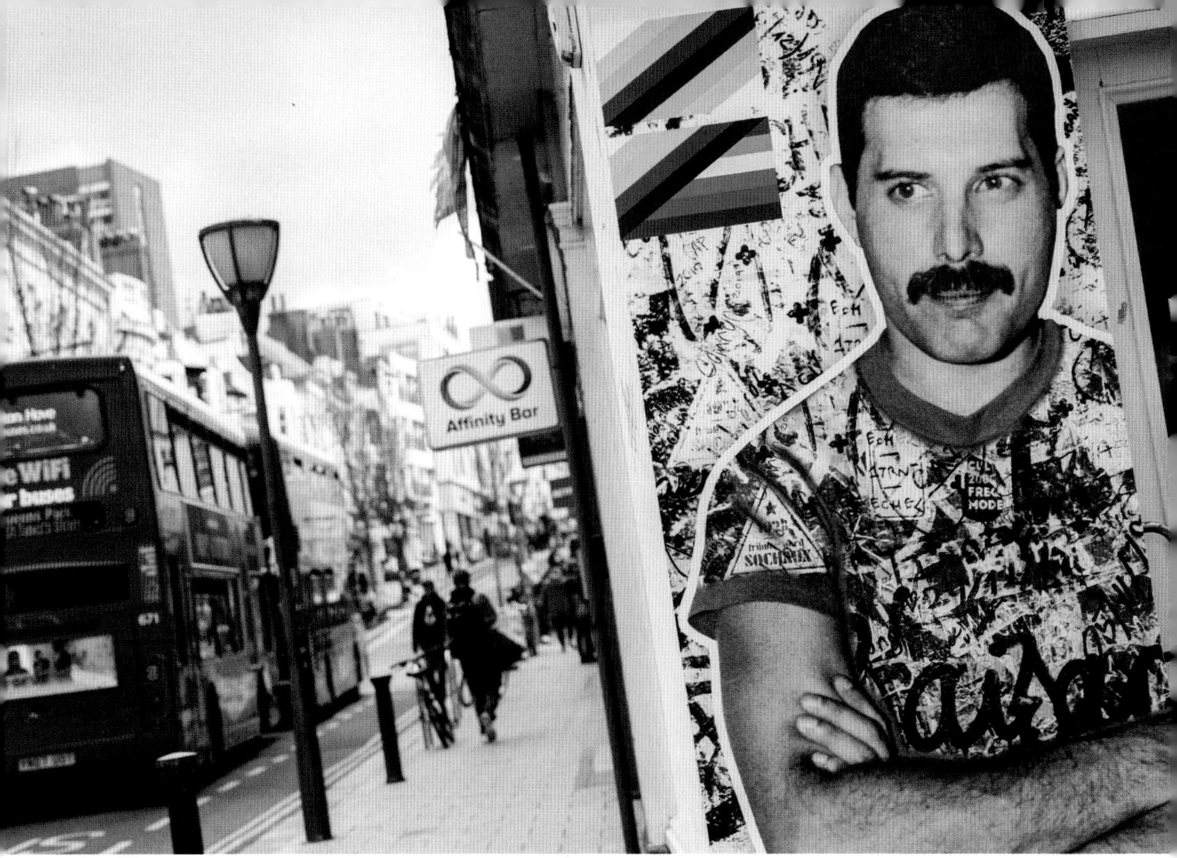

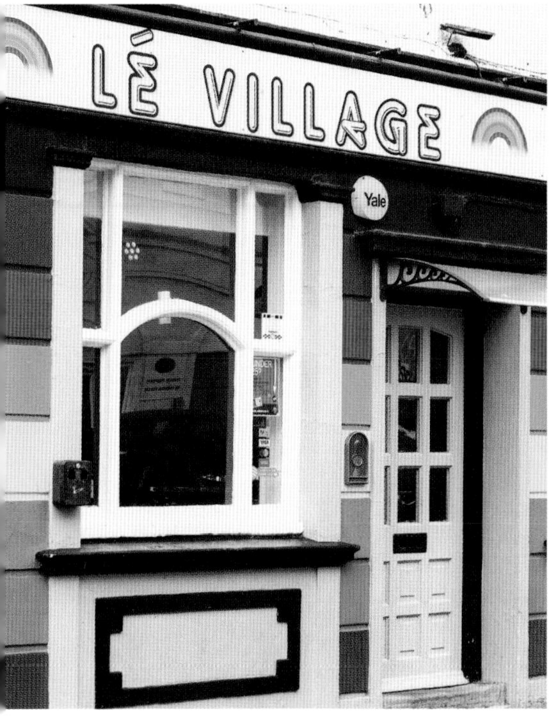

213 One night is not enough

Kemptown, Brighton, England

When to go: Any time
Best for: Choice

Kemptown is the vibrant LGBTQ+ area of Brighton and the heart of the party. Whether you're after a quiet boozer, a hip new bar, a cabaret club, or somewhere to dance the night away, you are spoiled for choice here. You could try to get round them all, but you'd need more than one night.

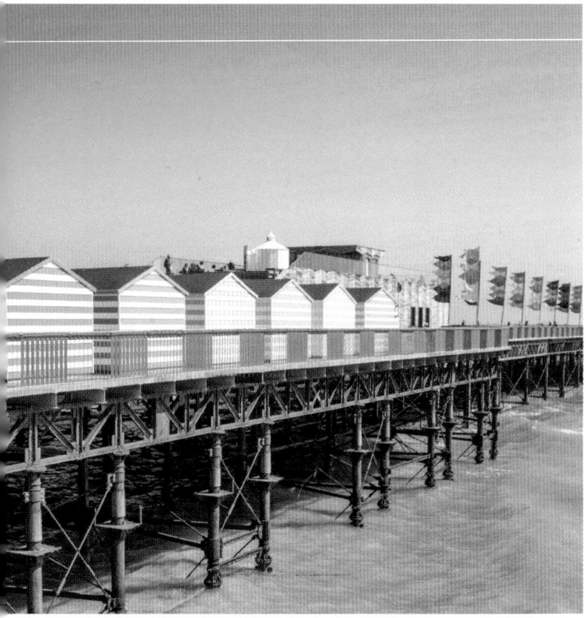

214 Queer eye for the pier guys

Piers and Queers Tour, Brighton, England

When to go: July to August
Best for: Tour of Brighton

Over two hundred years of queer history are covered in the 90-minute Piers and Queers walking tour. From an Edwardian drag king to a queer wedding in 1923, Brighton's queer history goes back way further than you might think.

215 Beer on the pier

▲ Queer on the Pier, Hastings, East Sussex, England

When to go: July
Best for: Drag, with fish and chips

The Queer on the Pier festival in the south-coast town of Hastings offers an Oktoberfest-type day out. It takes place on the town's main pier and features stage entertainment, DJs, and big, wooden picnic tables. You can understand why the organizers call it "the UK's largest beer garden."

216 Out with the locals

Moonlight Experiences, London and beyond, England

When to go: All year
Best for: Unique times

Navigating authentic, queer communities and spaces while traveling can be difficult. Moonlight Experiences is an award-winning travel and nightlife company run by queer women of color (QWOC) to tackle the lack of diversity in travel. Through them, you will not only be instantly immersed and connected with the local LGBTQ+ community, but also served unapologetic queer culture, history, art, thrilling underground parties, and vogue balls.

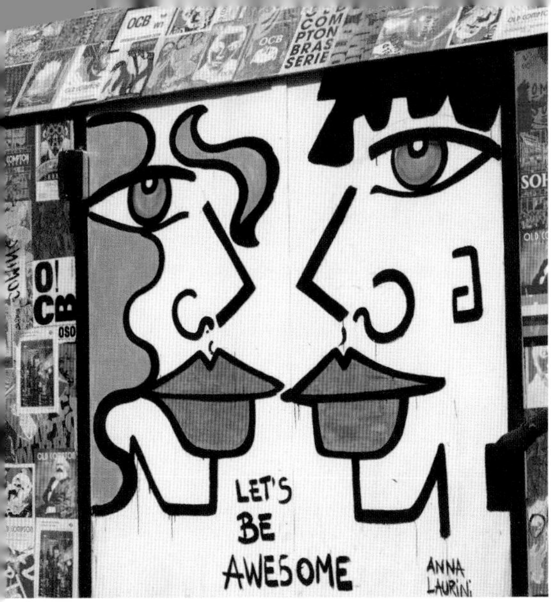

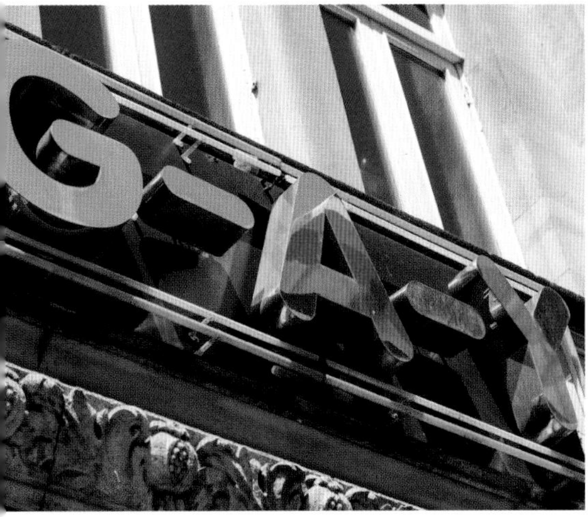

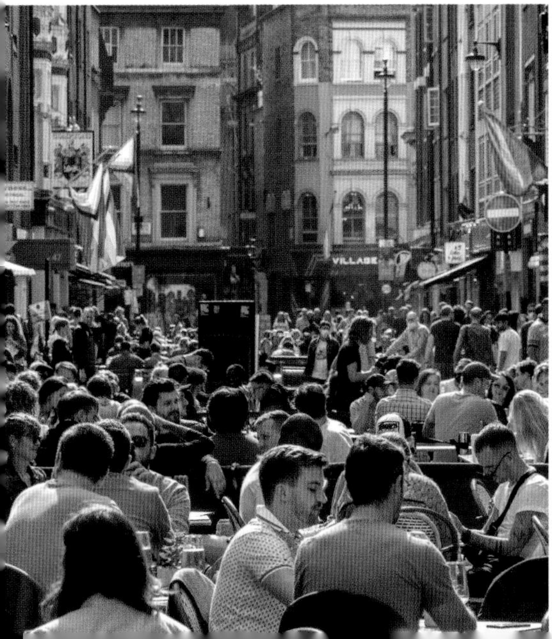

217 The heart of gay Soho

Old Compton Street, London, England

When to go: All year
Best for: People watching

London's gay neighborhood originated in what was originally one of its seedier corners. Soho enjoyed a reputation for strip clubs and sex work going back decades. However, it was also a magnet for artists and performers due to the nearby West End theaters. Gay men began to gather in its pubs in the early twentieth century. Comptons of Soho opened on Old Compton Street in 1986. Village Soho, with its sleek and modern design, appeared in the early 1990s. Both bars helped cement Old Compton Street's reputation as the number one destination for the city's gay boys, overtaking the more leather-oriented Earls Court. Nowadays, Old Compton Street offers several bars, including the G-A-Y, Admiral Duncan, and women's venue She Soho. Caffé Nero, on the corner with Frith Street, remains one of the most popular spots for coffee and people watching, while Balans Soho is open until 5 a.m. for the post-club crowds.

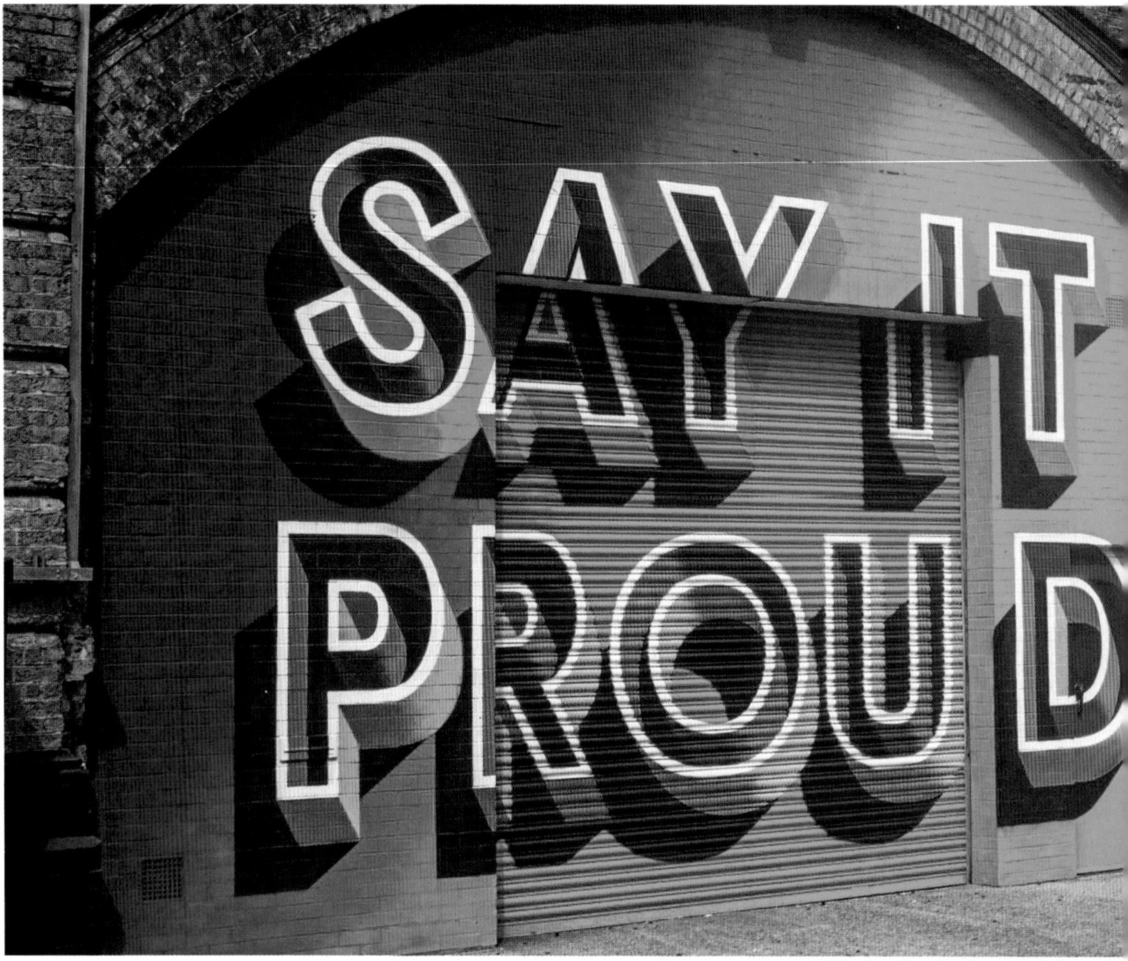

218 By royal command

The Royal Vauxhall Tavern, London, England

When to go: All year
Best for: An all-inclusive welcome

The Royal Vauxhall Tavern (affectionately known as the RVT) in South London holds a beloved place in the LGBTQ+ scene. It is known for its cabaret shows and long-running club events. The building dates back to the mid-1800s. No-one's sure when it first became known as a gay pub, but it hosted drag shows as far back as the 1950s. Drag legend Lily Savage, aka Paul O'Grady, used to be a regular, and there's even an apocryphal tale of Freddie Mercury taking Princess Diana here, incognito in male drag. On Friday nights, Beefmince is all about electro beats and burly bears, while the venue's Tuesday-night cabaret, Bar Wotever, is one of the most inclusive and welcoming nights out in London for anyone open-minded and up for a laugh.

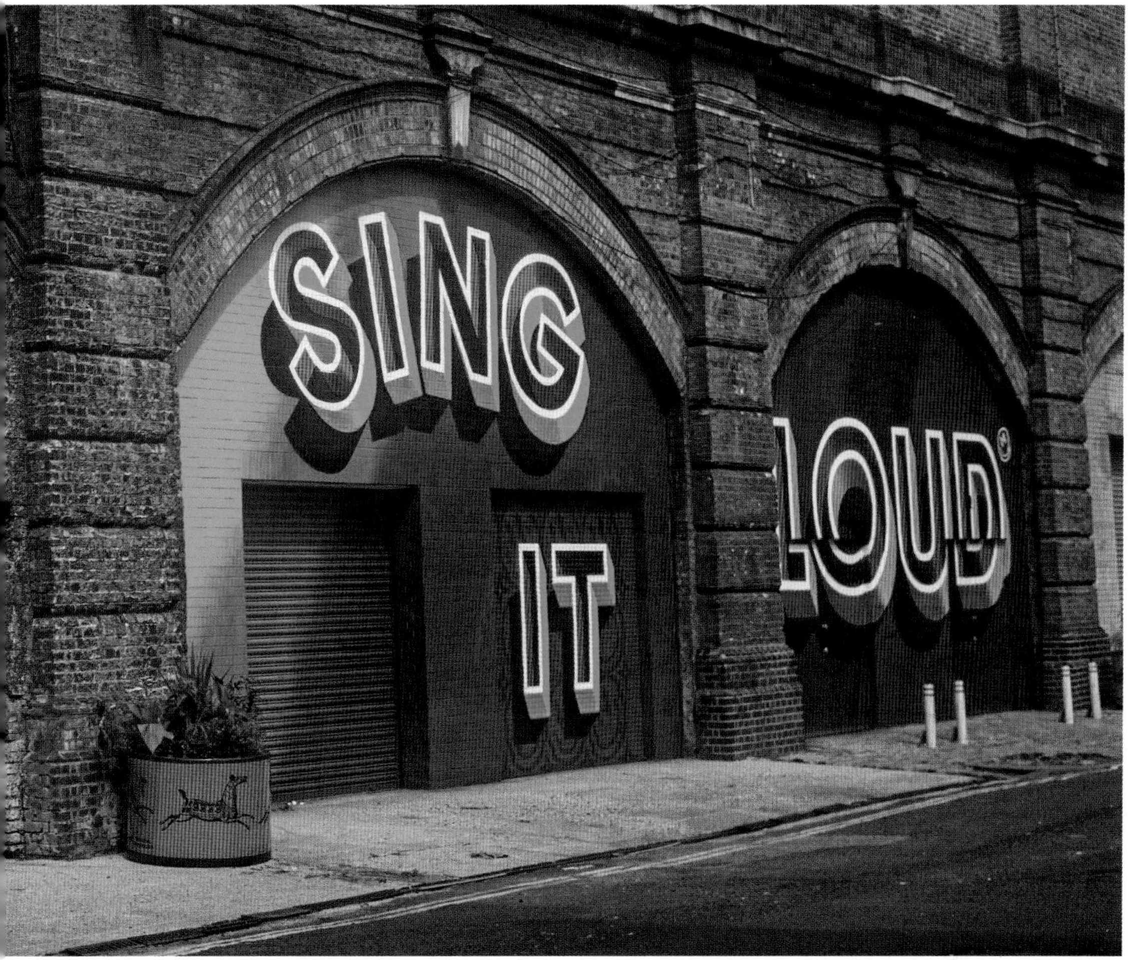
SING
IT
LOUD

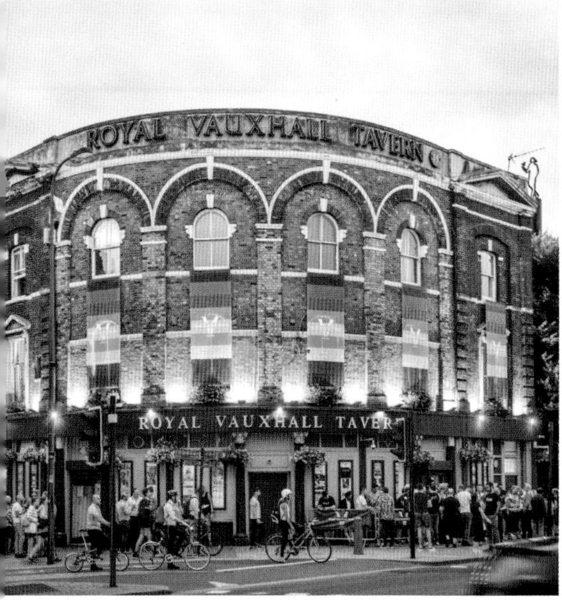
ROYAL VAUXHALL TAVERN
ROYAL VAUXHALL TAVERN

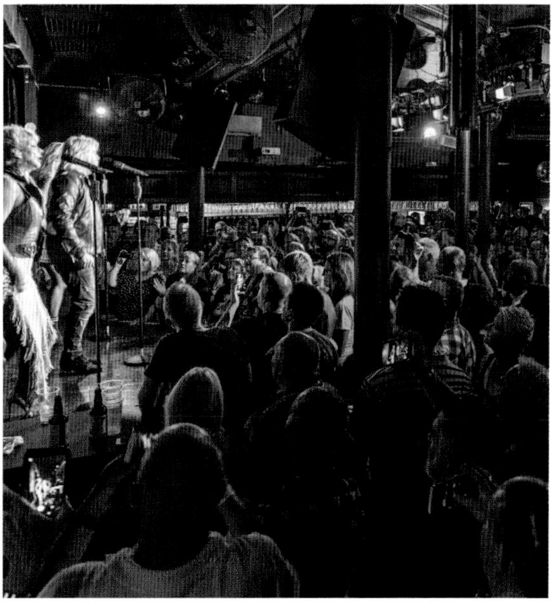

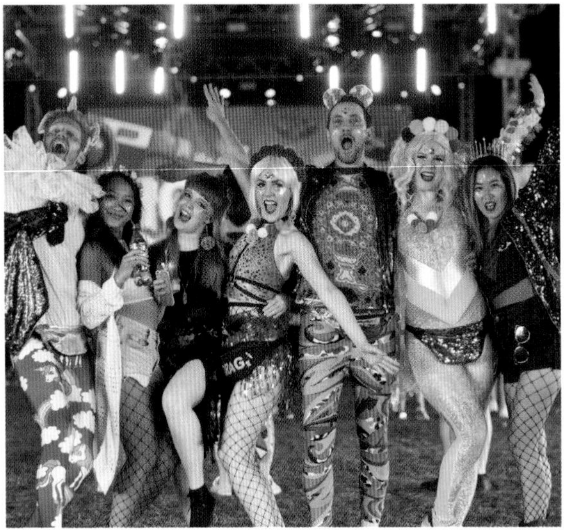

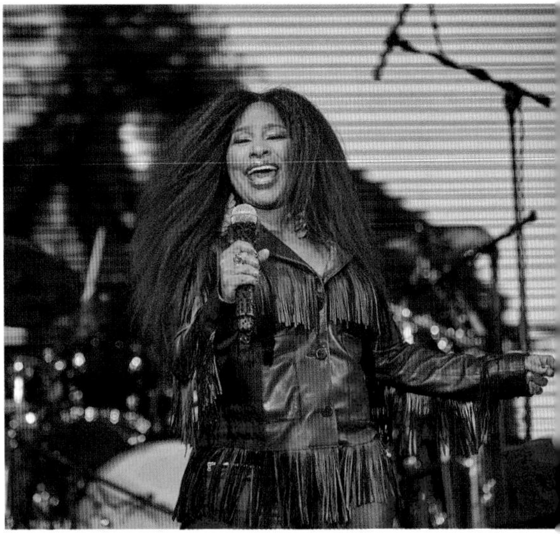

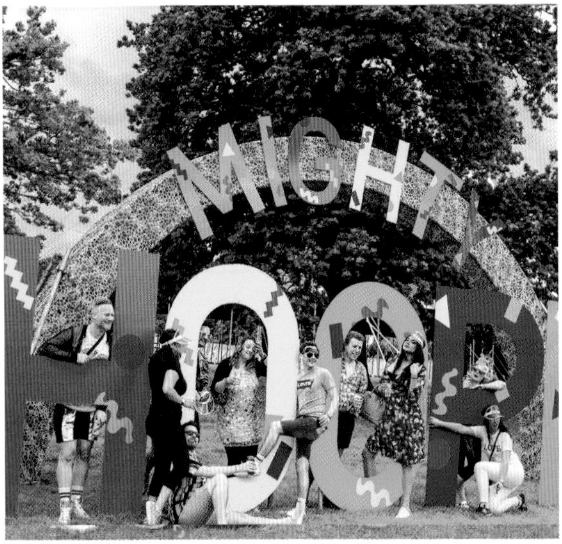

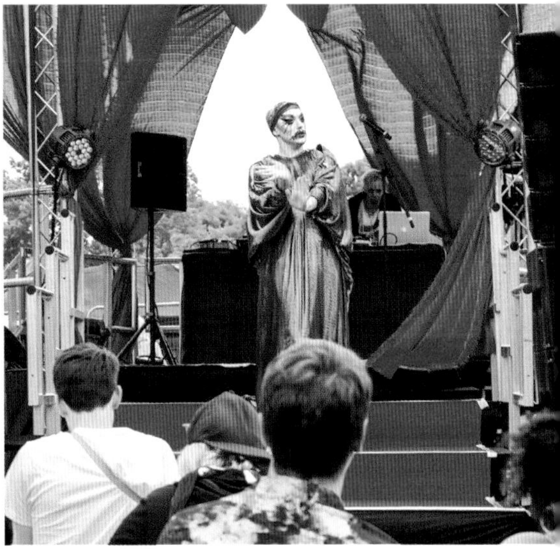

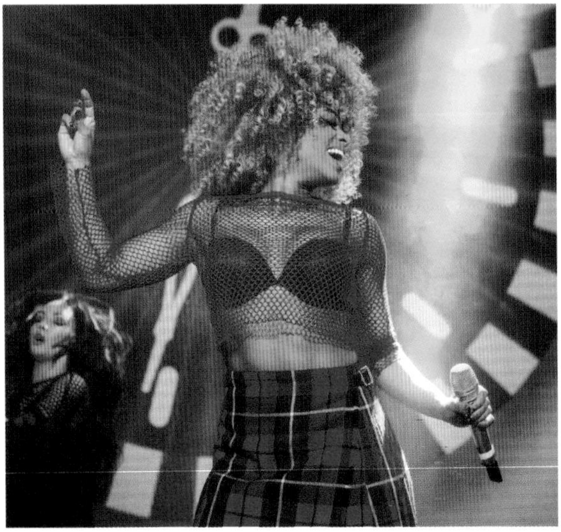

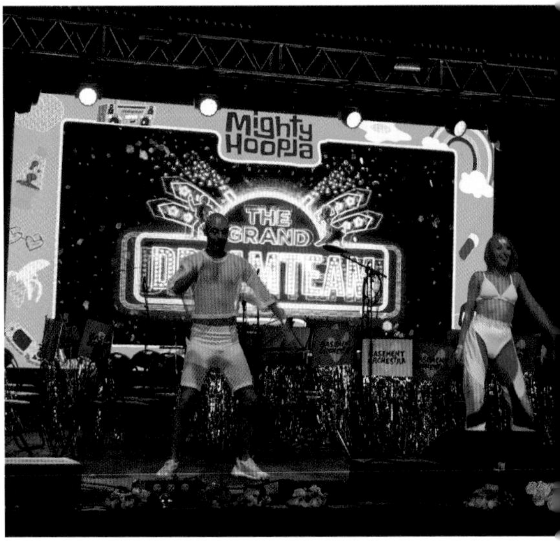
Mighty Hoopla
THE GRAND

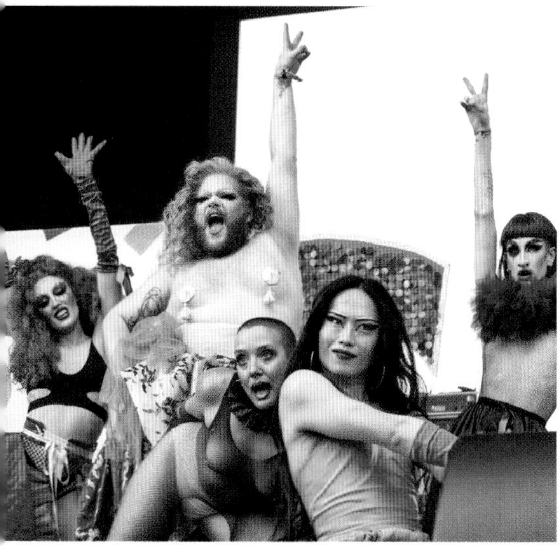

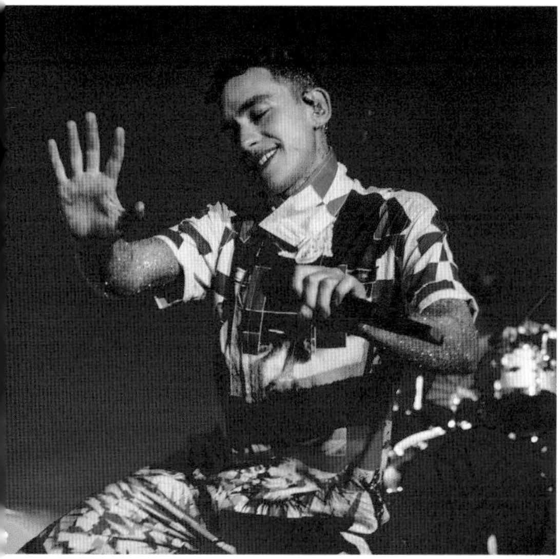

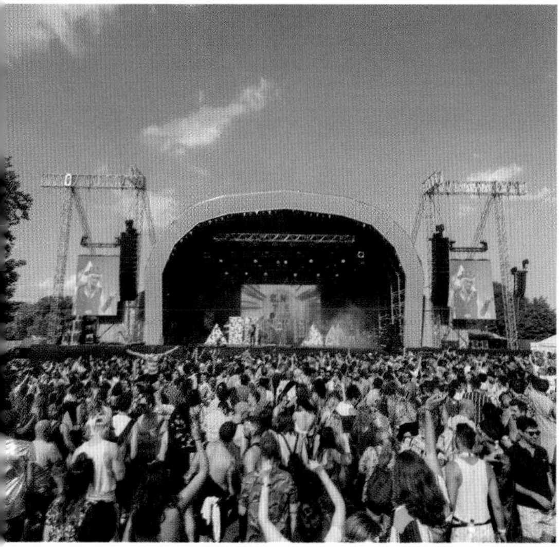

219 Jumping through Hooplas

Mighty Hoopla, London, England

When to go: June or August
Best for: Pop

This summer pop festival attracts 25,000 people every year. It showcases international artists, local queer artists, and performers from all across the community. Although London's weather can be awfully unpredictable and sunshine is not a given, what is guaranteed is an utterly fun-packed weekend full of nonstop entertainment and dancing at the most joyous pop-fuelled festival in the United Kingdom.

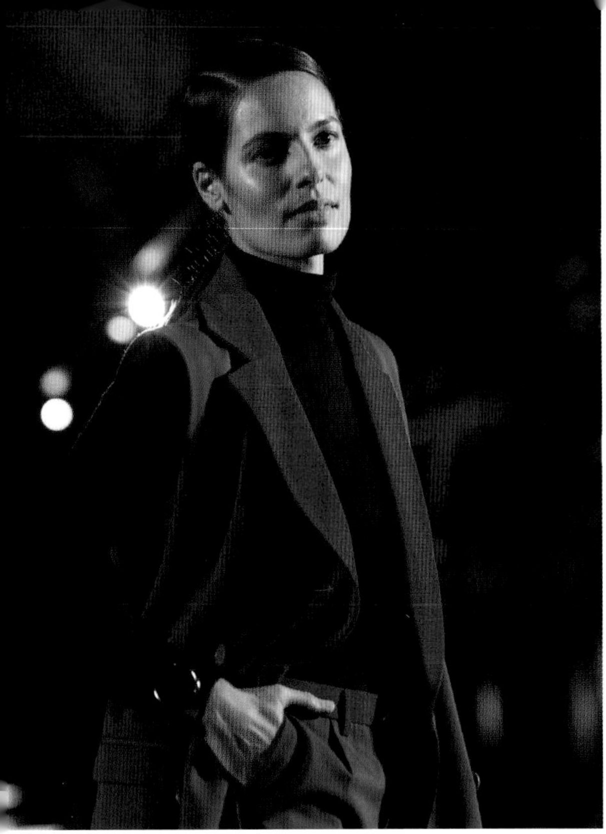

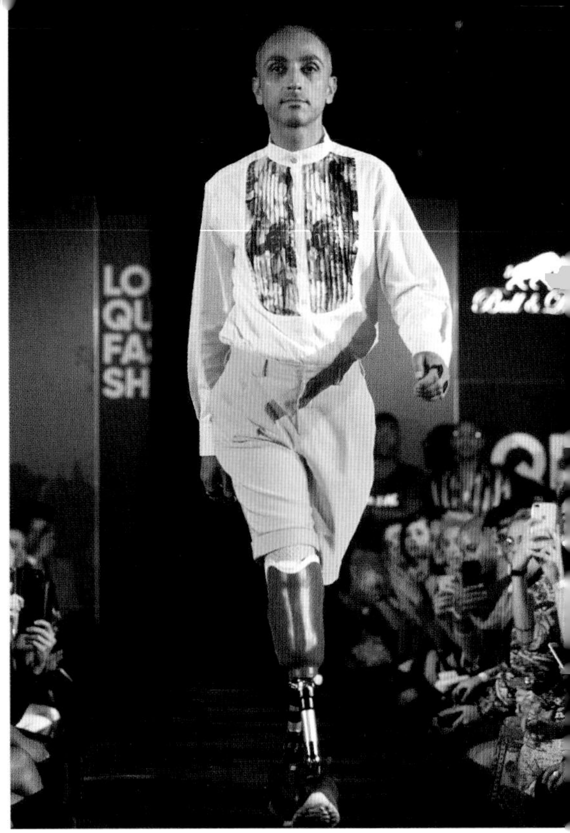

220 A la mode—queer style

▲ London Queer Fashion Show, London, England

When to go: September
Best for: Art, clothes, and community

Since 2017, the London Queer Fashion Show (LQFS) has been showcasing fashion, identity, and expression as part of London Fashion Week. Taking place in stunning venues across London, it supports and brings together talented queer designers and LGBTQ+ models of all body types. It's not your typical fashion show. It's also packed with performances, community leaders, and international models strutting their queer selves on the runway and disrupting the commercial fashion world as we know it.

221 Step back in time

The British Museum, London, England

When to go: All year
Best for: LGBTQ+ through the ages

The British Museum is over five hundred years old and houses one of the biggest collections of artifacts and antiquities in the world. You can view 15 items of specific LGBTQ+ interest with its "Desire, Love, Identity" walking trail. It includes marble busts of Emperor Hadrian and his lover, Antinous, and a carving of the Mesopotamian deity Ishtar, who worshippers believed had the power to assign gender. You can download an audio guide from various app stores. The museum also hosts special events for the UK's LGBTQ History Month each February.

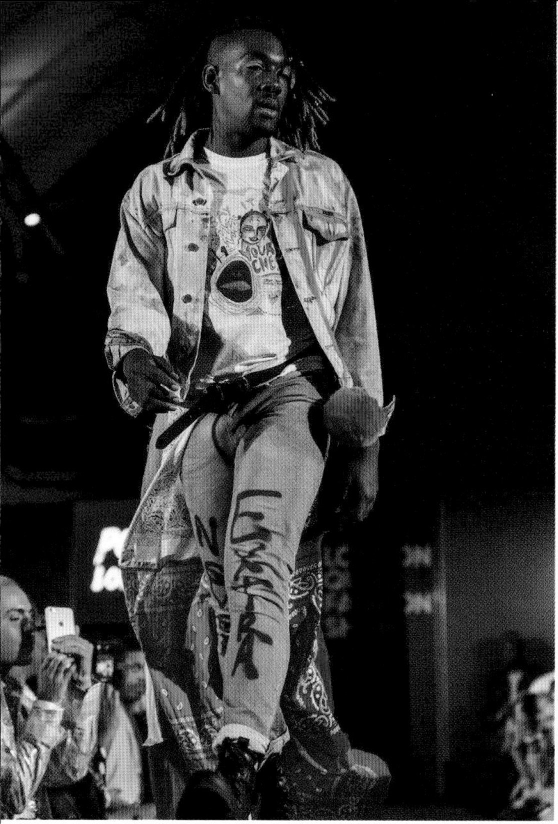

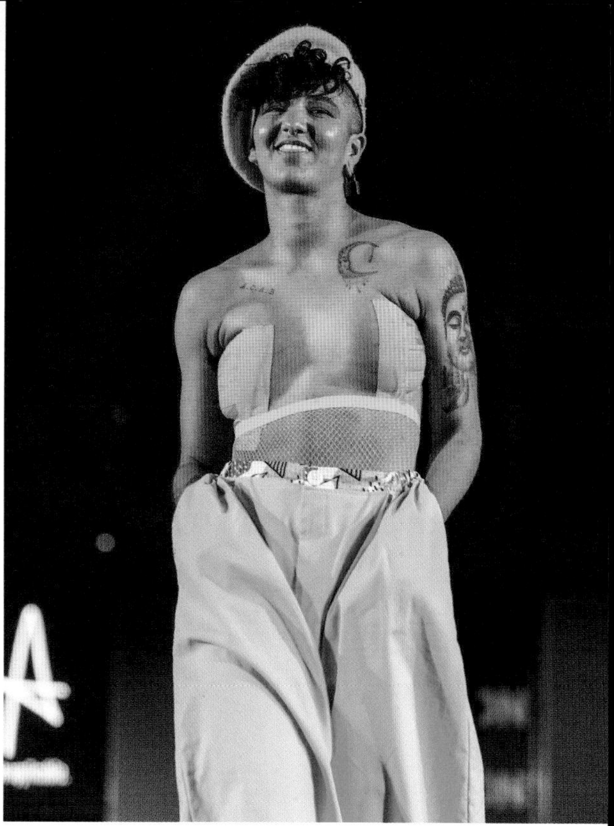

222 Learn all about it

Bishopsgate Institute, London, England

When to go: All year
Best for: Literature, exhibitions, and history

Bishopsgate Institute is a charming art-nouveau building that offers events and courses, and houses an expansive library and archive, including an extensive collection of LGBTQ+ history, politics, and culture. Opened to the public in 1895, this is a wonderful place to learn about the nineteenth and twentieth centuries up to the present day. The collection includes the UK Leather and Fetish Archives, which document the history and heritage of fetish, kink, bondage, discipline, and sadomasochism.

223 See it to believe it

Fringe! Queer Film and Arts Fest, London, England

When to go: September
Best for: Creative juices

Run by a team of incredible queer creatives and volunteers, the Fringe! Queer Film and Arts Fest offers interactive talks, eye-opening movies, experimental experiences, workshops, and wild parties.

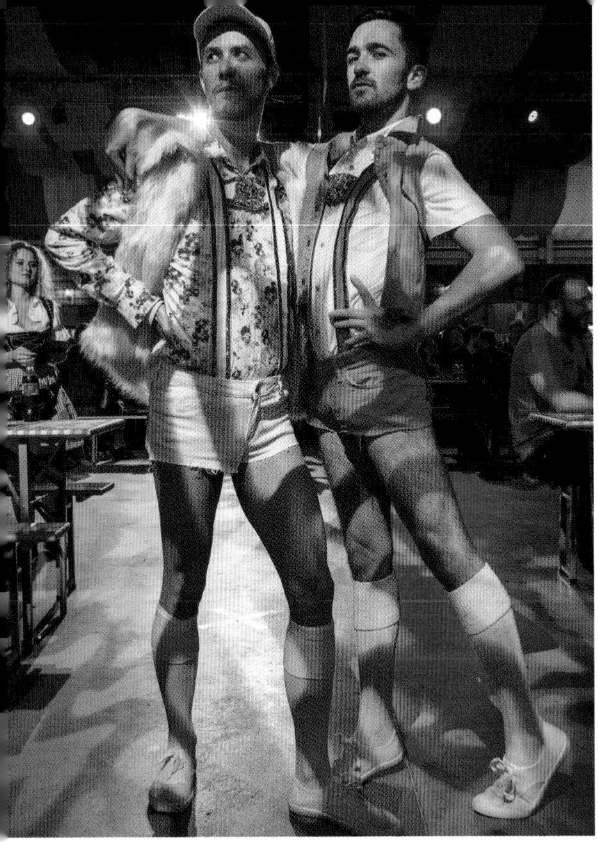

224 Who doesn't look good in lederhosen?

◀ ▼ Pink Oktoberfest, London, England

When to go: End of October or early November
Best for: Camp hangout

Pink Oktoberfest is the UK's largest gay party during Oktoberfest. It's camp, colorful, and filled with rainbows, drag queens, lip-sync battles, game shows, fire shows, and DJs. Oktoberfest authenticity is provided by German waiters, German sausage to munch on, and German crooners belting out songs for a jolly good time.

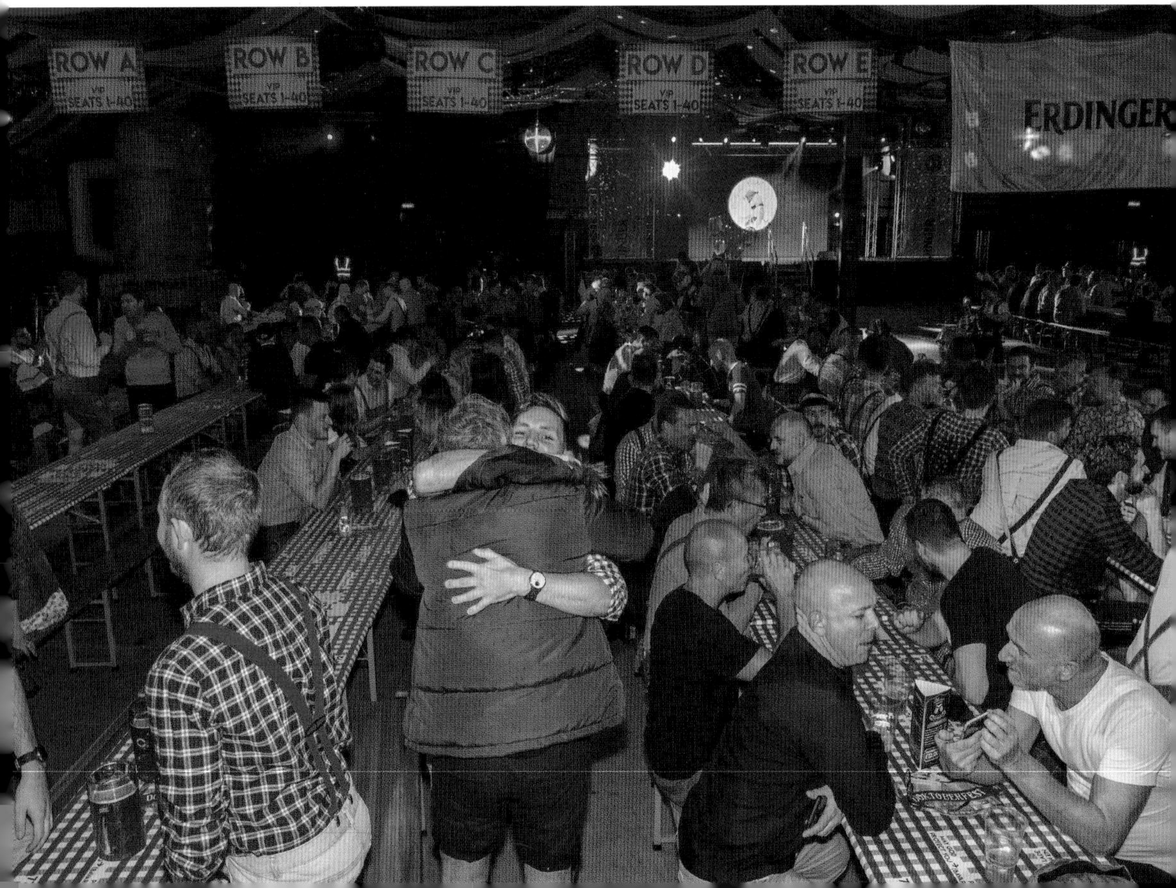

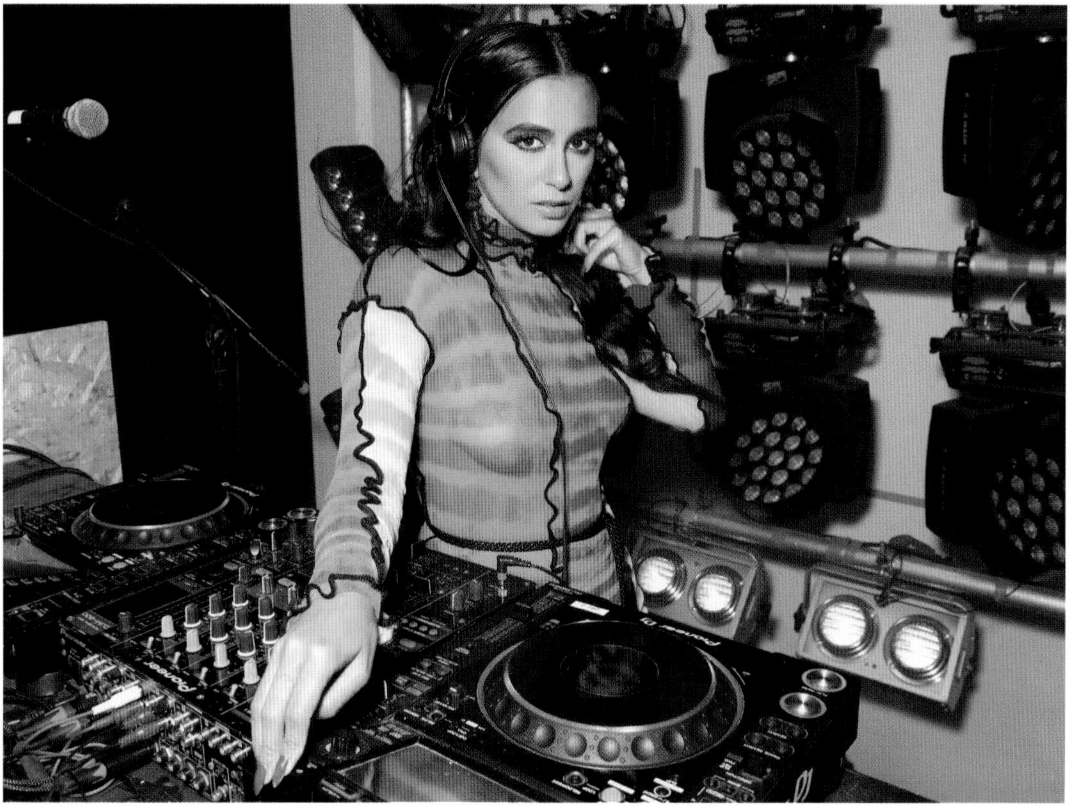

225 Safe night out, safe way home

▲ Pxssy Palace, London, England

When to go: All year
Best for: Unadulterated fun

Pxssy Palace is London's biggest community-led club night for queer, transgender, and intersex people of color (QTIPOC). The nights create a safe space for the QTIPOC community to dance and connect, with an emphasis on sexual freedom, pleasure, and the exploration of the full self. Brilliantly, there is a taxi fund for transgender women to get home safely after the party. The best way to enjoy a night out at Pxssy Palace is to come without prejudice and be respectful in your enjoyment.

226 Here come the girls

Lick Events, London, England

When to go: All year
Best for: Getting down

A groundbreaking London event and venue, launched by women for women. Each event hosts a unique array of DJs and artists, pumping out dancehall and hip hop. Lick is a safe space, where people of color are actively welcomed to come together and party. The event also offers an Instagram meetup group so you can make friends even before you step through the door.

227 Pan-Asia fantasia

The Bitten Peach, London, England

When to go: All year
Best for: Cabaret

The Bitten Peach, founded in 2019, is the UK's only Pan-Asian cabaret collective, made up of performers of Asian descent who work in a variety of genres, such as drag, burlesque, comedy, music, dance, and circus. The collective is increasing Asian representation and diversifying the drag and burlesque scene, at the same time as offering excellent nights out. It counts singer Jason Kwan, drag-artist Mahatma Kandi, and dancer Bolly Illusion among its finest Asian performers.

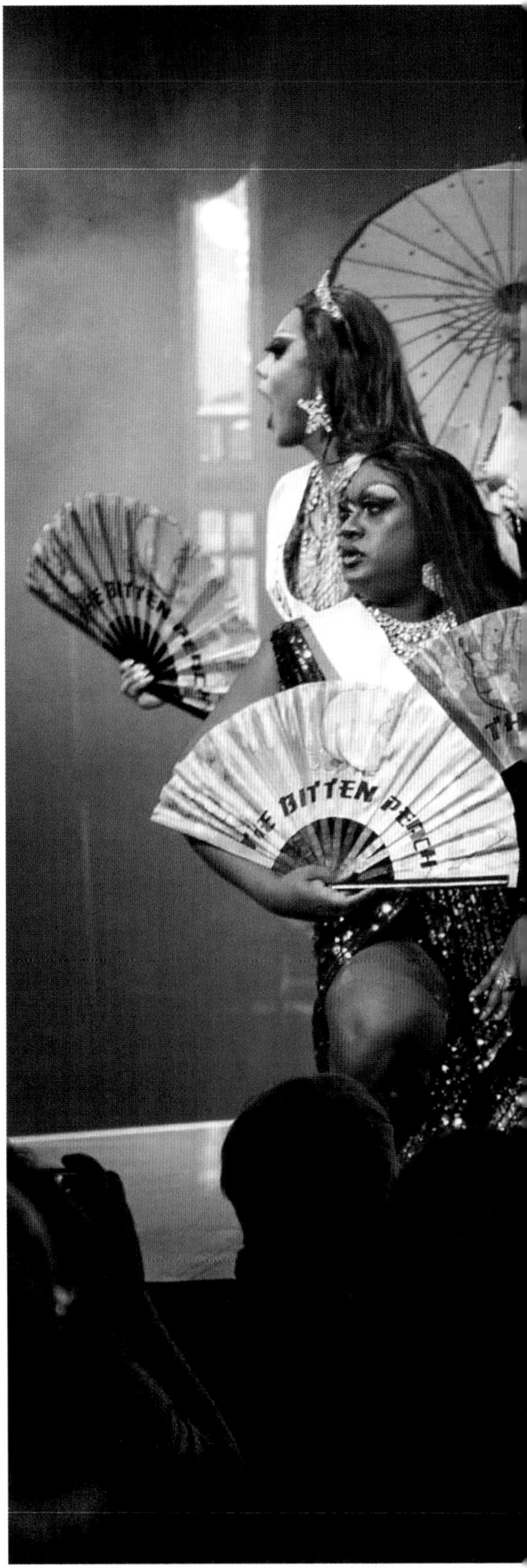

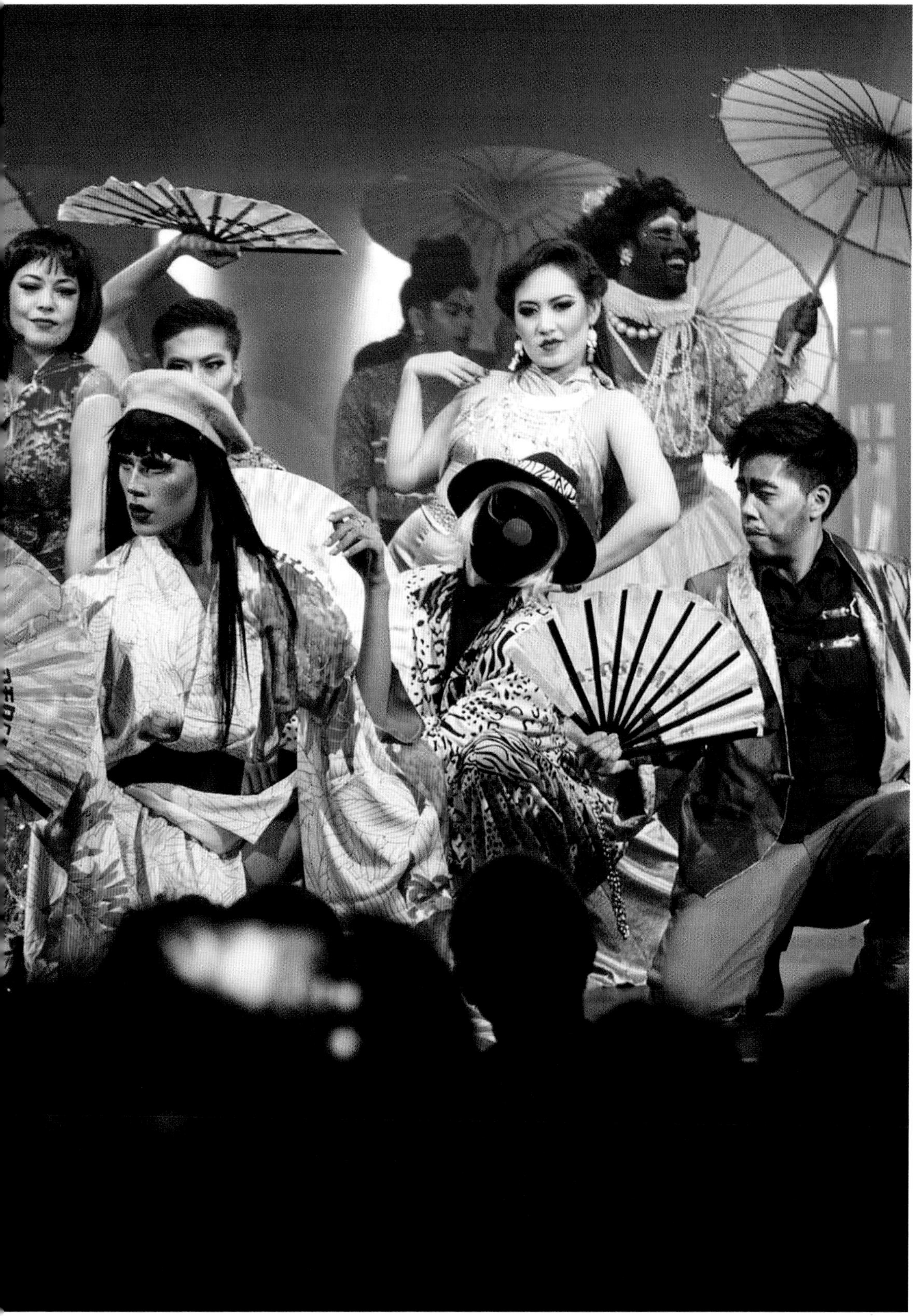

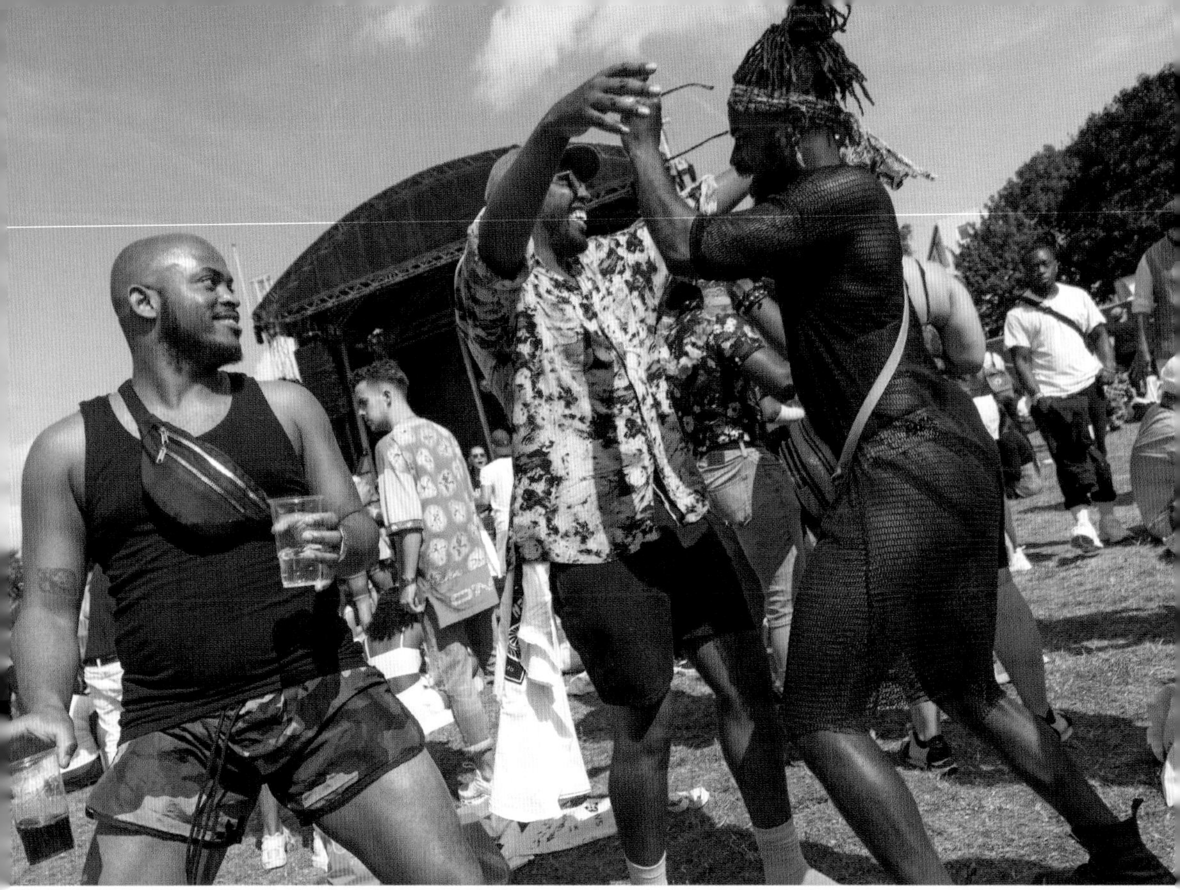

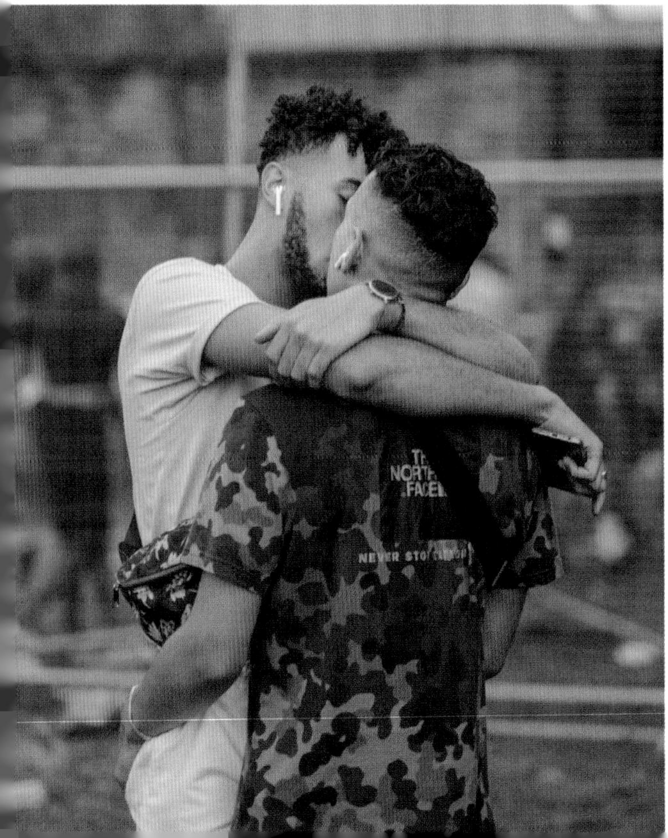

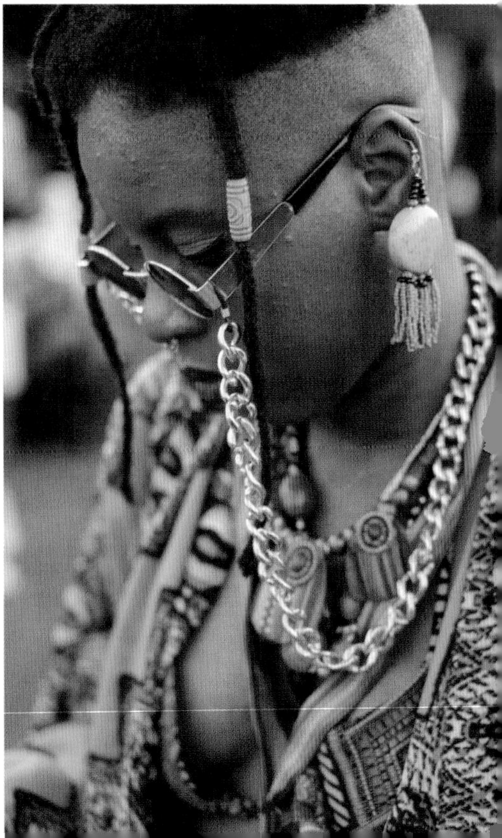

228 Say it loud, I'm Black and I'm proud

◀ UK Black Pride, London, England

When to go: August
Best for: Live performances

Europe's largest celebration for African, Asian, Middle Eastern, Latin American, and Caribbean-heritage LGBTQ+ people, UK Black Pride is a visible and inclusive event, as much about creating a community as fun. Singers, dancers, and poets give inspiration from the stage, while well-being–focused workshops, community stalls, and food and drink areas give nurture in a different form.

229 Out of the margins and into the spotlight

Queer Britain, London, England

When to go: All year
Best for: Queer history

Based in London's fashionable new development Granary Square, Queer Britain is the UK's first national museum dedicated to LGBTQ+ culture. With books, photos, and artifacts, it is making sure that the stories of the LGBTQ+ people and events that have impacted British culture are not left in the margins of the history books.

230 All things trans

Museum of Transology, London, England

When to go: All year
Best for: Celebrating trans lives

Packers, binders, hormones, stuffed toys, and protest placards are among the hundreds of items which comprise the Museum of Transology (MoT). Founded by E-J Scott in 2014, with the intention of preserving trans history, the MoT is one of the world's most significant collections representing trans, non-binary, and intersex lives. You don't want to miss the piece that started it all—E-J's very own breast tissue, from their top surgery, floating in alcohol-filled jars.

231 Tell me what's the word?

Gay's The Word, London, England

When to go: All year
Best for: Bookworms

Beloved as one of London's long-standing gems, Gay's The Word bookstore has a devoted and loyal following for whom it is more than a mere store—it's a refuge. In 1984, it became a meeting place for a group called Lesbians and Gays Support the Miners. The story of this small band of activists who raised money for pit-workers involved in the miners' strike of the 1980s made it onto the big screen in the acclaimed 2014 movie, *Pride*.

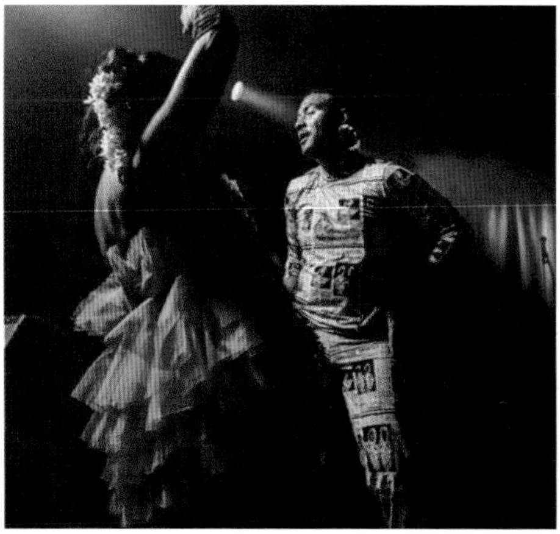

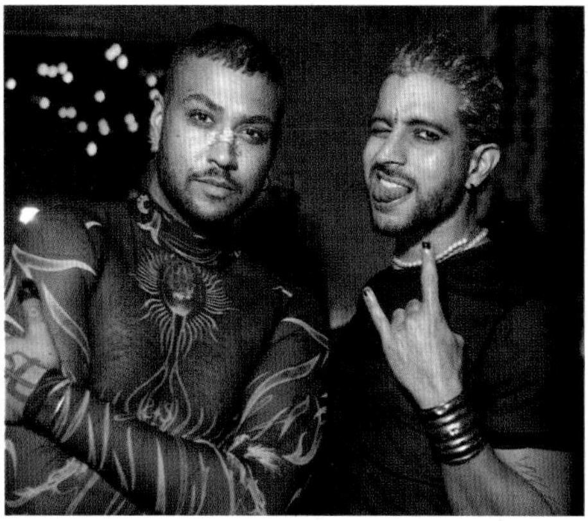

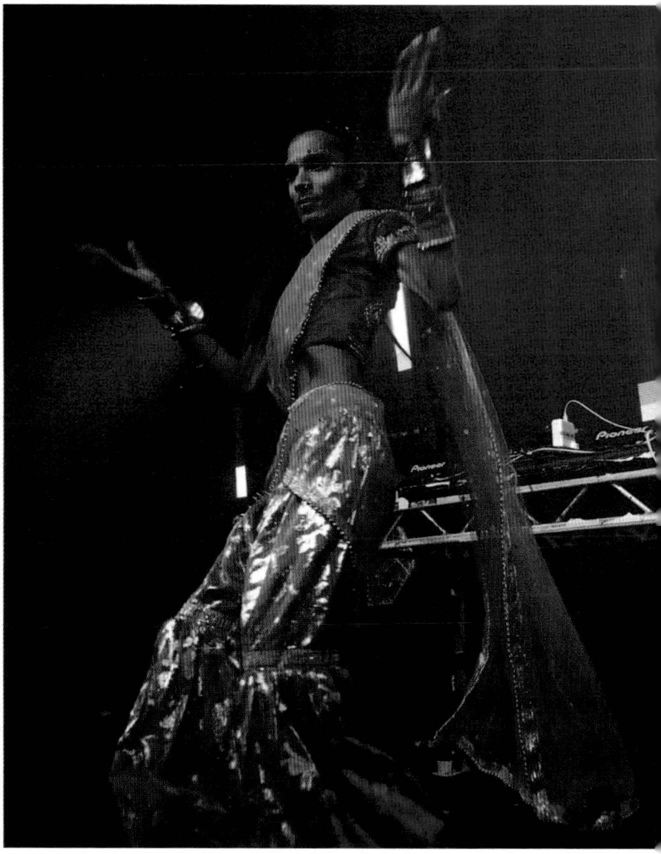

232 Bollywood nights

▲ Hungama, London, England

When to go: All year
Best for: South Asian art and club nights

Hungama is London's answer to queer Bollywood entertainment. Founded and hosted by Ryan Lanji, who is a DJ, curator, and producer, Hungama is not just a party, it's a movement that shines a light on sexuality in the South Asian community. Hungama hosts events throughout the year and while the South Asian community is at the forefront of the movement, everyone is welcome to the party.

233 Out for an ugly duck

▶ Ugly Duck, London, England

When to go: All year
Best for: Contemporary art shows

Ugly Duck is one of London's hidden gems. Tucked away near London Bridge, this venue is run by queer people who are challenging social issues and amplifying marginalized voices. This unique space hosts regular art exhibitions, artist residencies, and dreamy installations that are truly magical and should not be missed.

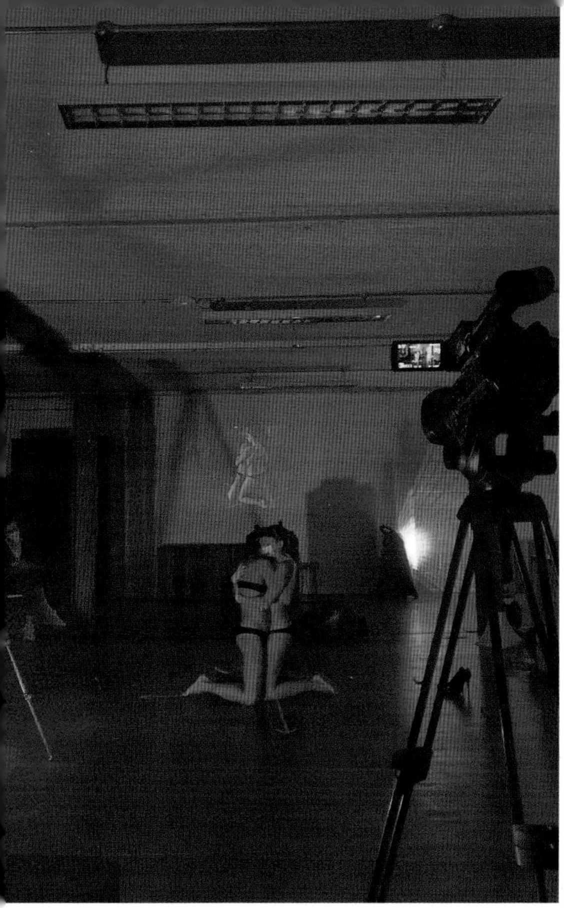
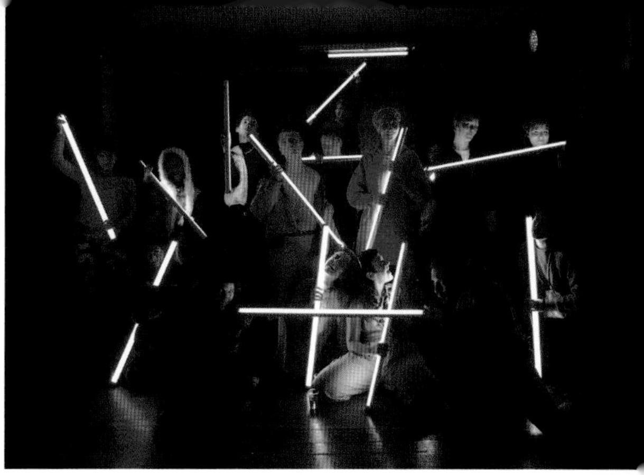
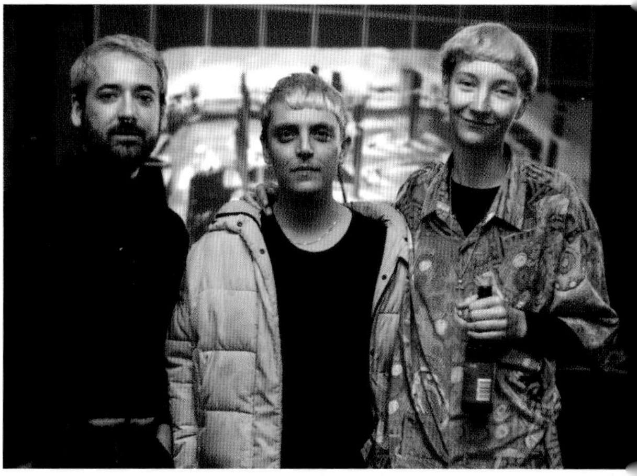
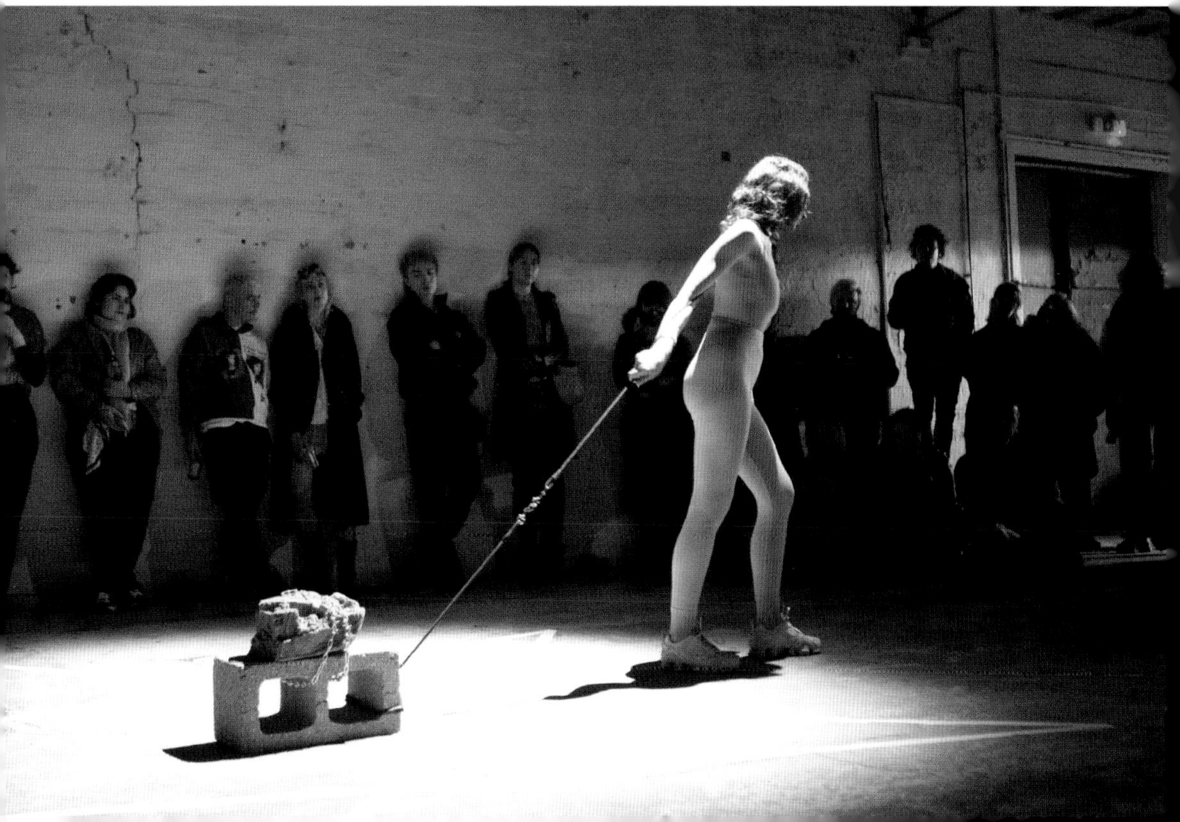

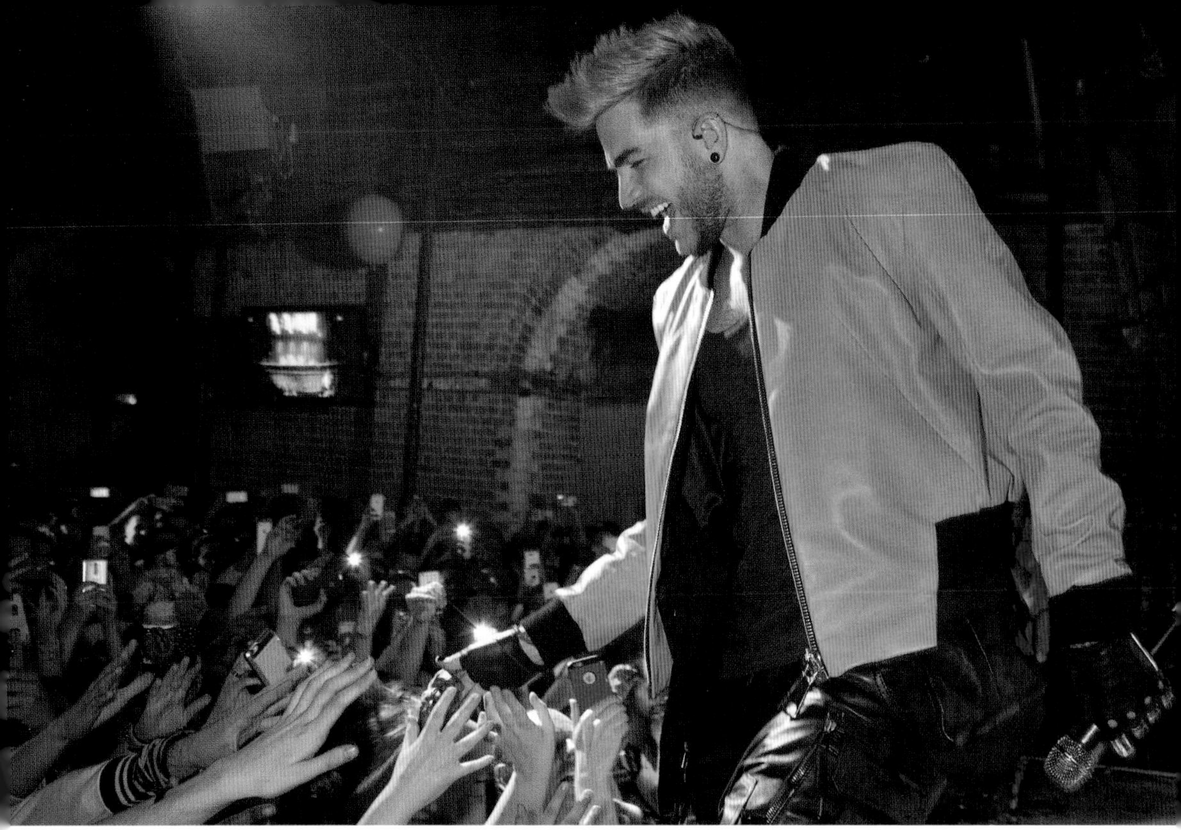

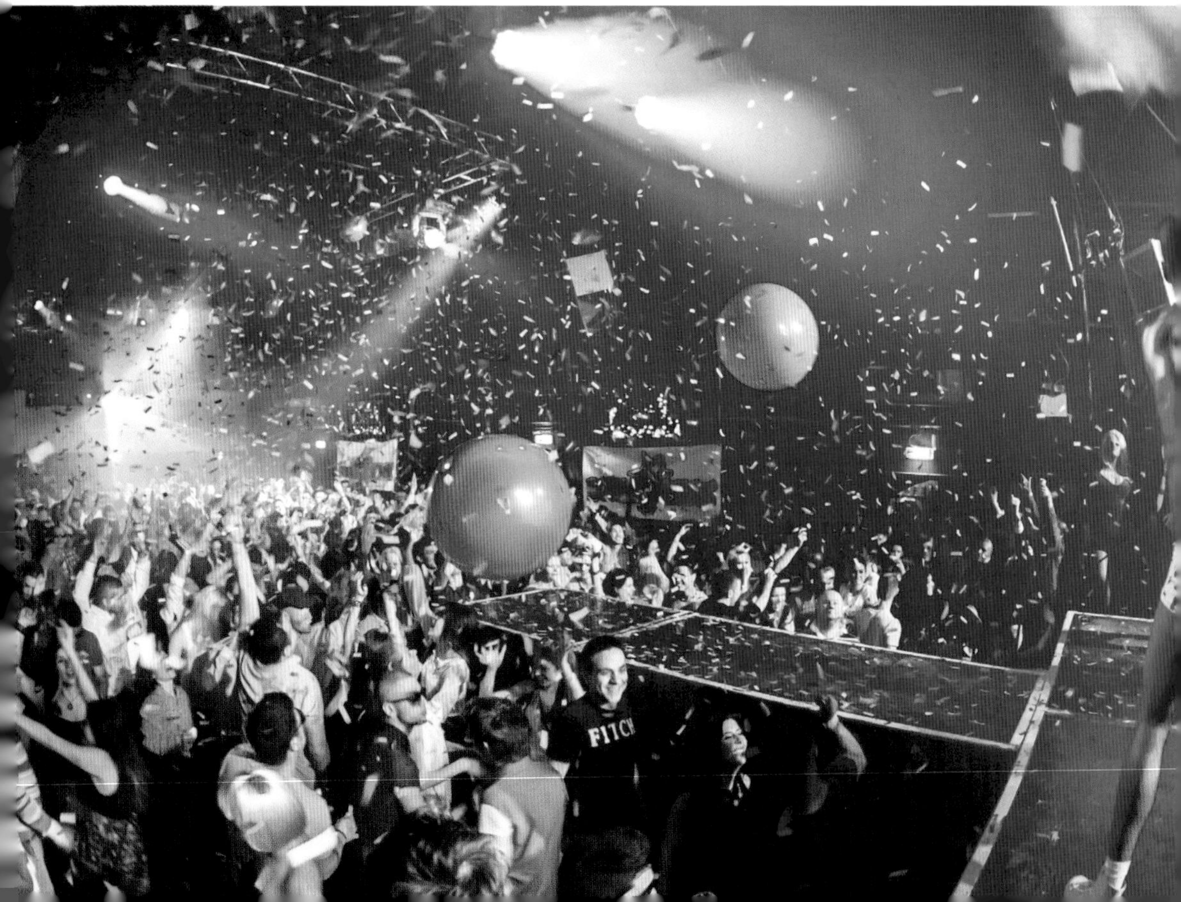

234 Heaven is a place on earth

◀ Heaven, London, England

When to go: All year
Best for: Big name personal appearances

Buried in two big railway arches beneath Charing Cross station, Heaven nightclub first threw open its doors in 1979. It instantly became the biggest and most brazen gay nightclub in London, as well as a 1980s breeding ground for hi-NRG and acid house. Heaven has remained gay London's most famous club for over four decades. Long-running Monday nighter Popcorn pulls in a young, mixed crowd heavy with students, while Friday nighter Camp Attack plays shameless camp classics. The signature G-A-Y night each Saturday is known for its high-profile special guests. Lady Gaga, One Direction, and Kylie Minogue are among the many to have thrilled audiences.

235 Spruce it up

▶ Open Barbers, London, England

When to go: All year
Best for: Affirming queer haircuts

Open Barbers is a hairdressing salon that welcomes people of all genders, sexualities, hair types, and lengths. Drop by for a fresh queer cut or dye, and make yourself at home with a cup of tea in their zine library. All of their hair services operate on a pay-what-you-can sliding scale and, in the back, they have a dedicated room for massage and therapy.

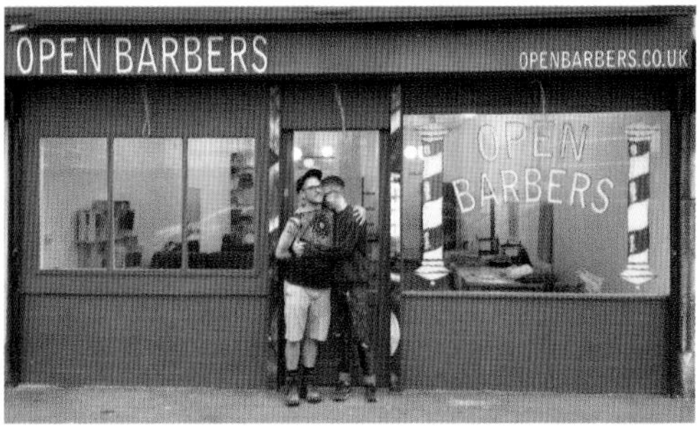

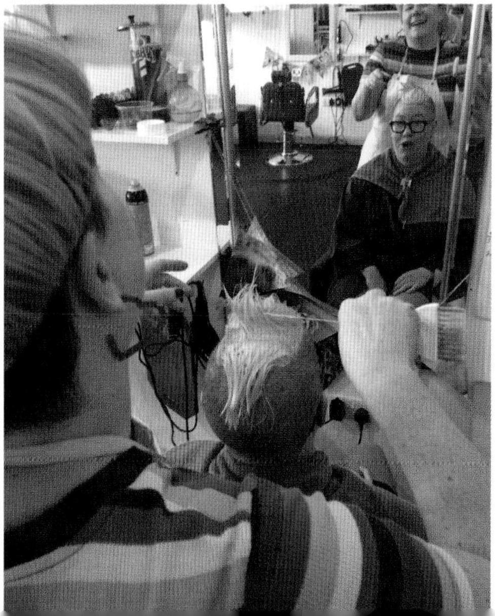

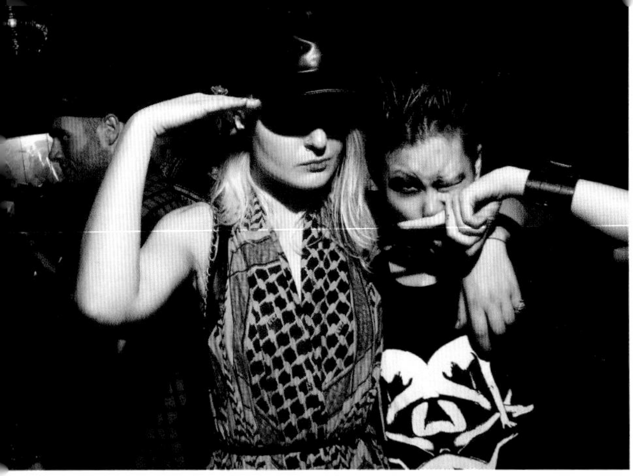

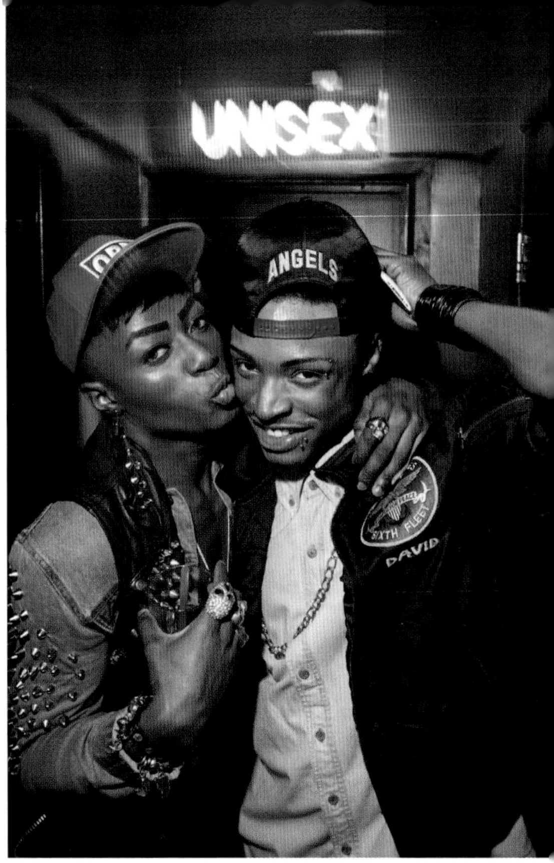

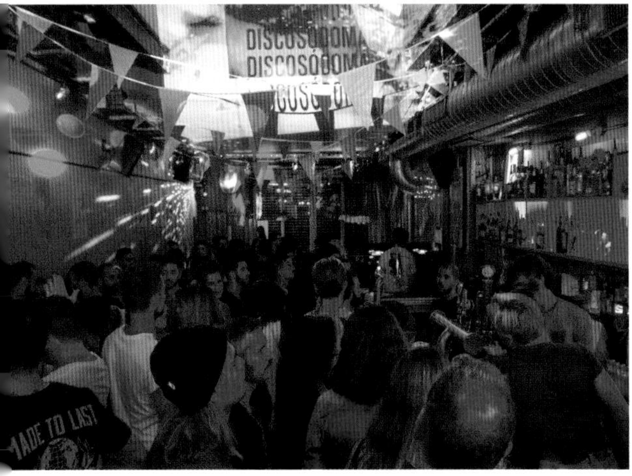

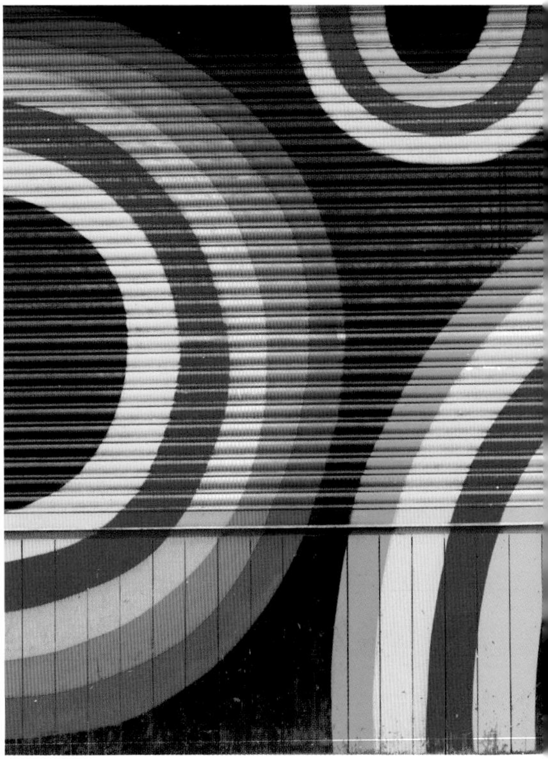

236 All day, and all of the night

▲ ▶ Dalston Superstore, London, England

When to go: All year
Best for: Feeling safe from brunch 'til dawn

Dalston Superstore is, to many, the ultimate underground queer space. It hosts events for everyone in the community, including unique occasions exclusive to trans people. It is not only a nightclub but a space to enjoy throughout the day, too. Enjoy drag brunches, daytime work spaces, or casual afternoon drinks. Stay all day and party all night.

237 She's so special

▼ SheSoho, London, England

When to go: All year
Best for: Queer women and non-binary folk

SheSoho is located in the heart of London's LGBTQ+ neighborhood and is a long-standing solo, permanent queer venue for women in the city. SheSoho has a unique bunker-style setting and not only hosts club nights, but also offers quiz nights, comedy, and cabaret. The array of queer events is enhanced by fabulous female or non-binary DJ's and stunning drag kings.

238 Find your batty buddy

Batty Mama, London, England

When to go: All year
Best for: Finding a place to belong

Batty Mama holds dynamic events around London that showcase the talents of People of Color and Black queer, trans and non-binary artists in an open and inviting way. There's everything from DJ events to movie nights and cabaret. "Batty Buddies," who are on-site to give hugs, reassurance, or support, really emphasize the safe space.

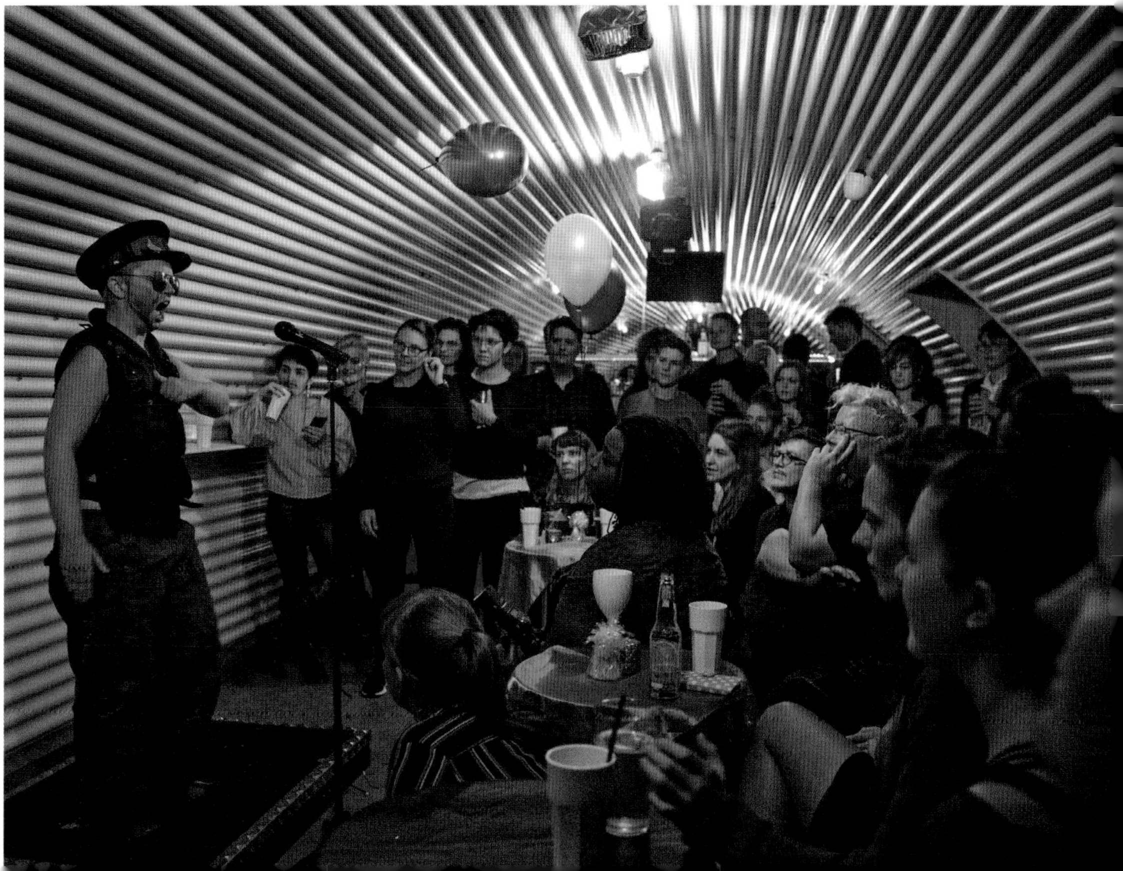

239 Northern pride

Manchester Pride, England

When to go: August
Best for: *Queer As Folk*–realness

After London and Brighton, the annual Manchester Pride is one of the biggest Pride gatherings in the UK. The festivities run over the extended, public-holiday weekend at the end of August. The parade heads through the city center, absorbing some of this northern city's former industrial heritage as well as its vibrant, newer quarters, while the city's gay village—Canal Street—hosts numerous stages for big-name acts as well as smaller performances, markets, and parties throughout its thronged streets.

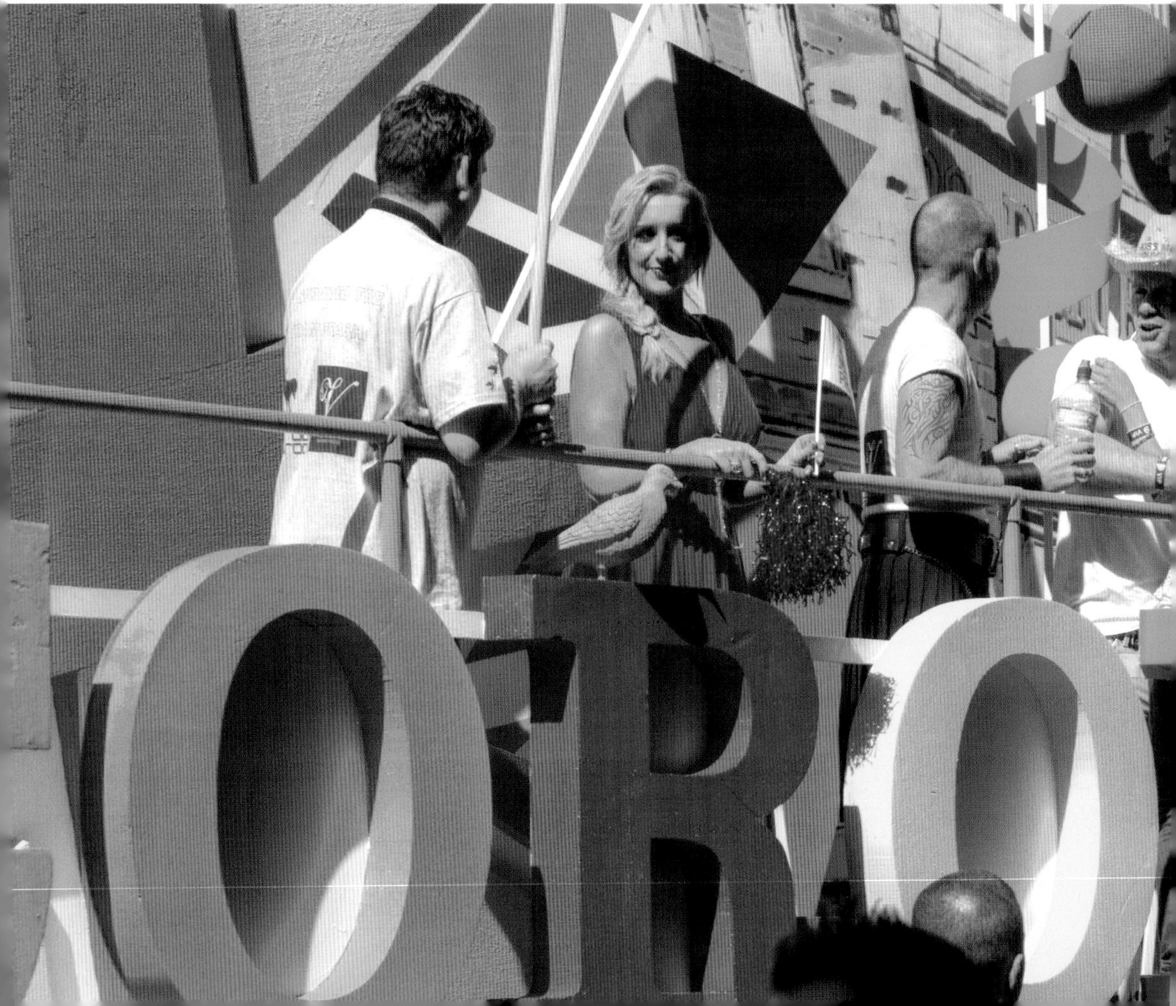

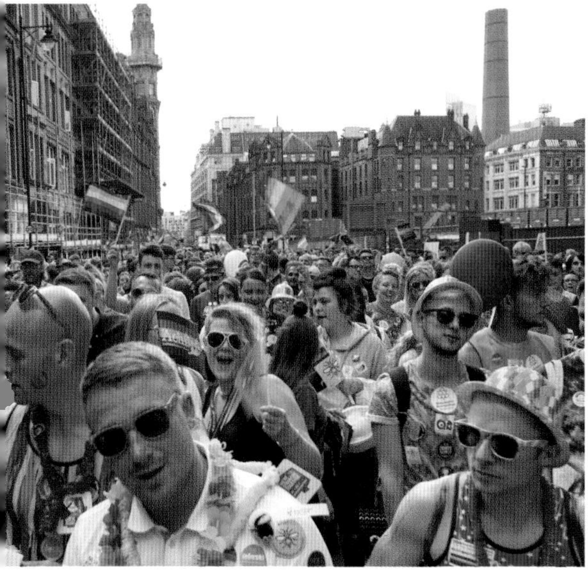

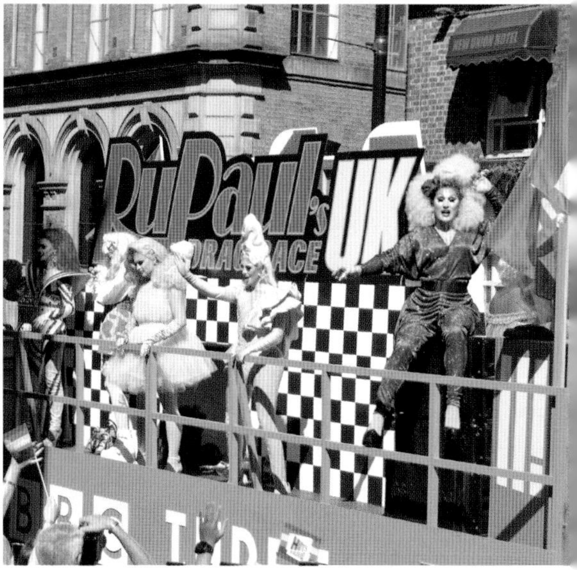
RuPaul's
DRAG RACE
UK

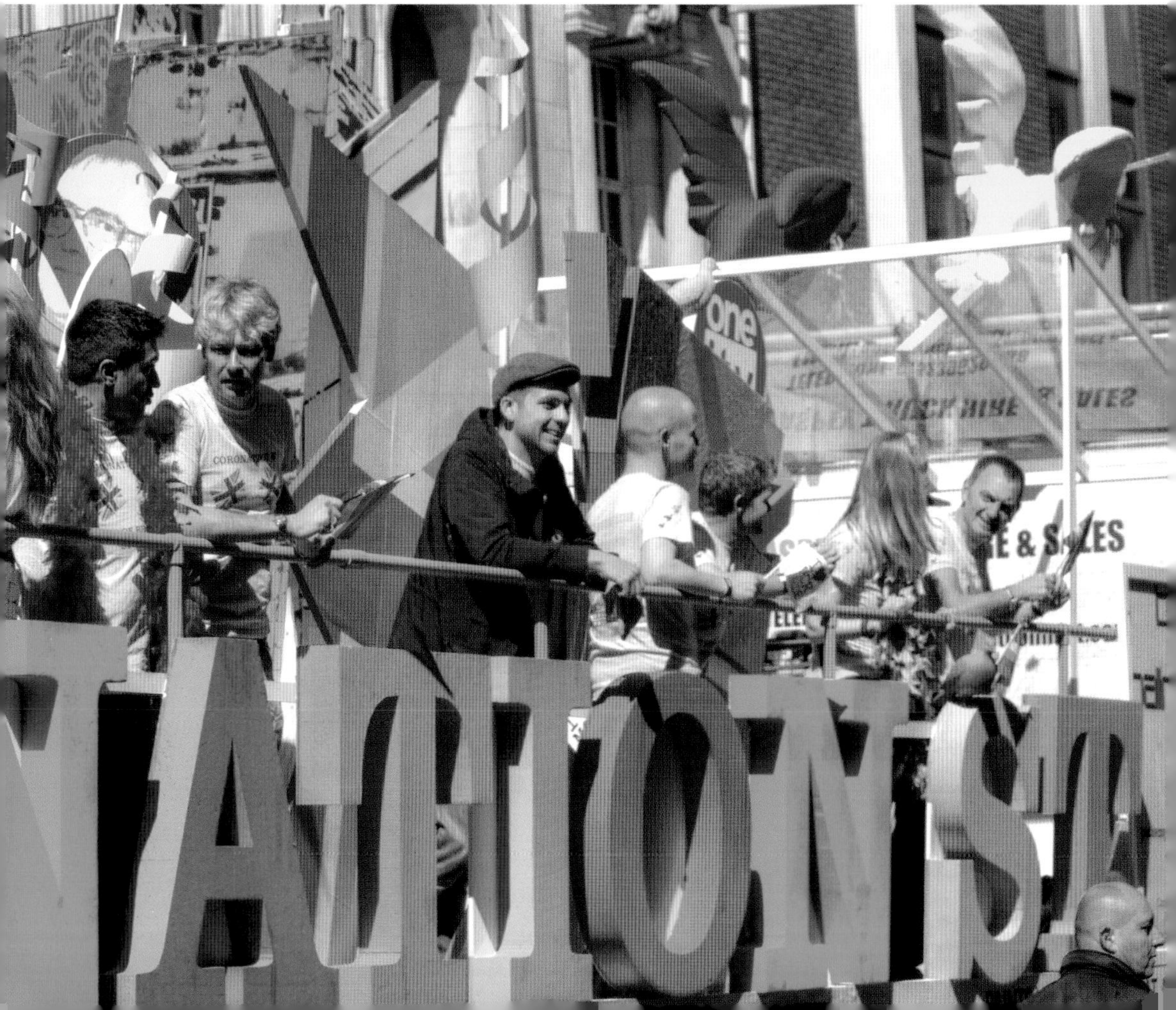

240 Break the code

Alan Turing Memorial, Manchester, England

When to go: All year
Best for: Remembering how far we've come

Alan Turing was a maths genius who played a key role in cracking the German Enigma code during World War II, and was also a pioneer in the field of modern computing. Despite these achievements, in 1952 he was arrested as a gay man and charged with gross indecency in 1952. He died by suicide two years later. Turing spent the period before his death as a researcher at the University of Manchester. A statue in his honor, by sculptor Glyn Hughes, stands in the city's Sackville Park, near the gay village.

241 Inside, outside, canal-side

▶ Canal Street, Manchester, England

When to go: All year
Best for: Northern England's exceptional hospitality

Outside of London, Canal Sreet, situated by the lovely Rochdale Canal, is known as the UK's LGBTQ+ center. There is a village-like community here with pubs, clubs, cafés, restaurants, and pop-ups that are all owned by and welcome LGBTQ+ people. These include Bar Pop, New York New York, and Manchester's leading lesbian bar, Vanilla.

242 Glitter, glow, and sparkle

Sparkle Weekend and Sparkle Bar, Manchester, England

When to go: July
Best for: Family fun

The Sparkle Weekend is a festival set up by the UK's volunteer-led, national transgender charity Sparkle. The weekender is held every year in Manchester's Gay Village and attracts a huge crowd to celebrate gender diversity. They also advocate and campaign for the rights of transgender women, transgender men, non-binary people, those with disabilities, and those from Black, Asian, and minority ethnic communities.

243 Any flavor you like, as long as its vanilla

Vanilla Bar, Manchester, England

When to go: All year
Best for: Meeting locals and partying

In the heart of Manchester's Gay Village is the award-winning lesbian bar Vanilla. Filled with contemporary photographic art decor, it has twice been voted as the best bar by DIVA magazine and is the destination of the north for the lesbian community. With the lack of queer-women spaces in the United Kingdom, Vanilla Bar has become iconic. Located just around the corner from Canal Street, it offers a good night out during the week and epic parties at the weekend.

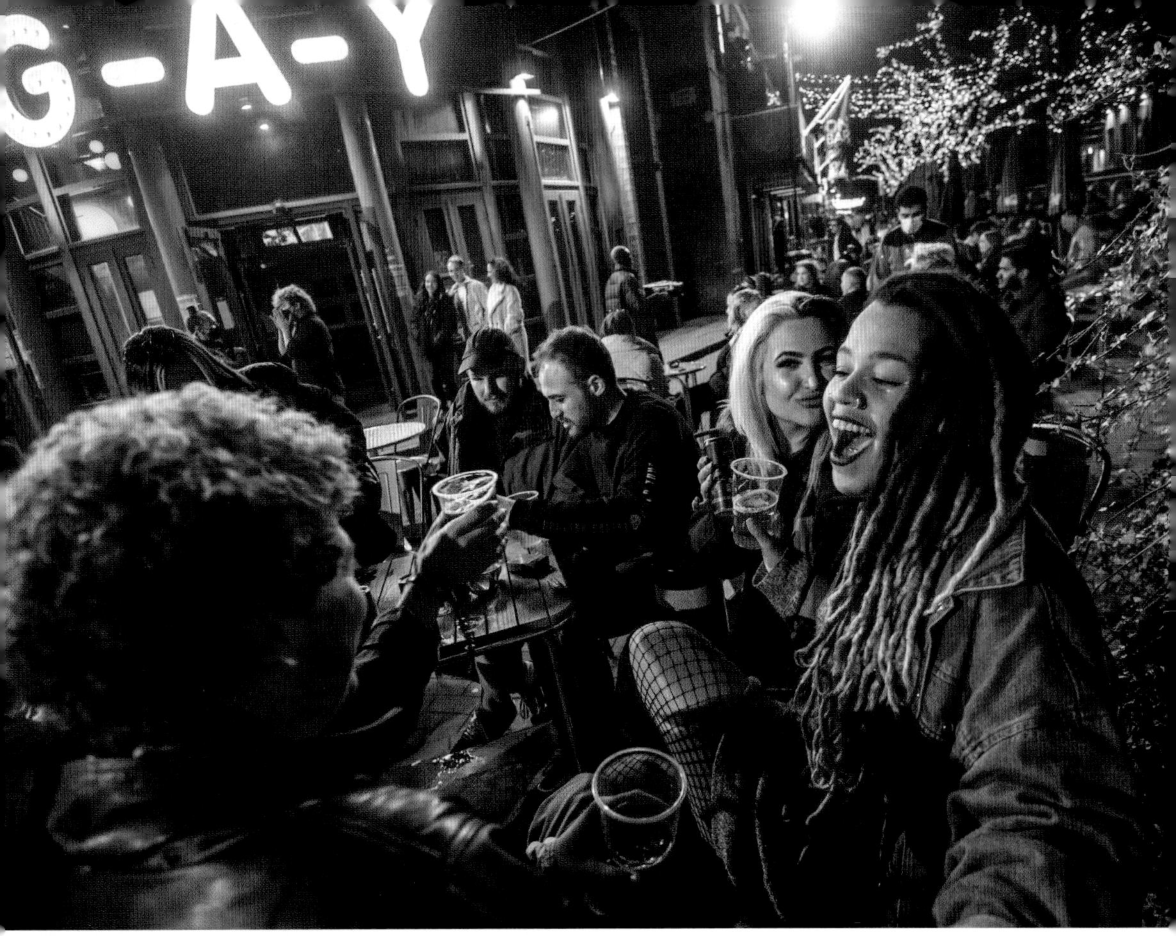
G-A-Y

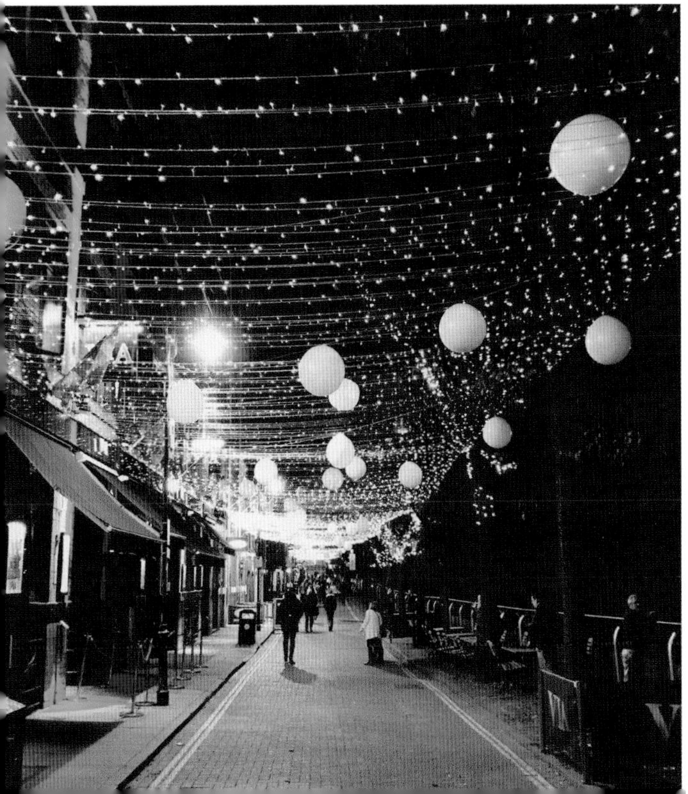

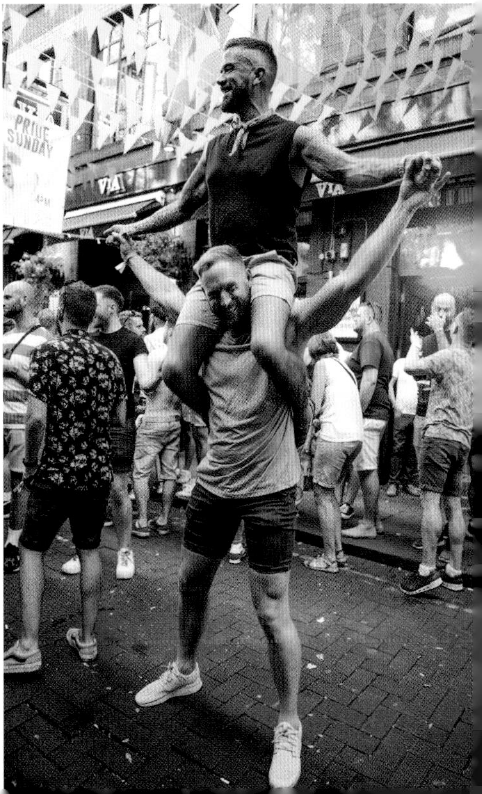
PRIDE
SUNDAY
VIA

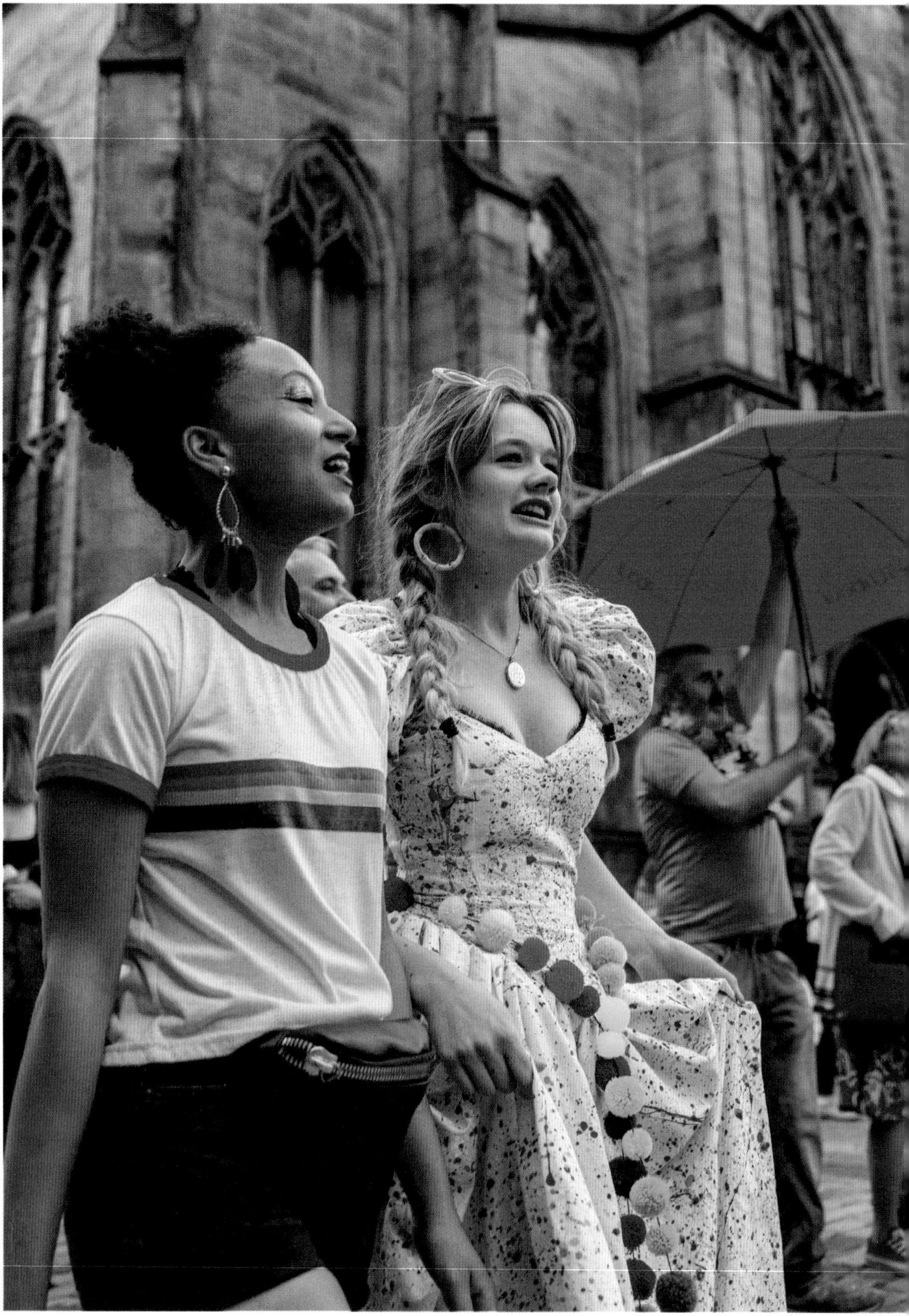

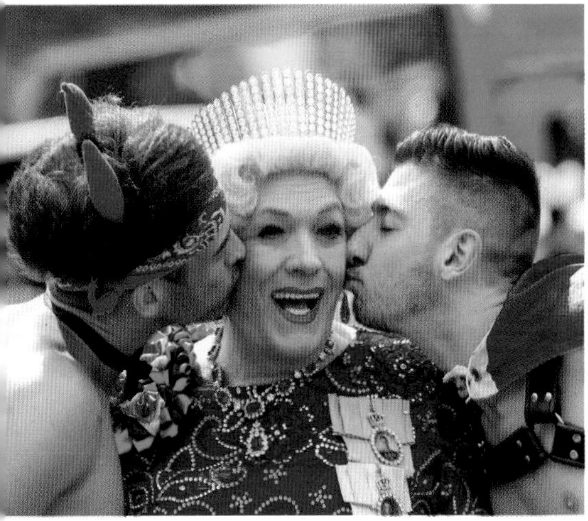

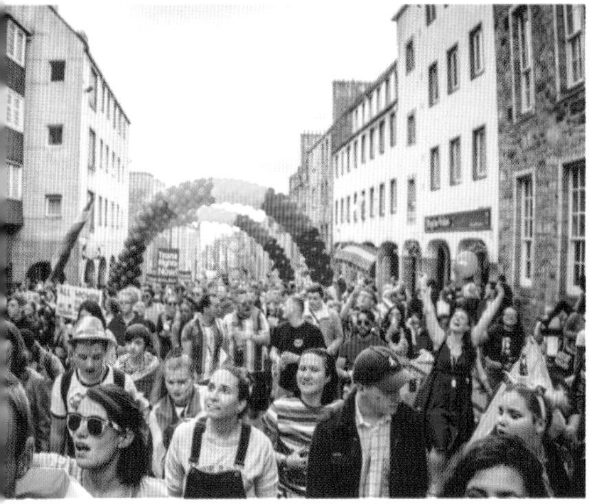

244 Party in pink

◀ Edinburgh Pride, Scotland

When to go: June
Best for: Shenanigans with charm

The people of Edinburgh are famous for loving a party and there is no exception for Scotland's biggest LGBTQ+ event. Expect the usual Pride parade shenanigans but with even higher energy and Scottish charm. The main action takes place around the "Pink Triangle," with many of the city's queer bars also hosting special Pride events.

245 Three corners

Pink Triangle, Edinburgh, Scotland

When to go: All year
Best for: Bar-hopping

Sing, dance, watch drag-performance acts, sip cocktails, nurse a pint. There is something for everyone in Edinburgh's "Pink Triangle," the LGBTQ+ area of the city around Leith Walk. With everything so close together, you can find exactly what you're looking for—or try them all.

246 Blooming marvelous

C.C. Blooms, Edinburgh, Scotland

When to go: All year
Best for: Local cuisine and gay culture

C.C. Blooms is Edinburgh's oldest gay bar. Launched in1994 and named after Bette Midler's character in the film *Beaches*, this historical bar is spread over two levels. It promises an unpretentious time with good vibes and a great list of drinks and food.

247 Drink in the history

▶ Waterloo Bar, Glasgow, Scotland

When to go: All year
Best for: Unpretentious hospitality

Just a stone's throw from Glasgow Central Station, this distinctive, purple-painted corner hostelry is regarded as Scotland's oldest gay pub. The venue dates back to Victorian times, and it's been welcoming gay drinkers since the early 1970s. The feel of the place is traditional, with a wood-paneled bar and stained-glass windows. Sedate earlier in the day, regular entertainment always ensures more of a party atmosphere in the evenings, especially at weekends.

248 And the category is . . .

Category is Books, Glasgow, Scotland

When to go: All year
Best for: Zine and badge collecting

You will find the cutest queer gifts at this fiercely independent bookshop in Glasgow's Southside area. Stocking comics, zines, cards, enamels, stickers, and (loads of) badges alongside new and secondhand books, this DIY gender-queer space has you covered. Don't forget to ask about local queer happenings and where you can catch the next Trigger Drag event.

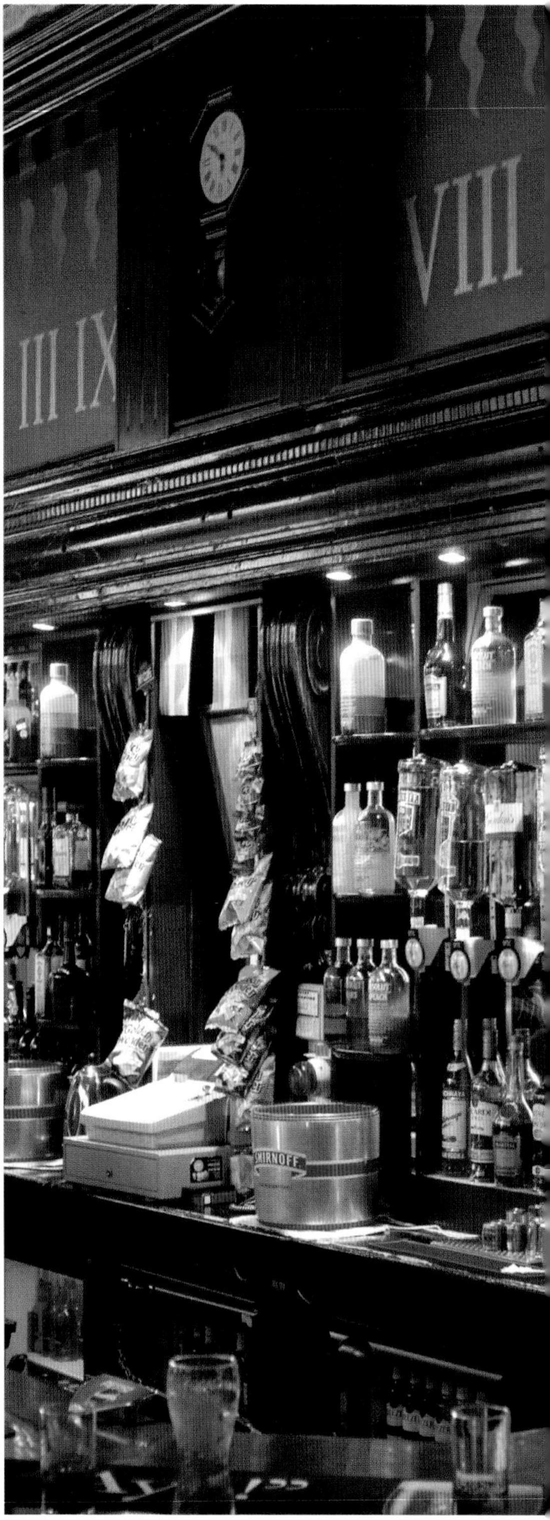

249 What Katie did next...

▶ Merchant City, Glasgow, Scotland

When to go: All year
Best for: Fun nights out

Merchant City is the hub of LGBTQ+ nightlife in Glasgow. Delmonica's has been providing nightly entertainment in the form of drag acts, games' nights, quizzes, and dancing since 1991, while relative newcomer Katie's Bar opened in 2013 and offers fun-filled, energetic, and vibrant nights. Think Bender Bingo hosted by drag artists, DJ themed-evenings, and karaoke late nights. Katie's has a loyal customer base that brings a relaxed and friendly atmosphere.

250 Stride with pride

Glasgow Women's Library, Glasgow, Scotland

When to go: All year
Best for: All things women

This whole library is dedicated to women's lives, histories, and achievements. But it's not just about coming here to find a book: there are courses for women, projects that delve deeper into the material held at the library, the UK's lesbian archive, and even maps such as *Stride with Pride*, which has used the archive material to create a walking route around sites significant to Glasgow's LGBTQ+ heritage and history.

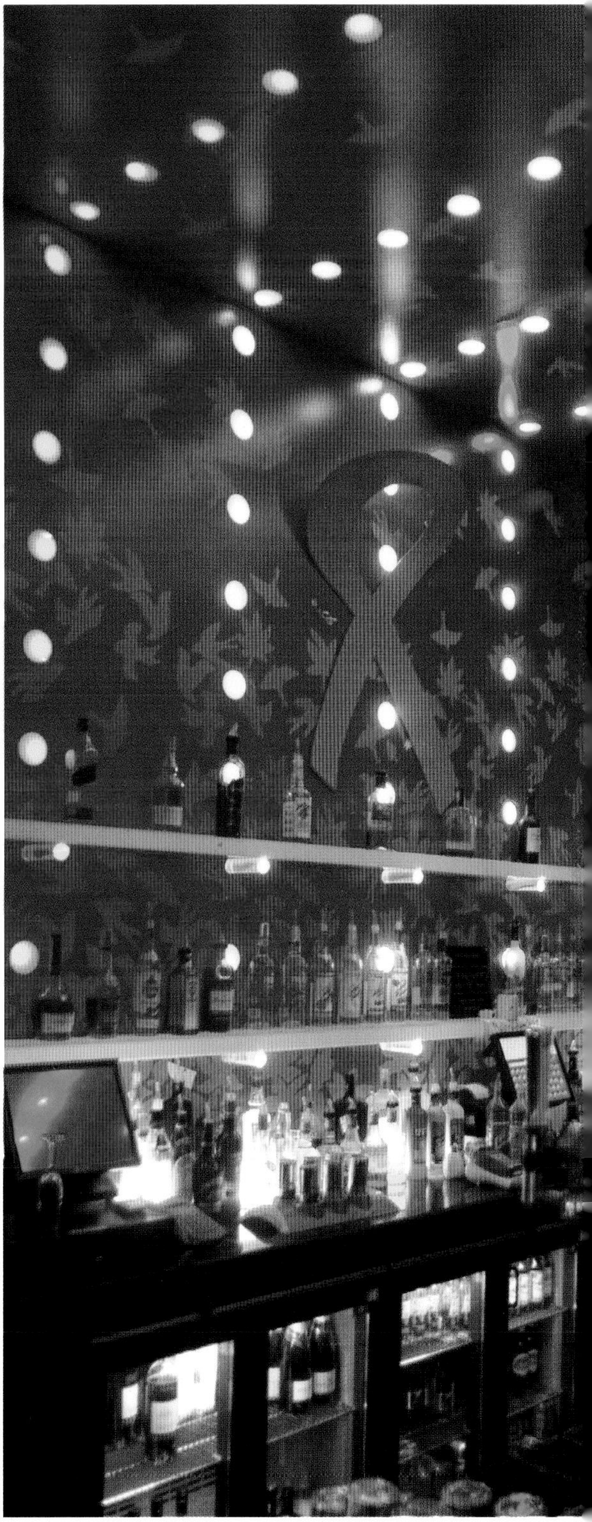

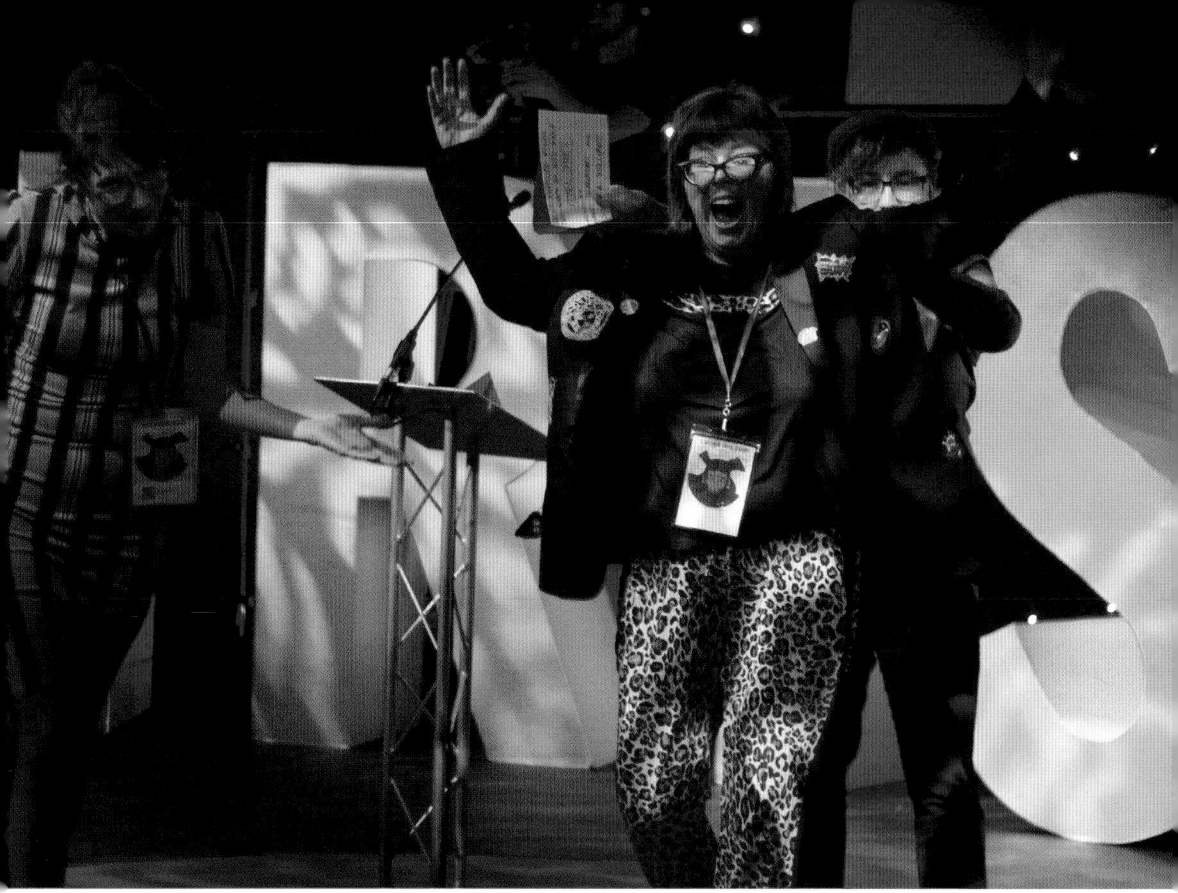

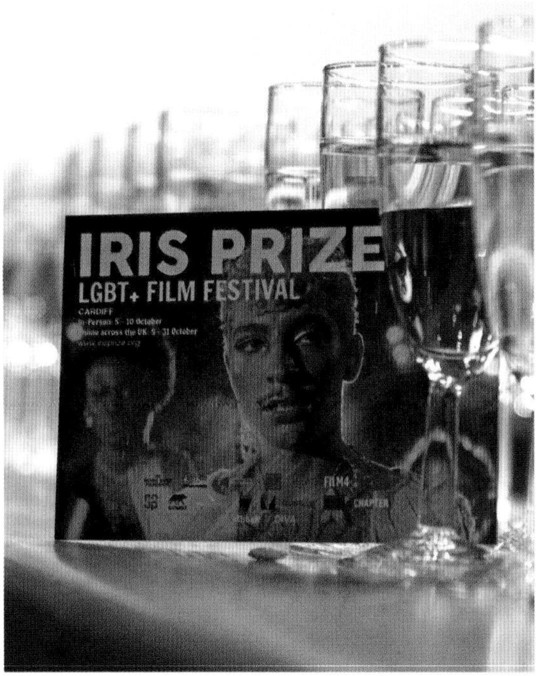

251 The Iris Prize

◀ ▲ Cardiff, Wales

When to go: October
Best for: Culture lovers

Welsh capital Cardiff is famed for its castle, shopping arcades, Bute Park, and the queer-oriented Iris Prize film festival. What makes this movie extravaganza different from other international LGBTQ+ film festivals is the fact it's dedicated to short films. First launched in 2007, the festival culminates with one bite-sized offering walking away with the coveted Iris Prize. This includes a cash injection to help fund the winning filmmaker's next project.

252 Written in black and white and rainbows

▼ Shelf Life Books and Zines, Cardiff, Wales

When to go: All year
Best for: Books and zines

A unique, not-for-profit, radical bookshop in Cardiff, Shelf Life Books and Zines brings together independent publishers and DIY-zine-makers in a space that amplifies marginalized and underrepresented voices. It is a thought-provoking shop full of undiscovered gems and irresistible book titles to purchase.

253 King of the Welsh frontier

The Kings, Cardiff, Wales

When to go: All year
Best for: Gay night out with locals

The Kings is Cardiff's busiest gay bar. Open all week long, the venue is spread over two floors, with a fireplace and a roof terrace. It is a bar that attracts a mix of queer crowds. If you want to feel immersed in Cardiff's gay scene, visit at the weekend to mingle with locals.

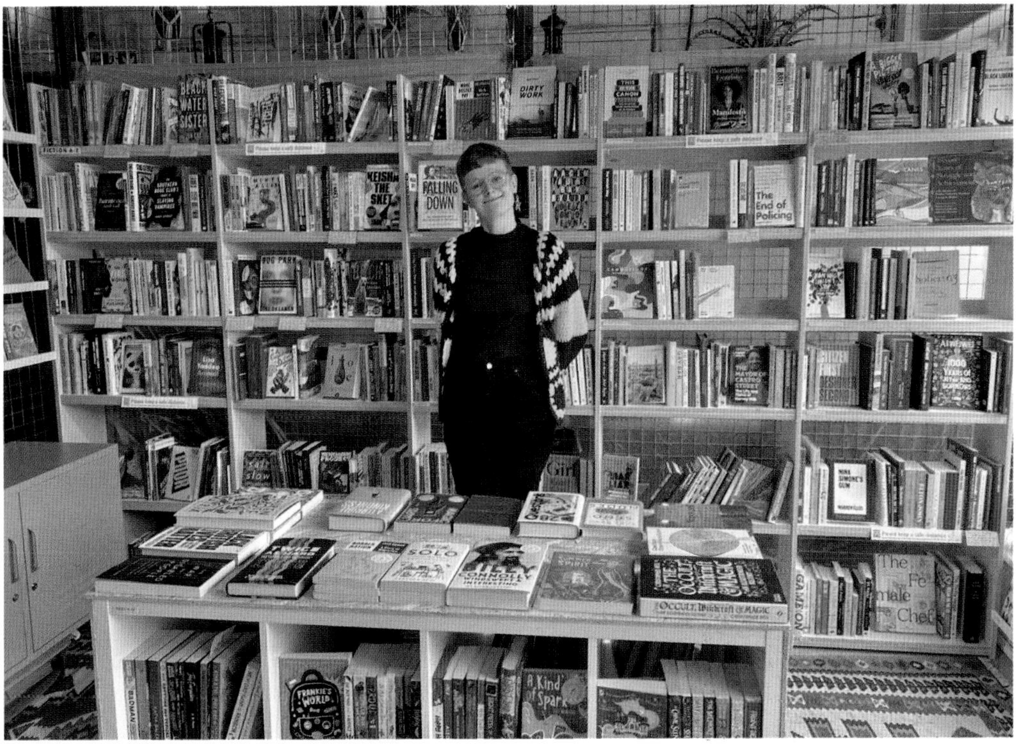

254 Best foot forward

The Boots, Antwerp, Belgium

When to go: All year
Best for: Leather lovers

Gay men looking to hook up in Antwerp, Belgium will often mention one specific LGBTQ+ haunt: The Boots. As its name suggests, this long-running, old-school leather club, which dates back to the early 1980s, is for those who enjoy the kink and fetish side of queer clubbing. Expect plenty of low-lighting, black walls, lingering glances, and atmospheric electro beats at one of the louchest clubs in Europe. The venue enforces a strict dress code at the door.

255 Chips and pride

▶ Antwerp Pride, Belgium

When to go: August
Best for: A fries-and-beer-fueled Pride

The vibrant and welcoming city of Antwerp is Belgium's second-biggest city, famous for being the diamond capital of the world. Each August it sparkles in a different way as Antwerp Pride comes to town. The city turns into a commemoration and celebration of LGBTQ+ culture for five days, with festivals, Pride nights, cultural events, and a spectacular parade. Pair the festivities with great food—especially Belgian fries—and Belgian craft beers.

256 Lez get this party started

L-week, Antwerp, Belgium

When to go: November
Best for: Connecting

Because gay men initially dominated the equal rights movement, lesbians established an annual Lesbian Day (L-Day) in Belgium in the 1980s. The event has grown from being one day long to ten days. L-week is a thriving festival where queer women and non-binary people come together to connect, have fun, and empower each other.

257 Here for it, queer for it

Het Roze Huis, Antwerp, Belgium

When to go: All year
Best for: Queer support

Pride parades are essential, but permanent and welcoming places for all LGBTQ+ people are even better; Het Roze Huis is such a place. It has been home to the queer community of Antwerp for over a quarter of a century. It hosts annual events such as L-week, as well as monthly board-game nights, community nights, and weekly support nights at queer Café Den Draak.

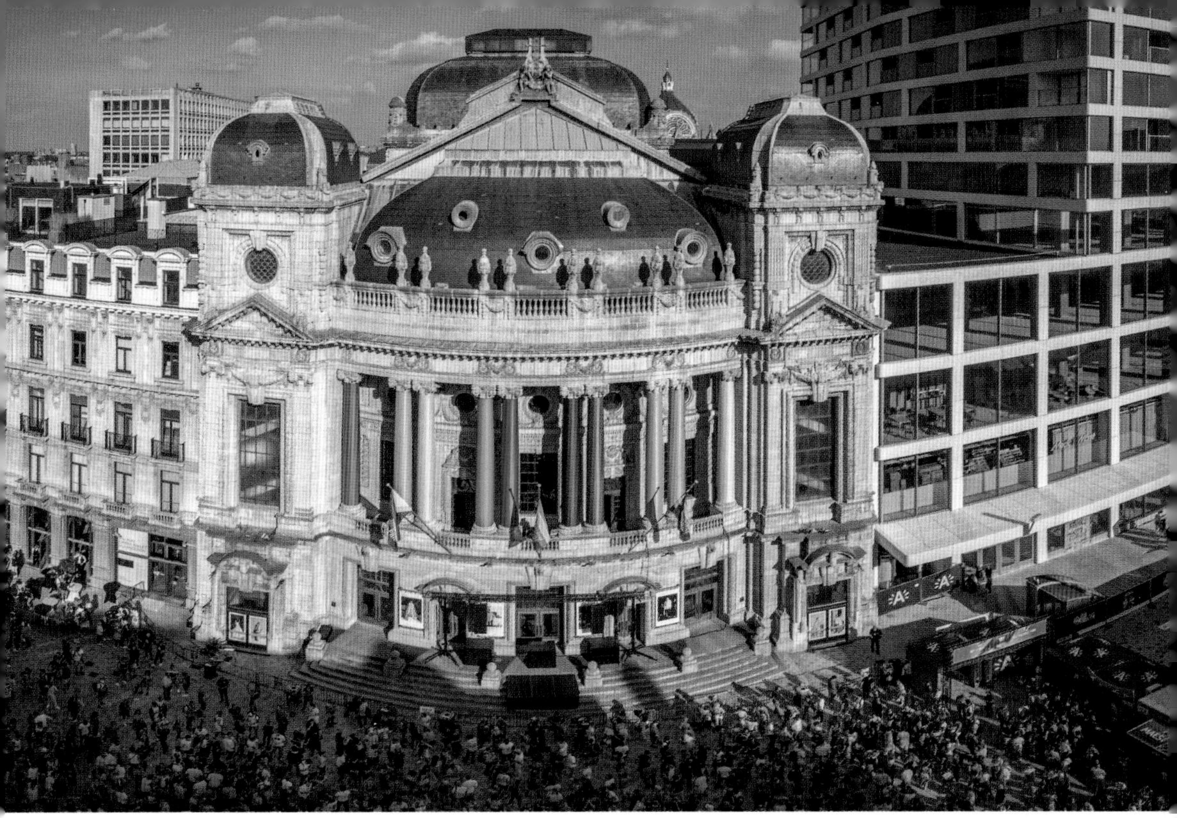

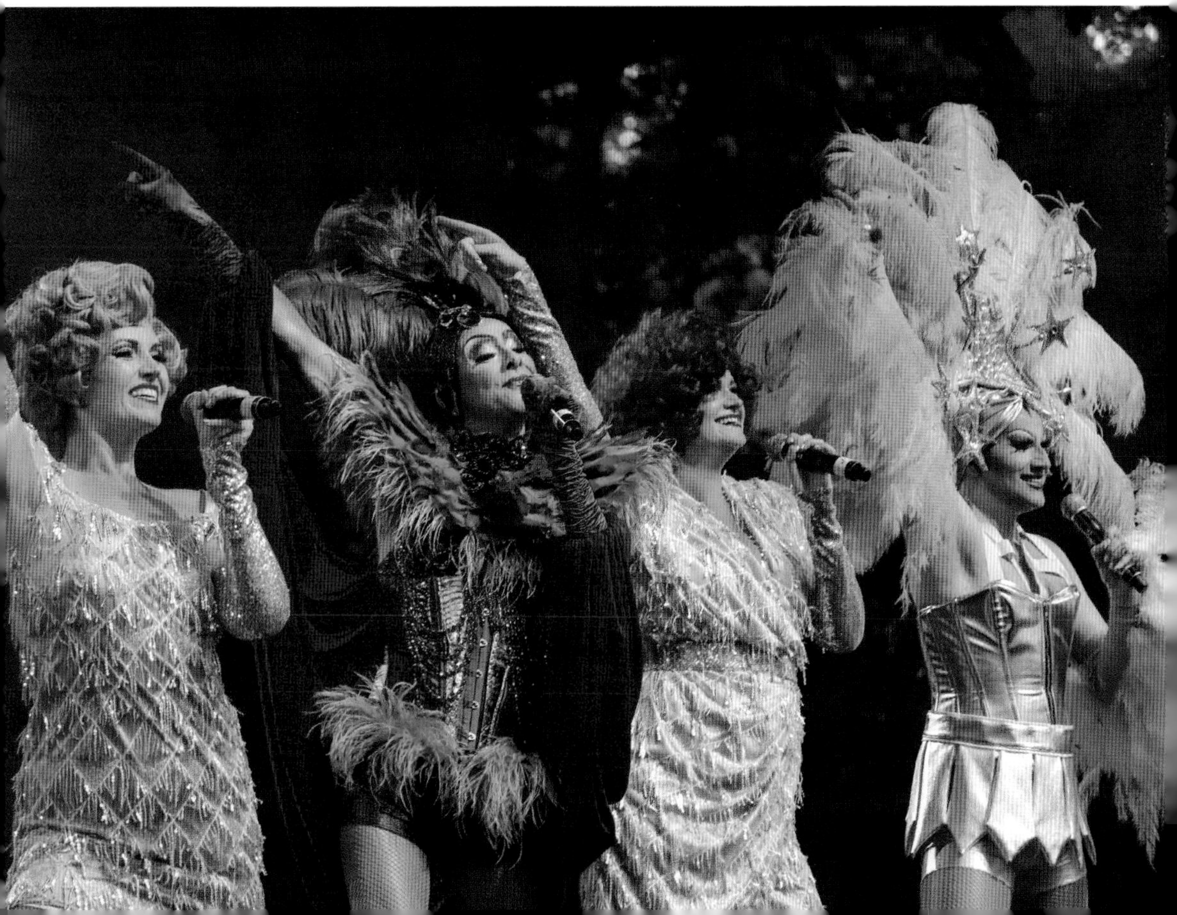

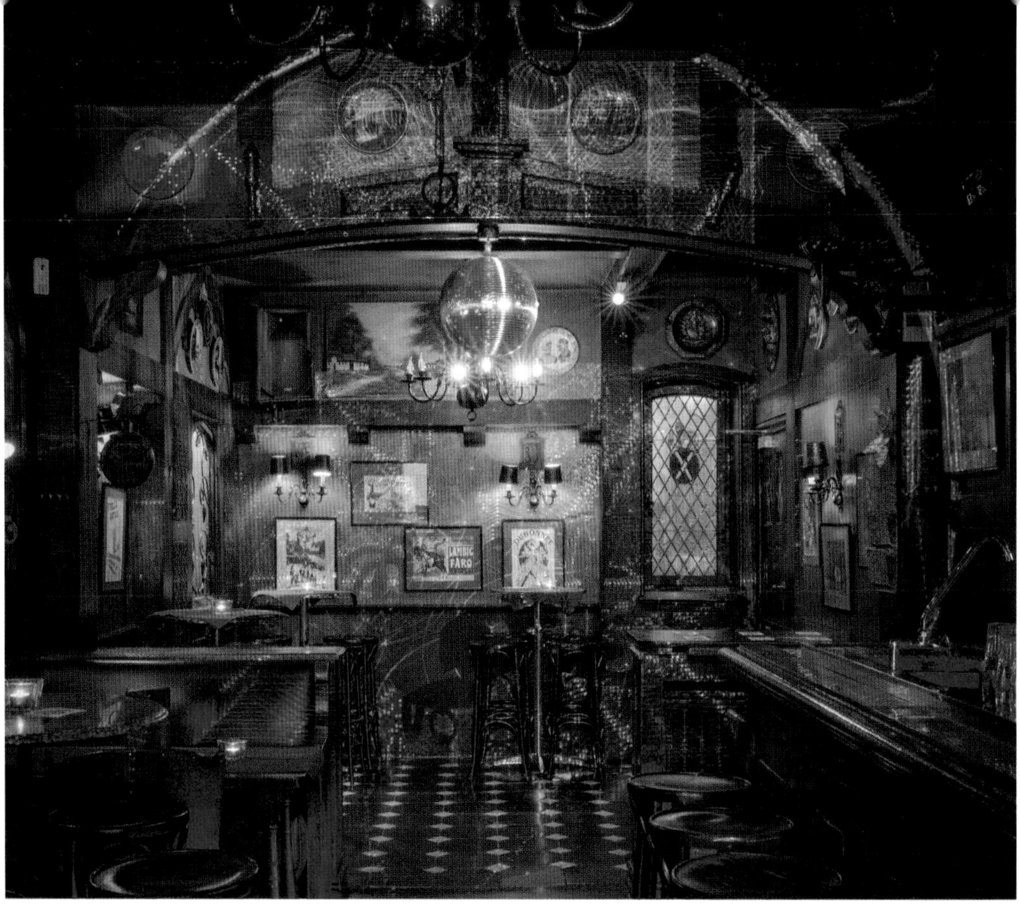

258 Do it by the book

Kartonnen Dozen, Antwerp, Belgium

When to go: All year
Best for: Representation in the written word

A stone's throw away from LGBTQ+ organization Het Roze Huis and queer Café Den Draak, you can find Belgium's only LGBTQ+ book and DVD store, Kartonnen Dozen. Don't be fooled by its small size; this shop offers an impressively extensive, intersectional collection—for all ages—of LGBTQ+ books (new and second hand), DVDs, magazines, and more.

259 Love and hoppiness

▲ La Reserve, Brussels, Belgium

When to go: All year
Best for: Beer

A short walk north of Rue du Marché au Charbon, you'll find Brussels' oldest gay bar, La Reserve. It's a small, old-fashioned brown café with an intimate atmosphere, a bunch of regulars, lots of dark-brown wood, and excellent Belgian beers. Its complete lack of "fabulousness" is all part of its charm.

260 The bustle of Brussels

▶ Quartier Saint-Jacques/Sint-Jacobswijk, Brussels, Belgium

When to go: All year
Best for: Queering around

Brussels might be the heart of EU bureaucracy, but the winding streets and eclectic businesses of Quartier Saint-Jacques—Sint-Jacobswijk in Flemish—have a very different heart. The area is famous for its queer nightlife and the unmissable bars, such as C'est ma Tournée, Le Fontainas, Dolores, and Le Belgica. All around the Rue du Marché au Charbon—Kolenmarkt—the sidewalks hum with LGBTQ+ venues.

261 Gay gals and non-binary pals

The Crazy Circle, Brussels, Belgium

When to go: All year
Best for: Open stage Wednesday nights

The Crazy Circle is a welcoming place for queer women, and trans and non-binary folks. Lesbian couple Laïla and Axelle transformed the small, former rum bar into a cozy, warm space, which is now well-known for its Wednesday night Femme Jam, empowering female and queer artists. Enjoy live music or an LGBTQ+ event with a cocktail, or get one of the solidarity beers and support LGBTQ+ organizations.

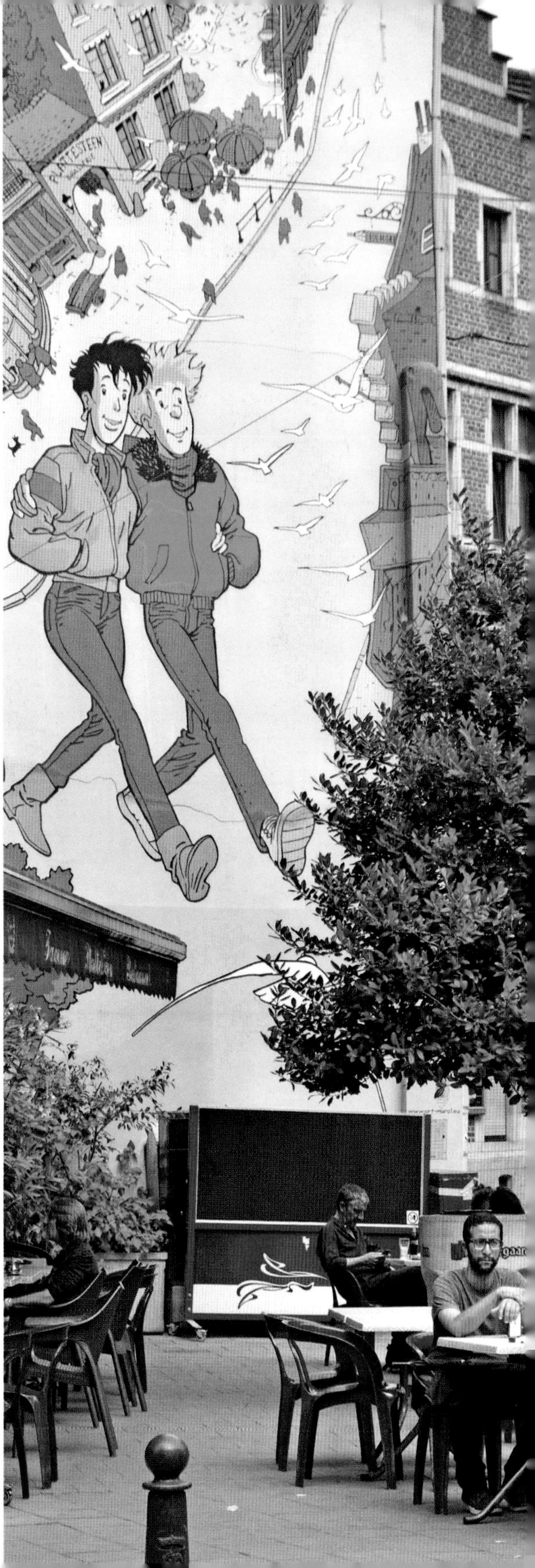

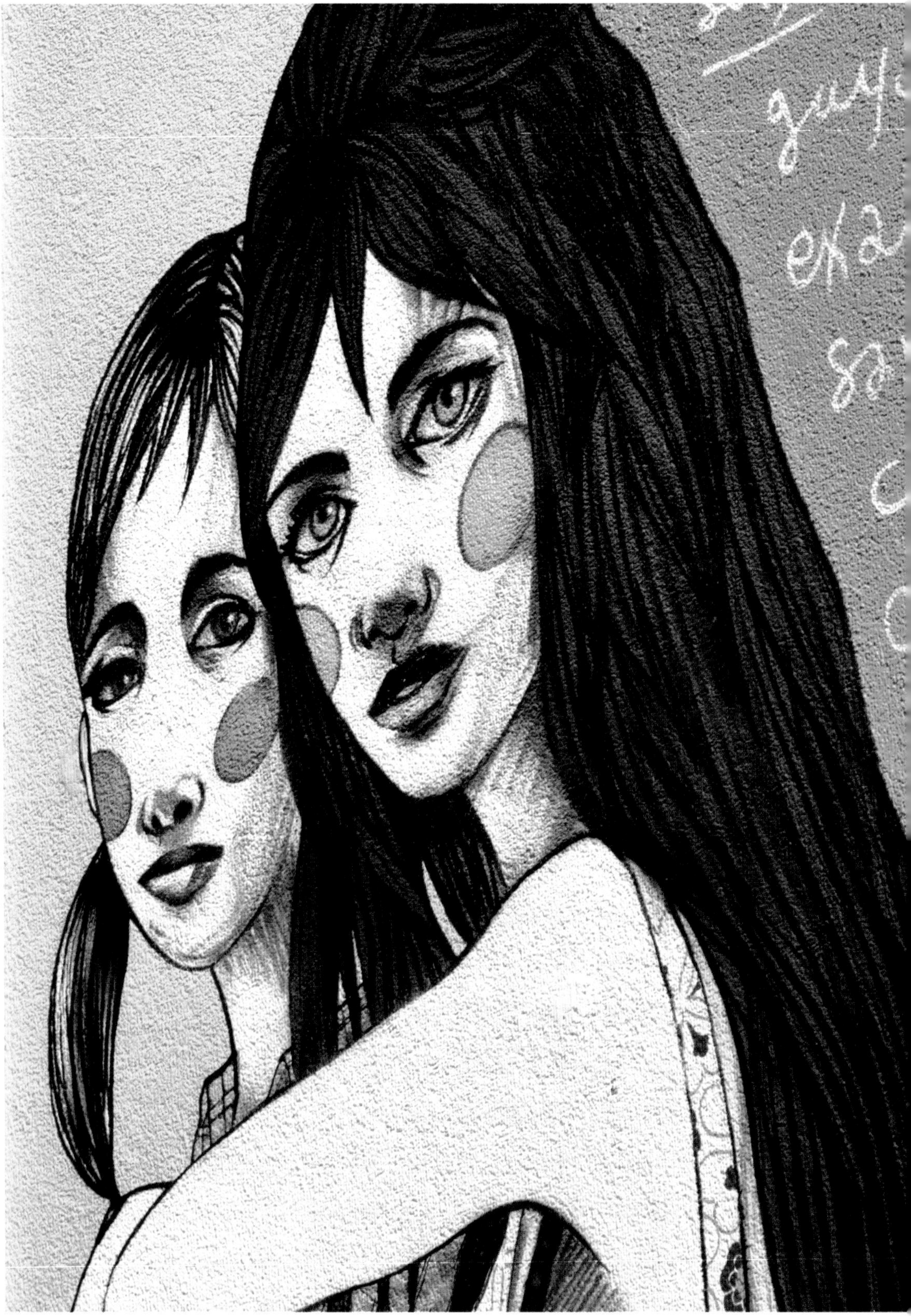

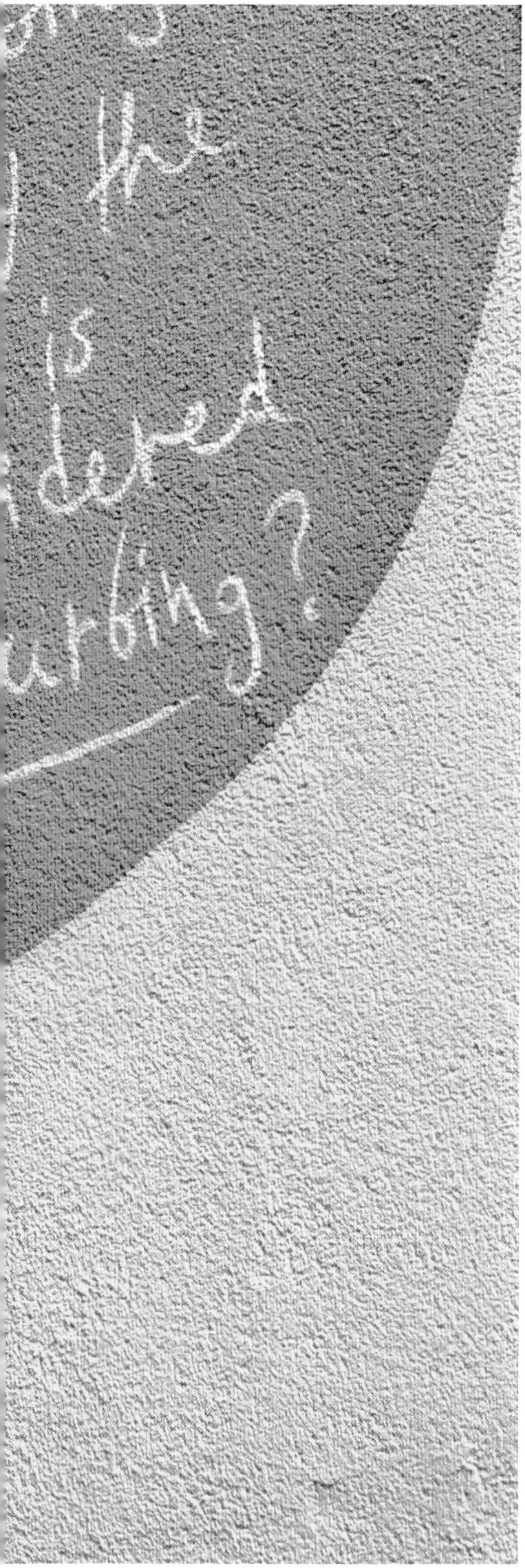

262 Out in the street

LGBTQ+ Murals Rue de la Chaufferette/Lollepotstraat, Brussels, Belgium

When to go: All year
Best for: Street art

Brussels has a lot of marvelous street art including LGBTQ+ murals. Found on Rue de la Chaufferette (Lollepotstraat), at the heart of Brussels' queer neighborhood, *Out in the Street* is a big wall strip that celebrates LGBTQ+ people publicly and addresses LGBTQ+ phobias. Eleven colorful portraits painted by Greek artist Fotini Tikkou cover the 131-ft/440-m-long walls, but alongside the portraits are clichés and abuse that LGBTQ+ people hear daily. *Love Remembers* on Rue Saint-Christophe/Sintkristoffelsstraat, by artist Anthea Missy, is a memorial to Ihsane Jarfi, who was the victim of a homophobic murder. You can pick up a mural map for a self-guided street-art tour, or arrange a guided tour with a local.

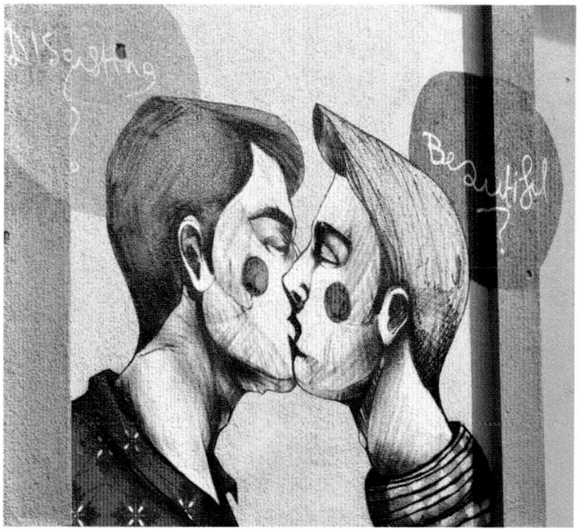

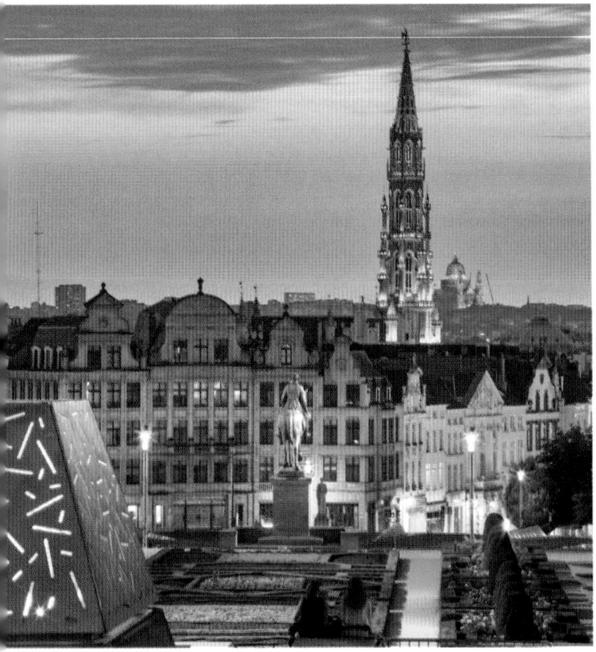

263 Beer-fueled boisterous bliss

◀ ▼ Belgian Pride, Brussels, Belgium

When to go: May
Best for: Marching for change

The Belgian Pride started as an LGBTQ+ protest march in the late 1970s—then called Pink Saturday—and traveled around for nearly two decades before finding its permanent place in Brussels. The colorful annual parade strides from Mont des Arts through the gayborhood of Saint-Jacques—the best area to find a queer bar with Belgian beers. Another annual queer event worth visiting is Brussels' LGBTQ+ film festival Pink Screens.

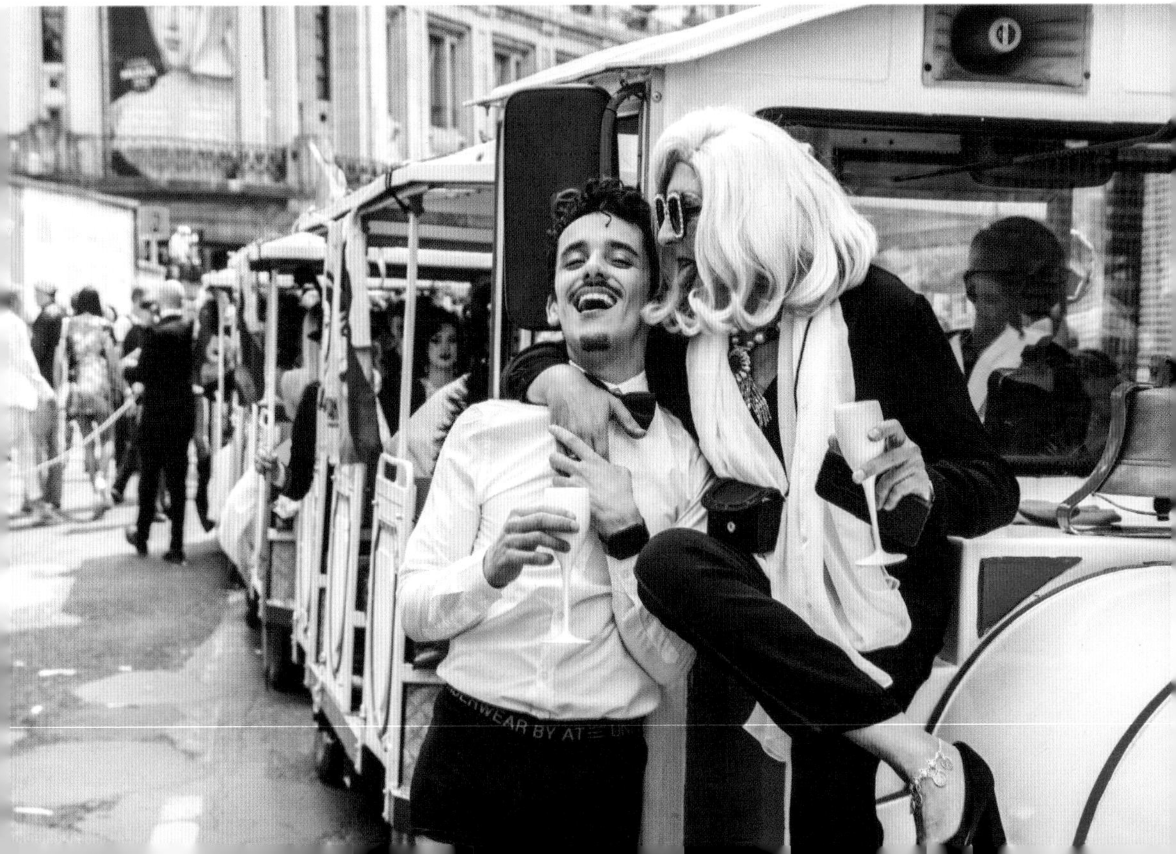

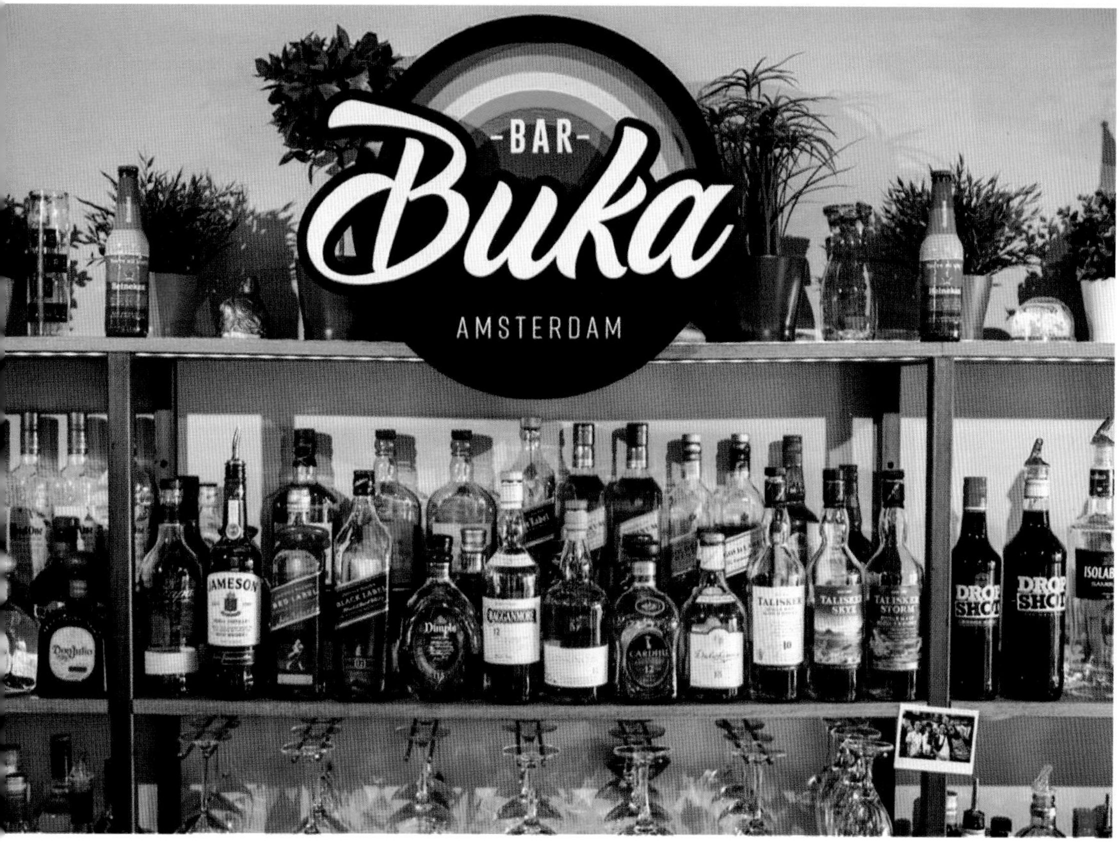

264 Sounds gay, I'm in

Luxembourg Pride, Esch-sur-Alzette, Luxembourg

When to go: July
Best for: A niche experience

As one of the world's smallest countries, Luxembourg doesn't have a massive queer scene, but it was the third country globally with an out, gay head of government and has progressive LGBTQ+ legislation. Luxembourg's week-long Pride in Esch-sur-Alzette attracts thousands of people, with exhibitions, movie nights, an equality march, and a Pride party. Throughout the year, there are vibrant events organized by FairyTails, Xxyz Luxembourg, Pink Ladies, and Banana.

265 Sip a gold star

▲ Bar Buka, Amsterdam, The Netherlands

When to go: All year
Best for: A haven for LGBTQ+ women

Amsterdam has only one LGBTQ+ women's bar: Bar Buka. *Buka* means "open" in Indonesian—founder Marianne's country of birth—and the bar is open to everyone. This cozy haven is where girl-gays and theys meet for good vibes, drinks, board games, and events. Try a lesbian-themed cocktail, beer by Gebrouwen door Vrouwen—a local women-led brewery—or support the local LGBTQ+ rights organization with a (rainbow) bottle of True Colours Cava.

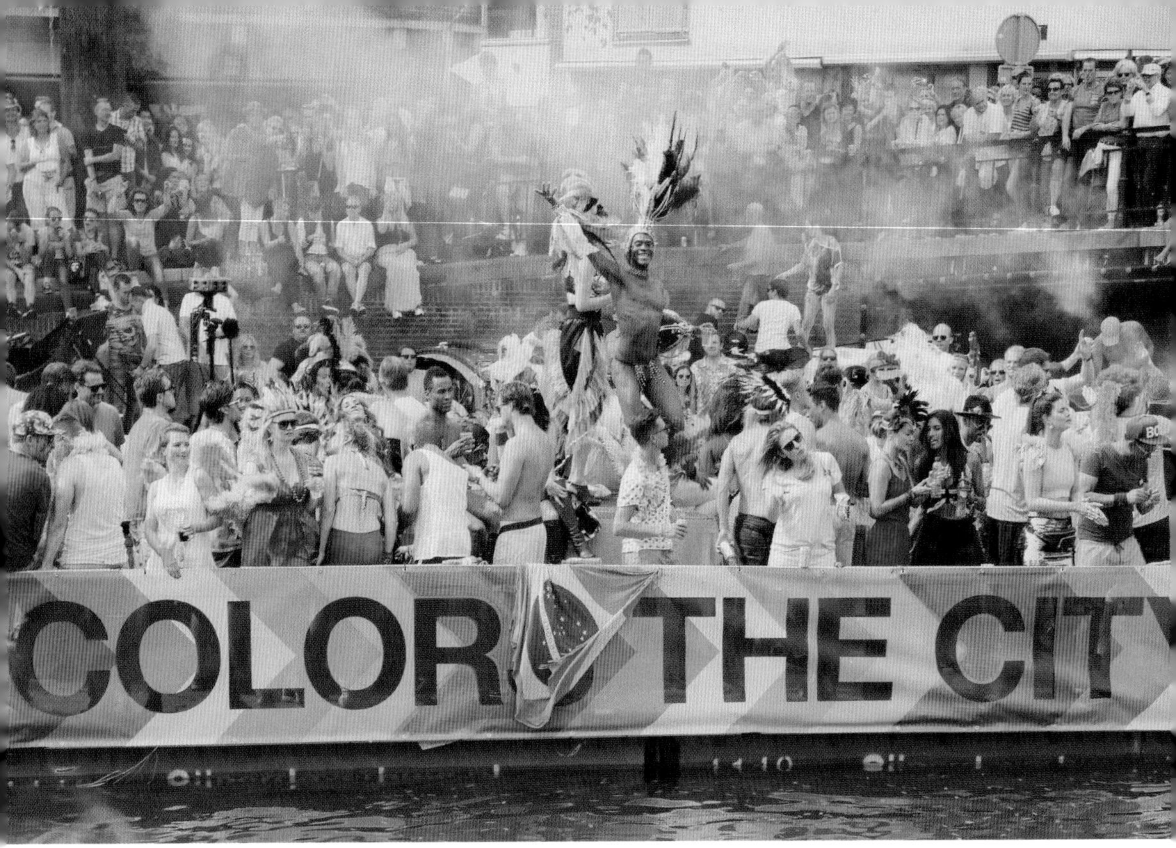

266 Dance on the canals like everyone is watching

Amsterdam Pride, The Netherlands

When to go: July and August
Best for: Pride on water

Pride Amsterdam has something most Prides don't have: a canal parade. Parade floats—actual boats—drive through the iconic Amsterdam canals in a long procession, while visitors watch from the banks. Besides celebrating LGBTQ+ rights, it's an excellent excuse for a party for Dutch people. After the parade, people join street parties held all over the city, with the Homomonument—a three-sectioned pink triangle in the center of town—as a significant spot. In the week leading up to the canal parade, you can attend film screenings, sports, and cultural events, exhibitions, parties, and lectures. If the commercialized canal parade isn't your jam, try the Pride Walk. It's an authentic Pride march to raise awareness of anti-LGBTQ+ violence globally, and the inequality LGBTQ+ people face.

267 Milkshake brings all the fun to the yard

Milkshake Festival, Amsterdam, The Netherlands

When to go: July
Best for: Fabulous festivaling

Things get wild at Milkshake Festival, which takes place in Amsterdam's Westerpark. Nothing's too extravagant for this fabulous, glittery event, with an eclectic atmosphere that blends playground, theme park, and dance club into one. Queer to its core, the festival is a safe space where anything goes, and diversity is celebrated, not alienated.

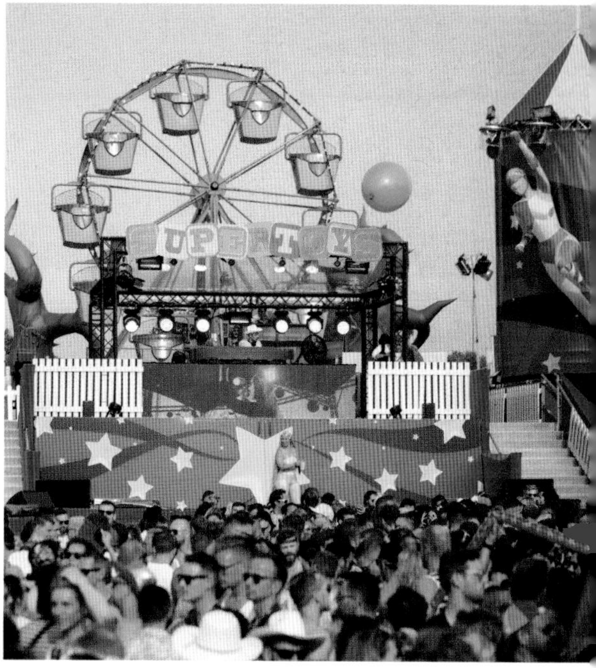

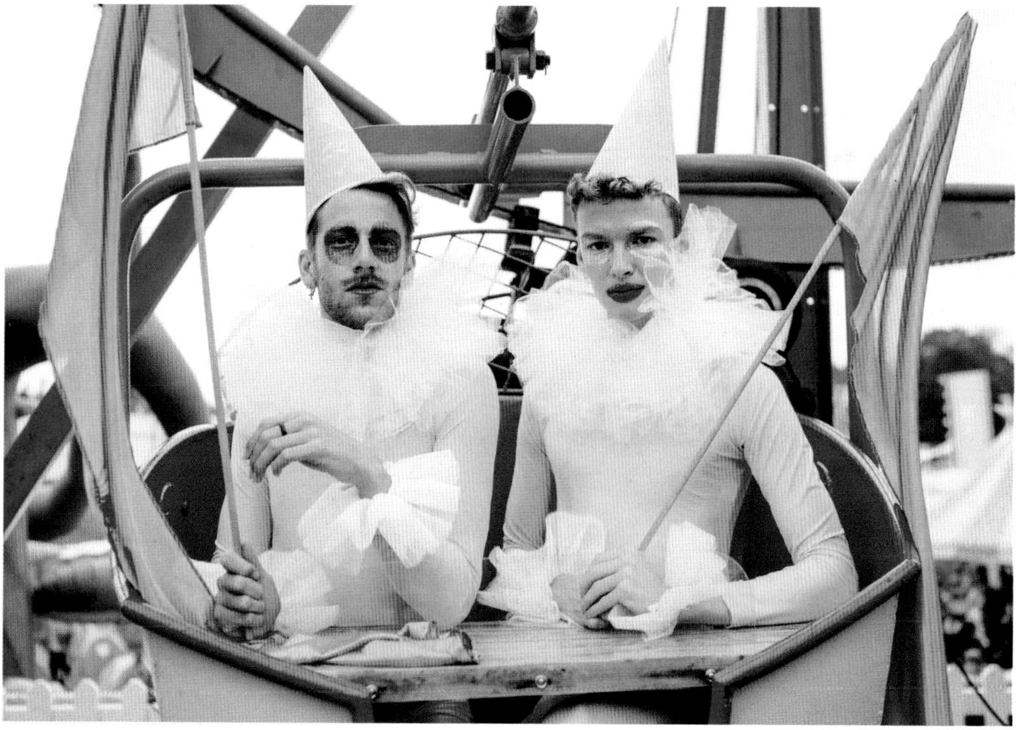

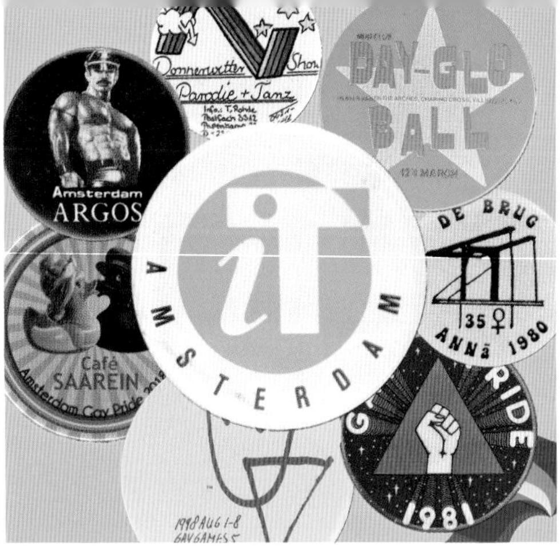

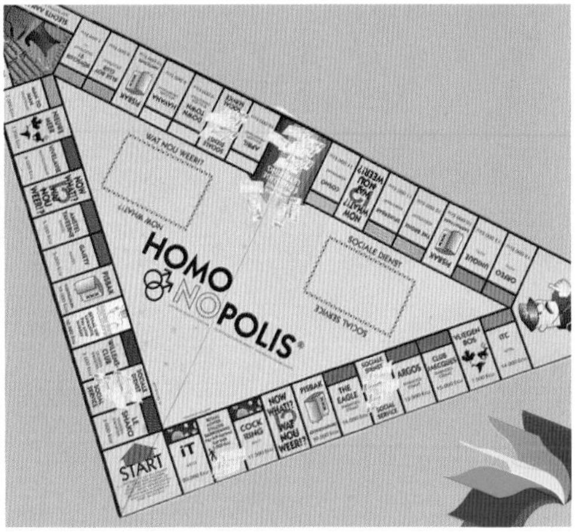

268 Baby, I was born to archive

◀ IHLIA LGBTI Heritage, Amsterdam, The Netherlands

When to go: All year
Best for: Researching LGBTQ+ history

On the third floor of the public library of Amsterdam, on Oosterdokskade, you can visit Europe's most extensive LGBTQ+ archive, IHLIA. The wide-ranging archive has books from four centuries ago, and magazines from last week. History is brought to life with exhibitions, panels, and workshops. A big issue with archives has been the systematic erasure of queer history (especially of people of color, transgender and intersex people, and women); IHLIA's program "Queering the Collections" is finding ways to change this.

269 'Dam(n) good hair

▶ Kindred Kuts, Amsterdam, The Netherlands

When to go: All year
Best for: Queer folks with hair

Amsterdam's only Black-owned queer barbershop, Kindred Kuts, is a safe space for all. In the cishet, male-dominated barber industry, founder Gray saw the need for gender-affirming haircuts for gender non-conforming, transgender, and non-binary people—especially Black folks and people of color. You can trust Kindred Kuts to make you feel and look good. Their salons always have good vibes and uplifting beats.

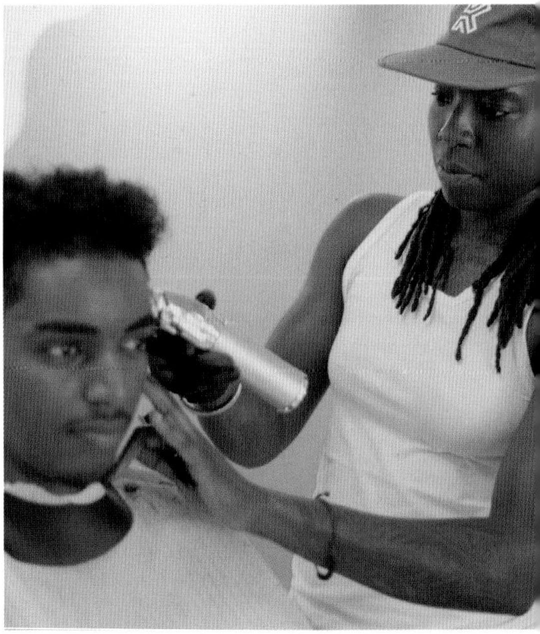

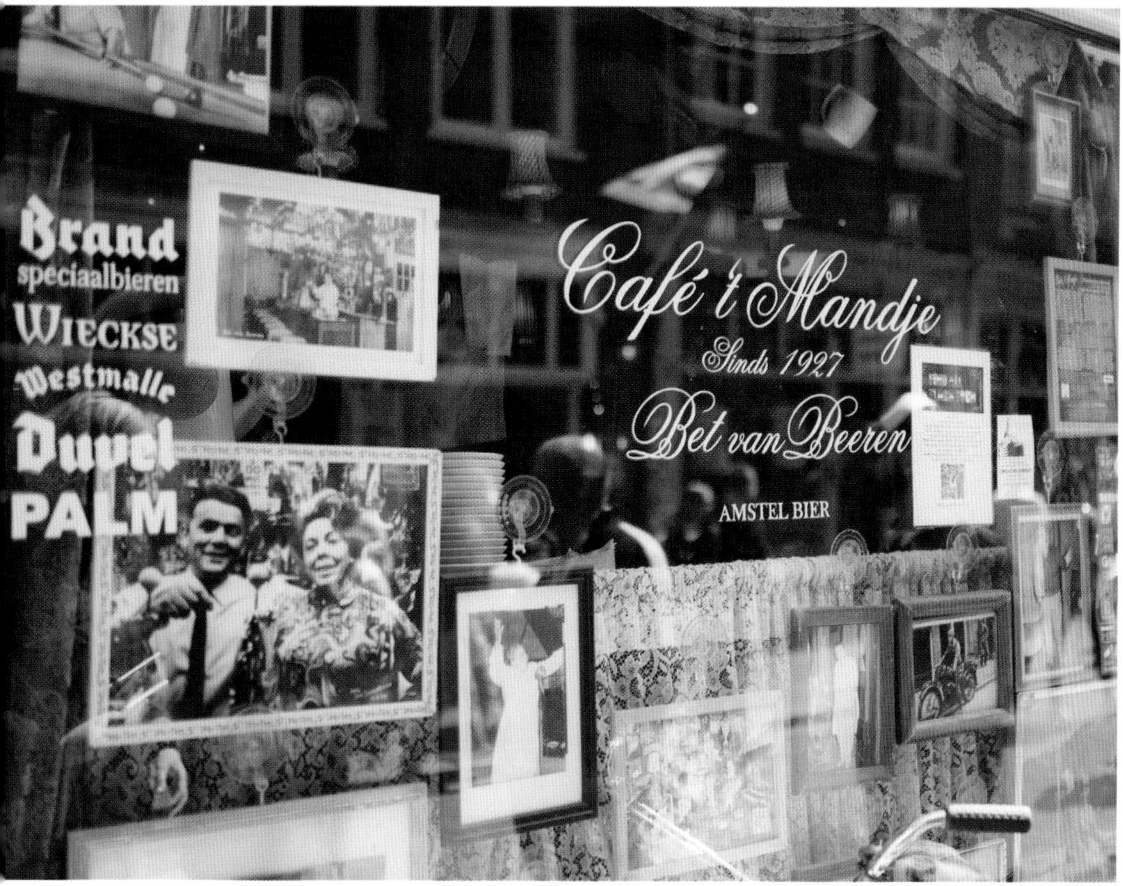

270 History on the ceiling

▲ Café 't Mandje, Amsterdam, The Netherlands

When to go: All year
Best for: A bar with history

Café 't Mandje is one of the world's oldest queer bars. In 1927, out lesbian Bet van Beeren took over her uncle's bar. At her dancing nights, LGBTQ+ couples could dance together. The interior remains almost as it was in Bet's day—including memorabilia on the ceiling that includes cut-off ties, pictures, and bras. Bet used to ask people to leave souvenirs, so bring something to leave behind when you visit.

271 Triangles point the way

Homomonument, Amsterdam, The Netherlands

When to go: All year
Best for: Honoring LGBTQ+ lives

Next to the Westerkerk lies the world's oldest monument to LGBTQ+ people who were killed by the Nazis, Homomonument. Three pink, granite triangles—symbolizing LGBTQ+ past, present, and future—form a larger triangle designed by lesbian Karin Daan. On holidays and during Pride, it's where LGBTQ+ people come together for street parties.

272 Pink is the warmest color

Roze filmdagen, Amsterdam, The Netherlands

When to go: March
Best for: Queer cinema in quaint theaters

While Netflix and other streaming services are now generating more LGBTQ+ movies, it hasn't always been easy to find and access queer cinema. Over a quarter-century, the Roze Filmdagen (translates to "Pink Film Days") has been fulfilling an essential role of increasing LGBTQ+ visibility with its annual, eleven-day-long LGBTQ+ film festival. Screenings happen in quaint, intimate theaters, and their program includes in-depth panels, award shows, and parties.

273 Queer by day and night

▶ Reguliersdwarsstraat, Amsterdam, The Netherlands

When to go: April to September
Best for: Dutch queer nightlife

The name is a bit of a tongue-twister, but the Reguliersdwarsstraat, just behind Amsterdam's iconic floating flower market, has been Amsterdam's most famous street for gay nightlife since 1980, with rainbow flags waving from either side. Start your adventures around 4:00 p.m. at Reguliersdwarsstraat's terraces, eat at one of the many great restaurants (food at the Vegan Junk Food Bar is delicious), have a casual drink at Exit Café, and end your evening getting dancey at Club NYX which has a queer night on Saturdays.

274 Trans on screen

TranScreen Film Festival, Amsterdam, The Netherlands

When to go: May
Best for: International trans films

Trans people travel from far and wide to come together for TranScreen's biennial multi-day film festival. It promises not only a stellar lineup of some of the best international trans films (of all genres), but also an engaging cultural program, including youth panels, self-defense workshops, and a raucous afterparty.

275 Nooks and books

Savannah Bay, Utrecht, The Netherlands

When to go: All year
Best for: Bibliophiles

In the heart of the historic center of Utrecht you can find Savannah Bay—a comprehensive, intersectional treasury of stories. Beyond a boutique bookstore, it's a living-room-like social space hosting workshops, readings, queer support groups, and their annual event, Queering the City of Literature.

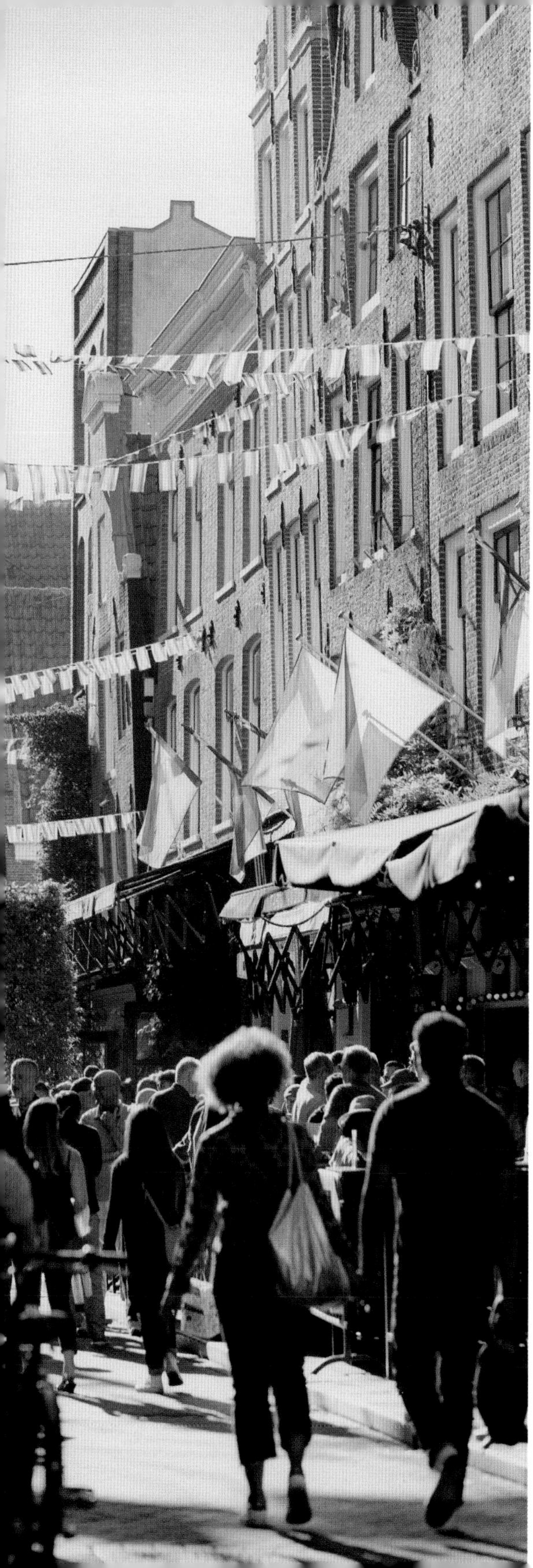
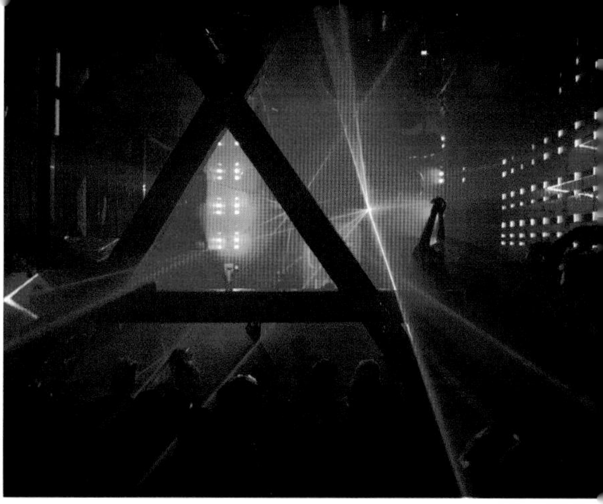
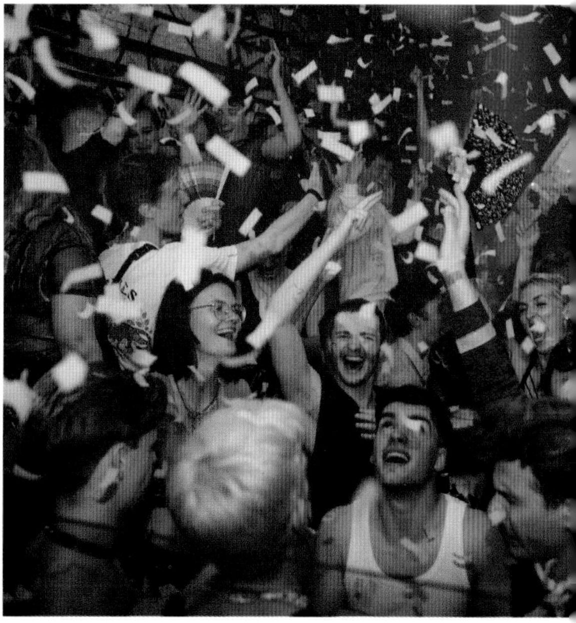
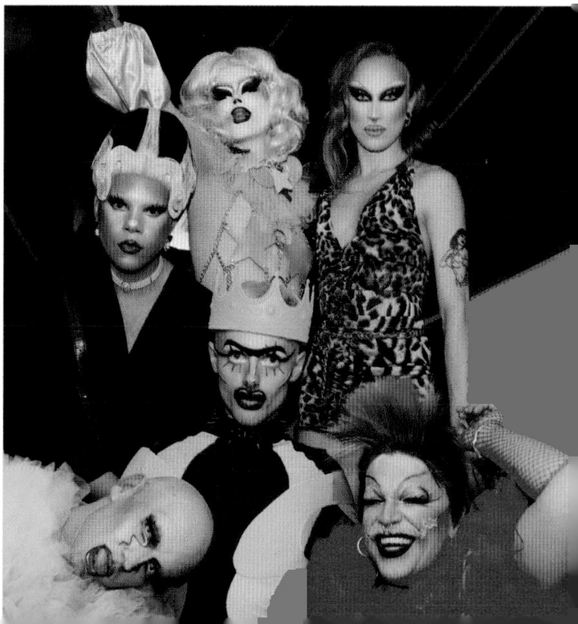

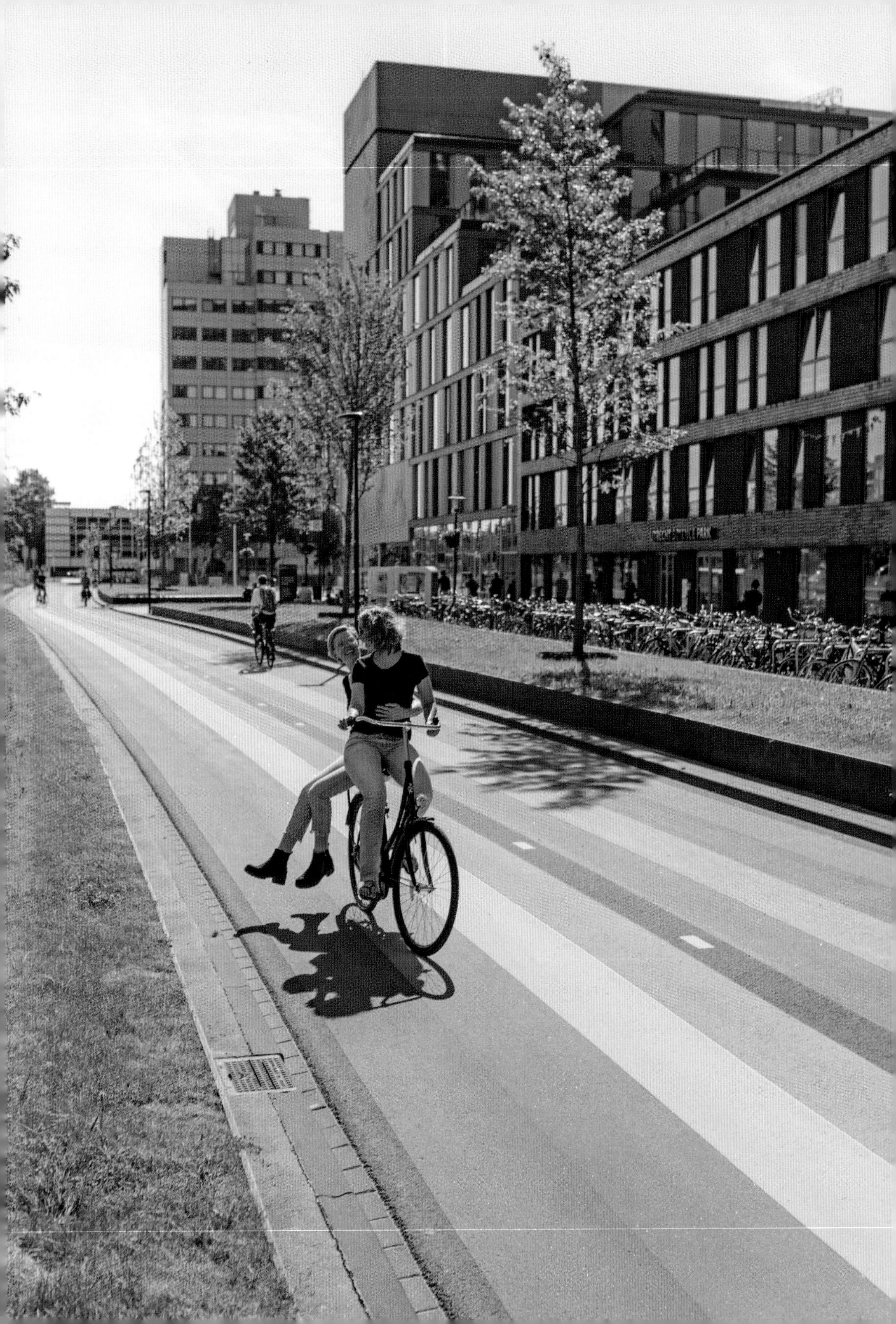

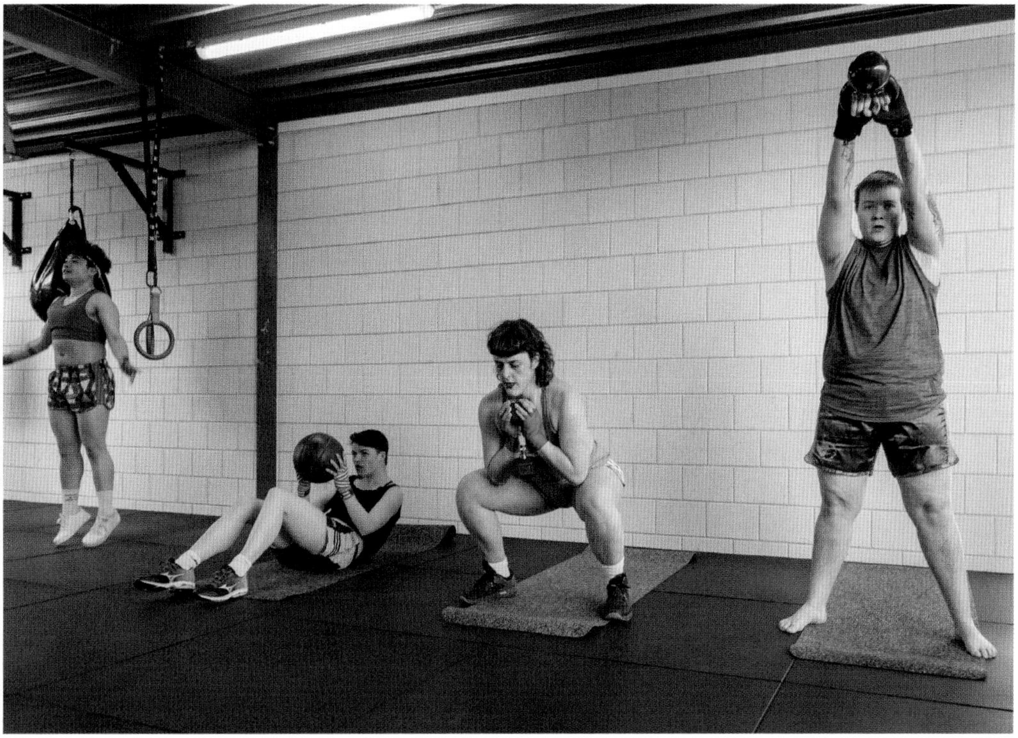

276 Ride rainbow road—on a bicycle

◀ Rainbow Bicycle Path, Utrecht, The Netherlands

When to go: All year
Best for: Colorful exercise

At Utrecht Science Park, a 1,870-ft/570-m-long rainbow—starting with the Progress Pride flag—was painted on a bicycle path. It's part of Utrecht University's goal to improve its inclusivity and diversity by creating visibility, raising awareness, and making policy changes. Rent a bicycle and ride the rainbow—after all, it's a classic thing to do in the country which allegedly has more bikes than residents.

277 Body beautiful

▲ Queer Gym, Rotterdam, The Netherlands

When to go: All year
Best for: Inclusive training

What happens if you mix queerness, fitness, and non-normative bodies? An inclusive gym for every body. During his transition, Romy Rockx found that a home-gym provided a safe place to discover his new body without the stress of heteronormative society. He wanted to offer others the same opportunity and opened the Netherlands' first queer gym. The aim is not training to fit Western beauty standards, but to gain strength and confidence in your new body and mind.

278 Wonderful, wonderful . . . Copenhagen Pride

Copenhagen, Denmark

When to go: August
Best for: Drag queens pedaling rickshaws

Denmark is one of the most LGBTQ-friendly countries in the world. It was the first country to legalize partnership equality back in 1989, followed by marriage equality in 2012. If there's no distinct queer neighborhood in Copenhagen, it's because you'll discover a welcoming atmosphere across the city. This is also evident at its annual Pride celebrations, which attract a huge and diverse crowd. Beside the usual floats and walking groups, you'll also find a broad and colorful array of cyclists—keep an eye out for the rickshaws offered by drag queens if you're looking to sit back and be pedaled around town. The parade takes you past the city's famous, pastel-painted old houses, and ends with a big concert in City Hall Square, followed by partying in the city's LGBTQ+ bars. The Pride celebrations spread throughout the city, and you'll find rainbow flags fluttering everywhere, including in the famed Tivoli Gardens—one of the oldest amusement parks in the world.

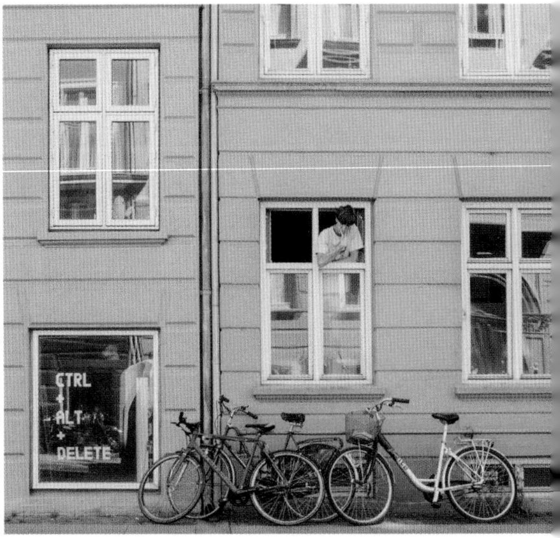

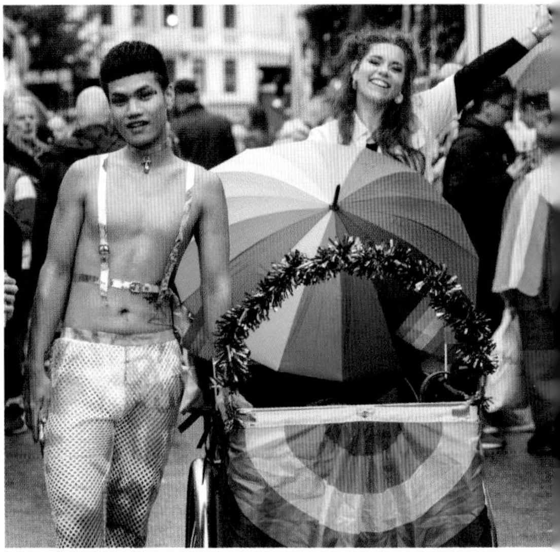

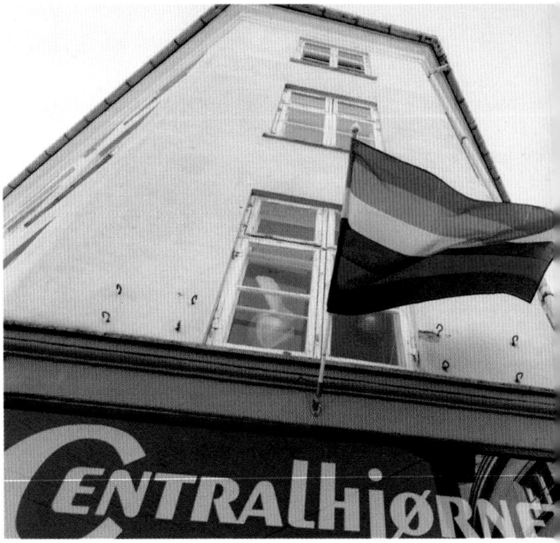

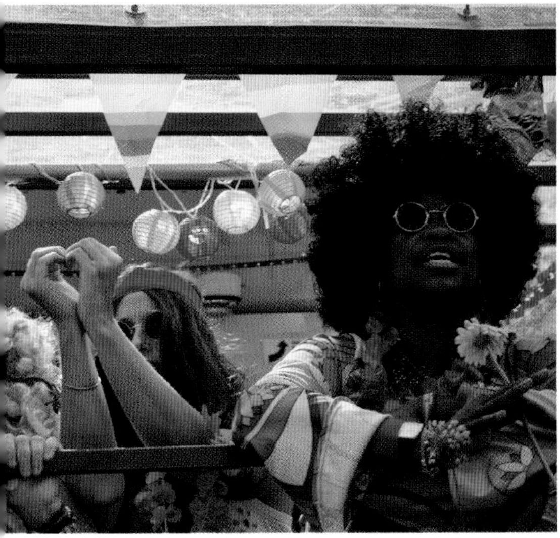
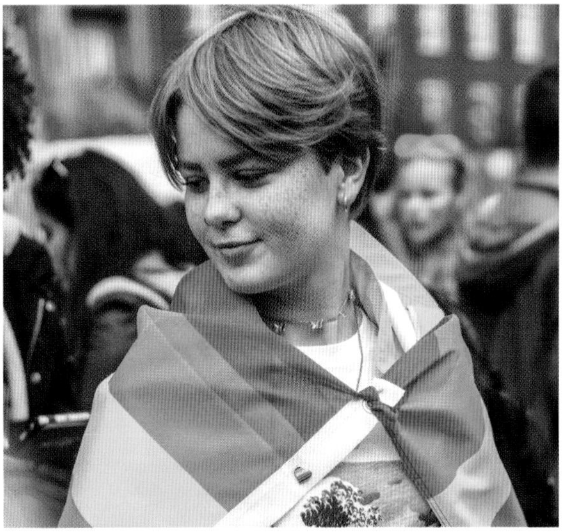
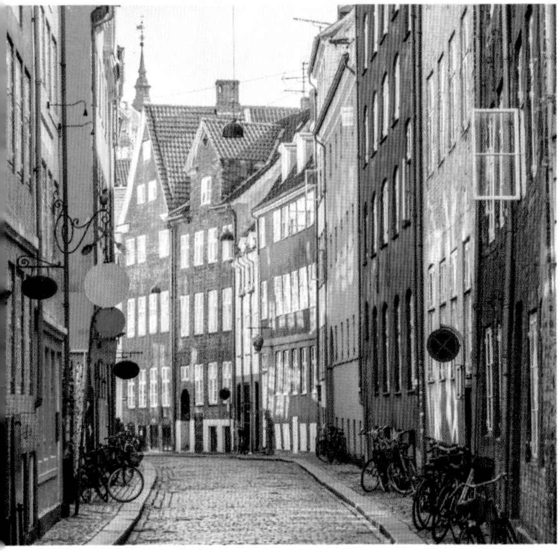
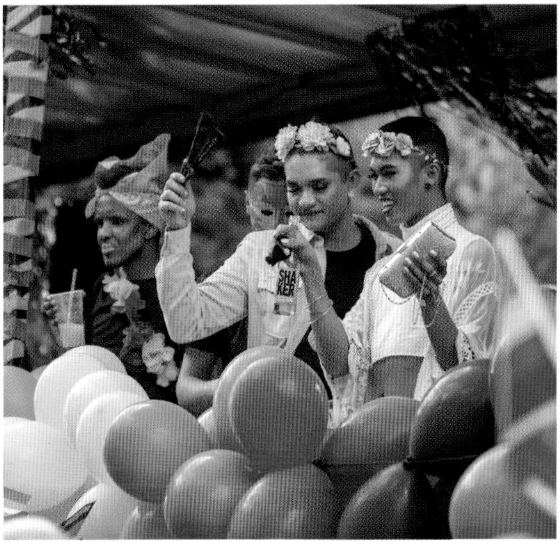
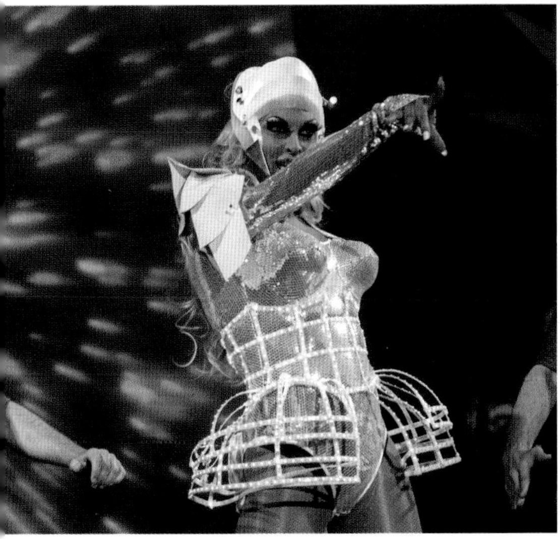
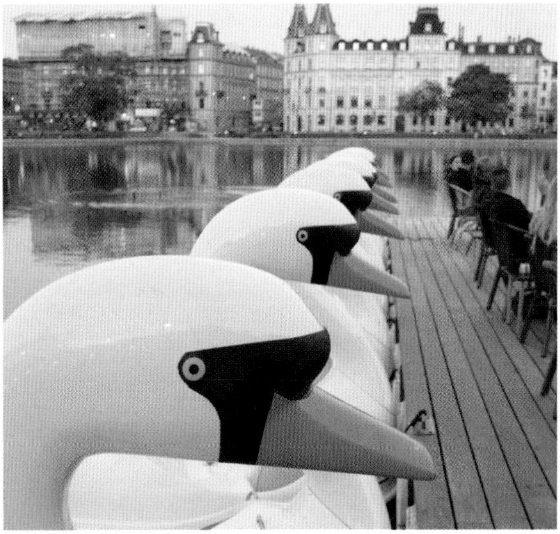

279 Enchanted harbor

▼ Nyhavn, Copenhagen, Denmark

When to go: All year
Best for: A stroll with stories

Copenhagen is colorful as a rainbow, both figuratively and literally. The iconic hot spot Nyhavn (New Harbor) has stunning canal houses with facades in all colors. That's not the only thing that makes this street queer. Danish fairytale writer Hans Christian Andersen, who was allegedly bi-romantic and asexual, used to live at Nyhavn 20. It is the place he wrote *The Tinderbox* and *The Princess and the Pea*.

280 Golden oldie

Centralhjørnet, Copenhagen, Denmark

When to go: All year
Best for: A chilled, neighborhood institution

This quaint little corner bar has been running since 1917 and it's easily the longest-running gay bar in Denmark. With its cozy and welcoming atmosphere and regular live entertainment, Centralhjørnet attracts a mixed crowd of locals and tourists. It offers a particularly warm welcome in the run-up to the winter holidays and is famed for its twinkling Christmas decorations. During the summer months, grab a beer and a seat outside to indulge in people watching.

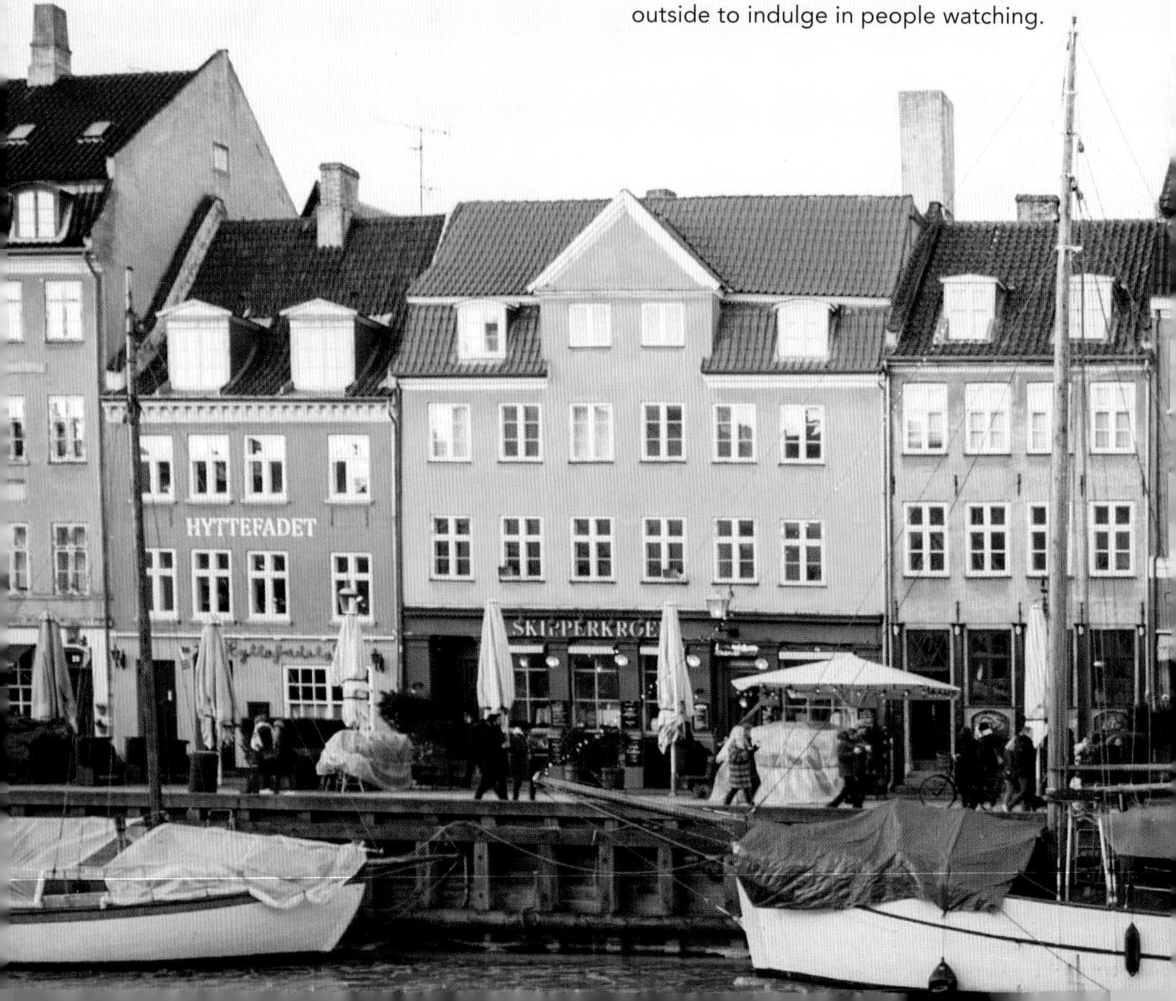

281 Class party

Latin Quarter, Copenhagen, Denmark

When to go: All year
Best for: Queer nights out in a historic area

The area around Studiestræde (Study Street) got nicknamed the Latin Quarter because the University of Copenhagen (founded here in 1479) predominantly used Latin. The old Copenhagen district is now famous for boutiques, cafés, and nightclubs, and it's where you'll find LGBTQ+ hot spots including Cosy Bar, prison-themed Jailhouse, or strip-club-turned-lesbian hot spot Vela.

282 Queers on film

MIX Copenhagen, Denmark

When to go: October
Best for: Queer cinema

With ten days of mainstream and independent queerness on screen, MIX Copenhagen is the Nordic's leading LGBTQ+ film festival. Its prominent award, the Lili Award, holds special meaning as it's named after Danish artist Lili Elbe, the first Dane to undergo gender-affirming surgery. Throughout the year, you can enjoy MIX's podcast, *Coming Out of The Celluloid Closet*.

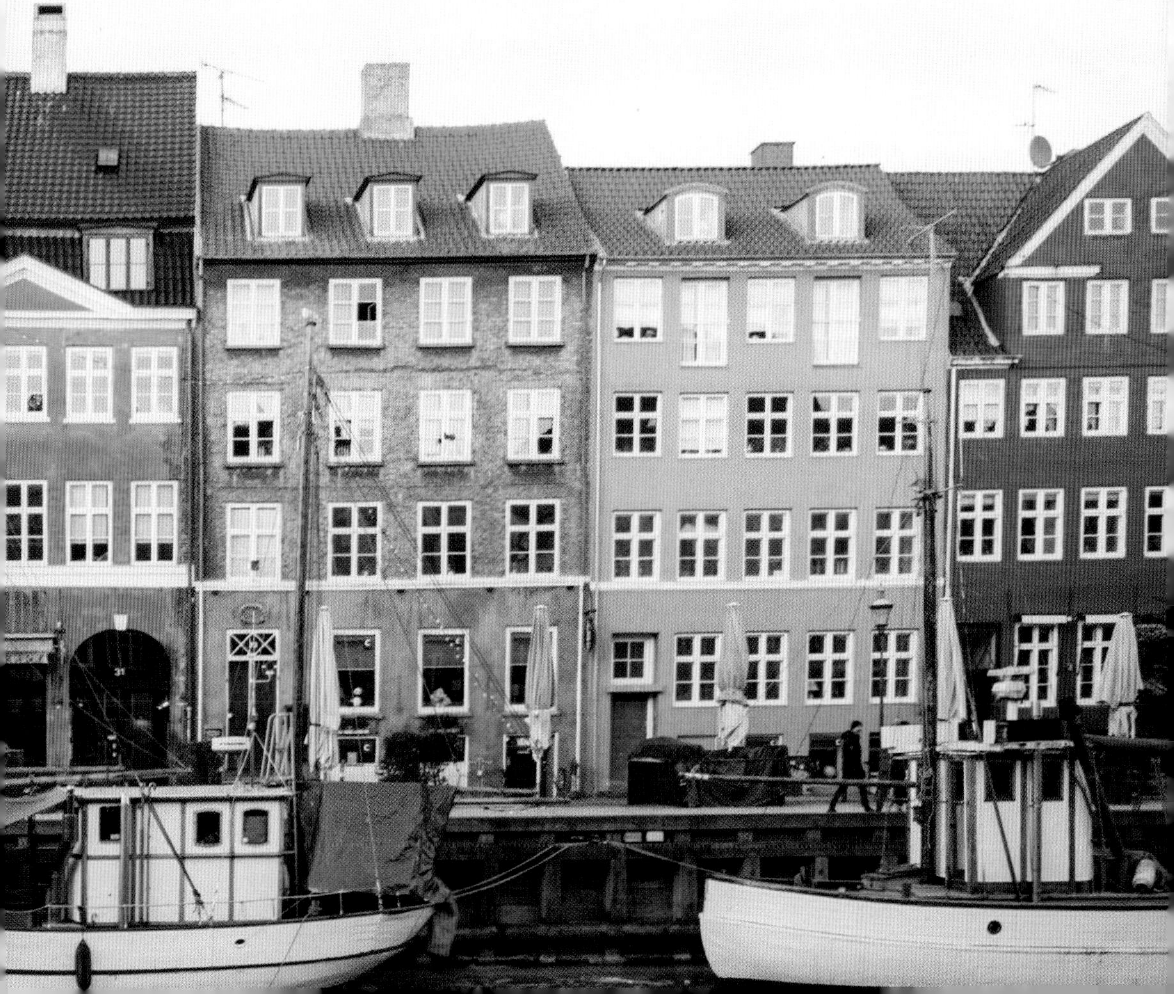

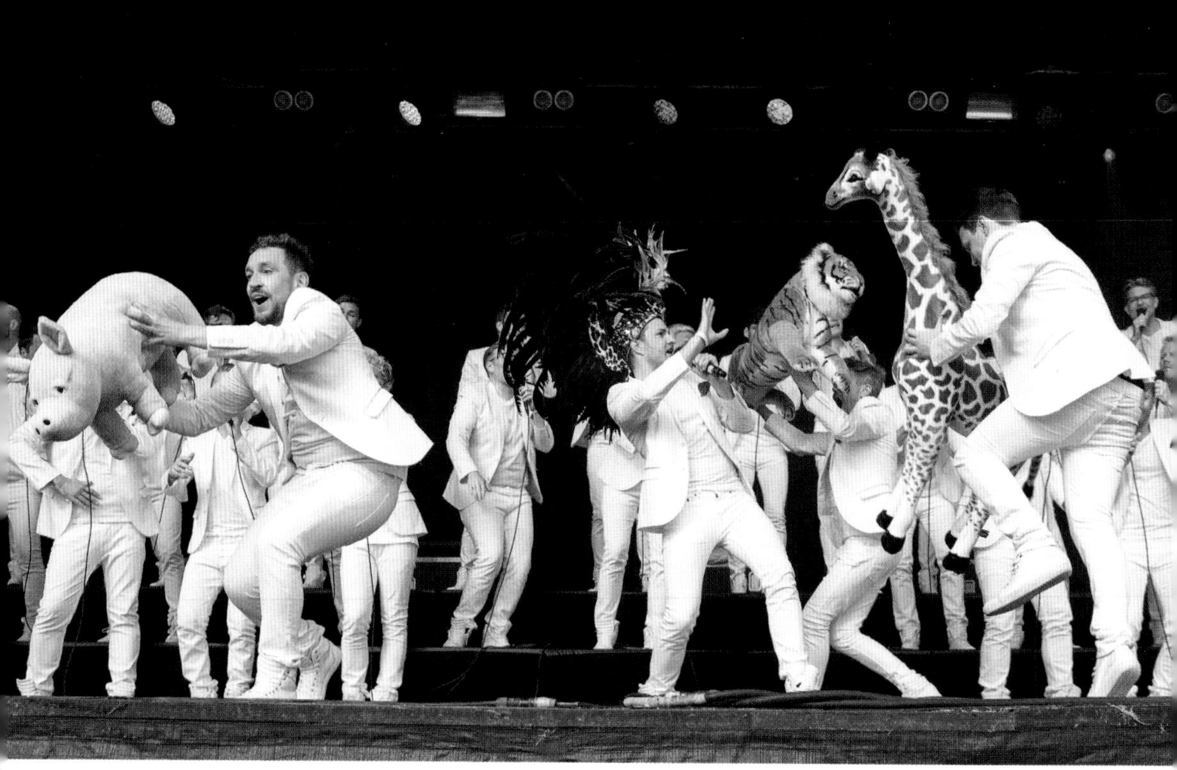

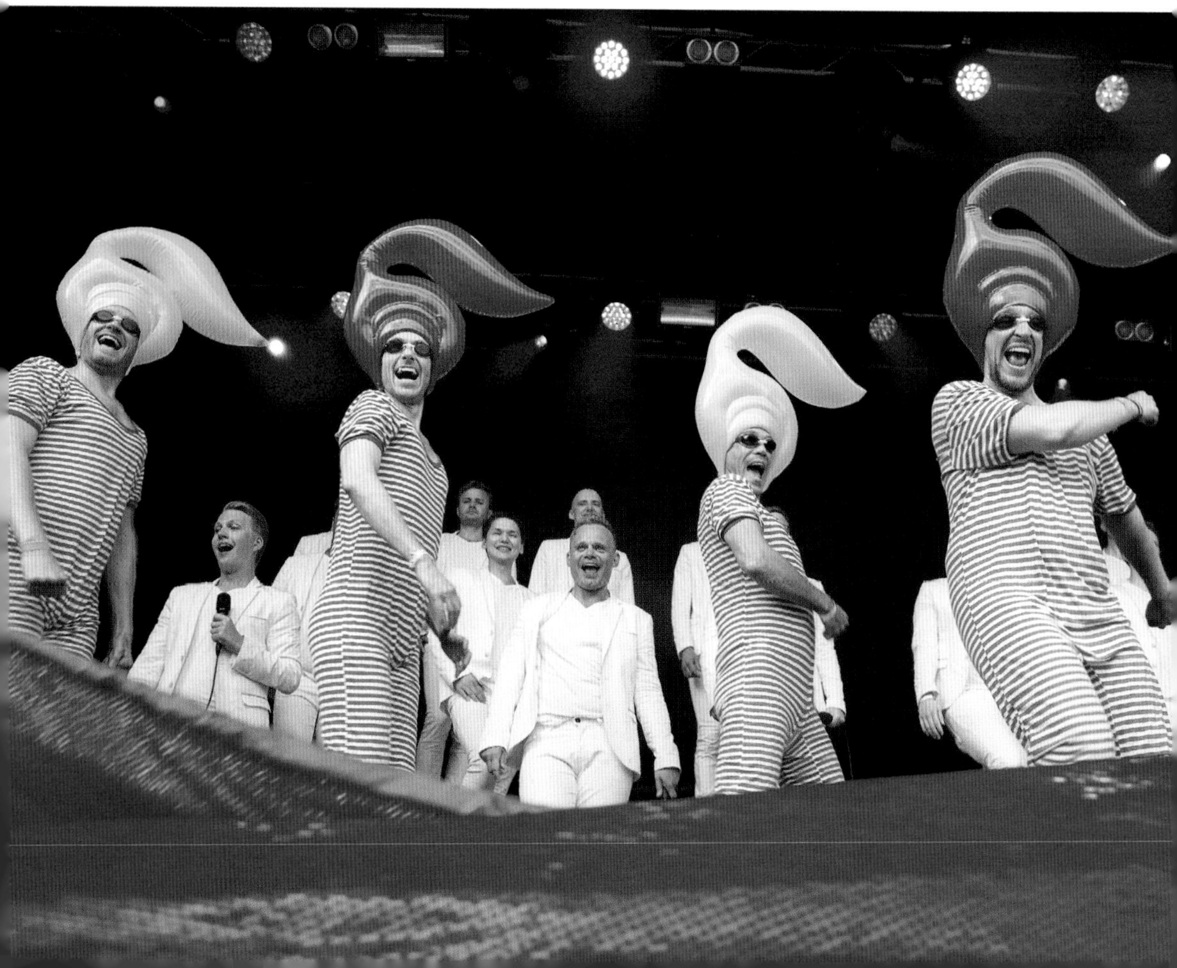

283 Slay on a sleigh

Winter Pride, Copenhagen, Denmark

When to go: February
Best for: Snowy parties

In Denmark in December, there can be 17 hours of darkness between sunset and sunrise. Queer folks decided to brighten things up with Winter Pride. Organized since 2015 by the Copenhagen Pride organization, the week-long Winter Pride feels comfortably familiar with its parties, performances, panels, and movie nights. Pride has a distinct celebratory vibe in Denmark—the first country in the world to recognize registered partnerships for LGBTQ+ couples.

284 Gender agenda

Genderhouse Festival, Aarhus, Denmark

When to go: September to October
Best for: Bold, interactive, and explicit queer art

With installations, performances, and exhibitions across Aarhus—Denmark's second city—the Genderhouse Festival will delight, surprise, and intrigue even the most seasoned queer-art connoisseurs. Taking gender as its starting point, this month-long arts festival presents some of the most innovative queer productions in Europe. Highlights from past festivals include Travis Alabanza's highly acclaimed *Burgerz*.

285 What's the difference between a bassoon and a gay guy?

◀ Oslo Fagottkor, Oslo, Norway

When to go: December
Best for: Christmas concerts

Oslo Fagottkor is the Norwegian gay choir you didn't know you needed in your life. In 2004, a group of men who loved men, music, and humor came together to sing. What started small became Norway's most famous gay choir. With a humorous approach, the ensemble has an eclectic repertoire. The choir's name is a fun word-play since *fagott* is Norwegian for the musical instrument bassoon, but also a reclaiming of the English slur "faggot."

286 Tales of the city, society, and more

Tronsmo Bokhandel, Oslo, Norway

When to go: All year
Best for: Bookworms

As a queer person, it can be freeing to escape society through books; it's why fantasy is a popular genre among LGBTQ+ bookworms. Whatever genre you're into, independent bookstore Tronsmo Bokhandel is a must-visit in Oslo. It's an alternative bookshop with books about politics, culture, subculture, feminism, music, photography, art, movies, and more. It has fiction and nonfiction books from nearly every continent, a dedicated LGBTQ+ section, and a legendary basement of comics.

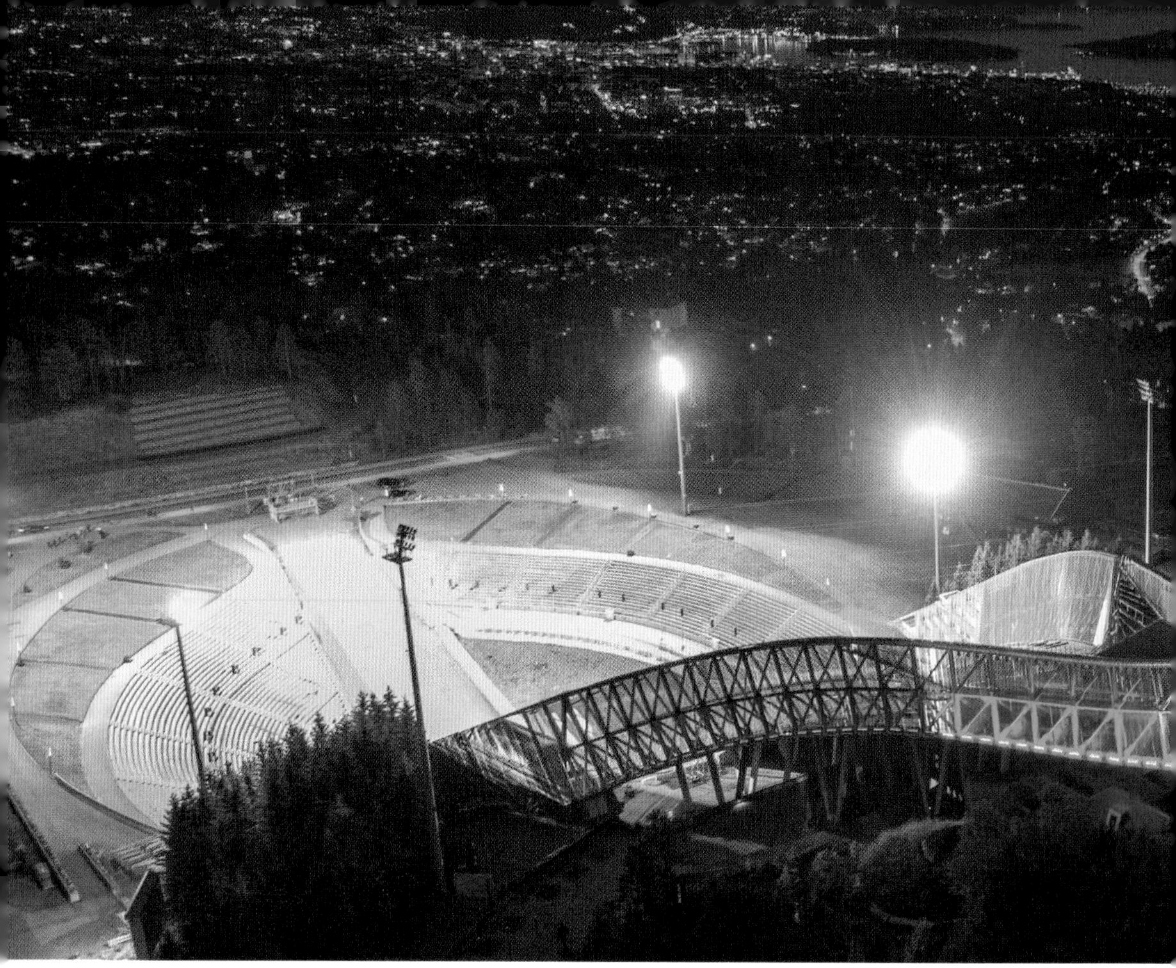

287 Walk it out

▲ Oslo Pride, Norway

When to go: June
Best for: Mountain flirting

Like its Nordic neighbors, Norway is a welcoming country for LGBTQ+ people. The capital, Oslo, is home to significant queer events and concepts, such as lesbian-founded DRAMAqueen, alternative Indieseksuell, nomadic Karmaklubb, and fabulous Open Drag Stage. Visit Norway's largest LGBTQ+ event in June: Oslo Pride. Its Pride Park, located at the heart of the city, is the epicenter of the ten-day-long event with shows, stages, restaurants, and mingling areas. For Norwegian Pride on another level, visit Fjellpride in the mountains. As an April Fool's joke, The Norwegian Trekking Association launched color-coded hats to stimulate flirting while hiking. But the joke proved popular, and soon after it launched a rainbow hat for queer hikers. It's the perfect accessory for the Fjellpride's parade—which, to be fair, is more of a hike.

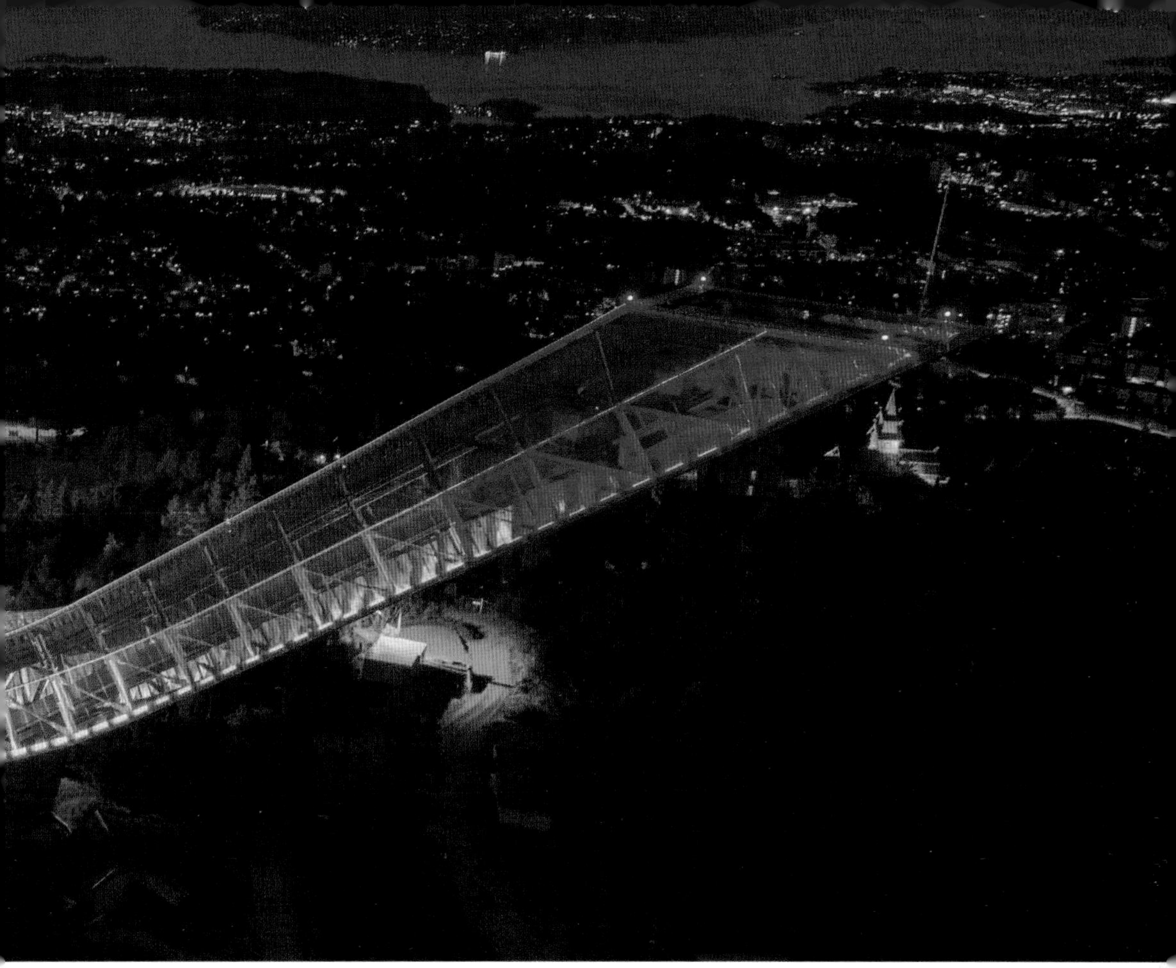

288 Hot and steamy

Finnish Sauna, Helsinki, Finland

When to go: All year
Best for: Sweating in company

Finns have used steamy rooms to survive freezing winters for centuries. The old Finnish saying, "First build the sauna, then the house," is true: Finland has roughly one sauna per two Finns—and only one gay sauna. The most LGBTQ+ friendly way to experience it is privately at your accommodation, or the public all-gender saunas at Löyly.

289 Karaoke is the great equalizer

Mann's Street, Helsinki, Finland

When to go: All year
Best for: Singing your heart out

Wet your whistle with happy-hour drinks and give Finnish and Euro-pop karaoke your best shot. In the center of Helsinki, the relaxed gay bar Mann's Street has an old-school vibe and crowd, and a small dance floor for their monthly dance nights.

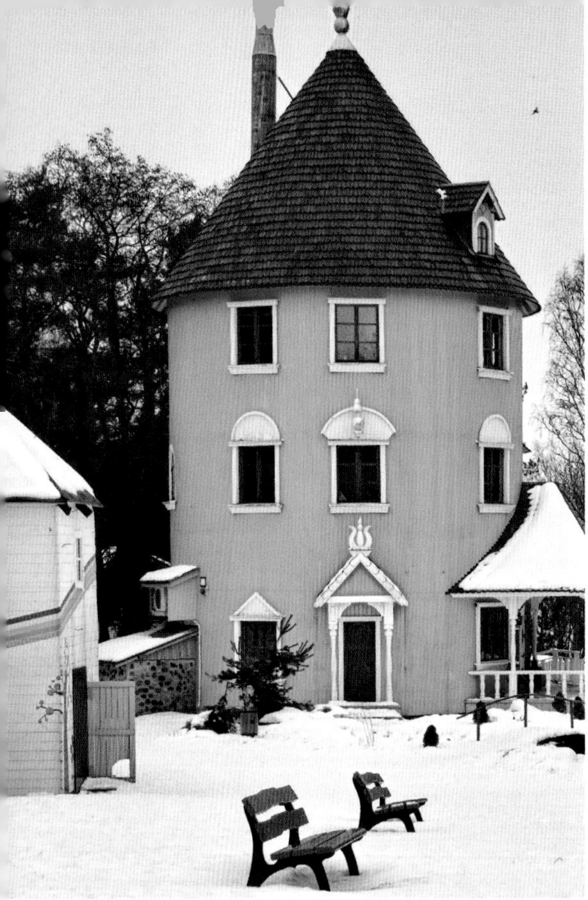

290 "Oh what happiness!" the Moomins are queer

◀ Tove Jansson's Finland

When to go: All year
Best for: Seeing the life of a queer artist

Step into the life of the queer icon, Finnish artist, and Moomin-creator Tove Jansson. See her art at Helsinki's Art Museum, walk by her childhood-home Katajanokka, indulge your inner child at Moomin World in Naantali, or visit Ateneum, where Tove and her life's love, Tuulikki "Tooti" Pietilä, studied. Tove and Tooti spent many summers on the Pellinki islands, where you can do a Moomin-inspired adventure walk. Lastly, visit the Moomin Museum to see the model of the Moomin House, crafted by Tove and Tooti.

291 Finnishing strong

Kvääristö, Helsinki, Finland

When to go: All year
Best for: Coming together

In Finnish, *kvääri* means queer, and the suffix *-stö* indicates a place; Kvääristö means queerhood, a place where queer people come together. Powered by crowdfunding, Kvääristö opened its doors in late 2022 in trendy Kallio—Helsinki's bohemian cultural district—as an accessible community bar-café run by and for LGBTQ+ women, transgender, and non-binary folks.

292 Show some shelf love

Kallio Library, Helsinki, Finland

When to go: All year
Best for: Queer fiction and education

Treat your-shelf with a visit to the Kallio Library in Helsinki. Since 2015, their *Sateenkaarihyllyjen* (Rainbow Shelves) proudly display LGBTQ+ books, films, comics, and information from queer organizations to increase visibility, representation, and awareness. The rainbow shelves help normalize queerness—the children's section includes books about rainbow families as an essential category. The library hosts a monthly *lukupiiri* (book club) to discuss a queer title from the shelves.

293 The shows must go on

Helsinki Gay Theater, Helsinki, Finland

When to go: All year
Best for: Theatrical activism

Since 2007, the amateur theater group Helsinki Gay Theater (HGT)—*Helsingin Gayteatteri*—has put on two or three productions a year. Their shows tell queer stories to advance equality in society through theatrical art. All art is a form of protest, and these men have a way of making it equally important and fun. Gays and theater go hand in hand, and naturally, HGT has become a staple in the Finnish gay community.

294 White nights and rainbows unite

▼ Juhannus and Helsinki Pride, Helsinki, Finland

When to go: June and July
Best for: Finnish fun

Finland gets two months of 24/7 daylight, known as "white nights." During the summer solstice, celebrate the whitest night, Juhannus, Finland's most important national holiday. Visit the open-air museum on Seurasaari Island for a big midsummer show with fire, water, music, and dance. During Juhannus, Finnish people also light bonfires, *kokko*, and go to the sauna together. Usually, Helsinki Pride happens the week after the Juhannus celebrations. Make your way back to the capital and enjoy a week of queer events, a parade, and a rainbow fair.

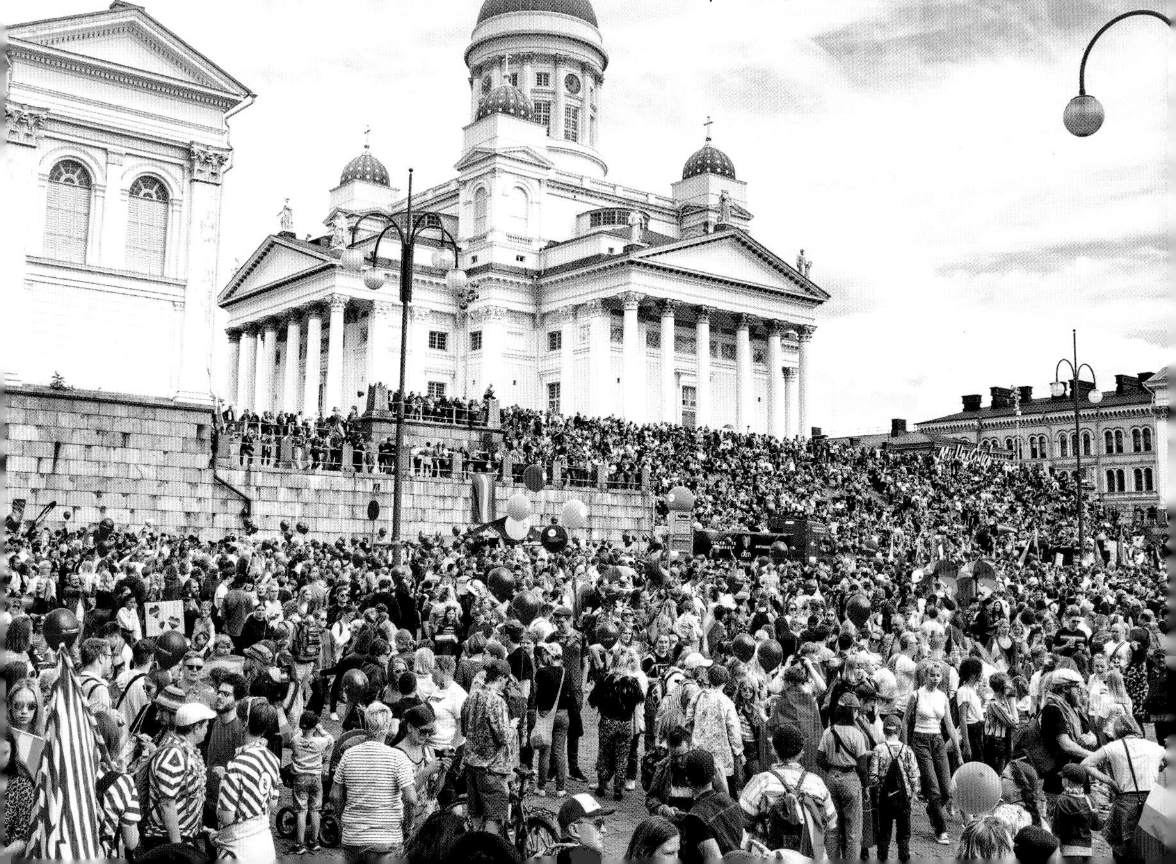

295 Rent a rainbow

West Pride, Gothenburg, Sweden

When to go: June
Best for: Small city rainbows

Sweden's second-largest city proves good things come in small packages. Gothenburg has a small but thriving queer scene—see devoutly updated Queerkalendern Göteborg (Queer Calendar GBG). Popular affairs are straight-venue-takeovers by Guerrilla Queer Bar, pop-up parties by Club Queer and Wish You Were Queer, and cultural events by Status Queer. Niche events include free haircuts at Salong Qlipp, mushroom picking with the Queer Outdoor Brigade, and trans *fika* meetings by Transammans. During West Pride, Gothenburg transforms into a rainbow city for over two weeks, with the unique option to rent Pride flags.

296 Out and outdoors

Luleå Pride, Sweden

When to go: June to September
Best for: The arctic way of life

Small-city Prides are something else. The sense of community and unity feels different at intimate events. Visit Swedish coastal city Luleå not only for its endearing, just-over-a-decade-old Pride, but also to explore the arctic outdoors and way of life. Visit over a thousand islands with iconic red-and-white cottages by boat. Learn about the borderless Sápmi region, the land of the Sámi, northern Europe's Indigenous people. Go hiking and kayaking during long summer days, or snowmobiling and ice skating under the aurora sky in winter.

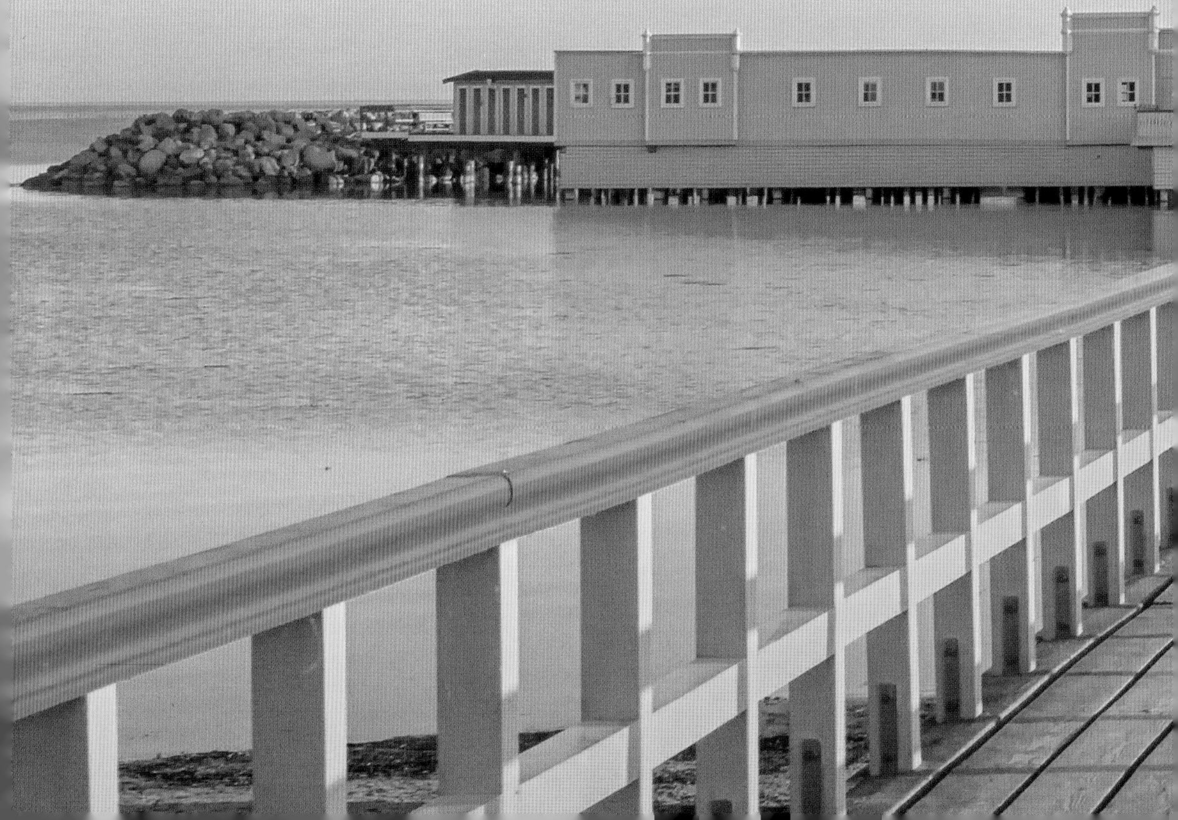

297 Bathe in the open

▼ Queer Kallis, Ribersborgs Kallbadhus, Malmö, Sweden

When to go: All year
Best for: Genderless saunas and skinny dipping

Every first Monday of the month is Queer Kallis at the historic Ribersborgs Kallbadhus bathhouse. During Queer Kallis, both areas of the open-air bathhouse on the beach are open to all people of all genders. Queer Kallis is a step toward creating a more inclusive, equal, accepting, and welcoming space for LGBTQ+ people in Malmö. It's the perfect Nordic-style sauna to relax year-round, with five saunas, two cold sea-baths, two wood-fired hot tubs, a sun deck and gorgeous sea views.

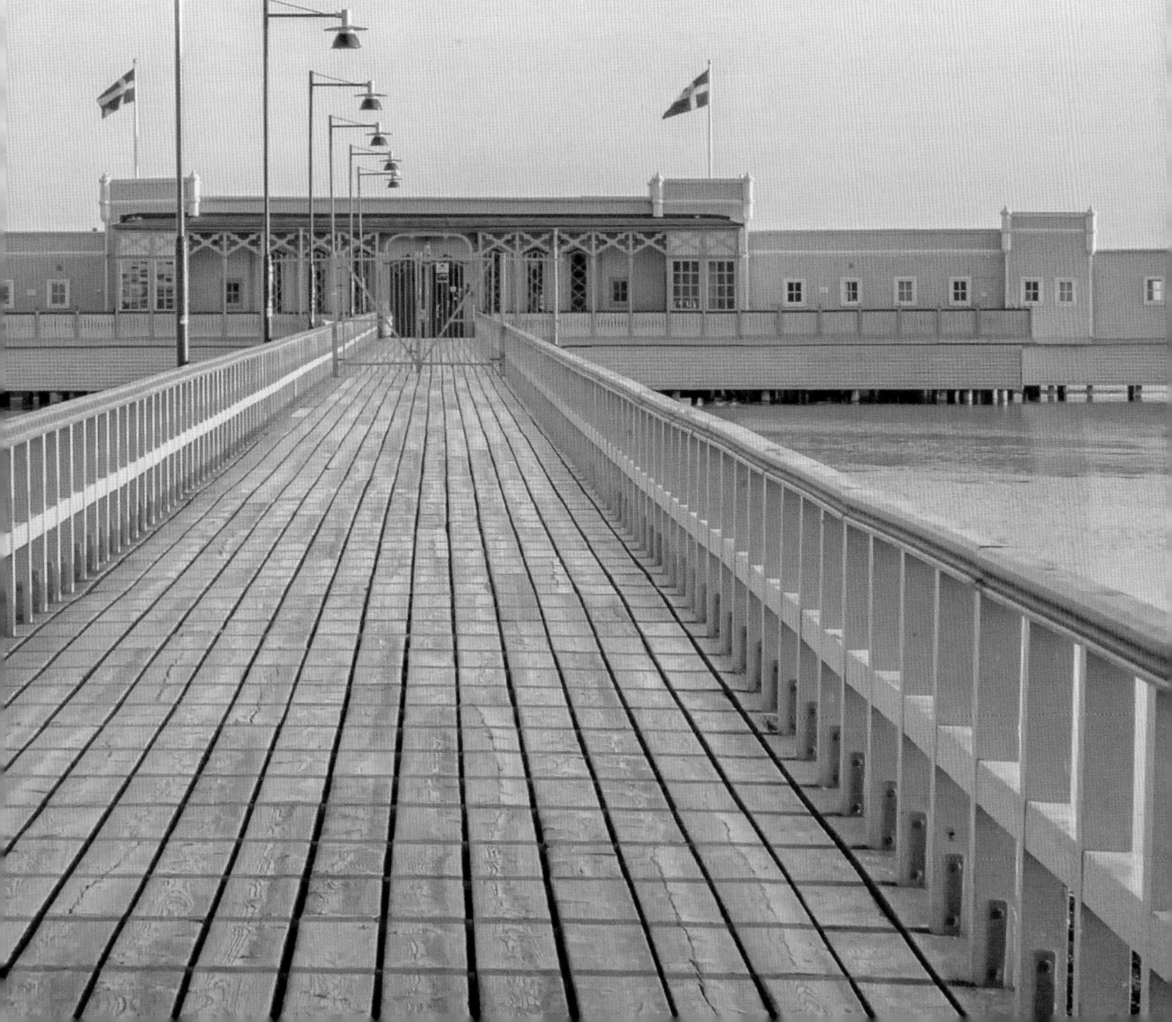

298 Twist and shout

▼ Malmö, Sweden

When to go: July
Best for: Nordic hospitality

The small, diverse, and friendly city of Malmö includes a thriving queer community among its young and international population. Find events via Queer Feminist Malmö, take the online audio-tour, *I'm Every Lesbian—Malmö* by Sam Hultin, join the monthly Queer Kallis, or visit Malmö Queer Film Festival in April. People of all ages—including young families—join the Pride parade through the city and continue the party in Folkets Park. In the heart is Sallys Kafé, perfect for *fika*: Swedish coffee-time.

299 Garden party

The Secret Garden, Stockholm, Sweden

When to go: All year
Best for: Botanical drinks

The Secret Garden, located in Stockholm's charming old part, is several venues rolled into one. This airy space is a gateway to three different bars in different rooms, offering something for everyone. The ambience is a mix of botanical gardens with fairy lights and rainbow accents that highlight the queer vibe. Get wild on the weekends when there's a DJ playing until the early hours, or go in the afternoon for a more low-key experience.

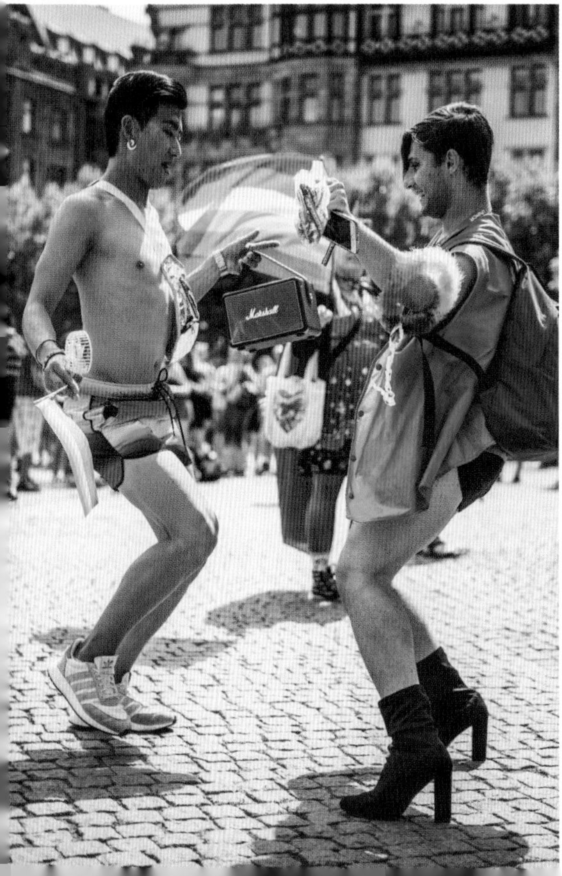

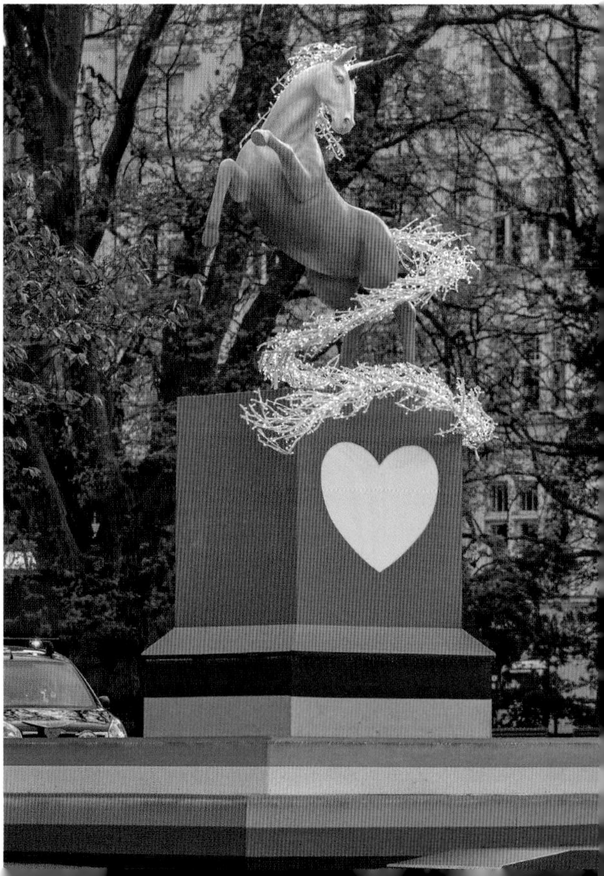

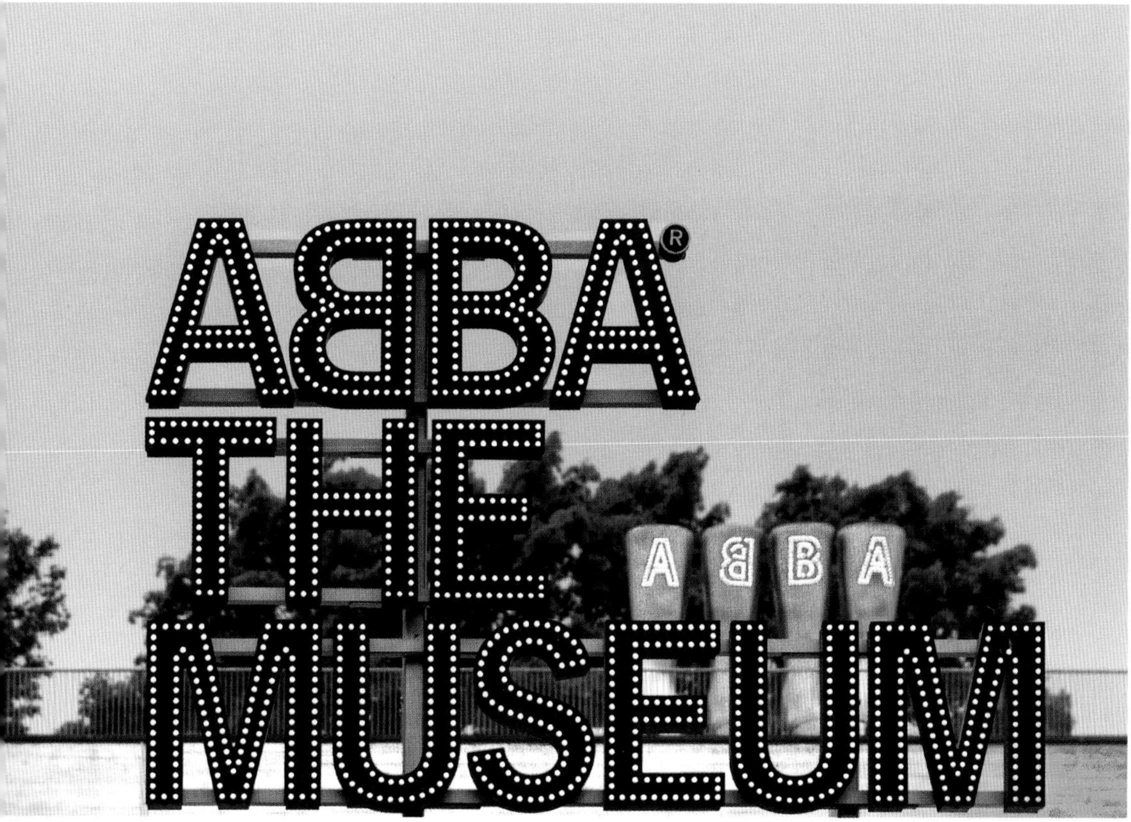

300 My, my, how can I resist you?

▲ Stockholm, Sweden

When to go: All year
Best for: All-round integration

Truly LGBTQ+ friendly places don't need to prove it with queer spaces, but rather, the opposite: true equality means queerness is normalized and integrated with society. Stockholm is one of those places. There are a handful of queer venues—lesbian club Moxy, fetish gay men's club SLM, old gay bar Side Track, Club Backdoor, The Secret Garden—but that's not what makes Stockholm distinctively queer. There's queer history in Stockholm's Royal Palace, with the seventeenth-century silver throne of Kristina—sometimes Kristine—of Sweden, who was gender-queer, and infamous for being intimate with women. Stockholm is also where queer-beloved pop group ABBA was born, Regnbågsfonden (Rainbow Fund) creates True Colors Cava, and Scandinavia's biggest Pride happens. But what stands out most in Stockholm is the welcoming attitude toward all genders. You find gender-neutral bathrooms nearly everywhere in Stockholm, and many gender-neutral shops on famous shopping streets.

301 Better than chocolate

▶ Chokladkoppen, Stockholm, Sweden

When to go: All year
Best for: Fabulous *fika*

There is no better place to go for *fika* than Chokladkoppen. *Fika* is the Swedish concept of coffee-time, and a state of mind as much as a time of day: a moment to slow down and connect with others while enjoying a coffee and something to eat—try a *kanelbullar* (cinnamon roll). LGBTQ-run café Chokladkoppen was the first place in Stockholm to wave a rainbow flag.

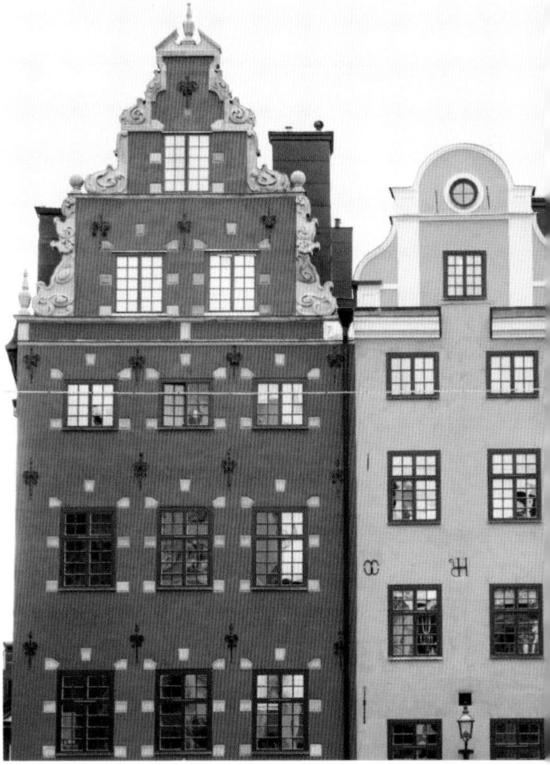

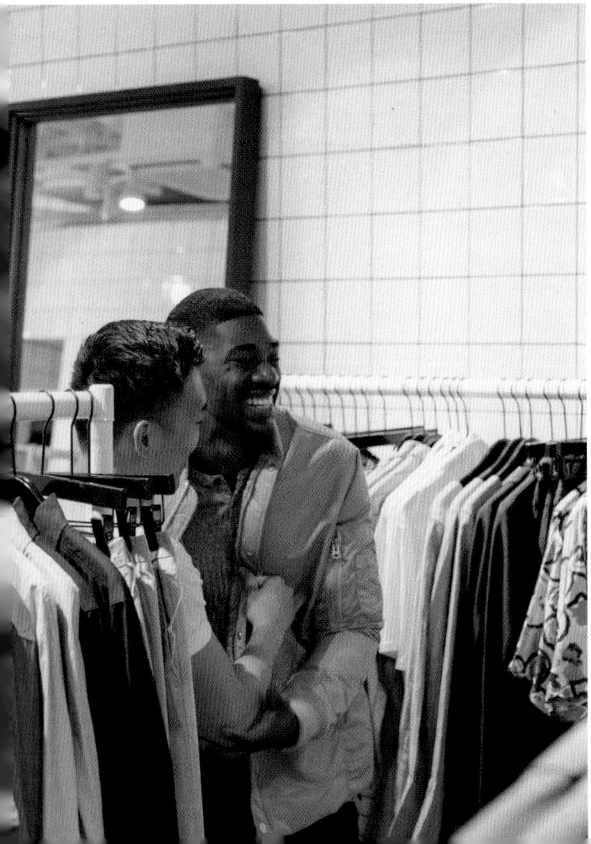

302 Closets are for unisex clothes

◀ Norrmalm, Stockholm, Sweden

When to go: All year
Best for: Gender-neutral shopping

Stockholm embraces the gender-neutral. Sweden was the first country in the world to legalize gender change, has transgender representation in government, and has a gender-neutral pronoun—*hen*—widely adopted since 2010. Fashion labels are taking note and Swedish labels Hope, Mini Rodini, Polarn O. Pyret, and Betón make all their clothes unisex, while Byredo offers gender-neutral fragrances. Find your fit in the shopping district of Norrmalm.

303 Somewhere in the crowd...

▼ ▶ Stockholm Pride, Sweden

When to go: July and August
Best for: Showing your *sanna färger* (true colors)

Stockholm Pride's three pillars are Pride House, Pride Park, and the Pride Parade. Pride House—the political and cultural center of the week-long festival—offers seminars, panels, workshops, screenings, and performances. Mid-week, Pride Park opens its gates, and you can enjoy stands, stages, shows, restaurant tents, shops, and exhibitions. And on Saturday, join Scandinavia's biggest Pride Parade and roll, dance, march, or strut with the crowd.

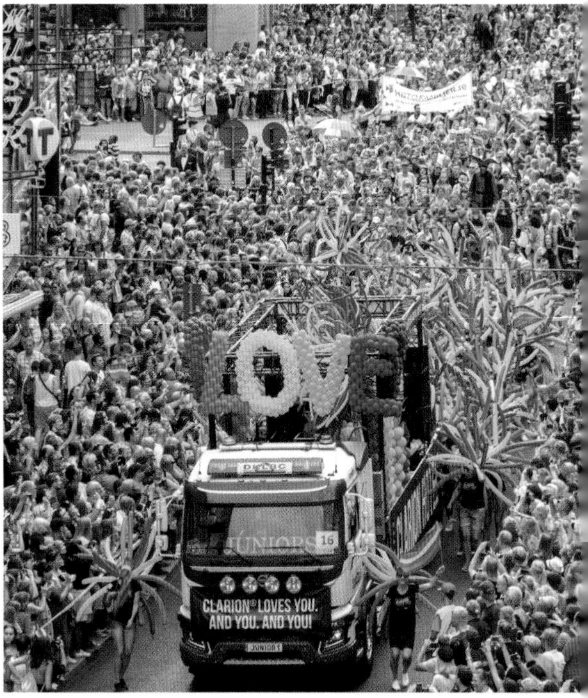

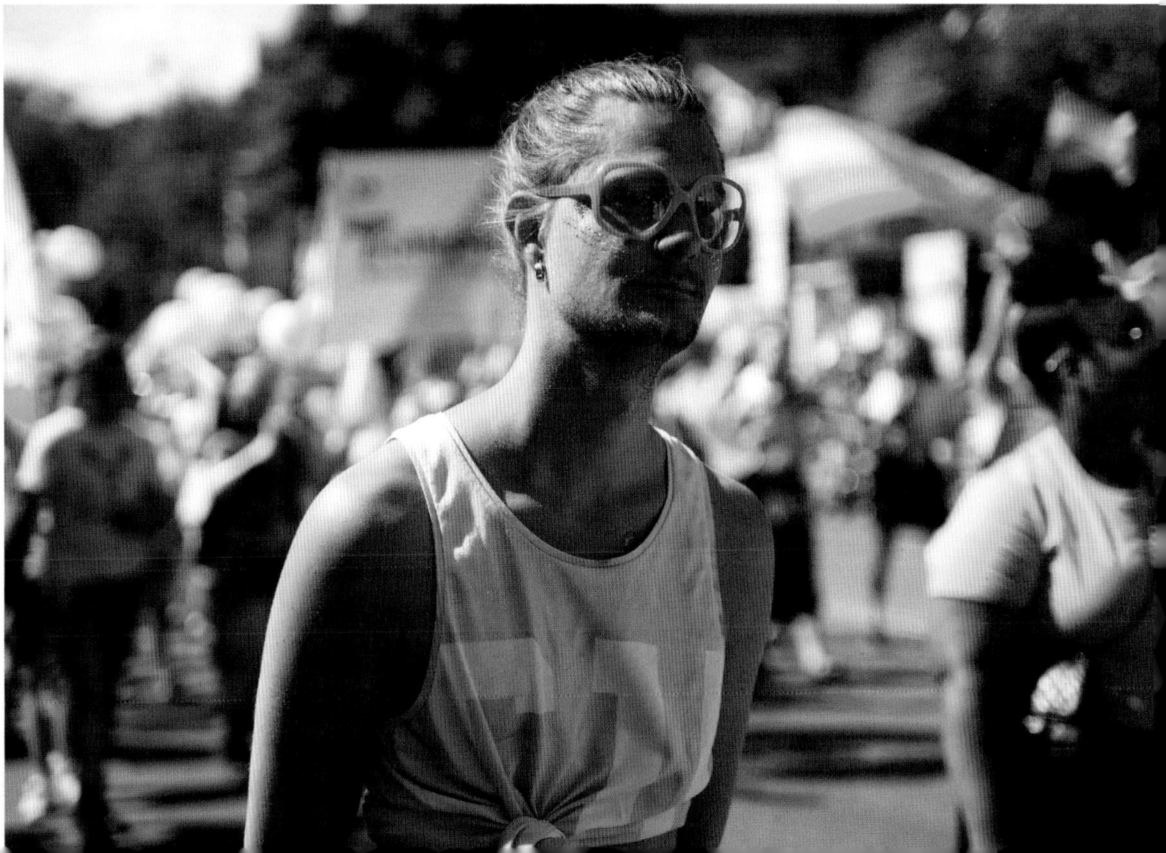

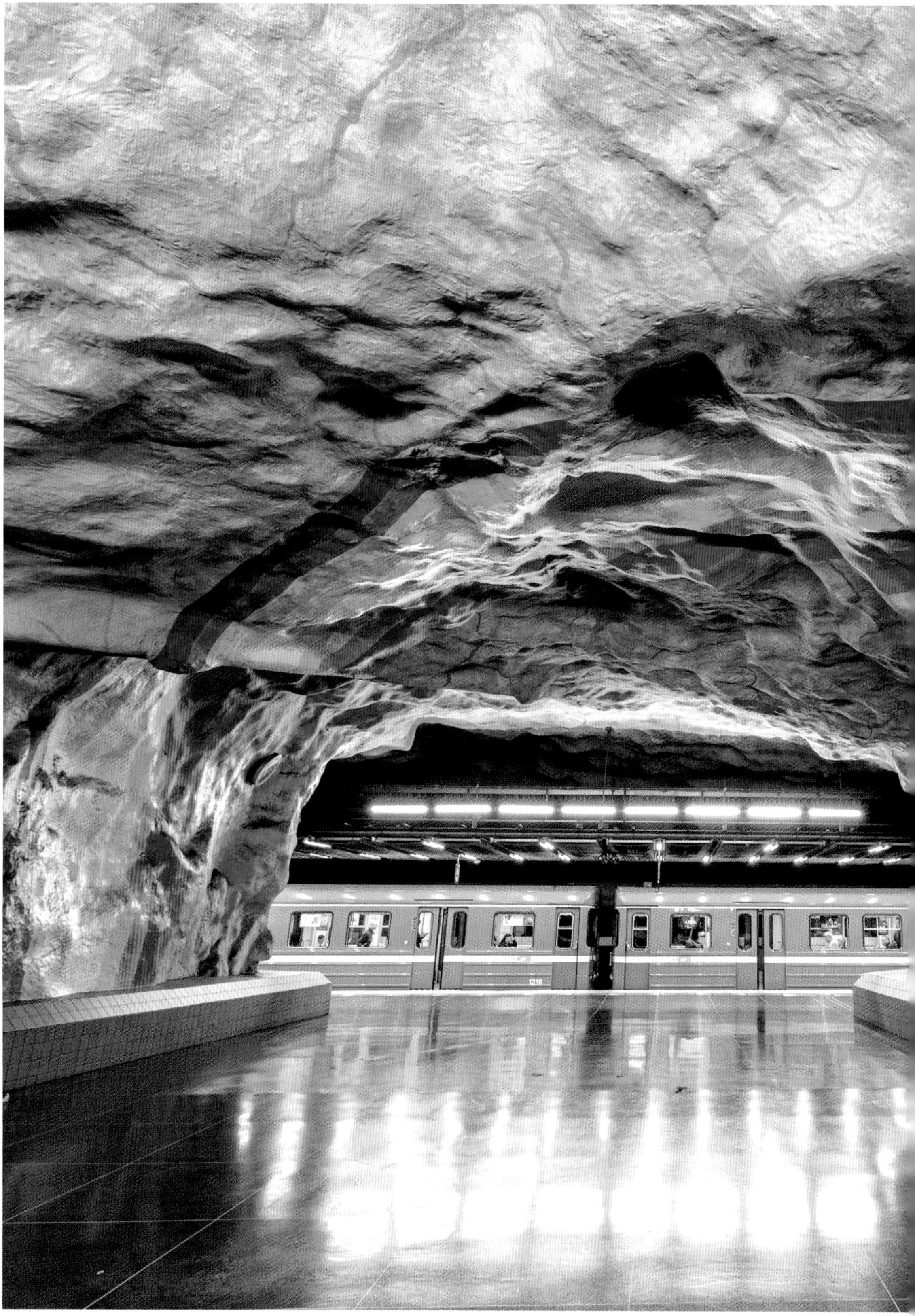

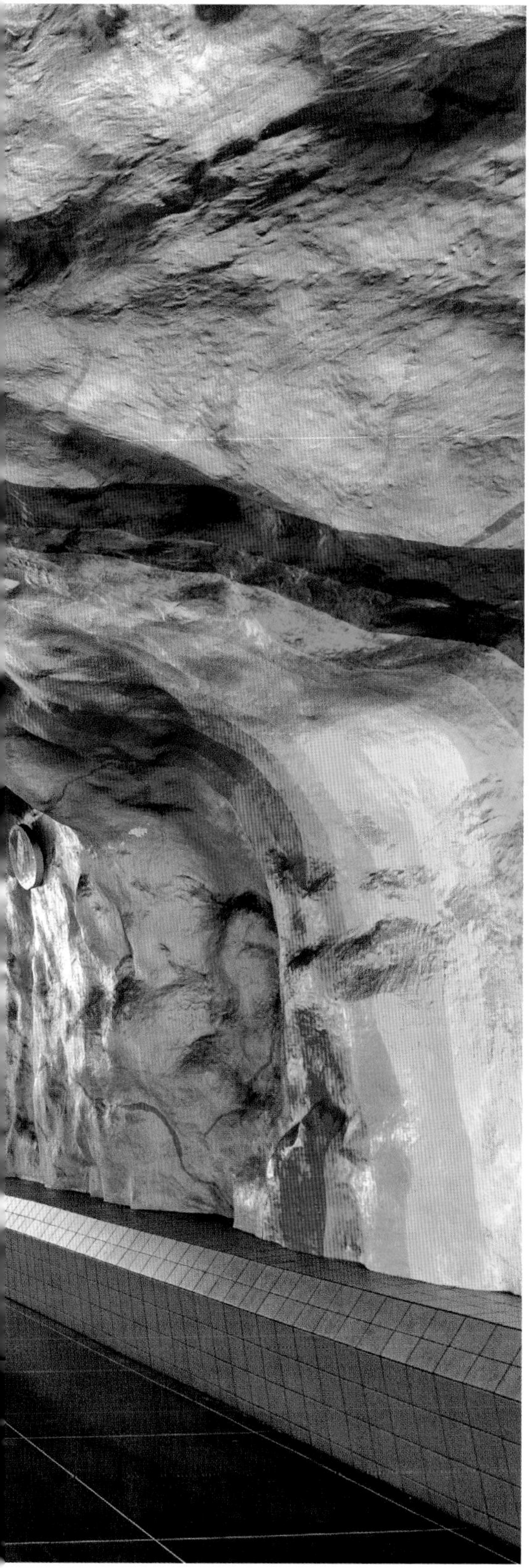

304 Underground art scene

Stockholm Metro Art, Sweden

When to go: All year
Best for: Accessible art

Enjoy the world's longest art gallery for the price of a metro ticket. Since the late 1950s, Stockholm's metro, or *tunnelbana*, invited artists to decorate the underground stations to make art more accessible. Today, 90 percent of the city's metro stations display the art of more than 150 artists in one form or another. Go on a self-guided tour—avoiding the morning and evening rush hours—by starting at the central hub T-Centralen, where Finnish artist Per-Olov Ultvedt created the first artwork for the blue line platform. And guess what colour the artwork is? Yes, it's calmingly blue—and flowery. Stadion Station was one of the first cave stations to open—the name given to the stations on the network which have the natural rock they are hewn from as their walls and ceilings. Close to Stockholm Pride's main area, Stadion has a large rainbow painted on bright-blue walls by Åke Pallarp and Enno Hallek, to remind people there's a sky not far above. At the end of the red line, Mörby Centrum station, there's another rainbow-like, cotton candy artwork by Gösta Wessel and Karin Ek, with colors changing depending on where you stand. And many stations, including T-Centralen, Östermalmstorg, Hallonbergen, Norsborg and Alby, have rainbow escalators.

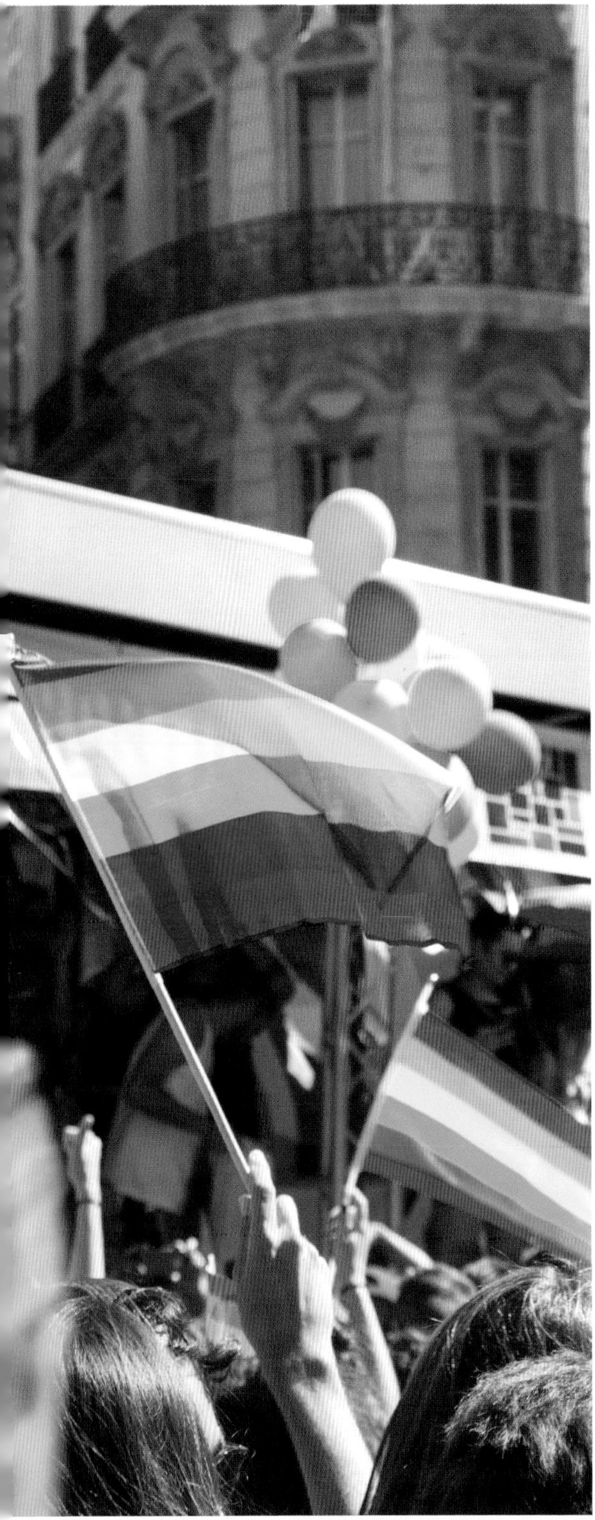

305 Sunny salty sailor city

◀ Marseille Pride, France

When to go: July
Best for: Ferocious *fiertés*

France's oldest and sunniest city, Marseille is also its most strategic port on the Mediterranean. And the city's character is as salty as the air. It has a rough-and-ready reputation as a port city with a seedy sailor history. But it is also a beautifully diverse, cosmopolitan melting pot, making it particularly LGBTQ-friendly. Marseille's Pride happens just after Paris Pride, and while Marseille's queer scene is low-key, thousands of people join the Marche des Fiertés parade and the Pride festival in the gardens of Palais Longchamp.

306 Laid-back lady bar

Aux 3G, Marseille, France

When to go: All year
Best for: Hooking up with lesbians

Nestled in the La Plaine district of Marseille, Aux 3G is more than just a lesbian bar. It's a lesbian, queer, and feminist bar and association, run by volunteers since 1995. When you enter the small, cozy space, you feel the welcoming, laid-back atmosphere and a strong sense of community. Grab yourself an affordable drink at the bar and enjoy the vibe. Aux 3G's eclectic events program includes poetry, music, karaoke, DJ nights, exhibitions, and workshops.

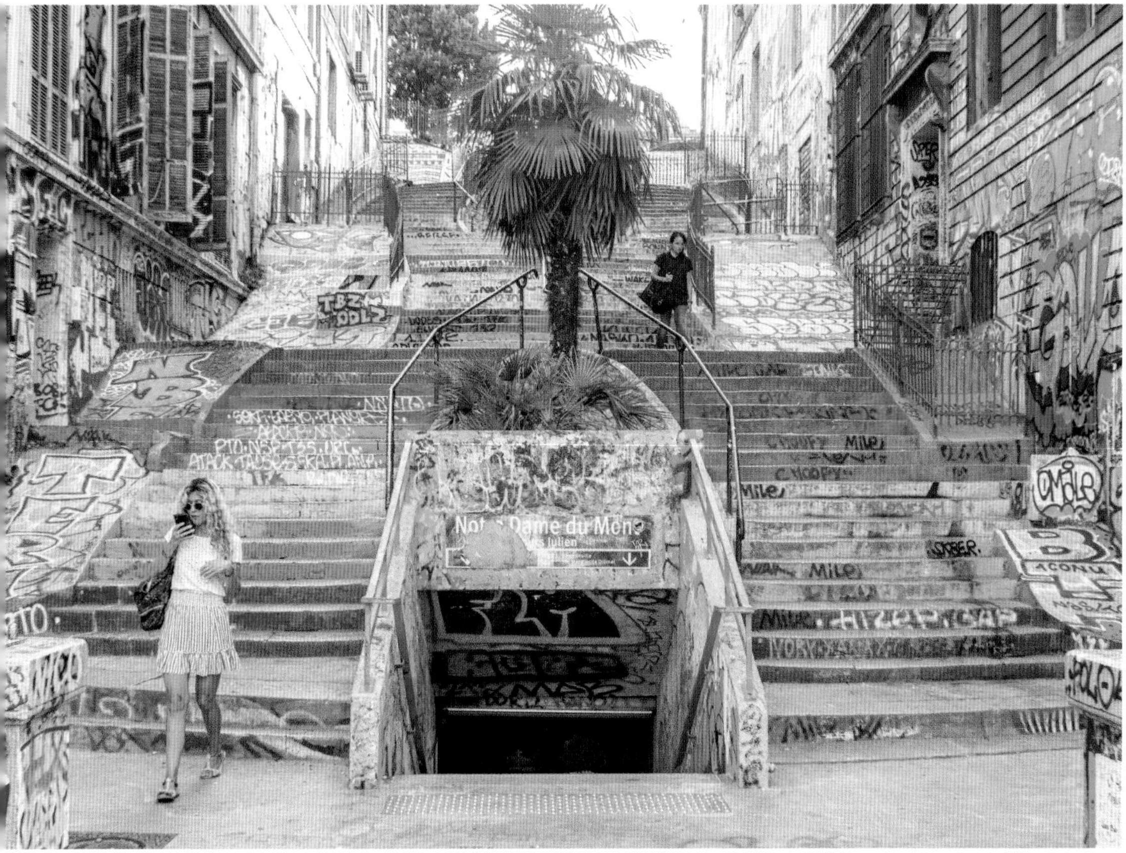

307 As queer as can be

▲ Cours Julien, La Plaine, Marseille, France

When to go: All year
Best for: Creators

Marseille's most lively and vibrant area is Cours Julien, or "Cours Ju." Known as *le quartier bobo*, the city's hipster district, it's where you find many artists, creators, musicians, and queer folks. By day, explore an abundance of street art by yourself or go on a guided tour. Wander around and visit art galleries and quirky local shops. If you're around on a Wednesday morning, get a glimpse into history; Cours Julien used to be the main trading area for fruit and vegetables, and its weekly organic farmers' market is iconic. By night, Cours Julien transforms into a trendy nightlife area. Visit The Espace Julien for live music, and Videodrome 2 for an alternative bar-cinema and media-store experience in one venue. Other LGBTQ-friendly spots to check out are Les Trois Rois, Caffénoir, Aux 3G, and Le Pulse. Marseille doesn't have an official queer neighborhood, but Cours Julien comes close.

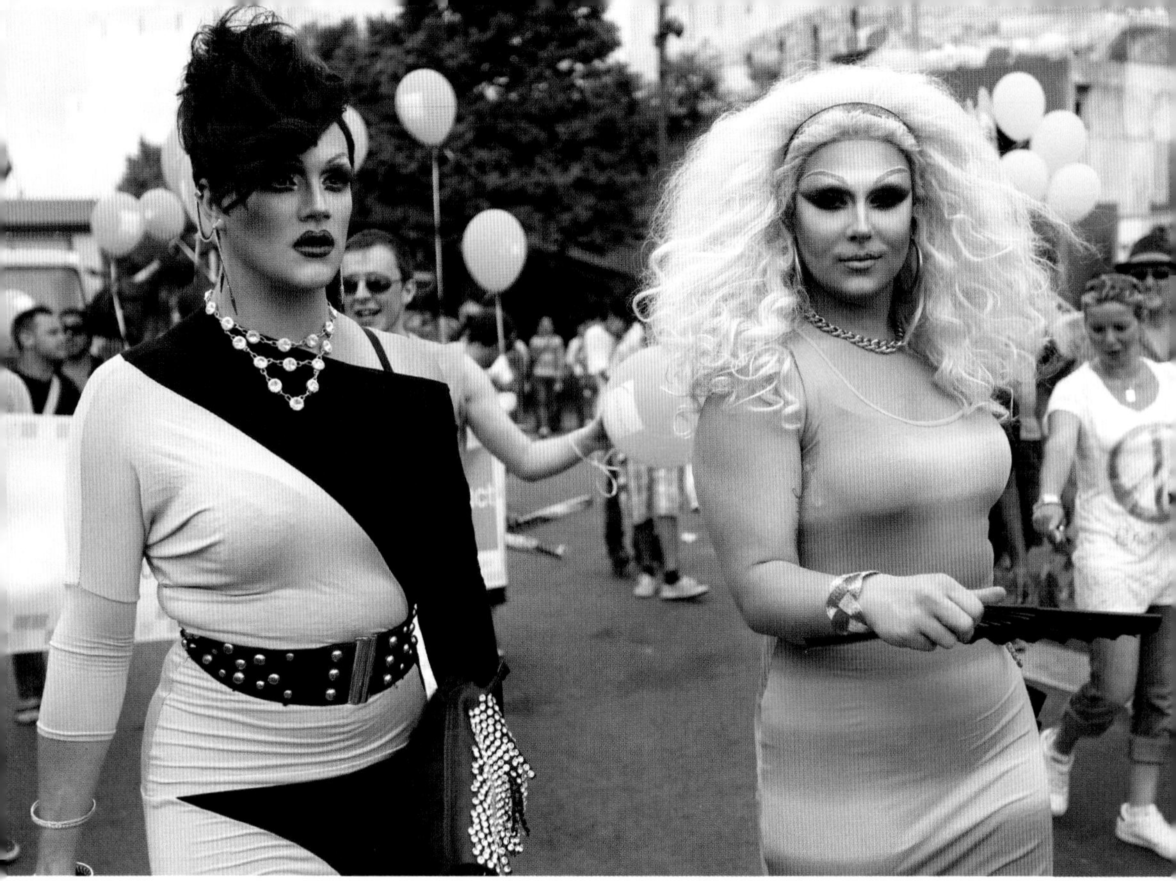

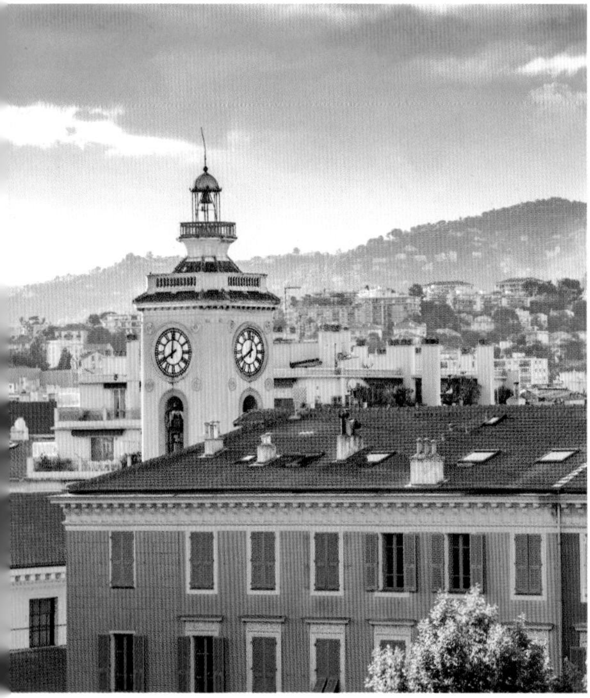

308 Twice as nice

◀ ▲ Pink Parade, Nice, France

When to go: July
Best for: Sea walks

The French Riviera's sun-drenched capital is home to a vibrant LGBTQ+ scene, with hot spots in Nice's old town such as Red Kafé, Le Glam, and Le Six. Step into lesbian-owned bookstore, Librairie Vigna, for the best queer and feminist information. Nice's Pink Parade, in summer, travels along Promenade des Anglais with an uninterrupted view of the azure sea and palm trees, before culminating in an outdoor Pink Drink party. In spring, there's Lou Queernaval—a queer carnival—and the LGBTQ+ In & Out film festival.

309 Steps in the right direction

▼ Les Marches de la Fiertés, Nantes, France

When to go: All year
Best for: Sashaying on a rainbow staircase

In French, *les marches* means both marches and a stairway. In 2018, local LGBTQ+ organization Nosig painted the steps on Rue Beaurepaire in rainbow colors for Nantes Pride, turning them into a literal Marches de la Fiertés. Only a few days later, the stairs were vandalized. The city filed an official complaint, and a heartwarming community of two hundred people came together to repaint them.

310 Forced out but not down

Les Mots à la Bouche, Paris, France

When to go: All year
Best for: Queer cultural heritage

LGBTQ+ bookshop Les Mots à la Bouche (words in the mouth) has been a queer landmark since 1980 that won't be silent or silenced. When soaring property prices forced the Marais staple—and many queer folk—to relocate, Les Mots à La Bouche took over 16,000 titles (LGBTQ+ books, DVDs, magazines, and comics) to a new location and reestablished its familiar, bright-blue façade and dazzling events calendar, not to mention its welcoming vibe.

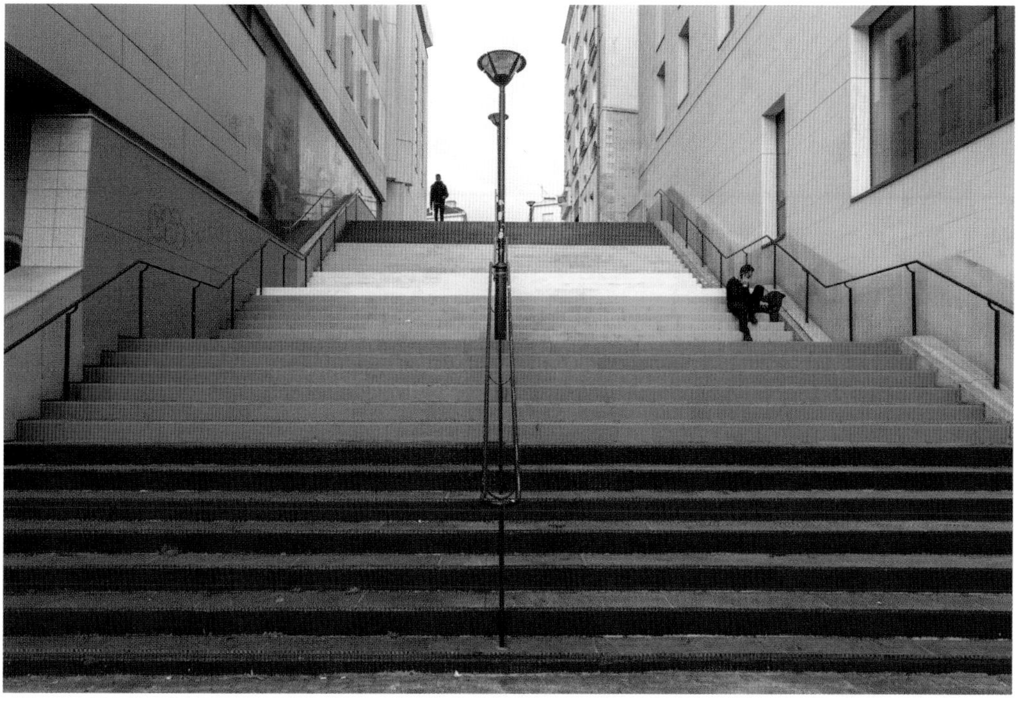

311 Give it your best shot

The Labo, Paris, France

When to go: All year
Best for: A truly Parisian night out

For sweet afternoons and wild nights, go to gay bar The Labo, famous for its happy hours and theme nights, including karaoke, drag shows, and date nights with toys. With each drink, you get a card, and if you find someone with a matching card, you get free shots.

312 *Joie de vivre*

▼ Rosa Bonheur, Paris, France

When to go: All year
Best for: Queer *joie de vivre*

When legendary lesbian club Pulp closed, its founder brought Pulp's spirit to a new venture; a *guinguette* chain named after LGBTQ+ artist Rosa Bonheur. *Guinguette* is a centuries-old French café concept, a rustic space where life is good. Rosa Bonheur's parkside and Seine-side venues boast queer *joie de vivre* and host exemplary events and activities.

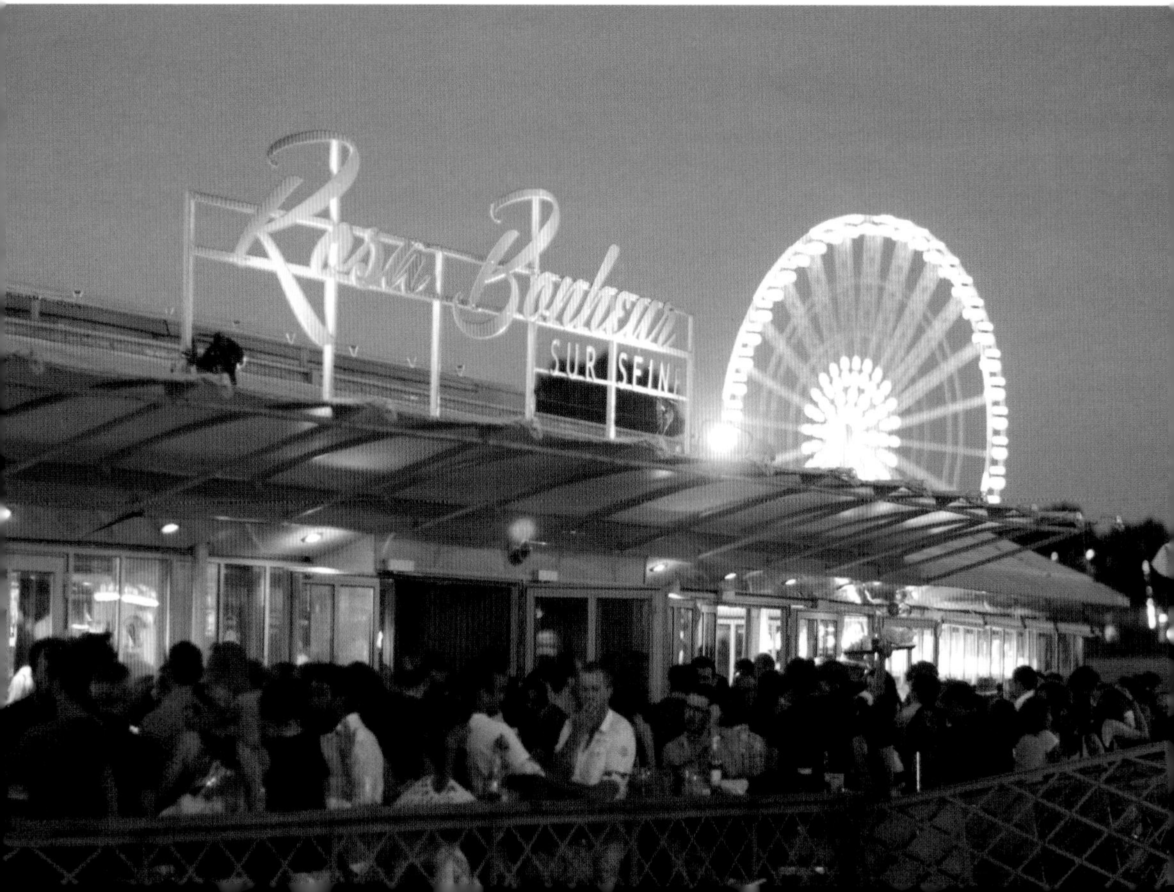

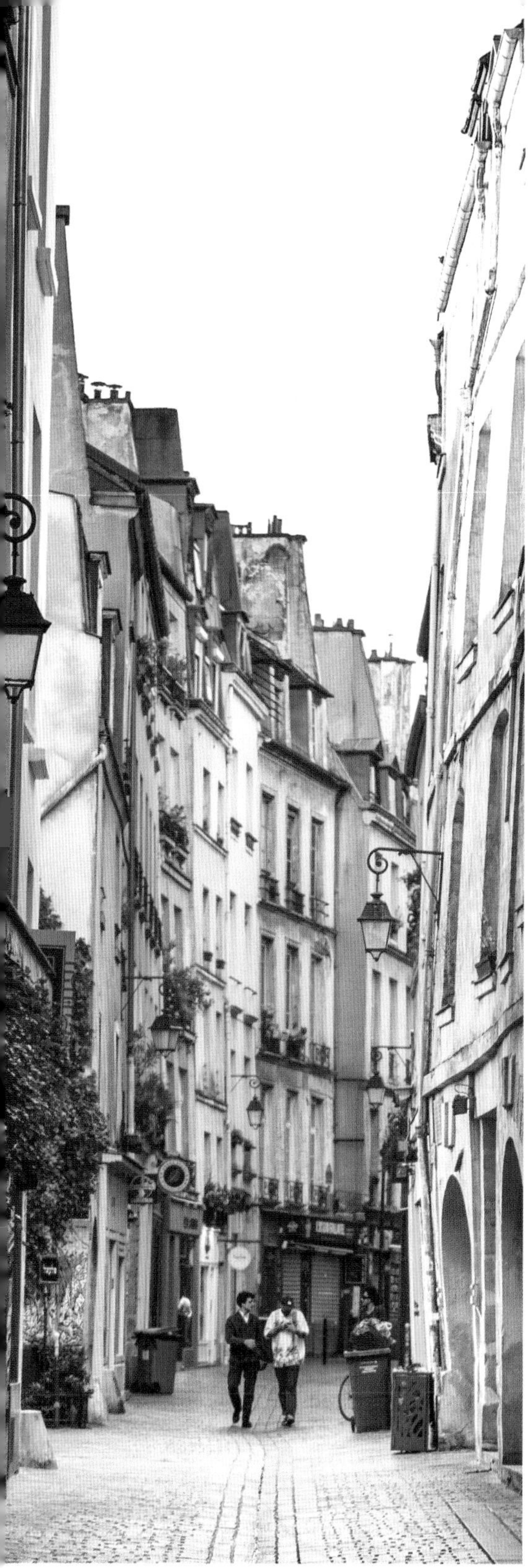

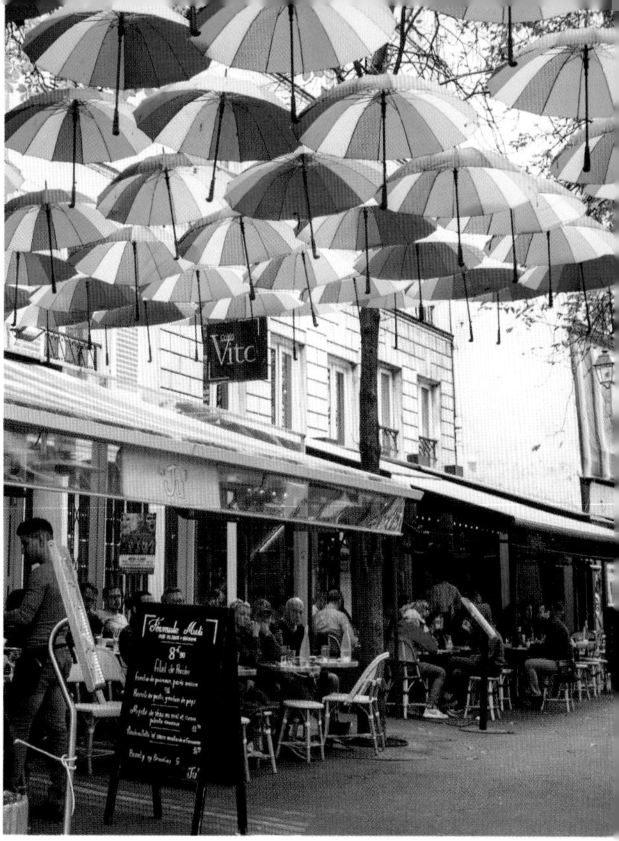

313 Gay Paree

◀ ▲ Le Marais, Paris, France

When to go: All year
Best for: Paris by gay and night

Dating back to the eighteenth century, Paris has a rich LGBTQ+ history, with a variety of gay neighborhoods. Since the 1980s, it is Le Marais which has taken the lead, with LGBTQ-named areas such as Place Harvey Milk. It is where you'll find the biggest street parties during Paris Pride. By day, it's a shopping paradise with trendy boutiques and vintage shops. At night, the food scene and nightlife come alive. Popular gay venues are COX, Who's, and Duplex Bar. You'll find a mixed crowd at Open Café and queer women at 3W Kafé, offering karaoke and drag nights.

314 Let your inner diva loose

Disneyland® Paris Pride, Disneyland Paris, France

When to go: June
Best for: LGBTQ+ families

For one magical night every year, Disneyland Paris is transformed into a celebration of diversity for LGBTQ+ folk and their families, with a parade, live performances, and attractions open until late into the night. From the moment you set foot through the gates, there's a vibrant and friendly party atmosphere bursting with Disney magic specially created for the occasion. It's a family-friendly event, so bring the kids and dive into this celebration surrounded by a welcoming crowd.

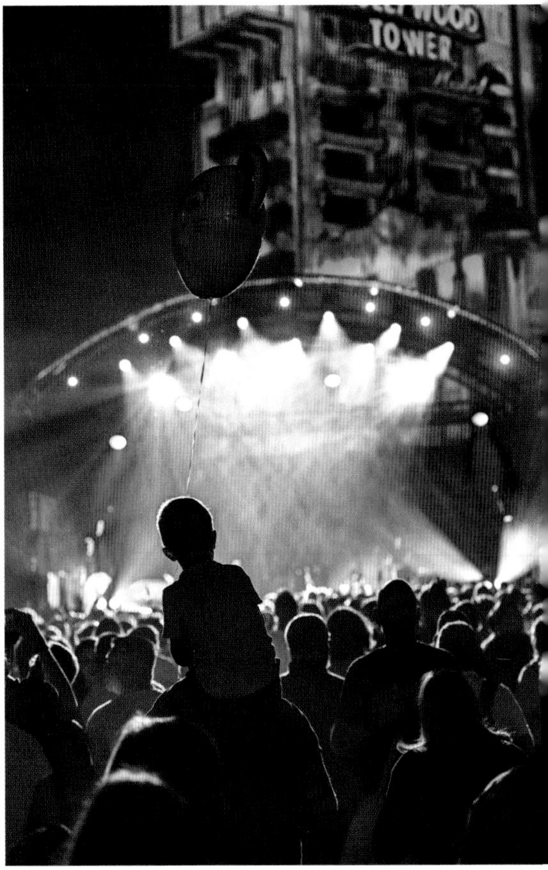

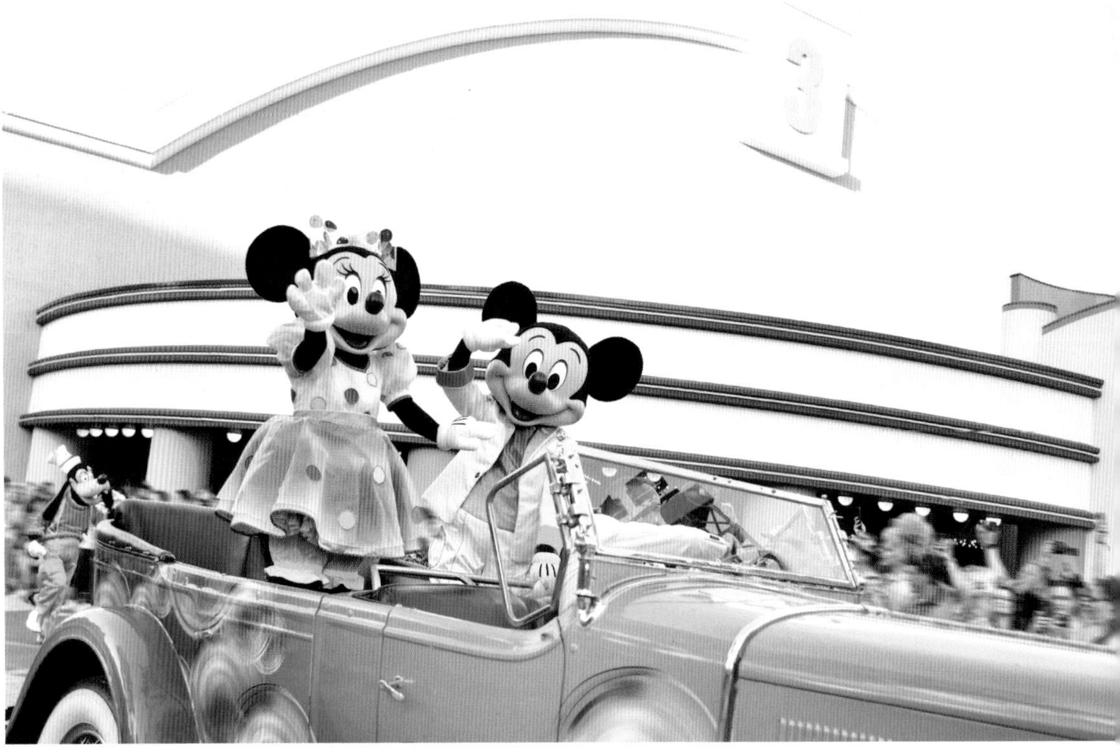

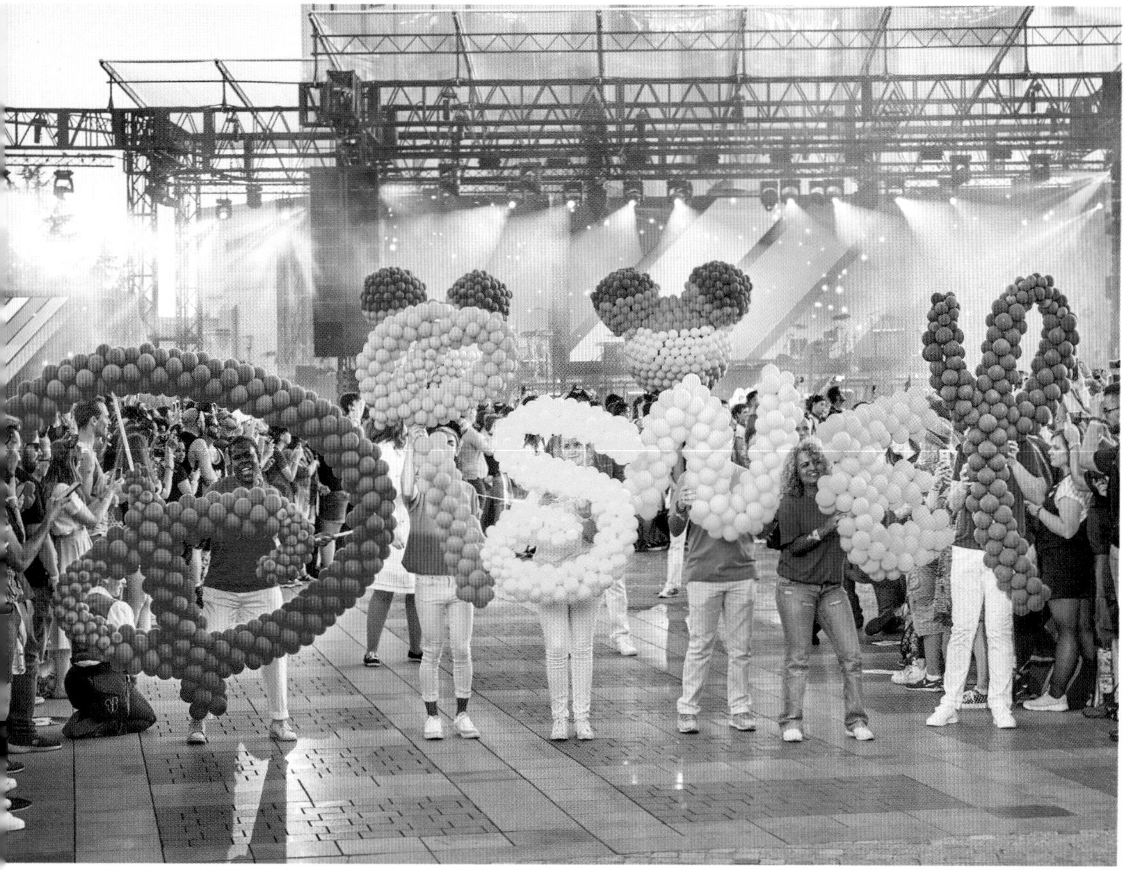

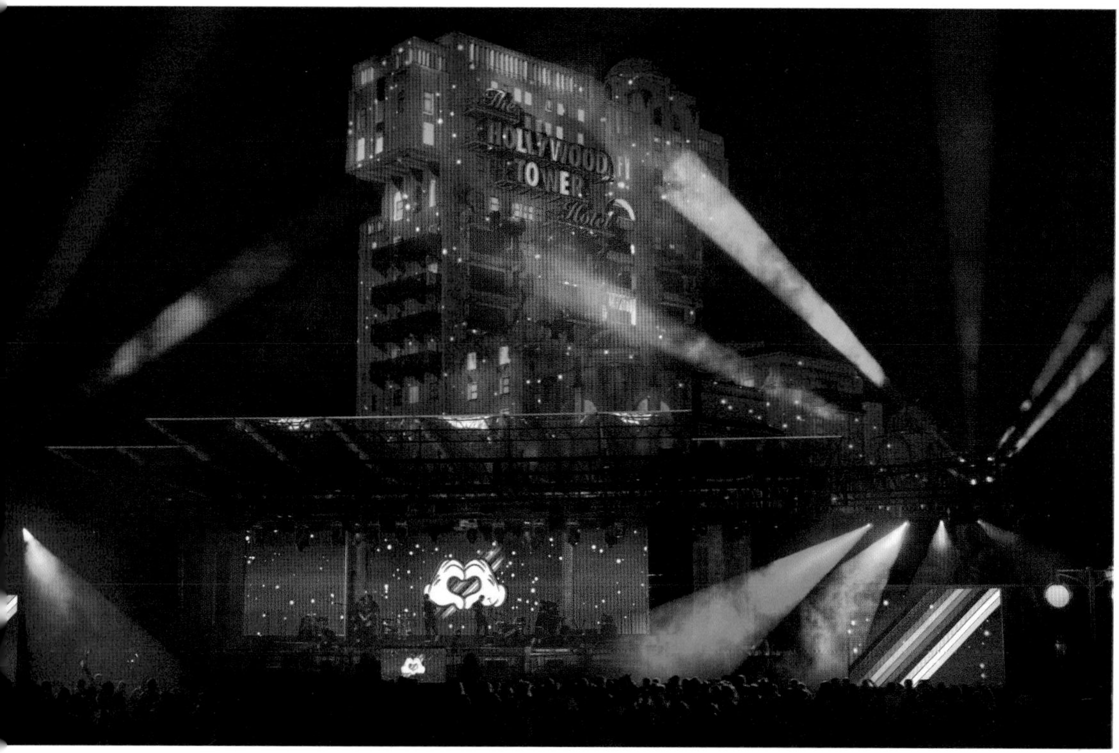
The
HOLLYWOOD
TOWER
Hotel

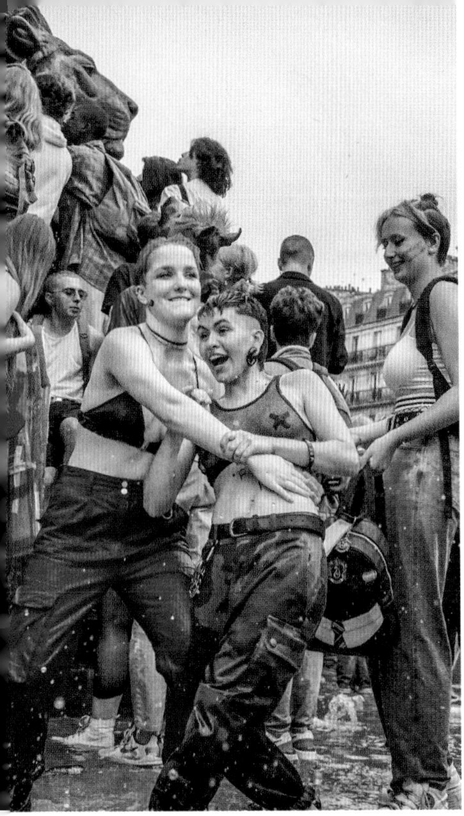

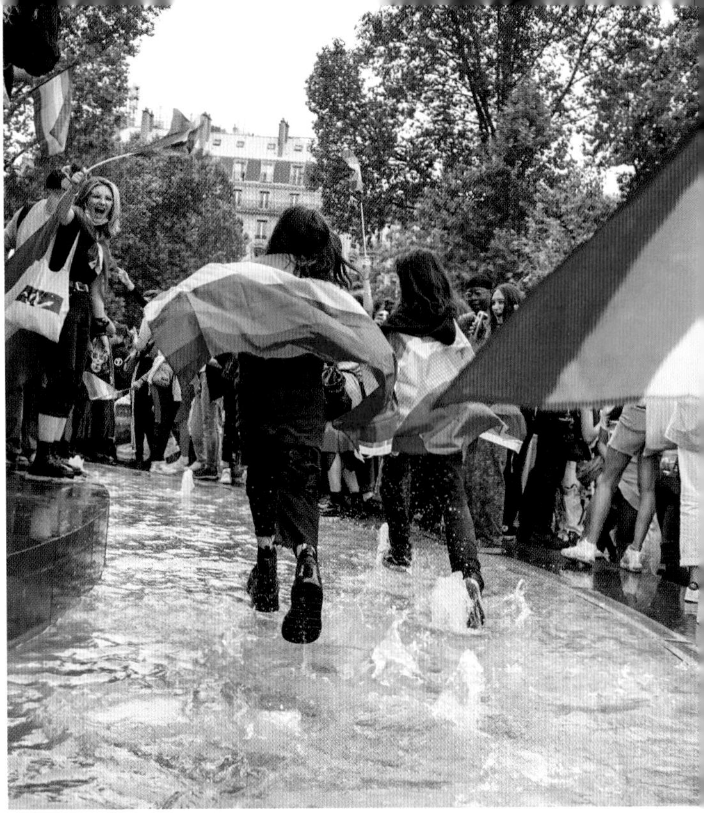

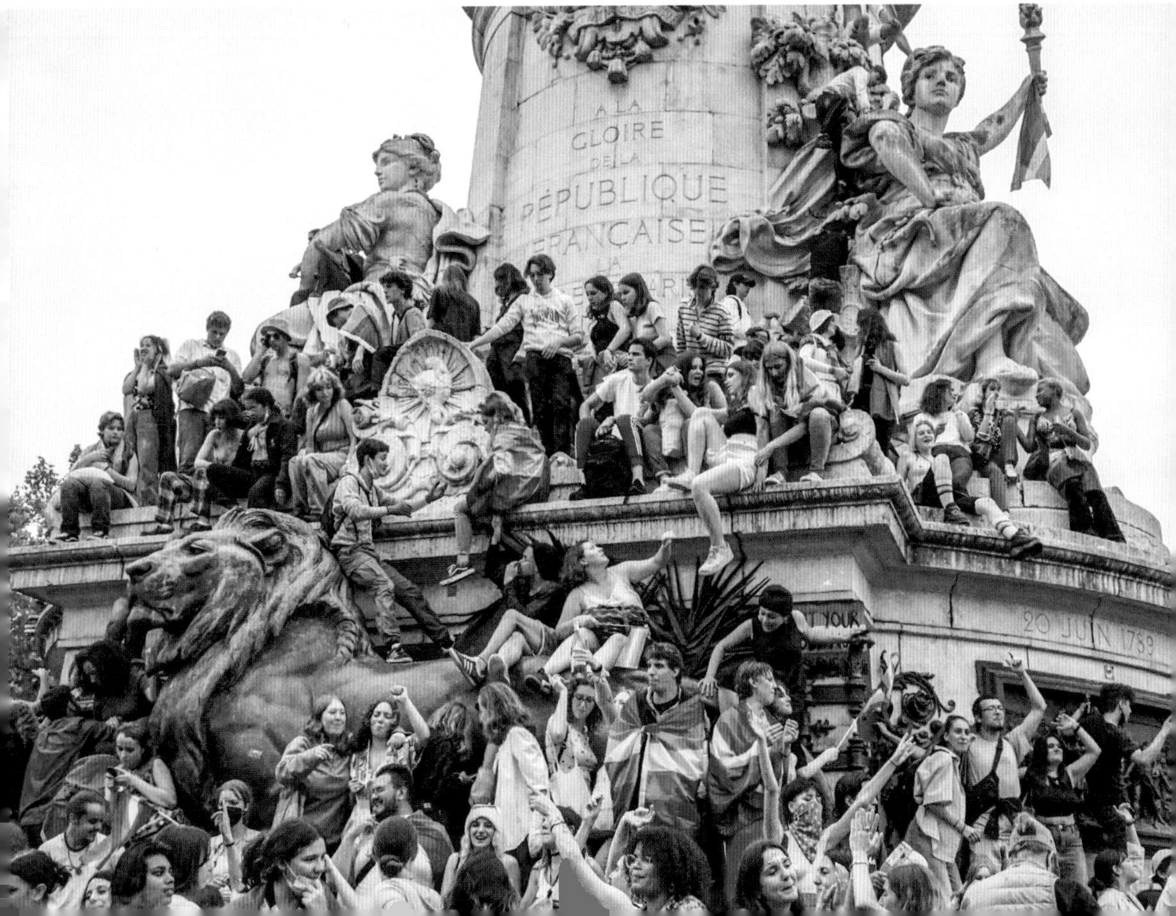
A LA
GLOIRE
DE LA
RÉPUBLIQUE
20 JUIN 1789

315 Summer in the city

◀ Quinzaine des Fiertés, Paris, France

When to go: June
Best for: Riverside Pride

Paris's festive summers are reason enough to visit France's capital, with the Seine riverbanks turning into city beaches, and parks with outdoor live music and dancing. Travel to Paris in June to be in time for Quinzaine des Fiertés, the multidisciplinary fortnight LGBTQ+ festival that culminates in the nearly half-a-century-old Marché des Fiertés (Pride parade), which retains a political edge. The parade is among the biggest in Europe, and while the route varies, Le Marais is always the popular place for after-parties.

316 Don't be a drag, just be a *gouine*

Mutinerie, Paris, France

When to go: All year
Best for: Mutiny and defiance

Run by and for queer women, *gouines* (dykes), and trans people, La Mutinerie is an anarchist harbor that has become the unofficial headquarters of lesbian and trans nightlife in Paris over the last decade. The space is small yet festive, the events are eclectic (dance/yoga classes, tattoo nights, drag performances, hacking and self-defense workshops), and the vibes are always intersectionally queer-feminist.

317 In remembrance of those gone before

Commemorative plaque Jean Diot and Bruno Lenoir, Paris, France

When to go: All year
Best for: Remembering

A century before Italy, and nearly two centuries before the United Kingdom, France decriminalized sodomy—including homosexuality—in the French Revolution. It was too late, however, for couple Jean Diot and Bruno Lenoir, who are believed to be the last gay people executed in France for homosexuality. A plaque commemorates where their arrest happened.

318 Seine-sational

Les Amarres, Paris, France

When to go: All year
Best for: Solidarity

Inspired by the utopian, pop-up, cooperative village of Les Grands Voisins (2015 to 2020), Les Amarres were port buildings on the Seine which have now been turned into a social space. The buildings house 14 social service organizations, which welcome people and families in precarious situations. Part of the building is the reception by day and a bar at night, with a gorgeous terrace overlooking the Seine. The bar area hosts cultural and festive events, including film screenings, concerts, artisans' markets, drag shows, yoga classes, and panels.

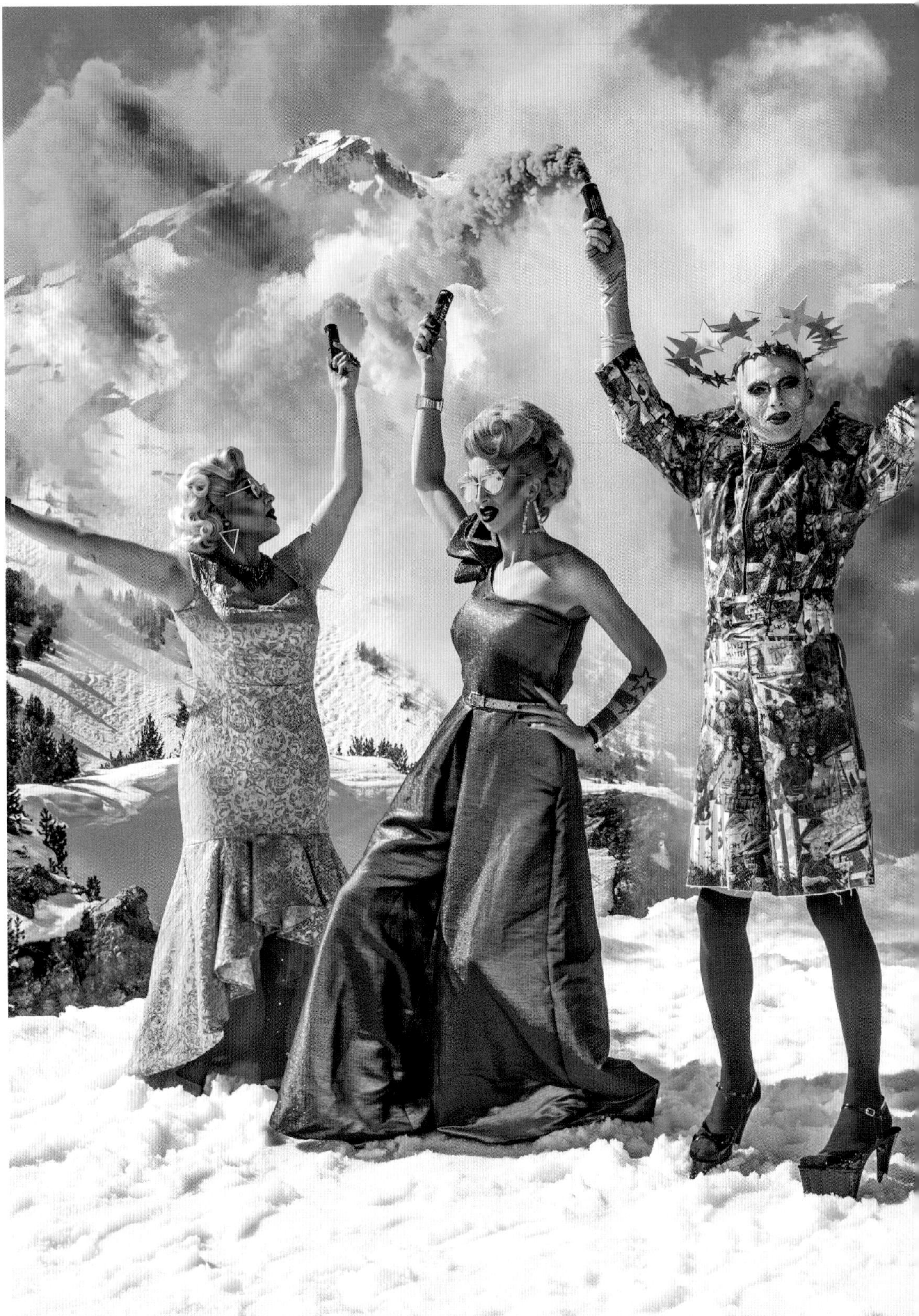

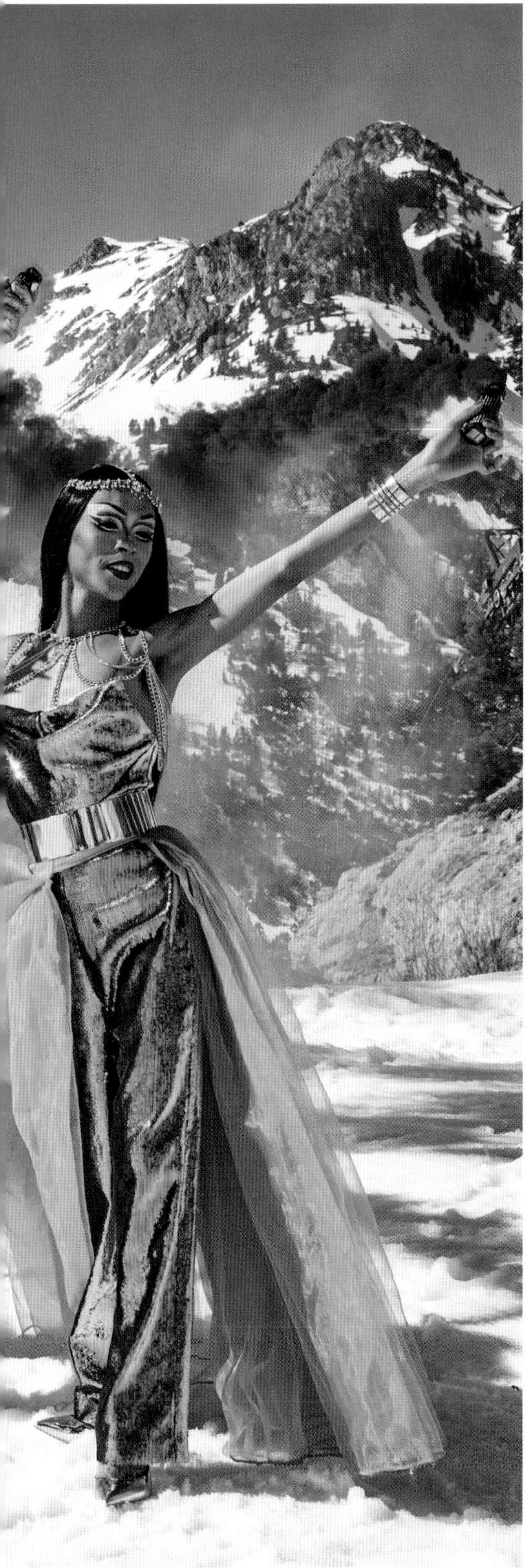

319 Peak performance

The French Alps

When to go: Late March
Best for: Skiing, snowboarding, and an abundance of après-ski fun

European Gay Ski Week began life in 2009 with just 50 guests. It has grown to become one of—if not *the*—biggest LGBTQ+ skiing and snowboarding events in Europe. It attracts people from the United Kingdom, United States, Brazil, France, Germany, Israel, Canada, and Russia to name a few. The host resort changes each year, but it tends to be somewhere high up in the French Alps. During the day—after a drag-queen–led warm-up session—there are exclusive LGBTQ skiing lessons, plus the opportunity to join groups if you're traveling solo. After a morning's skiing, rest and enjoy a hearty lunch at an Alpine lodge offering stunning views of the pristine mountains. Each evening, there are numerous après-ski events, with parties, discos, and entertainment. If you're not a big clubbing fan, there are quieter fondue and raclette gatherings. The event now attracts around one thousand fun-seekers across the week, with a wide mix of ages. Absolute beginners are always welcome. You're sure to leave with new skills, treasured friends, and some lifelong memories.

320 Beauty and the bratwurst

▼ Cologne Pride, Germany

When to go: June to July
Best for: Having fun while taking a stance

Cologne Pride is better known as Christopher Street Day, after the street on which the Stonewall Inn is located in New York. As well as the parade and music stages, there's also a political stage, where current social and political topics are discussed. A highlight of Cologne's Pride is also getting to soak in the charms of this beautiful city's historic Old Town.

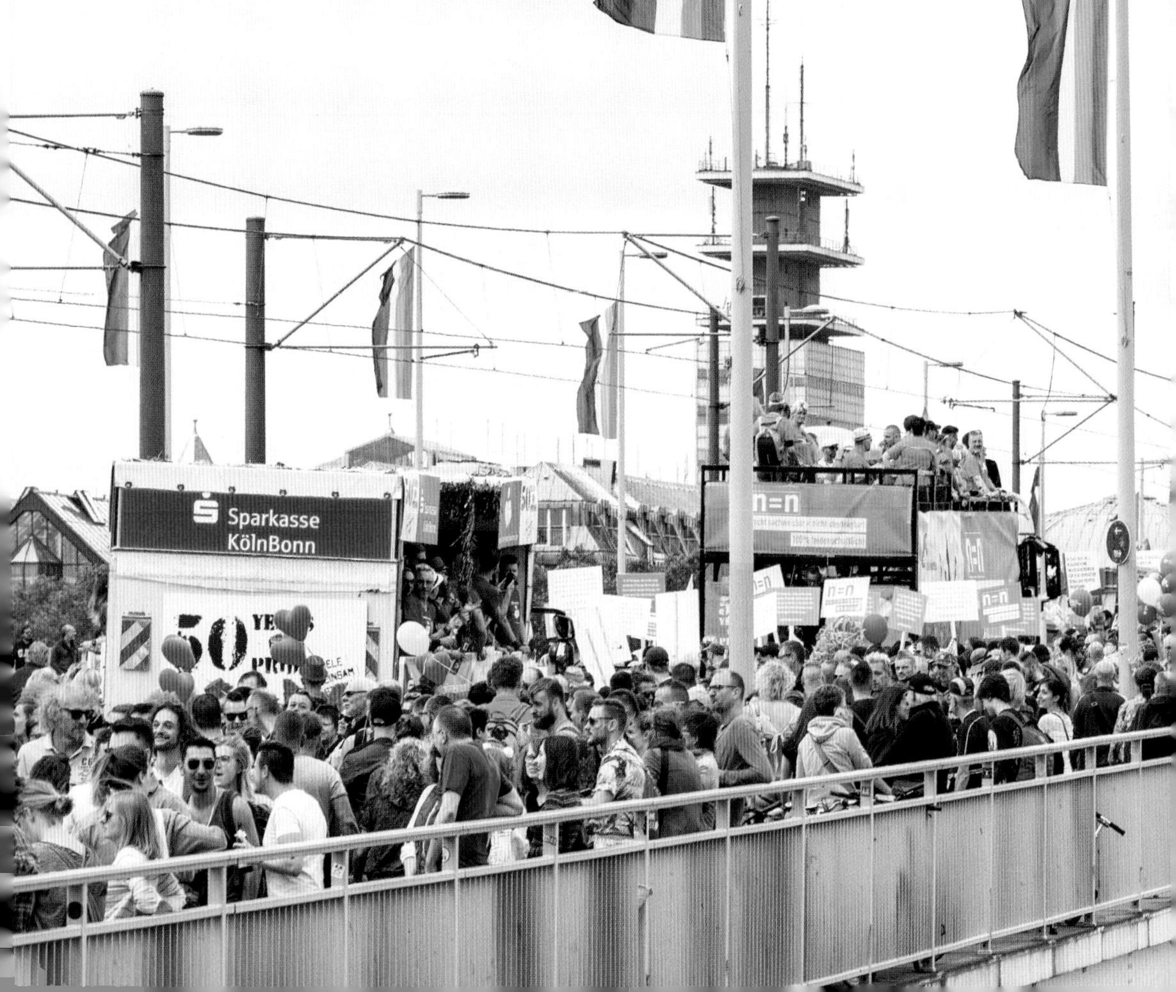

321 Turning policy into art

Frankfurter Engel, Frankfurt, Germany

When to go: All year
Best for: History in art

On Klaus-Mann-Platz there is a bronze, androgynous angel on an octagonal base, a reproduction of a destroyed angel from Cologne Cathedral. The base's inscription commemorates men-loving men persecuted under the German Criminal Code, enforced from World War II to 1968. The code's irreparable damage is symbolized by the angel's broken wings and fractured neck.

322 Fighting hate with love

Memorial to homosexuals persecuted under Nazism, Berlin, Germany

When to go: All year
Best for: Never forgetting

Opposite the 2,711 concrete columns of the Holocaust Memorial in the Tiergarten stands another memorial. This large, concrete cuboid has a small window through which visitors can see a short film on homosexual love. It is estimated that 100,000 gay men were arrested by the Nazis, 50,000 convicted, and between 5,000 and 15,000 sent to concentration camps, the majority of whom didn't survive.

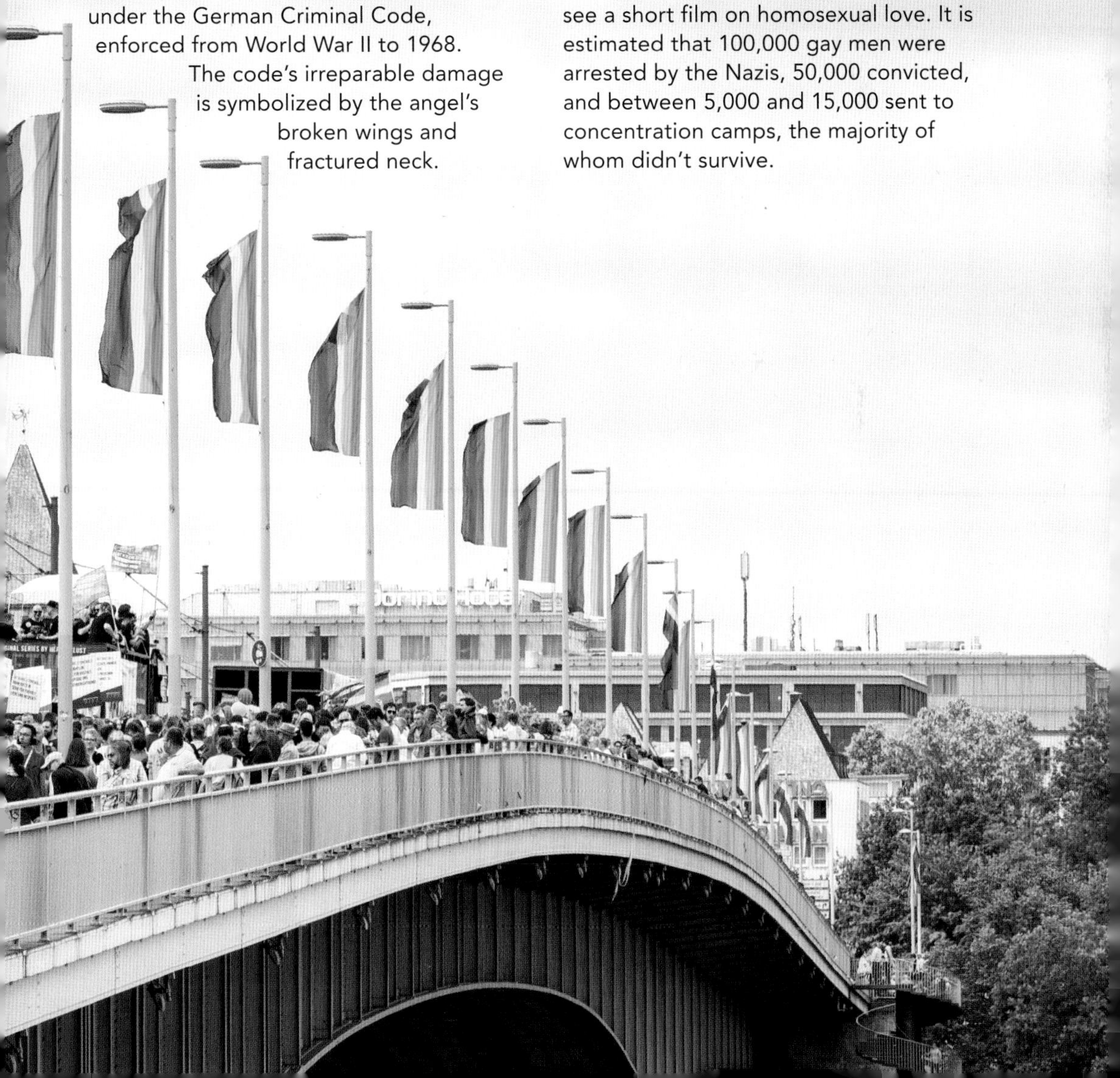

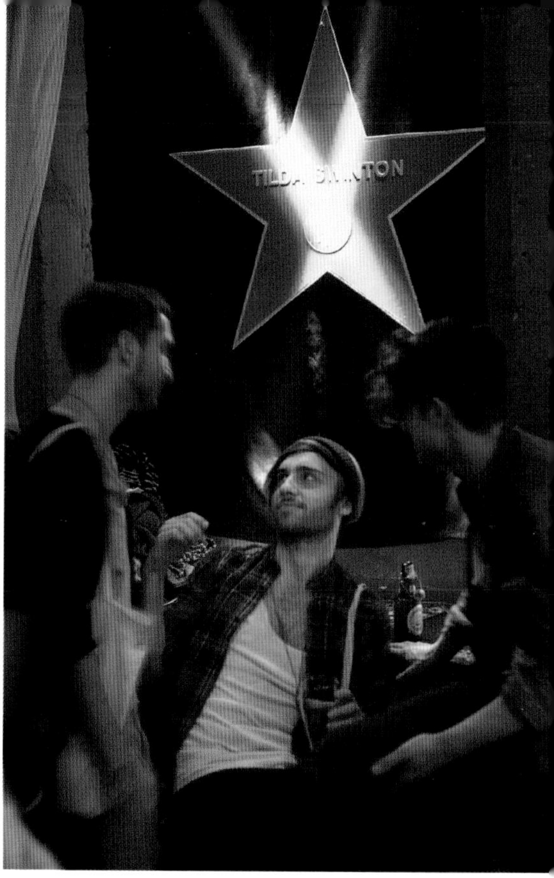

323 Boogie on the dance floors

▶ SchwuZ, Berlin, Germany

When to go: All year
Best for: Discoing the night away

Absorb Berlin's queer, industrial vibes in SchwuZ, Germany's oldest LGBTQ+ club. After relocating, SchwuZ found its present home in a former brewery in Neukölln. It is an open house for all and feels warm yet rebellious. The club isn't one thing; there's something for everyone, with different rooms and music styles.

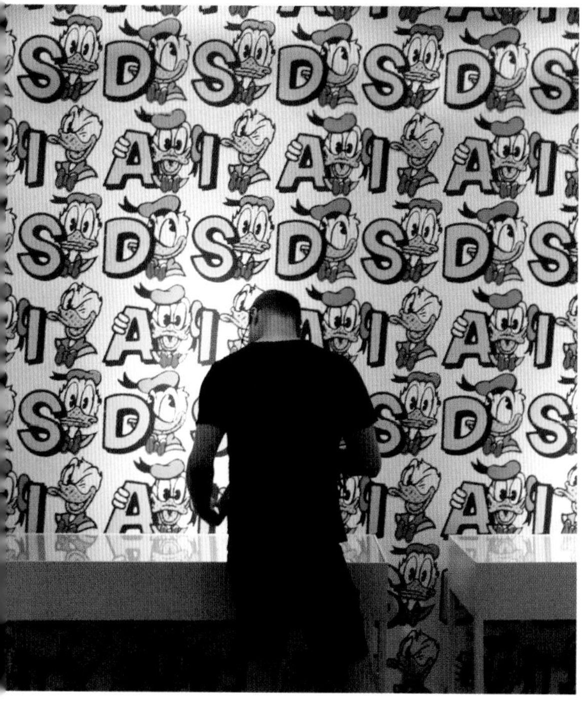

324 History, herstory, theirstory

◀ Schwules Museum, Berlin, Germany

When to go: All year
Best for: Exhibitions

Don't let its name fool you; the Schwules Museum (Gay Museum)—the world's first of its kind—is an intersectional LGBTQ+ powerhouse, with contemporary queer art and history exhibitions on the ground floor, archives in the basement, and a library on the first floor. Join a guided tour or events for a comprehensive experience.

325 Ad-mural-able art

▼ East Side Gallery, Berlin, Germany

When to go: All year
Best for: Sharing a gay kiss

When the Berlin Wall fell in 1989—coinciding with the premiere of East Germany's first gay feature film, *Coming Out*—more than a hundred artists started painting a section of the wall, creating the East Side Gallery. Dmitri Vrubel's larger-than-life artwork *Bruderkuss* became world famous. The real kiss between Leonid Breshnev, General Secretary of the Soviet Union, and Erich Honecker, General Secretary of the Socialist Unity Party of East Germany, was nothing more than a fraternal kiss, but over time, the mural has become a symbol of Berlin's open-mindedness and present-day freedom.

326 Hipster queen of the scene

The Silver Future, Berlin, Germany

When to go: All year
Best for: A vision of future queer nightlife

"For Kings and Queens and Criminal Queers," The Silver Future embodies what future queer nightlife looks like, leaving heteronormativity behind. It's small, chill, quirky, friendly, artsy, hipster, and not dominated by men. The interior of this queer dive bar is pink and colorfully lit. The decorations keep your eyes busy: flyers, posters, pictures, and campy kitsch. The crowd is queer, alternative, and young. It's well worth visiting for great cocktails, whisky, drag shows, and dating events.

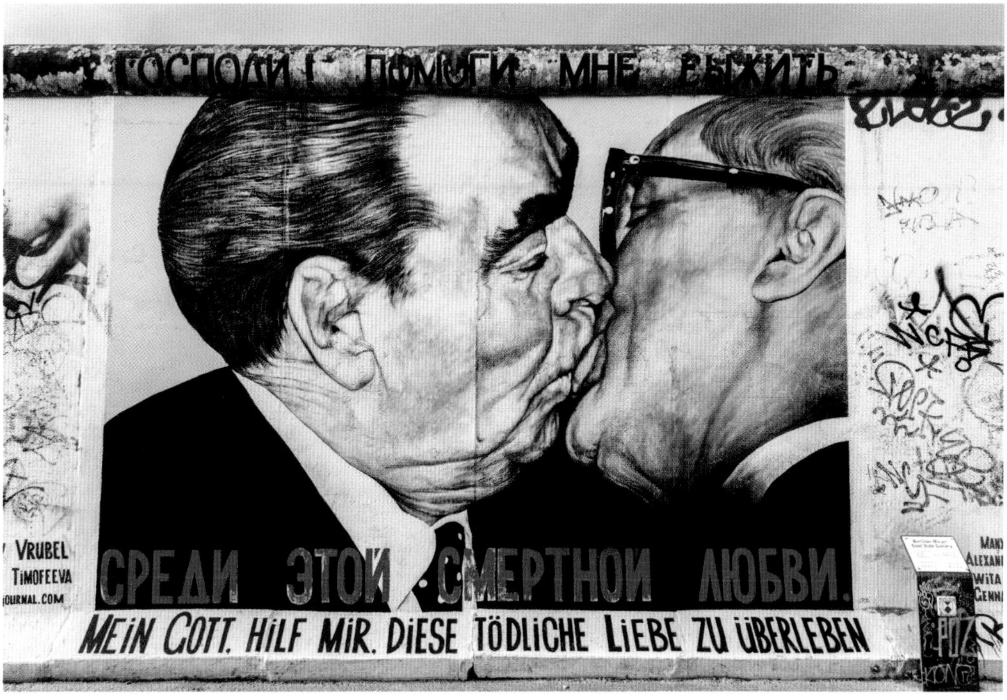

327 The greatest cultural extravaganza

▼ Schöneberg, Berlin, Germany

When to go: All year
Best for: Historic gay village

Berlin is home to the world's first gayborhood: Schöneberg. From the 1920s, the area was home to many LGBTQ+ venues. After a painful interruption during the Third Reich, the scene recovered and maintains its charm. When David Bowie lived here in the 1970s, he described it as, "the greatest cultural extravaganza that one could imagine." Old-but-gold Tom's Bar is an iconic meeting place. Younger, hipper venues are Hafen and Prinzknecht. Begine is a lesbian bar and Xenon Kino is an LGBTQ+ cinema.

328 Where the Wilde things are

Prinz Eisenherz Buchladen, Berlin, Germany

When to go: All year
Best for: Literature lovers

Founded in 1978 in Schöneberg, Berlin's Eisenherz bookshop's collections outgrew the shelves quickly, and the shop moved twice in three decades before coming home on Motzstraße. With every move, the shop became more inclusive. Nowadays, Eisenherz offers LGBTQ+ books, magazines, movies, special events, and exhibitions in its gallery space.

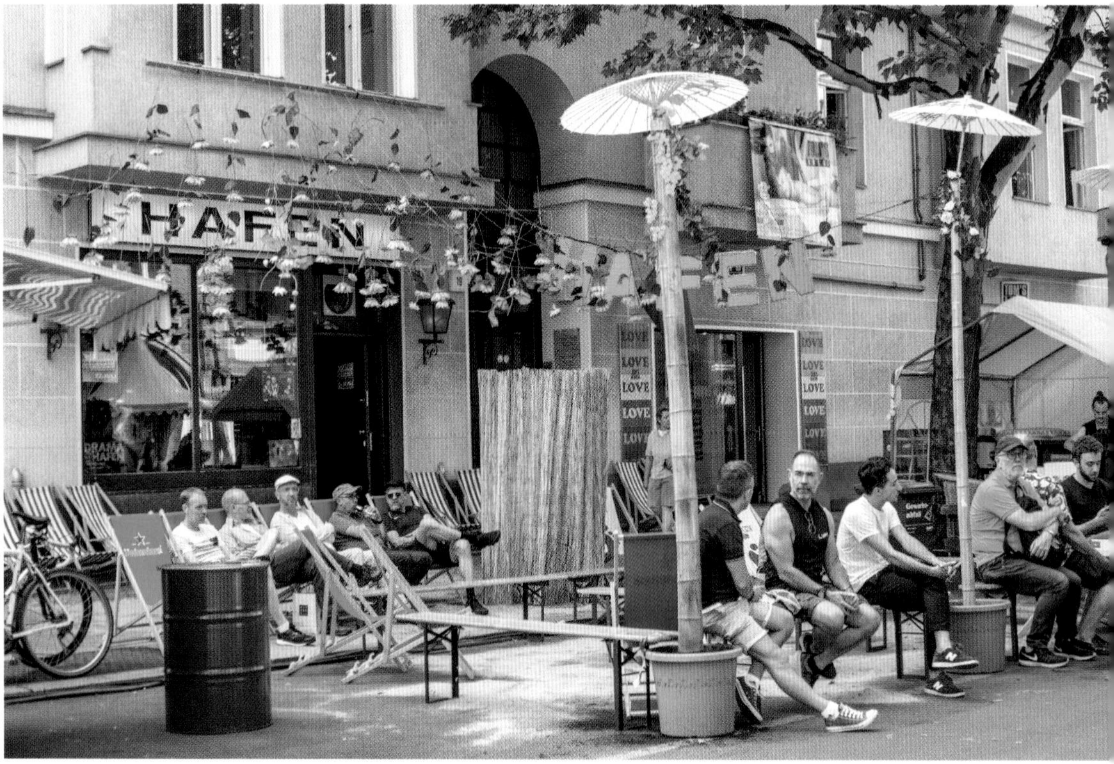

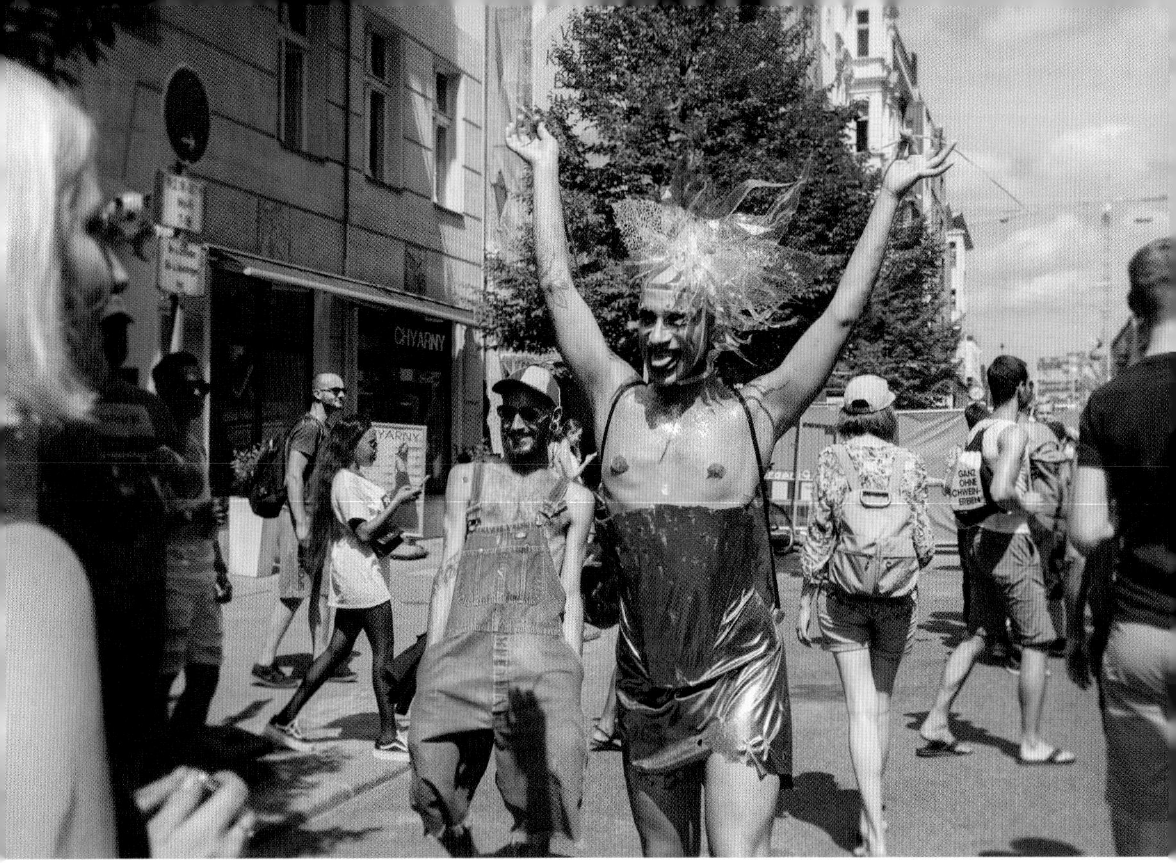

329 Nonstop demonstrating

▲ ▶ Christopher Street Day, Berlin, Germany

When to go: July
Best for: Berlin's *stolz* (Pride)

A week before Berlin's main Pride parade, Schöneberg's main street, the Motzstraße, hosts a giant, two-day festival. The following Thursday, you can join the canal-side Christopher Street Day *auf der Spree*, a sightseeing tour, party, and demonstration all at once. The big Pride parade on Saturday—Christopher Street Day Berlin—honors the Stonewall Riots on Christopher Street in New York. More than 50 floats and half a million people join the march.

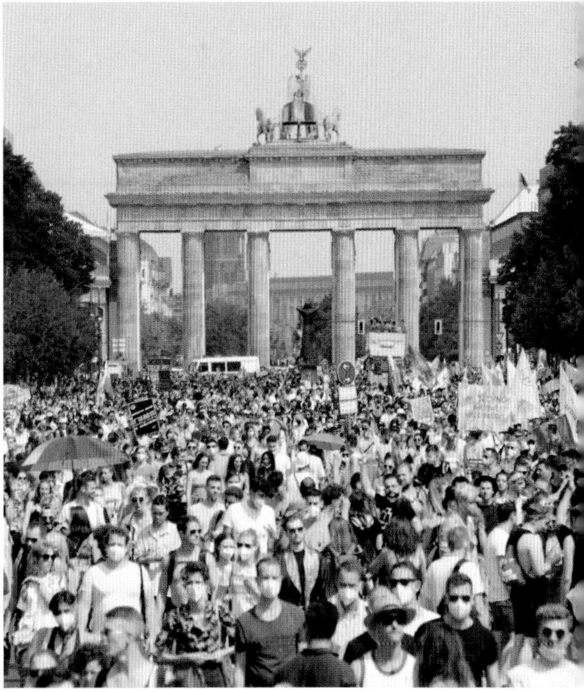

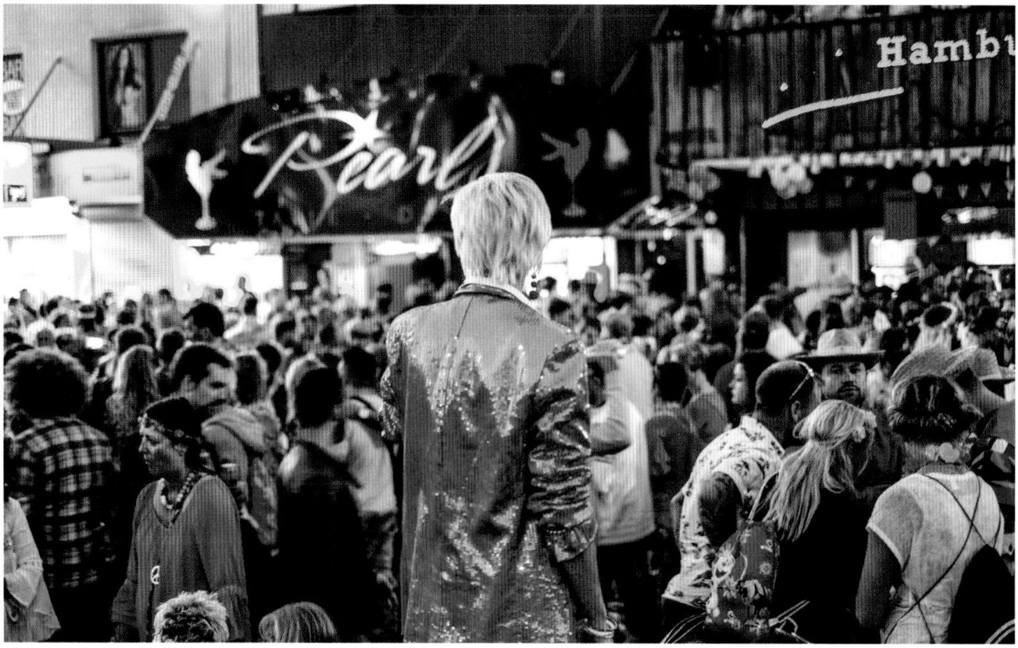

330 Queer all year

Hamburg, Germany

When to go: All year
Best for: Year-round events

Germany's second-largest city is queer all year with two queerborhoods and the iconic events Queerball and Vogelball; there's also a film festival, HIQFF; Queer Cup; and Hamburg Leather Party. Reeperbahn—Hamburg's historic red-light district—is the beating heart of the city's nightlife, Talstraße being particularly queer. But the area of St. Georg takes Hamburg's queer crown, and Lange Reihe is the queen of the scene—with popular gay bar M&V Bar and lesbian-founded Kyti Voo. Every May, it's the festival ground for Stadtfest St. Georg; in August, CSD Hamburg (Pride parade) kicks off here; and it transforms into a queer Christmas village during Winter Pride.

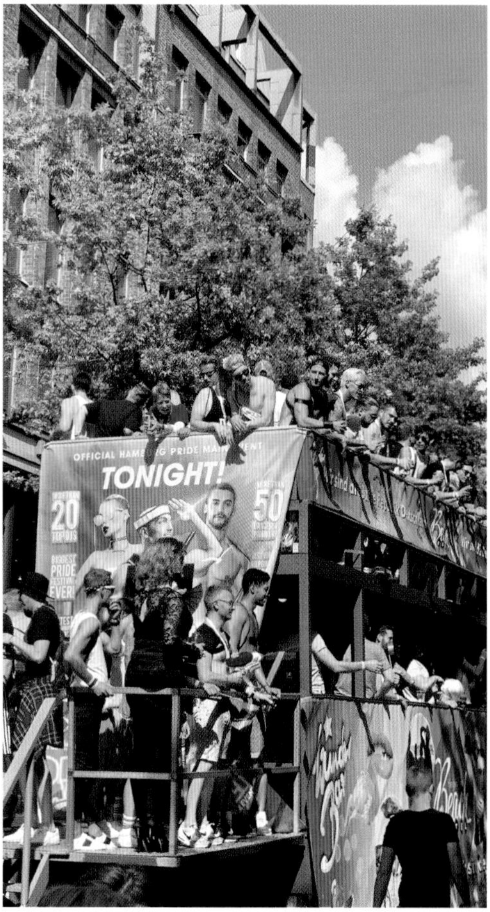

331 Get intoxi-gay-ted

Pink Inc., Hamburg, Germany

When to go: All year
Best for: No tea, no shade, just pink well-played

Pink Inc. organizes the best regular queer parties in Hamburg. Drag queen, singer, host, and DJane Valery Pearl joined forces with lesbian party organization Alpha Girls and gay venue WunderBar over a decade ago. Their regular takeovers left a queer mark throughout Hamburg, and Pink Inc. found its home at Schmidt's Tivoli in Reeperbahn. The parties are boisterously popular, the vibe is euphoric, and the crowd is a well-balanced representation of the LGBTQ+ community.

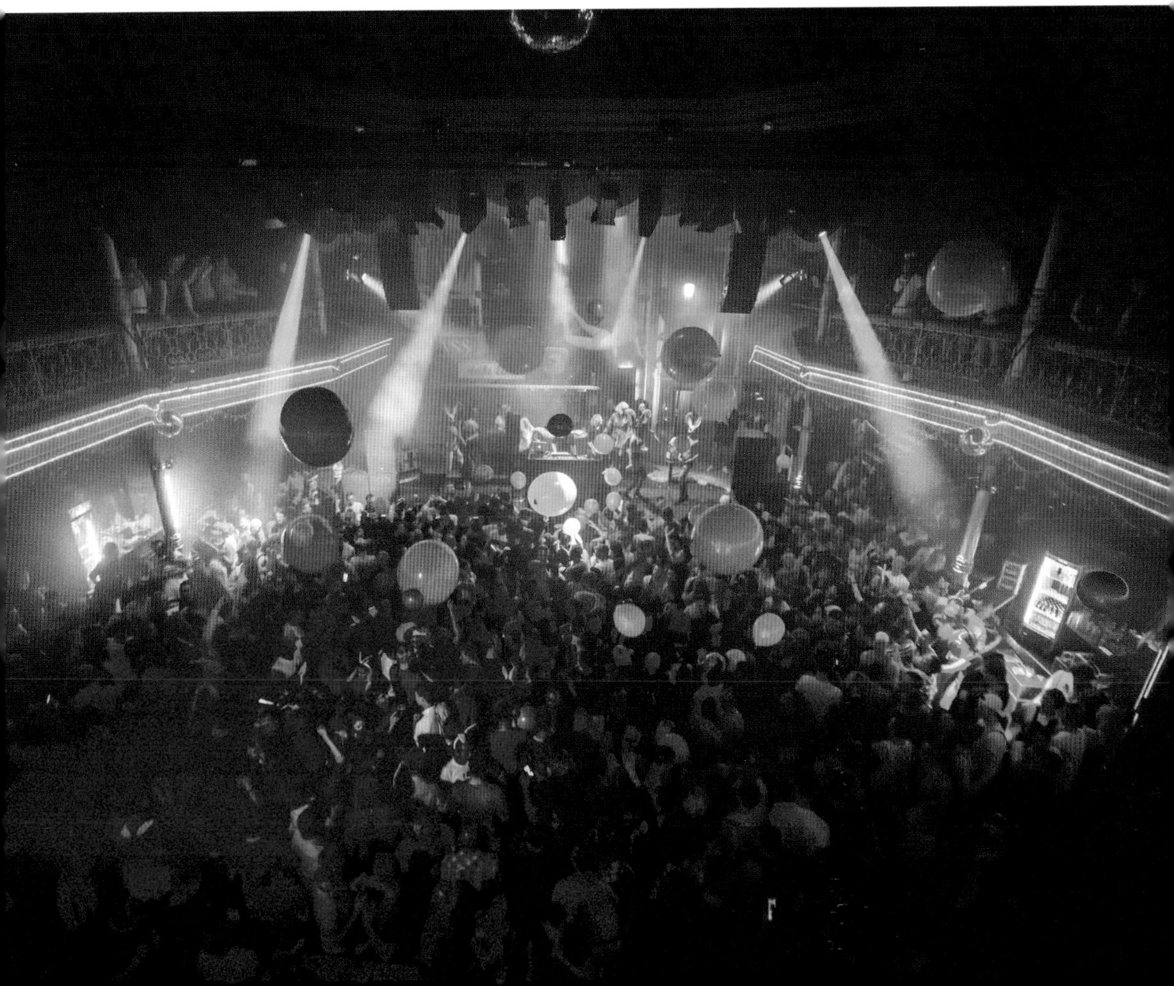

332 If you're fond of sand dunes and salty air

Gran Canaria, Canary Islands, Spain

When to go: All year
Best for: Getting lost in the sand dunes

The Spanish island of Gran Canaria is one of the most popular destinations for LGBTQ sun-seekers in Europe. It actually lies 93 mi/150 km off the coast of northwest Africa (approximately 840 mi/1,352 km from Europe), and offers year-round sunshine and acres of Sahara-like sand dunes around its coast. Queer visitors—predominantly gay men—flock to the dedicated gay beach in Playa del Inglés, and the nearby Yumbo Center in Maspalomas. The latter is a shopping mall by day, but when the sun sets, it comes alive with around two dozen different gay bars and clubs. It's not all about the beach and the clubbing, you can also take a jeep excursion into the volcanic mountains, or take advantage of the perfect stargazing opportunities. The island offers two big, annual Pride festivals: Gay Pride Maspalomas tends to take place in early-to-mid May, while Winter Pride Maspalomas takes place six months later, in early-to-mid November.

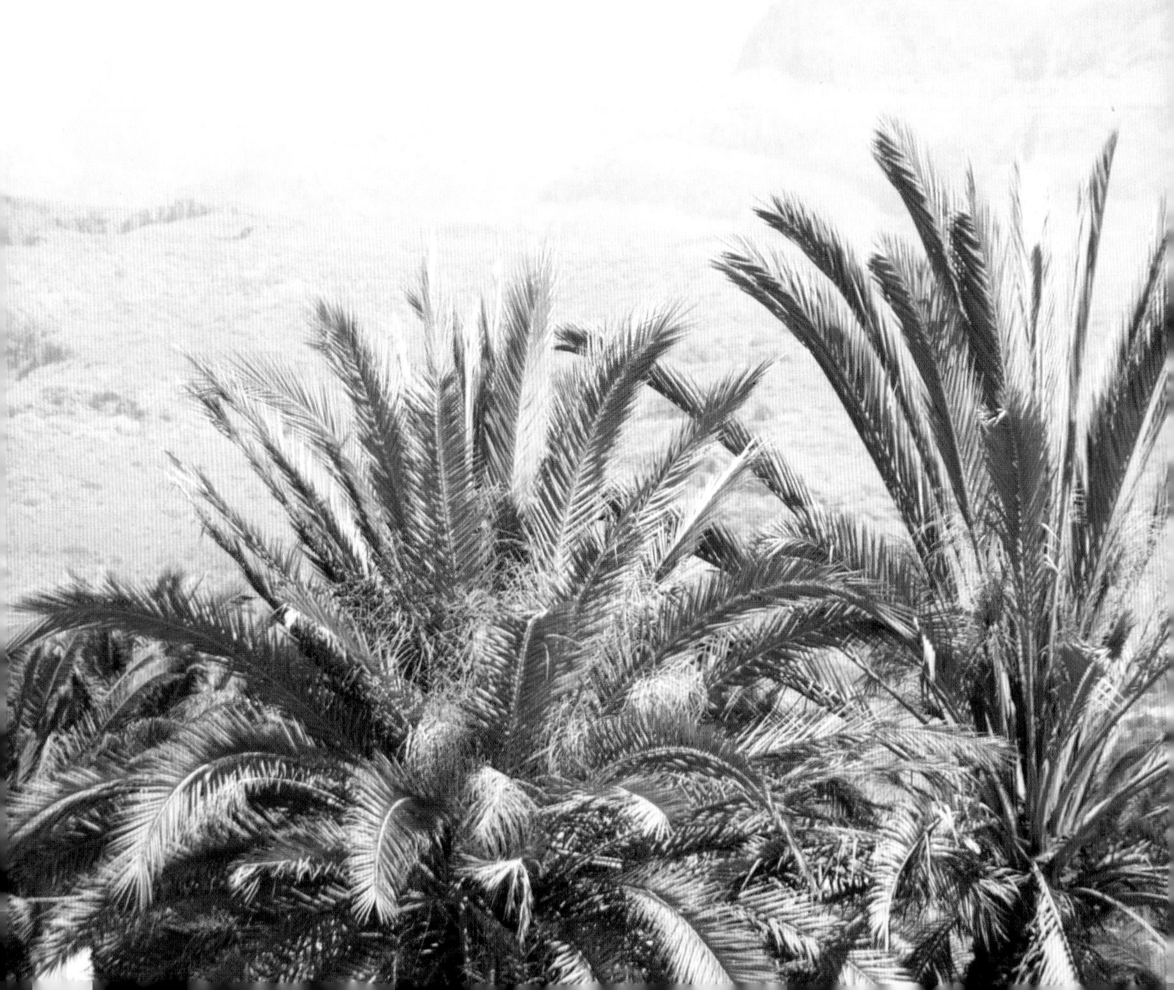

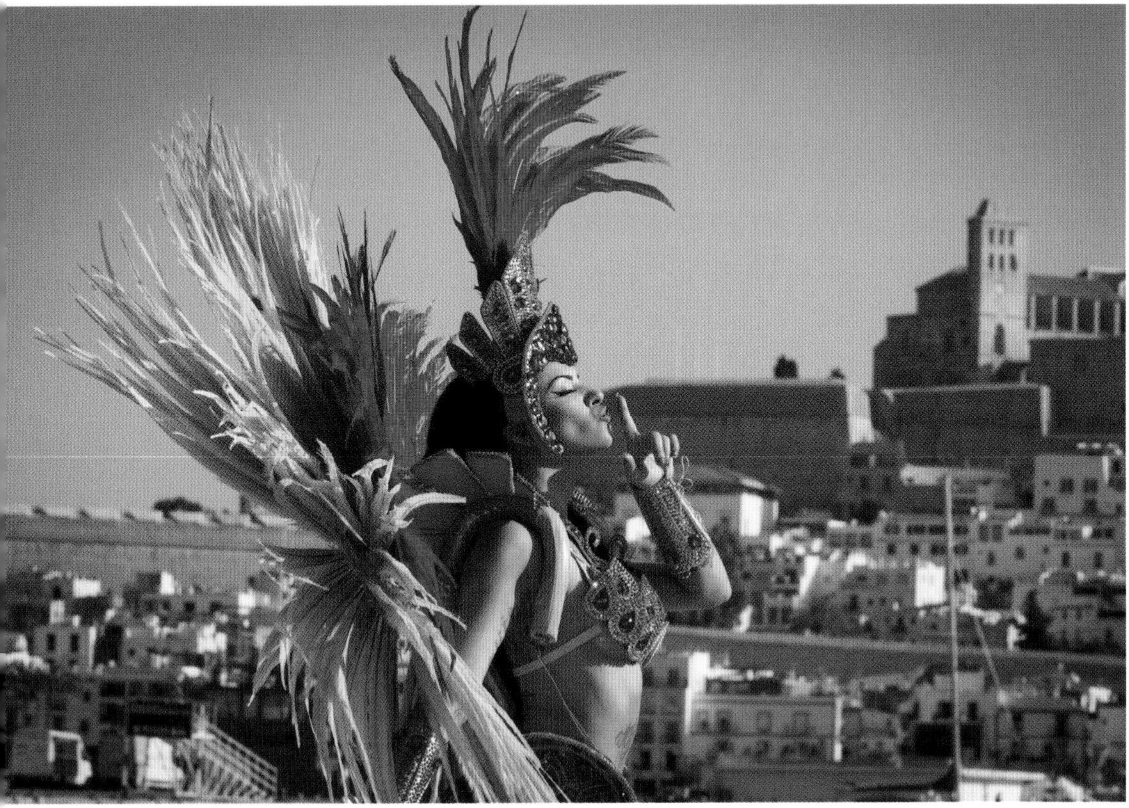

333 More than an island, it's a state of mind

Ibiza Pride, Ibiza, Spain

When to go: June
Best for: Hedonistic tropical parties

The party capital of the world, Ibiza, has an inclusive nightlife scene with a laid-back, captivating atmosphere. Thanks to artists and bohemians migrating here over the last century, the Mediterranean island has become charmingly hedonistic. Life gets colorful during Ibiza Pride—four days of cultural events and a packed clubbing agenda. On the last day, join the march and continue partying on Ibiza's gay street Calle de la Virgen (Carrer de la Mare de Déu).

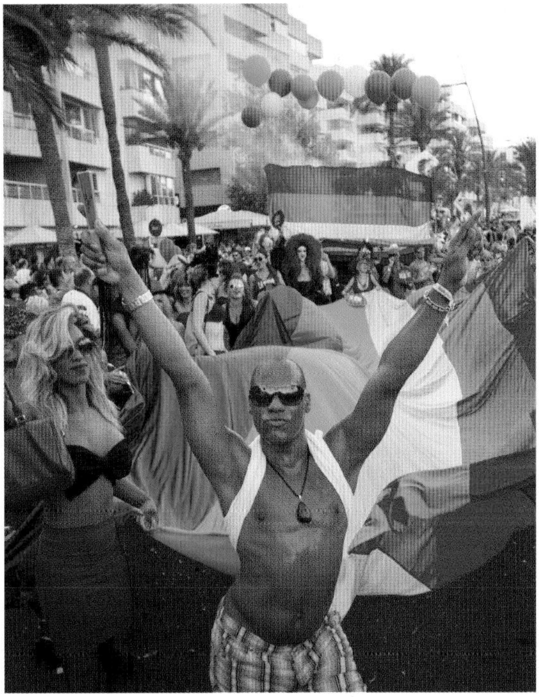

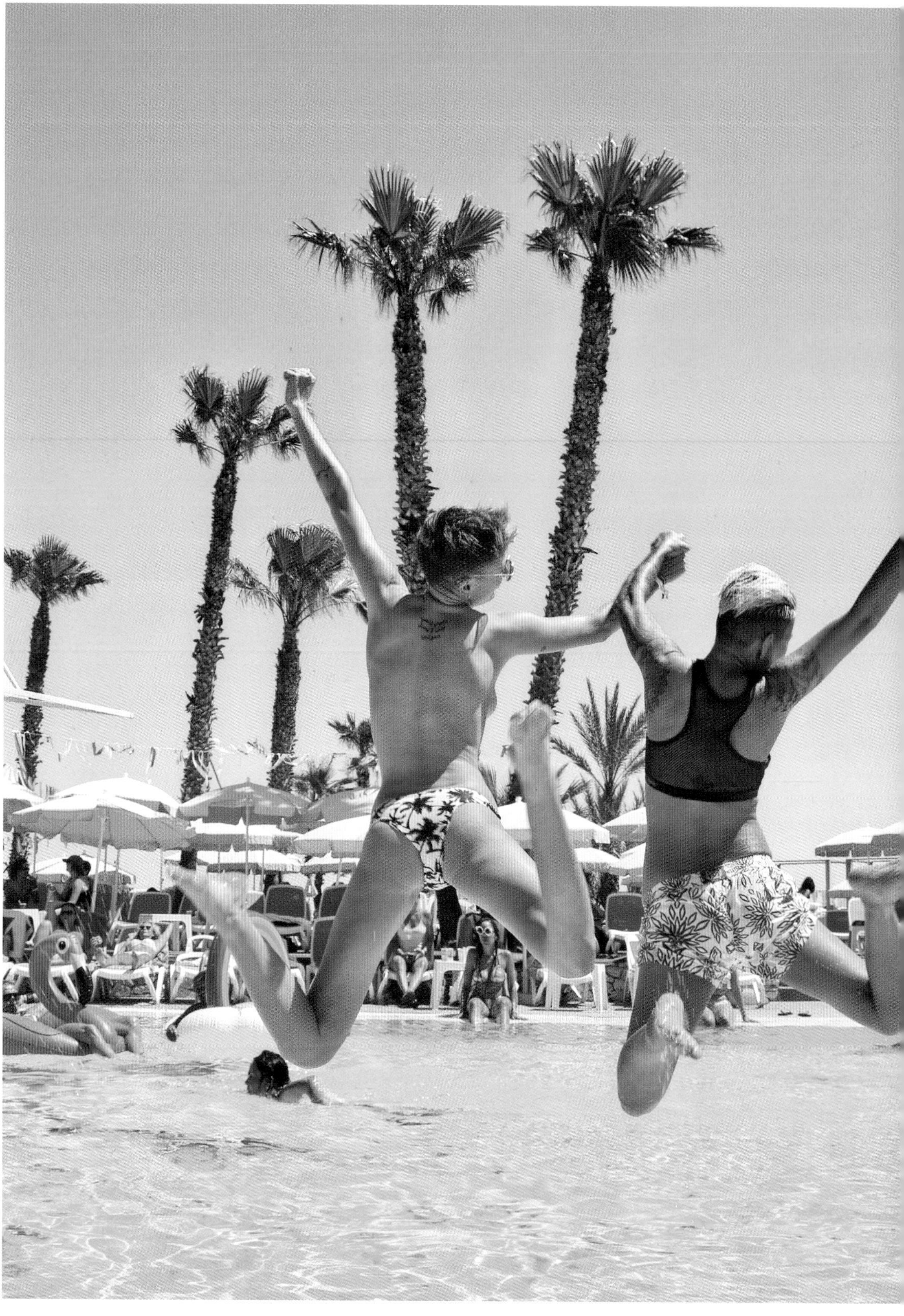

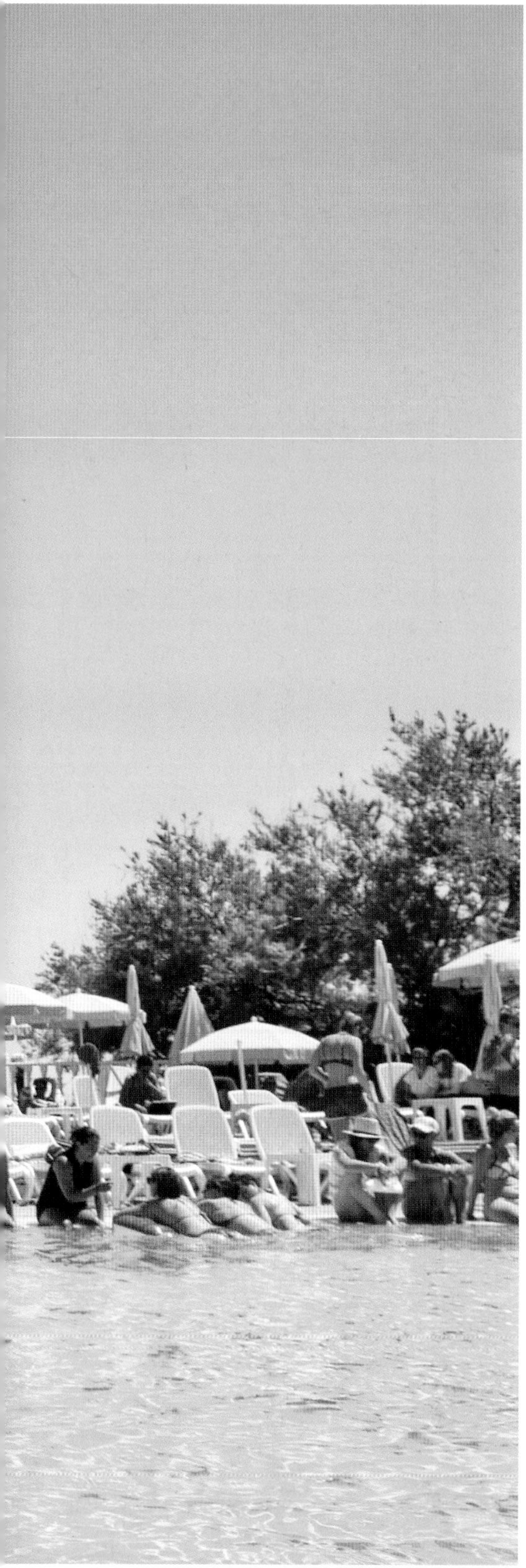

334 Girls just wanna have sun

Velvet Ibiza, Ibiza, Spain

When to go: May
Best for: A wild women's weekend

There's a wide range of bars, clubs and events for LGBTQ+ men in Ibiza, but the options for queer women are (as is so often the case) more limited. Belgian trailblazer Carine De Mesmaeker, who owned a lesbian bar in Brussels and launched the Brussels' women's event Velvet Sixty Nine, challenged this when she launched Velvet Ibiza, the multi-day festival in the sun, in 2015. It was the Mediterranean island's first-ever queer women's event. The wild women's weekend of pool parties, beach activities, and clubbing has since grown into an established five-day all-in resort festival attracting a diverse, international crowd of LGBTQ+ women. It's like Palm Springs's The Dinah—which inspired De Mesmaeker—but European, with free-spirited Ibiza as the sunkissed star.

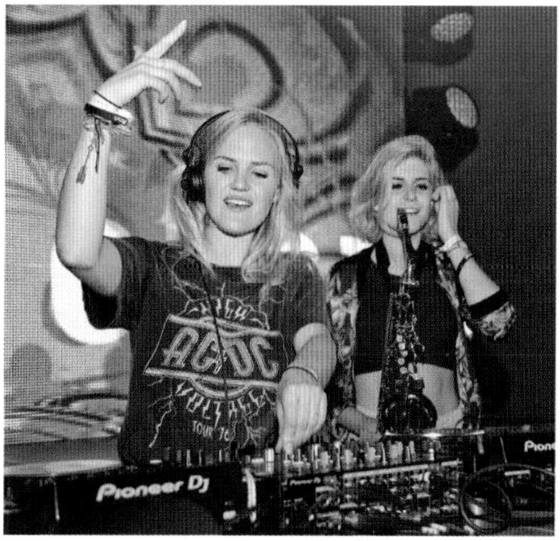

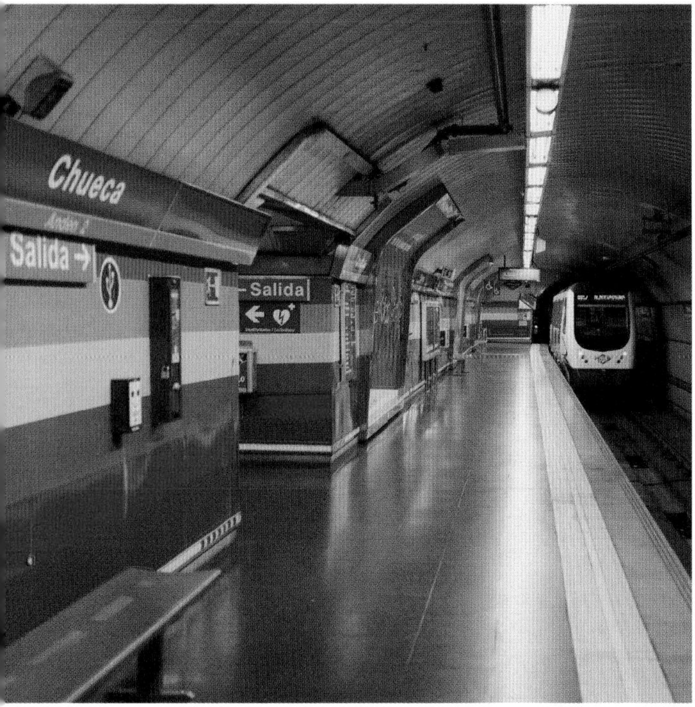

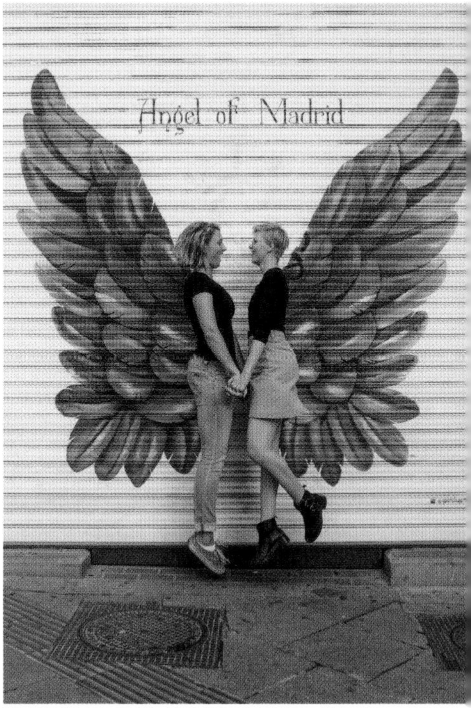

335 Let's c-ella-brate

ELLA Festival Mallorca, Palma de Mallorca, Spain

When to go: August
Best for: Sunkissed partying

The Balearic Islands' capital is home to a legendary lesbian festival: the original ELLA Festival. For one week every summer, the seaside city of Palma de Mallorca is turned into a queer women's and non-binary paradise, with ELLA Beach as its epicentre. The week-long festival is a full-grown, sexy event, mixing culture, music, sports, workshops and art. Beyond the festival, the ELLA Global Community is a comprehensive community-building organization with an online community platform that organizes mini festivals around the globe.

336 Eureka, eureka, Chueca!

▲ Chueca, Madrid, Spain

When to go: All year
Best for: Madrilenian queernergy

Exiting the rainbow-colored Chueca metro station, you emerge into Spain's queer heart, Plaza de Chueca. Rainbow flags welcome you in every direction; the ambiance juxtaposes a mix of the funky, chic, trendy, and traditional. In summer, MADO (Madrid Pride) is the area's highlight, but throughout the year, Chueca's shops, art, food, and nightlife draw visitors. Head to Diurno for brunch, Mercado de San Antón for tapas, Berkana for LGBTQ+ books, or L.L. Bar for a classic drag-show night.

337 Discover deviant diverse downtown

Lavapiés, Madrid, Spain

When to go: All year
Best for: Drawings, drinks, devouring, and dancing

Melting-pot Lavapiés is colorful in the broadest sense of the word, with colorful street art, lively tapas bars, flavorful global cuisines, and an alternative spirit. Home to a younger LGBTQ+ community (particularly lesbians), this Bohemian neighborhood has plenty to keep you busy both day and night, from a feminist cultural center, to cafés, bars and legendary clubbing at Club 33, La 80, or quirky La Noche Boca Arriba.

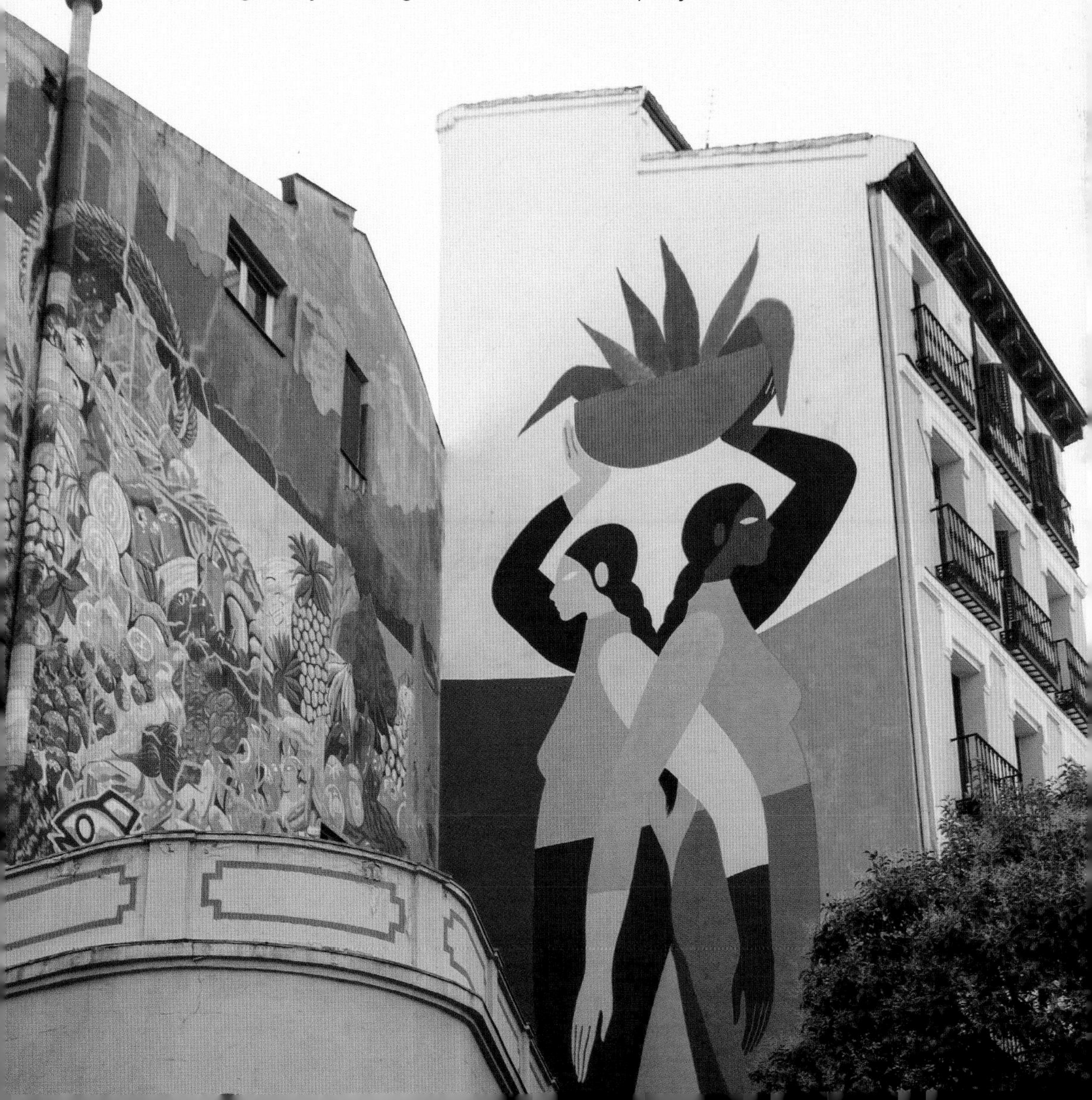

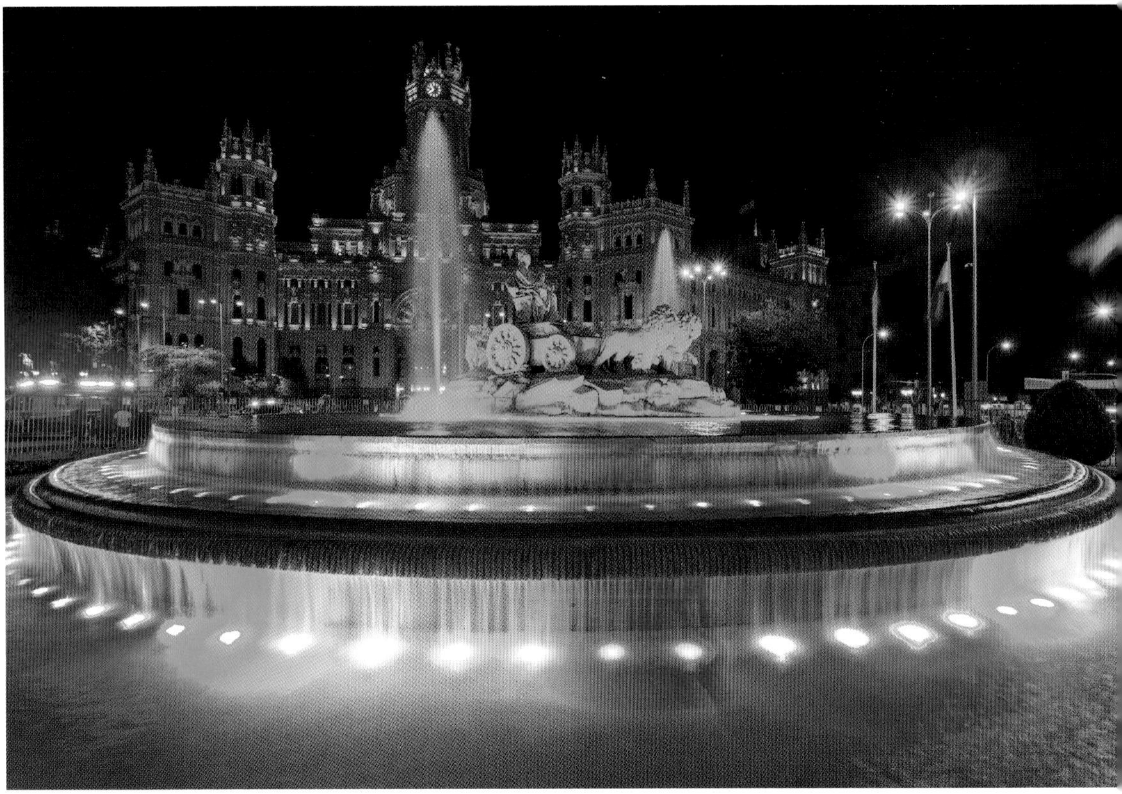

338 Sometimes size matters

Madrid Pride, Spain

When to go: Early July
Best for: Feeling part of a huge LGBTQ+ family

Madrid Pride is the largest LGBTQ+ Pride celebration in Europe. When the city played host to World Pride in 2017, attendance is believed to have topped two million. The celebrations begin on a Wednesday, with events in and around Chueca Square in the gay neighborhood. These culminate with the Orgullo Gay de Madrid (MADO) parade on the Saturday. The sight of hundreds of thousands of LGBTQ+ people making their way down Paseo Del Prado is awe-inspiring.

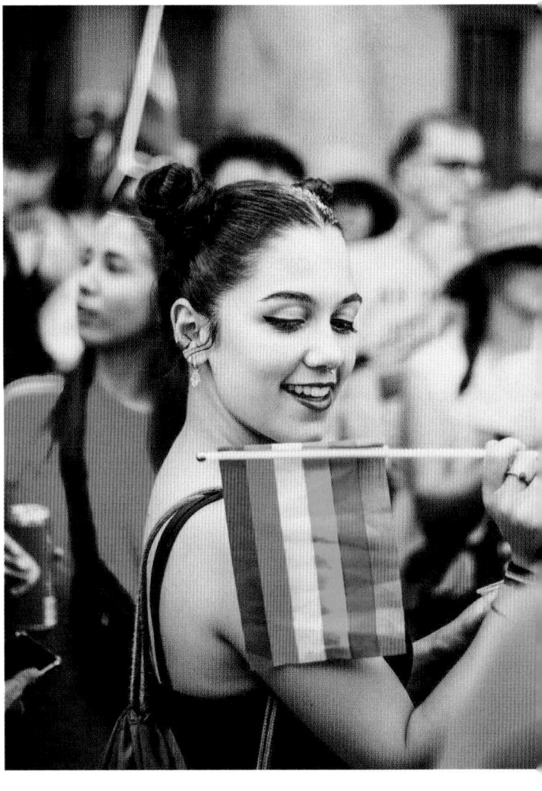

339 Catalytic Catalonian celebration

Barcelona Pride, Spain

When to go: June
Best for: Family-focused Pride

Catalonia's capital Barcelona has a historic Pride; two years after Spanish dictator Francisco Franco's death, around four thousand people gathered on Las Ramblas to protest against Franco's remaining anti-LGBTQ+ laws. It was Spain's first Pride, catalyzing the LGBTQ+ liberation movement across the country, and resulting in the first law changes two years later. Nowadays, the two-week-long Barcelona Pride draws a vast amount of people with diverse events, a focus on rainbow families, and a big parade.

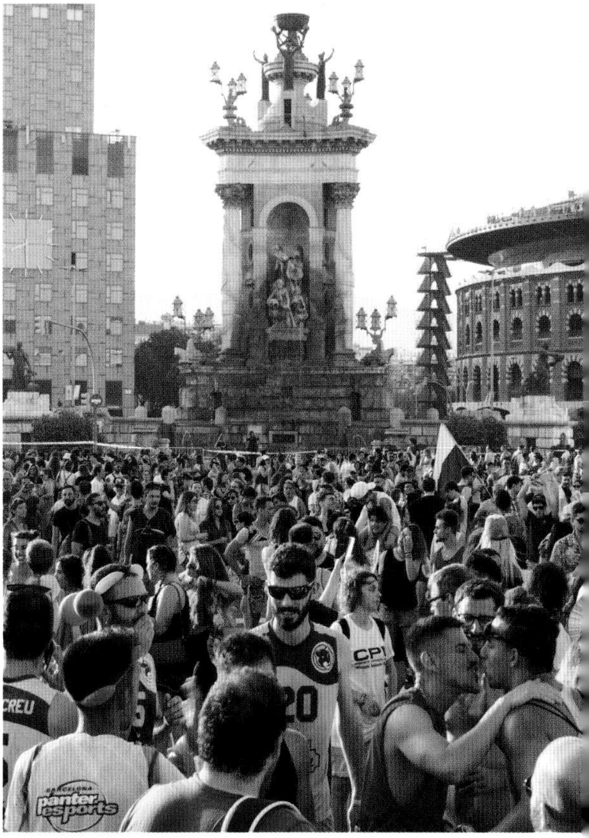

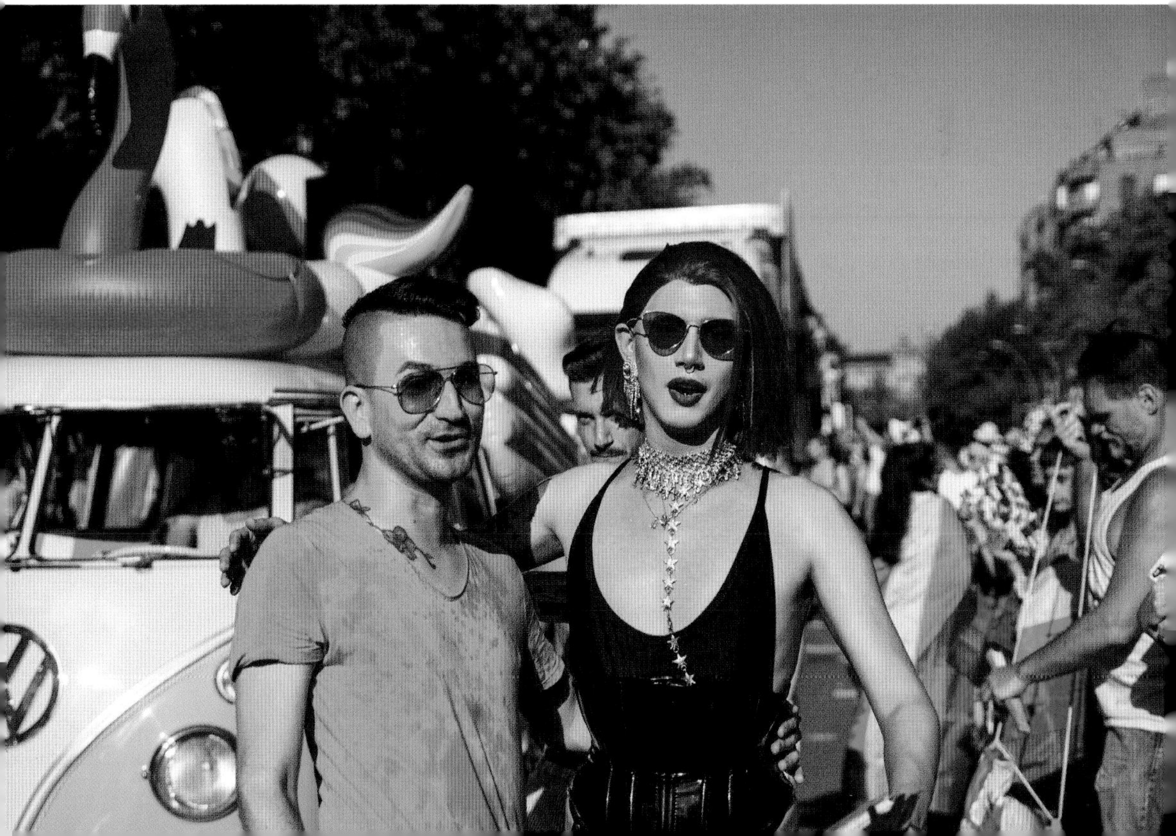

340 Suite dreams are made of this

▼ Axel Hotel, Barcelona, Spain

When to go: All year
Best for: (Not) sleeping

"Are you sure you don't want separate rooms?" is not a question queer couples hear at the Axel Hotel. Strategically located in the center of Eixample—dubbed Gaixample because it's so gay—with a stunning rooftop, and "Please Disturb" signs, the hotel is well-placed for sightseeing, and stumbling home from a late night out.

341 Taking a stand

La Glorieta de la Transsexual Sonia, Barcelona, Spain

When to go: All year
Best for: Commemorating queer and trans lives

Ciutadella Park is home to the first monument dedicated to gay, lesbian, and transgender people in Spain. Installed in 2011, this pink-bordered granite triangle is located near to the bandstand where Sonia Rescalvo Zafra, a trans woman, was murdered in 1991. This bandstand "glorieta" was officially renamed La Glorieta de la Transsexual Sonia in 2013, making Barcelona the first city in Europe to name a public space after a trans person.

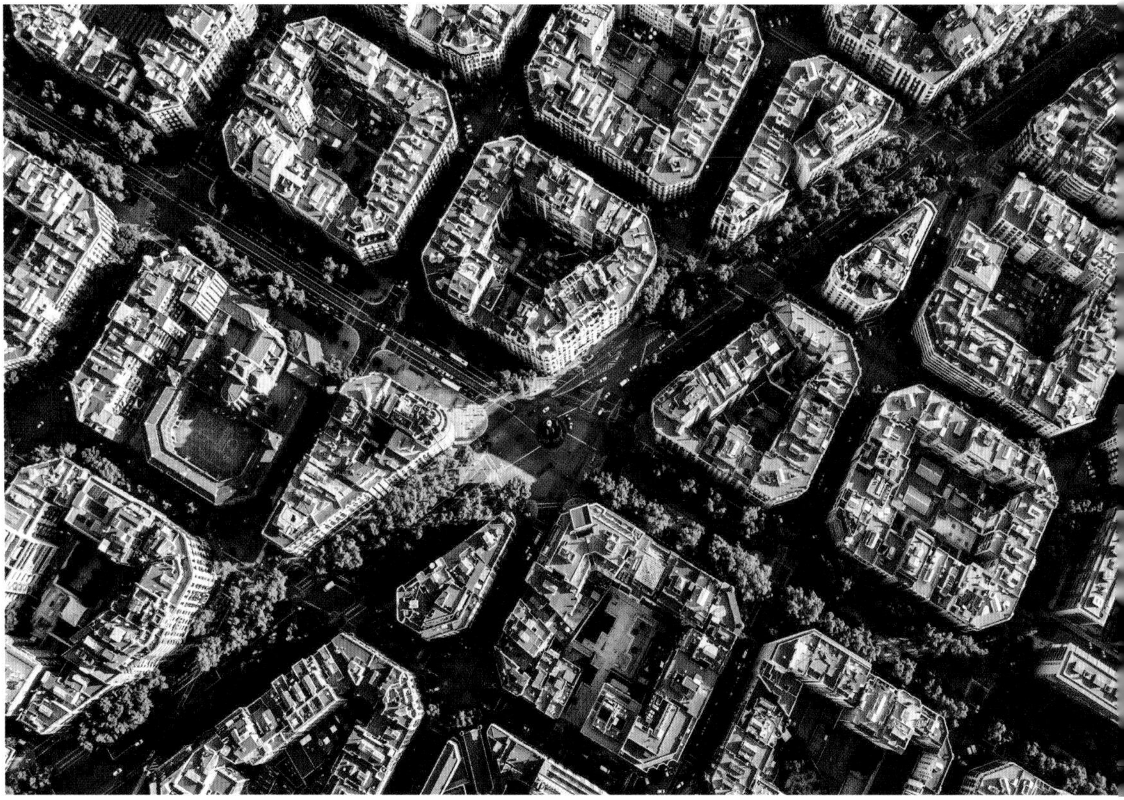

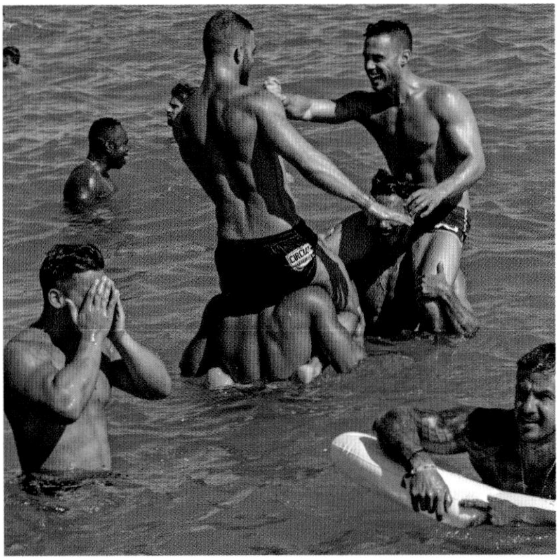

342 Sun's out, buns out

◀ Platja de la Mar Bella, Barcelona, Spain

When to go: Summer
Best for: Nude bathing

Possibly one of the most popular gay beaches in Spain, Platja de la Mar Bella is where you will find local gay men and women during the summer months. Located on the northern end of Barcelona's beachfront, this dreamy spot is clothing optional.

343 Fun, friendly, flirty fiesta

▶ Benidorm Pride, Spain

When to go: September
Best for: Fabulous queer fiesta

There's always a party atmosphere in the Costa Blanca's capital Benidorm, so it's unsurprising that it hosts a fabulous fiesta for Pride. Over a dozen years, it has grown from a small gathering into a multi-day event. Recurring events include an open-air opening party, a sensational High Heels Race, a colorful parade, and a classic White Party. There's a good selection of LGBTQ+ venues dotted along the coast and a thriving community around the Old Town.

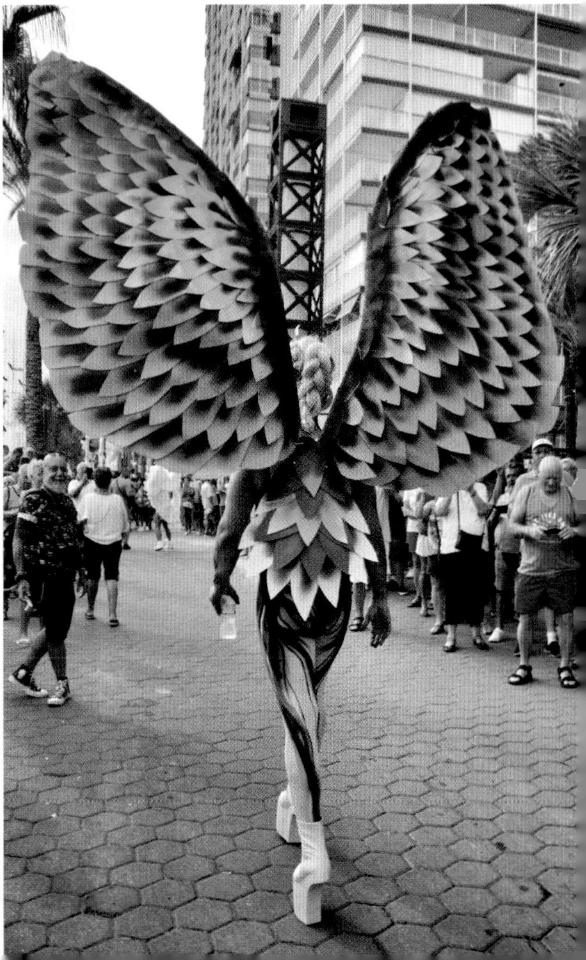

344 Spain-sational sunbathing

▼ ▶ Sitges, Spain

When to go: April to September
Best for: Beach-town fun

Thirty minutes south of Barcelona lies gay haven Sitges, a small beach town jam-packed with gay bars. In the dark days of Franco's dictatorship, Sitges—like Ibiza—became an epicenter for Spain's counterculture movement, a liberal antidote, and a secret gay haven. Over time, Sitges's vibrant gay scene came out of hiding and took over the coastal town. One of the town's main streets—Carrer Primer de Maig—became aptly known as *Carrer del Pecat*, Sin Street.

Legendary square Plaça de la Indústria is home to two large terraces from Sitges institutions, Parrots Pub and Central Bar. The famous LGBTQ+ beach Platja la Bassa Ronda lies a short walk away, while gay nude beaches Playa del Muerto and Playa de las Balmins are a bit farther. Worthwhile annual events to visit are Sitges Carnival in spring, Sitges Pride and Bears Week in summer, and Sitges Film Festival in fall.

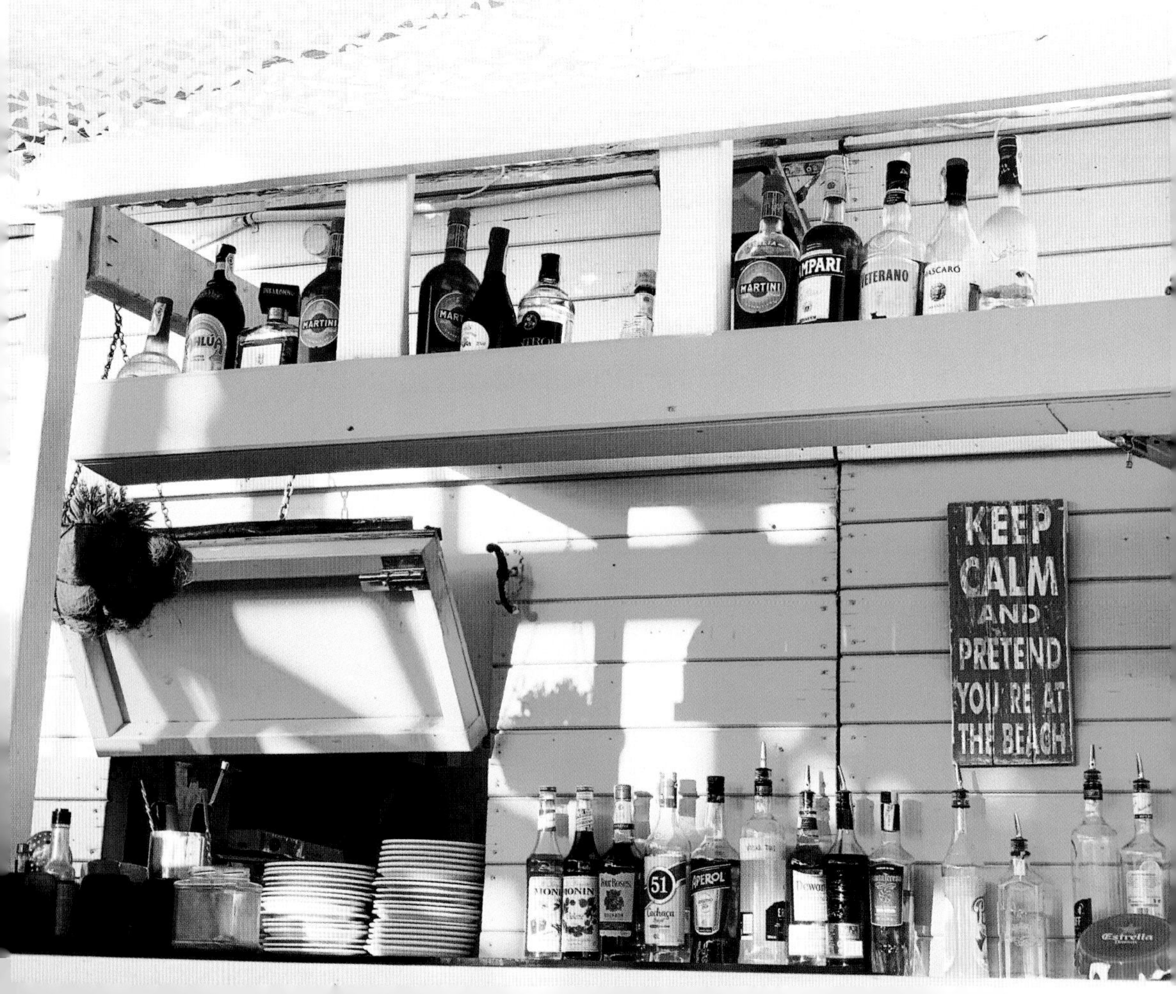

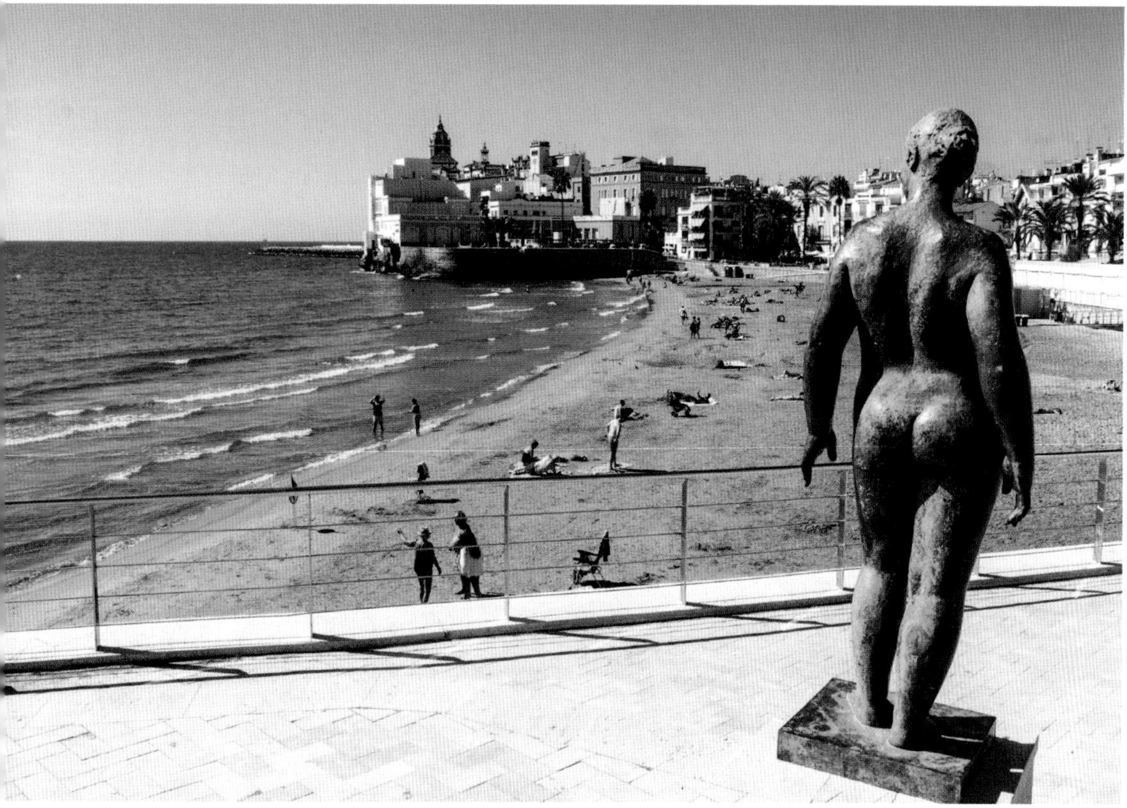

345 **Equal-actually, triangle**

▶ Pink Triangle Monument, Sitges, Spain

When to go: All year
Best for: LGBTQ-friendly town

Sitges is home to the very first LGBTQ+ monument in Spain: the Pink Triangle Monument. The triangle was installed in 2006 to mark ten years from when police in Sitges specifically targeted gay men, which eventually resulted in public outcry and riots. It has "Sitges against homophobia—never again" inscribed on it.

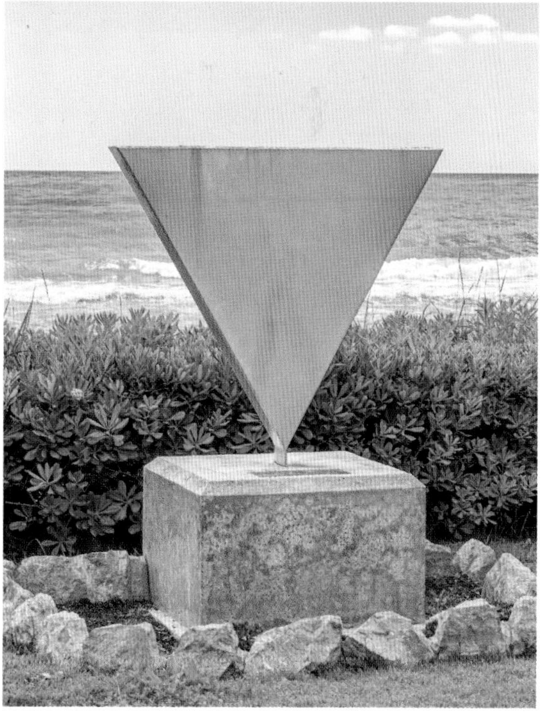

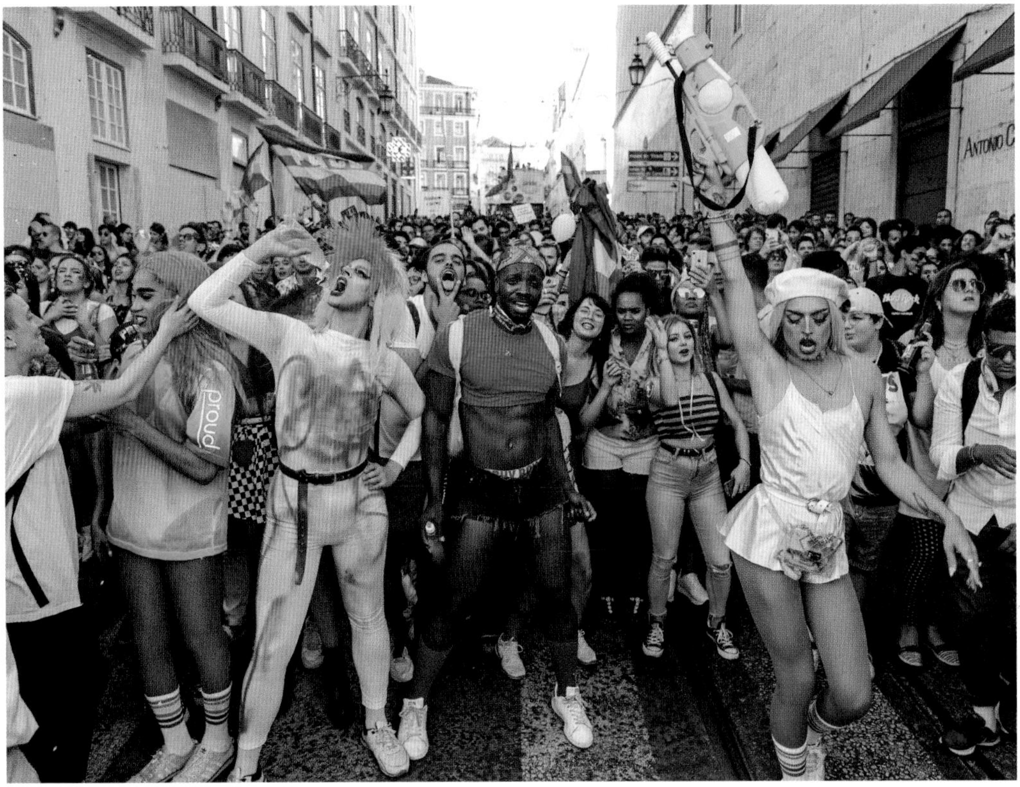

346 Live laugh Lisbon

▲ Lisbon Pride, Portugal

When to go: June
Best for: Being double so proud

The uniqueness of Lisbon's two-fold Pride is that the political parade—*Marcha do Orgulho LGBTI+ de Lisboa*—comes first. The second event—Arraial Lisboa Pride—usually happens the following weekend at the city's largest square, Praça do Comércio. This free-for-all festival, also dubbed Pride Village, features plenty of music, drinks, food, and fun. For more queerness, visit the areas of trendy Bairro Alto, or predominantly gay Príncipe Real.

347 Watch and learn

Queer Lisboa, Lisbon, Portugal

When to go: September to December
Best for: Queer movie nights

The LGBTQ+ movie festival Queer Lisboa has been running for more than 25 years and draws people to the city's old-school movie theaters. With its lavish art-deco style, Cinema São Jorge is one of the only historic cinemas in Lisbon still in use, while Cinemateca Portuguesa also houses a bookshop and museum. Queer Lisboa's program offers around one hundred movies—focusing on titles less seen on the regular circuit. And since 2015, the festival has a younger sibling up north: Queer Porto.

348 It's only natural

▼ Algarve, Portugal

When to go: April to October
Best for: Nature lovers and beach hoppers

Portugal is a top destination for queer travelers, partly thanks to its exemplary LGBTQ+ legislation. The southern region of Portugal is a paradise for nature lovers; the Algarve has a mild and sunny climate all year, a 96-mi/155-km-long rocky coastline, clear blue waters, large sandy beaches, and dozens of hiking trails. Get romantic and find the "Heart of the Algarve" at Praia da Marinha, between gay-popular cities Albufeira and Portimão. Eat fresh seafood, admire natural and historical sights, or visit the gay beaches sprinkled along the coast.

349 From horror to hope

Porto Pride, Portugal

When to go: July
Best for: Giving a voice to the most marginalized

The murder of trans woman Gisberta Salce Júnior in 2006 provoked the first Marcha do Orgulho LGBT do Porto (MOP). Commemorating all Gisbertas of Portugal, five hundred people marched for human rights for the most marginalized LGBTQ+ people; recent parades drew thousands, culminating in *O Arraial Mais Orgulhoso do Porto* (Porto Pride Festival).

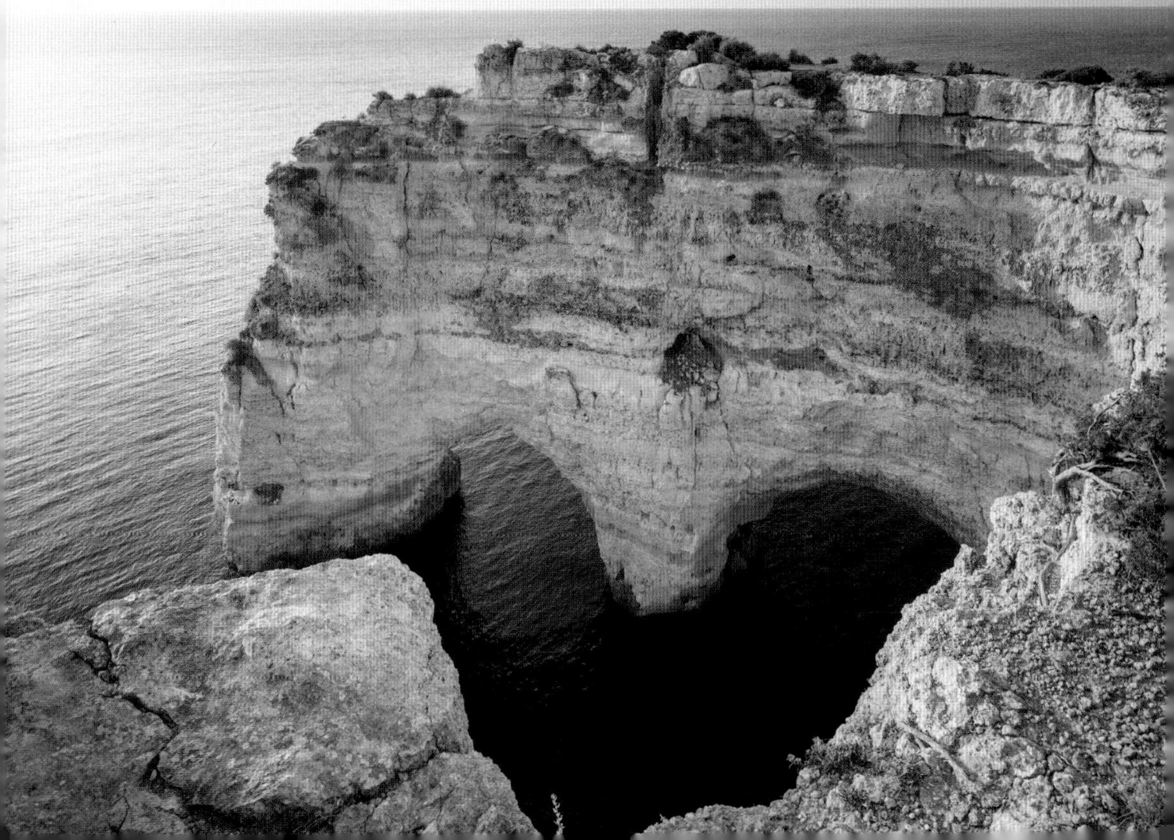

350 Don't worry, beach happy

Beach 19, Lisbon, Portugal

When to go: May to October
Best for: Nude sunbathing and gay cruising

Across the Tejo river, 14 mi/22 km south of Lisbon, lies the pristine and secluded gay nude beach, Beach 19, on Costa da Caprica. Bordered by dunes and forest, it's one of Europe's largest casual and natural gay beaches, perfect for sunbathing, cruising, and swimming.

351 Fado-lous music

▼ Fado Bicha, Lisbon, Portugal

When to go: All year
Best for: The power of song

Expressive, melancholic, heartfelt *fado* is the soul of Portuguese music. But traditional *fado* doesn't include queerness. Vocalist Tiago Lila—Lila Fadista on stage—and guitarist João Caçador decided it was time to shake things up, to bring the noise to a music genre that requires silence. The queer-duo forms Fado Bicha (loosely translated as "queer *fado*") and makes intersectional, provocative, experimental *fado* music, with the Portuguese *guitarra* replaced by an electric one. Find Fado Bicha performing in alternative spaces of Lisbon's nightlife or catch one of their nationwide concerts.

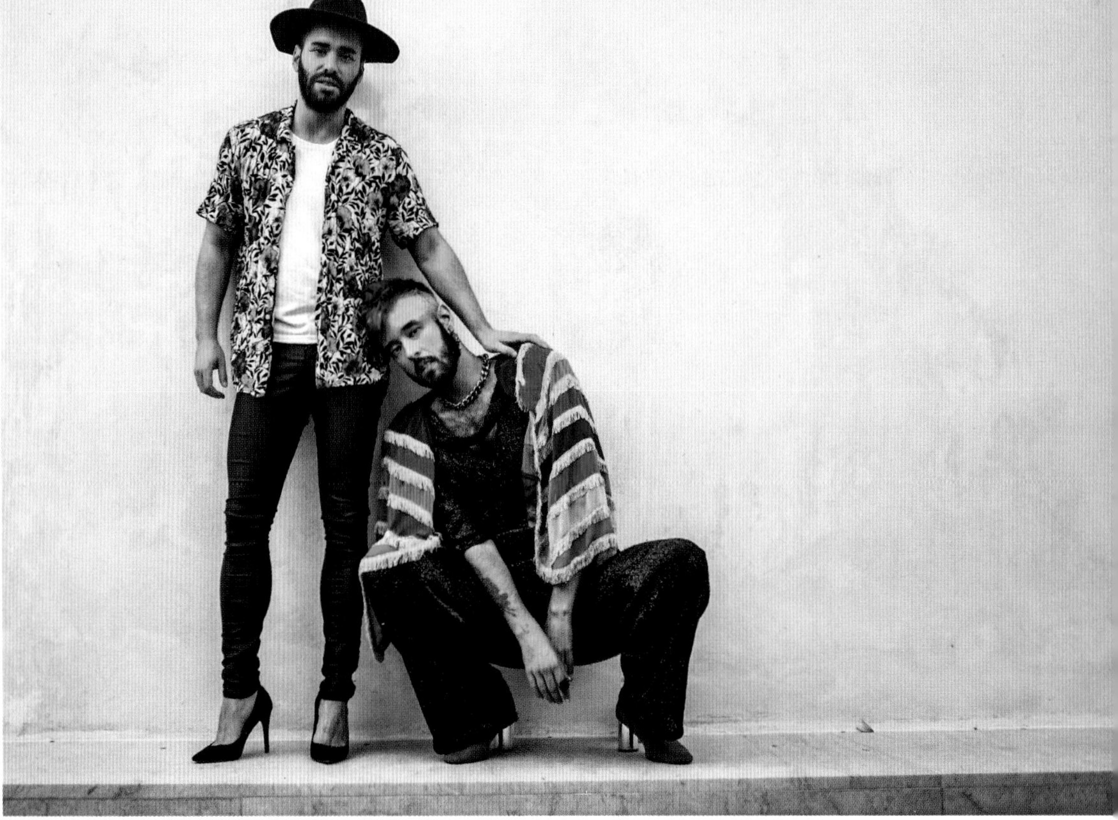

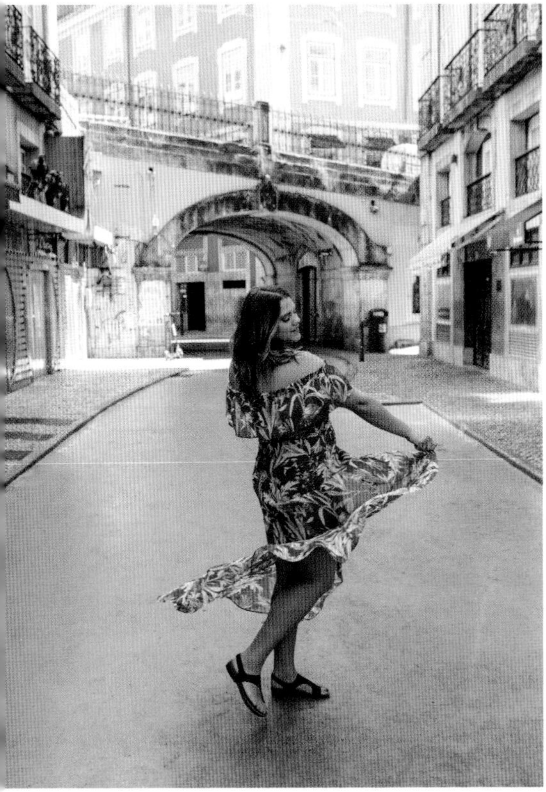

352 Pretty in pink

◀ Pink Street, Lisbon, Portugal

When to go: All year
Best for: Erotic history

Rua Nova do Carvalho, in Cais do Sodré, was once infamous for its brothels, gambling dens, and unsavory bars. In 2011, architect José Adrião painted the street bright pink. Now known as Rua Cor-de-Rosa (Pink Street), it has become a vibrant hot spot. By day, it's picturesque; by night, it's fantastically vulgar, sensual, and diverse. Visit the quirky, soft erotic-themed venues Pensão Amor and MEL (Museu Erótico de Lisboa) to catch a glimpse of raunchy history.

353 Ain't no district high enough

▶ Bairro Alto, Lisbon, Portugal

When to go: March to October
Best for: Partying like a Lisboeta

When evening falls in Lisbon, take the iconic Bica Funicular up from Cais do Sodre to explore Bairro Alto. Jam-packed with bars, the maze of narrow, car-free streets comes alive at night. Traditional *fado* music fills the air, and people from all over visit the quaint district for food and drink—particularly caipirinhas and caipiroscas. All bars are queer-friendly, particularly lesbian-popular PUREX, old tavern Portas Largas, cozy Espaço 40e1, and famous Friends Bairro Alto.

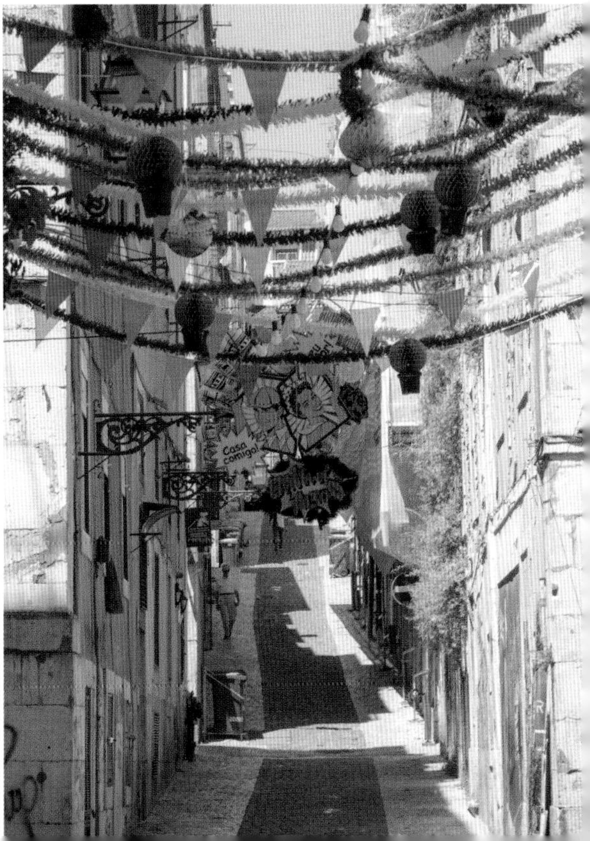

354 A piste of my heart

Arosa Gay Ski Week, Switzerland

When to go: January
Best for: Snow much fun

The lack of color in a snowy landscape could get boring, but not when you add some rainbow color. Bring your LGBTQ+ flags and winter flair, and join Arosa Gay Ski Week. Since 2005, hundreds of gays of all genders have joined the annual Arosa Gay Ski Week, making it one of Europe's most prominent gay, winter events. Arosa is a small village with sweeping views, nestled on a wide sunny plateau in the Swiss Alps. The whirlwind seven-day event is fun-filled with parties, concerts, dinners, drag performances, skiing, and snowboarding. The sparkling alpine Arosa Lenzerheide slopes—140 mi/225 km in total—offer something for everyone, and there are instructors if you want to learn more. For the nonskiers there are also plenty of options, with hiking trails, sledding, ice skating, cozy ski huts, warm mulled wine, and sunbathing opportunities.

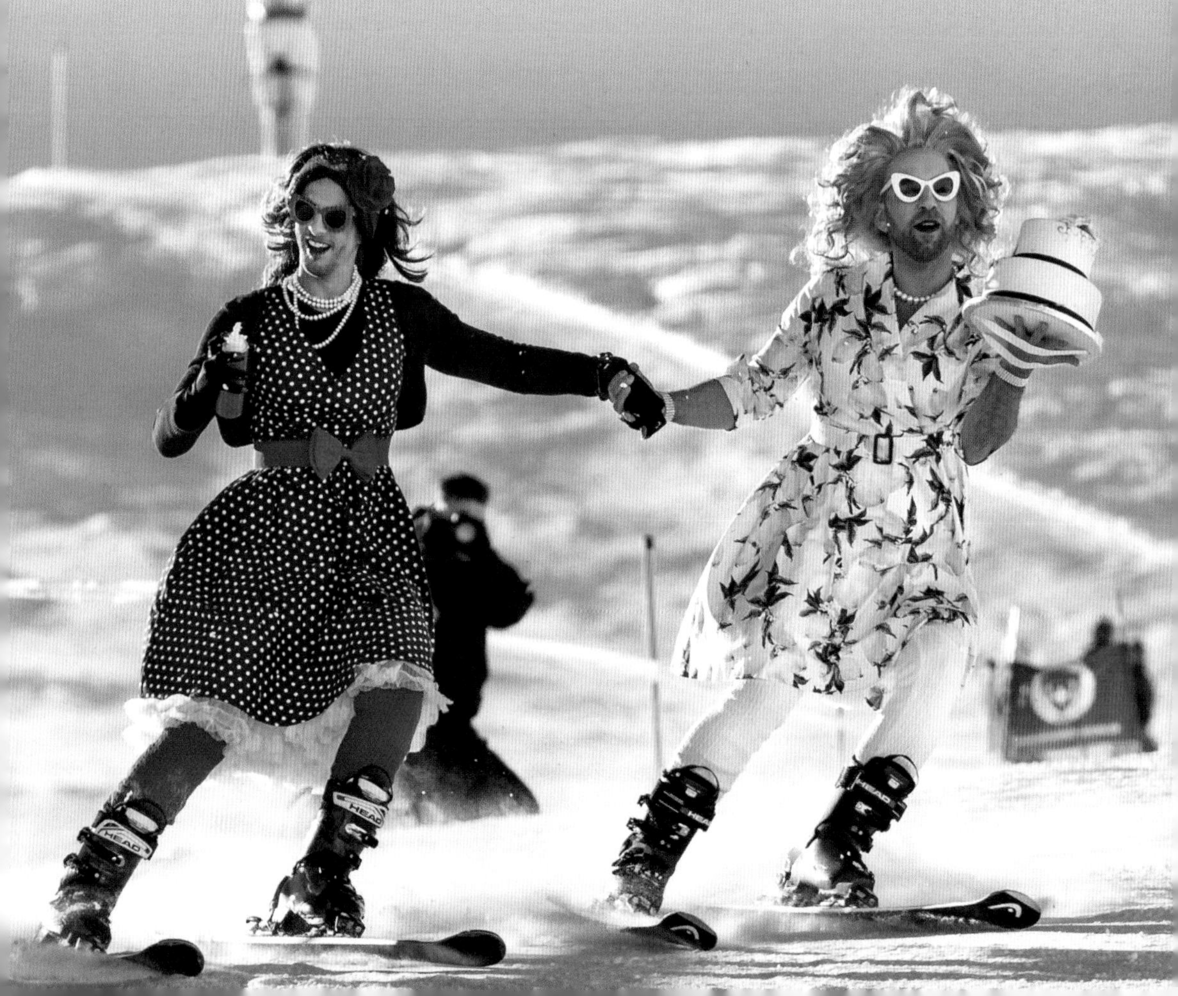

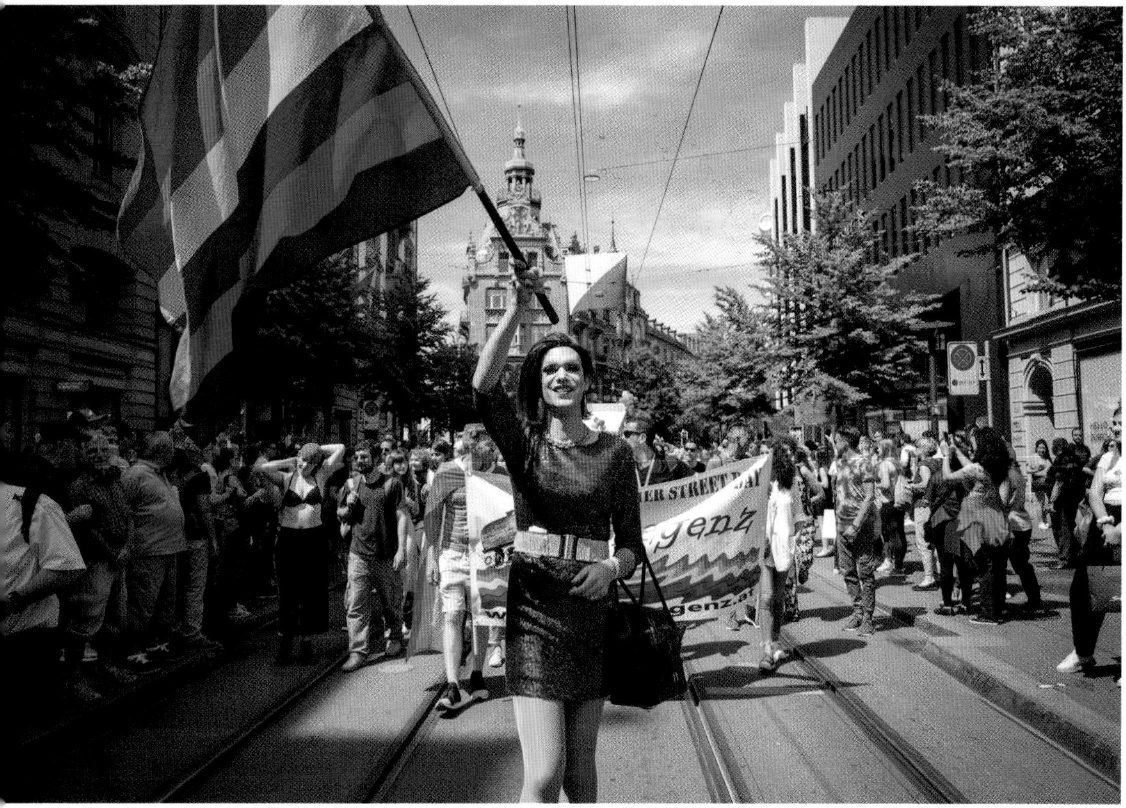

355 Together we rise with allies in Schweiz

Zürich Pride Festival, Switzerland

When to go: June
Best for: Fourteen days of diversity

With two weeks of Zürich Pride, culminating in a roaring two-day Zürich Pride Festival, Zürich has attracted thousands of queer visitors annually since 1994—it's the country's largest queer event. Formerly Christopher Street Day, Zürich Pride offers a diverse range of events leading to the big peaceful, political demonstration parade and free-for-all festival at the barracks area, Kasernenareal. When you're in town, keep an eye out for concerts by Cor Rosa, Switzerland's queer choir.

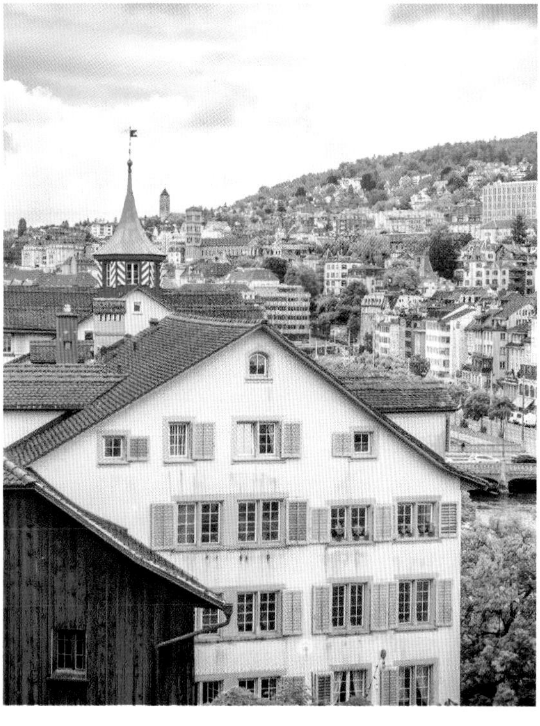

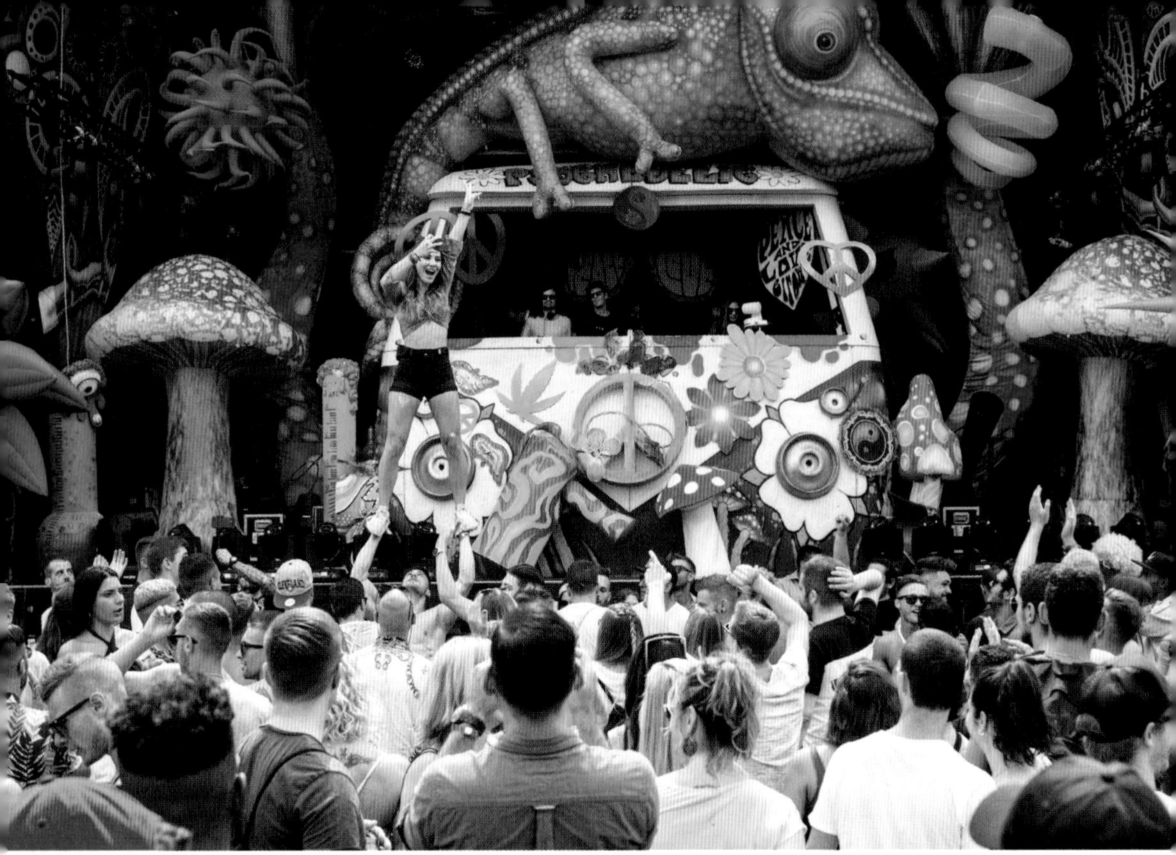

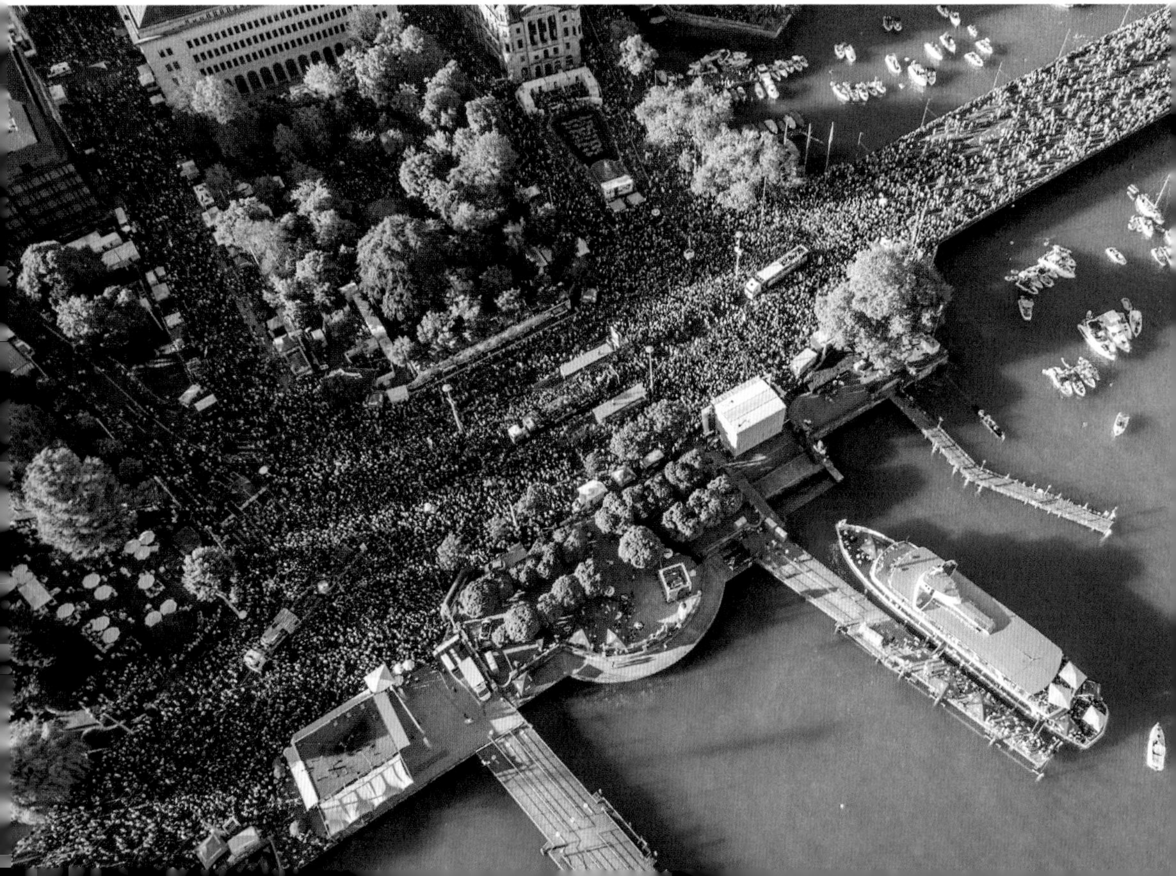

356 Don't tech-no for an answer

◀ Street Parade, Zürich, Switzerland

When to go: August
Best for: An exhilarating street-party

Every second Saturday in August, Zürich hosts one of the world's largest techno parties. The first parade's motto, in 1992, was "demonstration for love, peace, freedom, generosity, and tolerance." It's an exhilarating party. Thirty moving stages called Love Mobiles take you around the Lake Zürich basin, with additional stationary stages along the route. Join the afterparty at queer bars in Niederdorf, or one of the legendary Angels gay events.

357 Simply irre-Swiss-tible

Angels Events, Zürich, Switzerland

When to go: All year
Best for: Meeting boys

Leading gay-party organizer since 1994, Angels Events organizes enthralling LGBTQ+ events with fabulous people, international DJs, and phenomenal shows. Their legendary events include the Black Party, White Party (during Zürich Pride), Kitsch Party, and Flash Party (following the Street Parade). The perfect events to meet boys and, increasingly, all manner of queer folks.

358 Rock-solid flint

Tanzleila, Zürich, Switzerland

When to go: All year
Best for: A women-dominated party

Lighting up Zürich women's nightlife since 1987, Tanzleila has become an established noncommercial party series for all *FLINT*—Frauen, Lesben, Intergeschlechtliche, Nonbinäre, und Transpersonen (women, lesbians, intersex, non-binary, and trans people). The venue (Club EXIL) is glitzy, the DJanes' music eclectic, and your money is well spent, with proceeds going to LGBTQ+ and women's projects.

359 Apple of your eye

Pink Apple Film Festival, Zürich and Frauenfeld, Switzerland

When to go: April and May
Best for: Queer cinema-lovers

Founded in the apple-growing region of Switzerland (the Canton of Thurgau) in 1997, the Pink Apple Queer Film Festival's first edition screened just 10 films for a few hundred guests in Frauenfeld. Over the years it has become the country's largest intersectional LGBTQ+ film festival, with thousands of guests, screening around 120 Swiss and international films with just as many side events, shared across the Swiss cities of Zürich and Frauenfeld.

360 Make a füss

▼ ▶ Niederdorf, Zürich, Switzerland

When to go: All year
Best for: Queer and quaint nights

Niederdorf—locally known as Dörfli (Little Village)—is Zürich's historic center of the LGBTQ+ community and home to one of Europe's oldest gay bars, Barfüsser. Wander the medieval car-free streets and charming squares of the historic quarter, stroll along the Limmat river, and admire the colorful architecture. Get sushi and drinks at the iconic Barfüsser, a stone's throw away from its original location (Spitalgasse 14), or a cocktail at the award-winning Cranberry Bar. For more queerness, the former red-light district, Langstrasse, is the place to be.

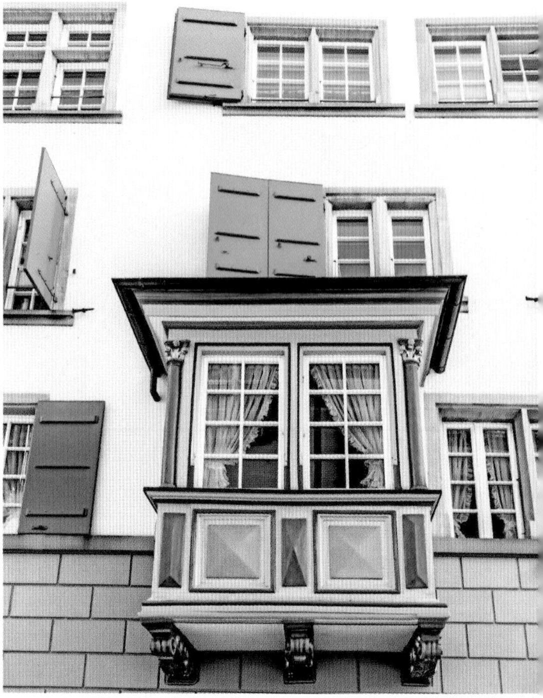

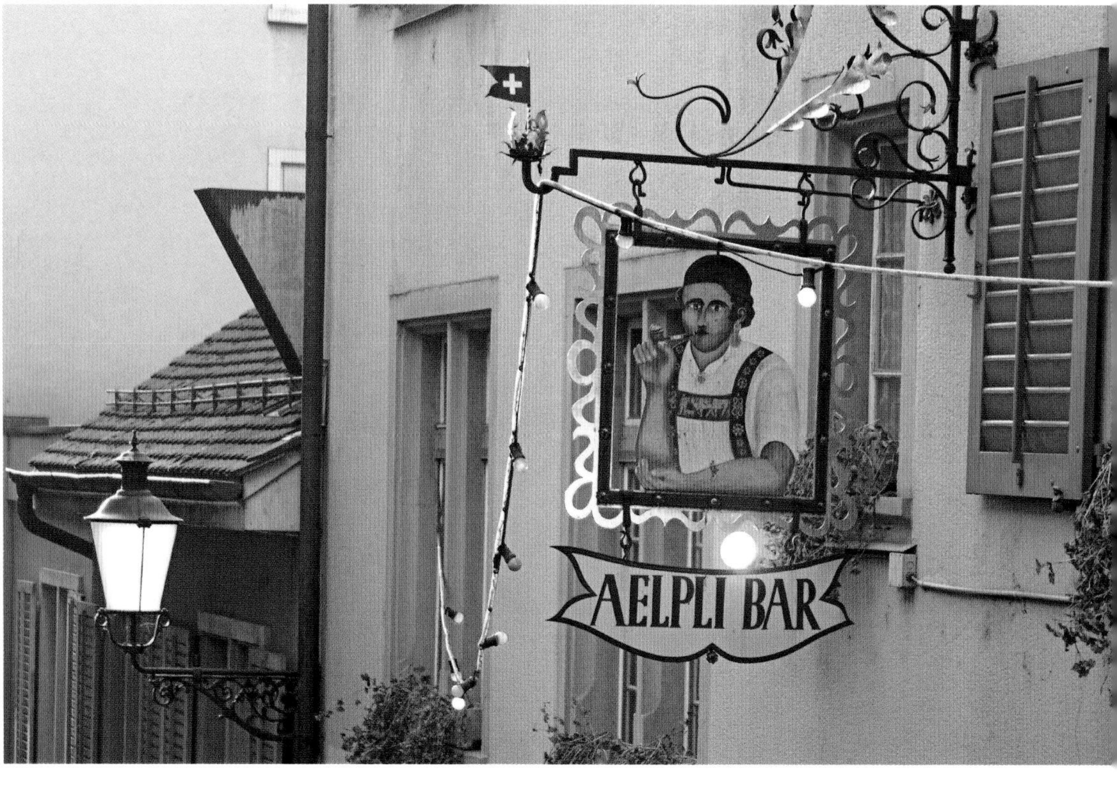

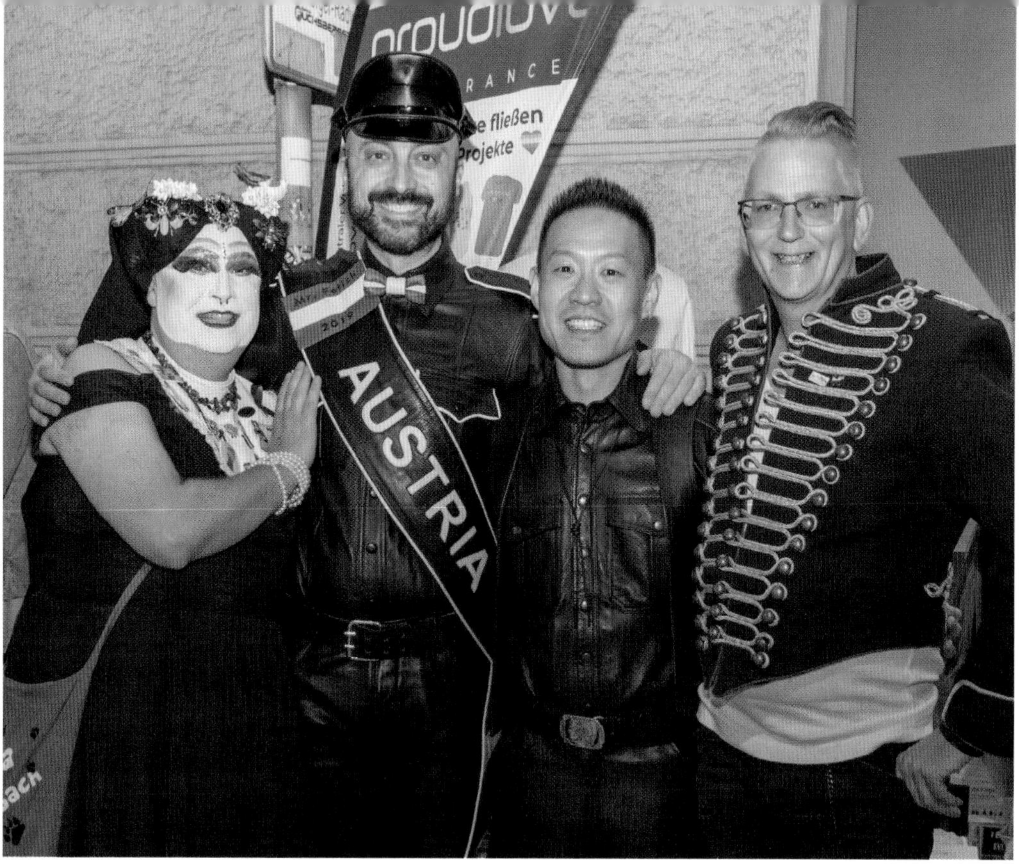

361 Follow every rainbow

Salzburg Pride, Austria

When to go: September
Best for: Sounds of music and pride

On the Salzach river lies the idyllic, alpine city of Salzburg. Backed by mountains, it is dominated by the impressive clifftop fortress of Hohensalzburg and famous as the city of music: both for being the birthplace of Wolfgang Amadeus Mozart and the film location of *The Sound of Music*. Bordering the romantic, historic center, Altstadt, you can find Salzburg's queerborhood Andräviertel, home to gay-popular spots Mexxx Bar, Dark Eagle, and HOSI bar.

362 Feel blessed at HOSI Fest

▲ HOSI Fest, Salzburg, Austria

When to go: All year
Best for: Good vibes

In the heart of queerborhood Andräviertel, on Franz-Josef-Straße 22, you can find the multifaceted LGBTQ+ organization HOSI (Homosexual Initiative) Salzburg, founded in 1980. It's a bar, a community center, and an organization that hosts legendary events. One of these is HOSI Fest, Salzburg's biggest LGBTQ+ clubbing event, that takes place at ARGE Kultur, attracting queer folks from Austria, Southern Germany, and beyond.

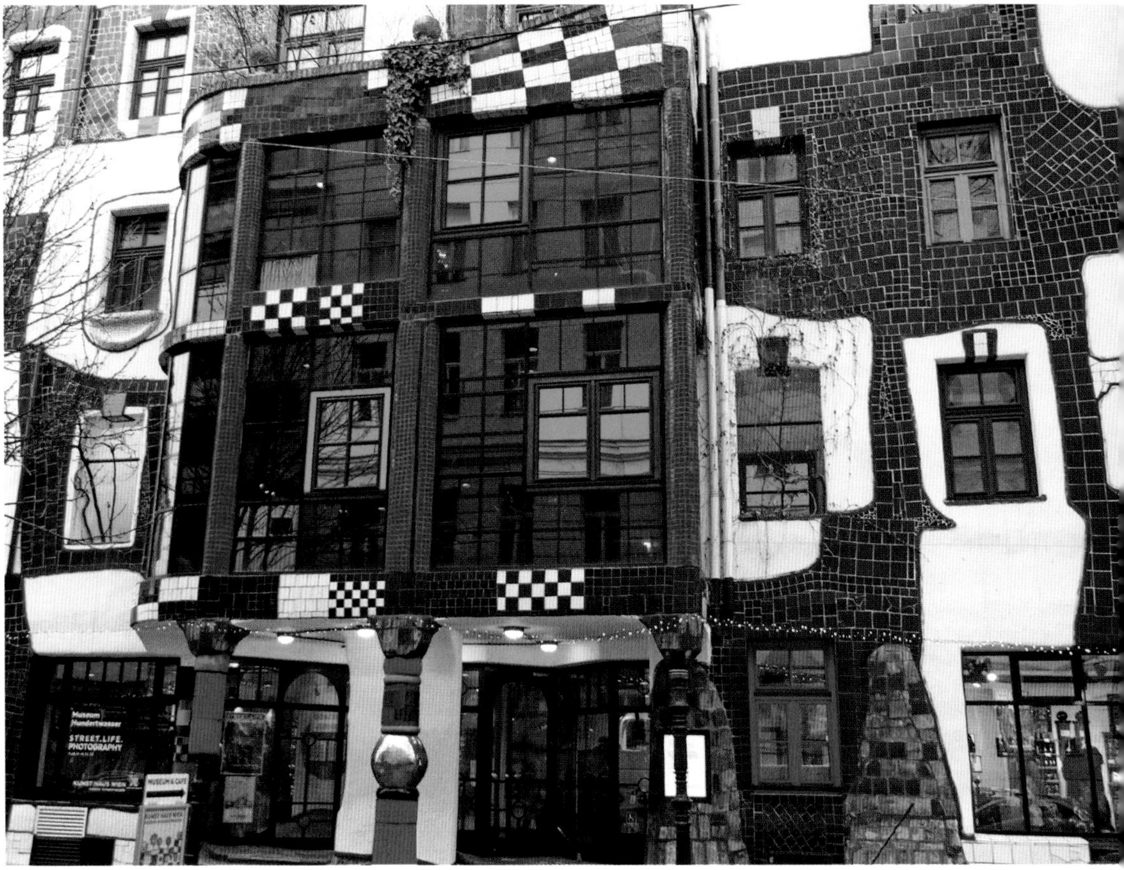

363 Where straight is ungodly

Kunst Haus Wien, Vienna, Austria

When to go: All year
Best for: Non-straight building and art

Most buildings are straight, but this one isn't. Legendary artist Friedensreich Hundertwasser thought the straight line was ungodly and designed the five-story museum, Kunst Haus Wien, as a bastion against the grid system, monotony, and standardization. If you stand in front of the facade, you notice it is wavy, colorful, irregular, and green—with live vegetation. The inside isn't straight either, with curved walls and uneven tiled floors mixed with wooden floorboards. Discover the museum's permanent Hundertwasser exhibition on the first two floors, and temporary exhibitions dedicated to photography of the twentieth and twenty-first centuries on the third and fourth floors. Temporary exhibitions are often LGBTQ-themed, and include queer artists like Mapplethorpe and Pierre & Gilles. Are you looking for more non-straight buildings? Visit Hundertwasserhaus nearby, another iconic building designed by Hundertwasser.

364 Take a Viennese whirl

Vienna Pride, Austria

When to go: June
Best for: Viennese flair

Austria's capital is home to a lively and diverse queer scene. The Naschmarkt and the Rathausplatz areas are where you'll find some of the city's best LGBTQ+ venues. Near Naschmarkt, inside the legendary queer space Türkis Rosa Lila Villa—or the Villa for short—there's the Black-woman-owned, queer, community café Villa Vida. Café Savoy brings queer people together for brunch and Viennese flair, while Village Bar and Mango Bar are busy at night. Rathausplatz is the star during Vienna Pride, hosting a multi-day Pride Village, and acting as the start and endpoint of the Regenbogenparade (Rainbow Parade).

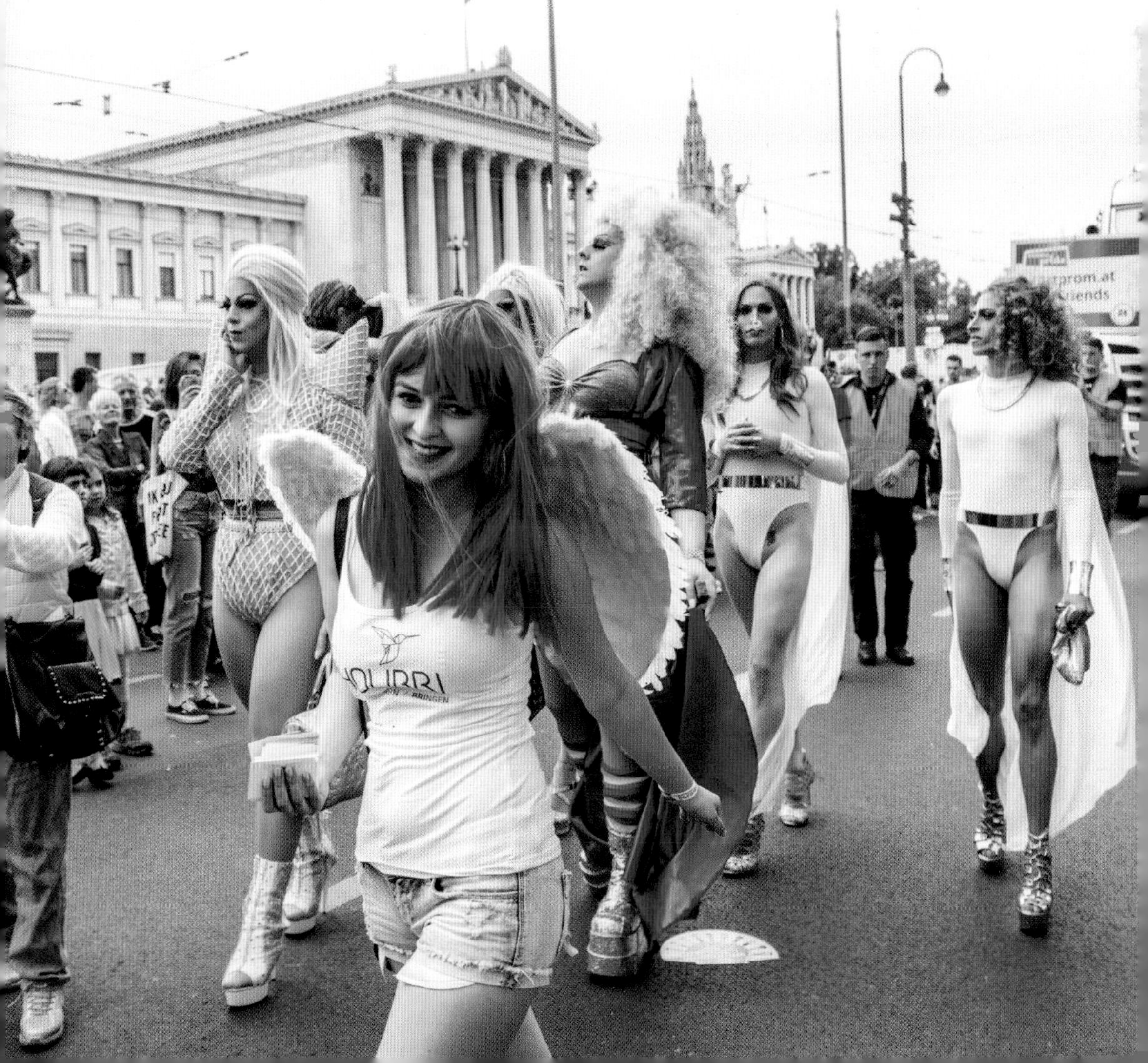

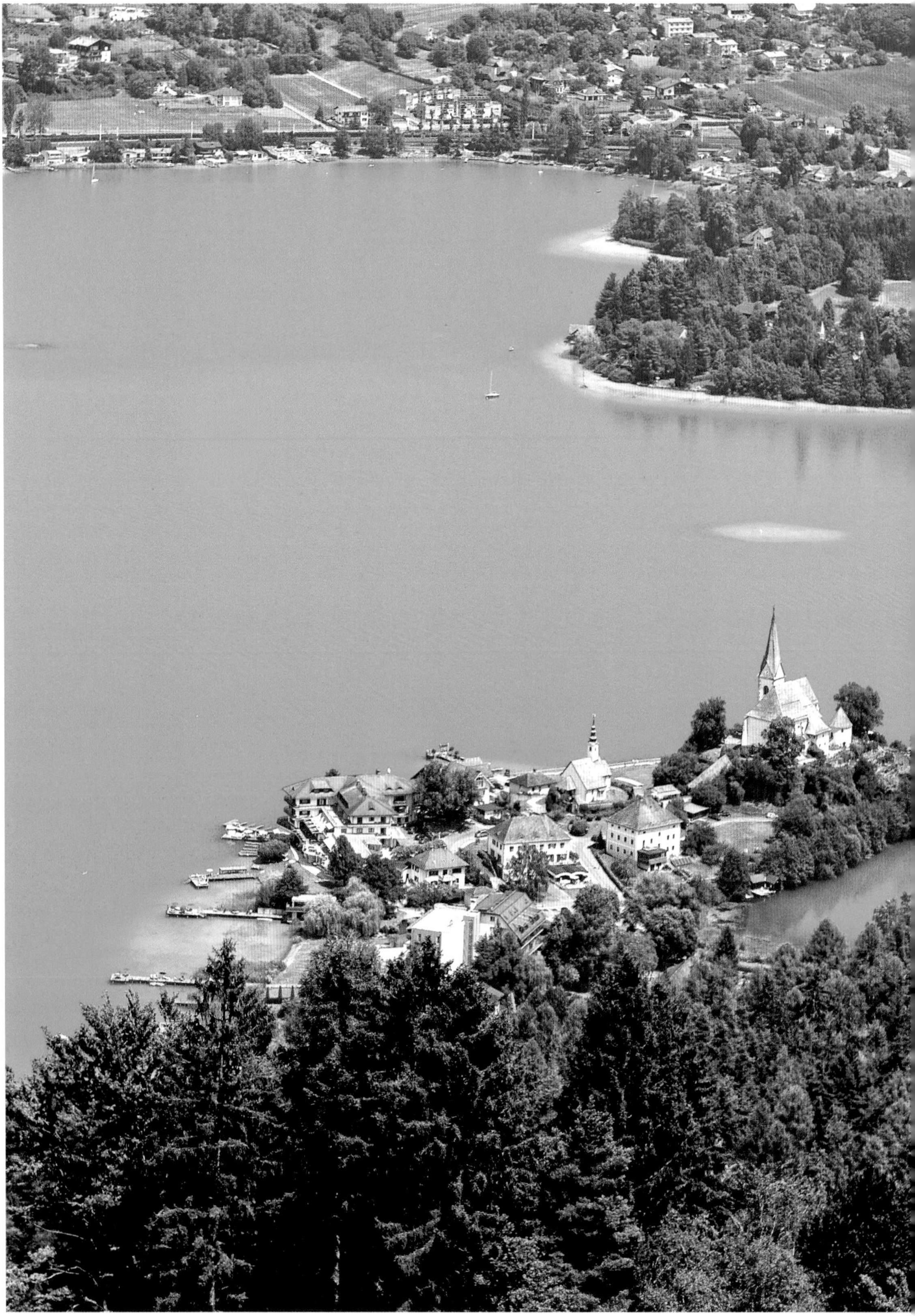

365 Because you're worth it

Pink Lake, Pörtschach am Wörthersee, Austria

When to go: August
Best for: Lakeside fun

There's no shortage of lakes in Austria's southernmost state, Carinthia. This alpine region is an outdoor lover's paradise, with over 1,200 lakes and gorgeous mountains. Wörthersee—Lake Wörth—is the biggest lake in the area, located south of the Alps and close to the Italian and Slovenian borders. Thanks to the mild climate, Wörthersee is one of the Alps's warmest lakes, with rich shades of green and blue. Naturally, people flock here in the summer, gays in particular. Since 2007, Wörthersee has turned (metaphorically) "pink" in the summer for the Pink Lake festival. The days are fun-filled, with beach days, games, and watersports on Pink Island. And the nights are wild and colorful with a Dirndl and Lederhosen (traditional Austrian clothes) party, a boat-cruise party (on multiple tied-together ships), and drag and club nights. For essential beauty-napping, the lakeside towns offer plenty of LGBTQ-friendly accommodation. Hotel Schloss Leonstain—where the "Almdudler Almrausch Party" takes place—in Pörtschach am Wörthersee is closest to the festival.

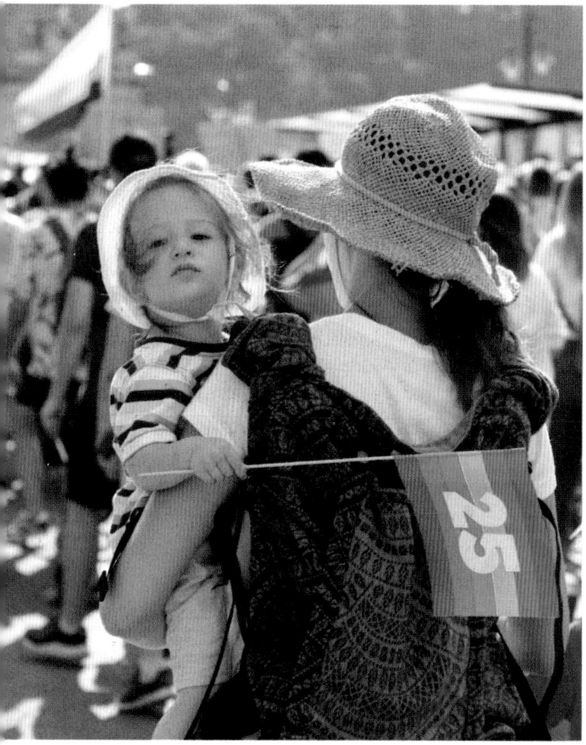

366 Leave Hungary for more

◀▼ Budapest Pride, Hungary

When to go: July
Best for: Living your Buda-pest life

Hungary is a conservative country, but Budapest is home to a "queer bubble." The enchanting city is famous for thermal baths, ruin bars (bars in abandoned buildings), and festivals. Sziget Festival is loved by many; its queer stage, Magic Mirror, welcomes all with shows and performances—from cabaret to burlesque. Every July, Budapest Pride brings the community together for over one hundred events, including a political, nongovernmental march, culminating in Rainbow Party in Budapest Park.

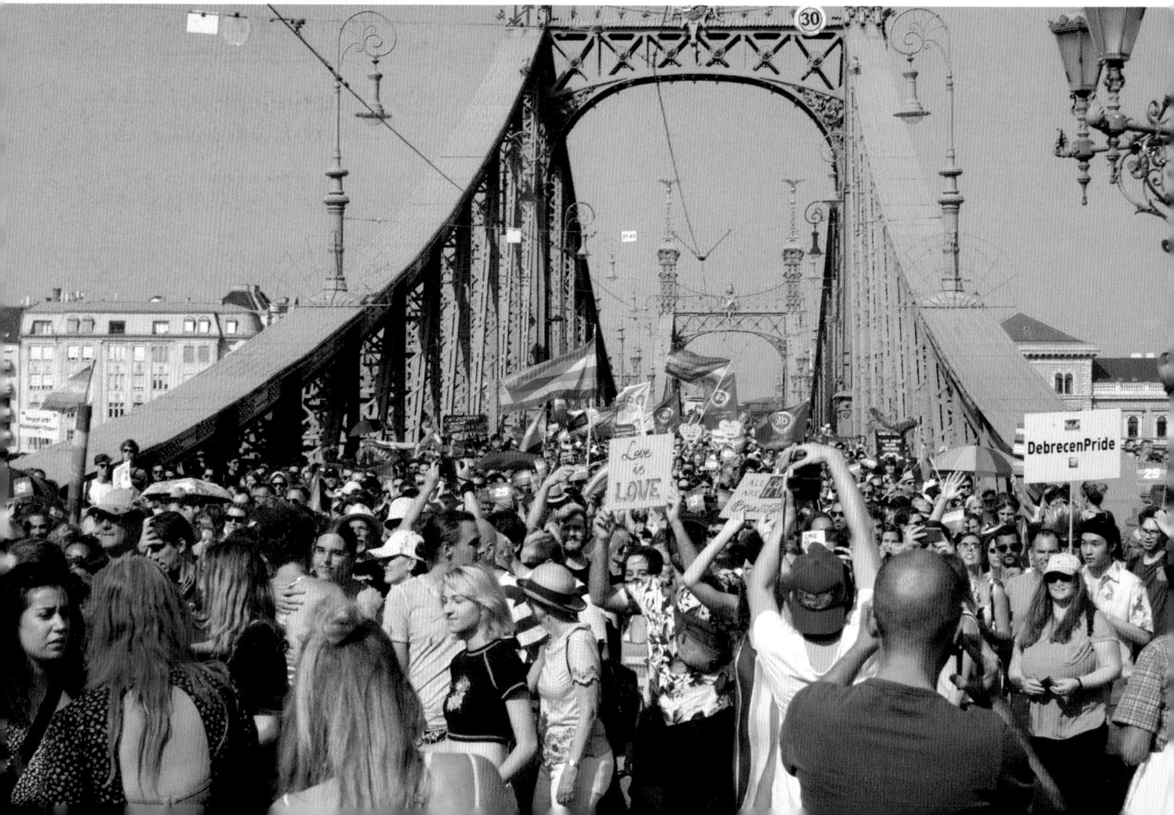

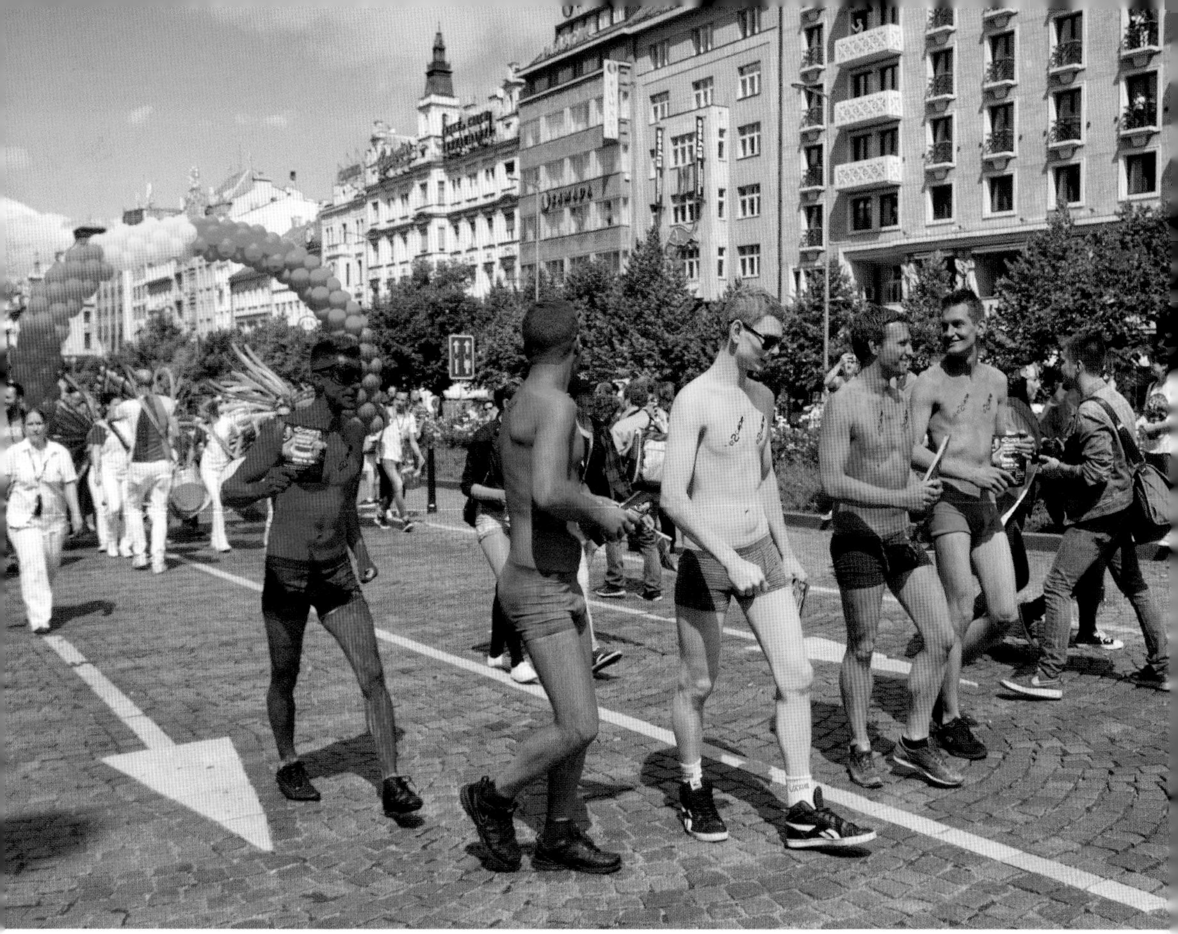

367 Czech out the scene

▲ Prague Pride, Czech Republic

When to go: August
Best for: Pride in a gothic city

Prague, with its striking gothic architecture, is an amazing city to visit. For a week each summer, the city hosts hundreds of events as part of Prague Pride. A crowd-favorite since it started in 2011 is Pride Village on Střelecký Island, which has everything from yoga, games, and spiritual spaces to hairdressers, picnics, and mini-markets.

368 Choose any style, as long as it's yours

Barberette, Prague, Czech Republic

When to go: All year
Best for: Getting the hairstyle you'd like, no questions asked

Originating in London, Barberette has expanded to Prague. This gender-neutral barbershop has a no-judgement policy, and prices are listed by style and length—not by gender—allowing people to get whatever hairstyle they truly love.

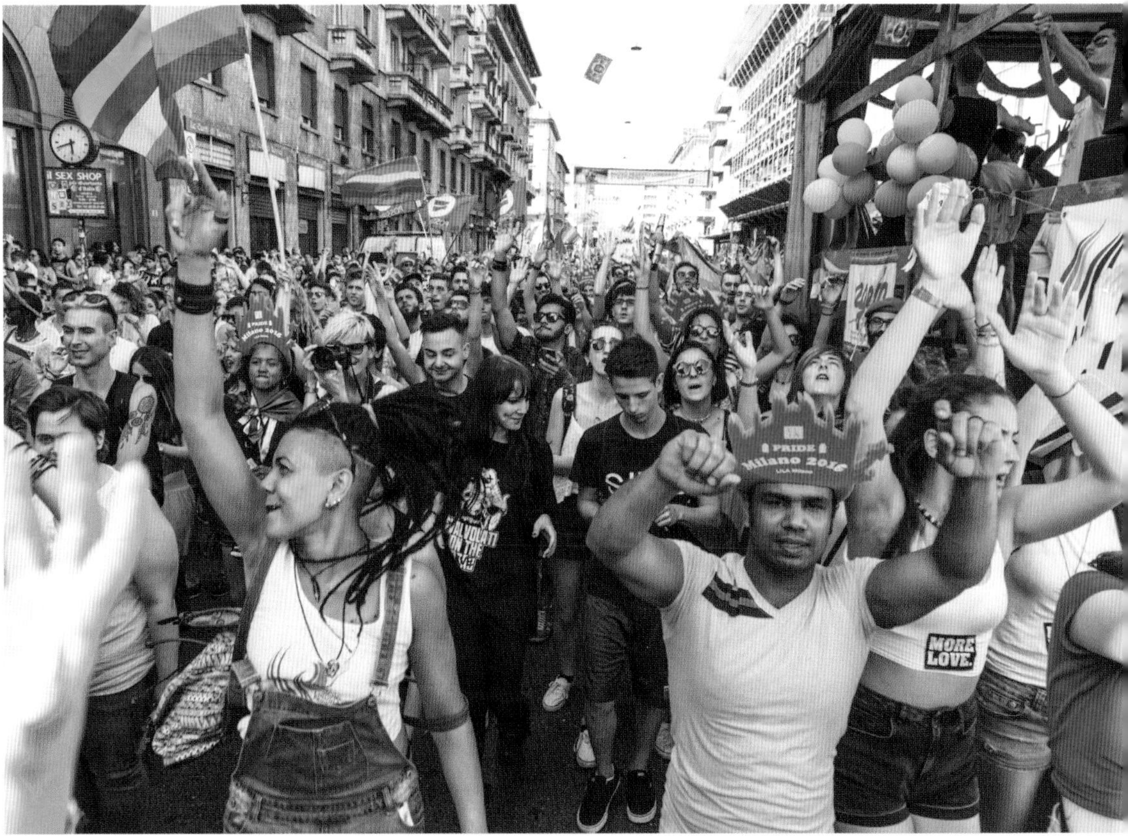

369 Never out of fashion

Milan Pride, Italy

When to go: June and July
Best for: Fashionable queerness

Italy's fashion capital, Milan, has a vibrant LGBTQ+ scene and a heartfelt Pride. Milan Pride adds color to the city in late June with multiple Pride Squares, concerts, film screenings, a traditional *sfilata* (parade), and a rainbow-illuminated Palazzo Marino (city hall). More events and parties happen in the LGBTQ+ neighborhood of Porta Venezia, and specifically on Via Lecco—home to most of the city's queer venues and a gay Christmas market in winter.

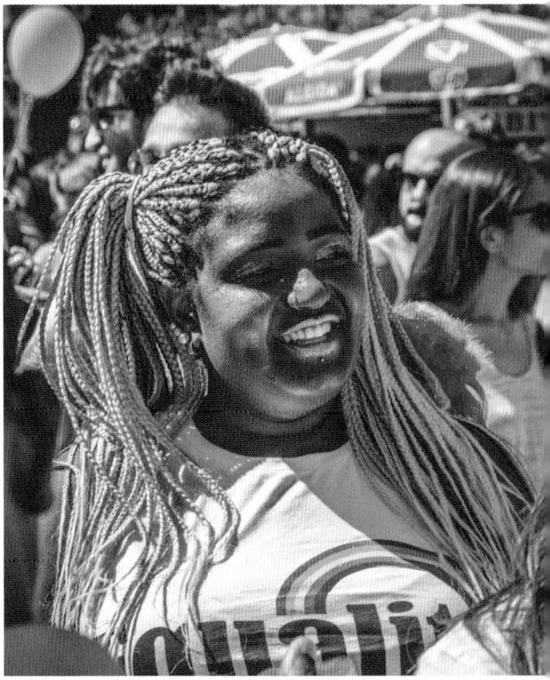

370 Take a pizza your heart

Napoli Pride, Naples, Italy

When to go: June and July
Best for: Pizza and espresso

The pizza- and espresso-capital of Italy is Napoli (Naples); it's where pizza was born, and the espresso machine found its roots (thanks to Neapolitan flip coffee pots). Part of Napoli's charm is that it is curiously chaotic, graffiti-covered, and a little rough around the edges. Napoli Pride is a meaningful happening in summer, with a parade through the historic center toward the Ovo Castle. Connect with LGBTQ+ locals on Piazza Bellini at gay-popular Bar Fiorillo or low-key literary café Intra Moenia.

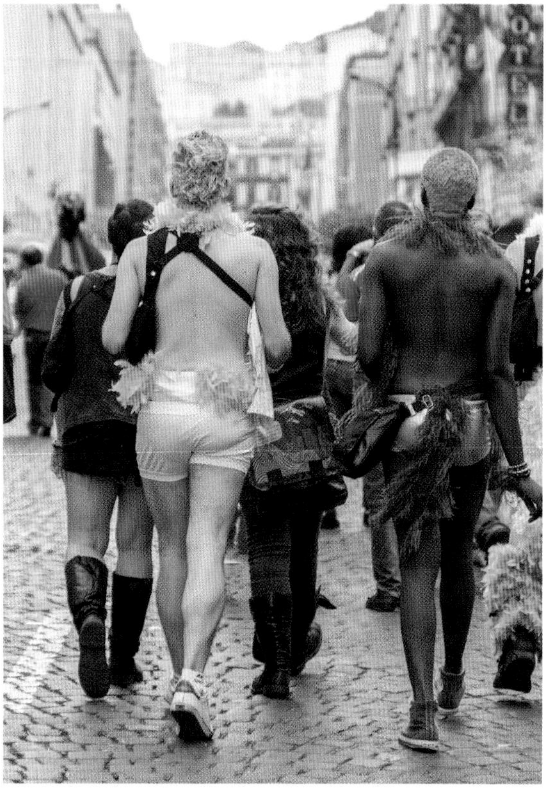

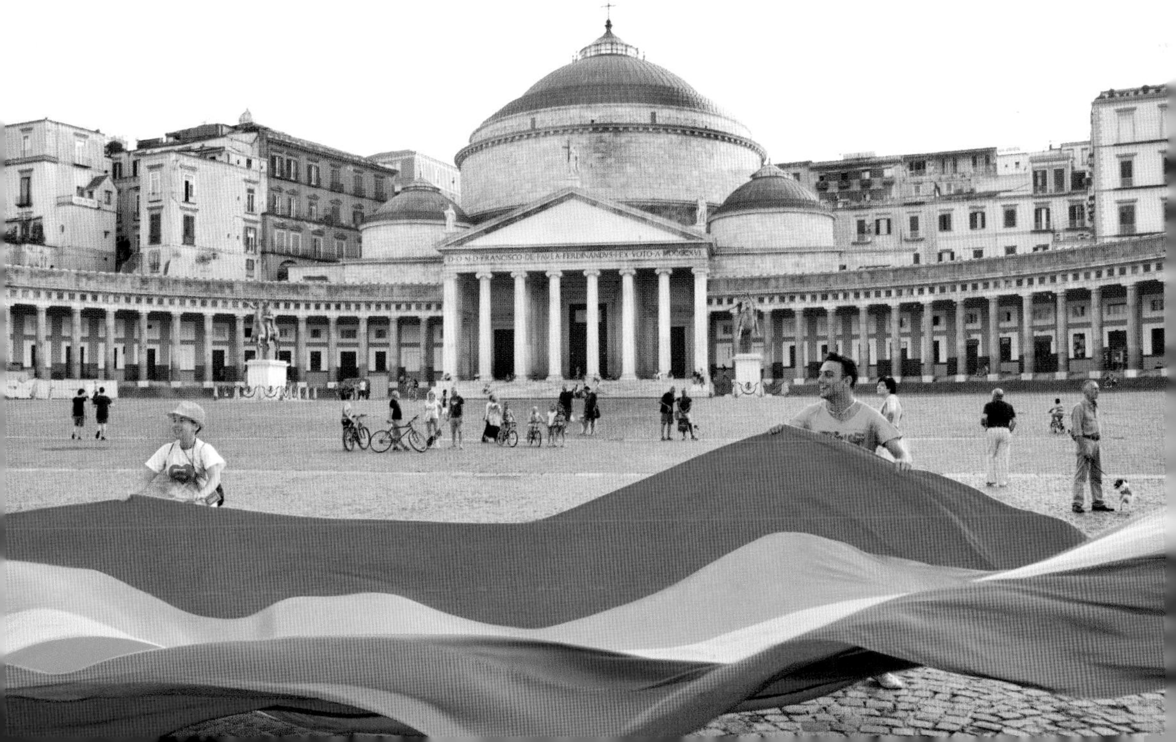

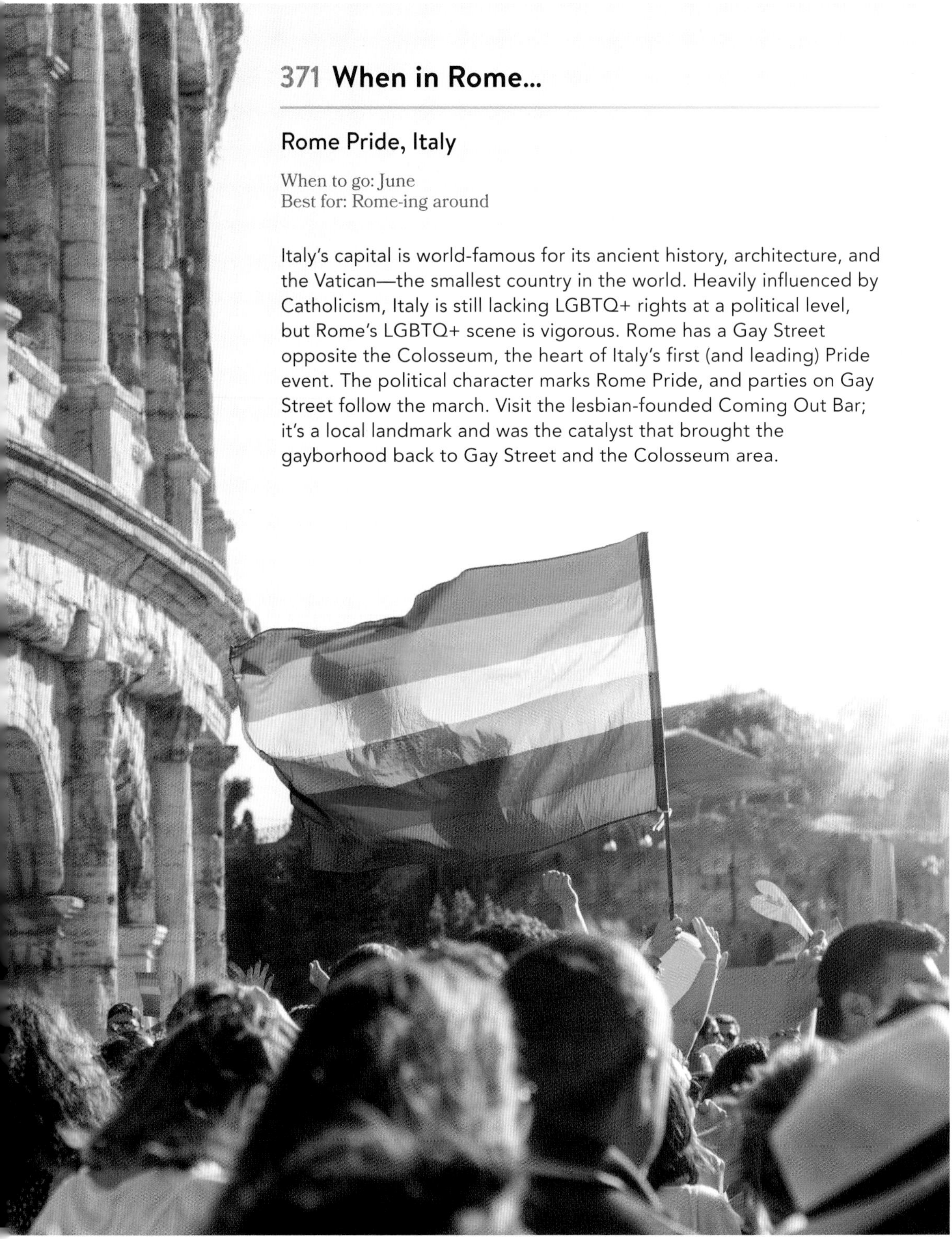

371 When in Rome...

Rome Pride, Italy

When to go: June
Best for: Rome-ing around

Italy's capital is world-famous for its ancient history, architecture, and the Vatican—the smallest country in the world. Heavily influenced by Catholicism, Italy is still lacking LGBTQ+ rights at a political level, but Rome's LGBTQ+ scene is vigorous. Rome has a Gay Street opposite the Colosseum, the heart of Italy's first (and leading) Pride event. The political character marks Rome Pride, and parties on Gay Street follow the march. Visit the lesbian-founded Coming Out Bar; it's a local landmark and was the catalyst that brought the gayborhood back to Gay Street and the Colosseum area.

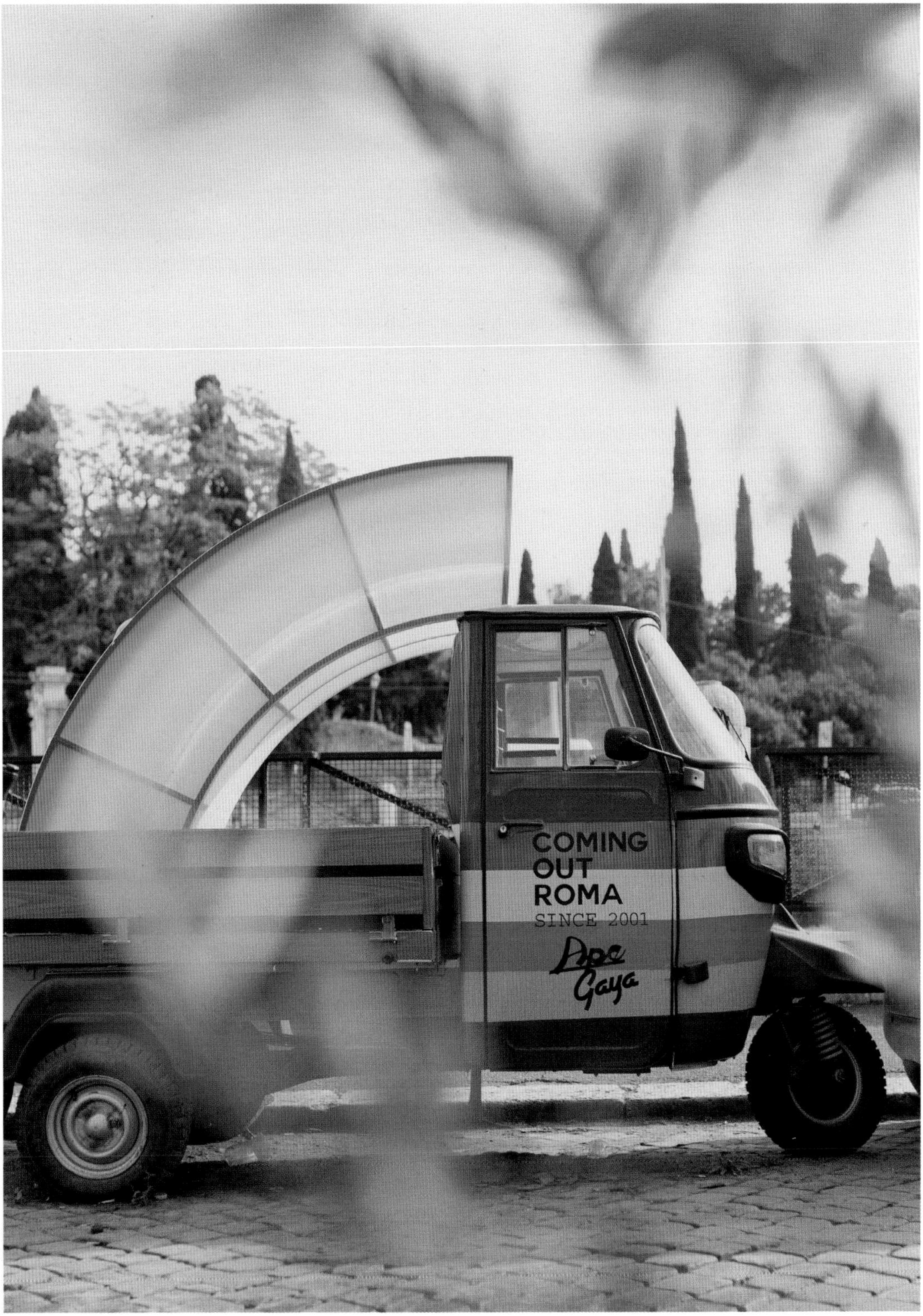
COMING
OUT
ROMA
SINCE 2001
Ape
Gaya

372 Dogs, cats, and beer

▼ Maori Bar, Valletta, Malta

When to go: April to September
Best for: A chill and casual evening out

Not everyone can find this hidden gem (clue: look for the tunnel on Old Bakery Street), but Maori's queer owner, Simone, and her pets welcome you to their alternative seaside space when you do. The best way to enjoy this quaint, living-room-style bar is on a warm spring or summer night with friends—and a cold Cisk beer.

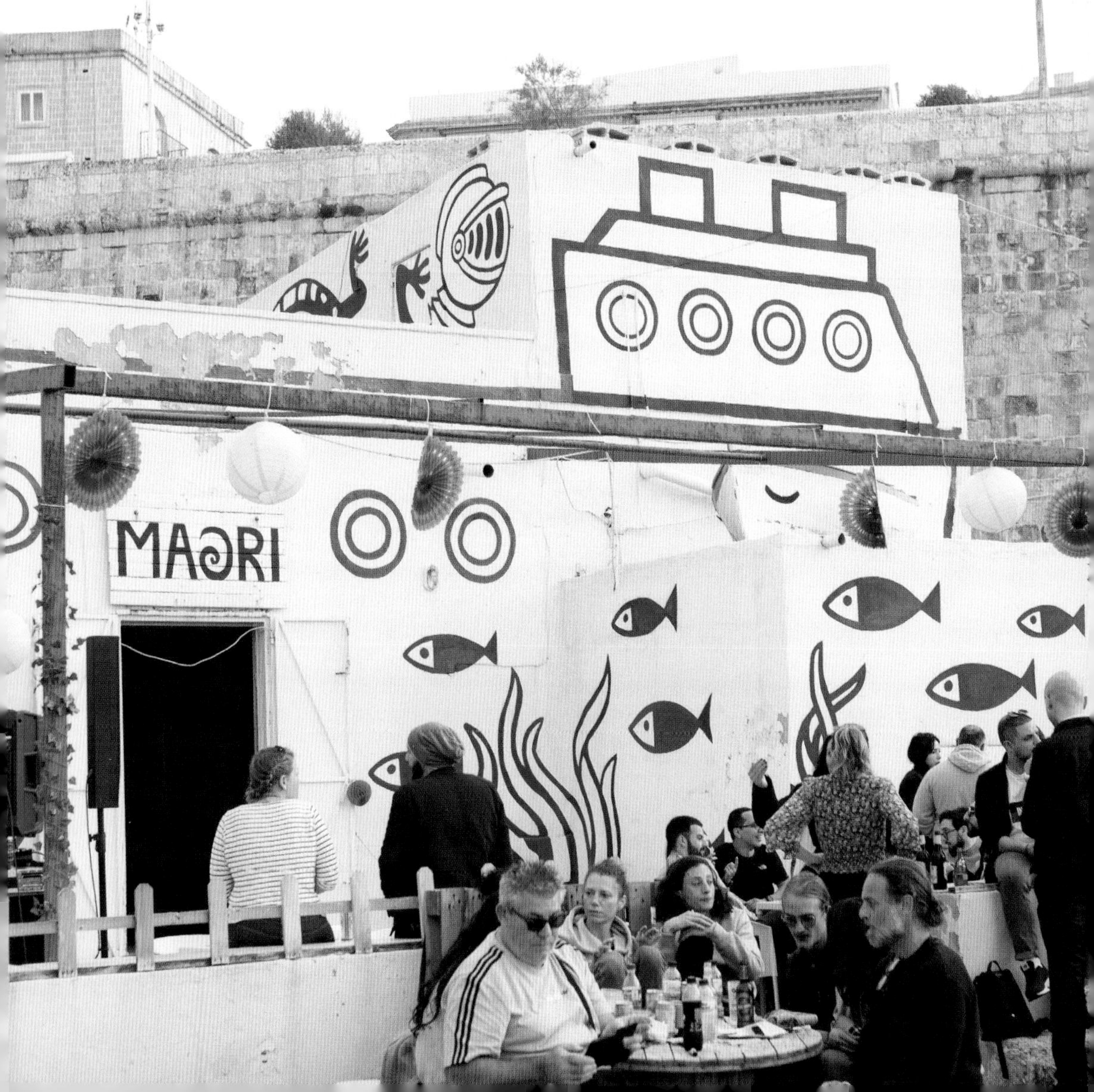

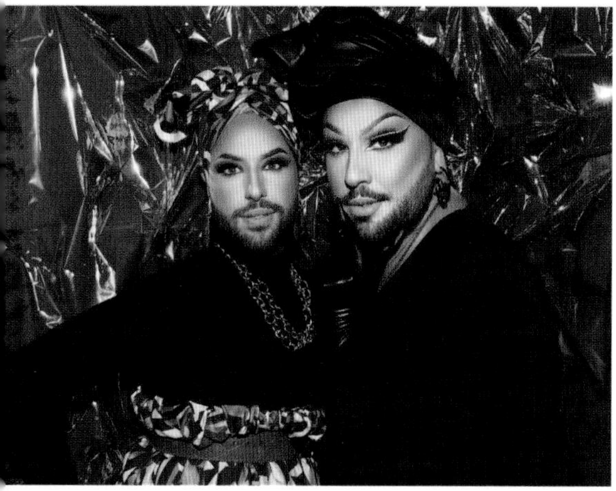

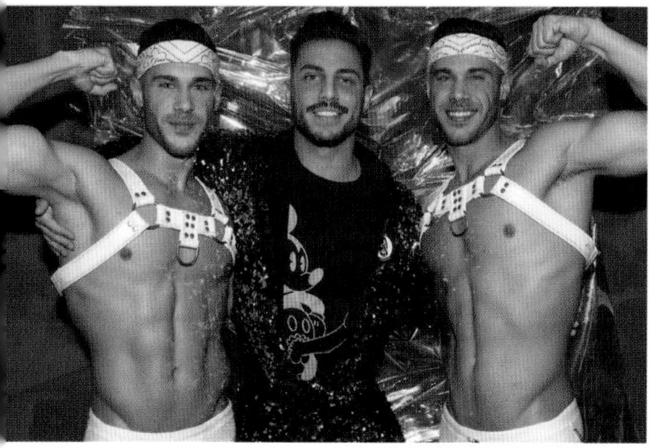

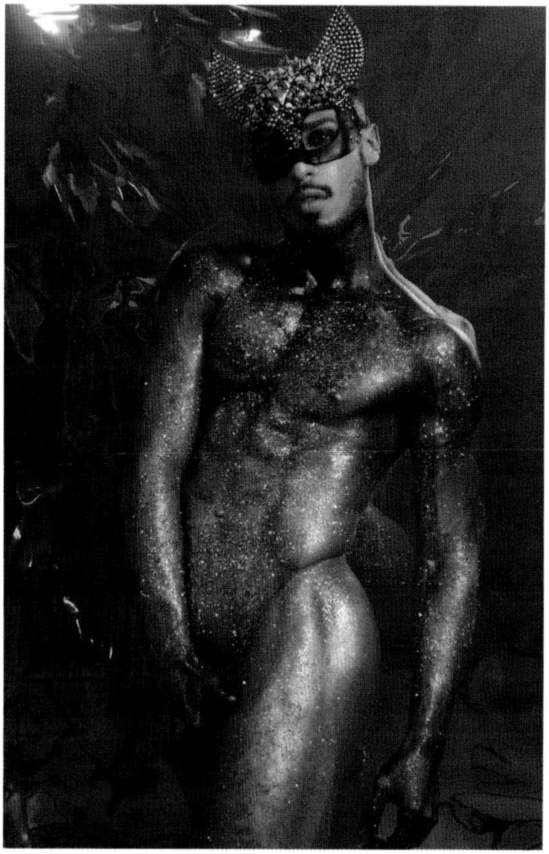

373 Sweet as candy

▲ Lollipop, Malta

When to go: All year
Best for: Clubbing to pop, house, and tech-house music

Malta—a predominately Catholic archipelago in the Mediterranean Sea—is a country of contrasts. Divorce wasn't legal until 2011—and abortion still isn't—but the country now has some of the most progressive LGBTQ laws in Europe and queer people feel comfortable everywhere. Since 2016, Lollipop's monthly parties and events at various venues in Malta have been bringing the community together. Their disco nights attract a hot and diverse LGBTQ+ crowd.

374 Leave a Smudge on your heart

Smudge's The Falcon Bar, Buġibba, Malta

When to go: All year
Best for: Affordable drinks at a relaxed, friendly bar

In the lively coastal village of Buġibba, there's a small, relaxed, corner bar where the queer owner, musician, and natural bodybuilder Smudge welcomes you. She welcomes everyone. As well as its wonderful, inclusive atmosphere, Smudge's The Falcon Bar also hosts special women's events and LGBTQ+ meetups.

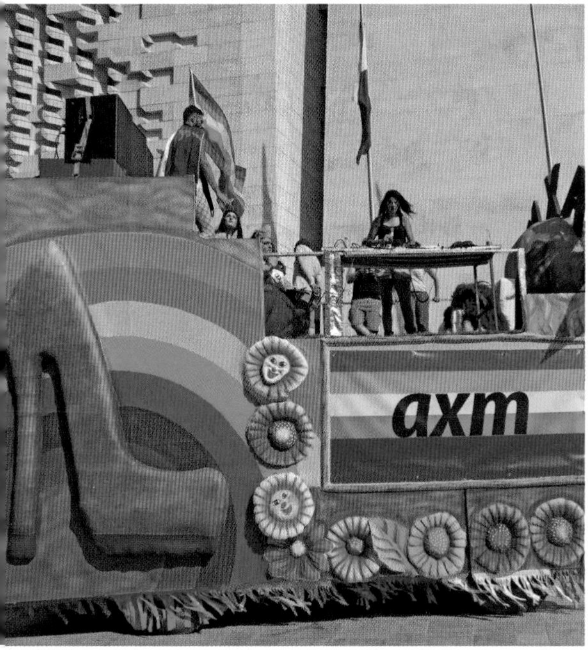

375 Small but mighty

◀ Malta Pride, Malta

When to go: September
Best for: Queer Mediterranean vibes

Malta Pride may have only started in 2004, yet its dreamy island vibes and the LGBTQ+ friendly attitudes of the island have gained huge popularity in recent years. Malta Pride now hosts a wide variety of parties throughout Pride Week (the Disco Tits pool party is a lot of fun). It also includes two Pride marches: one in the capital, Valletta, and another in Gozo, the small northern island which is also home to the blue lagoon.

376 Za-grab yourself a drink and chill

▶ Zagreb Pride, Croatia

When to go: June
Best for: Coastal and capital fun

Croatia has been leading the queer way in southeast Europe since 2002 when Zagreb—Croatia's capital—hosted the region's first Pride march. Zagreb Pride events have significantly improved Croatian LGBTQ+ rights and acceptance. Croatia's alluring coastal destinations—Dubrovnik, Split, Rab, and Hvar—now openly market themselves as LGBTQ-traveler friendly. LGBTQ+ popular spots in the capital city are Hotpot and low-key cultural club Kic Klub. LGBTQ-friendly music festivals—like SUNcéBeat—are another great reason to plan a visit.

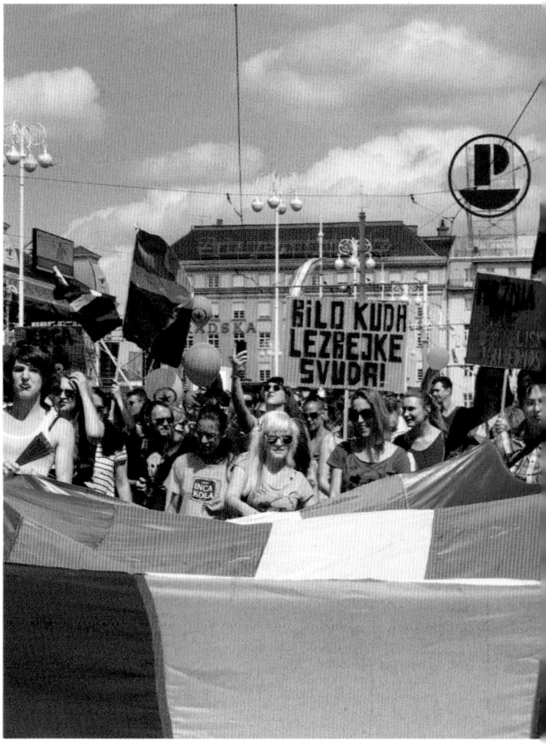

377 In the birthplace of lesbian love

▼ Lesbos, Greece

When to go: March to October
Best for: Poems for the ultimate lesbian

"Someone will remember us, even in another time," wrote Greek poet Sappho, and she was right. More than two thousand years after her birth on the island of Lesbos, people honor her poems celebrating love between women. Lesbos is charming, with quaint fishing villages, rustic beaches, rich mythology, and hospitable islanders. Residents call themselves lesbians (unrelated to their sexuality), and queer terms *sapphic* and *lesbian* come from this island.

378 Sapphic seduction

International Eressos Women's Festival, Lesbos, Greece

When to go: September
Best for: Live love lesbian

The remote coastal "lesbianville" Skala Eressos is home to many queer-women-owned venues and the long-running International Eressos Women's Festival. The two-week-long queer women's festival packs laid-back vibes, alternative events, nude beaching, breathtaking sunsets, and lively parties. The festival goes beyond tolerance and acceptance; it celebrates queer women.

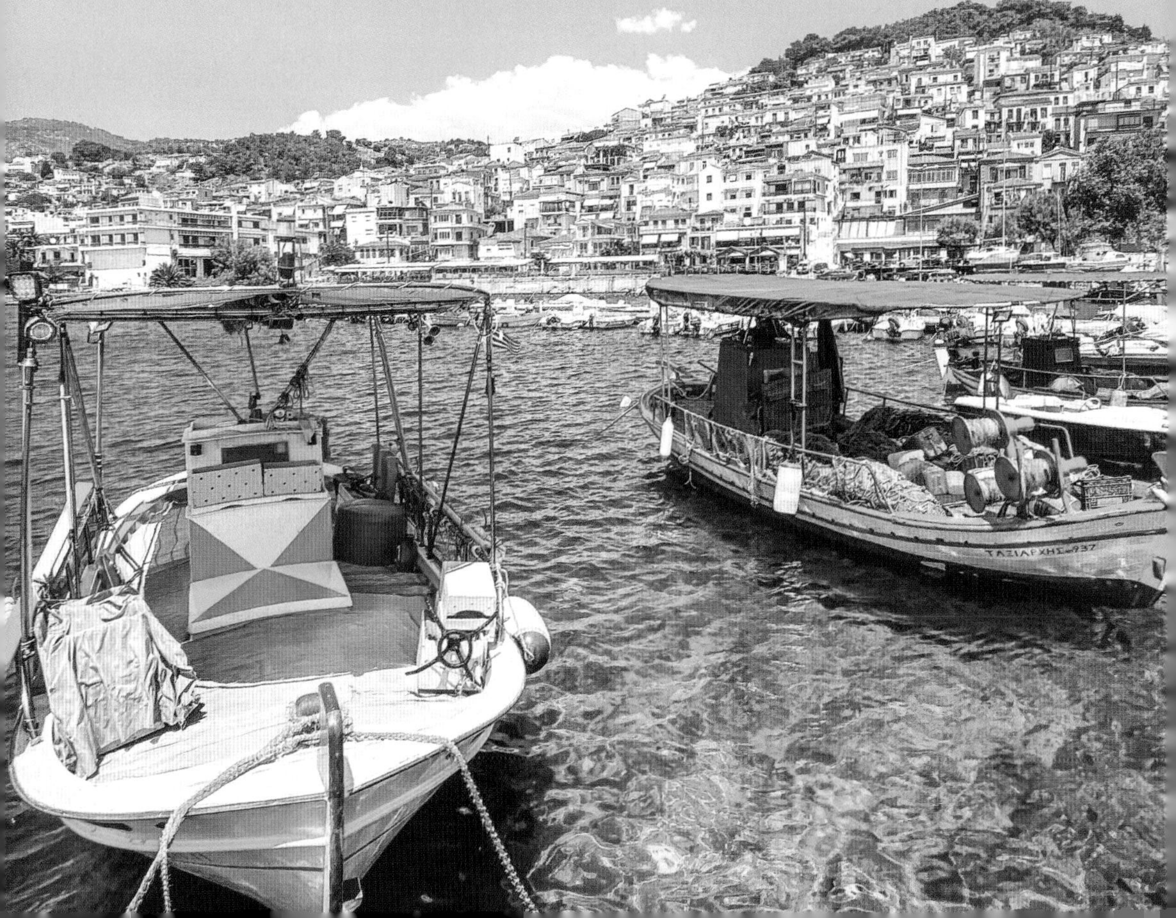

379 Bag the big four

Mykonos, Greece

When to go: April to October
Best for: Greeking out

Ibiza, Gran Canaria, Sitges, and Mykonos are Europe's "Big Four" destinations for gay men. Mykonos's *chora* (old town) is picturesque by day and wild at night, with most gay venues in Little Venice. JackieO' Bar is legendary, taking its name from Jackie Onassis, who frequented Mykonos in the 1970s and the gays followed. There's also a Jackie O' Beach on Super Paradise Beach, an infamous gay beach.

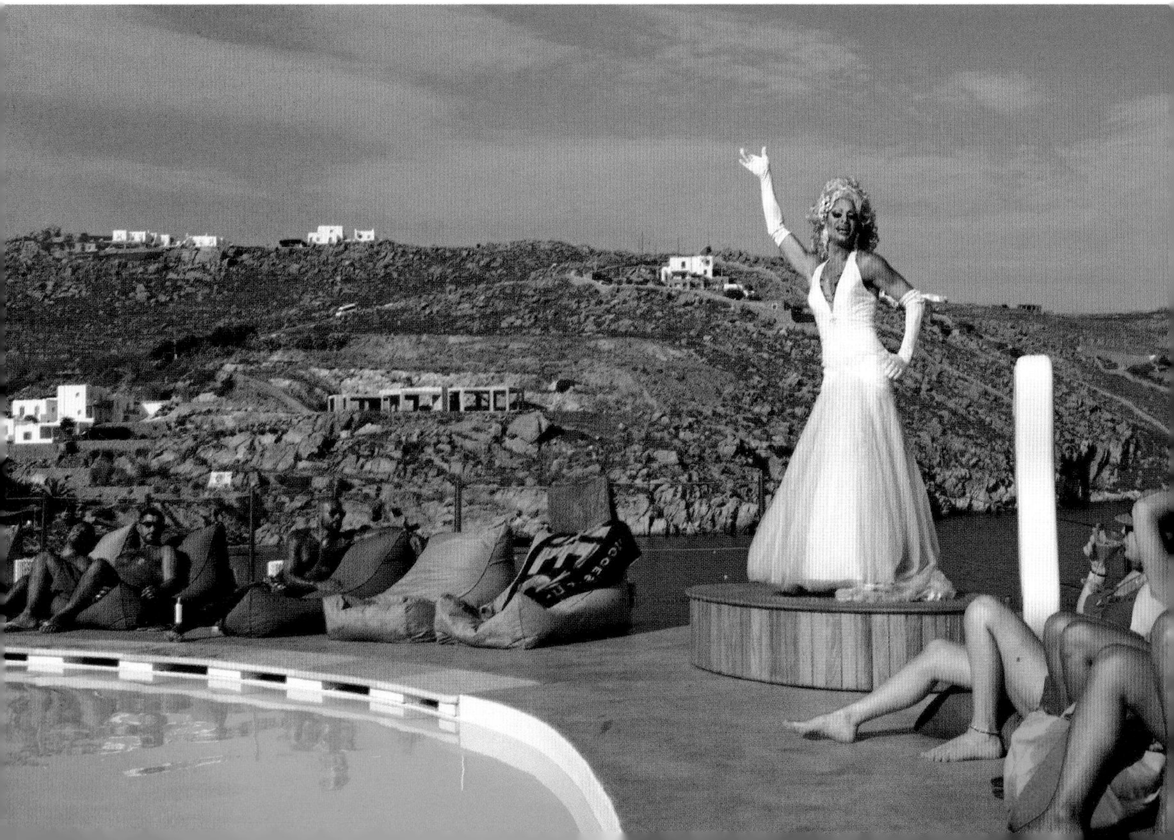

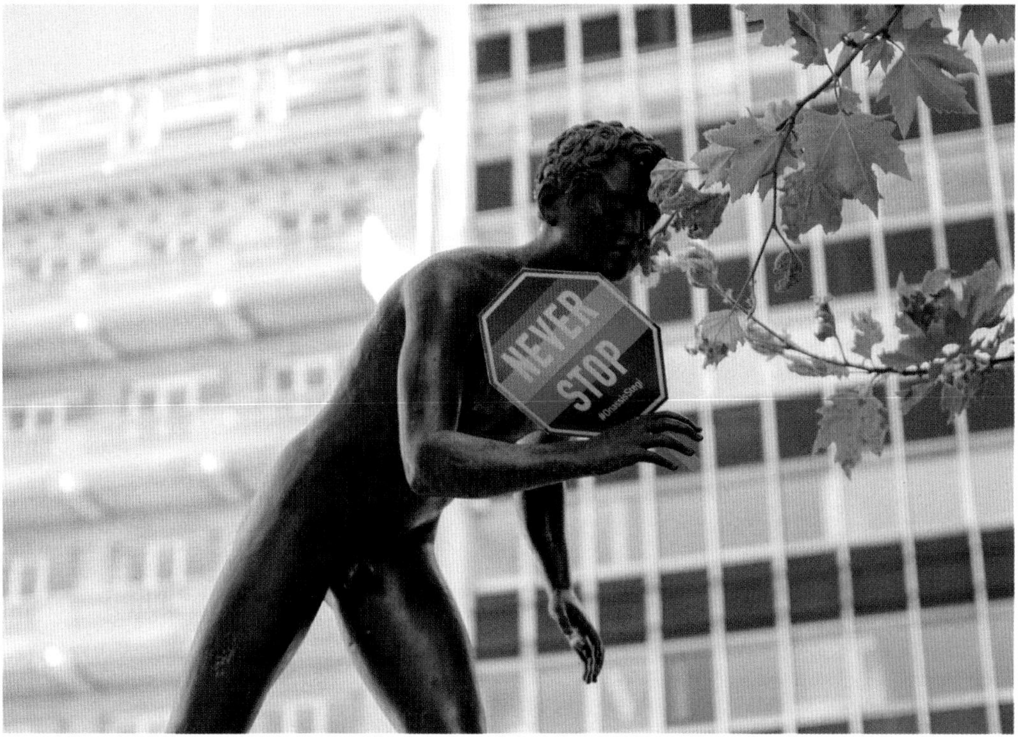

380 What Athens in Greece, stays in Greece

Athens Pride, Greece

When to go: June
Best for: Pride among landmarks

Greece's capital is famous for its philosophers, legendary landmarks, and being the birthplace of Western democracy. It also has a thriving LGBTQ+ scene. Bohemian Athenian neighborhood Gazi—near the Acropolis—offers a plethora of queerness. Get Greek coffee at queer-women-run co-op Beaver; dance the night away at staple Sodade2, alternative BeQueer, or diverse Shamone Club. And visit the pinnacle of the Athenian LGBTQ+ scene, Athens Pride at iconic Syntagma Square.

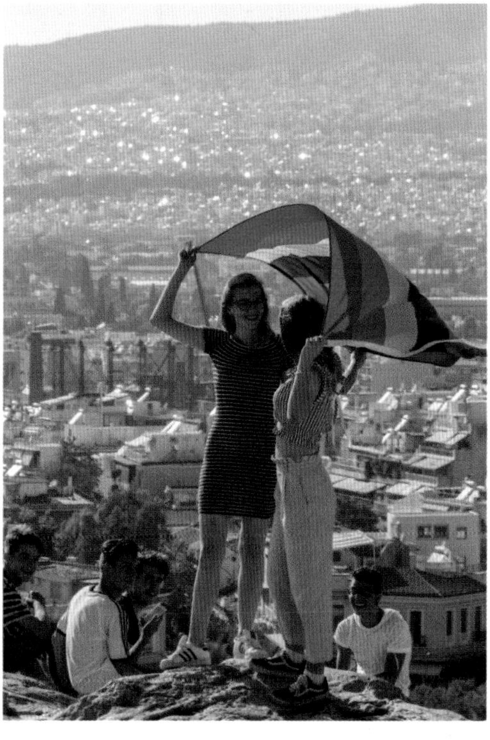

381 Looking for luxury?

Santorini, Greece

When to go: May to October
Best for: Picturesque romanticism

Santorini is one of the most picturesque places to enjoy a romantic getaway without setting foot outside your hotel. Contrary to other Greek Islands, Santorini is not a famous beach destination. People come here for the high level of luxury and the most romantic sunsets. The white and blue cliffside village of Oía (pronunciation "ee-a") in the north of Santorini is dazzling. Book one of the cave hotels with a caldera view and a pool for the complete experience. Queer-owned accommodation Santorini Sky offers levels of luxury that are as high as the location, 2,000 ft/610 m above the Aegean Sea. Are you feeling adventurous? Hire a buggy or a moped and explore the island's cutest villages and sights; there's much more to Santorini than Oía.

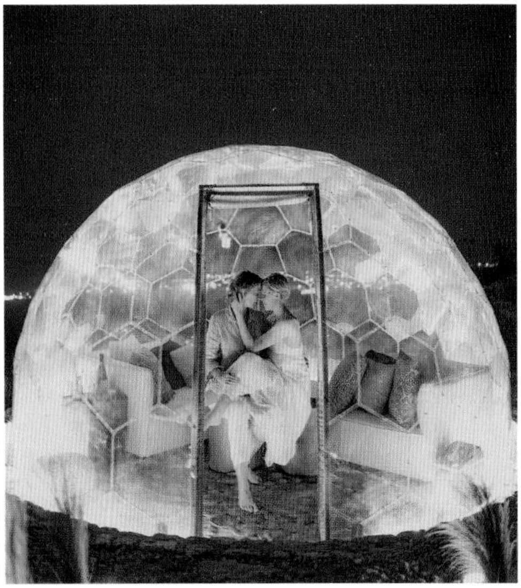

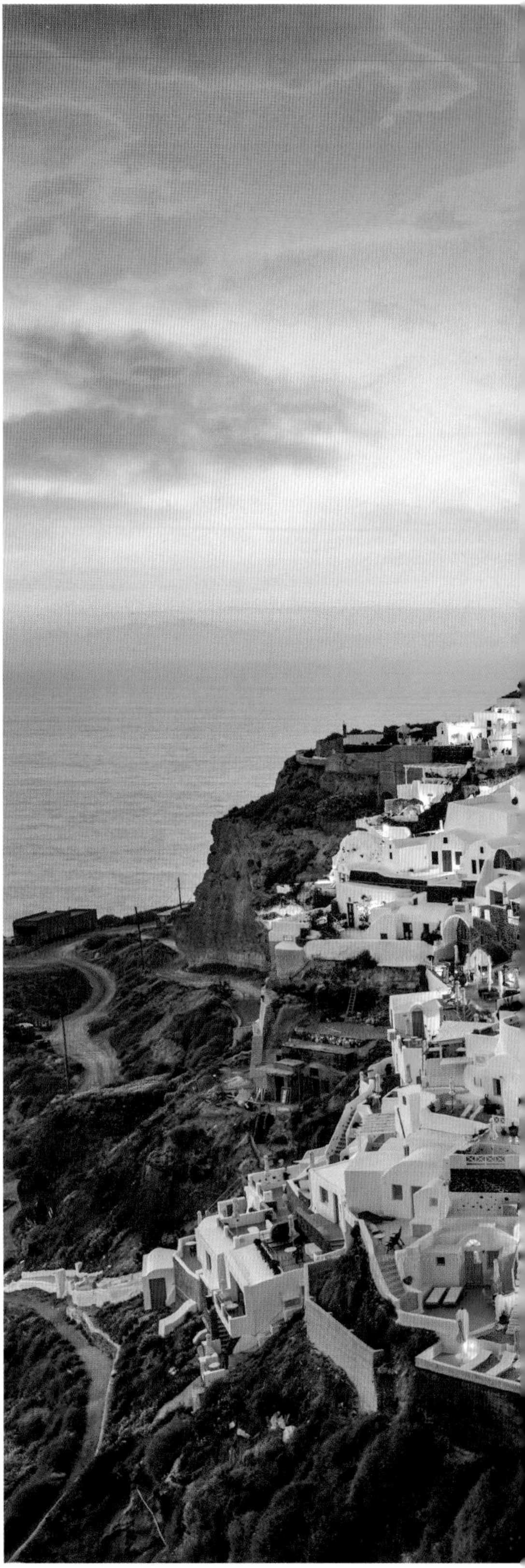

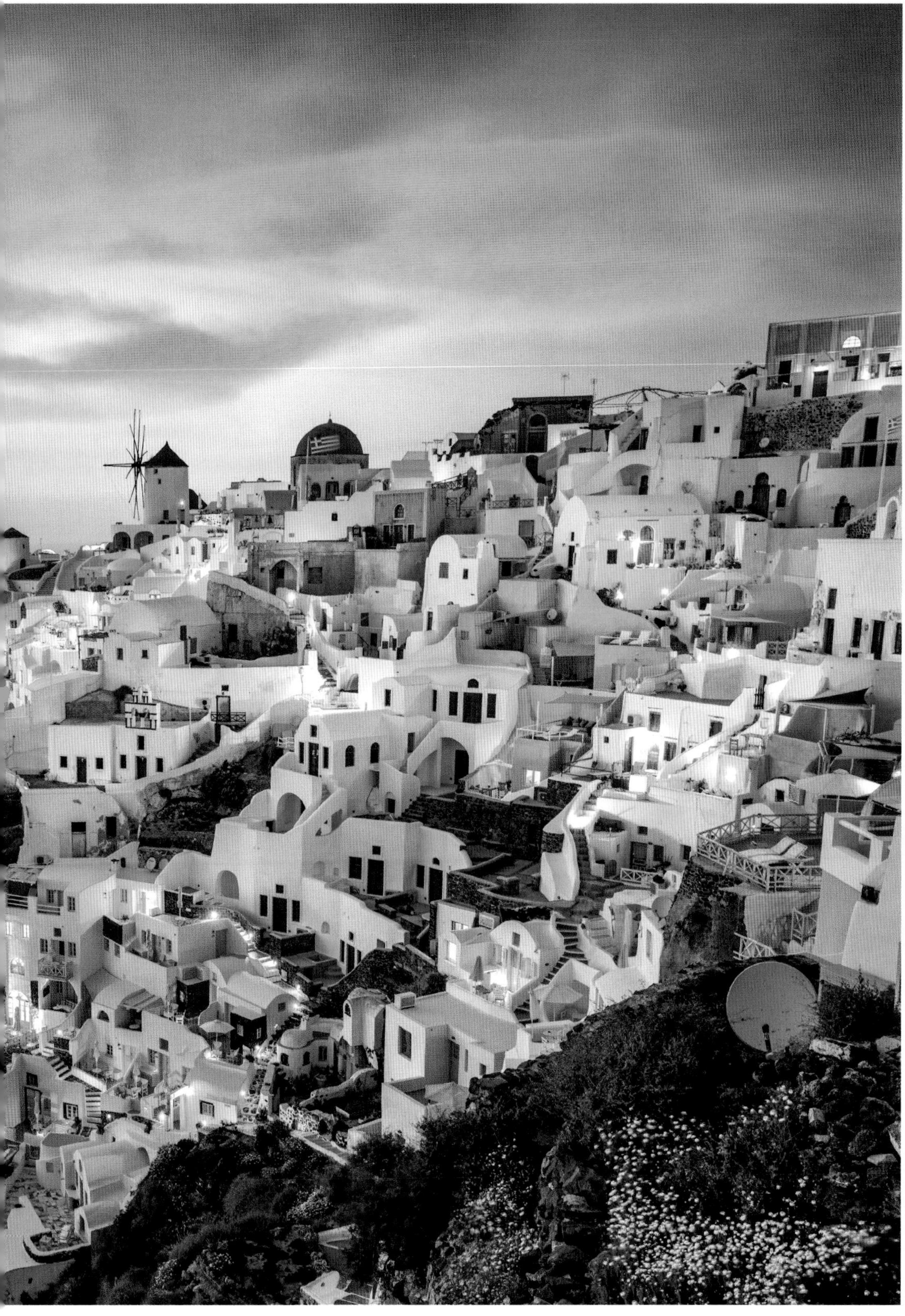

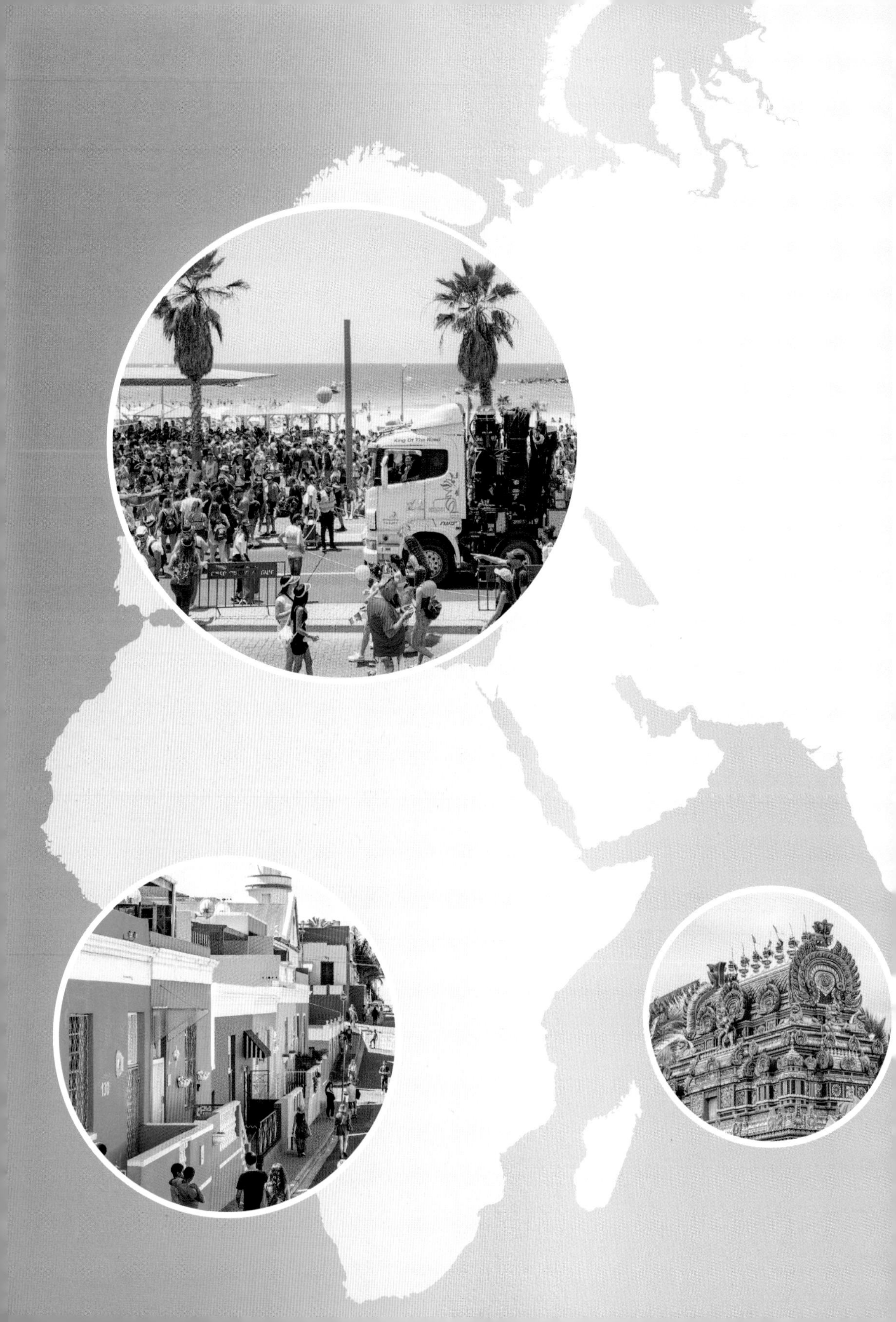
King Of The Road

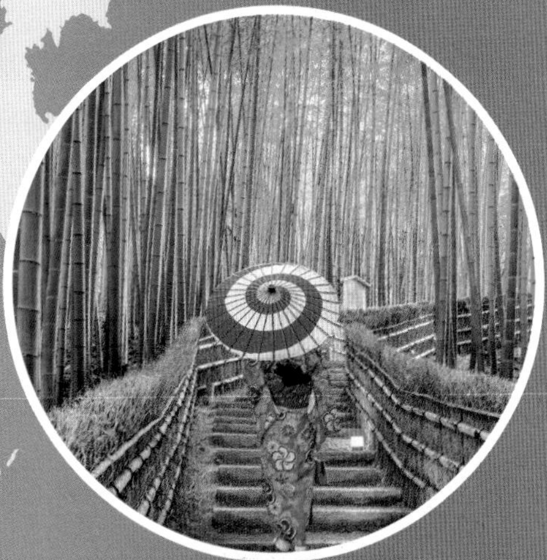

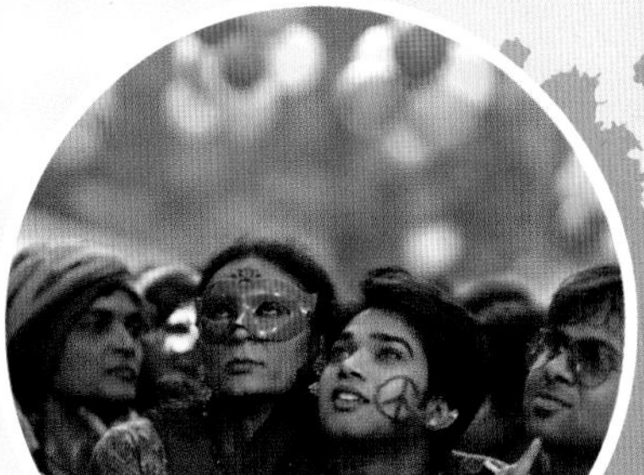

CHAPTER FOUR

AFRICA, MIDDLE EAST, AND ASIA

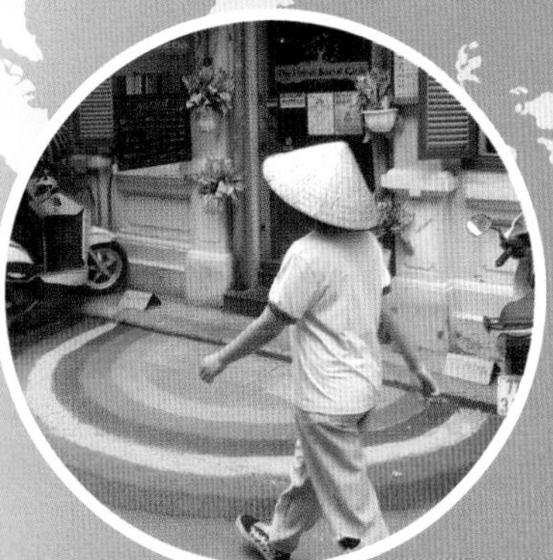

382 Find balance at Imbala

Imbala, Jerusalem, Israel

When to go: All year
Best for: Changing the world

Founded by Jerusalem activists, Imbala is a multilingual, political co-op, vegan café, library, and LGBTQ+ safe space with many queer events. Imbala—"if she wills it" in Hebrew and "actually, yes" in Arabic—has a mission to create a more welcoming Jerusalem.

383 Everyone has rights

▼ Jerusalem Pride, Jerusalem, Israel

When to go: June
Best for: Keeping the fight alive

While Tel Aviv Pride celebrates LGBTQ+ achievements, Jerusalem Pride is still fighting for rights to be recognized. Jerusalem is a holy site for Judaism, Islam, and Christianity, and religious fervor runs high. LGBTQ-organization Jerusalem Open House has served the queer community since 1997, birthed Palestinian LGBTQ+ organization Al-Qaws, and has run Jerusalem Pride since 2002. The Pride march starts at Liberty Bell Park, with ultra-Orthodox and far-right extremist protestors and police bolstering the highly charged event, revealing the complexity of queerness here.

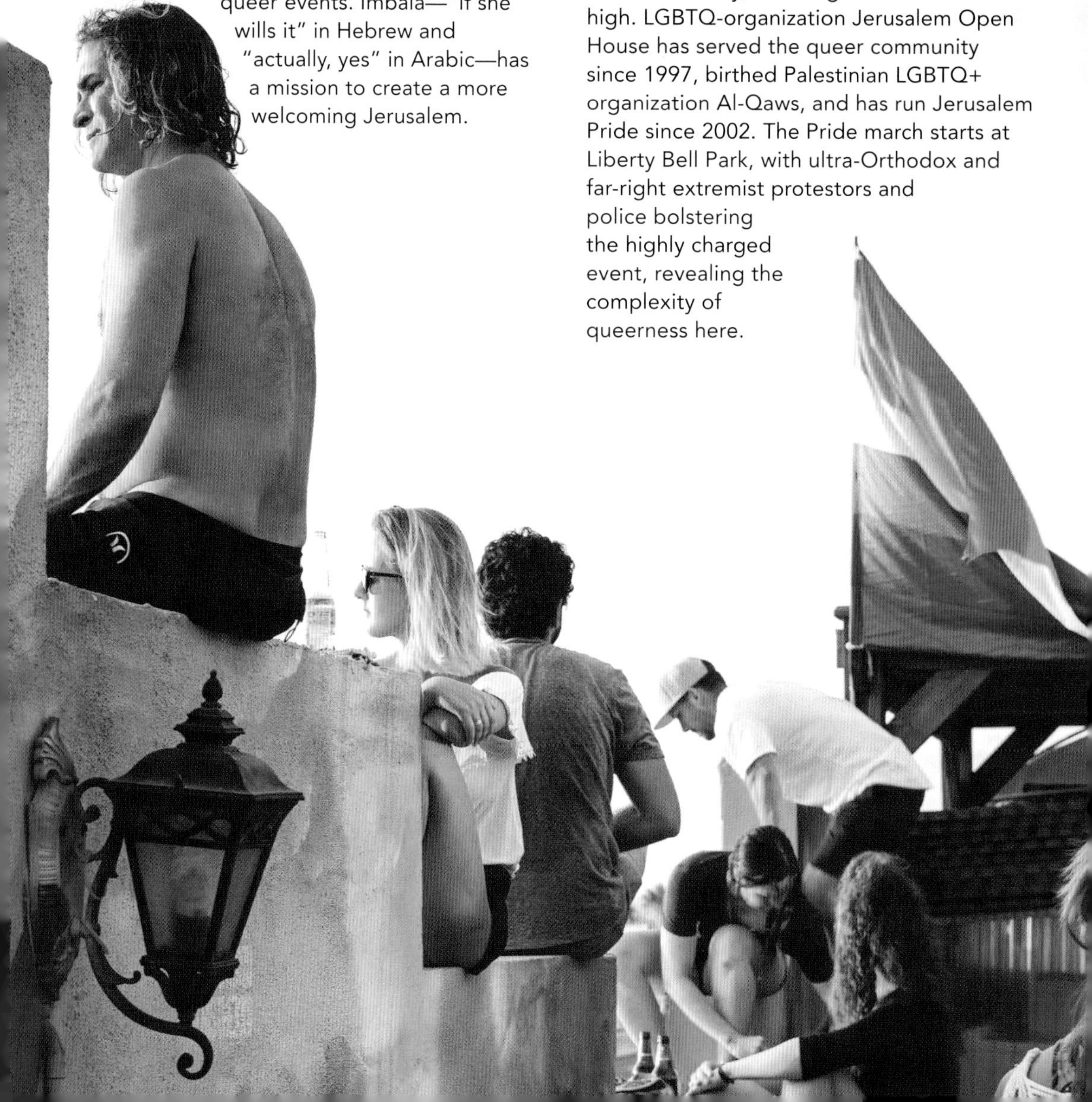

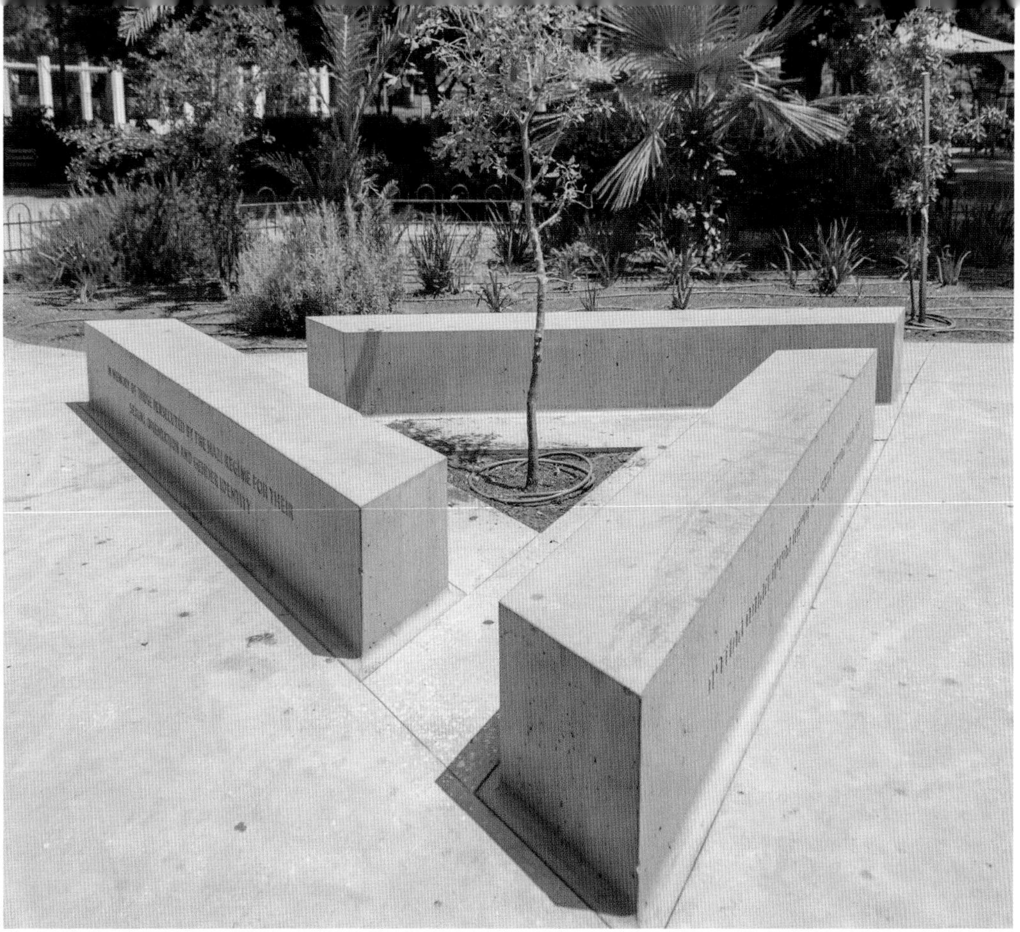

384 Take a moment to reflect

▲ The Memorial for LGBT Victims of the Nazi Persecution, Tel Aviv, Israel

When to go: All year
Best for: Remembrance

Besides the LGBT Center, a calming pond, and an adorable dog park, green oasis Meir Park is home to an important pink, iron triangular memorial. Inspired by Amsterdam's Homomonument, it honors the Jewish and non-Jewish gay victims of the Holocaust, holding special significance in the Jewish State of Israel.

385 Come on in, the café's lovely

LGBT Center, Tel Aviv, Israel

When to go: All year
Best for: All things queer

Tel Aviv's lush Meir Park is where you find the bustling heart of the local LGBTQ+ community. At its southern end, a large rainbow flag flies from the LGBT Center, a big, inviting building which has been welcoming queer folk since 2008, with a casual café and terrace, cultural activities, workshops, and support groups and services.

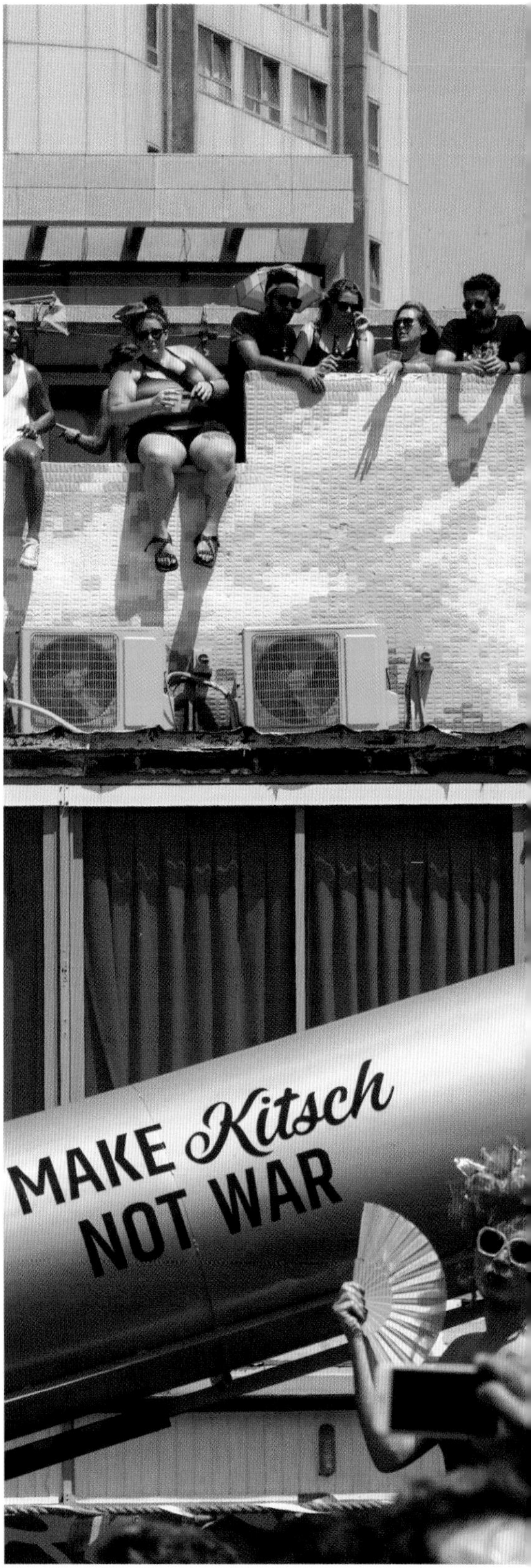

386 Are we there yet?

Tel Aviv Pride, Israel

When to go: June
Best for: Celebrating conflicting progress

Well known for its municipal and governmental support, Tel Aviv is loudly out and proud, often oversimplified as a gay paradise. About 25 percent of the city's population identifies as gay, the city hosts Asia's largest Pride, and gay rights are the most advanced in the region. On the other side, Israel has been criticized for boasting of its gay image while lacking intersectionality, including support for trans people, and Arab and Palestinian LGBTQ+ people. Where Jerusalem Pride is a fight for what hasn't yet been achieved, Tel Aviv Pride celebrates what has. The big parade kicks off near Meir Park and hundreds of thousands of people—including young families and older people—make their way to the beachfront. The parade's scenic route along the seafront culminates in a big party in Charles Clore Park.

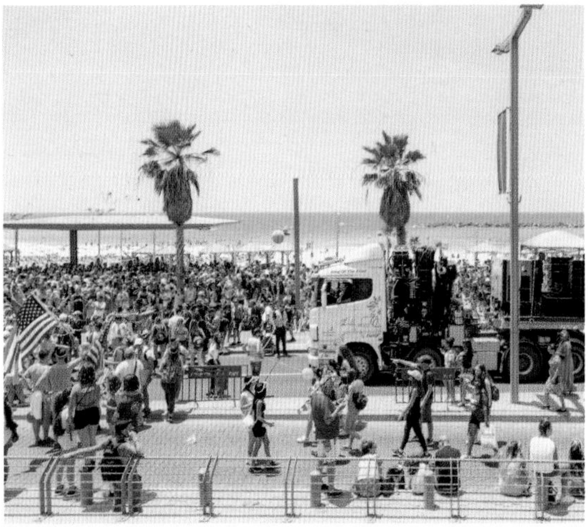

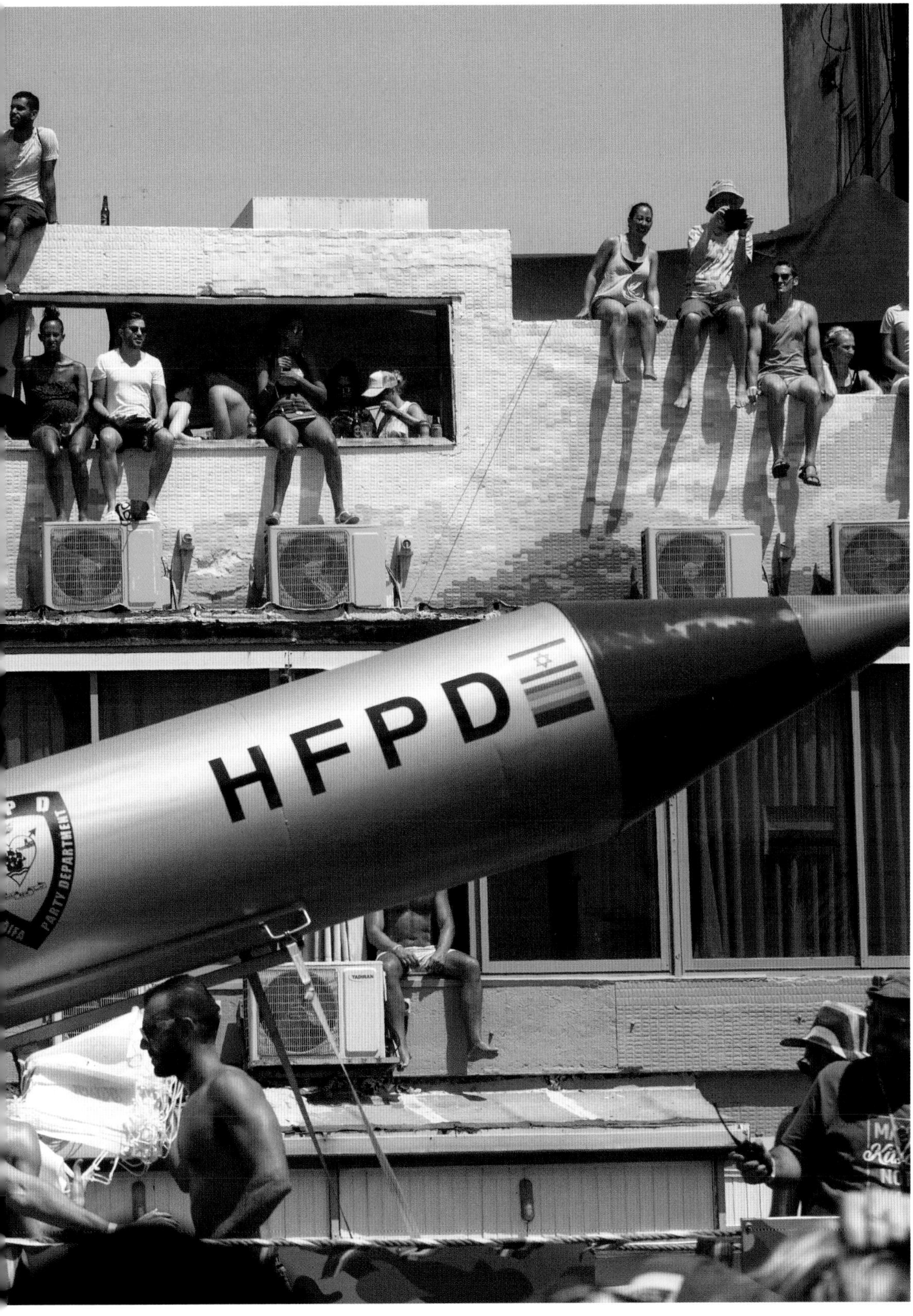
HFPD
PARTY DEPARTMENT
TADIRAN

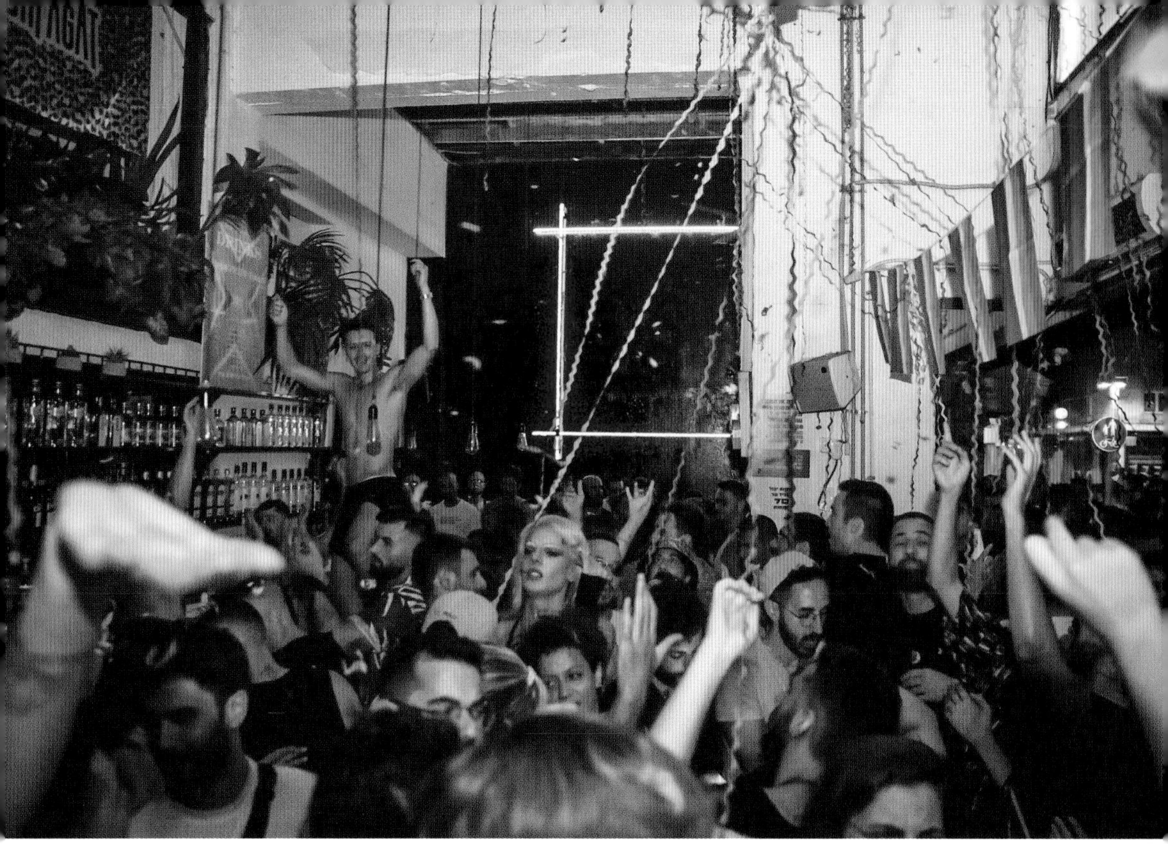

387 Do the splits

▲ ▶ Shpagat, Tel Aviv, Israel

When to go: All year
Best for: Shpa days and nights

The trendy and artsy Nachalat Binyamin Street—a cultural hot spot in Tel Aviv's city center—will keep you entertained with its colorful architecture, regular craft markets, and abundance of shops. It's also home to the heart of Tel Aviv's queer nightlife: Shpagat (Hebrew for "splits"). Over a decade old, Shpagat is a casual café and terrace by day that turns into a lively LGBTQ+ dance floor at night. It's famous for delicious cocktails, tasty food, occasional art exhibits, vibrant DJ nights, and events that cater specifically to LGBTQ+ women—like Shpagirls.

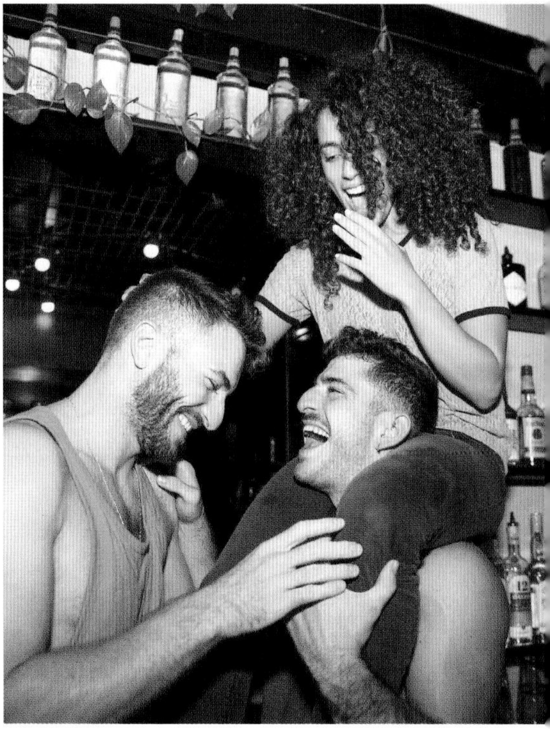

388 Ready, set, take action

TLVFest and Queer Cinema for Palestine, Israel

When to go: October and November
Best for: Queer Israeli and Palestinian cinema

The ten-day TLVFest, the first LGBTQ+ film festival in the Middle East, has showcased queer cinema in Tel Aviv since 2006. The coinciding global Queer Cinema for Palestine (QCP) was born in 2021, following a boycott by LGBTQ+ filmmakers of the Israeli-government-sponsored TLVFest, to show solidarity with the Palestinian queer community. QCP is a platform for Palestinian filmmakers.

389 Burgers with extras

▼ Beefcakes, various towns, South Africa

When to go: All year
Best for: Feasting with your eyes and your stomach

This popular LGBTQ+ establishment in South Africa has venues in Cape Town, Johannesburg and Pretoria. Promoting itself as "drag dining at its finest," each night plays host to a wide variety of drag acts while serving staff, chosen for their sex appeal, dish up your burgers, beers, and cocktails all night. There's an ever-changing list of events, from bingo, quiz nights, and set-menu dinners.

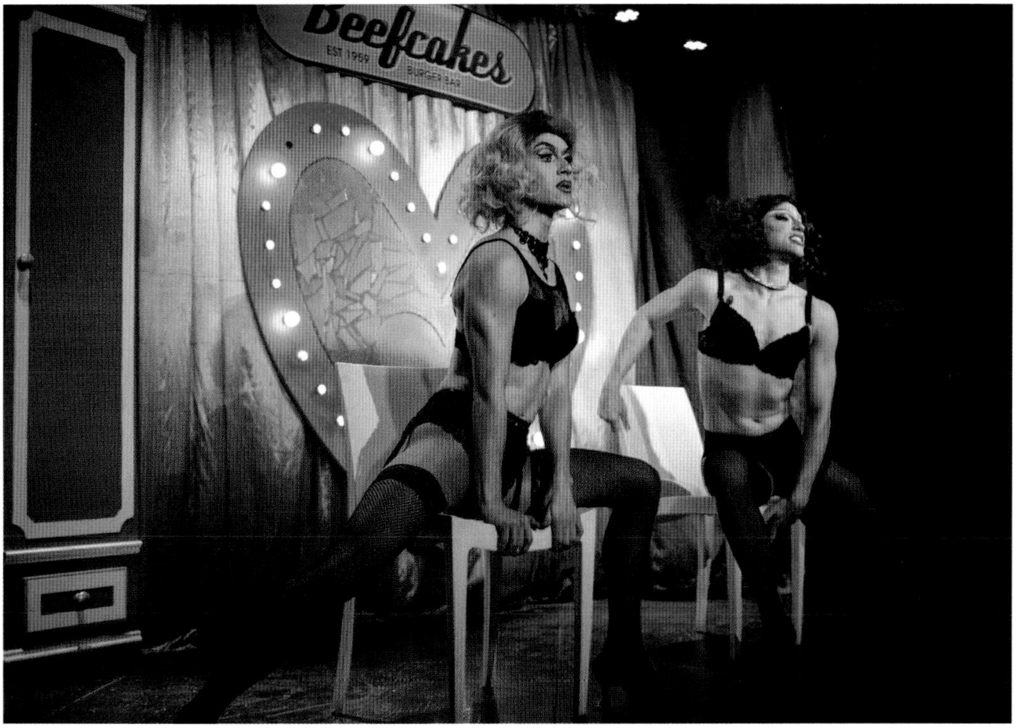

390 Somewhere over the rain-Bo-Kaap

Bo-Kaap, Cape Town, South Africa

When to go: All year
Best for: Learning colorful history

Wandering the hilly, cobblestone streets of Bo-Kaap—"above the Cape" in Afrikaans—you'll pass the most brightly colored homes. Nestled on the slopes of Signal Hill, bordering the city center to the south and LGBTQ+ neighborhood Waterkant to the north, it's Cape Town's oldest-surviving neighborhood, and the Iziko Bo-Kaap Museum (IBKM) here is one of the oldest surviving homes, built in the 1760s. Originally, the Dutch and Georgian-style lease-houses were painted white. During apartheid, Bo-Kaap was a neighborhood for "Cape Muslims only." The residents allegedly painted the houses rainbow colors in the 1990s, expressing freedom and individualism in the post-apartheid Rainbow Nation.

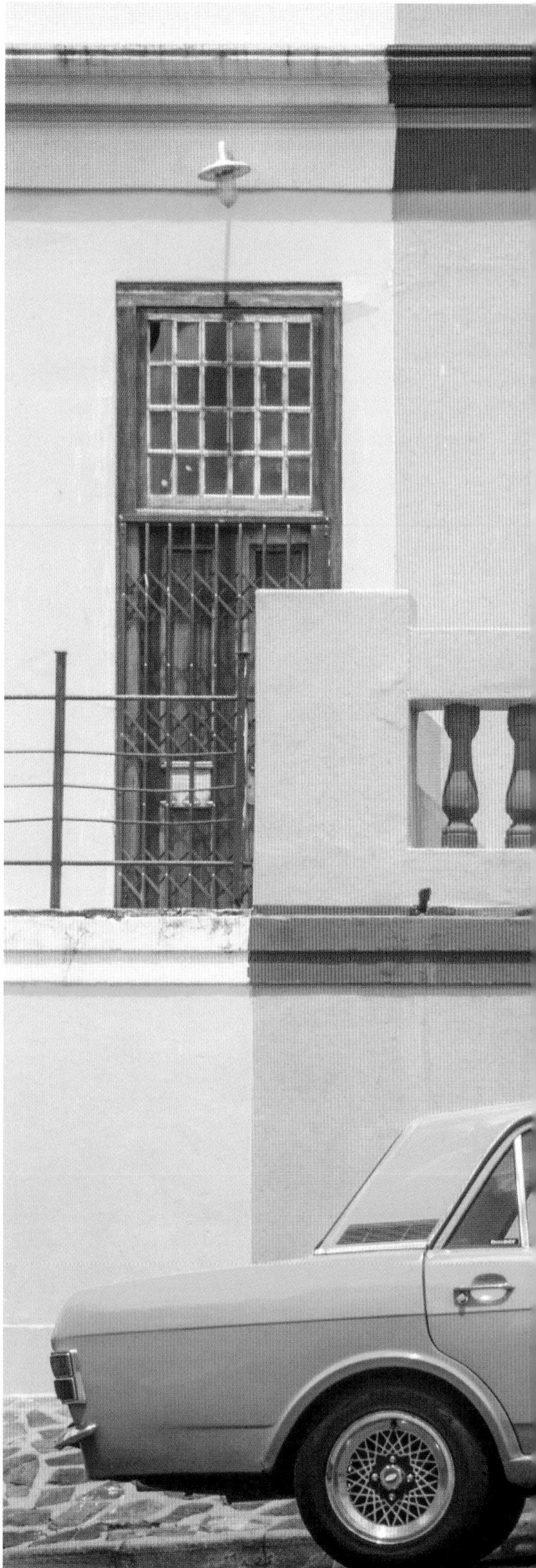

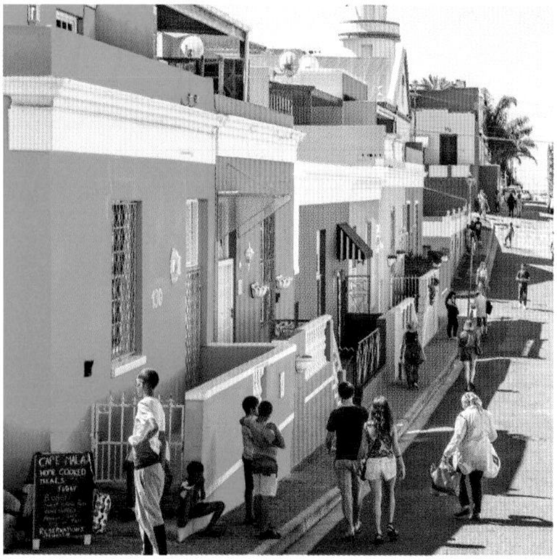

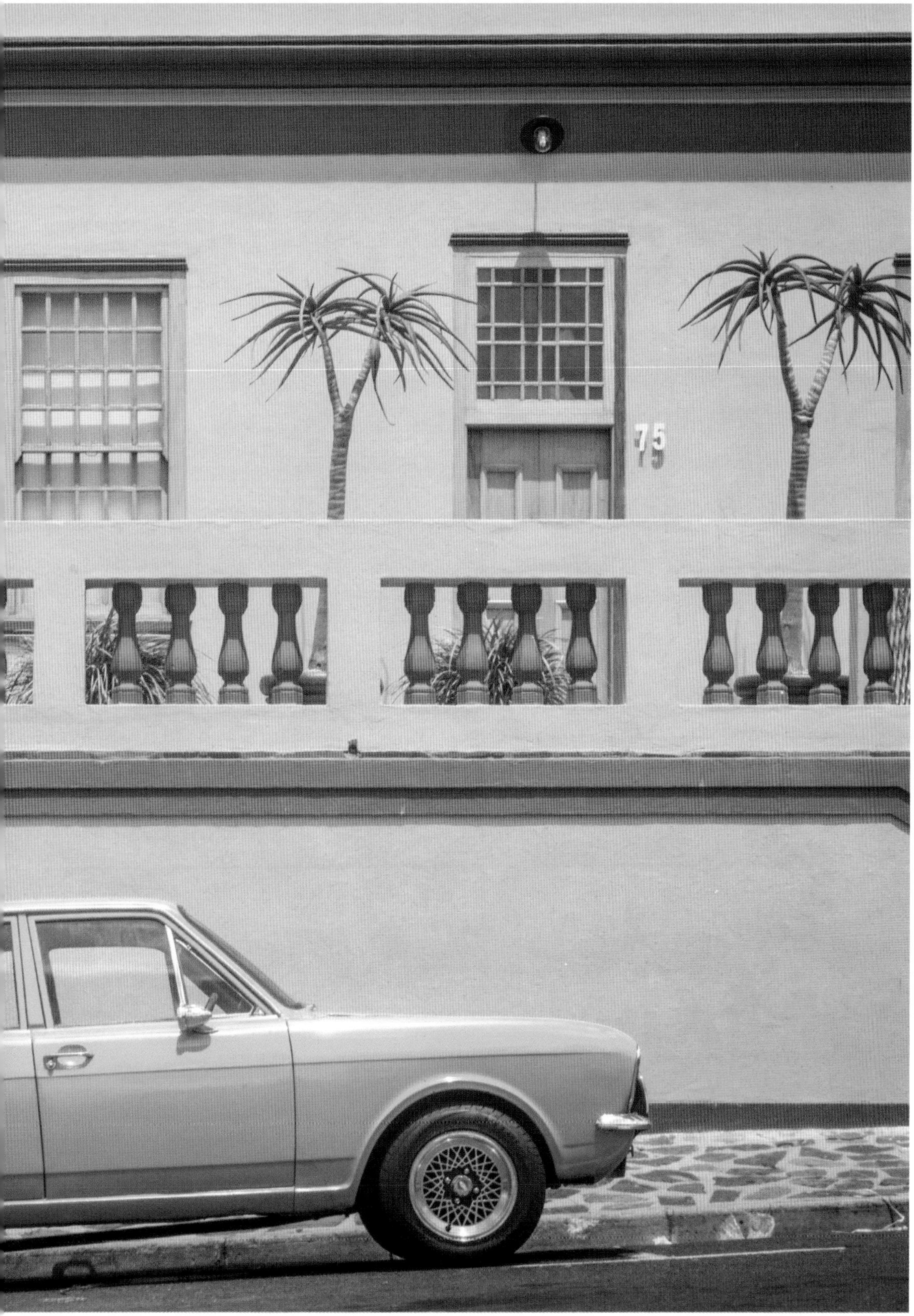
75

391 Escape to the city

De Waterkant, Cape Town, South Africa

When to go: All year
Best for: City break

The beating heart of LGBTQ-beacon Cape Town is the chic, trendy neighborhood of Waterkant, north of colorful Bo-Kaap. It's popular with LGBTQ+ travelers and home to many welcoming bars, hotels, restaurants, and shops. Somerset Road—The Strip—has a lot of LGBTQ+ venues, including iconic burger-bar Beefcakes. The oldest LGBTQ+ venue is laid-back Café Manhattan, and the best clubbing happens at Pink Candy. The lesbian-popular The 2 Eves and mixed-culture Zer021 Social are also worth a detour.

392 Put on your cape and celebrate

▶ Cape Town Pride, South Africa

When to go: February and March
Best for: Celebrating gay the South African way

In the dry and bright days of late summer, the queer community from Cape Town and beyond come together for a glittery, unifying Cape Town Pride, a more-than-a-week-long celebration of cultural heritage and LGBTQ+ rights. In 1996, South Africa was the world's first country to outlaw discrimination based on gender and sexual orientation, and the world's fifth—Africa's first—to extend marriage to LGBTQ+ couples. Iconic Pride events include hikes, the crowning of Pride royalty, and the costume-rich parade.

393 Educate yourself

Durban Gay and Lesbian Film Festival, South Africa

When to go: Late September to early October
Best for: Cutting-edge East African culture

Durban is South Africa's third-largest city and besides being a haven for surfers, has a thriving LGBTQ+ scene centered around the Morningside neighborhood. One of its queer calendar highlights is the Durban Gay and Lesbian Film Festival (DGLFF). Established in 2011, it's now the longest-running queer film festival on the continent. In addition to dozens of screenings, there are also workshops, Q&A events, and debates, with a particular emphasis on Durban and KwaZulu-Natal filmmakers.

394 Strip off and jump in

Sandy Bay Beach, Cape Town, South Africa

When to go: December to February
Best for: Nude sunbathing

Sandy Bay Beach, on the coast between Cape Town and Cape Point, is not officially a nudist spot. However, because it's a 20-minute walk from the nearest parking lot, across the Hout Bay dunes, it takes quite an effort to visit and has largely been taken over by naturists and LGBTQ+ sun-worshippers. Enjoy tranquil sunbathing against the stunning, mountainous backdrop, or skinny-dip in the beautifully clear waters.

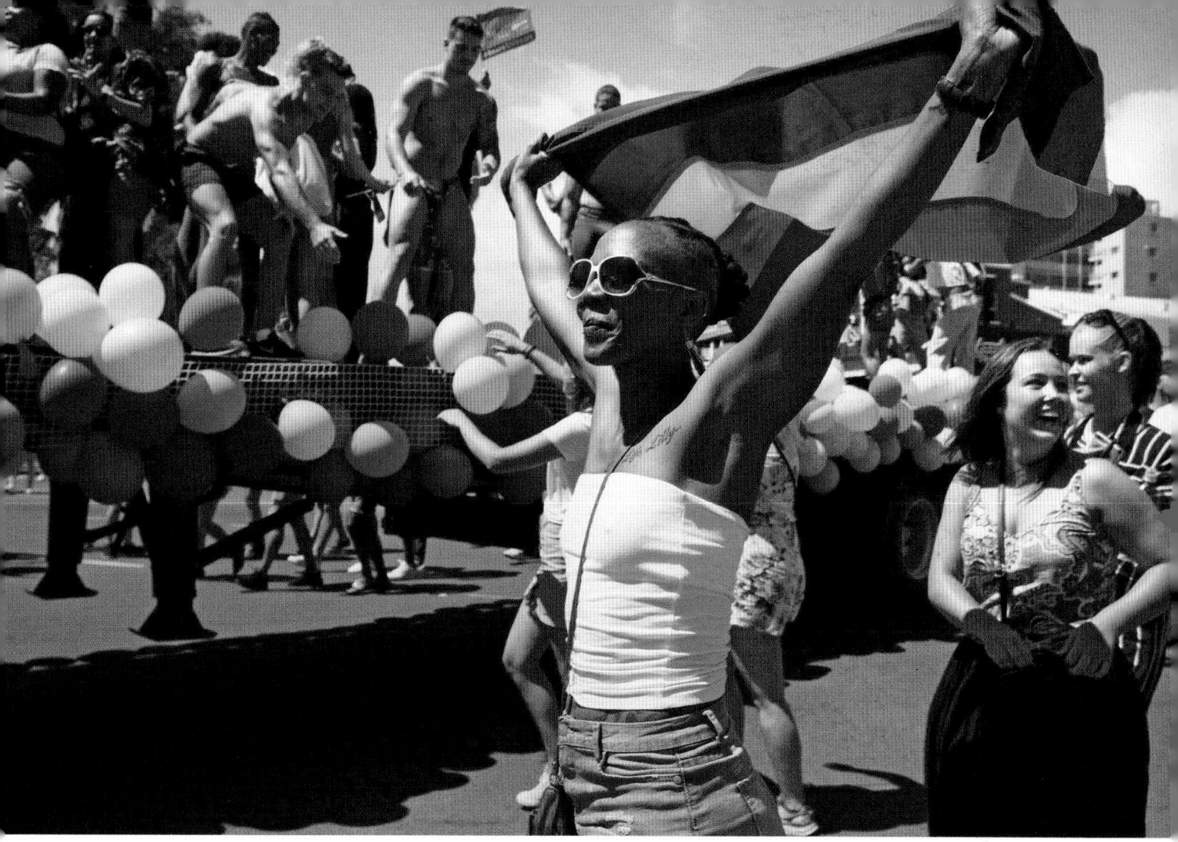

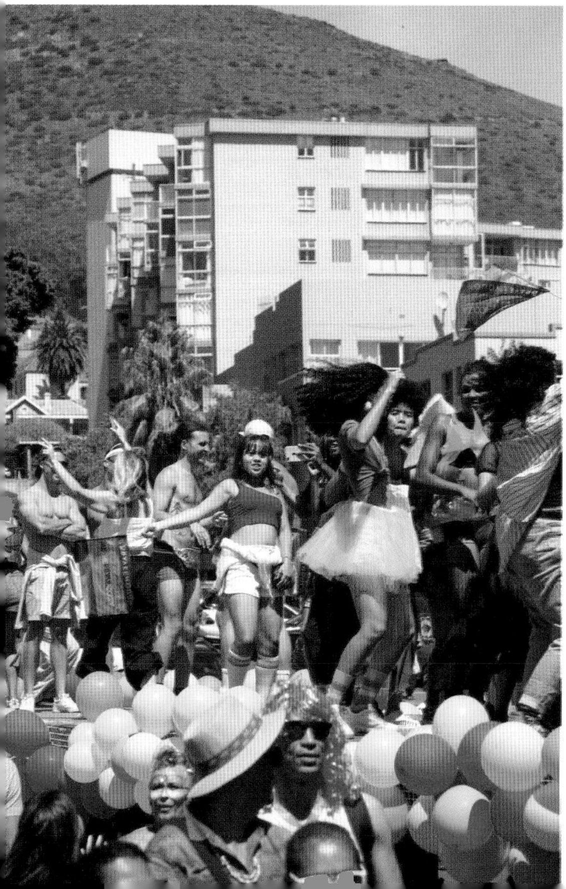

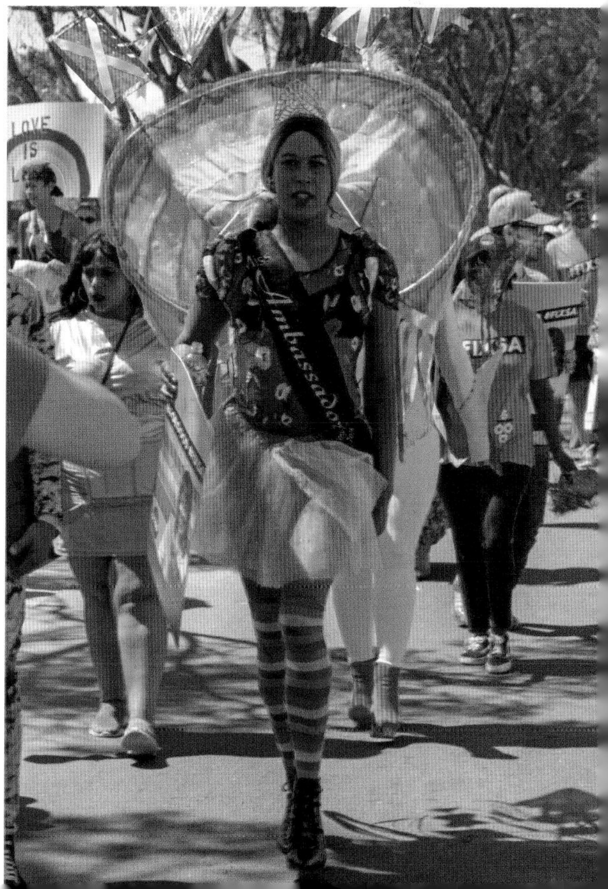
LOVE
IS

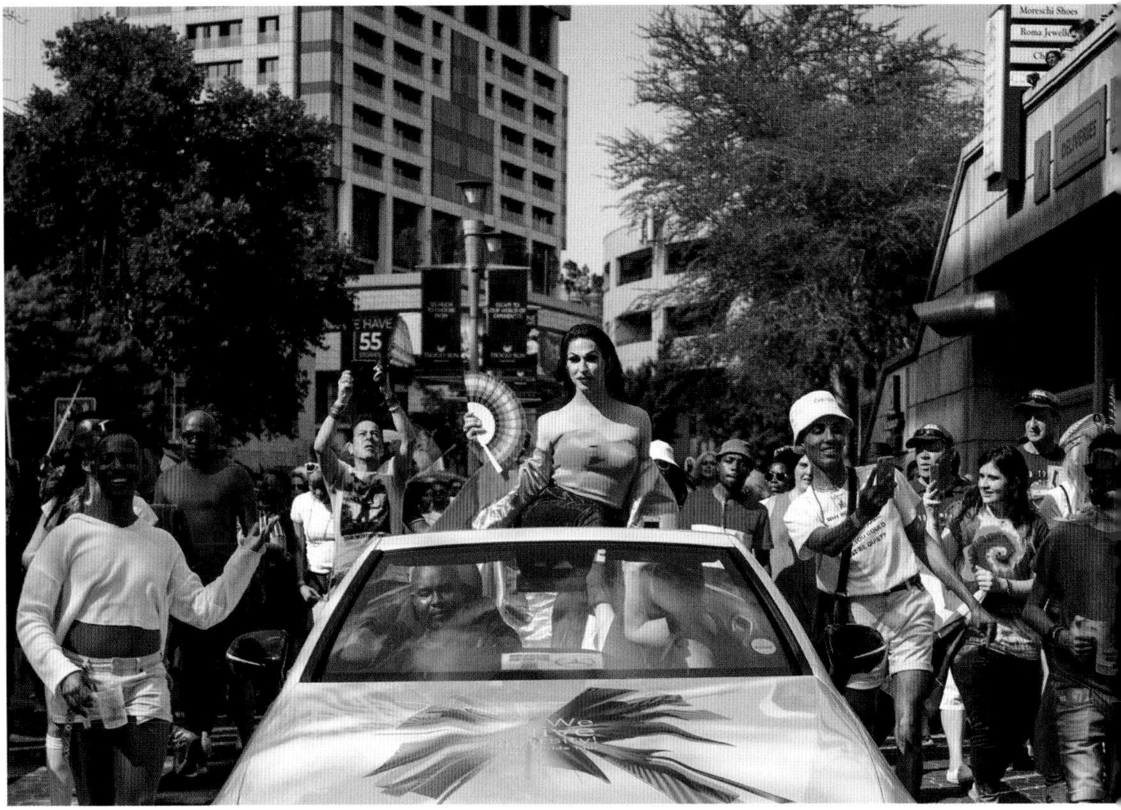

395 Along for the Pride

▲ Johannesburg Pride/Pride of Africa, South Africa

When to go: October
Best for: Diverse, progressive, African queerness

Johannesburg is known for its decolonizing-activism and optimism. It is where South Africa first made LGBTQ-rights history in 1996, accelerated by the Gay and Lesbian Organization of Witwaterstrand (GLOW). Six years prior, during the apartheid, GLOW—led by Simon Nkoli—organized Africa's first Pride. Nkoli's words, "I am Black, and I am gay. I cannot separate the two parts of me into primary or secondary struggles," mark the intersectionality that characterizes inclusive Johannesburg Pride, Pride of Africa.

396 Spread your wings

Pink Loerie Mardi Gras and Arts Festival, Knysna, South Africa

When to go: April and May
Best for: Feeling free

This culturally aware and uniquely South African carnival isn't just festive—it's a rejection of the oppression brought to Africa by colonizers, including anti-LGBTQ+ laws and stigmas. Named after the African green turaco bird—*knysna loerie* in Afrikaans—the Pink Loerie Mardi Gras & Arts Festival flies away from traditional, Western Pride. Coastal township Knysna is the perfect location for this flight to freedom, on the "Garden Route," surrounded by lush rainforest.

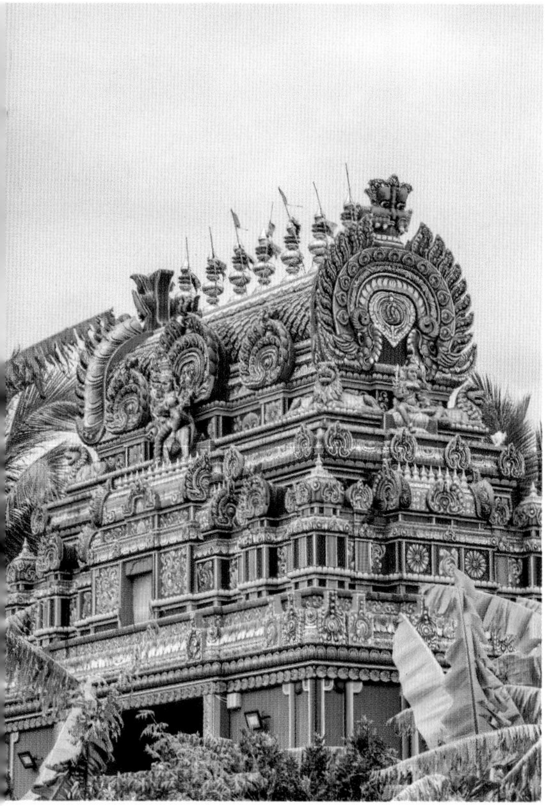

397 Lava's all you need

◀ ▼ Réunion Island

When to go: April to November
Best for: Island life

The three-million-year-old volcanic island Réunion is famous for its rugged landscape, tropical rainforest, scenic beaches, and active volcano Piton de la Fournaise. It's one of the more welcoming islands in the Indian Ocean because of its French legislation. Indulge yourself in Creole culture and cuisine, soak up the sun in the lagoon, get active in the great outdoors, visit gay nudist beaches, dance at Le Loft and Zanzibar Café, and connect with locals at events by Requeer.

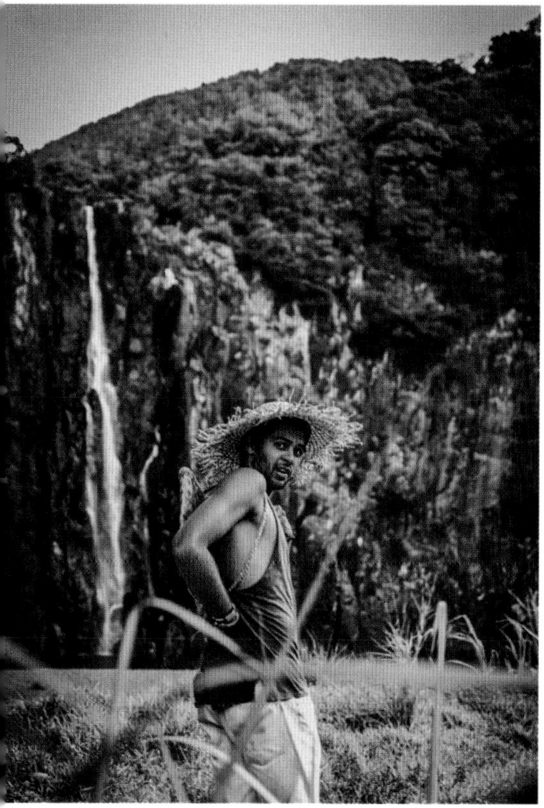

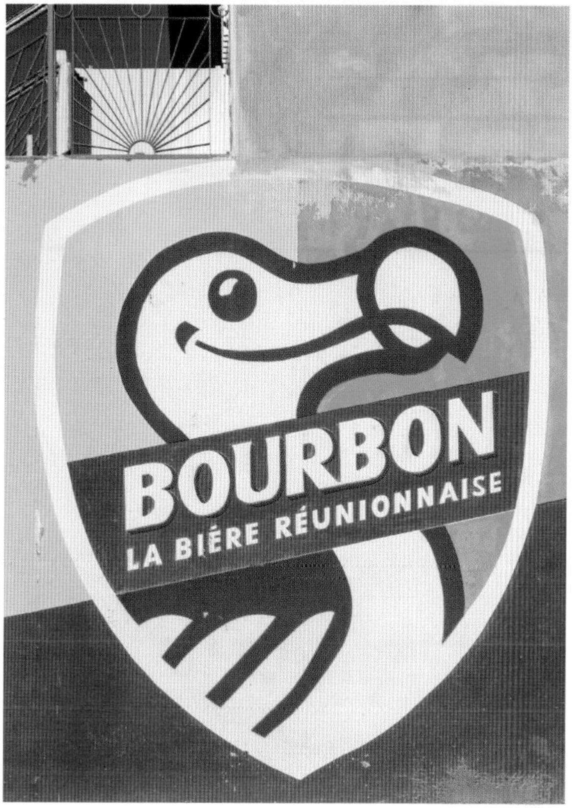

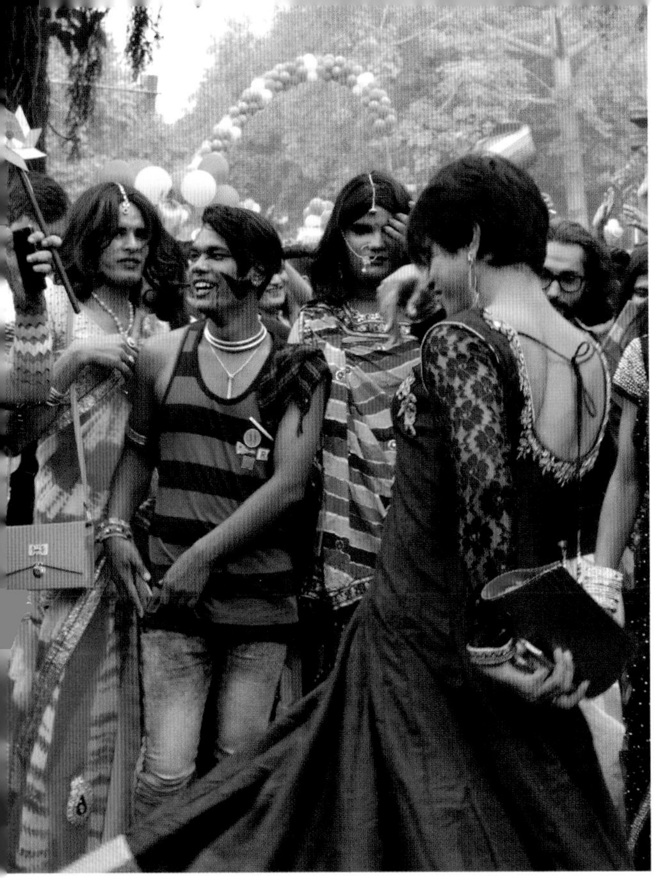
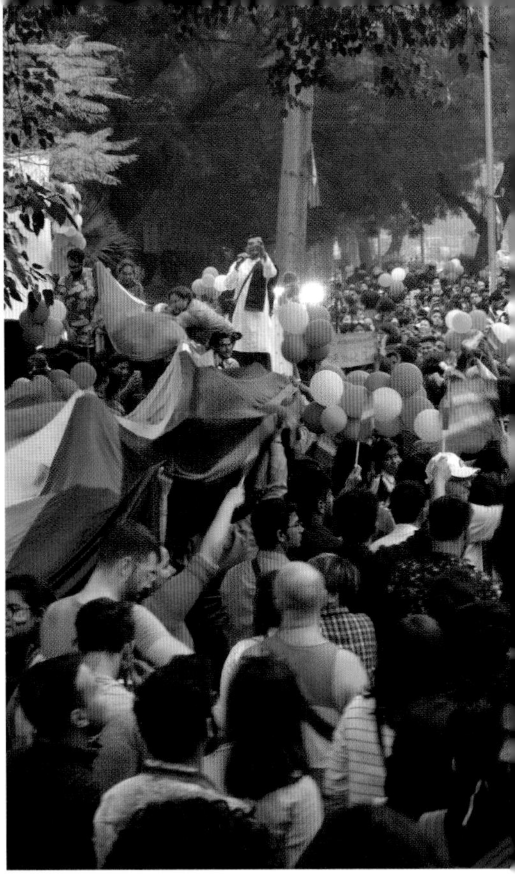
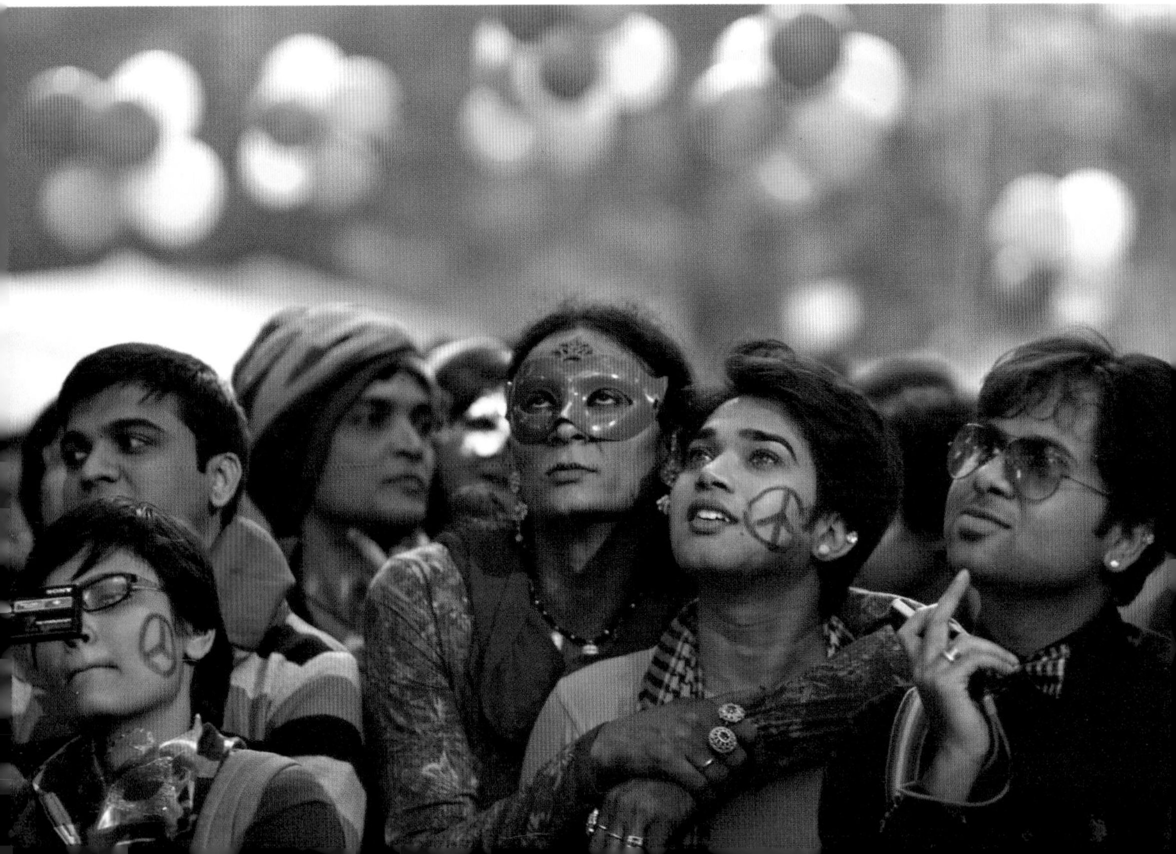

398 Bask in queer love in Delhi

◀ Delhi Queer Pride Parade, India

When to go: Fourth Sunday of November
Best for: Grassroots activism

Started in 2008, Delhi's Queer Pride Parade is one of India's biggest queer events. Held on the fourth Sunday of November each year, the parade honors and celebrates the diverse queer communities and their allies in India. A grassroots community event organized by local queer groups, Delhi's annual Pride parade is a great atmosphere to bask in queer love and joy.

399 Love after death

Jamali Kamali Mosque and Tomb, Mehrauli, Delhi, India

When to go: All year
Best for: Indian LGBTQ+ history

Before colonization, the Indian subcontinent was very queer: its religious scripts and history are full of LGBTQ+ representation. Known as "the gay Taj Mahal," the sixteenth-century Jamali Kamali *dargah* (a tomb for Sufi saints) is a shrine where Sufi poet Jamali was buried with his male lover Kamali, in the manner of married couples at the time. Not far away, Hijron ka Khanqah, another 500-year-old dargah, honors about 50 *hijron* (Indian subcontinent's third gender) who were believed to have special powers and were held in high regard.

400 E-quality dining

Covai/Madurai Trans Kitchen, Pollachi and Madurai, India

When to go: All year
Best for: Delicious supportive food

Get a taste of local Indian food while also supporting the trans community. The two kitchens are managed entirely by local trans people, who are trained and supported by charity organization Swasti, which works to address health inequality in vulnerable communities.

401 Feed your mind

Amra Obdhuth, Kolkata, India

When to go: All year
Best for: Community workshops

Amra Obdhuth is a queer space with a drop-in library that hosts community events, zine-making, body-mapping workshops, film screenings, and live performances. A venue for local and international artists—poet and public speaker ALOK has performed here—it is an enriching space to feed your mind.

402 Wake me up before you Goa-Goa

Goa, India

When to go: November to April
Best for: Beach parties

The beach and party capital of India, Goa, has a long and diverse known-history dating back to the third century BC. After 450 years of Portuguese colonization, there followed a bohemian influx as hippies gathered along the welcoming coast of northern Goa. The result is the laid-back lifestyle, welcoming attitude, and wild parties that characterize modern-day Goa. With 78 mi/135 km of beaches, yoga retreats, hippie markets, and lush countryside, Goa offers something for everyone. The LGBTQ-friendly Bardez area is home to the queer-allied restaurant and bar Flying Dolphin. Get into queer arts, permaculture, and healing at SanQtuary Goa, and keep an eye out for Bollywood-centric parties by Queer Kinara and Pink Pill events. At some, you'll be served a drink by transgender barman Fay Barretto, who trains women and LGBTQ+ bartenders with Mr. Bartender & Crew.

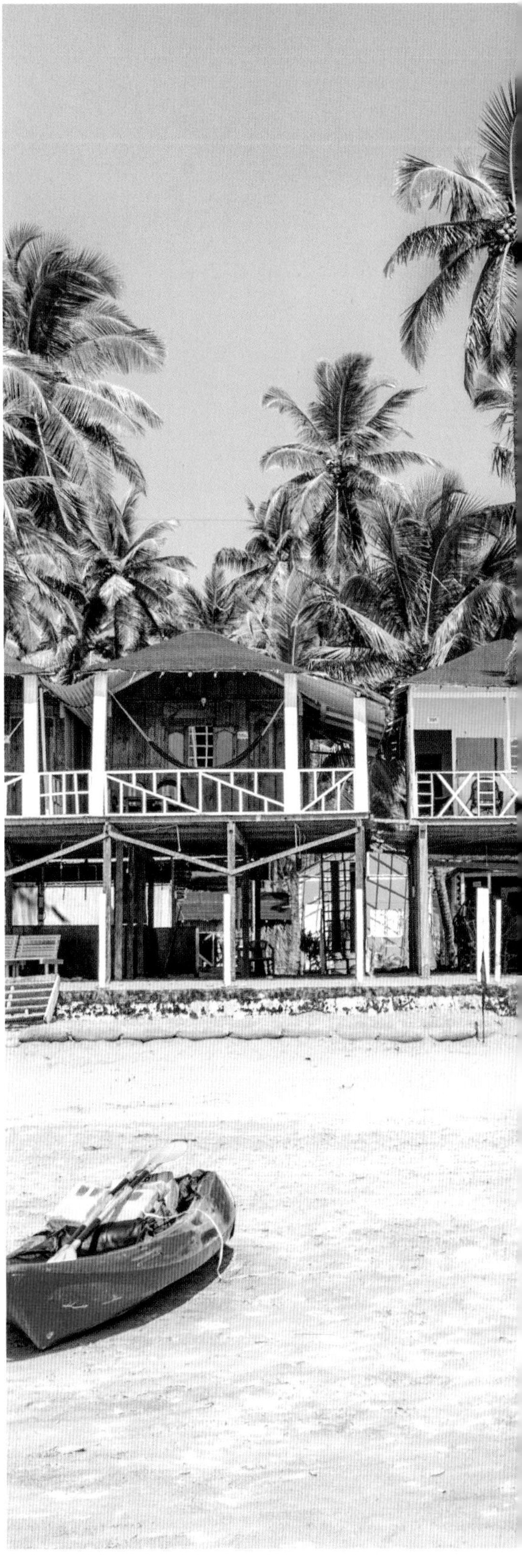

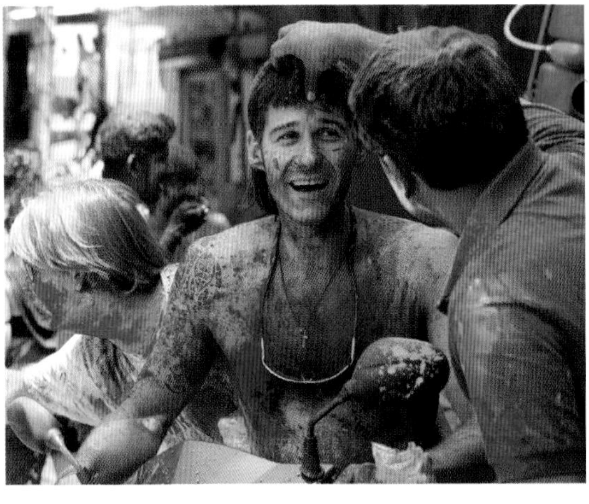

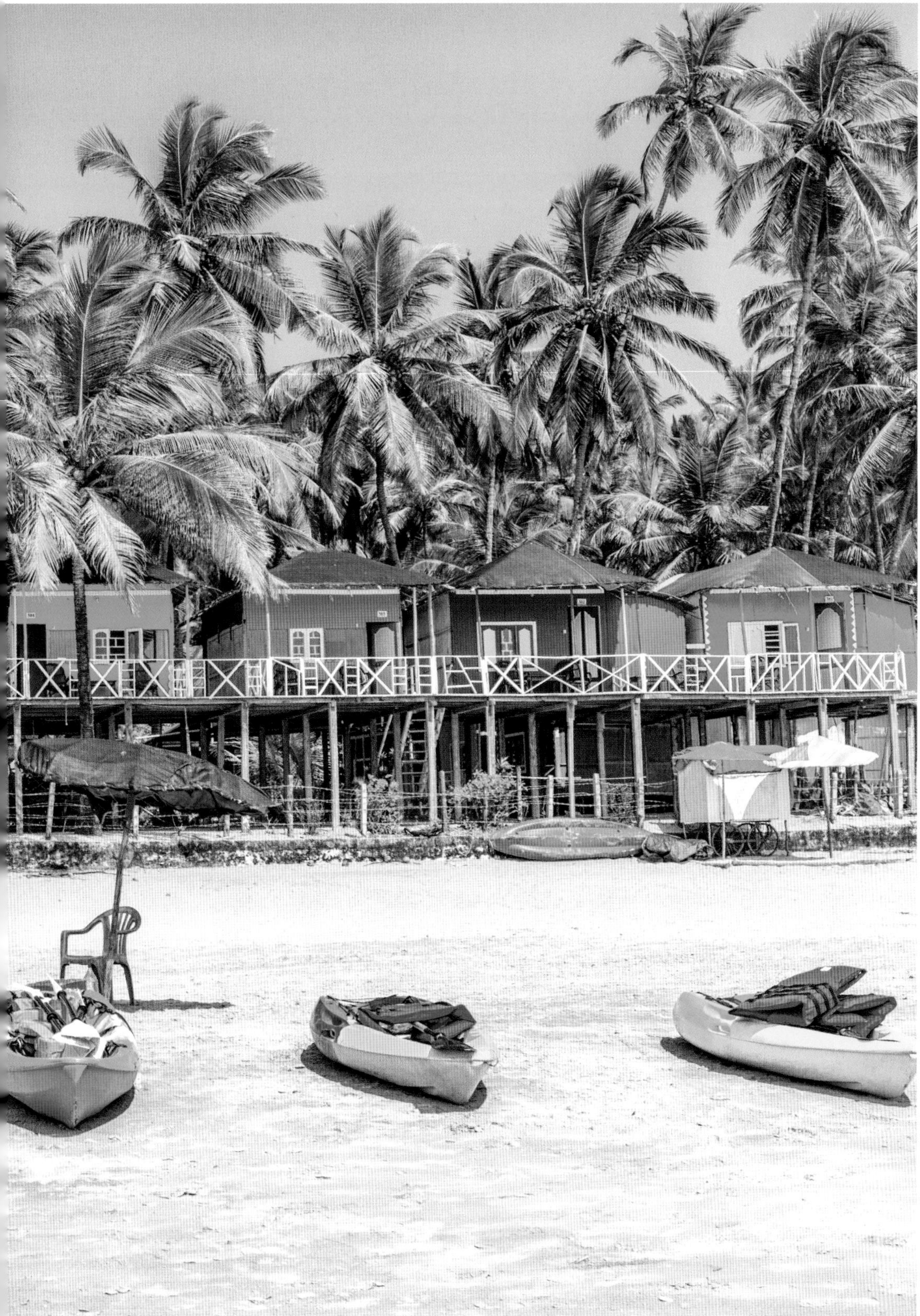

403 You're my salvation

Salvation Star, Mumbai, India

When to go: All year
Best for: Partying in the city of dreams

The Bollywood capital of the world, and the economic capital of India, Mumbai is known for many things, including ancient sites and modern skyscrapers. India's rich history of queerness, condemned in colonial times, is slowly returning to Mumbai one hot, queer soirée at a time. Salvation Star has been the city's foremost queer-event organizer since 2007, hosting significant events for New Year's, Pride, Diwali, and other parties at queer-popular venues such as Kitty Su.

404 A nice cup of tea

Café Guftagu, Mumbai, India

When to go: All year
Best for: Tea

Queer legends Sumit Pawar and Apurva Paithane opened Café Guftagu—meaning "dialogue"—in the suburbs of Mumbai as a place run by and for queer people. Enjoy a cup of chai or coffee and mouthwatering food with a vibe that initiates conversations. It's home to an affirmative rainbow theme, shelves of LGBTQ+ books, board games, discussion events, and open mic nights.

405 Grab your popcorn and take a seat

KASHISH Mumbai International Queer Film Festival, India

When to go: May or June
Best for: The full LGBTQ+ spectrum of life

The KASHISH Mumbai International Queer Film Festival is a five-day celebration of LGBTQ+ movies. KASHISH (which means "attraction or allure" in Urdu) has been running since 2010. Each year, besides screening around 160 different movies, organizers run a poster-design competition, which brings in entries from queer designers throughout Asia and beyond. KASHISH is well-recognized as an empowering hub for Indian queer filmmakers to promote their visions to an international audience.

406 I see you and ICT

▶ Bengaluru Namma Pride March, India

When to go: September
Best for: Tech heads

Running since 2008, the Bangaluru Namma Pride March is a culmination of a month of Pride events, from wild parties to casual games nights and fun runs. The information and communications technology (ICT) industry has drawn a young and progressive crowd to Bengaluru and it is one of India's more LGBTQ-friendly cities. The Pride march draws thousands of participants, and ends with a party and dancing outside the town hall.

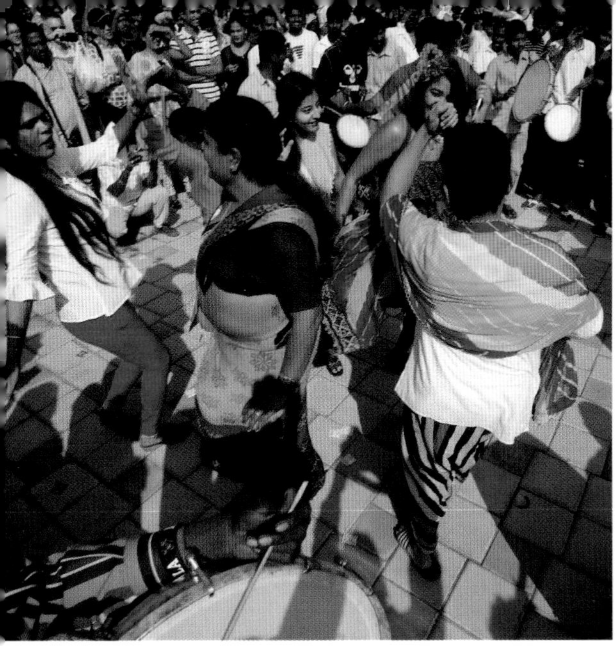
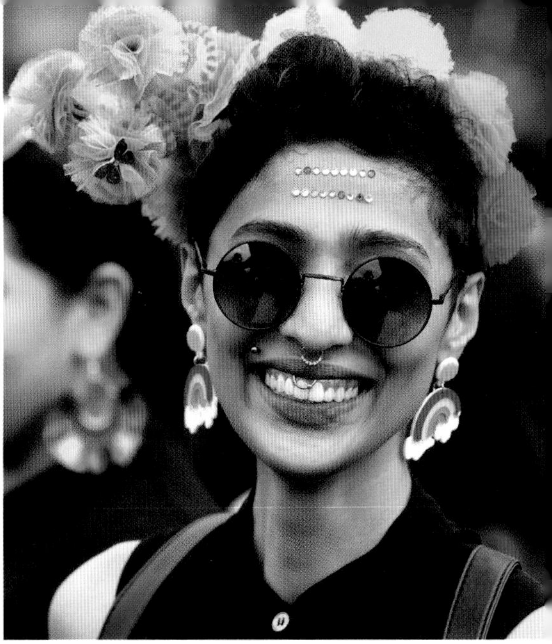
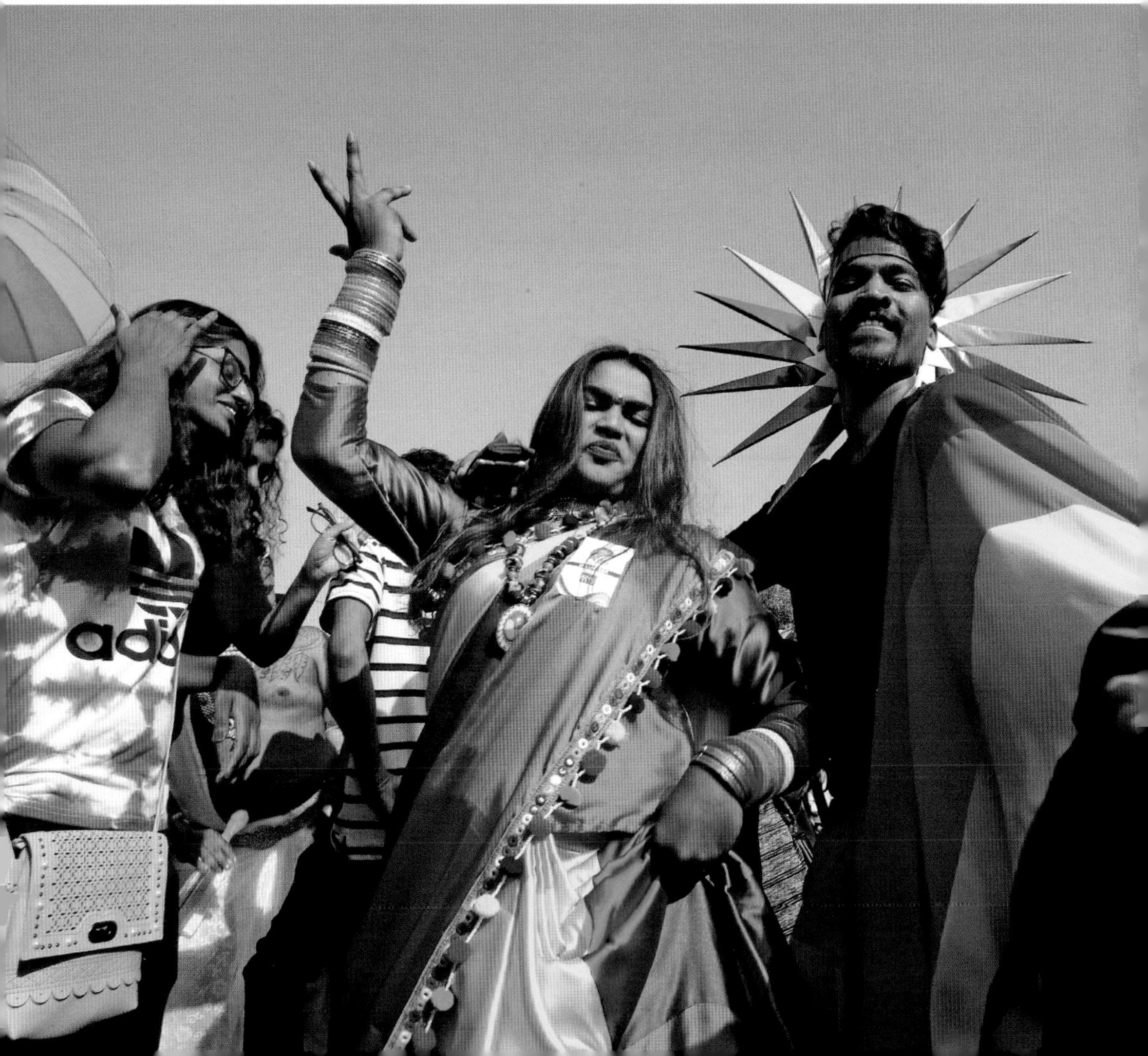

407 Move over Bollywood

Bangalore Queer Film Festival, Bengaluru, India

When to go: February
Best for: Non-Western independent cinema

The Silicon Valley of India, IT-hub Bengaluru, is a welcoming, green city in southern India and has been home to the large Bangalore Queer Film Festival (BQFF) since 2008. BQFF highlights queer, non-Western, south Indian, and independent cinema, and is a hub for queer arts and culture, with exhibitions and performances as well as movies.

408 Putting the G&T in LGBTQ

▼ Pink Tiffany Restaurant & Bar, Kathmandu, Nepal

When to go: All year
Best for: Trans nights out

Surrounded by the Himalayas, Kathmandu—Nepal's capital—is home to an old, maze-like center filled with ancient Newari, Hindu, and Buddhist architecture. In the buzzing nightlife zone of Thamel, you can find a queer gem: Pink Tiffany. Transgender model and activist Meghna Lama opened Nepal's first LGBTQ+ bar and restaurant in 2015 because she had difficulties finding welcoming spaces. Pink Tiffany has since become a cozy, colorful beacon for queer folk.

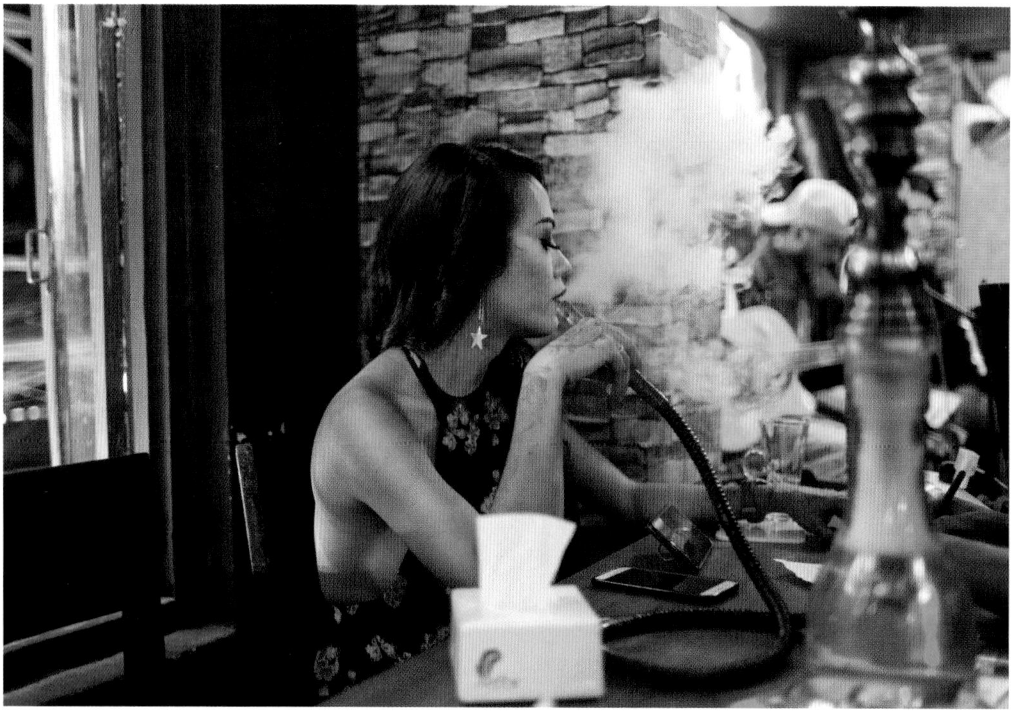

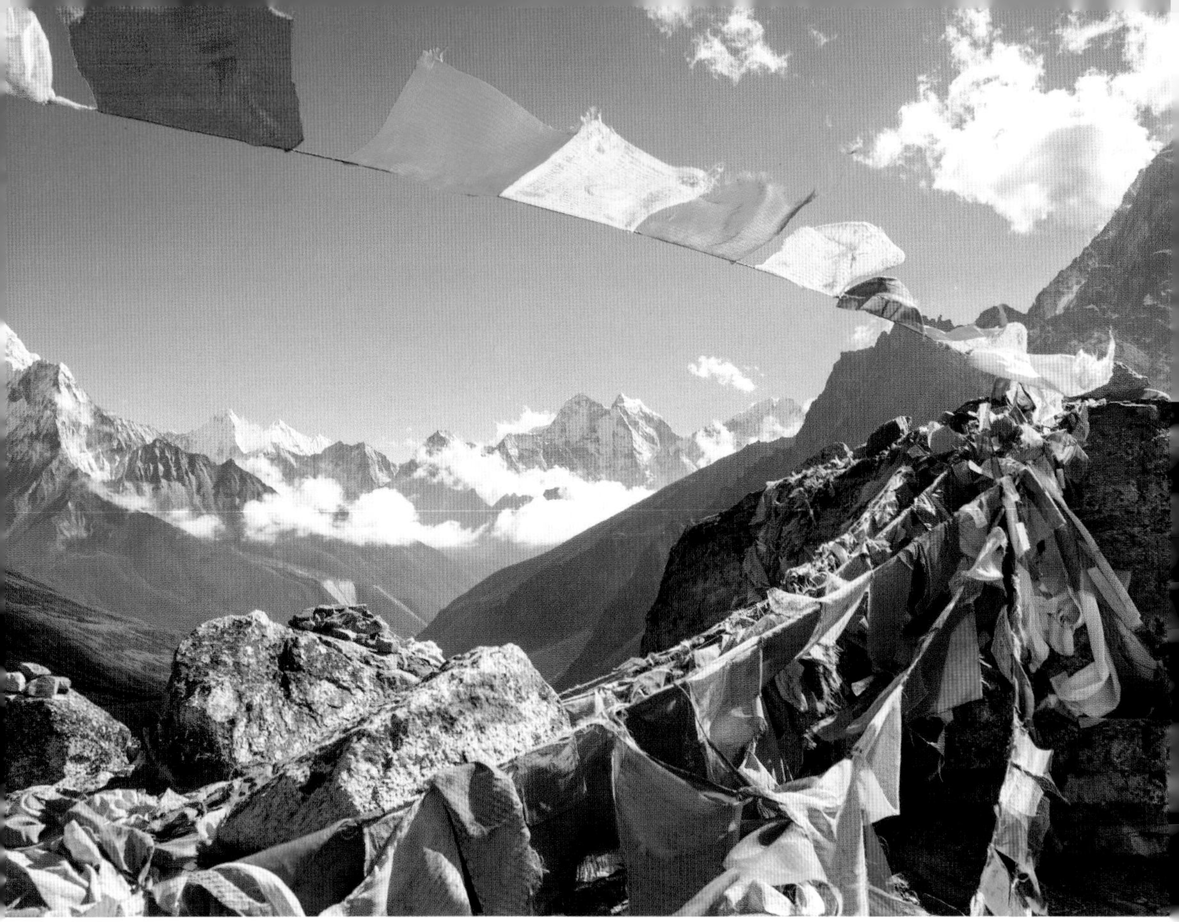

409 Head for the hills

▲ Pink Mountain Treks, Nepal

When to go: March to June or September to December
Best for: Himalayan trekking and historical tours

Operating across Nepal, Bhutan, India, Myanmar, and Tibet, Pink Mountain Treks offers tours for LGBTQ+ travelers seeking adventure, culture, and community. From one-day excursions such as rafting, to three-week cultural cross-country tours, or two-month-long Everest treks, Pink Mountain Treks serves the needs of sightseers and nature-lovers with an outdoorsy spirit.

410 Movie magic

Abhimani Queer Film Festival, Sri Lanka

When to go: Dates change each year
Best for: South-Asian queer films

Established in 2006 and originally affiliated with Colombo Pride, the Abhimani Queer Film Festival is the oldest queer film festival in South Asia. Dedicated to increasing the visibility of queer people in Sri Lanka, the Abhimani Queer Film Festival showcases both local and international short and feature films.

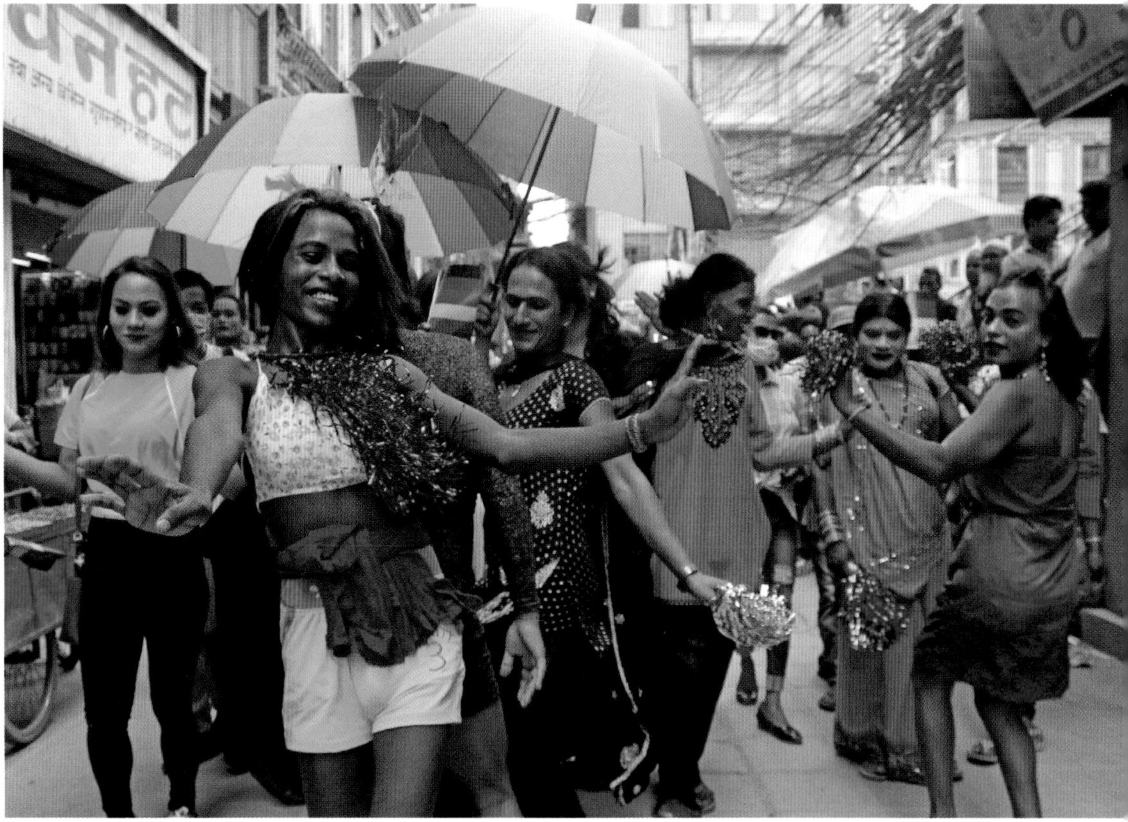

411 Everyone out

▲ ▶ Nepal Pride Parade, Kathmandu, Nepal

When to go: Second Saturday of June
Best for: Pride Parade

Started in 2019, Nepal's Pride Parade kicks off Pride season in the country. Although Nepal decriminalised homosexuality in 2007, this parade is about recognizing and celebrating people of marginalized sexual orientation, gender identity, and sex characteristics. Nepal Pride Parade sees a diverse group of people and identities coming together.

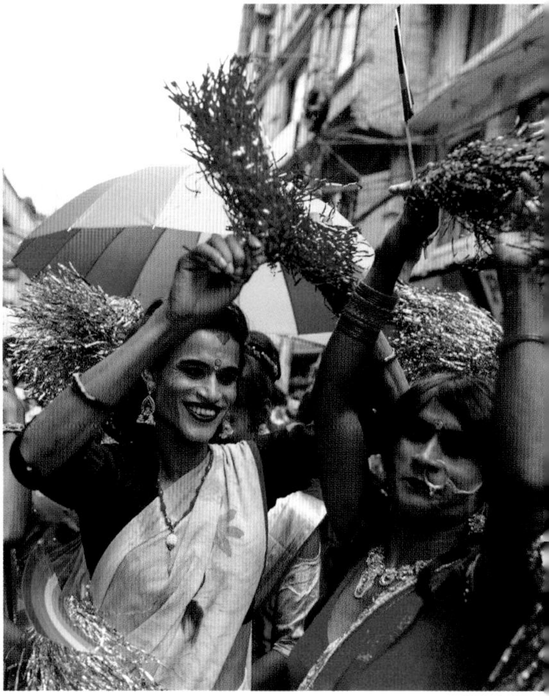

412 Out among the skyscrapers

▼ Central District, Hong Kong

When to go: All year
Best for: Partying

The gay scene in Hong Kong is mostly focused around the Central District, also known as SoHo (South of Hollywood Road). Central is home to the famed Lan Kwai Fong entertainment district, one of the city's most popular nightlife and expat hot spots. This is where you'll find some of the city's most inclusive gay and non-gay bars. Drop by Petticoat Lane for the city's best drag shows.

413 Animal attraction

Zoo Bar, Hong Kong

When to go: October to December
Best for: Meeting LGBTQ+ locals and visitors

Zoo Bar is one of Hong Kong's most popular gay bars, located on Jervois Street, right across the road from FLM, another well-loved gay hangout. Zoo Bar is very much the place to be seen, especially on Friday and Saturday nights, when it is usually so busy the crowd spills out into the street.

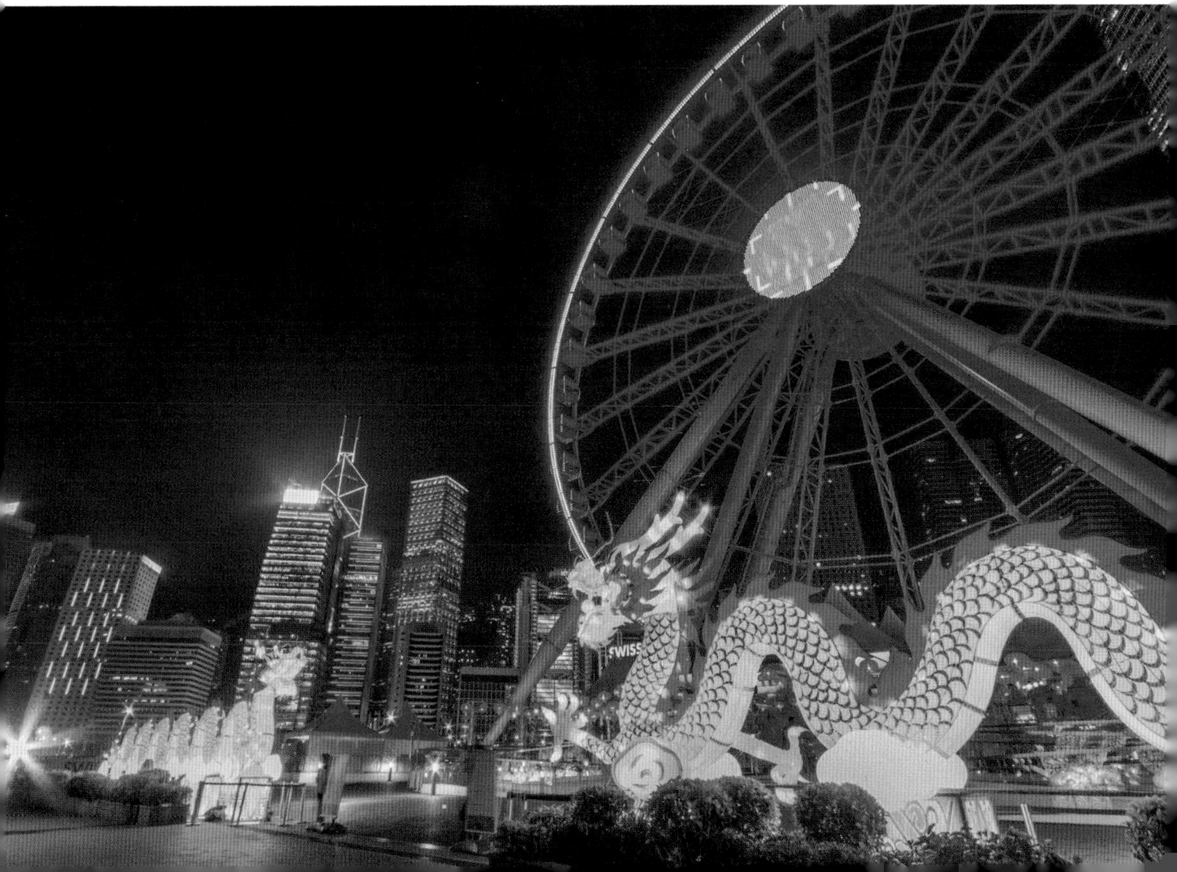

414 Parade with a theme

▼ Hong Kong Pride Parade, Hong Kong

When to go: November
Best for: Themed costumes

Started in 2008, Hong Kong's Pride parade sees thousands of people marching down Victoria Park every year. Each year's parade has its own theme and dress code, such as "workplace outfits" and "proud purple," which address important causes for the local queer community. The event also features performances, entertainment, vendors, and after-parties.

415 No place for pettiness

Petticoat Lane, Lan Kwai Fong, Hong Kong

When to go: All year
Best for: Drag and nightlife

Featuring some of the city's biggest drag performances, this queer bar is in the heart of Hong Kong's famed magical nightlife spot, Lan Kwai Fong. A queer and inclusive space, Petticoat Lane is a great place for fun and promises a good time for all who visit.

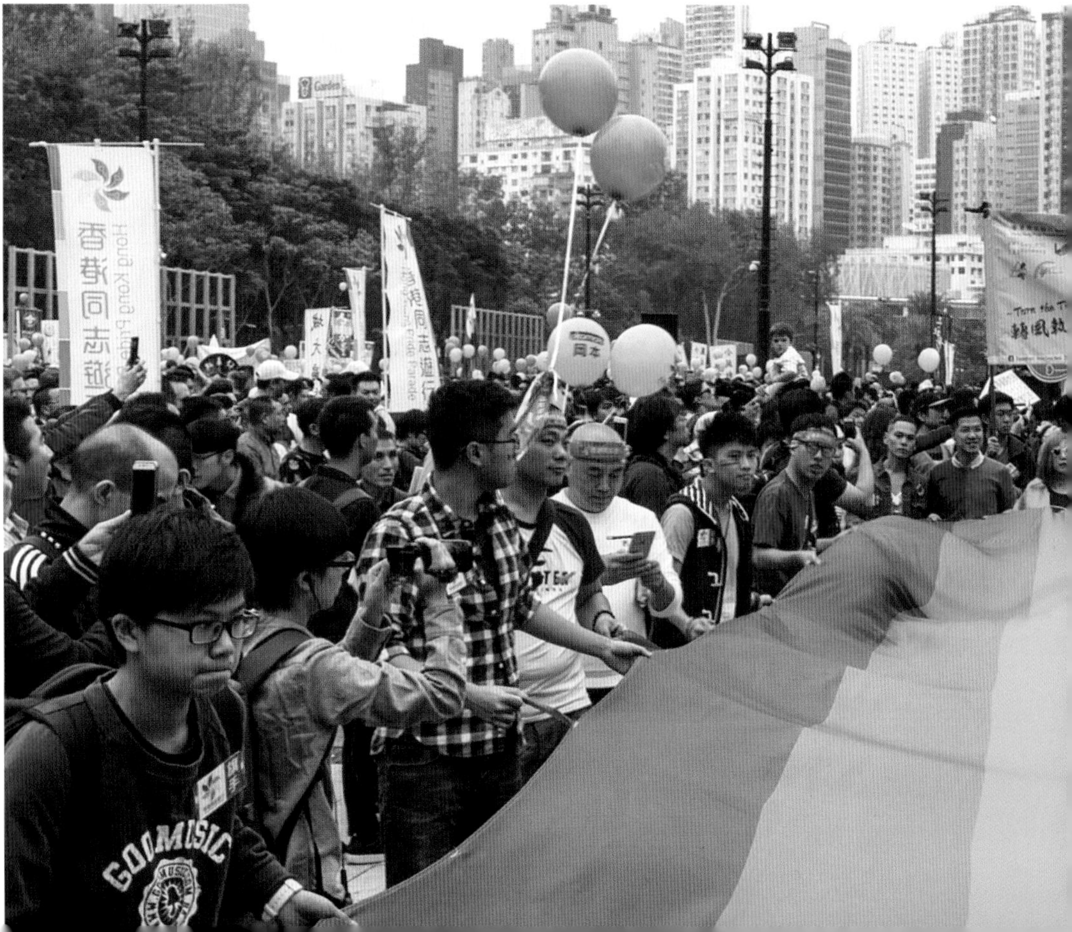

416 What the FLM...

FLM, Hong Kong

When to go: October to December
Best for: Dancing

FLM is one of the few gay clubs where you can dance on the first floor and have a quiet drink on the second floor. It has become a gay institution and remains one of the most popular gay bars in Hong Kong. FLM hosts fun themed nights, karaoke, bingo, quizzes, and live performances by singers, drag queens, and dancers. It also offers a two-for-one happy hour every night so don't be late.

417 Game, set, and match?

L'Paradis, Hong Kong

When to go: All year
Best for: Drinking and games

Although L'Paradis is one of the few lesbian bars in Hong Kong, it is welcoming of all LGBTQ+ people for a relaxed night of drinks, darts, beer pong, and table-top dancing.

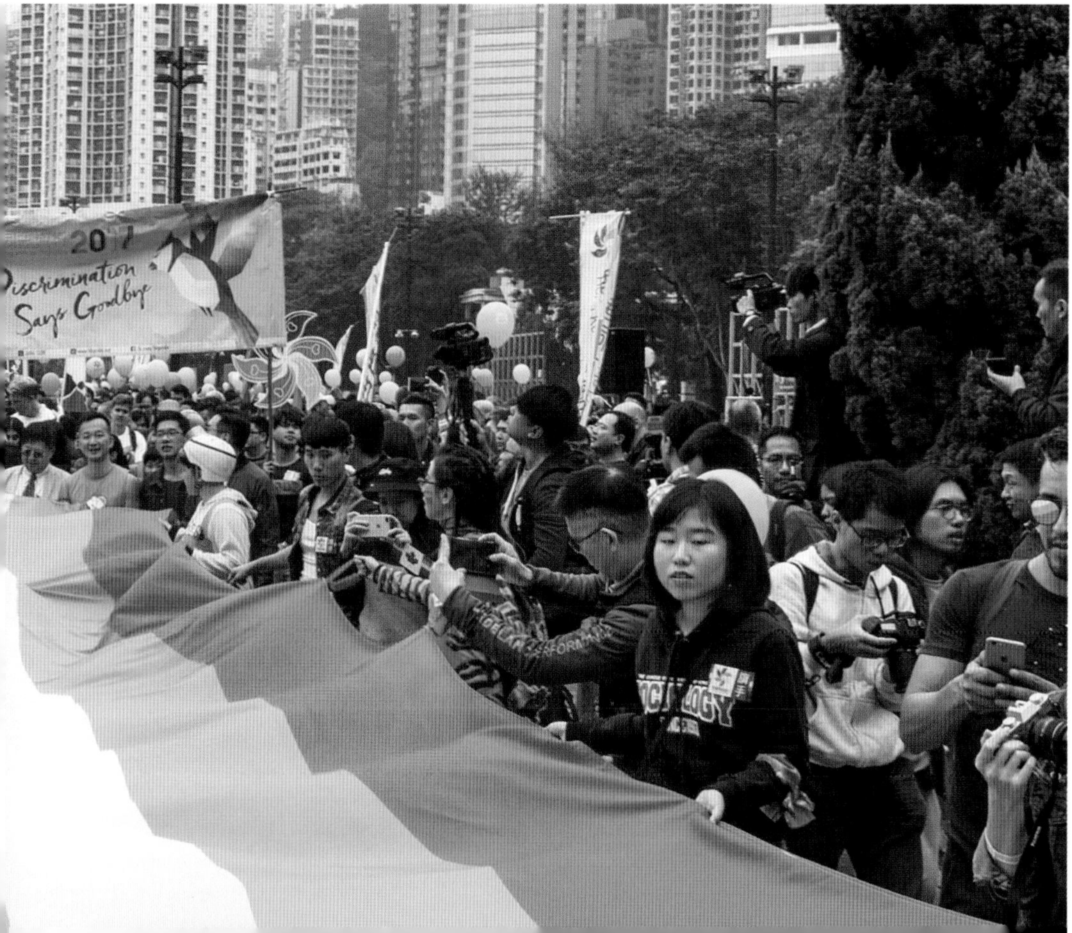

418 Coming out of the... cloakroom

The Cloakroom, Causeway Bay, Hong Kong

When to go: All year
Best for: Theme nights for queer women

Describing itself as a "mystical girls cocktail lounge," this lesbian bar is located in the shopping district of Causeway Bay. With theme nights and events for occasions such as Halloween, where everyone dresses up, this is a fun bar for queer women to meet and have a great night out in the city. Known for their tailor-made cocktails, be ready to try new flavors.

419 In the town of Taipei

▼ Ximending, Taipei, Taiwan

When to go: All year
Best for: Queer bars and nightlife

Ximending is one of the most popular areas in which queer travelers choose to stay when visiting Taiwan. Home to many of the country's gay bars, shops, and restaurants, Ximending is Taiwan's main gay district. This vibrant and culture-rich area is easy to get to with the Ximen train station located close by. For travelers looking to immerse themselves in queer culture in Taiwan, Ximending is a great place to start.

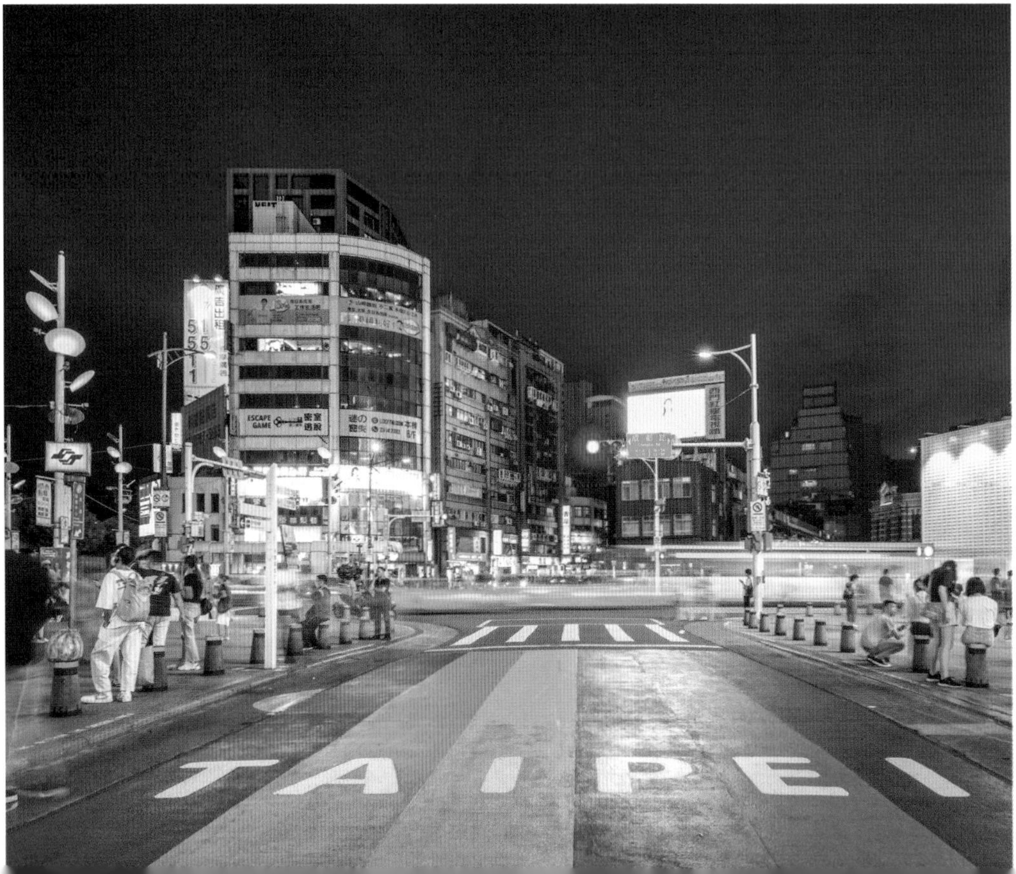

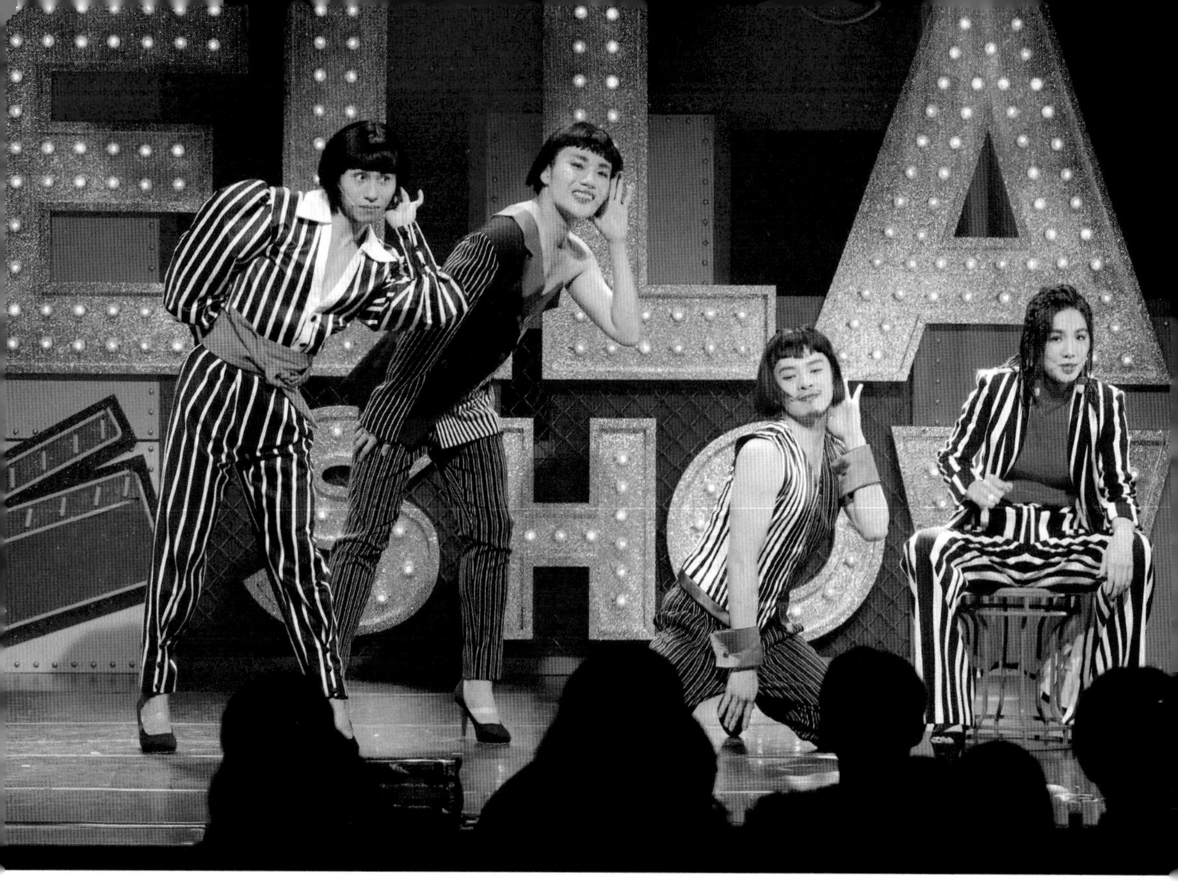

420 Paint the town red

▲ ▶ The Red House, Ximending, Taipei, Taiwan

When to go: All year
Best for: Queer bars and local art

The Red House, as the name suggests, is an iconic red-brick, octagonal building built in 1908, located in Taiwan's main gay district, Ximending. A few souvenir and craft stalls line the front of this theater, while most of Taiwan's most famous gay bars and drag shows are found right behind it. There is also usually a weekend market where you will find local artists selling their wares.

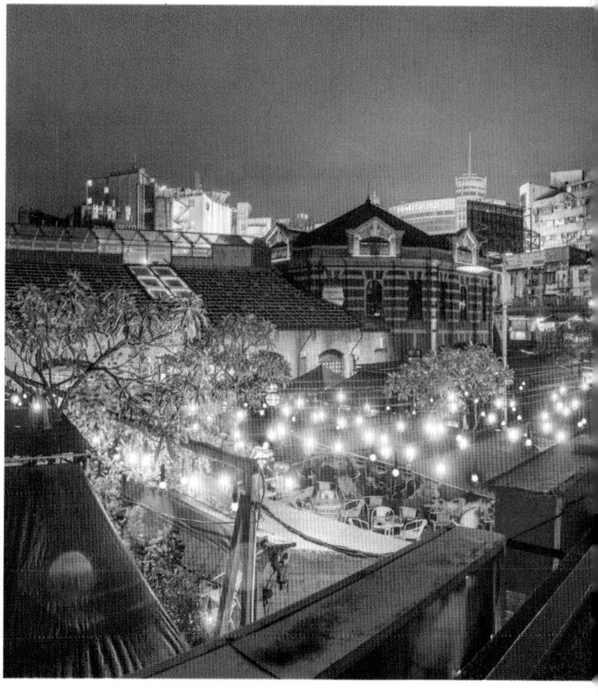

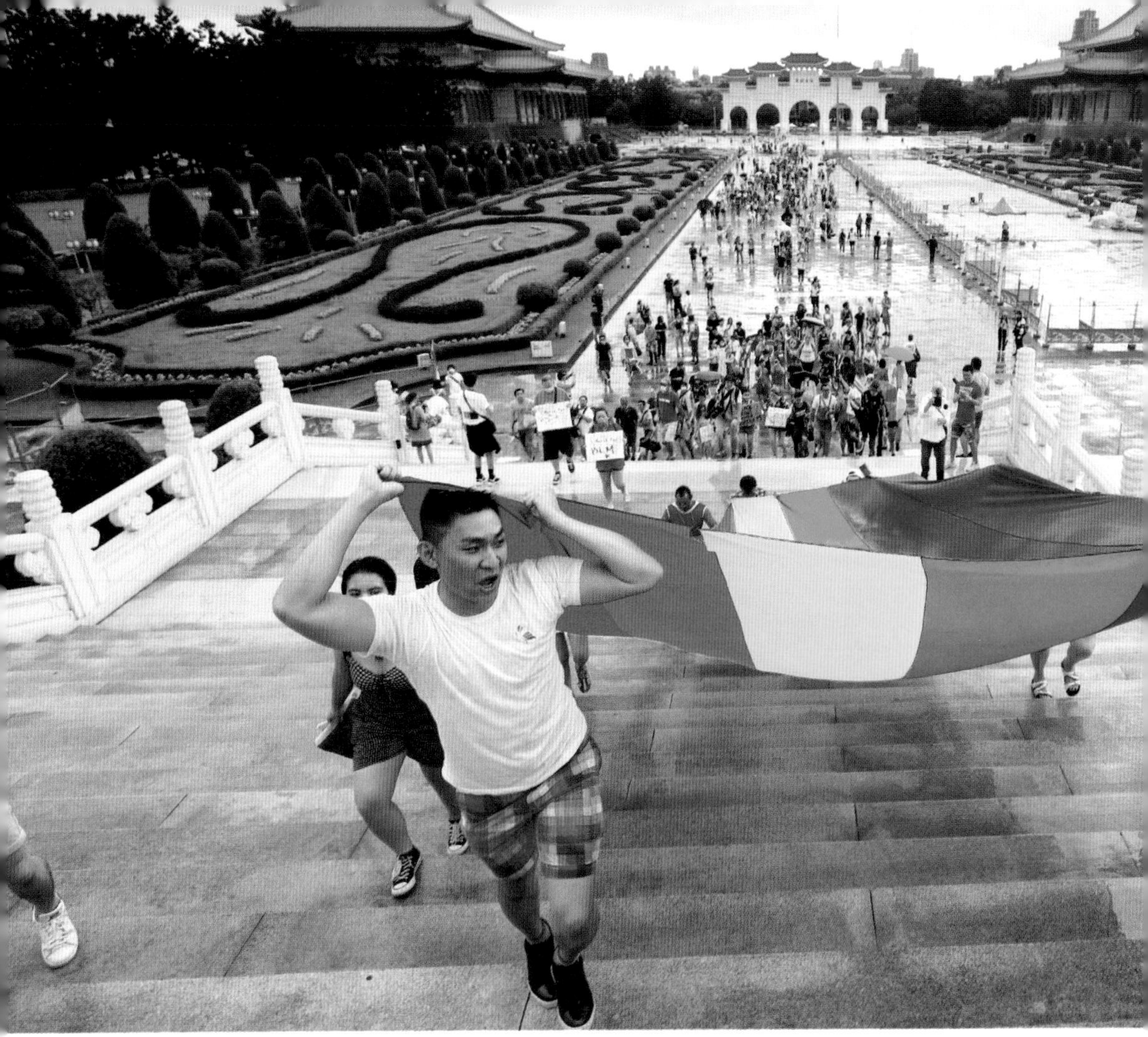

421 Uplifting upholstery

ShiDa, Taipei, Taiwan

When to go: Any time
Best for: Queer fashionistas

ShiDa night market is the central hub located between two of Taipei's biggest universities. The market is brimming with popular street-food stalls and trendy fashion boutiques. There are also several LGBTQ+ stores near ShiDa, and The Witch House Bar, which features seats decorated with bras.

422 Books and binders

GinGin Store, Taipei, Taiwan

When to go: All year
Best for: Mandarin queer lit

Stocked with a whole range of queer literature, including sexy magazines, GinGin Store has been serving Taiwan's queer community since 1999. It also sells clothes and binders, and hosts small art exhibitions in the summer months.

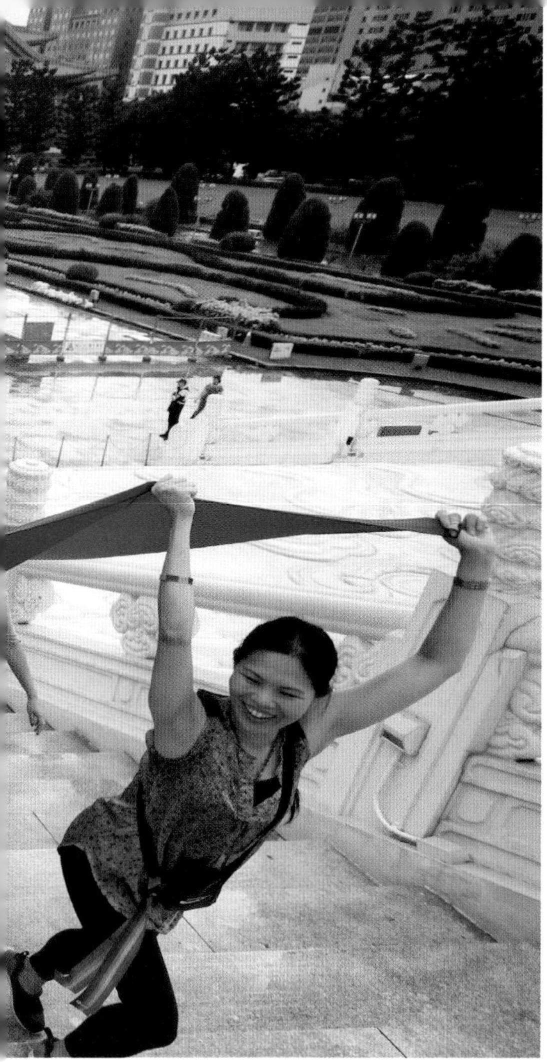

424 Cuddles and bubbles

◀ ▼ Taiwan Pride, Taipei, Taiwan

When to go: October
Best for: a taro-fic time

Whether you're into *boba* (Taiwanese slang for "big boobs"), balls, or neither, Taiwan is the place for you. The country is famous for its bubble tea (also pearl tea, boba tea, or tapioca milk tea), mouthwatering street food, enchanting lantern festivals, bustling night markets, enriching cultural diversity, lush national parks, and affirming LGBTQ+ acceptance. With ancient queer history, it's one of the few countries that has never had anti-LGBTQ+ legislation and is leading the way in eastern Asia with a female president, egalitarian marriage, and protective LGBTQ+ rights. And while public displays of affection are generally frowned upon for all couples, the younger generation is more expressive. Taiwan Pride, in Taipei, is east Asia's biggest, and the parade is a social movement rather than a commercial occasion.

423 Make me blush

Blush, Taipei, Taiwan

When to go: Check in advance
Best for: Drag balls for queer and non-binary folk

Blush organizes drag balls for anyone and everyone to enjoy. The only rule seems to be that there are no rules. A platform for queer folks to express, experiment, and be their extraordinary selves, this event's an inclusive space for everyone.

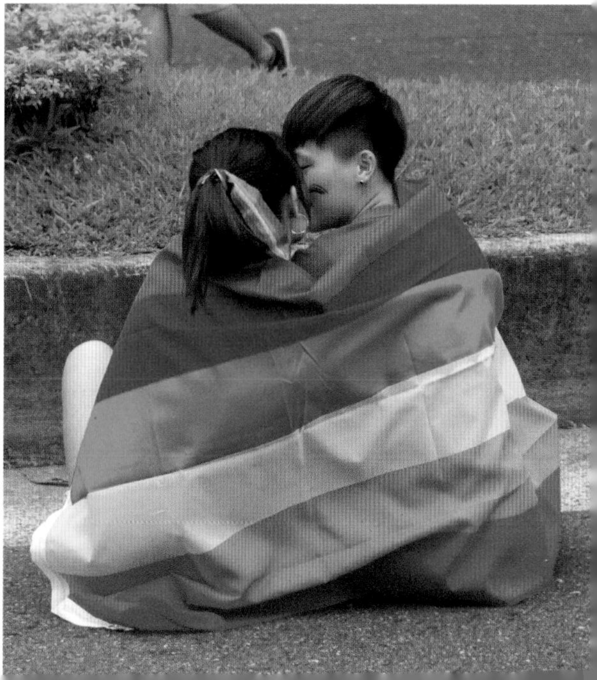

425 Visible visual voices

Taiwan International Queer Film Festival, Taiwan

When to go: August to November
Best for: Advancing queer Taiwanese cinema

Taiwanese gay activist and movie-producer Jay Lin founded Taiwan's first LGBTQ+ film festival in 2014 to increase queer visibility and acceptance in Taiwan's movie industry. Taiwan International Queer Film Festival (TIQFF) grew into a significant event, with screenings, Q&As, and workshops in Taiwan's biggest cities of Taipei, Kaohsiung, and Taichung. Additionally, Lin founded the LGBTQ+ movie-streaming service GagaOoLala, focusing on Asian-Pacific cinema.

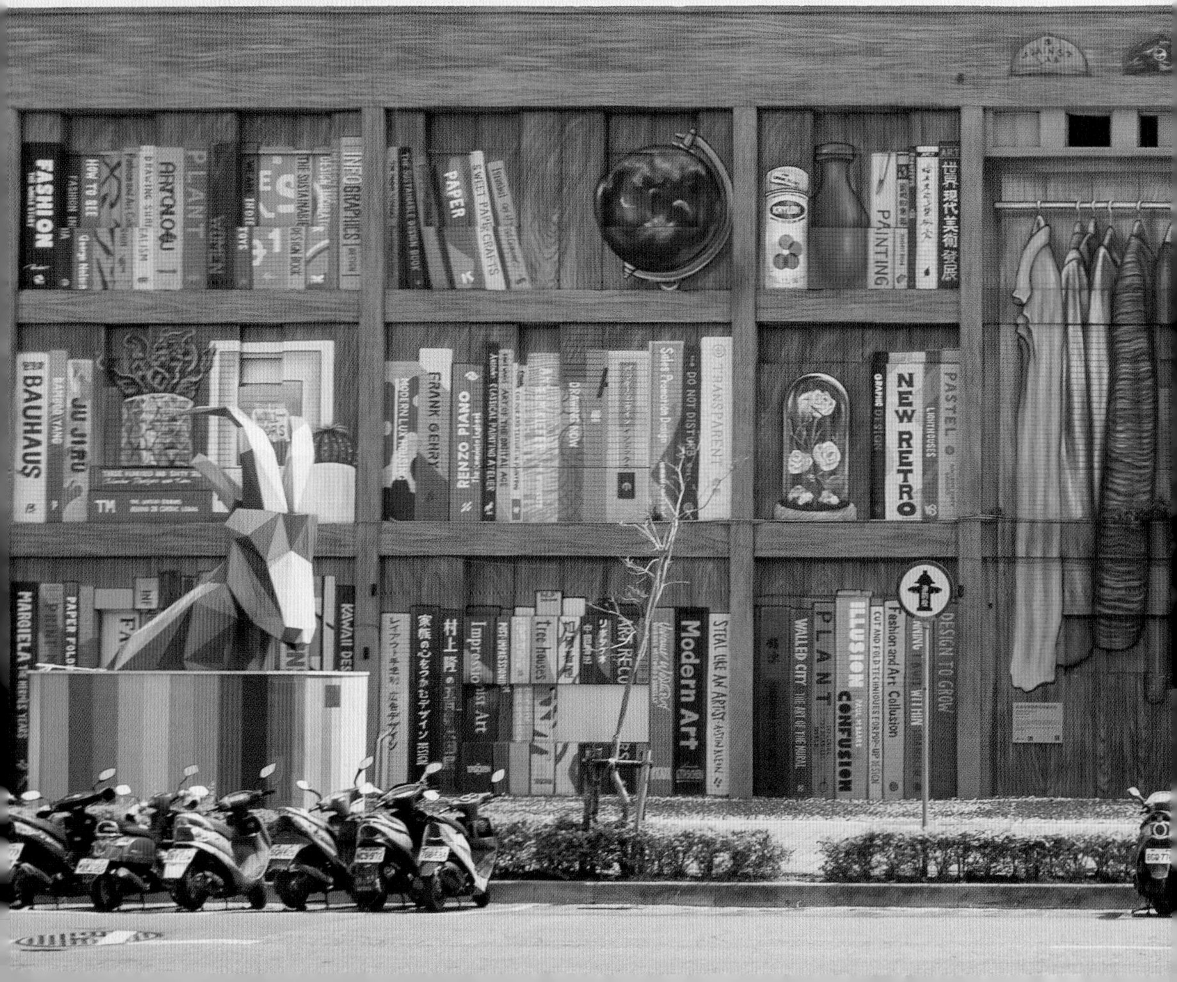

426 Follow your art

▼ Kaohsiung, Taiwan

When to go: All year
Best for: Street-art lovers

The harbor-city of Kaohsiung lies one hundred minutes away from Taipei via the high-speed rail link. Over the last decade, it has become a vibrantly colorful place that has hosted an annual Pride parade since 2010. The streets themselves are colorful, with the city council proactively encouraging street art that can be seen on Jiuru Street, at the Pier-2 Art Center, and in the Lingya District. Find contemporary art installation "Rainbow Church" on Cijin Island and mesmerizing stained glass "Dome of Light" in the Formosa Boulevard Station.

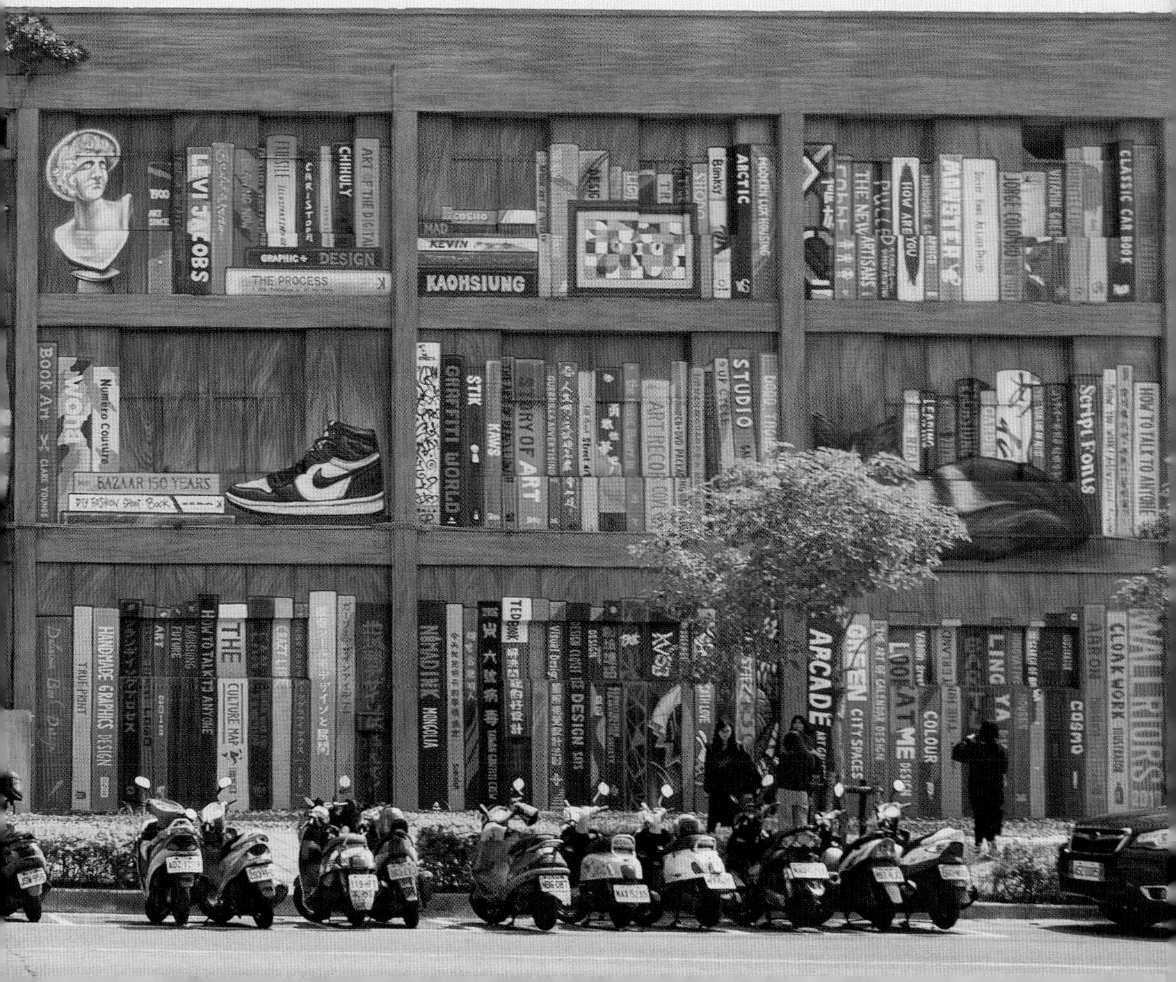

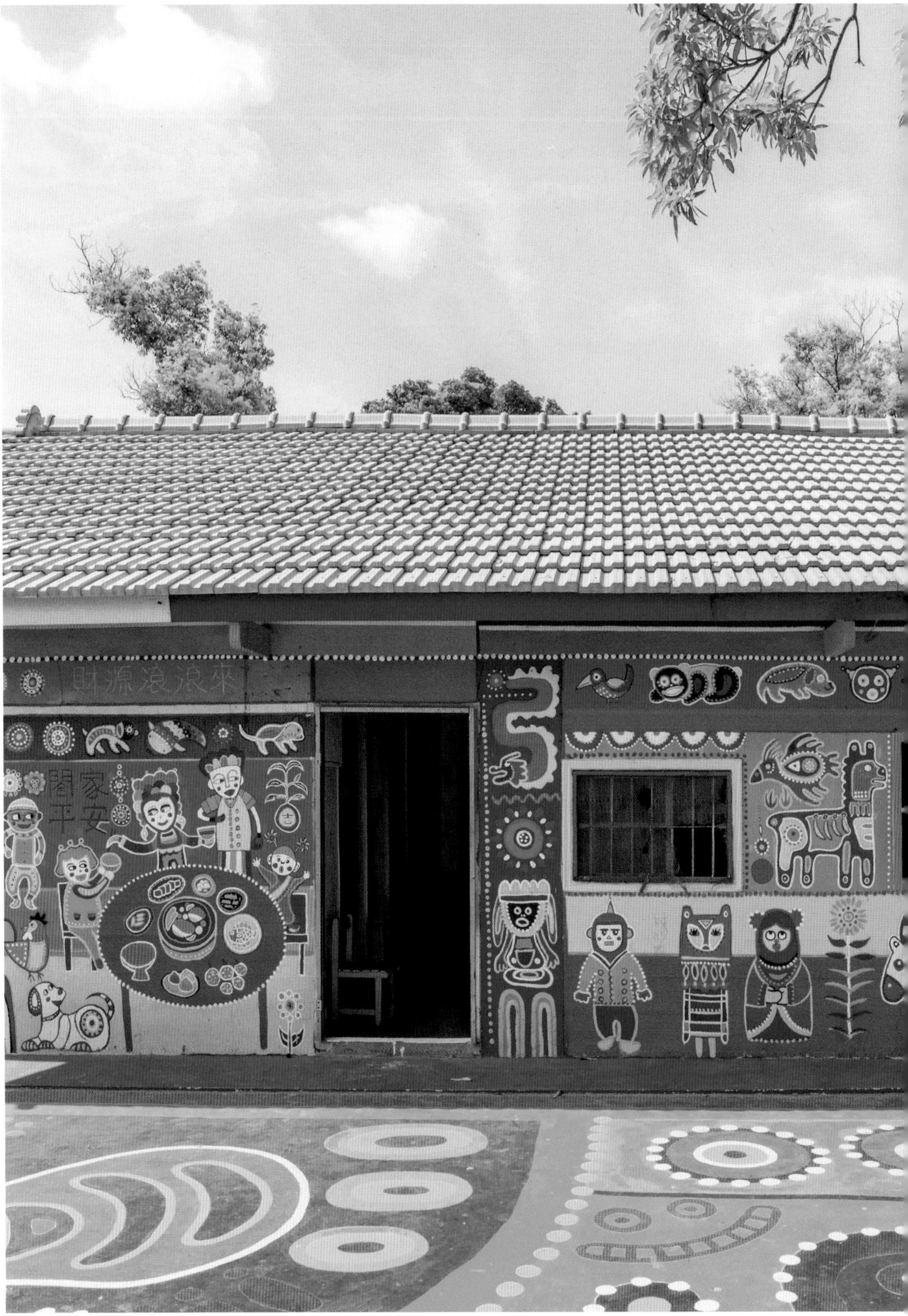

財源滾滾來
闔家
平安

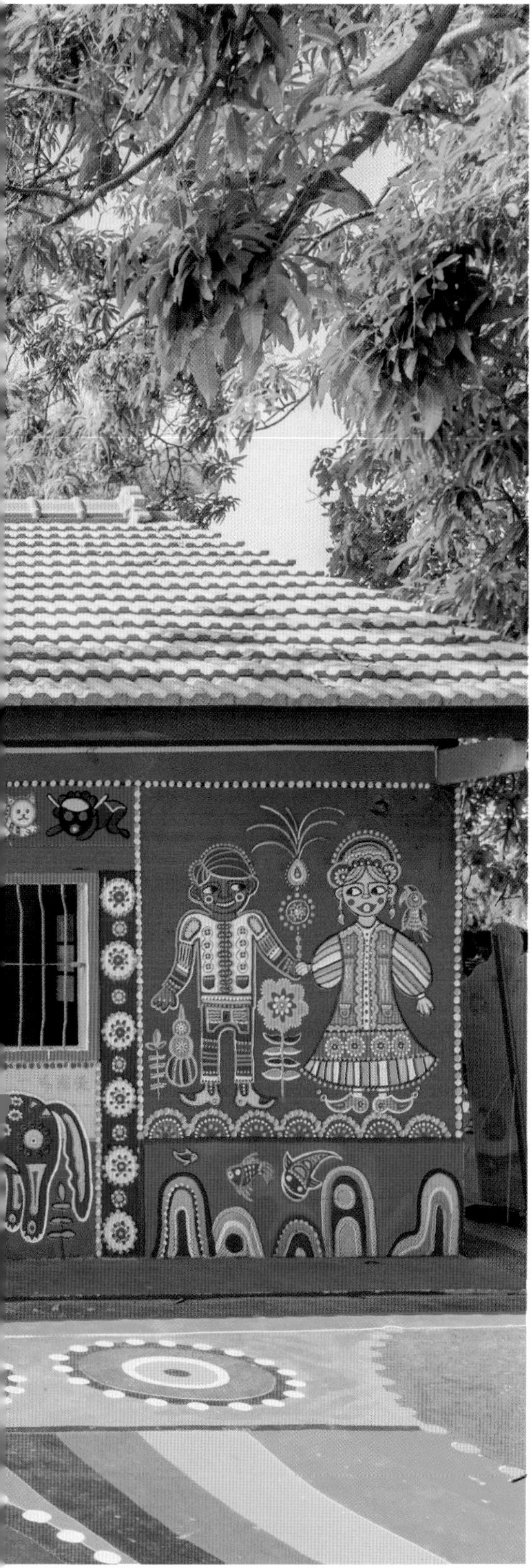

427 A town called rainbow

Rainbow Village, Taichung, Taiwan

When to go: All year
Best for: Painted houses

Taiwan's third-largest city, Taichung, is the island's colorful cultural center and home to the renowned National Taiwan Museum of Fine Arts. The city also has a small but vibrant queer nightlife scene, with famous gay club Plaza, Kudos gay bar and restaurant, karaoke-bar First Floor, student-popular Gong High, funky lesbian bar Funway T Bar, and queer-friendly No Boundary. Taichung's over-a-decade-old Pride parade colors the streets every year, and on the eastern side of the city—in the Nantun District—there's a splash of color to visit year-round: Rainbow Village. Rainbow Grandpa—the Chinese-born veteran Huang Yong-fu—started painting to save his tiny home in a military dependents' village from demolition. Of the 1,200 homes, only 11 remained by 2008. His first painting was a colorful bird as a protest. But when he started painting, he found his happily ever after. With rainbow colors, he generated change, found happiness, and built a community that's keeping the legacy alive. Doesn't that sound familiar?

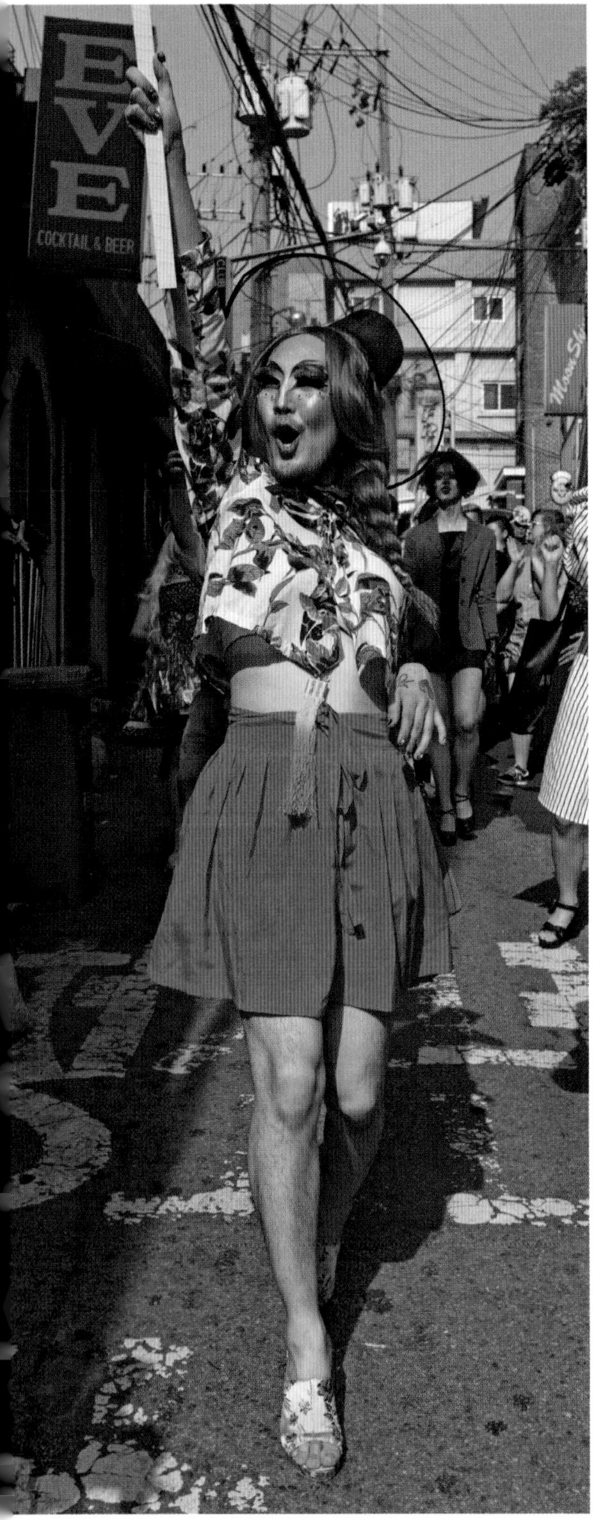

428 Heart and soul of drag

◀ Seoul Drag Parade, South Korea

When to go: May to July (dates change)
Best for: Community drag

One of the first of its kind and the largest annual drag parade in Asia, Seoul Drag Parade features drag queens and kings on a march through Itaewon, home to Seoul's "Homo Hill." Held as part of Seoul Queer Culture Fest, but separate from the main Pride parade, Seoul Drag Parade is community- (rather than party-) focused, with the aim of bringing drag out from the bars and onto the streets.

429 Parades, parties and K-Pop

▶ Seoul Queer Culture Festival, South Korea

When to go: May to July (dates change)
Best for: Pride Parade

Since 2000, the Seoul Queer Culture Festival has grown from a march of 50 to a multi-week event attracting over 100,000. Home to South Korea's biggest Pride parade—which marches past the City Hall—and the nascent Seoul Drag Parade, Seoul Queer Culture Festival is equal parts community, party and K-Pop. You can also catch a film at the Korea Queer Film Festival and you won't want to miss the after-parties at "Homo Hill."

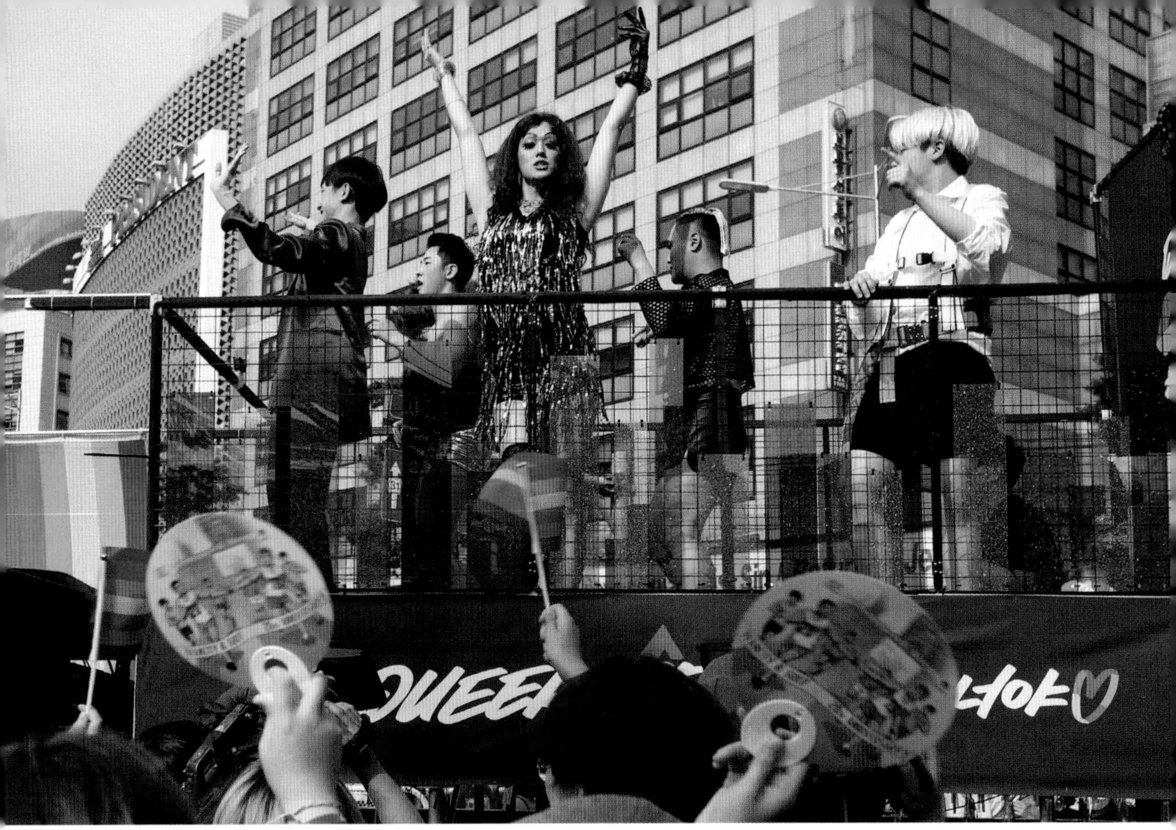

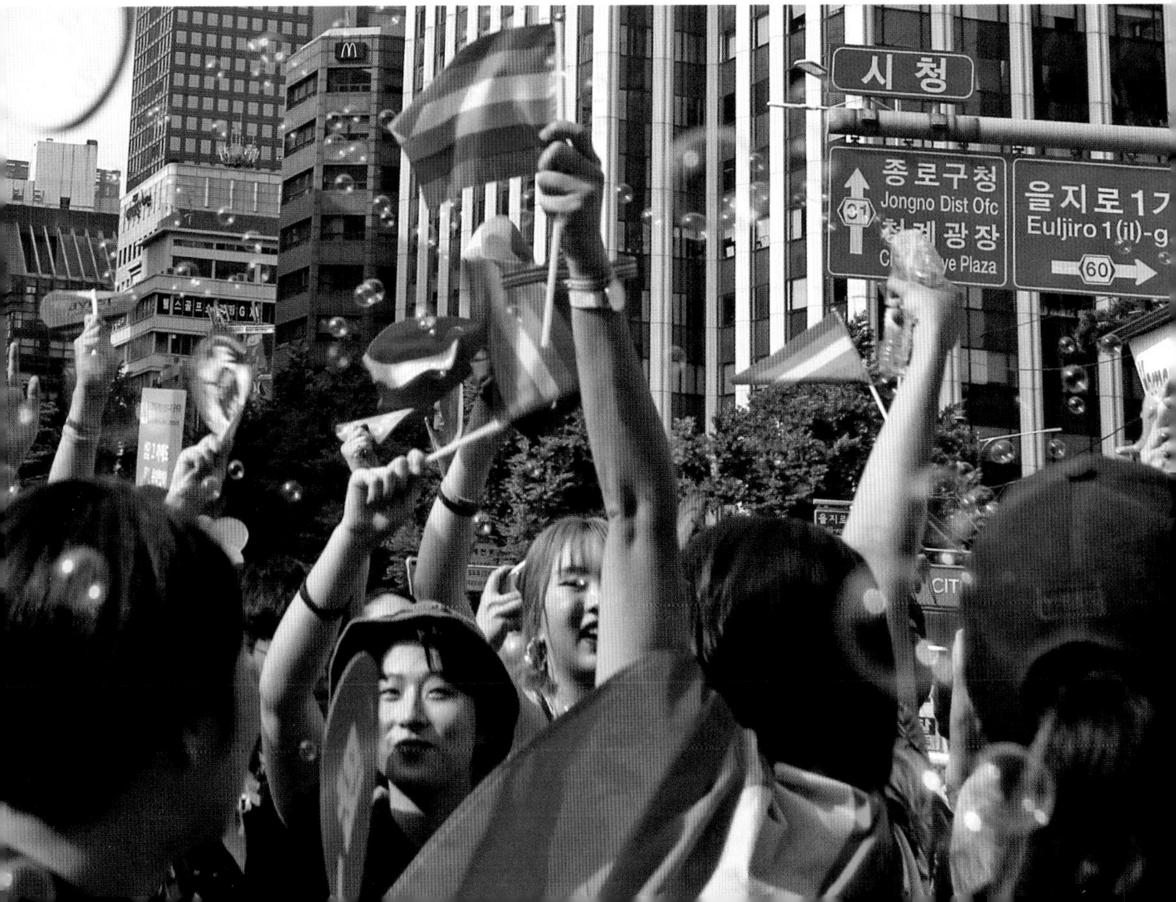
시청
종로구청
Jongno Dist Ofc
60

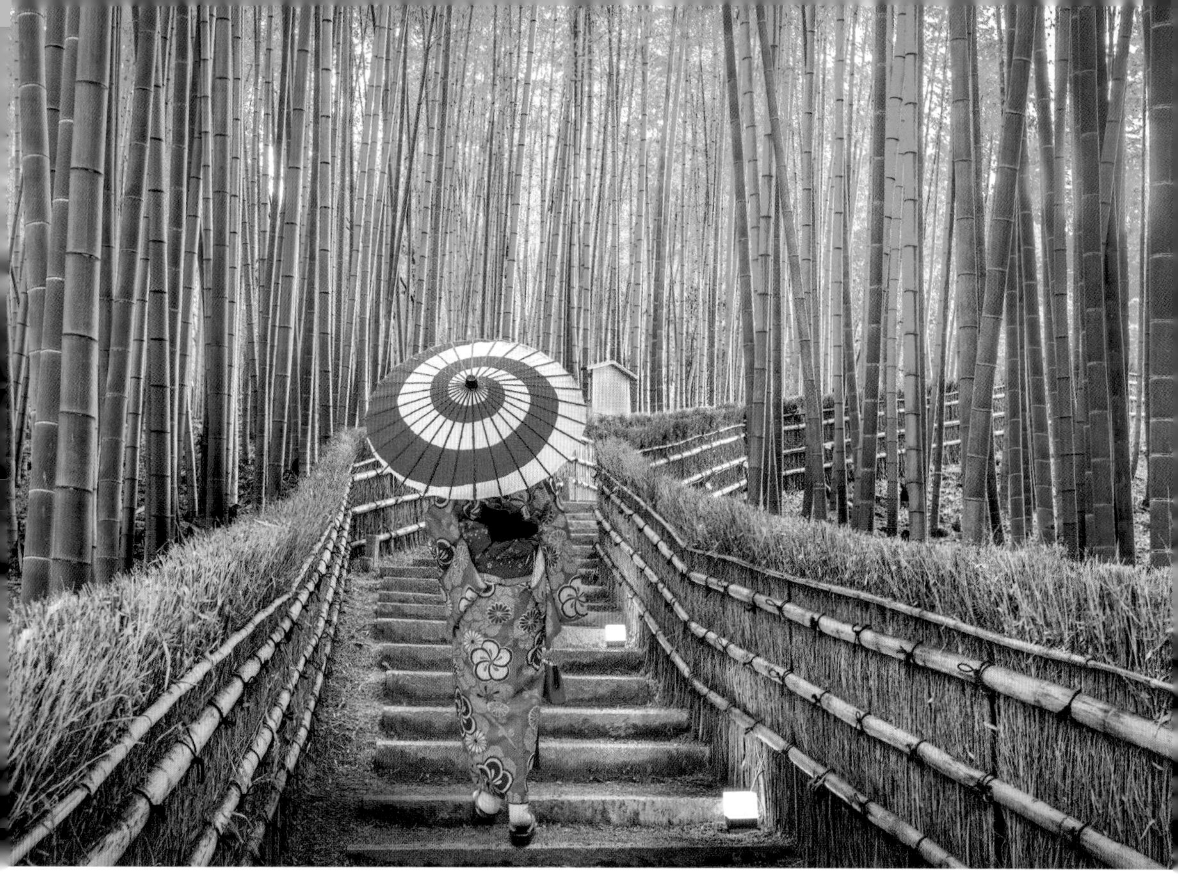

430 Let's go to Kyoto

▲ Kyoto, Japan

When to go: March to May and
September to November
Best for: Culture and cafés

Kyoto is home to a bamboo forest, geisha culture, and hundreds of temples, palaces, shrines, and gardens. Go on a geisha tour to learn about the highly skilled and well-respected entertainers—historically they were men known as *taikomochi*. Modern-day geishas are female and known as a *geiko* (meaning "woman of art") or *maiko* (a geiko in training). End your day in the trendy Pontocho area at gay-popular bars Azure and Apple, or lesbian-popular Bar Look Me.

431 It's raining rainbows

Kansai Rainbow Festa, Osaka, Japan

When to go: October
Best for: Queer performances

Attracting over 10,000 attendees annually, Osaka's weekend-long Kansai Rainbow Festa is the gayest way to ring in the fall. Join locals and local celebs in a parade along the famous Tenjinbashisuji shopping street, which ends at a city park filled with community stalls and live performances. Get your fill of vegan food served by local lesbian bar WaaGwaan, or feast on myriad rainbow treats as you wait for the famed release of rainbow balloons.

432 Keen to sing-o

Susukino, Sapporo, Japan

When to go: All year
Best for: Welcoming spaces

Sapporo is the largest city on Japan's northernmost island of Hokkaido, and it has a lively LGBTQ+ scene, mainly found in the nightlife hotspot of Susukino. Bar Orb is open to everyone, but especially welcoming for lesbians with a women-only night on Saturdays. Bar Sign Oh! offers great views over the city, lively pop music and dancing, while gay men looking to indulge their karaoke habit should head to Bar Hammer.

433 Rainbow Tokyo

▼ Tokyo Rainbow Pride, Japan

When to go: April
Best for: Pride event and parade

Held at the Yoyogi Park every April, the Tokyo Rainbow Pride is a celebration of Tokyo's queer community. Spanning several days, the event features music performances, booths by LGBTQ-friendly businesses, and drag shows. The 2-mi/3.2-km parade starts at Shibuya, with participants marching in colorful attire, proudly waving rainbow flags alongside others riding on floats. Here's an opportunity to surround yourself with other queer folk and experience pride, queer joy, and acceptance in Tokyo.

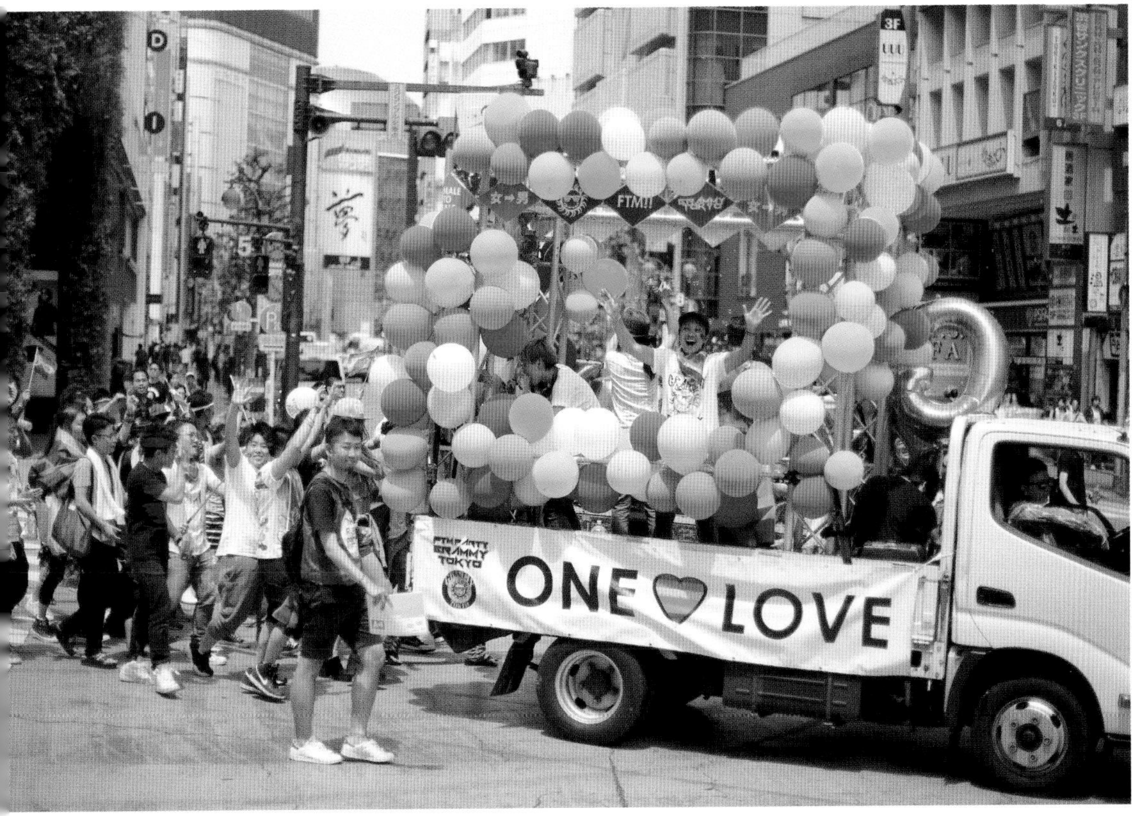

434 Roam in Ni-Chōme

▼ Shinjuku Ni-Chōme, Tokyo, Japan

When to go: All year
Best for: Queer bar-hopping

Shinjuku—one of Tokyo's 23 wards—is famous for its buzzing nightlife, neon lights, and LGBTQ+ district Ni-Chōme. East Shinjuku's queer district has about 300 queer venues. Local queer people frequent small, unassuming Japanese-style bars where "mama-san" (the bar manager) chats and drinks with customers. Traveler-friendly gay bars include Aiiro Café Bar, Arty Farty, and Campy! Bar. The iconic New Sazae disco (since 1966) has a fun, mixed audience. Queer women connect at Goldfinger, Dorabune, Diamond Holic, or Adezakura, and trans folks find each other at FTM Bois Bar at GF and FTM Bar 2's Cabin.

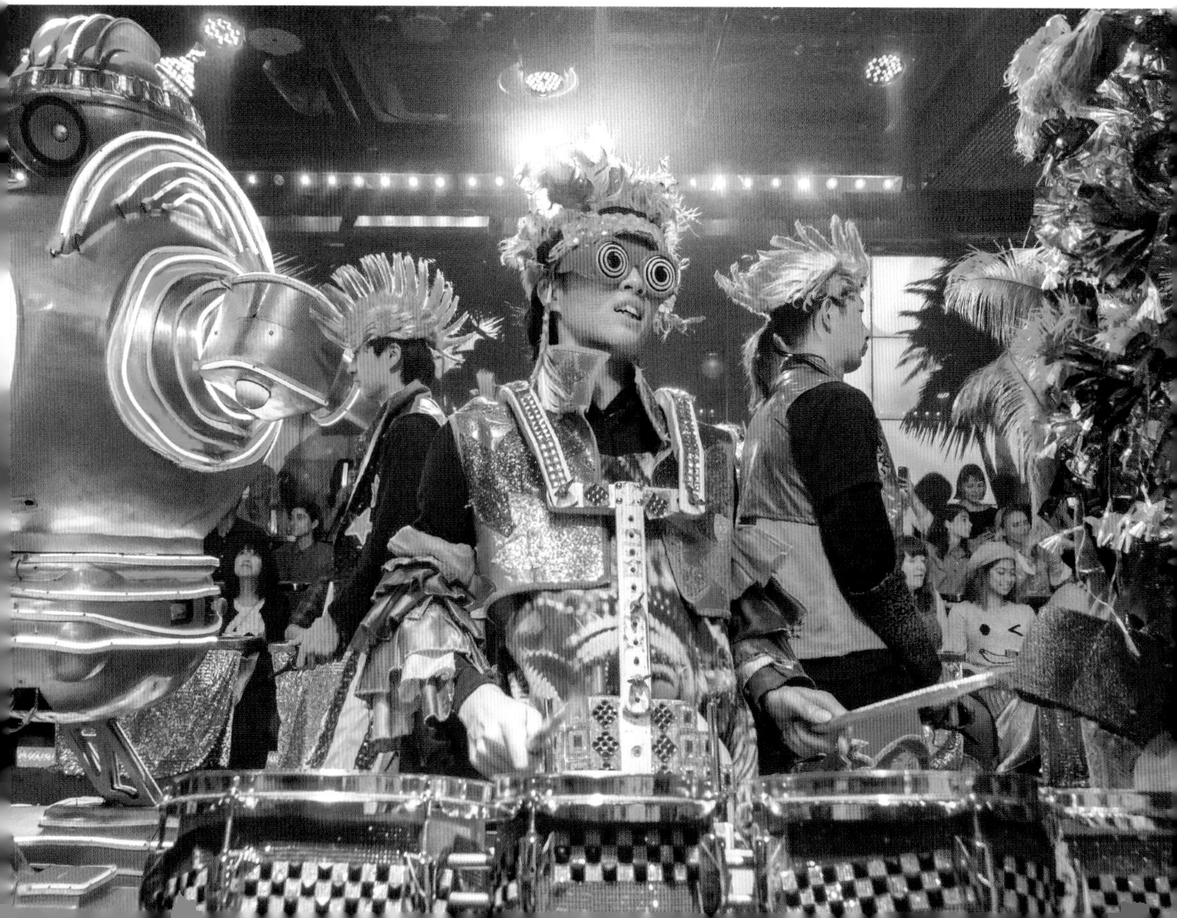

435 Too many cooks . . . make a party

FTM bars, Tokyo, Japan

When to go: All year
Best for: A trans-tastic night out

Onabe bars are unique to Japan's queer nightlife. *Onabe* (literally meaning "cooking pot") is a term for masculine lesbians and transgender men. Part of the (underground) queer scene since the 1960s, these bars now openly advertise as being trans-men-run and can be found throughout Tokyo, including the famous FTM Bois Bar at GF and FTM Bar 2's Cabin.

436 Putting on a show in Tokyo

Rainbow Reel Tokyo, Tokyo, Japan

When to go: July
Best for: Queer Asian short films

Operating in both Tokyo and Osaka, Rainbow Reel has been a leading queer film festival in Japan since its inception in 1992. Screening Japanese and international films (all with English subtitles), Rainbow Reel welcomes locals and tourists alike. Don't miss their annual QueerxAPAC program, which showcases the best queer films from emerging talent across the region.

437 My big gay Asian dance festival

▶ GCircuit Songkran, Phuket/ Bangkok, Thailand

When to go: April
Best for: Nightlife

Attracting gay men from all over the world, GCircuit is Asia's biggest, gay dance festival that takes place for Thai New Year. Featuring some of the most popular DJs in the world, you can expect a splashing good time at this four-day event. A bucket-list item for many gay men, this pool-cum-dance party is an eclectic ensemble of Gogo dancers, heart-thumping music, and water fights.

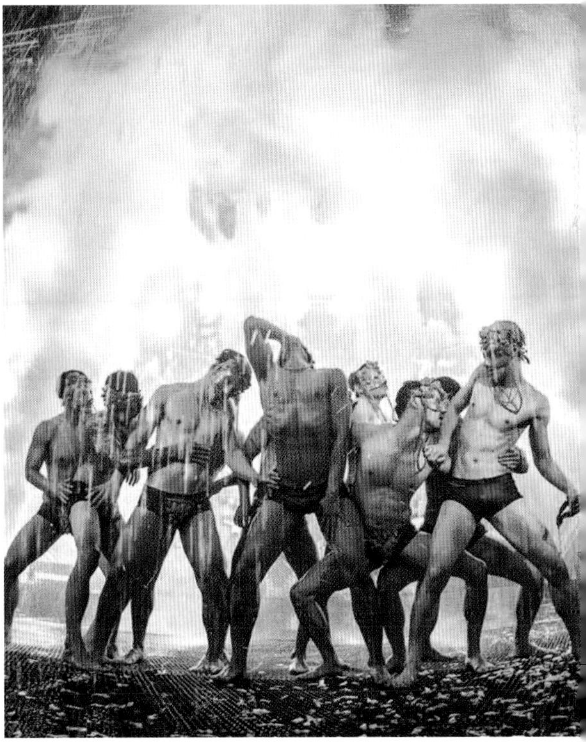

438 Lip-synch the night away

▶ Calypso Cabaret, Bangkok, Thailand

When to go: All year
Best for: Transgender performers

For an entertaining night out and a meaningful engagement with Bangkok's transgender community, hit up Calypso Cabaret—a transgender cabaret that has been running for over 20 years. Featuring a talented cast of transgender women lip-synching their way through all-time favorites and contemporary show tunes, the stars of Calypso Cabaret will delight and surprise with their costumes, dance, and decor.

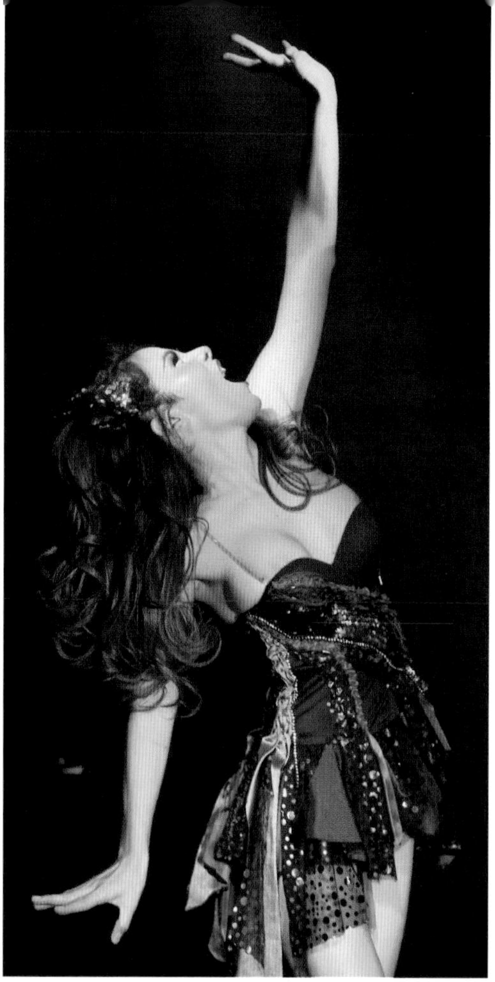

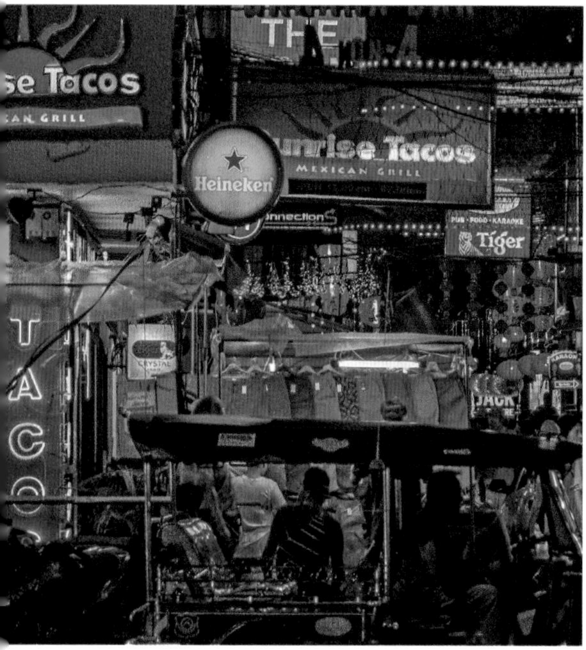

439 Wild times

◀ Silom Soi 4 and Soi 2, Bangkok, Thailand

When to go: All year
Best for: Nightlife

Find Bangkok's epicenter of LGBTQ+ nightlife in the party-central Silom district. The relaxed Soi 4 street has many gay bars and restaurants including the city's oldest gay bar, Telephone Pub. As the night gets wilder head to Soi 2, two streets where you'll find the famous DJ Station dance club.

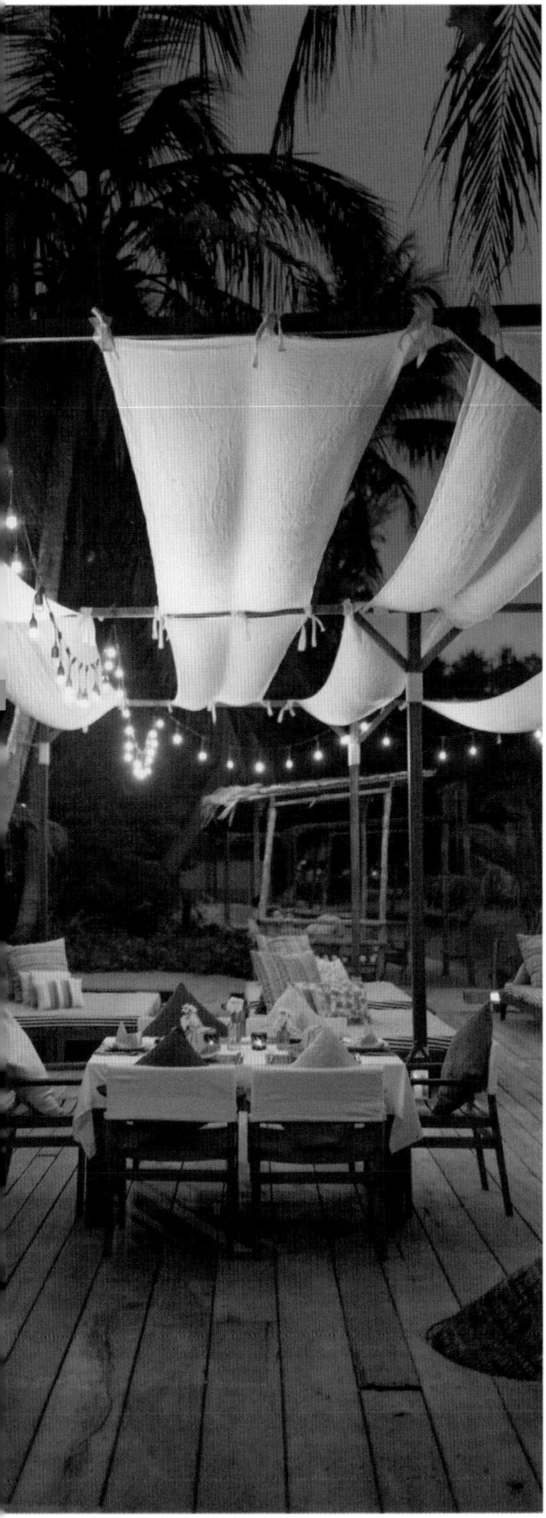

440 Gorgeous, gorgeous Grrrls

Go Grrrls, Bangkok, Thailand

When to go: All year
Best for: The whole she-Bangkok

Founded a decade ago by three iconic queer female Thai DJs (Dookie, Mae Happyair, and Cleo P), clubbing collective Go Grrrls unites queer folk with epic, inclusive parties. Not only is the crowd diverse, but the music too. Each DJ specializes in a different genre, resulting in a vibrant mix of indie, techno, and hip hop.

441 Put your money where your heart is

◀ Koh Phangan, Thailand

When to go: December to August
Best for: Supporting queer-owned businesses

The stunning island of Koh Phangan in the Gulf of Thailand is famous for its hedonistic full-moon parties, but the island offers much more. The island is home to natural beauty, snorkel- and dive-perfect waters, queer-friendly beaches, rich Thai culture, a significant health and wellness scene, and lovely queer-owned businesses. Visit the relaxed and cozy bar and bistro L'Alcove, run by a French lesbian couple. Stay at the romantic, lesbian-owned Thai hotel and spa Chantaramas, affordable gay-owned For You Guesthouse, or OUT! Hostel.

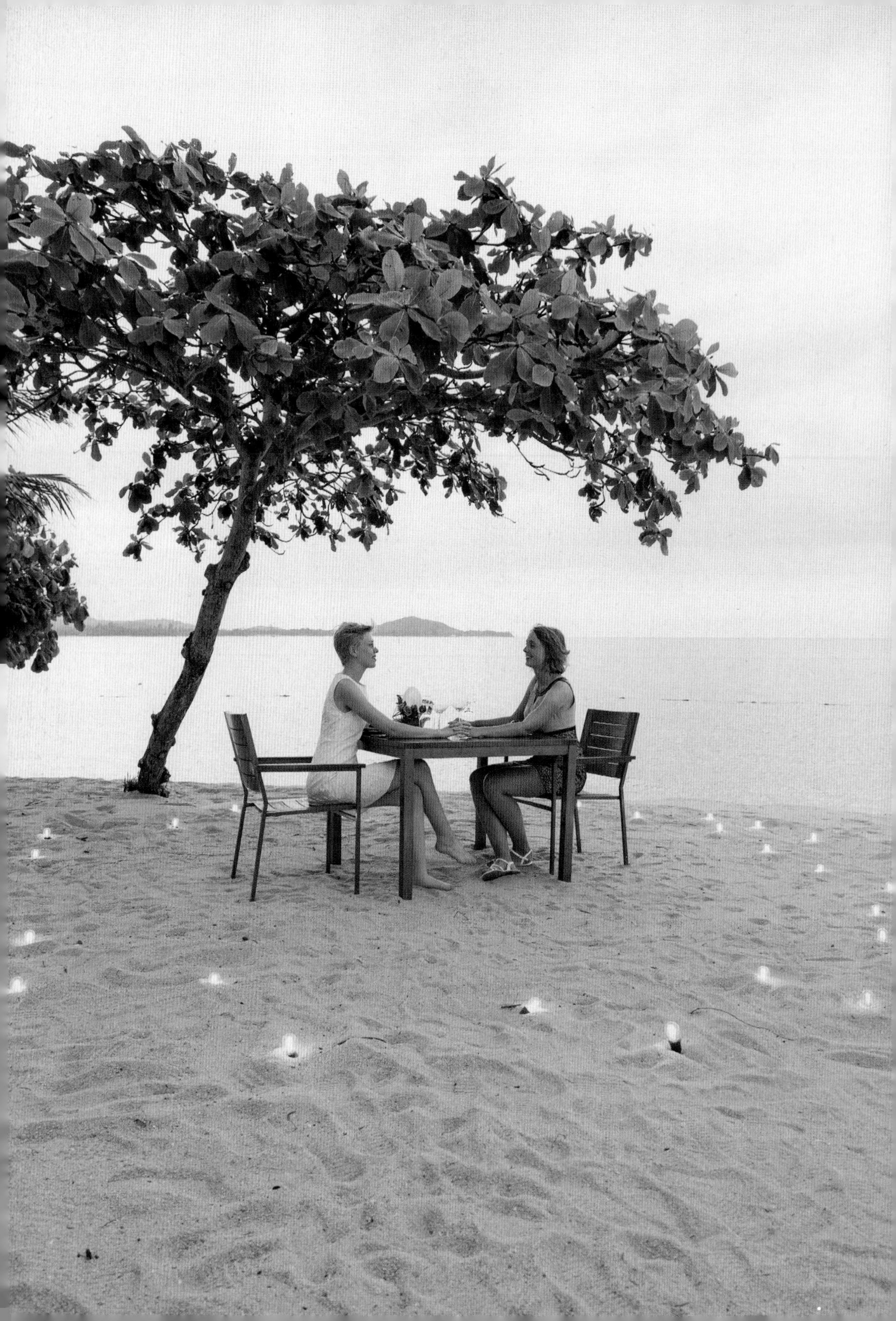

442 Beach bar, hurrah!

▶ Chaweng, Koh Samui, Thailand

When to go: December to August
Best for: Laid-back gay scene

Besides natural beauty and relaxing vibes, Koh Samui is home to a lively gay scene. The island's gay heart is in the buzzing beach area Chaweng in Bo Put, with most LGBTQ+ venues dotted along Chaweng Beach Road. Pride Bar is a welcoming, relaxed café and bar, while ARK bar is famous for fire shows and gay clubbing. Divas Cabaret offers unique, family-friendly shows by Thai *kathoey* (Thai term for a third gender and transgender women) performers, combining Western pop divas with Thai cultural dance.

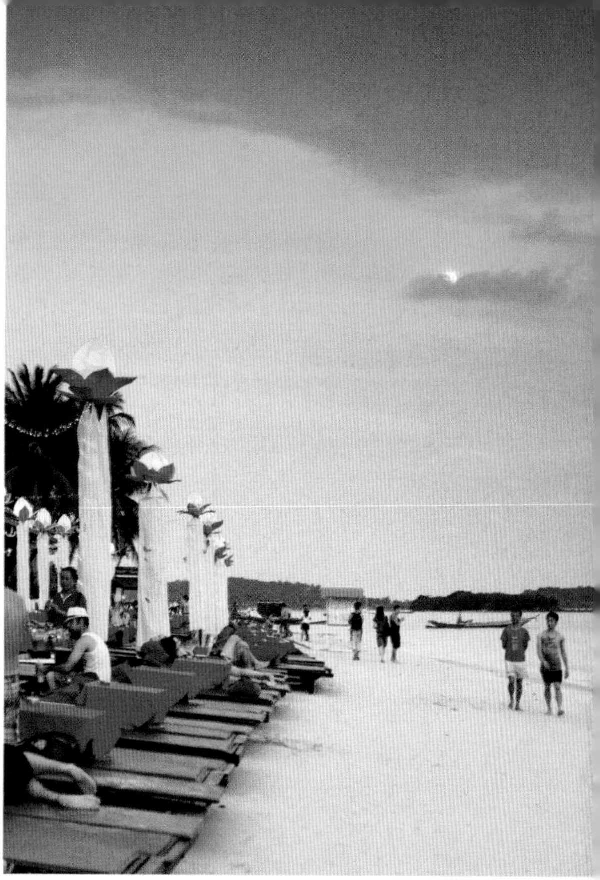

443 Love island

◀ Koh Samui, Thailand

When to go: December to August
Best for: Romantic queer-cation

Koh Samui, Thailand's second-biggest island, boasts palm-tree-lined, white sand beaches, crystal-clear blue waters, lush mountainous rainforest, and luxurious resorts and spas. Add Thailand's LGBTQ-friendly attitude and you've got yourself a perfect tropical getaway. If you're done with relaxing, go on a day trip to pristine archipelago Ang Thong Marine Park, get your diving certificate at nearby Koh Tao, or visit lively neighbor Koh Phangan.

444 Sun, sea, and sequins

Phuket Gay Carnival, Thailand

When to go: April
Best for: A wild Pride

Patong in Phuket is well-known for its nightlife. The area is brimming with bars and clubs, and Phuket Gay Festival brings even more fun in April. There are all manner of activities throughout the festival but one of the main highlights is the Parade—and its extravagant outfits.

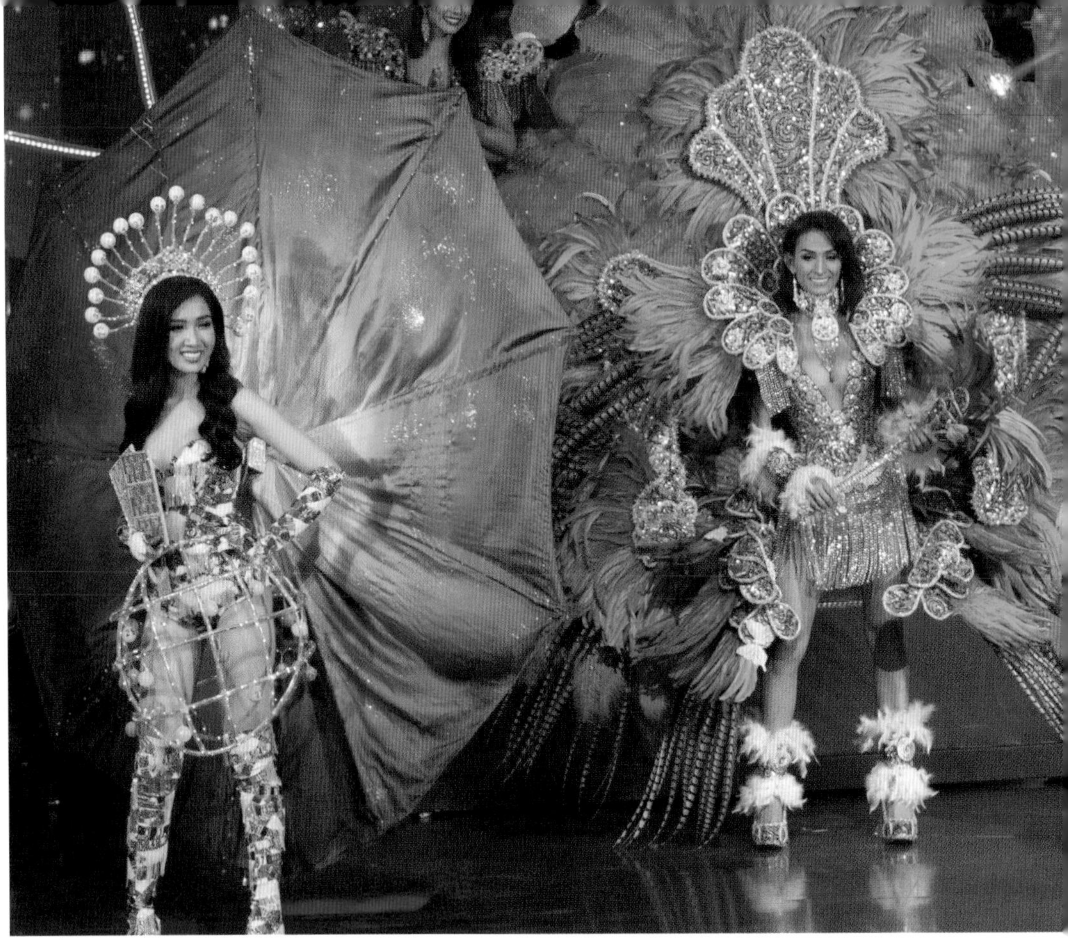

445 Cleaner, safer, way more fun

▲ Pattaya, Thailand

When to go: November to May
Best for: Transgender shows

Thailand's Sin City, Pattaya, has long been infamous for its go-go bars, sex shows, and gay beaches. But Pattaya is changing, with authorities cleaning the beaches, pedestrianizing the city, and regulating the sex industry, making for a safer, more welcoming destination. Travel south for the vibrant gay scene in Jomtien, or attend a Pattaya cabaret with world-class transgender performers.

446 Good on you

La Chhouk Recycled and Creative Fashion, Phnom Penh, Cambodia

When to go: All year
Best for: Queer fashion

Environmental and LGBTQ activism is central to the work of La Chhouk fashion collective. Much of their clothing is made from materials such as plastic bottles, wire, and cement bags. See their collections at one of their self-hosted fashion shows throughout the year, featuring queer models, or at bigger events such as the Earth Day Fashion Show.

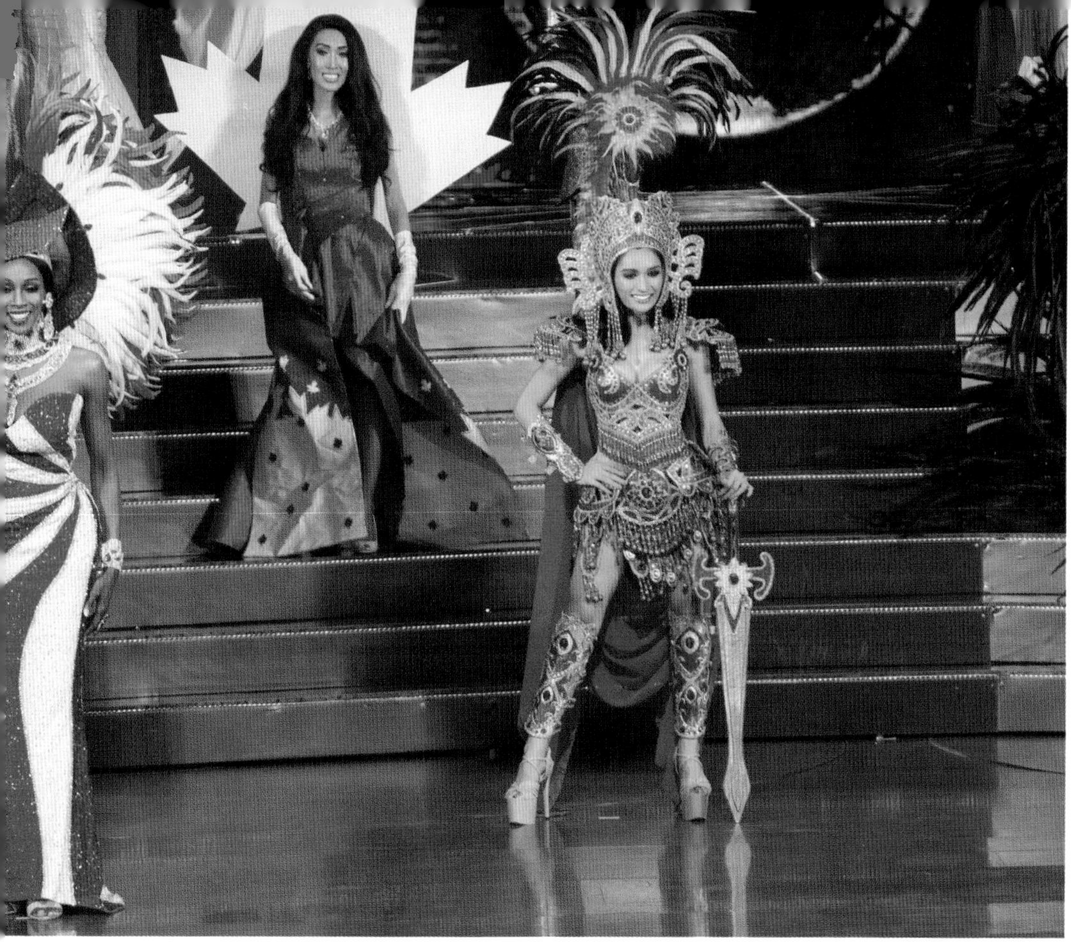

447 Where there's only men's rooms

Arthur and Paul Hotel, Phnom Penh, Cambodia

When to go: November to April
Best for: Relaxing

For a luxurious, gay getaway, check yourself into the men-only Arthur and Paul Hotel in the heart of Phnom Penh. Located within tuk-tuk distance from the Central Market, National Museum, and Royal Palace, and fully equipped with a chlorine-free pool, spa, and massage services, the Arthur and Paul Hotel is the perfect base to explore the city and your lover (or lovers).

448 Sing the blues

Blue Chilli Bar, Phnom Penh, Cambodia

When to go: All year
Best for: Queer karaoke

While spending time in Phnom Penh (which is the best place in the country for queer nightlife), you won't want to miss Blue Chilli Bar, Cambodia's longest-running gay bar. From 11 p.m. every Thursday to Saturday, catch their drag-queen shows, or else swing by on Mondays and Tuesdays for karaoke night.

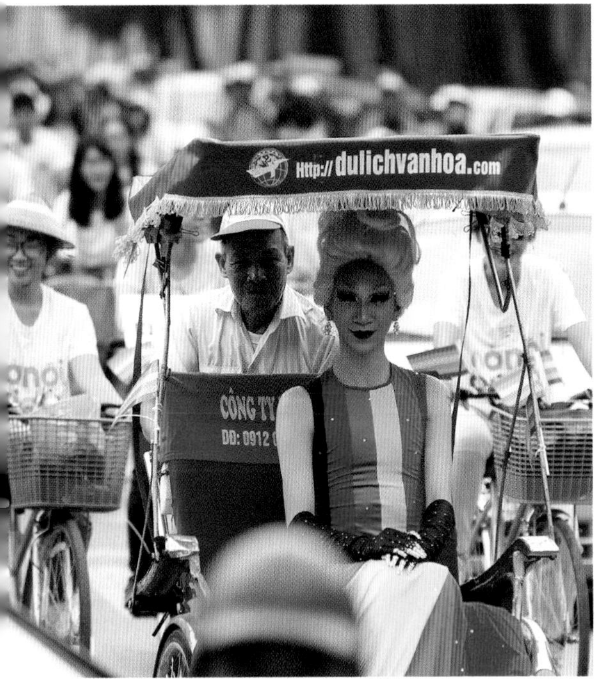

449 Putting the ride in Pride

◀ VietPride, Hanoi, Vietnam

When to go: August
Best for: Flexing your pride

VietPride in Hanoi is quite unlike any other Pride festival because this annual event relies on pedal power. Many of those attending ride bicycles and rickshaws, often flying rainbow flags and other banners. The bikes are then followed by a small walking parade. The event began in 2012, and now normally attracts over one thousand people. It might be one of the world's smaller Pride festivals, but it's definitely one of the most unique. Its success has prompted further VietPride celebrations in other cities.

450 Good morning, queer Vietnam

▶ Hanoi Social Club, Hanoi, Vietnam

When to go: All year
Best for: Hanging with old and new friends

Vietnam's capital, Hanoi, is full of charm and has come a long way with its LGBTQ+ rights. It now recognizes the legal right to change genders, among other triumphs. One of the most popular LGBTQ-friendly spots is Hanoi Social Club. This is a trendy café with a rooftop bar, serving delicious food and cocktails in an openly comfortable space.

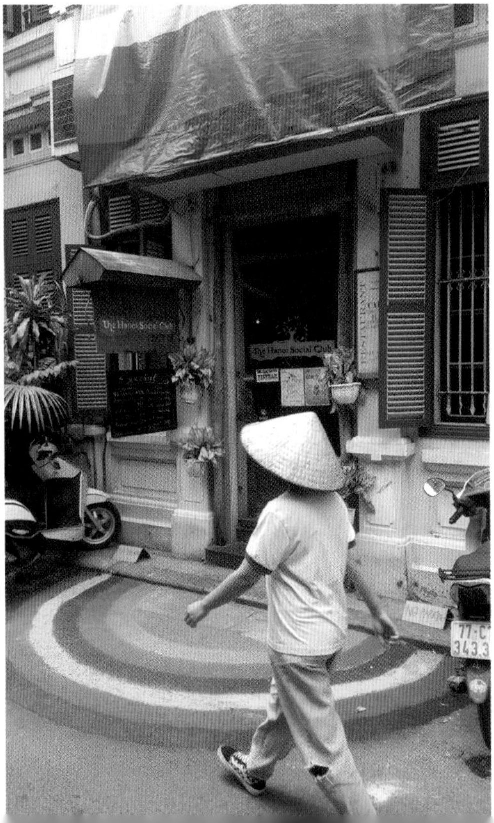

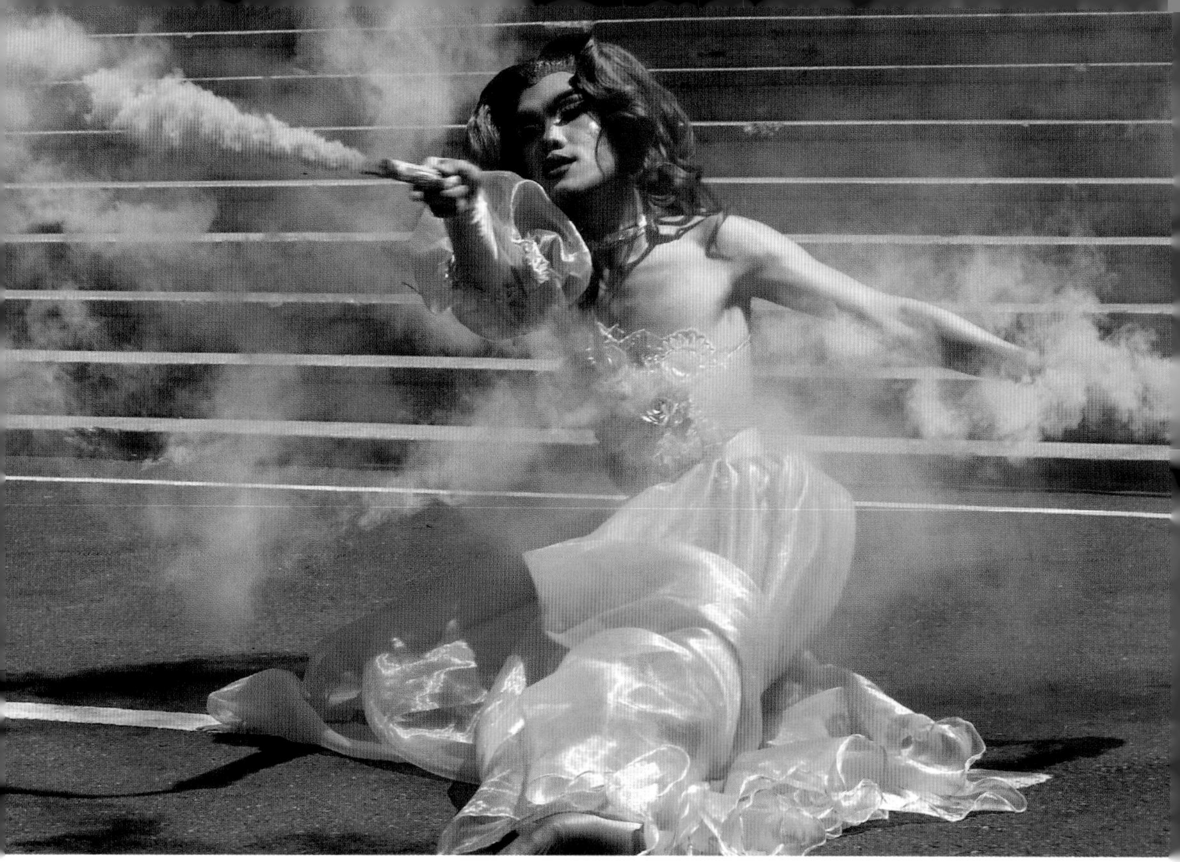

451 Nothing's vanilla in Manila

▲ ▶ Metro Manila Pride, Philippines

When to go: June
Best for: Filipino queerness

Metro Manila's queer scene is ever-changing. The Malate district was the original thriving queerborhood, but has now scattered to Cubao, Makati, and Taguig. The Metro Manila Pride March and Festival brings the Filipino LGBTQ+ community together with educational and arts programs, and a large Pride parade. Year-round, queer people connect at homey Commune Café and welcoming Food for the Gays by day. By night, head to the trendy Nectar Nightclub, iconic O Bar, or laid-back Fred's Revolucion.

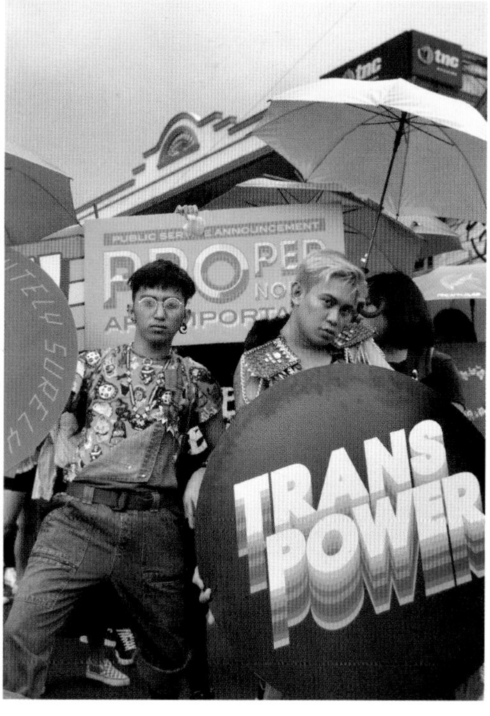

452 Join the dots

▼ Pink Dot Festival, Hong Lim Park, Singapore

When to go: June
Best for: Making a pink statement

The Pink Dot festival in Singapore began in 2009. LGBTQ+ people and allies gather at Speaker's Corner in Hong Lim Park; wearing pink, they stand together to create one huge, pink dot, visible from the sky. It's a *de facto* Pride celebration, even if it doesn't have "pride" in its name. The event has proved so popular that it has prompted similar events in cities around the world.

453 Tantalizing good times

Tantric Bar, Singapore

When to go: All year
Best for: Feeling tantric

Home of the Blue Spin, one of Singapore's most famous cocktails, Tantric Bar is the biggest and most popular gay bar in the city. Weekdays see the after-work crowd stopping by for a quick drink, while on Fridays and Saturdays everyone sweats it out on the dance floor.

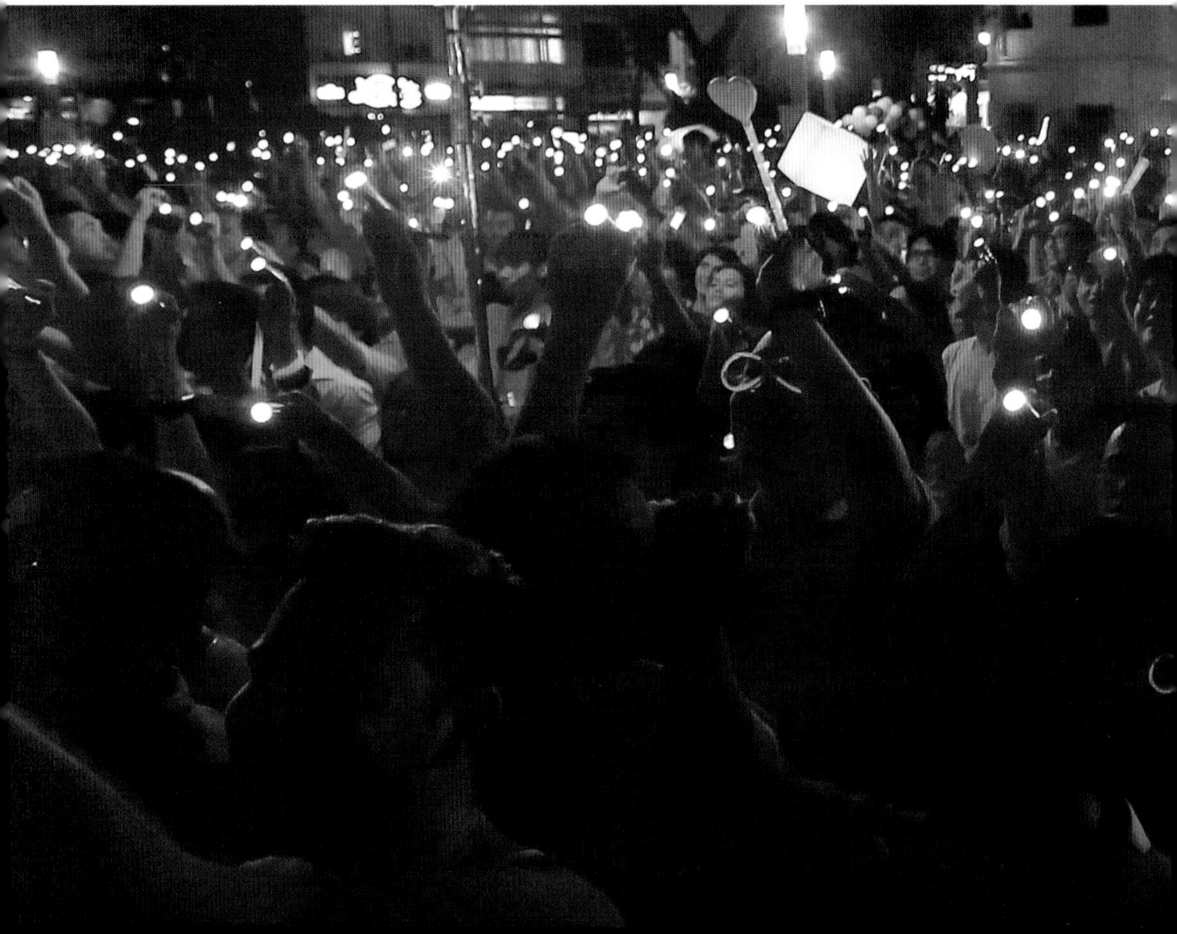

454 Have a riot

Riot Drag Show, Singapore

When to go: All year
Best for: Local drag and comedy

Hosted and produced by one of Singapore's biggest drag queens, Becca D'Bus, these weekly drag and burlesque shows are a celebration of wit, humor, queer joy, and sex appeal. Featuring a changing lineup of Singapore's most popular drag queens, performing dance numbers to pop songs with a tongue-in-cheek homage to queer life in Singapore, Riot is a great way to immerse yourself into local queer culture.

455 Dress up, go out

OUT Bar, Singapore

When to go: All year
Best for: Gay bar-hopping

If you are bar-hopping around Tanjong Pagar in Singapore, make sure OUT bar is on your list; a funky gay bar which regularly hosts events and performances by guest DJs. With decor inspired by Hollywood, it is a place to dress to the nines and have a good time.

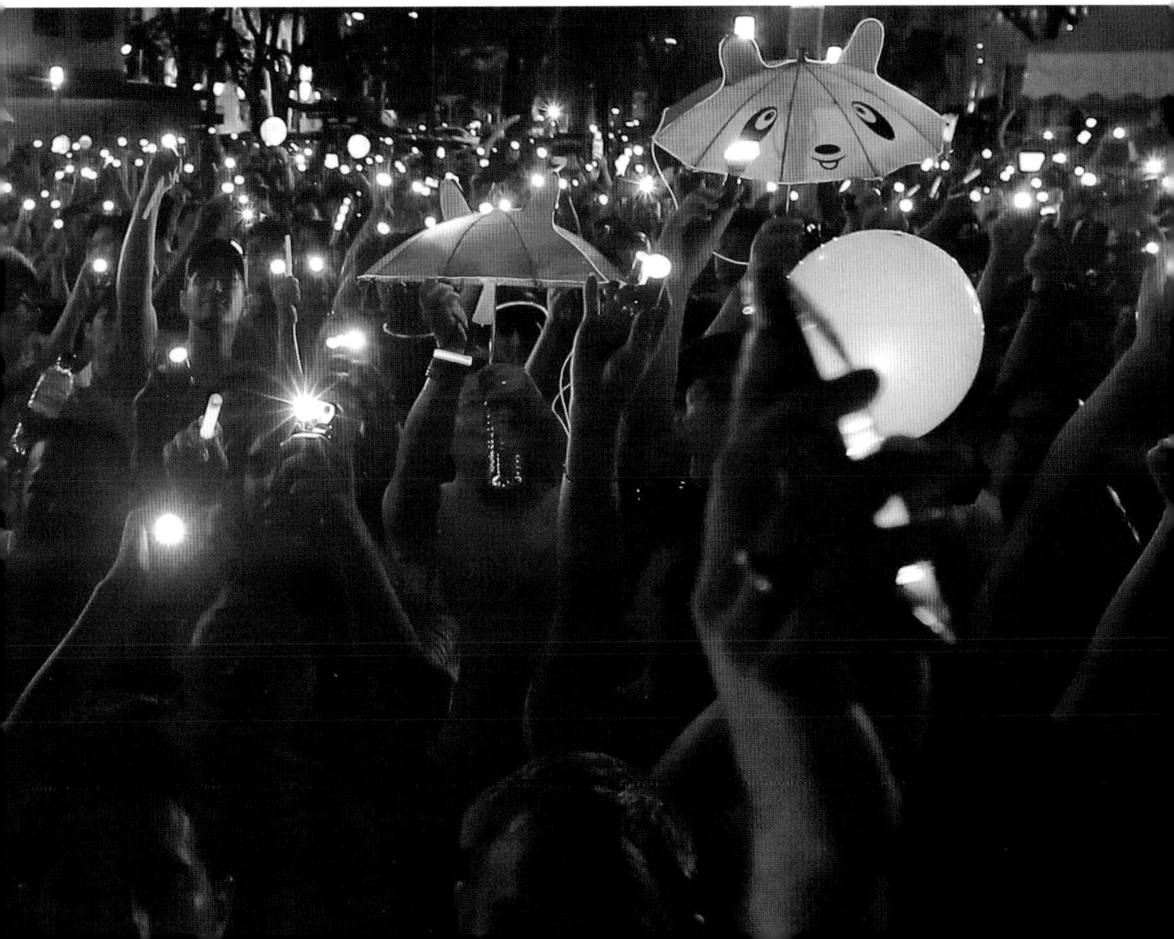

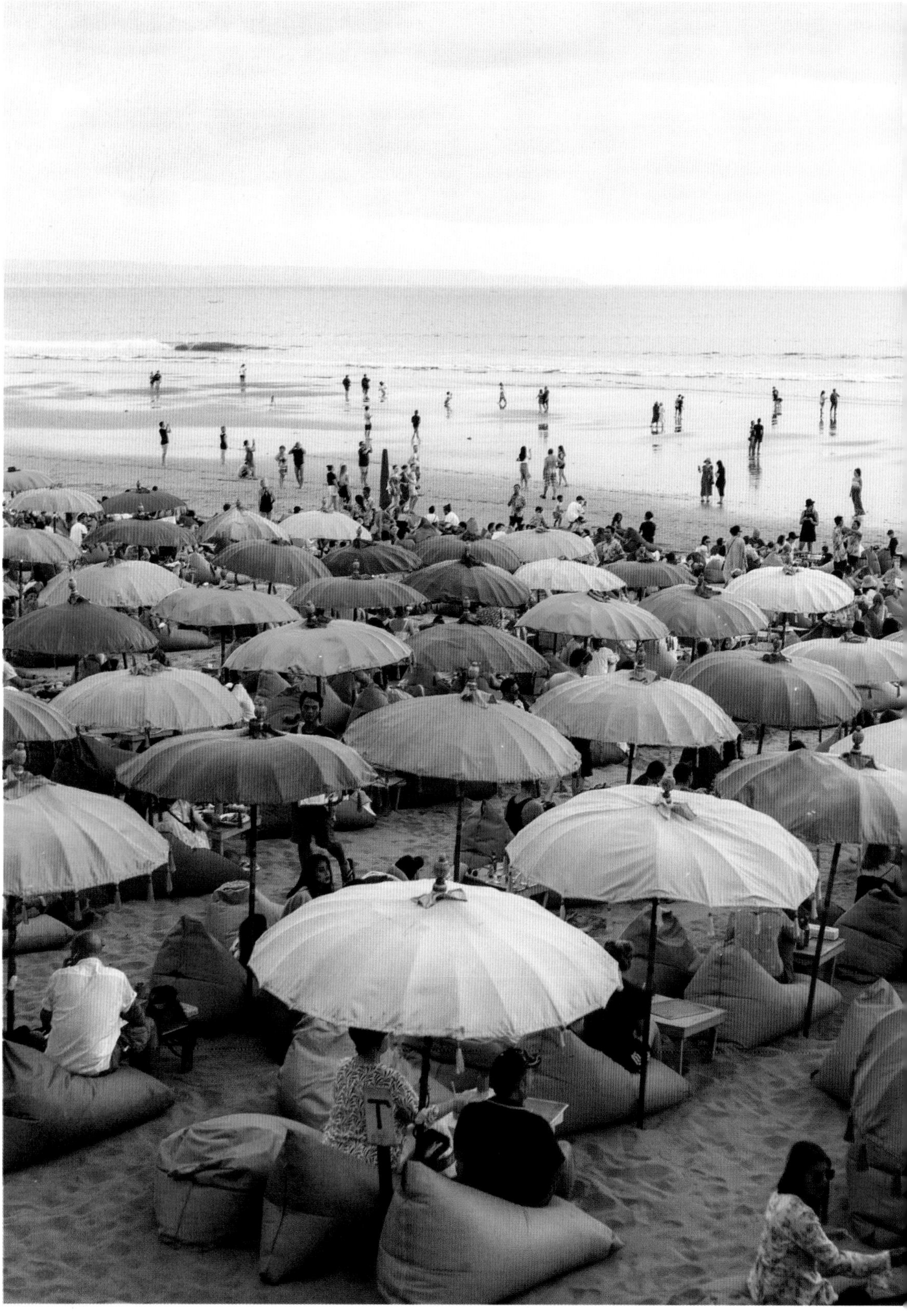

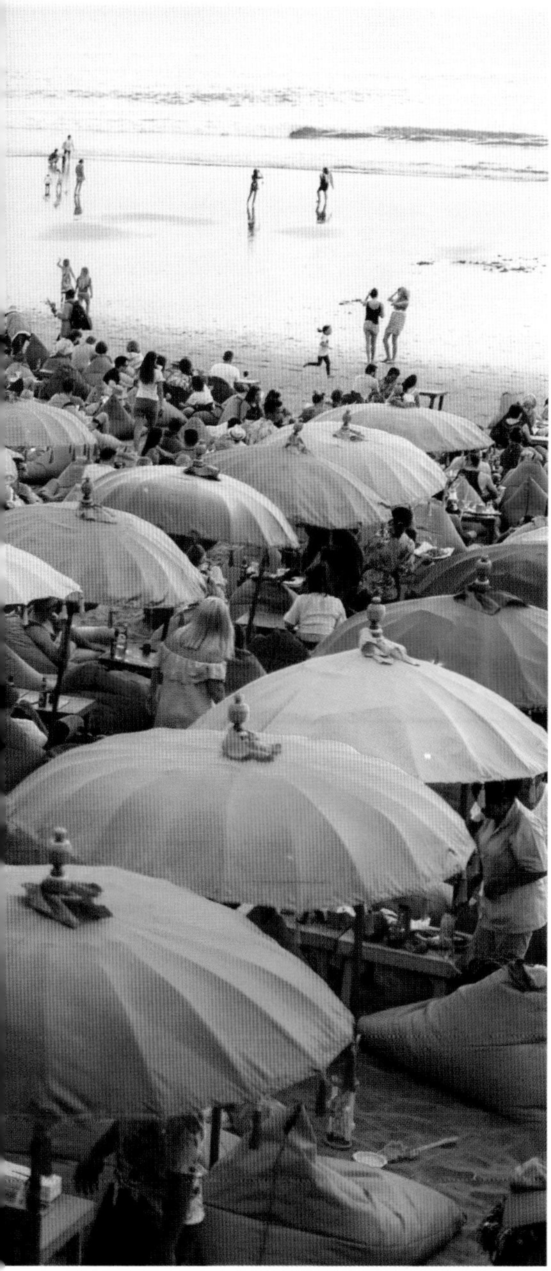

456 Seminal Seminyak

Seminyak, Bali

When to go: April to October
Best for: Peace and party

Famous for its cultural and natural beauty, Bali—locally dubbed "the Island of the Gods"—is loved by many. Home to terraced rice fields, active volcanoes, diverse beaches, cultural temples, and countless waterfalls, it's a dream destination for nearly every traveler, with affordable options for low-budget backpackers and high-end offerings for travelers wanting to go all out. Contrary to the rest of Indonesia, Bali is a relatively liberal, queer bubble, thanks to its Hindu culture and tourism-dependent economy. Visit sophisticated Seminyak in the southwest of the island for the best beach bars and clubs, cute cafés, chic boutiques, relaxing spas, and Bali's gay street, Jalan Camplung Tanduk. Seminyak's chill beach vibe characterizes its vibrant nightlife. In the north, busy gay-owned restaurant La Lucciola sits on one of the best beaches, close to queer-friendly Desa Potato Head and Ku De Ta in Canggu. Continue the night at Jalan Camplung Tanduk, home to many gay bars and clubs, including the legendary Mixwell, F Bar, and Bali Joe.

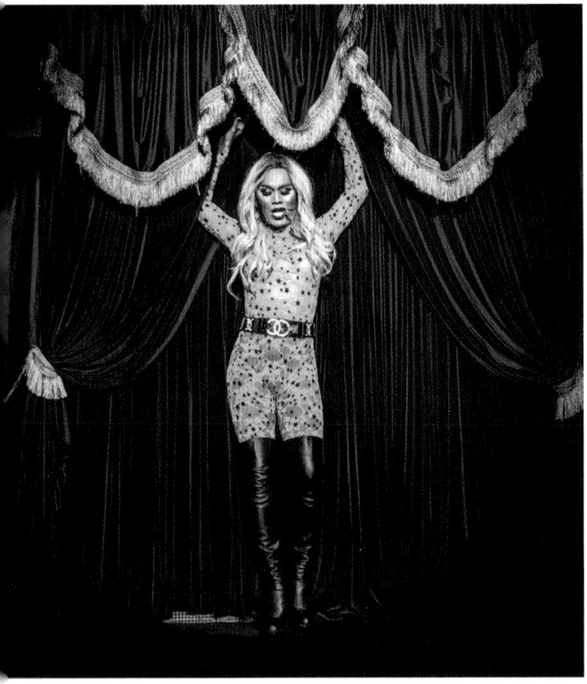

457 In the mix

◀ Mixwell Bar, Seminyak, Bali, Indonesia

When to go: All year
Best for: Meeting others

With mixed drinks, mixed music, and a mixed crowd, Mixwell Bar is a popular LGBTQ+ spot on Camplung Tanduk Street in Seminyak. With go-go boys and diva performers, there's something for everyone at the nightly shows at this bar, which is equally as popular with queer locals as with tourists.

458 Unwind and undress

Bali au Naturel, Bali, Indonesia

When to go: All year
Best for: Nude bathing in the tropics

Escape the partying and tourist haunts and instead head to this nudist resort in northern Bali. Located on the beachfront, Bali au Naturel invites guests to bathe and lounge nude around their shared garden and living area, two outdoor pools, gym, and waterfront restaurant. Attracting bounteous gay men, this gay-owned resort is welcome to all looking to unwind and undress in a remote paradise.

459 Dance like an icon

Club Icon, Guam

When to go: January to June
Best for: Sunsets

In the heart of Guam's tourism industry, Tamuning village, you'll find the most stunning beaches, lavish accommodation, a palm-tree-lined boulevard, and vibrant nightlife spots. Queer-friendly Guam Beach Bar is the best place to catch a sunset while enjoying cocktails and mouthwatering food, and the nights never end at the island's biggest club, The Globe, which hosts queer parties during Guam Pride in June. The highlight of Guam's queer scene is Club Icon, with its karaoke nights, and Gender Bender Thursdays with fabulous drag shows.

460 Paradise in the Pacific?

▼ Guam

When to go: January to June
Best for: A little bit of everything

In the Pacific Ocean—closer to Japan than to the United States—the blissful US Territory of Guam is famed for its warm, hospitable Håfa Adai spirit. The Indigenous people of Guam, CHamoru, have a four-millennia-long history of LGBTQ+ acceptance. Guam was also the first U.S. territory to legalize egalitarian marriage in 2015 and elect a female governor, out gay vice governor, and transgender woman to government, in 2018. With breathtaking wedding venues along its coastline, honeymoon-perfect resorts, and unique adventure opportunities, Guam might be the ultimate paradise island for queer lovers. Relax on the pristine beaches, explore the underwater world, hike magnificent trails full of waterfalls, or shop tax-free—Guam offers something for everyone.

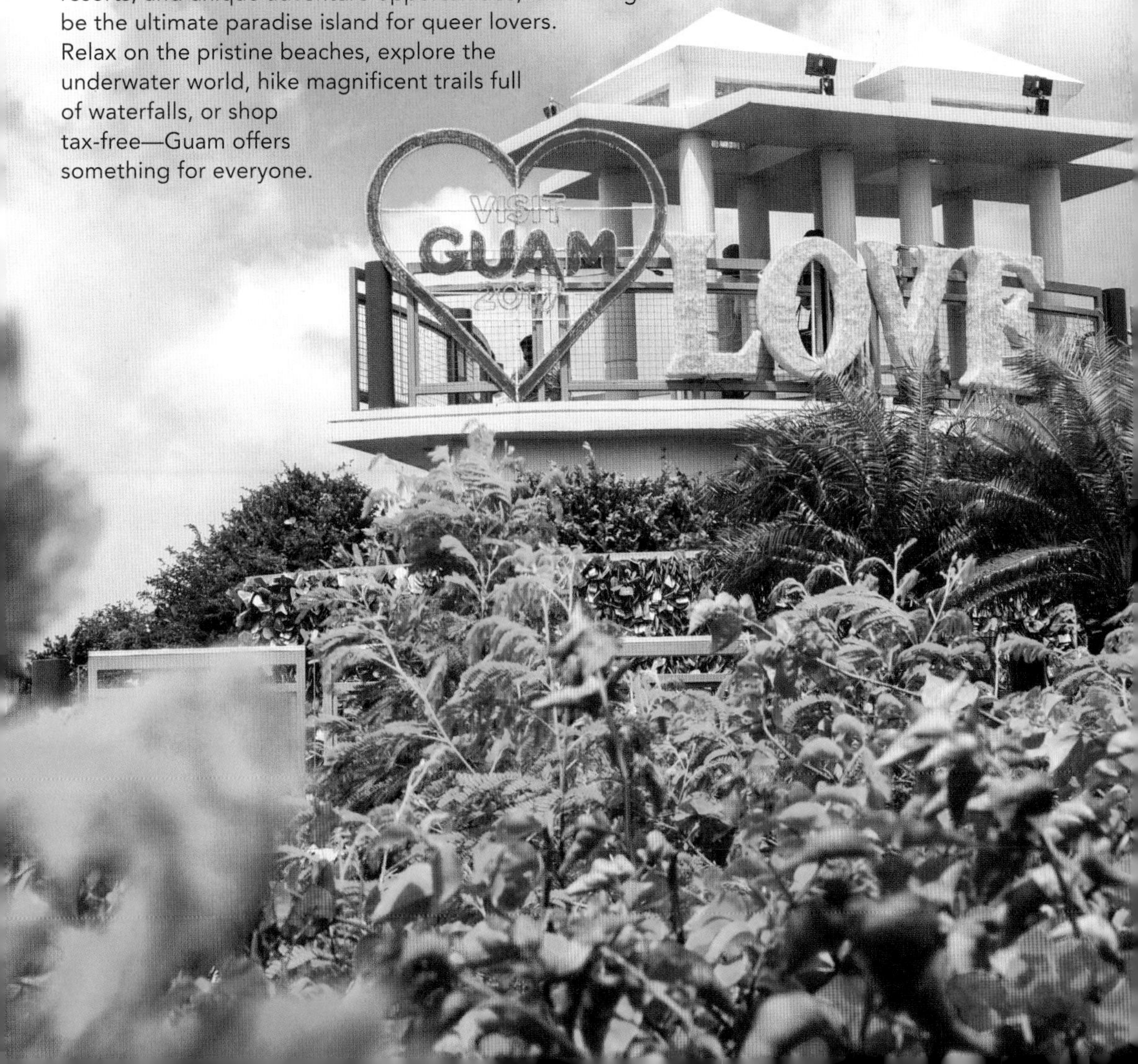

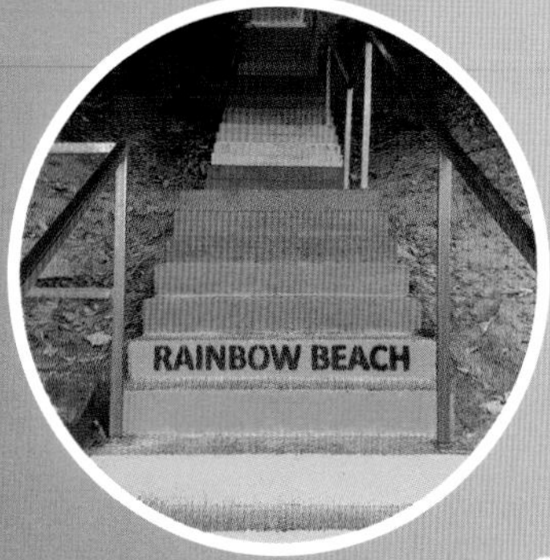
RAINBOW BEACH

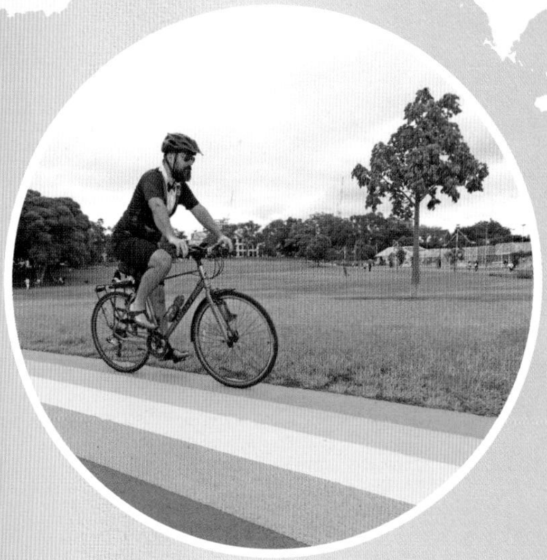

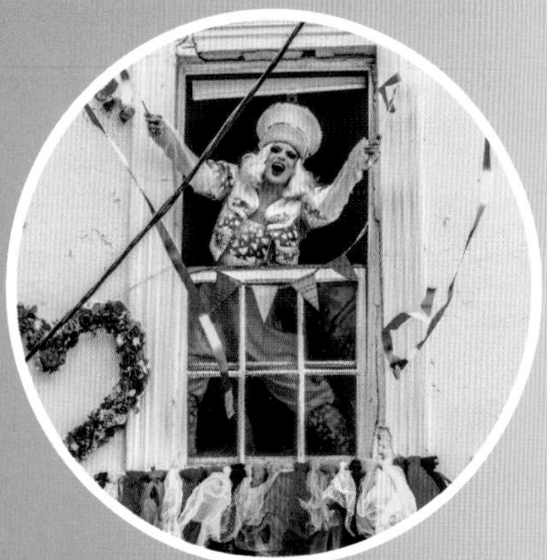

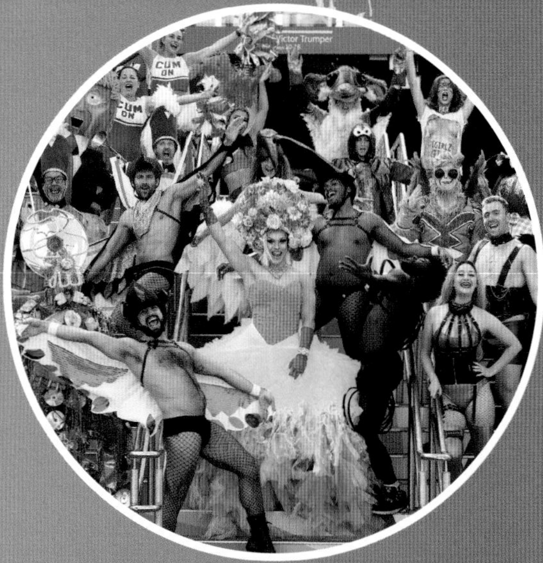

CHAPTER FIVE

AUSTRALASIA

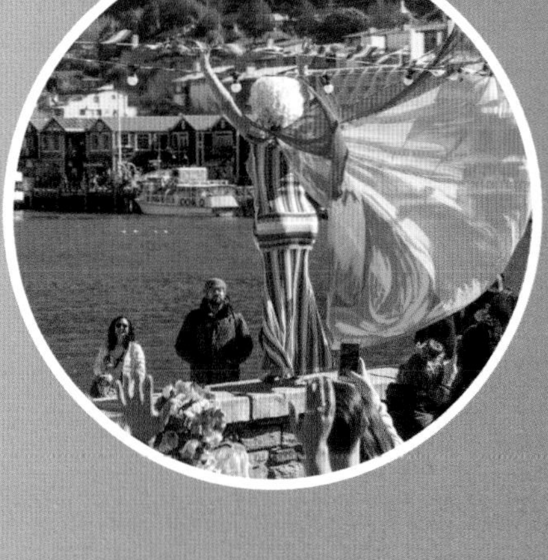

461 That's a-Bora-Bora-ble

▼ French Polynesia

When to go: May to October
Best for: Revitalizing romance

If the cishets have the Maldives, the queer folk have French Polynesia. This archipelago of over one hundred islands is popular among LGBTQ+ travelers because of both the French equality rights and the ancient culture of Māhū, a divine gender that goes beyond the Western gender binary. The islands aren't known for their thriving nightlife scene, although there are a few welcoming venues in the capital Papeete. Instead, French Polynesia is famed for its isolation, and grandeur. The idyllic volcanic islands of Tahiti, Moorea, Taha'a, and Bora Bora are the best places for a romantic getaway. Beaches with soft white sand, palm trees, and lush volcanic landscapes create a stunning tropical vibe. Stay in an overwater bungalow ringed by the bluer-than-blue Pacific, and admire the jaw-dropping views, including the colorful life under the sea.

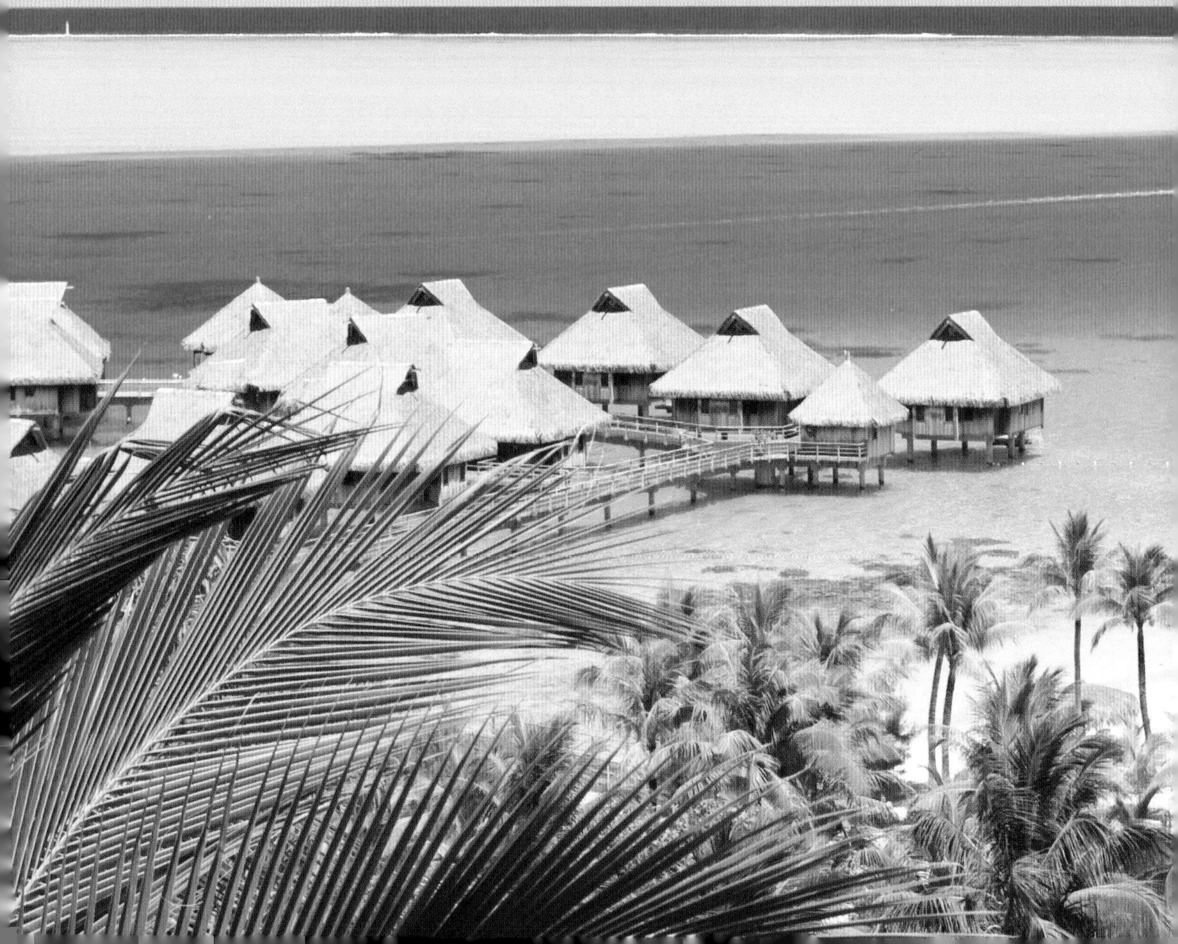

462 Nourishing Nouméa

Nouméa, New Caledonia

When to go: May to October
Best for: Vitamin sea

About 900 mi/1450 km east of Australia, you can find the French Territory of New Caledonia (Kanaky) in the Coral Sea. In the cosmopolitan capital of Nouméa, visit the Tjibaou Cultural Center—named after the independence movement leader—and learn about the archipelago's Indigenous Kanak people. Enjoy the city's idyllic beaches, relaxed atmosphere, and emerging LGBTQ+ scene at welcoming venues XO Club, MV Lounge, and La Bodega del Mar. Or join the colorful Nouméa Carnival in September.

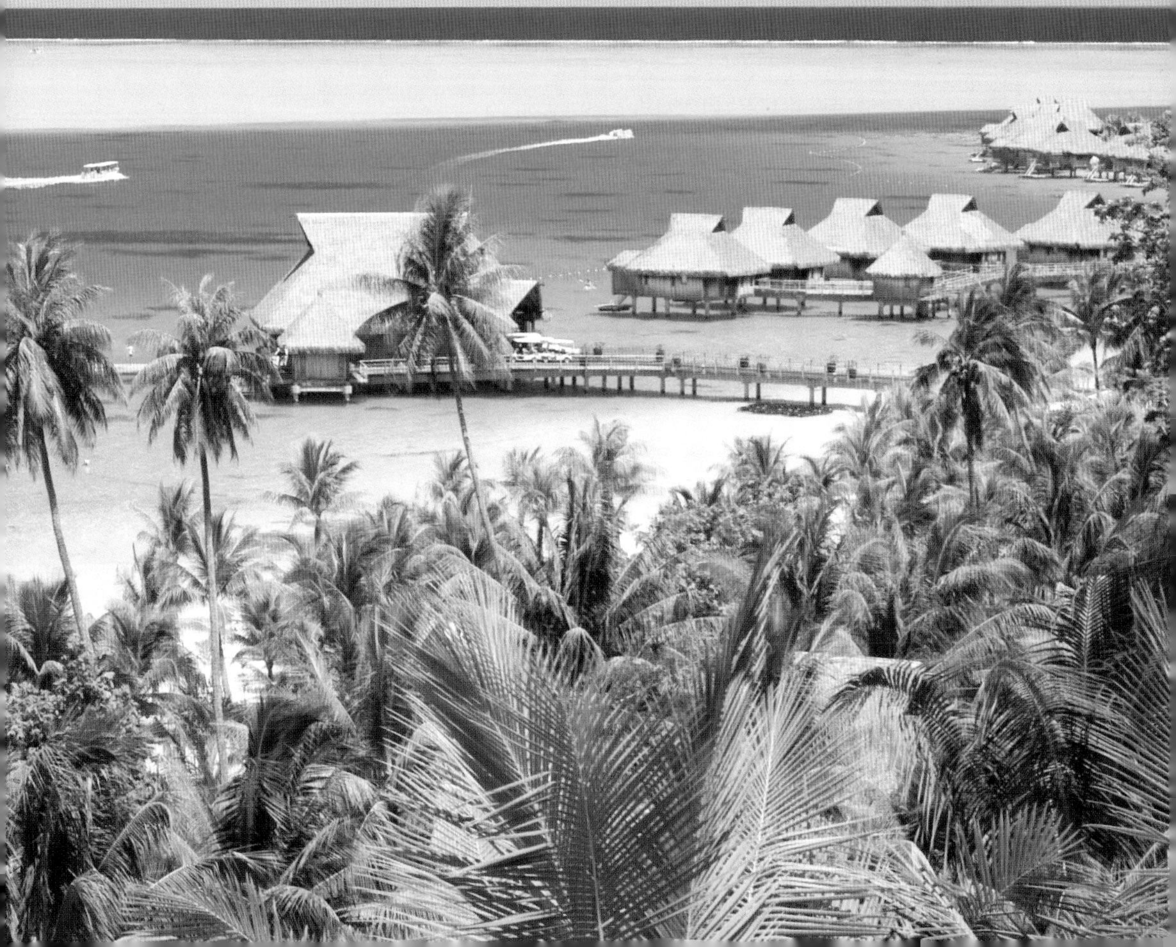

463 New on the scene

▶ New Caledonia

When to go: May to October
Best for: Tropical state of mind

Although the archipelago of New Caledonia isn't outspokenly queer, and modesty is a key feature of the local culture, the LGBTQ+ scene is increasing. With France's legalization of marriage equality in 2013, New Caledonia has become an increasingly popular wedding and honeymoon destination for all couples. The Loyalty Islands Lifou (Drehu), Maré (Nengone), and Ouvéa (Iaaï), and Isle of Pines (Kunyié) are the perfect places to enjoy pristine beaches, diverse and colorful marine life, and well-preserved South Pacific traditions. Join one of the islands' cultural festivals and try *bougna*, possibly the most iconic Kanak meal. And whether you're looking for luxurious resorts for all-day chilling or somewhere to camp below the starry sky and get active by day, these islands offer something for you.

464 Good connections

Connections, Perth, Australia

When to go: Wednesday to Saturday
Best for: Partying in history

Connections is the oldest LGBTQ+ nightclub in Australia, and possibly the southern hemisphere. It originated in 1975 as a safe space for then-illegal queer relationships to gather, and all cameras were banned inside its walls for its first 14 years. Now, more than 40 years later the nightclub still stands in the same venue with the same name it began with. Some of the original patrons still visit, too!

465 Life on the open road

Van Dykes, Australia

When to go: Check the Facebook group
Best for: Camping

Van Dykes is a Facebook group aimed at anyone who identifies as a lesbian or queer in Australia and also loves the outdoors and camping. The group hosts regular meetups across Australia, and provides a welcome space for the community to seek fellow adventurers and advice for van-life living.

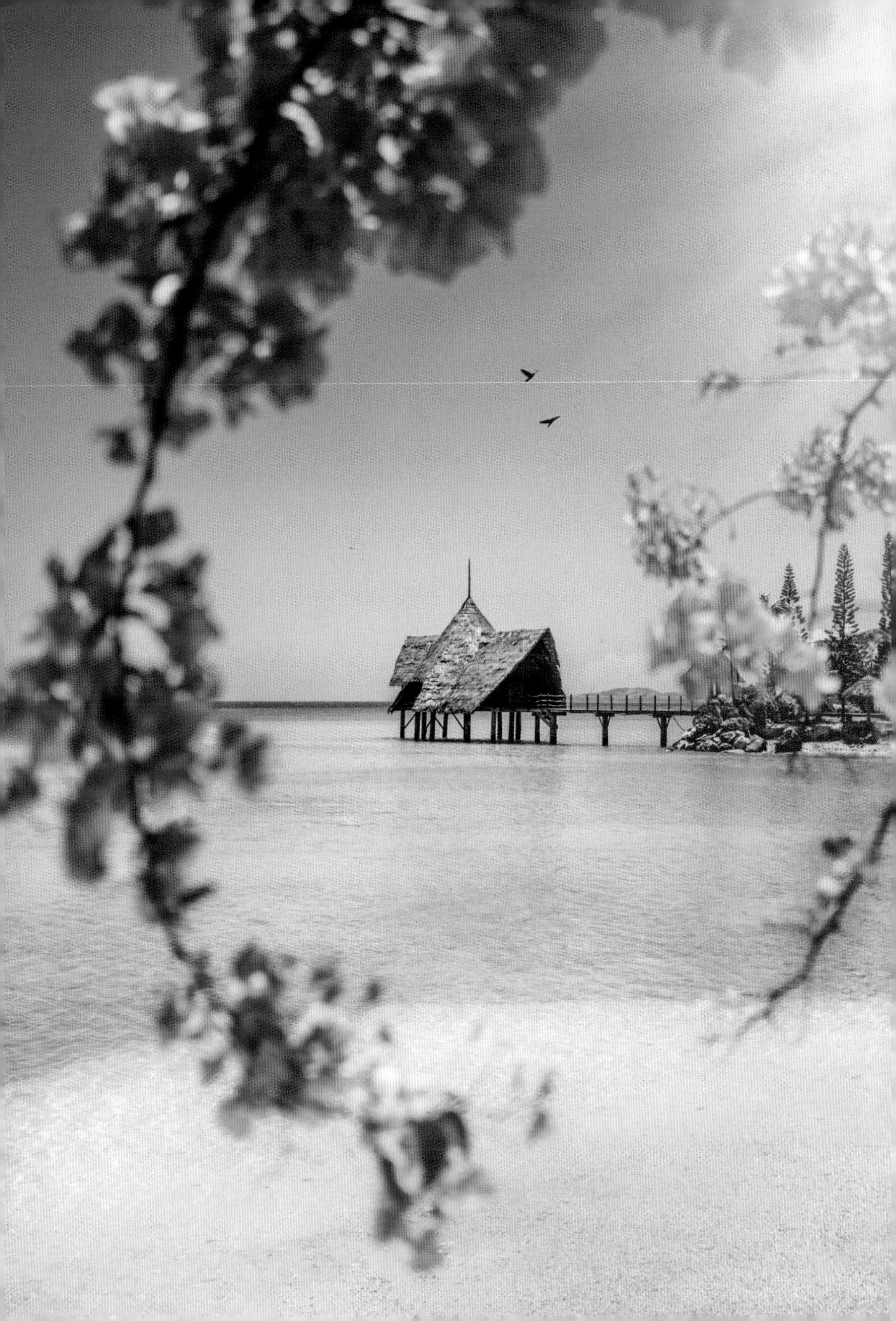

466 A town like Alice

▼ Alice Springs, Australia

When to go: All year
Best for: Finding queer culture in the outback

Alice Springs is home to one of the largest communities of lesbians per capita in the world. Hundreds of queer women have made Alice Springs their home, after a protest in 1983 led them to this outback town in Central Australia, near to Uluru and the Macdonnell Ranges. It is a queer hub filled with welcoming bars and its very own FABAlice Pride festival held in March every year.

467 What a feast

Feast Festival, Adelaide, Australia

When to go: November
Best for: Expression through art and culture

South Australia is also known as the "Festival State," as it has so many events held throughout the year. One such event is Feast Festival, which is held in the state's capital, Adelaide. This LGBTQ+ Arts and Cultural Festival is held over the course of a month and has been running since 1997. The program is always jam-packed with comedy, workshops, theater, cabaret, and more.

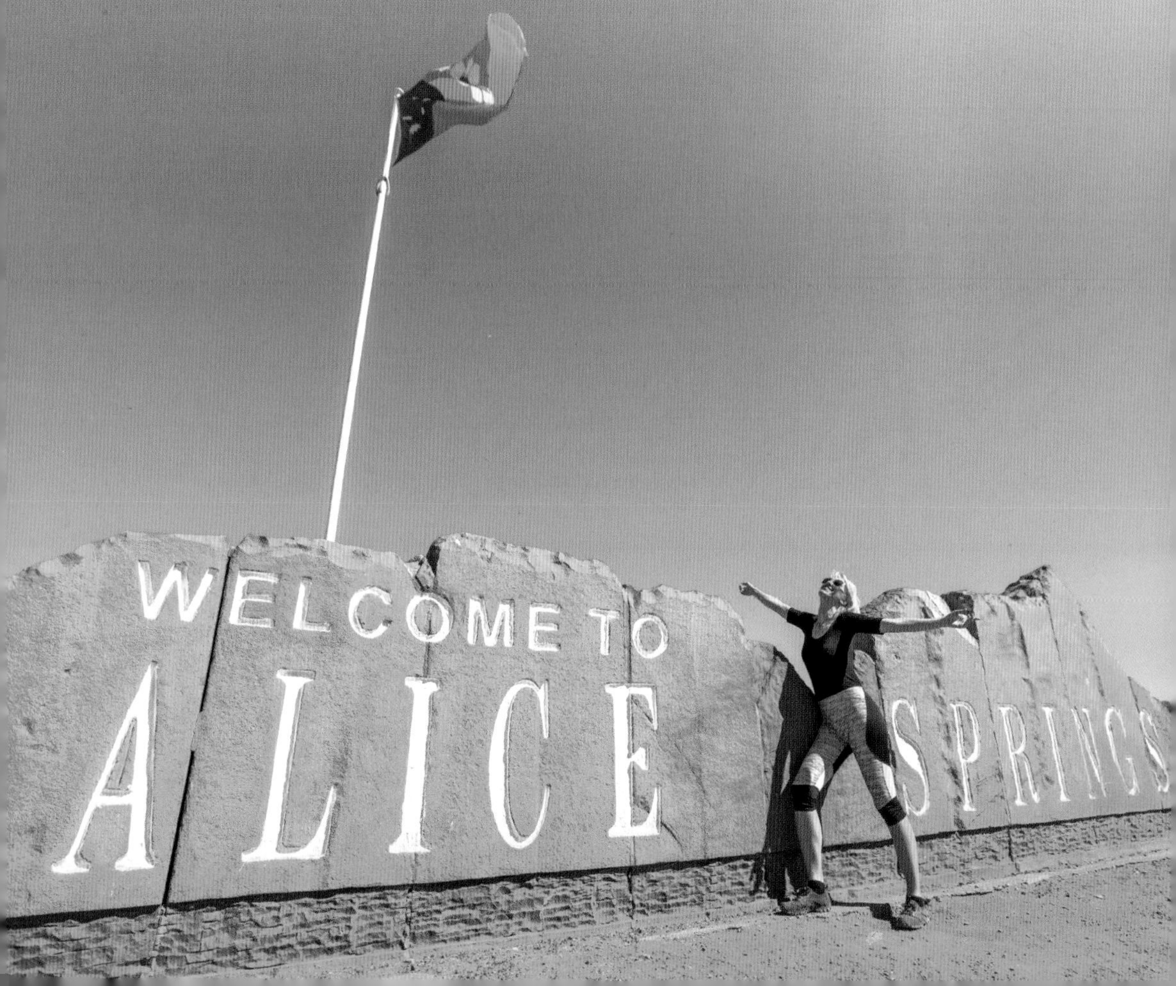

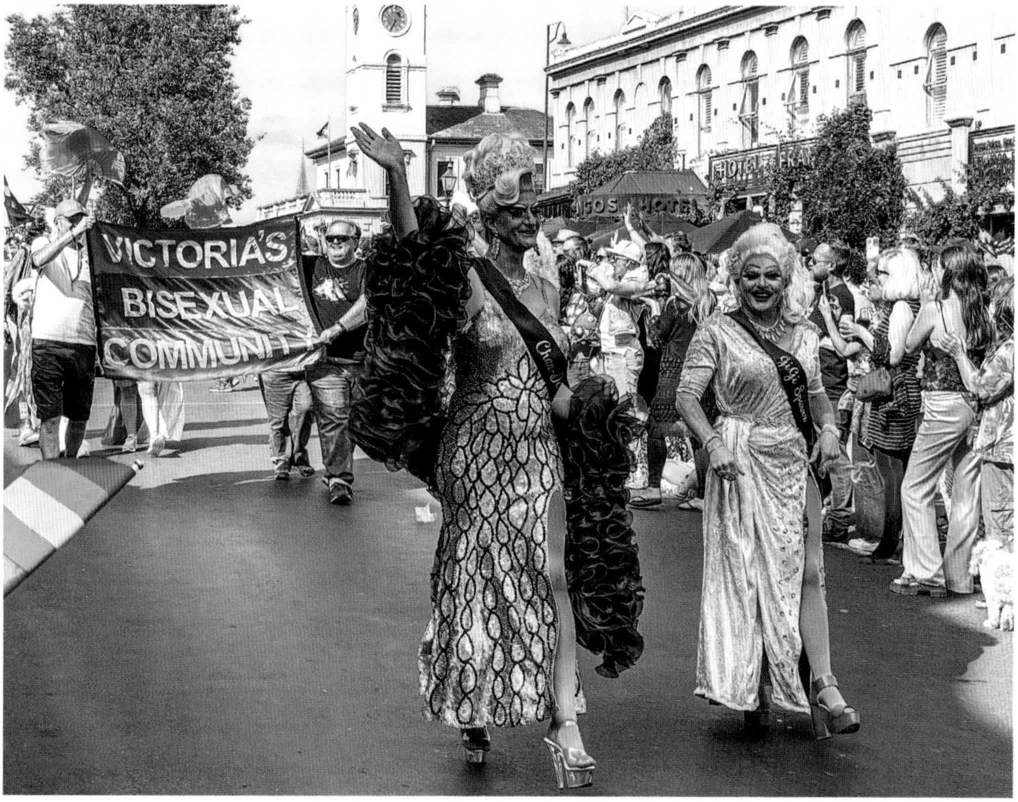

468 The snow must go on

Australia Gay Ski Week, Falls Creek Resort, Victoria, Australia

When to go: September
Best for: Slope fun

Based at Falls Creek Resort, Victoria, Australia's Gay Ski Week is a huge festival of queerness in a unique ice-cold setting. Events throughout the week include cocktails, karaoke, late-night cabaret lounge, and a Falls Creek Pride event.

469 Small place, big heart

▲ ChillOut Festival, Daylesford, Victoria, Australia

When to go: March
Best for: Inclusivity in an unexpected place

With a population of around 2,500 people, Daylesford—lovingly nicknamed Gaylesford—is not the sort of place where you would necesssarily expect a big LGBTQ+ event. However, this idyllic lakeside spa-town is very inclusive and has hosted the ChillOut Festival for more than 25 years, with activities including tree planting, parades, bush dances, shows, picnics, and more.

470 Outrageous outback

▼ Broken Hill, New South Wales, Australia

When to go: September
Best for: Camping it up

The Australian movie, *The Adventures of Priscilla, Queen of the Desert*, proved an unexpected and enduring worldwide hit following its release in 1994. The tale of three Sydney-based drag queens on a road trip across the outback later spawned a hit stage musical … and its own annual tribute gathering. The aptly titled Broken Heel Festival is a five-day event that takes place in and around the Palace Hotel, which featured in the movie. You'll find it in the small town of Broken Hill, 715 mi/1,150 km west of Sydney or 310 mi/500 km from Adelaide. Expect five days of cabaret, a drag parade through the town, plenty of food, cocktails, and glamping opportunities, and the chance to enjoy your own unique, outback adventure, with added glitter and sparkle.

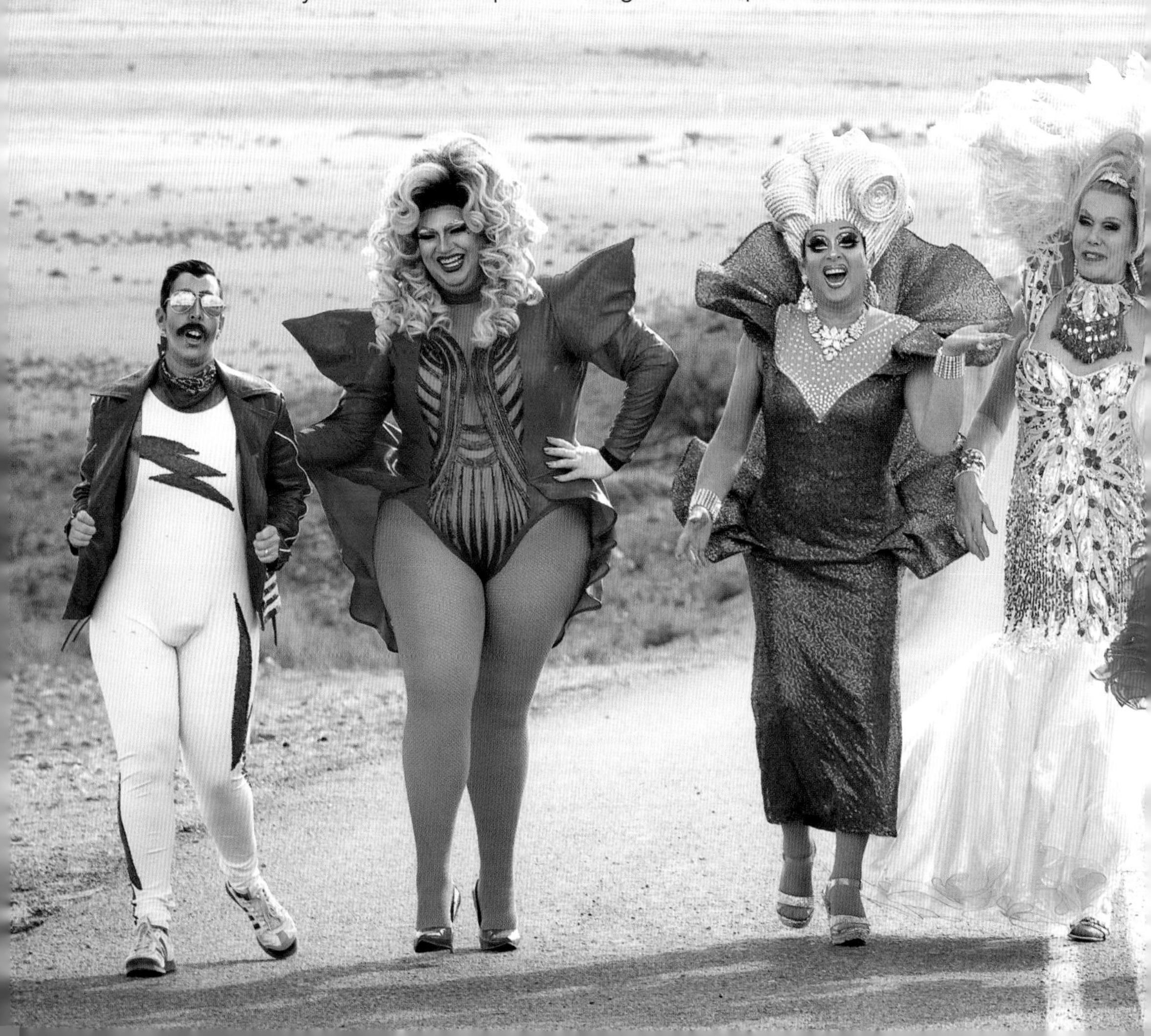

471 Brokeback Melbourne

Melbourne Queer Film Festival, Australia

When to go: November
Best for: Being educated and entertained

With more than 140 showings of LGBTQ+ movies, Melbourne Queer Film Festival is the biggest queer film festival in the southern hemisphere, as well as the oldest. The festival celebrated 30 years in 2020, after starting out in the back room of Melbourne's queer bookstore Hares and Hyenas. In addition to the movies, there are Q&A panels with discussions of LGBTQ+ issues.

472 A real page turner

Hares and Hyenas, Melbourne, Australia

When to go: All year
Best for: Getting lost in books

Based inside the Victorian Pride Centre in Melbourne, this unique bookstore offers an all-queer selection of fiction, nonfiction, coffee-table books, erotica, and magazines. Whether you're looking for coming-out self-help or for non-binary or transgender literature, you'll find it here.

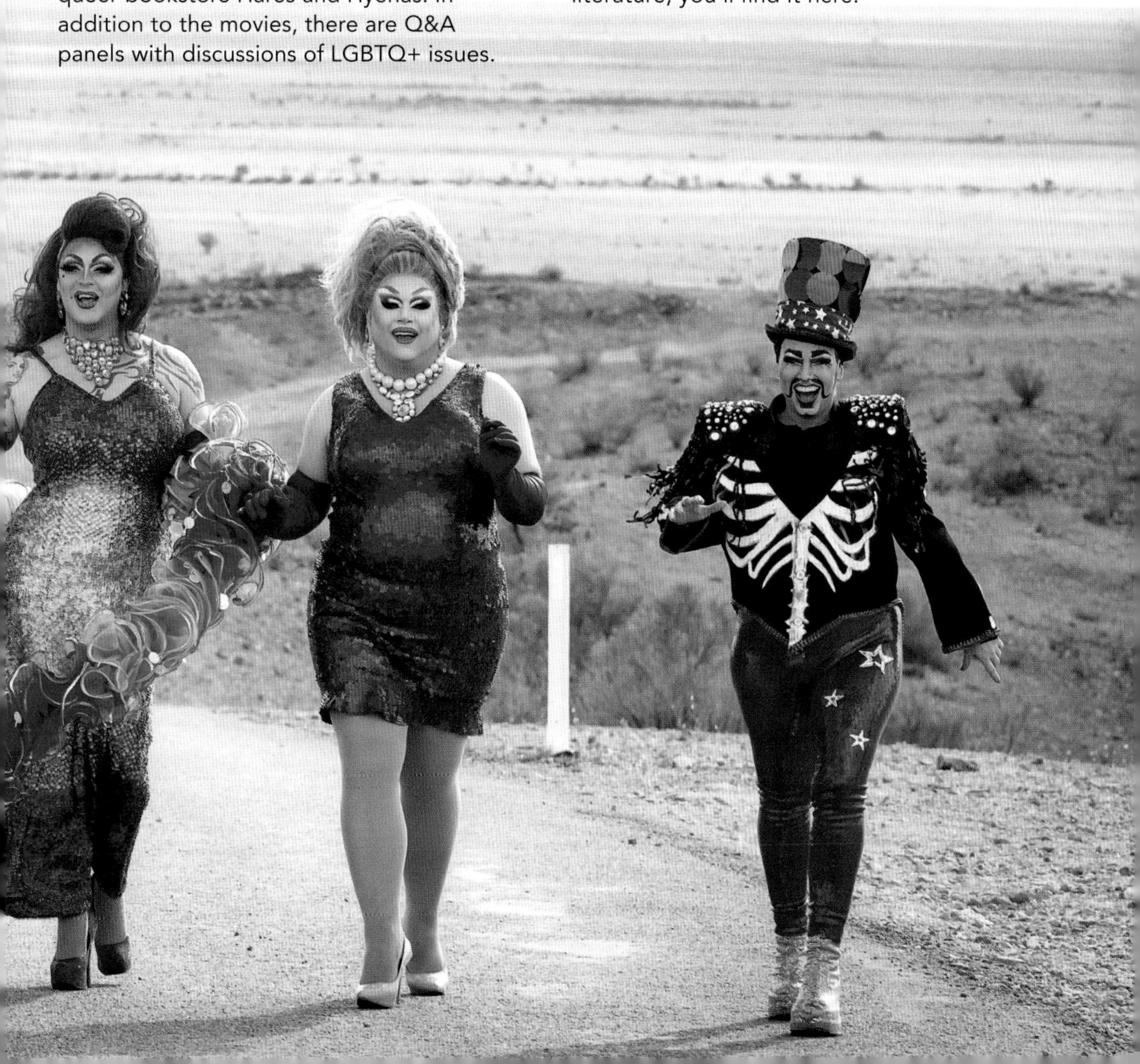

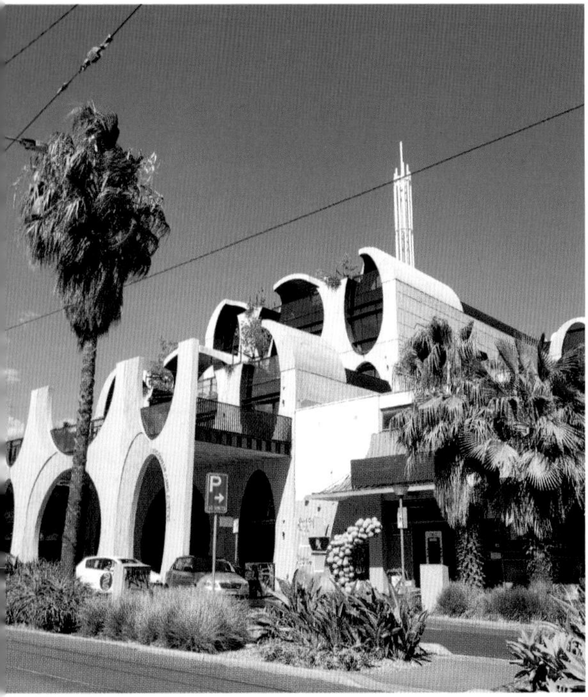

473 **Pride by design**

◀ ▼ Victorian Pride Centre, St. Kilda, Melbourne, Australia

When to go: All year
Best for: A warm welcome in a cool environment

The Victorian Pride Centre in Melbourne opened its doors for the first time in July 2021. Although there are other LGBTQ+ centers in Australia, they usually take up space in old buildings. This is the country's first purpose-built LGBTQ+ center designed and built from scratch and the architecture is eye-catching. Inside, the center hosts numerous events and services, and works to amplify LGBTQ+ voices.

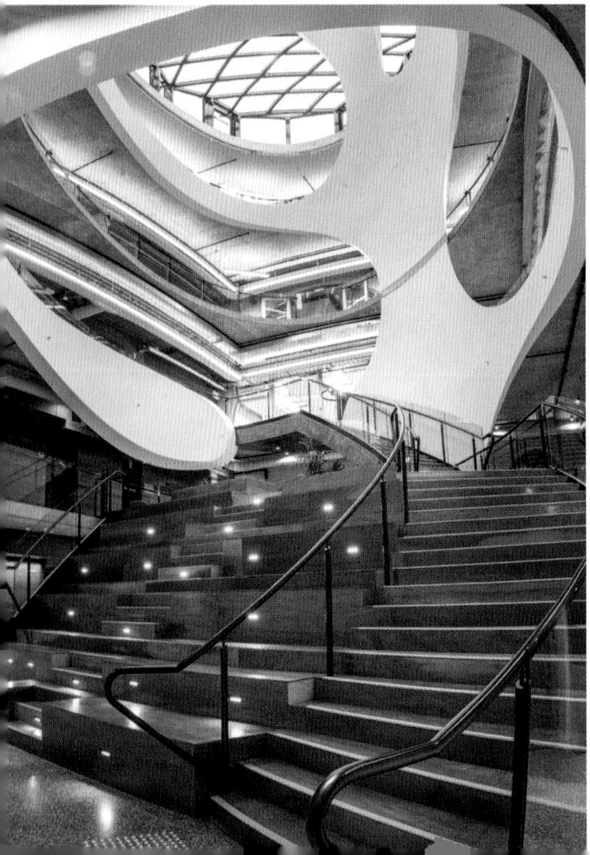

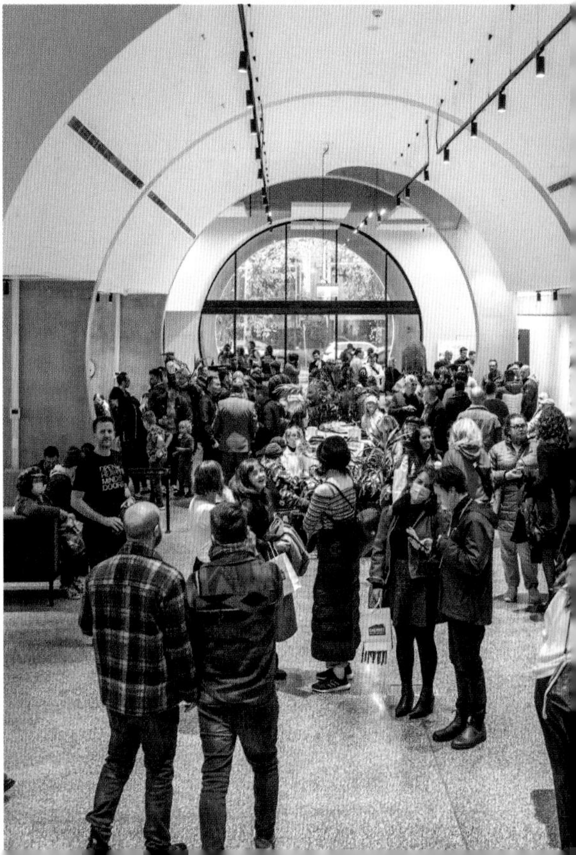

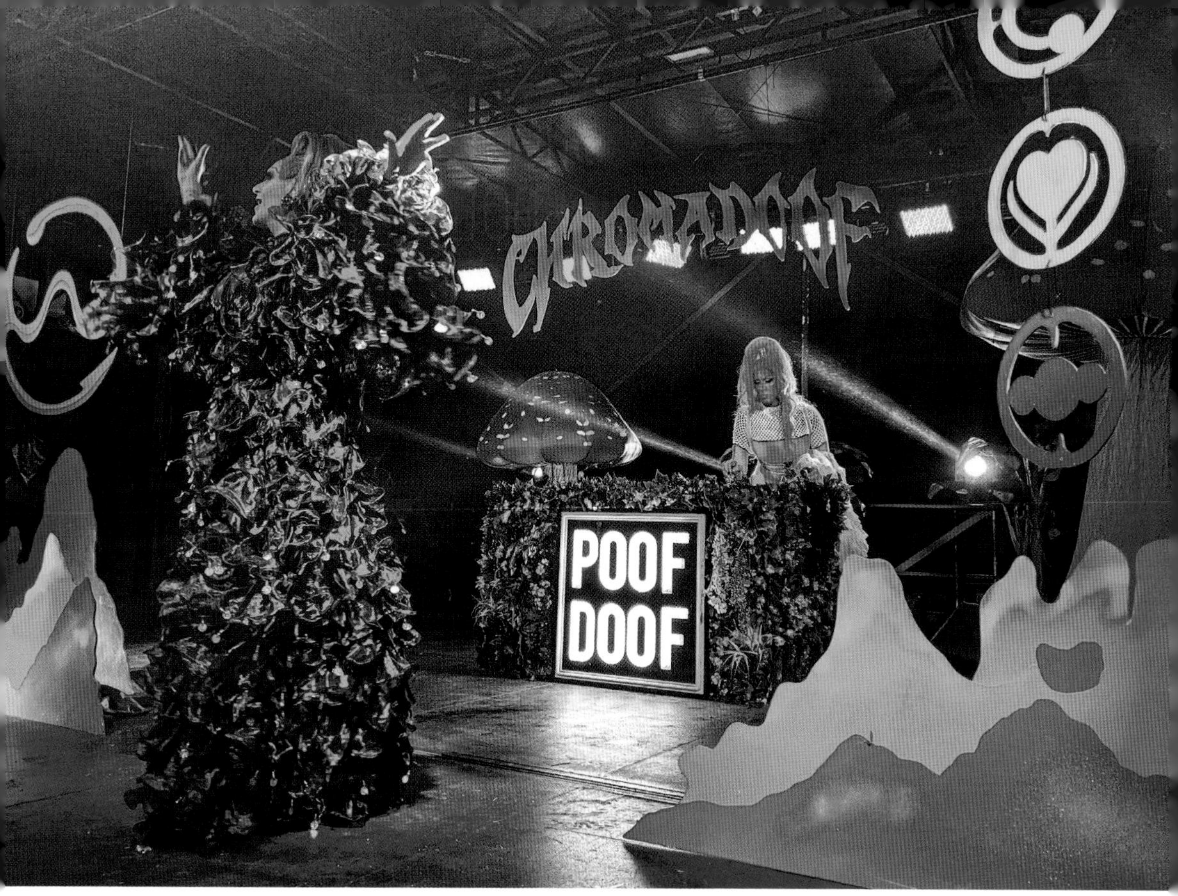

474 Putting the "poof" in doof

▲ Poof Doof, Australia

When to go: All year
Best for: Queer parties

A large party is known as a "doof" in Australia, and so "Poof Doof" is a fun LGBTQ+ spin on this favored Australian pastime. Poof Doof events are held in Melbourne, Sydney, and across the country. Drag queens will welcome you in and host performances, while electro house beats keep your feet moving all night long.

475 Keeping it reel

Queer Melbourne Stitch 'n' Bitch, Australia

When to go: Alternate Sundays
Best for: Knitters and crocheters

Every other Sunday, queer bookstore Hares & Hyenas hosts a get-together for those in the LGBTQ+ community who are passionate about—or keen to learn more about—all forms of needlework, while enjoying a good old-fashioned natter.

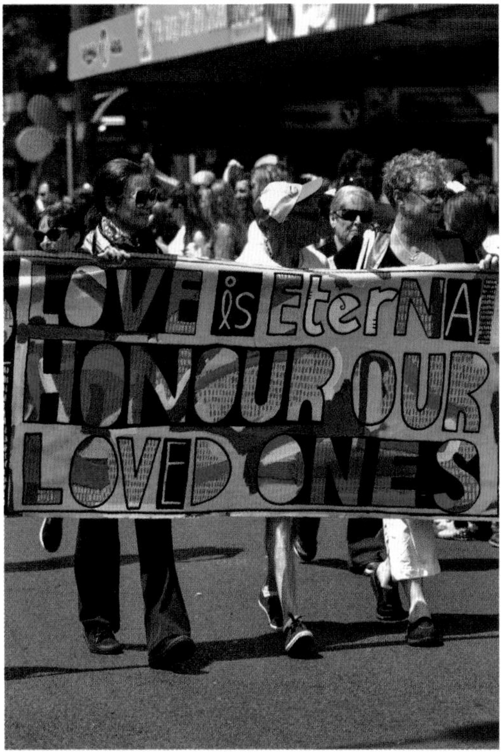
LOVE is
HONOUR OUR
LOVED ONES

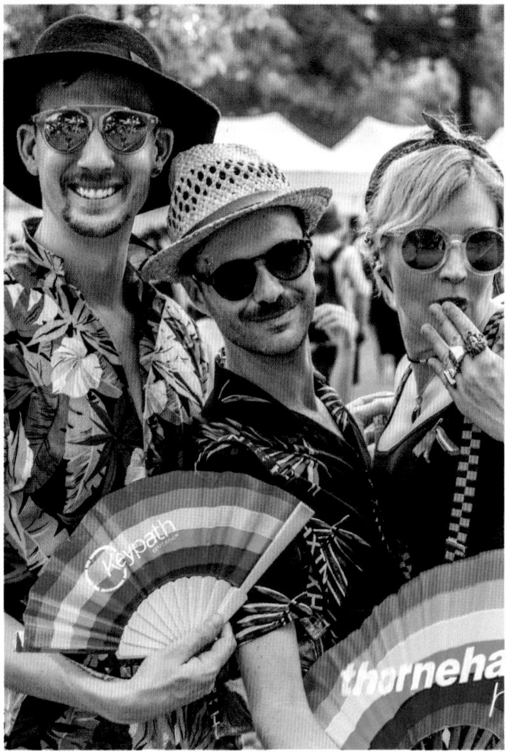
Keypath

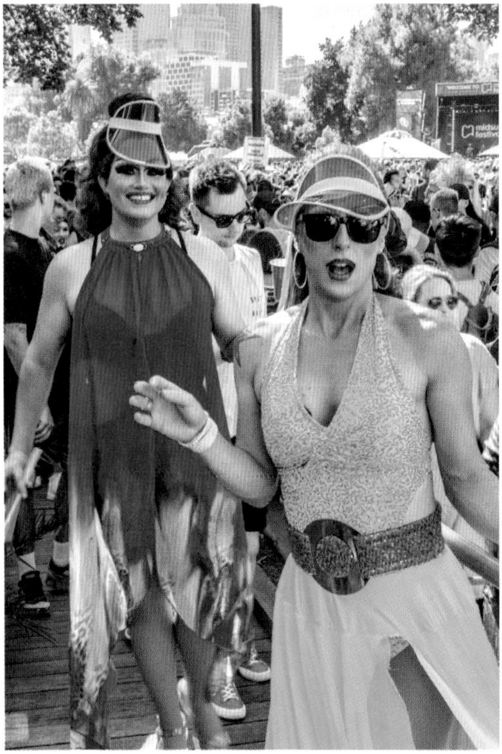

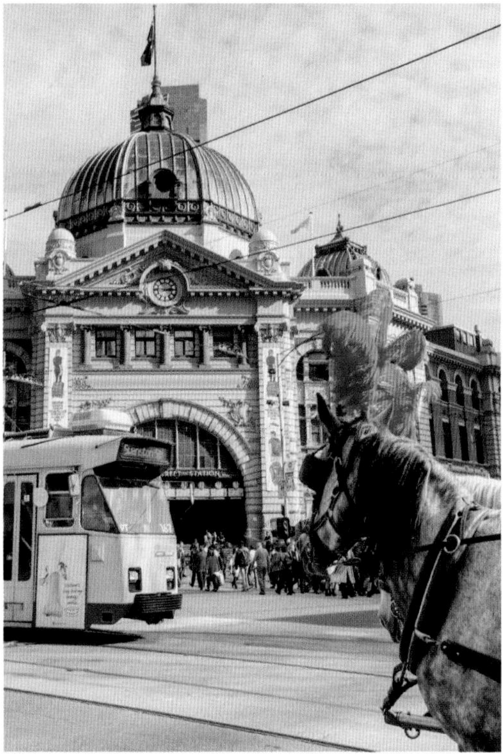

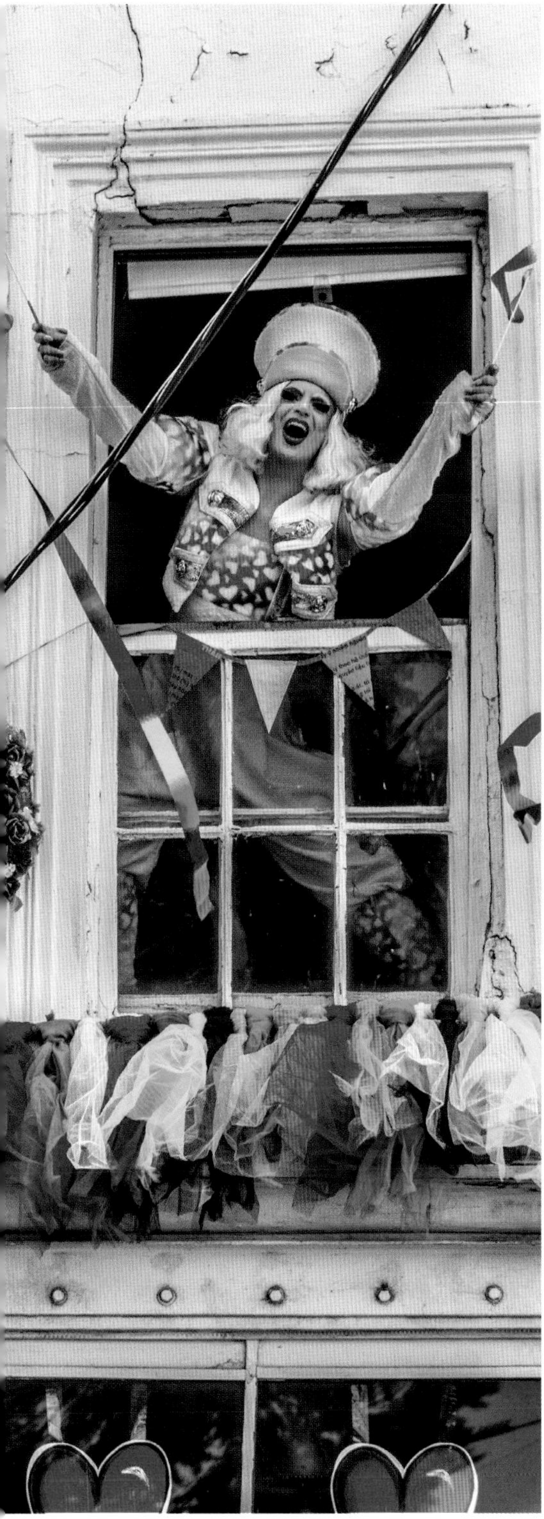

476 The one not to be missed

Midsumma Festival, Melbourne, Australia

When to go: January to February
Best for: Queer summer vibes and trailblazing queer art

An explosion of queer art fills Melbourne for three weeks each summer during its annual Midsumma Festival. Spread over one hundred venues and involving more than five thousand culture-makers, the Midsumma Festival delights with its program of visual arts, live music, spoken word, cabaret, theater, film, and even sport. Opening the festival each year is the Midsumma Carnival, an outdoor party located in a parking lot, with bite-sized stage performances that offer a sneak preview of the upcoming program. Audience participation is fully encouraged in the headlining Lip Sync Limelight and Dog Show (if you happen to be traveling with your pooch), where fun prizes are up for grabs. Running for more than 30 years, and featuring both local and international artists, the Midsumma Festival is a highlight of Australia's queer calendar.

477 Twist and shout

▼ Coastal Twist, Woy Woy, Central Coast, New South Wales, Australia

When to go: October long weekend
Best for: Immersing in diversity

The quirky Coastal Twist LGBTIQA+ Arts and Culture Festival is quite a newbie to the scene with the first festival held in 2019. It expected 800 people, but more than 7,000 joined the celebrations. Its popularity means it has now extended its week-long program of out-there events across multiple Central Coast locations. These include a beach picnic, the world's first LGBTQ+ surf event, theater, music, cabaret, film, family activities, and international headliners at the festival's highlight the Coastie Carnie Fair Day. Inclusivity and diversity are key, with events for people of all ages, backgrounds, and abilities, and a strong focus on First Nations voices and perspectives.

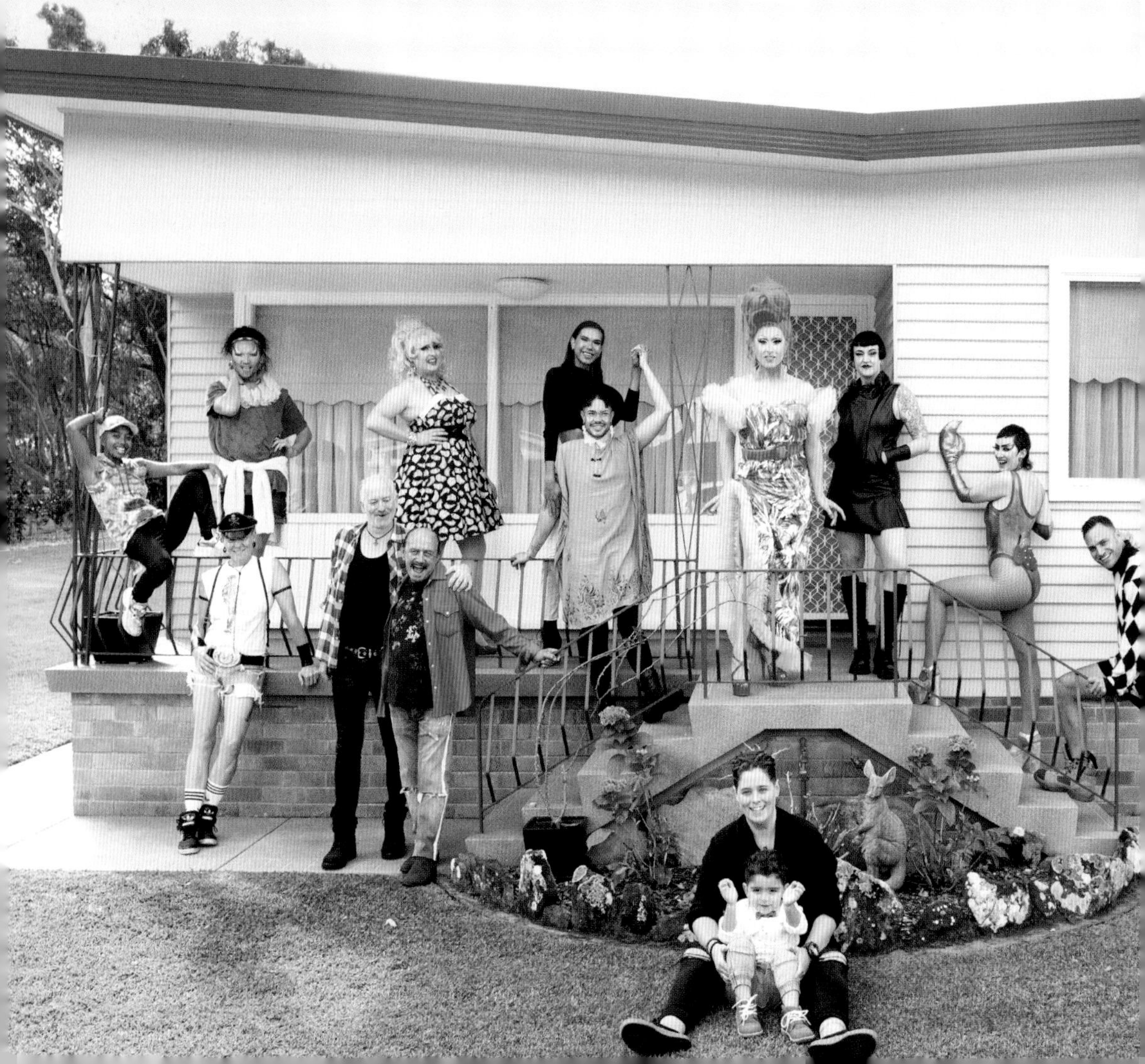

478 Where it really is all sunshine and rainbows

▶ Rainbow Beach, Queensland, Australia

When to go: All year
Best for: Colorful backdrops

Rainbow Beach is one of the most stunning beaches in sunny Queensland and is also the gateway to the biggest sand island in the world: Fraser Island. The beach coined its name from its backdrop of multicolored rock sediments. These have now been joined by a set of rainbow stairs that were painted by Team Rainbow as a "legacy from Australia's first Pride House."

479 Turn turtle

Turtle Cove Resort, Port Douglas, Australia

When to go: May to October
Best for: Inclusivity, surrounded by palm trees

Port Douglas in the far north of Queensland is a beautiful area of turquoise seas and palm-fringed, sandy beaches. And where better to stay on a visit than Turtle Cove Resort. This charming LGBTQ+ adult-only resort has its own private (clothing optional) beach, a pool, hot tub and spa. Staff are all part of the LGBTQ+ community, and if you're traveling solo, the Turtle Table in the restaurant is a communal table for guests who want to meet other guests.

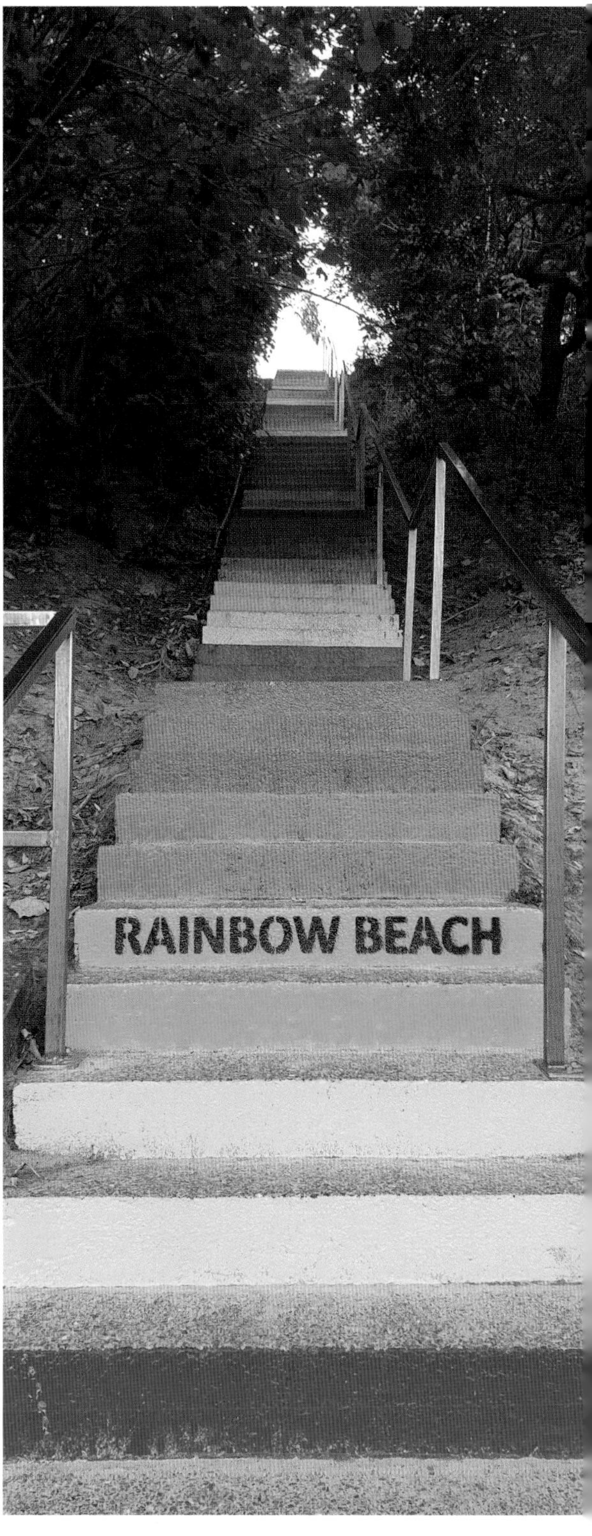

480 Get angry, then party

Sydney Gay and Lesbian Mardi Gras, Australia

When to go: February
Best for: Big celebrations

Sydney Gay and Lesbian Mardi Gras is Australia's biggest demonstration of LGBTQ+ Pride. Its history dates back to June 1978, when campaigners held a gay-rights march to commemorate the Stonewall riots in New York. Police attempted to break up that first event, resulting in the arrest of 53 people. The charges against all but two individuals were dropped. The needless arrests not only angered many in the LGBTQ+ community but also helped accelerate much-needed law reform. The event has grown exponentially since that time. In the 1980s it moved from June to February and was renamed Sydney Gay and Lesbian Mardi Gras. The most high-profile event of the three-week festival is the Oxford Street parade. It's watched by hundreds of thousands of spectators live and also live-streamed to even more. A massive post-parade party follows later in the night.

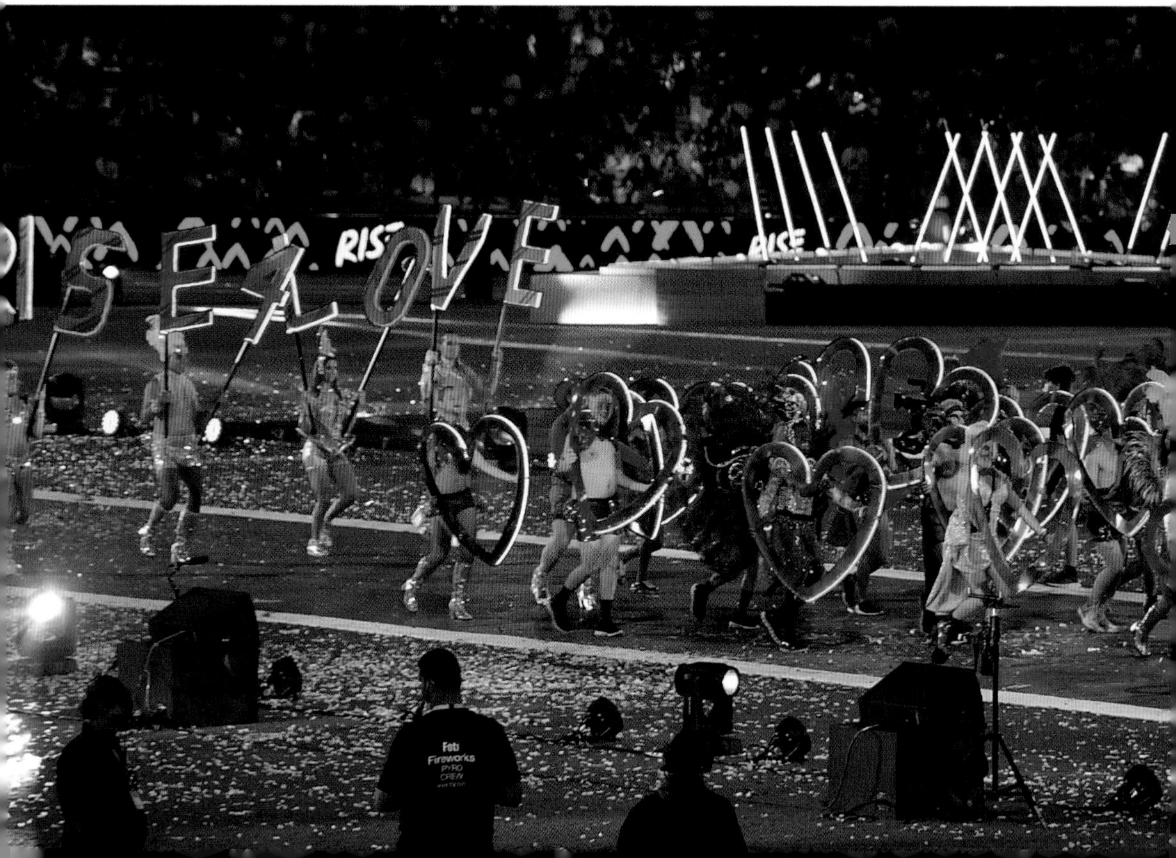

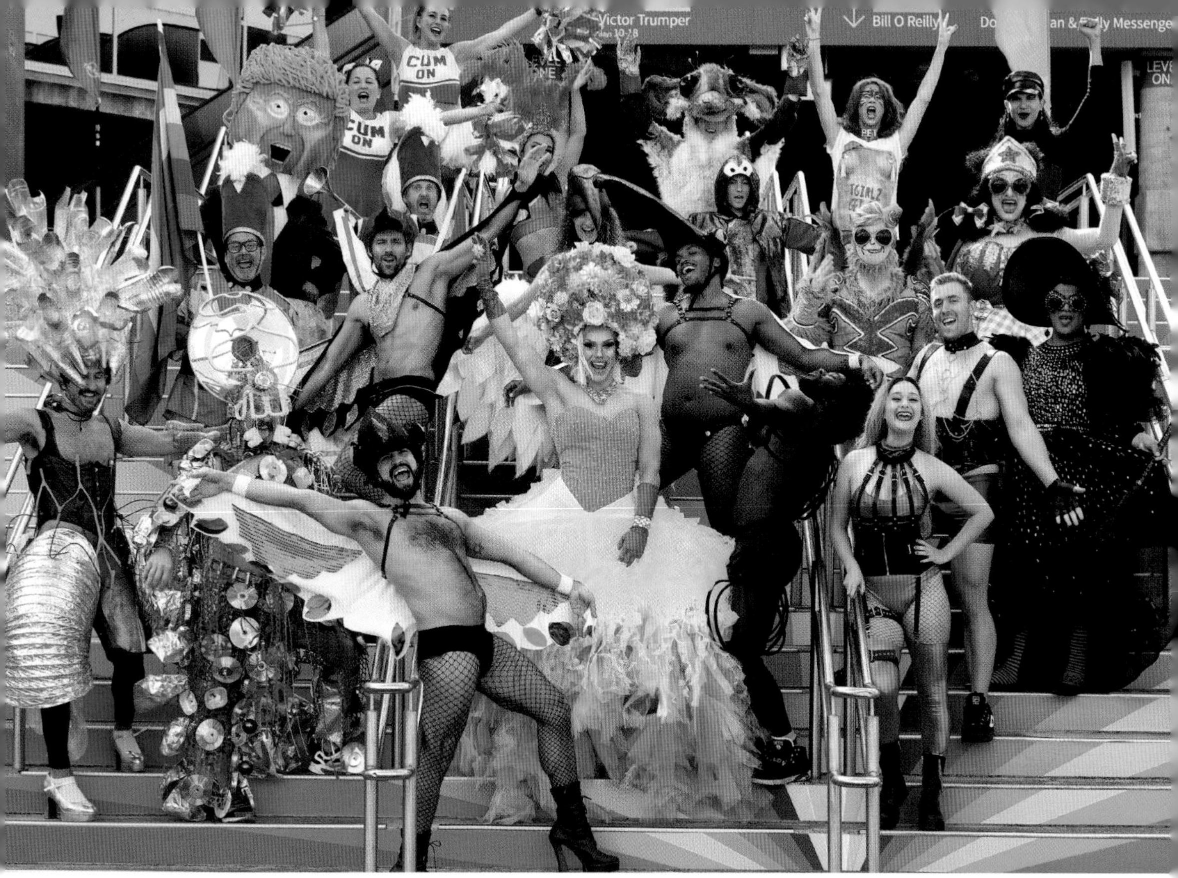
Victor Trumper
Bill O Reilly
CUM ON
CUM ON

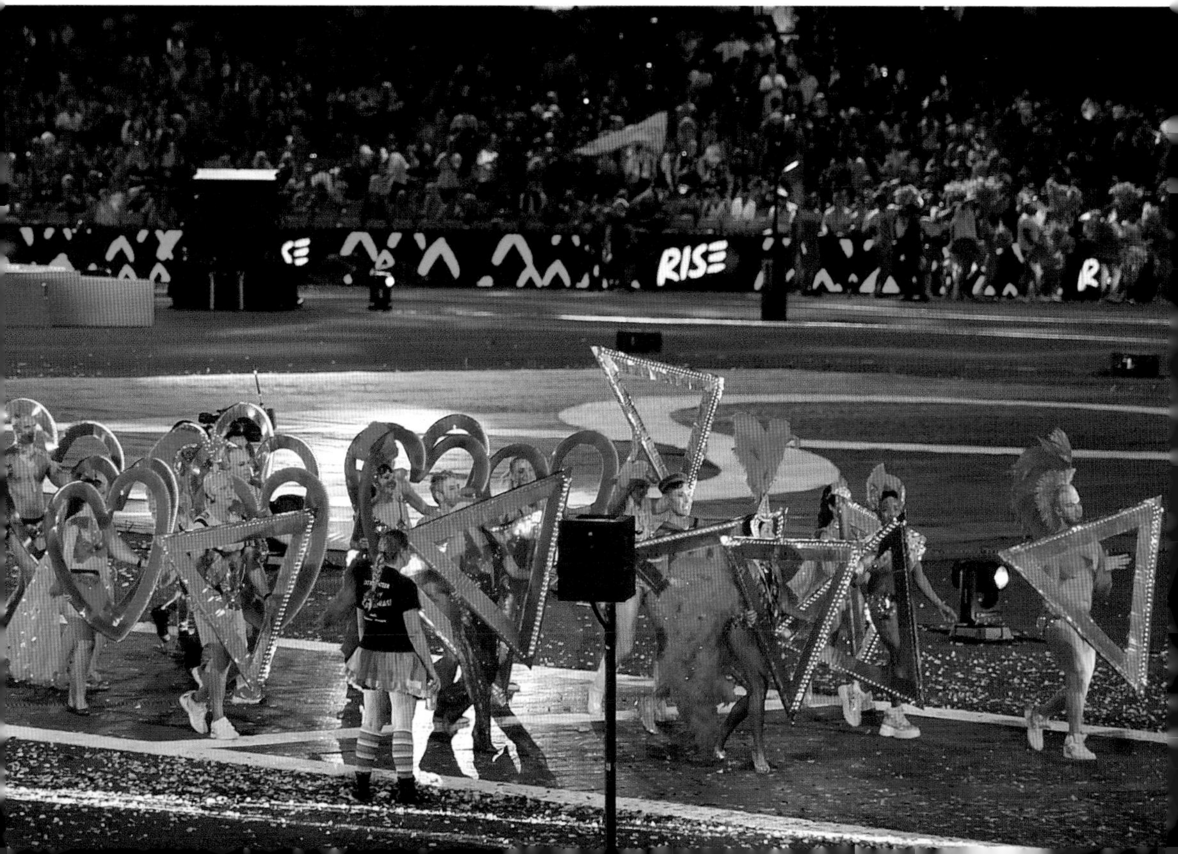
RISE

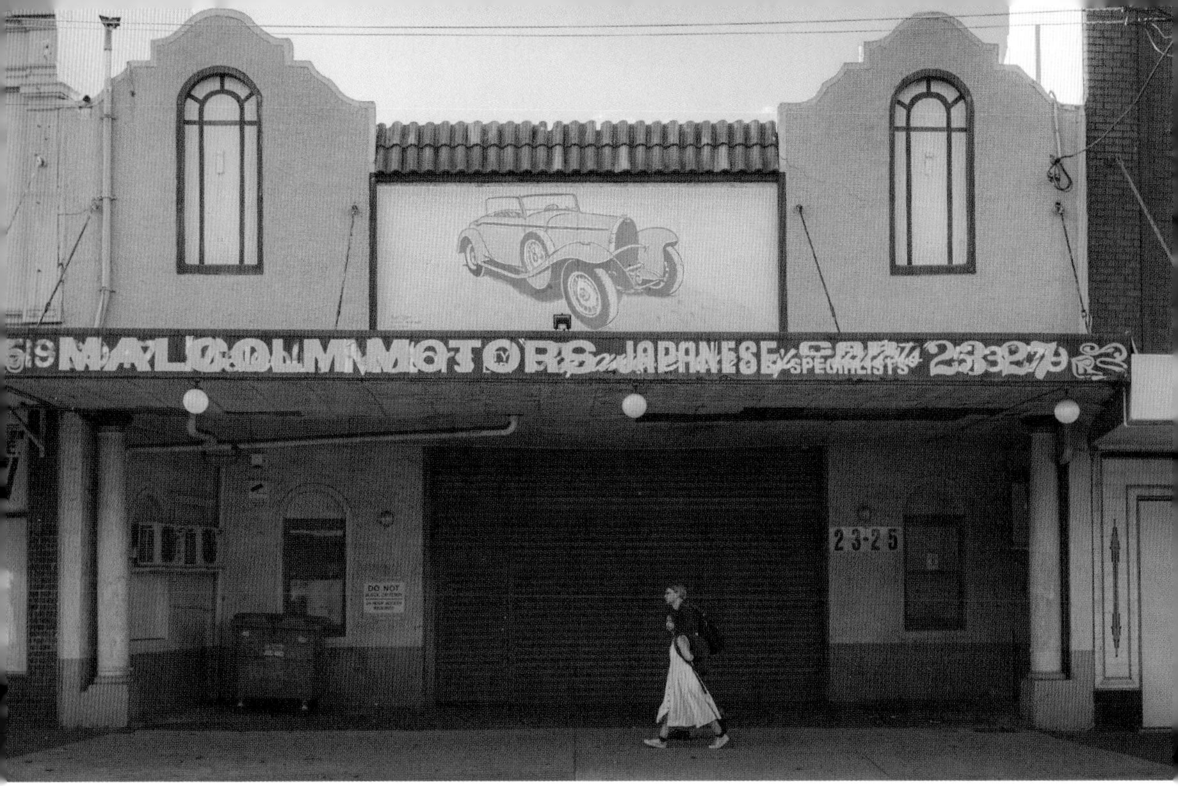

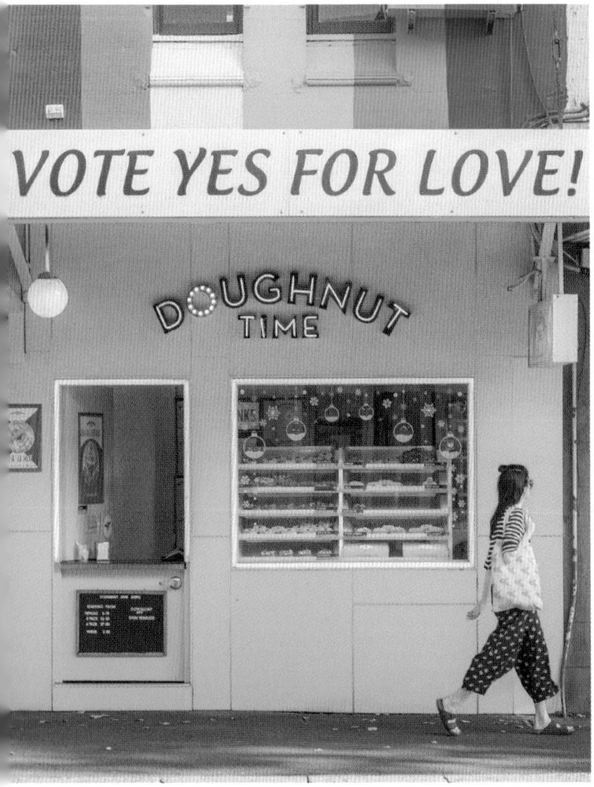

481 Bring on the queer

◀ ▲ Newtown and Enmore, Sydney, Australia

When to go: All year
Best for: Food, bars and lesbians

The Sydney hot spots for lesbians, Newtown and nearby Enmore are brimming with funky coffee shops, organic markets, and a plethora of food options to suit all diets. The weekly girls nights at the Imperial Hotel bring in the crowds, as do the many independent theaters for both live performances and movies. The queer vibes are felt everywhere; Newtown even has a Women's Library, a safe space for all who need it.

482 Furever friends

▼ Harbour City Bears, Sydney, Australia

When to go: All year
Best for: Hairy gay men

With over 140 events held every year, Harbour City Bears makes the most of being Australia's only community group for bears. There's something for every bear and their allies, with activities including a monthly gaymer event, movie nights, picnics, bowling, and dance parties; as well as two annual festivals—Bear Essentials and Bear Pride.

483 Six steps to remember

Bondi to Coogee Coastal Walk Memorial, Sydney, Australia

When to go: All year
Best for: Ocean views and commemoration

In Marks Park, along the stunning Bondi to Coogee coastal walk, you will find the Bondi Memorial: Rise, a six-level stone terrace that represents the six bands of the Pride flag. A popular queer hook-up space in the late 1990s, Marks Park was a site of much homophobic violence. Rise is for the victims and survivors of this violence.

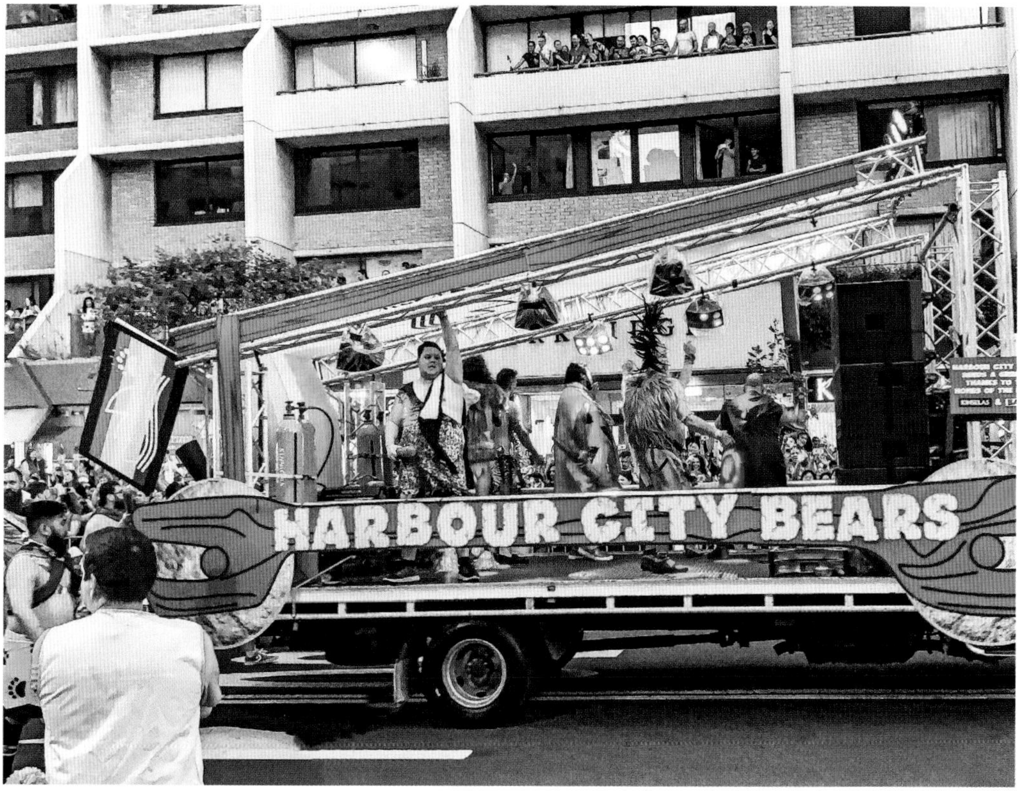

484 What's in the mail?

▼ Stonewall Hotel, Sydney, Australia

When to go: All year
Best for: "Malebox" Wednesdays

Stonewall Hotel is a mainstay of the Sydney LGBTQ+ scene. It offers cocktails, trivia quizzes, drag karaoke, and some of the best theme nights around. The "meals on heels" service will look after you across the three levels of bars and dance floors. And if you're looking for the man of your dreams, don't miss the legendary, weekly "Malebox" event—the hottest pick-up night in Sydney.

485 A name that speaks volumes

The Bookshop, Sydney, Australia

When to go: All year
Best for: Digging deeper into queer life

The Bookshop is the oldest LGBTQ+ bookstore in Australia and is an amazing hub not just for queer books and magazines, but also for information, advice, and community.

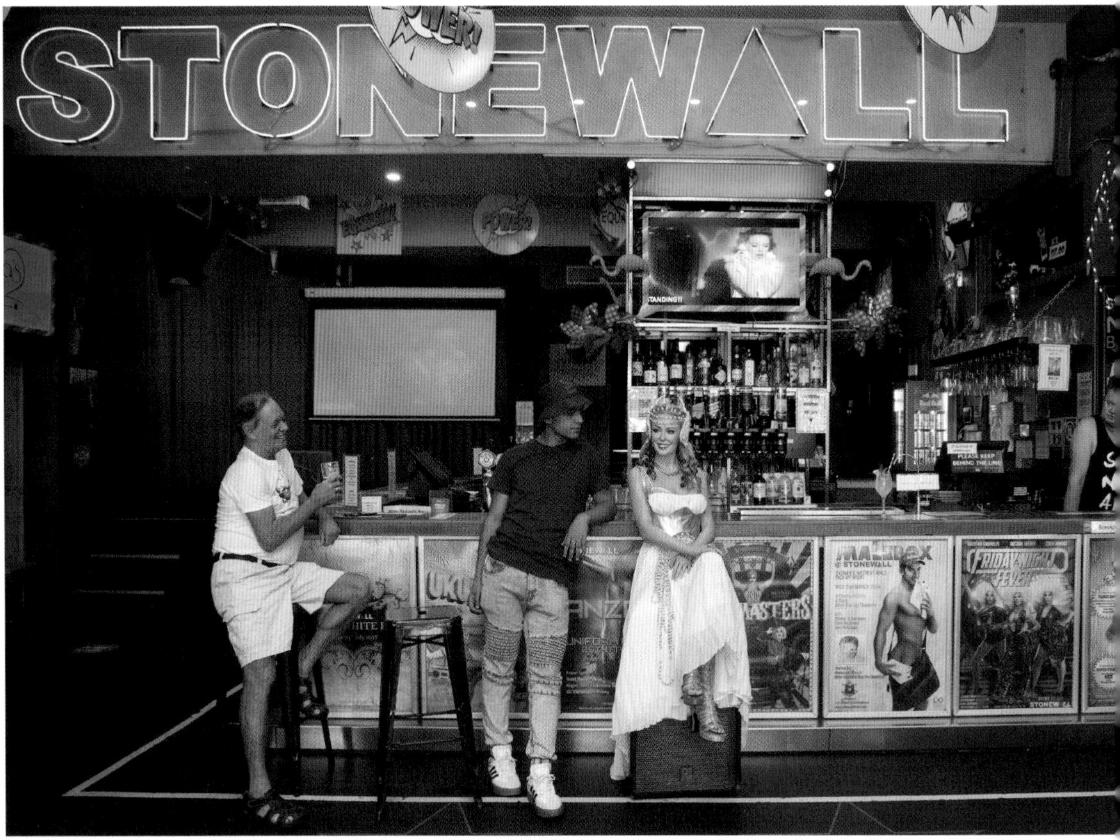

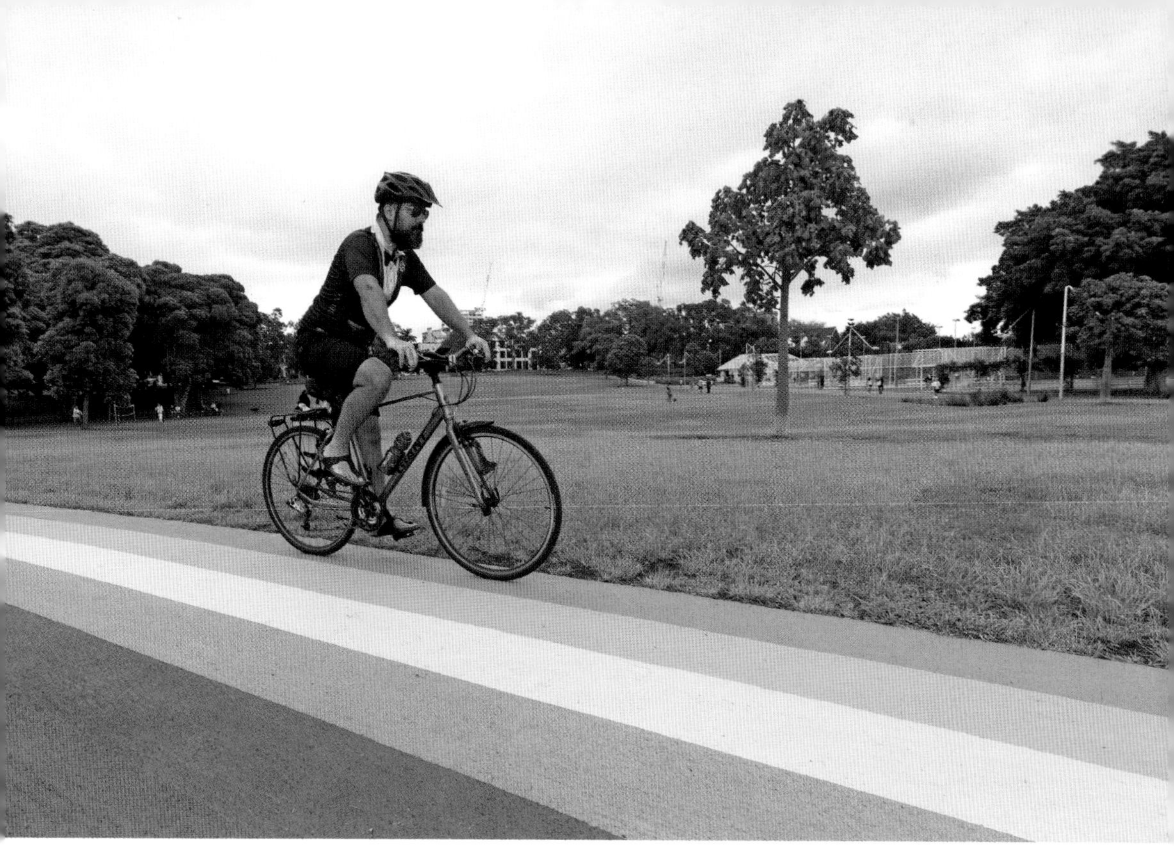

486 Follow the rainbow

▲ Prince Alfred Park, Sydney, Australia

When to go: All year
Best for: An "Off To See The Wizard" hop, skip, and dance

This beautiful rainbow path lies in Prince Alfred Park, in the Surry Hills neighborhood of Sydney. The 90-ft/27-m pathway commemorates the legislation for marriage equality in Australia. The site was chosen to honor the moment in November 2017 when 30,000 people gathered on the lawn—now renamed Equality Green—to hear the results of Australia's marriage equality postal survey. The result was a resounding "yes" and just weeks later, marriage equality was enshrined in law.

487 Violence remembered

Sydney Gay and Lesbian Holocaust Memorial, Sydney, Australia

When to go: All year
Best for: Paying respects

Located in Darlinghurst, this memorial recreates symbols used in the Holocaust to represent gay men and lesbian women: pink and black triangles are combined to form a fractured Star of David. Situated near the Sydney Jewish Museum, this memorial honors those oppressed during the Nazi Holocaust, but also all those in the queer community who are still victims of violence for their sexuality today.

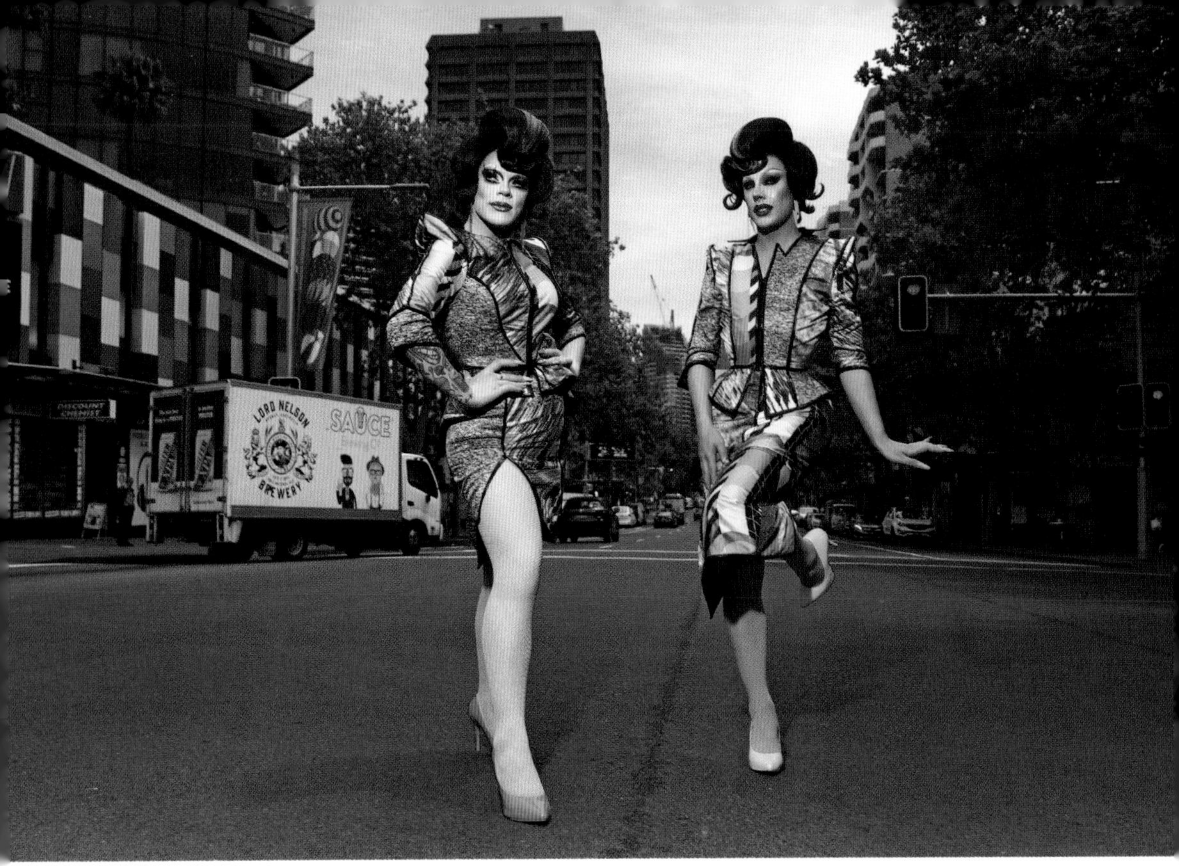

488 Look up and down for rainbows

▲ Oxford Street, Sydney, Australia

When to go: February to March
Best for: Mardi Gras Parade

Home to some of Sydney's most iconic queer venues, such as the Stonewall Hotel, Oxford Street is the heart of Sydney's "gayborhood." You can't miss myriad rainbow flags, including a giant progress flag at Taylor Square. Just off Oxford Street, there's the only rainbow-shaped rainbow-crossing in the world. Most famously, Oxford Street is the site of the annual Mardi Gras Parade, where you will be awed by Sydney's world-renowned floats.

489 Pride through the ages

▶ Brisbane Pride, Australia

When to go: June
Best for: All ages

Brisbane Pride kicks off with a march and rally along Brunswick Street. It appeals to all ages, with an inclusive prom-themed party for the LGBTQ+ school leavers and the Queens Ball for those over 18. Queens Ball is possibly the longest-running queer event in the world, started over 60 years ago. As well as a meal and party, it is also an awards night for achievements in the LGBTQ+ community.

490 **Laugh out loud**

No Homo: Queer Comedy, Auckland, New Zealand

When to go: All year
Best for: Giggles

The monthly queer comedy nights of No Homo began by bringing a regular dose of laughter to Auckland in 2018, at the intersectional activist venue Basement Theatre. Since then it has evolved into a country-wide event, promoting queer comedy talent across New Zealand.

491 **Crystal queer**

Garnet Station, Auckland, New Zealand

When to go: All year
Best for: Versatile vibrant venues

In the suburbs of Auckland you can find queer gem Garnet Station, run by lesbian-founders Verity George and Lisa Prager. What started as a pizza restaurant transformed into a lively meeting venue, with an art bar, spaces-for-rent including a tiny theater, and a gallery displaying Lisa's art alongside other female artists. Their Sappho Disco and comedy events are well worth dropping in for.

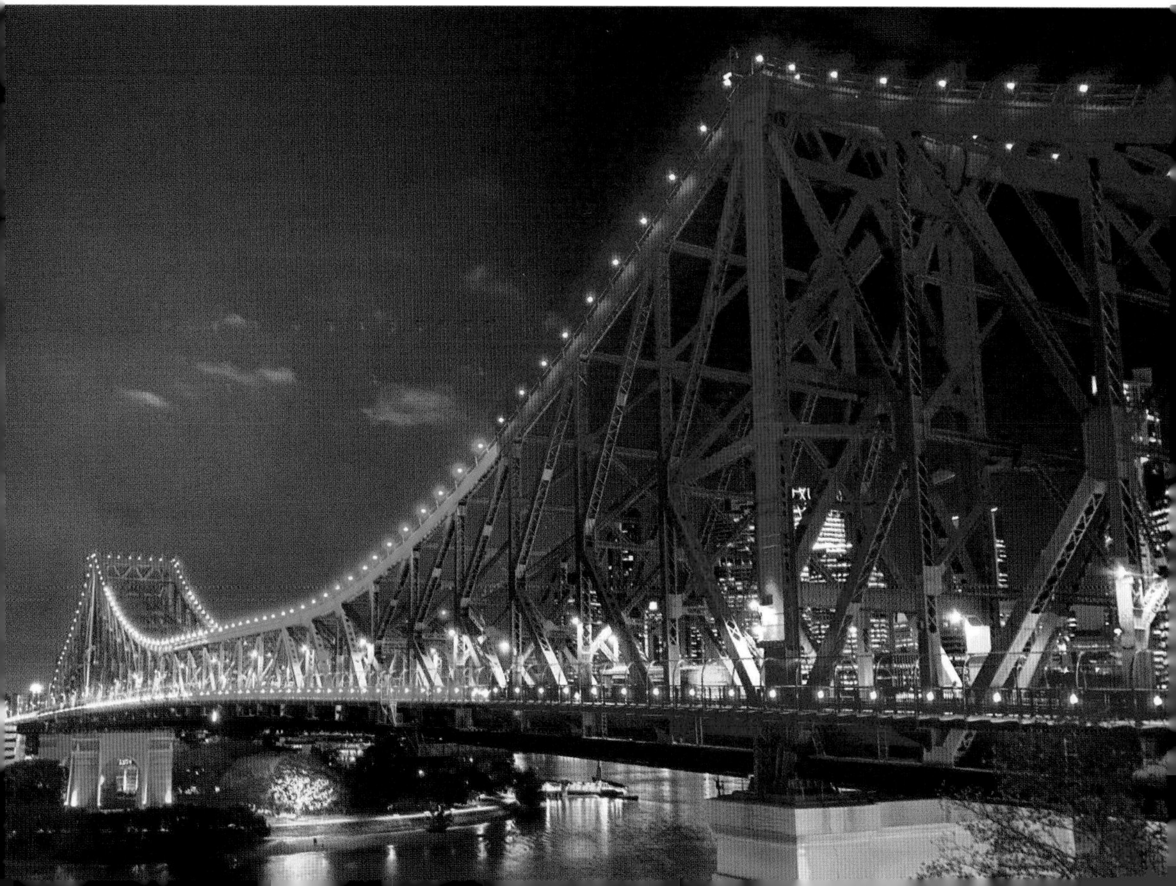

492 Ponderable Ponsonby

▼ Ponsonby, Auckland, New Zealand

When to go: All year
Best for: Queer life

Trendy, residential Ponsonby is where many of Auckland's queer community live, eat, and shop. As a result, the eclectic suburb has a welcoming atmosphere and many queer-friendly businesses line Ponsonby Road (Te Rimu Tahi)—which gets packed with love, light, and color during the city's Pride parades. Queer-popular spots include Salta for coffee, The Women's Bookshop for feminist lit, Studio One Toi Tū for art, SPQR or Prego for dining, Bedford Soda & Liquor for cocktails, and Eat Drink Laugh for brunch.

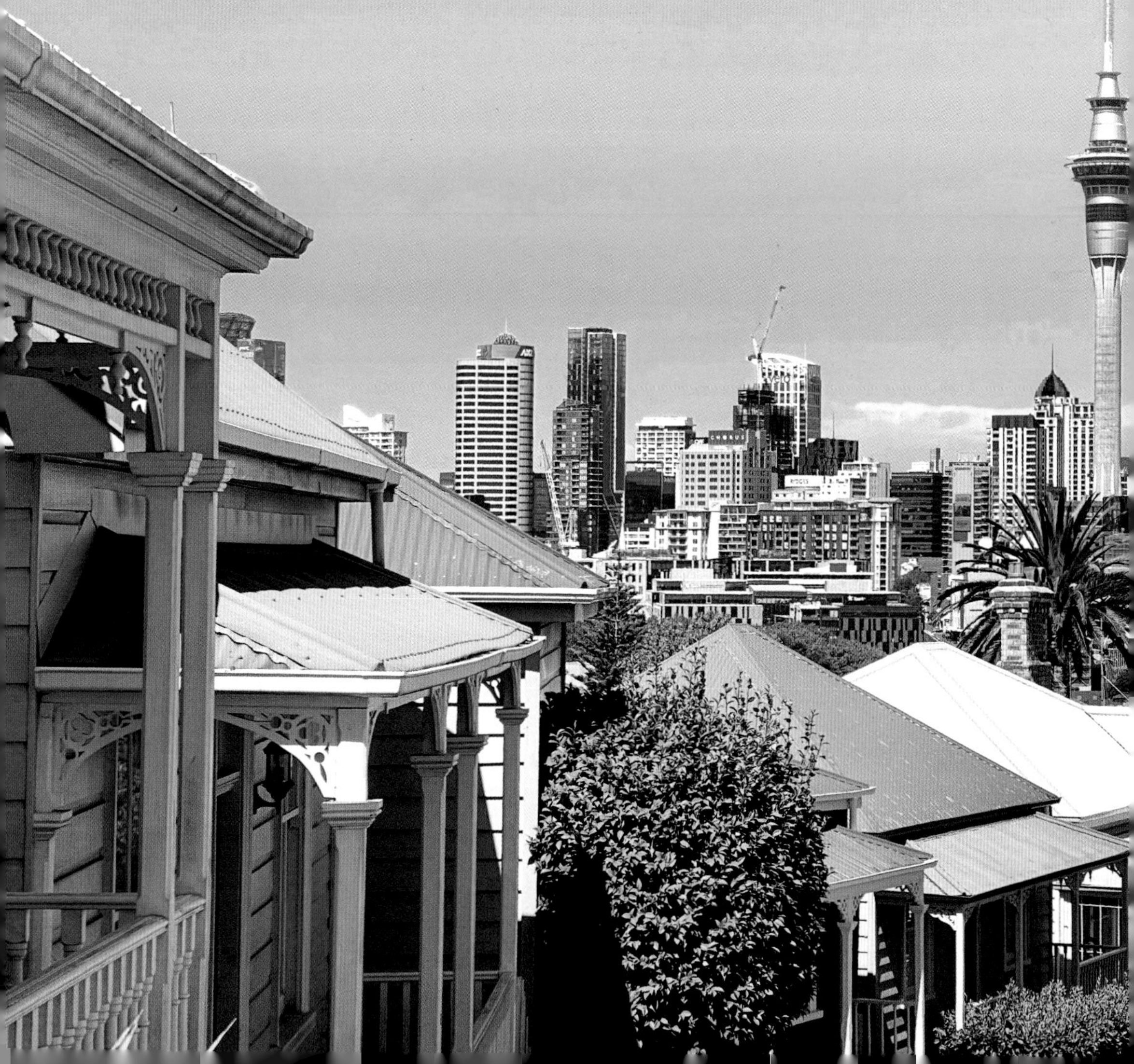

493 Positive queernergy

Queer AF events, Auckland, New Zealand

When to go: All year
Best for: A good vibe with your queer tribe

Olivia Coupe set up Queer AF to organize inclusive social events, club nights, and markets showcasing work by queer creatives and makers, after she found that queer spaces were increasingly attracting a cishet audience. Queer AF's Queers and Wares market is a powerful platform for queer-owned businesses, with themed editions throughout the year.

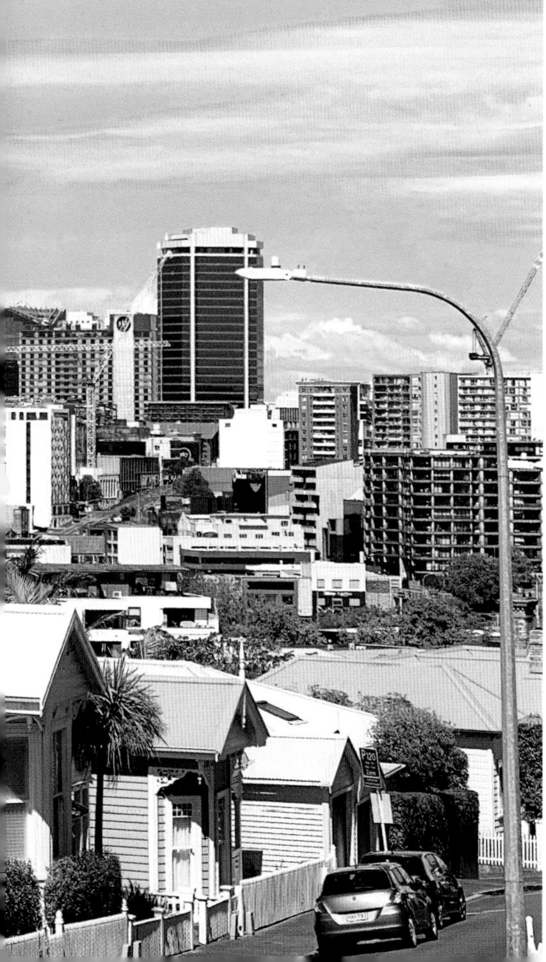

494 Yaaasss queen!

Caluzzi Cabaret, Auckland, New Zealand

When to go: All year
Best for: Yassifying brunch

Entertaining LGBTQ+ audiences for nearly three decades, Caluzzi Cabaret is Auckland's original drag-queen dinner-show on the city's raunchy, colorful Karangahape Road—K'Road for short. What started as a humble café with two drag queens grew into a legendary, award-winning experience.

495 Heart of the glitter ball

Family Bar & Club, Auckland, New Zealand

When to go: All year
Best for: Partying

A short four-minute walk up K'Road from Caluzzi Cabaret, you find another staple for the queer community, Family Bar & Club. The large, gay-owned and run venue with four levels of different bars and music feels like many spaces all rolled into one. With sister-bars Saloon Bar and G.A.Y. right next door for karaoke and more clubbing, this spot on K'Road is the epicenter of the city's queer scene with entertainment all night long.

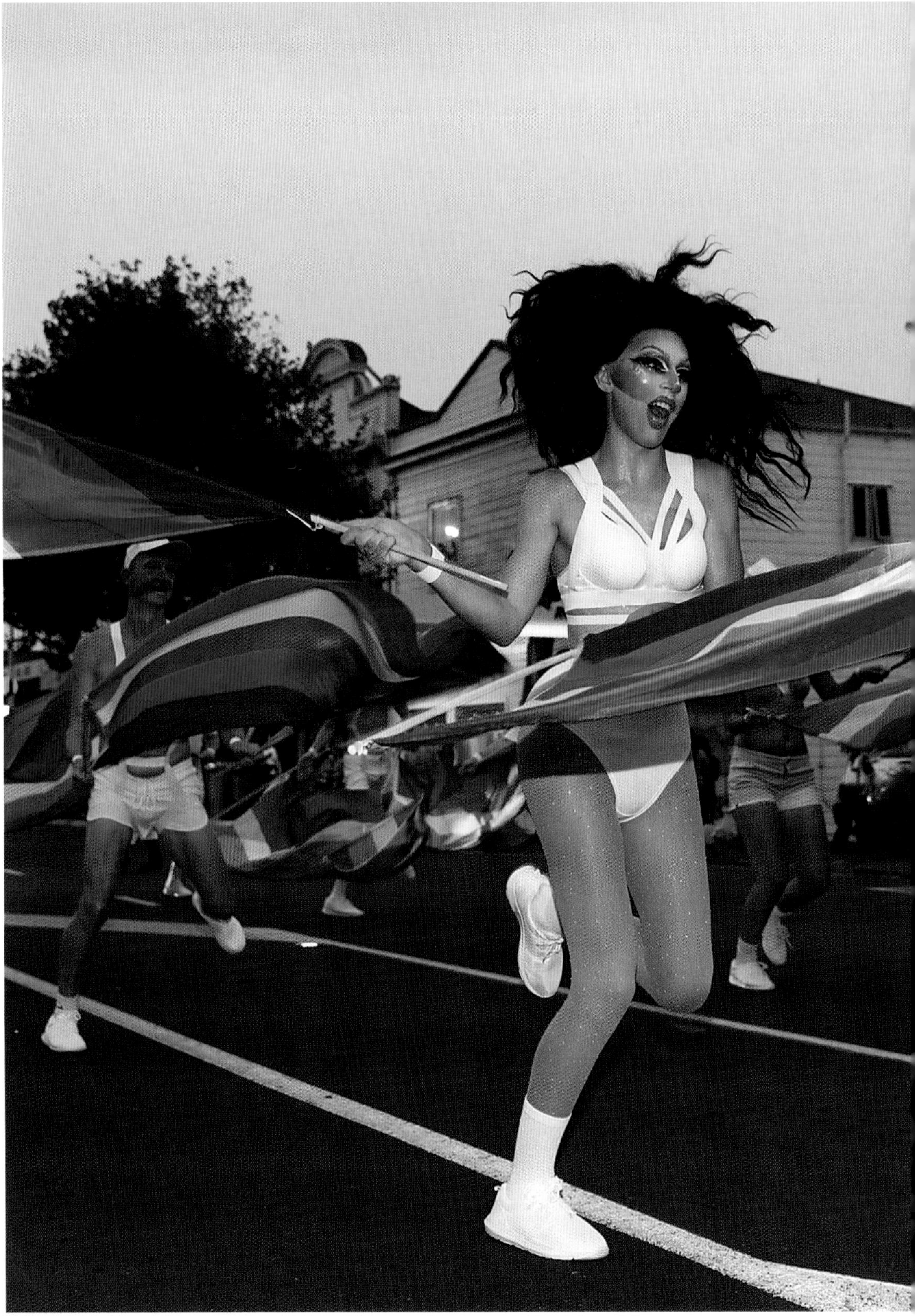

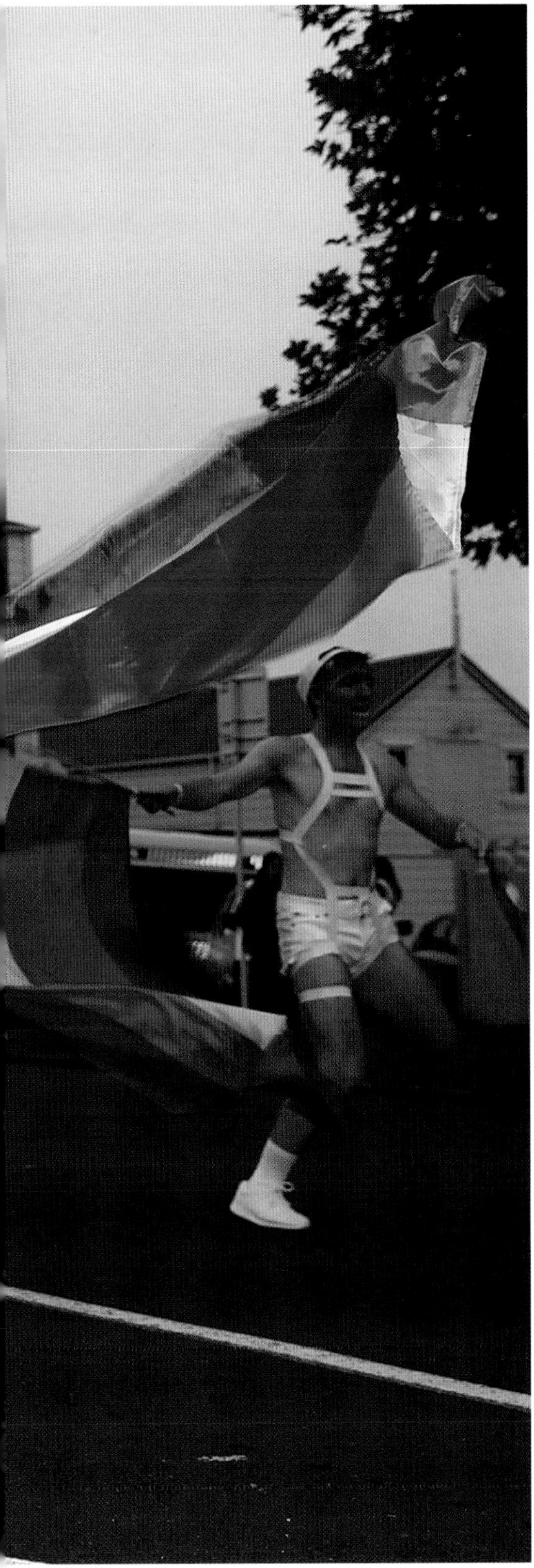

496 View a double rainbow

Auckland Pride and Rainbow Pride (Whakahīhī), New Zealand

When to go: February
Best for: Partying and protesting

Auckland has not one but two Pride events connecting and celebrating the *takatāpui* (Te Reo Māori umbrella-term for "rainbow community") and the LGBTQ+ community. The city hosted one of New Zealand's first annual LGBTQ+ parades in 1991 on Ponsonby Road, running for a decade and significantly advancing LGBTQ+ rights in the country. A dozen years later, Auckland Pride returned annually, but shifted its focus in 2019 by reclaiming the Pride march as an intersectional, grassroots march and banning police in uniform. The launch of Rainbow Pride Auckland—a week apart from Auckland Pride—restored the historic Pride parade on Ponsonby Road. Plenty of Pride activities happen leading up to the marches, including the LGBTQ+ queer literary festival Samesame but Different. Auckland Pride's The Queer Agenda features queer events year-round.

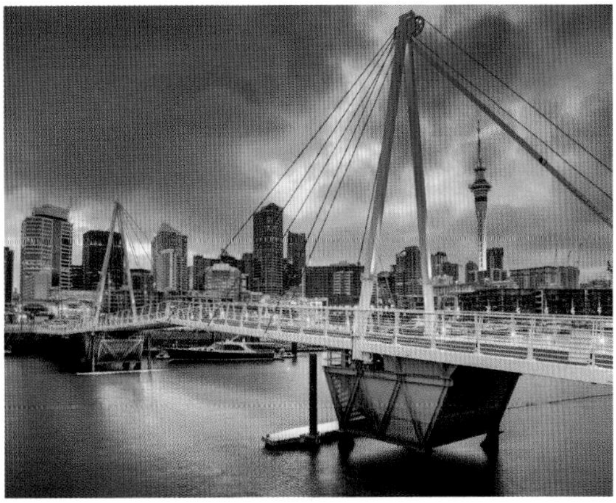

497 Discover her-story...

Charlotte Museum, Auckland, New Zealand

When to go: Any time
Best for: Learning about lesbians

Charlotte Museum is one of the very few museums dedicated entirely to lesbians. Each floor is packed with lesbian artifacts and queer exhibitions. Wander around taking in the queer culture, or seek out the huge range of LGBTQ+ books and articles in the reading room, which is equipped with bean bags and comfy chairs.

498 Color counts

Ōtautahi Christchurch Pride, New Zealand

When to go: June
Best for: Artsy queer scene

The third-largest city in New Zealand, Christchurch might not have a prolific queer scene but it is colorful. The city has a vibrant and growing arts scene with iconic street art, and hosts a fabulous Pride week annually, with a parade, festival, cultural events, and parties.

499 Themme fatale

Ivy Bar, Wellington, New Zealand

When to go: All year
Best for: Queertertainment

New Zealand's capital, Wellington, is home to LGBTQ-powerhouse Ivy Bar. Originally founded in a department store basement, Ivy Bar has proudly hosted and entertained queer folk for more than a dozen years. Its drag, burlesque, comedy, karaoke, and poetry shows are spectacular, with the annual Mx Capital drag pageant hosted by Mx Aotearoa taking the crown. For more (queer) showbiz in the Te Aro district, head to Circa Theatre and BATS Theatre, and keep an eye out for productions by Butch Mermaid Ghostlight Wellington.

500 A Rainbow Shade of Winter

▶ Gay Ski Week, Queenstown, New Zealand

When to go: August to September
Best for: Spectacular scenery

Queenstown is the adventure sports capital of the world; there's bungee jumping, skydiving, zip-lining, whitewater rafting, quad biking, canyoning, and paragliding to mention some. There's also relaxing vineyards, stunning wildernesses, hot springs, and spa options for those after something more relaxing. And somewhere in between is Gay Ski Week—or Winter Pride—with skiing, snowboarding, games nights, and epic parties at the southern hemisphere's biggest LGBTQ+ winter festival.

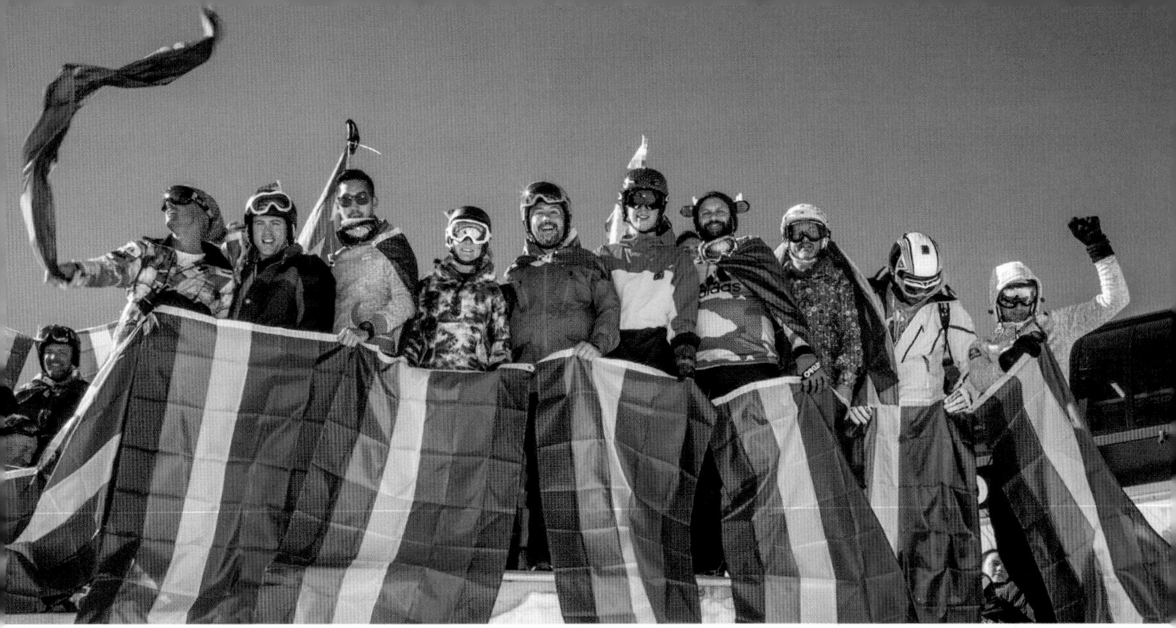

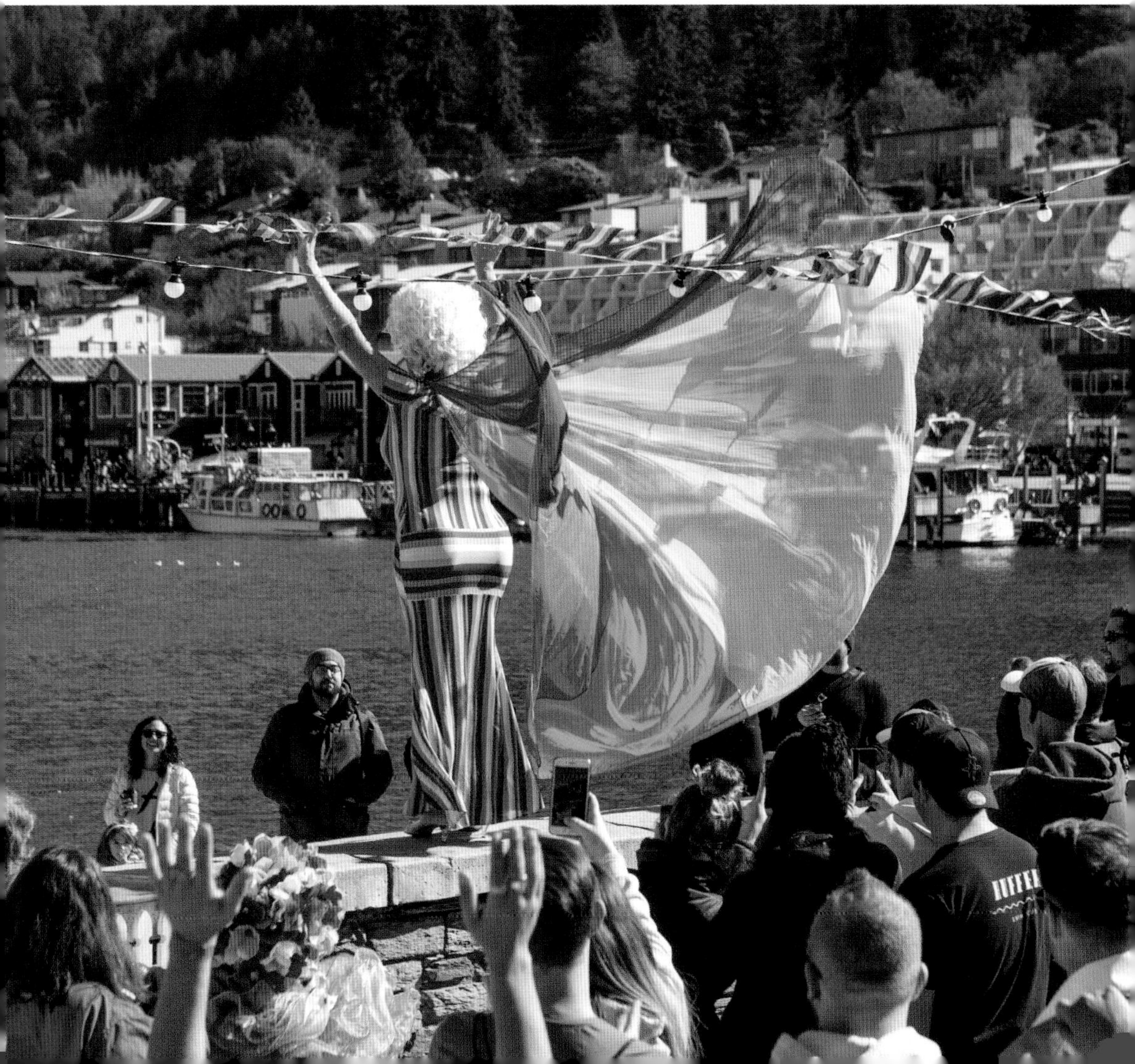

INDEX

DECOLONIZING QUEER TRAVEL

In this book we have used official city and country names of which many are settler labels because colonialism is an ongoing process. We want to take this space to acknowledge that these countries were built on land originally inhabited by Indigenous peoples.

The Pride Atlas acknowledges and recognizes, among others:

- First Nation, Métis, and Inuit as Indigenous groups of Canada.
- The traditional territories of all Indigenous American tribes, Alaska Natives, and Pacific Islander Americans.
- Indigenous peoples and mestizos/mestiços in South America.
- The Sámi as the original inhabitants of Sápmi (parts of Finland, Russia, Norway, and Sweden).
- Khoisan (Khoekhoen and San Peoples) as Indigenous peoples of Southern Africa.
- Palestinians as Indigenous peoples with an Indigenous connection and right to their ancestral land.
- Seafaring Austronesians and the local Indigenous populations of the places to which they've migrated.
- Aboriginal and Torres Strait Islander peoples (Australia's First Nations) as the traditional owners of the land Australia was built on.
- Māori as tangata whenua (First People) of Aotearoa New Zealand.

This is no comprehensive list, and land acknowledgments are only a tiny part of disrupting and dismantling colonial structures. Ensuring factual accuracy is difficult because Indigenous voices and cultures have been systematically erased, causing a great loss of records of Indigenous land and resources.

Revitalization of Indigenous culture is essential for LGBTQ+ liberation worldwide. Decolonizing queer travel means challenging and resisting the mainstream culture that reinforces colonial oppression.

Mainstream travel culture is white- and cishet-centered, but we should reframe travel to consider all migratory experiences and highlight the importance of decolonizing queer culture and travel.

We encourage readers to be mindful travelers and to look deeper into a place's history.

Doing better

We have done our best to make this book as comprehensive as possible, but we know that language, ideology, culture (including LGBTQ+ culture), and social climates are subject to change, and we strive to keep learning. If we have missed or misrepresented something, please email us at **hello@prideatlas.com** so we can do better in future reprints.

IMAGE CREDITS

t = top, b = bottom, l = left, m = middle

Cover: Unsplash, Alexandra Mitache front t; Tristan B. front br; Luis Cortés back and spine. Getty Images, JAIME REINA front bl.

Also: Maartje Hensen @onceupon ajourney @maartjehensen 2, 3, 4t, 7t, 9, 10, 11, 72 tl, bl, br, 73, 77, 92, 94, 95, 99t, bl, 102, 104t, 112b, 115, 121mr, 122,123, 132tl, tr, bl, br, 133t, b, 170tl, b, 172, 174t, 224, 226b, 227, 229l, 230, 246t, b, 267t, 274l, r, 275, 301, 302, 308bl, 310br, 313, 314bl, 340, 341, 348t, 351, 352, 360, 361;
Cayla Nimmo 12b, 49t, b; Copyright New Hope Celebrates, Inc. 13t, 105; Tess & Chey 16tr; Fairy Tales Queer Film Festival 17; Whistler Pride and Ski Festival / Photos by DCO Digital 18t, m, b, 19tl, tr, ml, mr, bl, br; Brasserie Harricana and Anne-Marie Pellerin 24l, r; Spade & Palacio 25t, m, b; image+nation 26l, r; Devenae Bryce 31t, bl, br; Julie Riemersma 32t; Glad Day Bookshop 32b; Kegan Marling (keganmarling.org) 34bl, 35; Chris Collins @chriscollins mix 37t; Gay Wine Weekend at Out in the Vineyard 43b; Shawn Mac Lean and Matthew Buchta 48t, b; Reginald D Allen 50; Lisa Whiteman (www.lisawhitemanlens.com) 51; The Dinah 56t, m, b, 57tl, tr, ml, mr, bl, br; Justin Kim @jkimisyellow 58t; The Hole in the Wall San Diego 59t, b; Lukas Volk, NHxDesigns.com 62ml, bl; -RADskillZ 69t, b, 76b; One Magical Weekend 75t, bl, br; @bossbrittx djexel 76t; Muffy Fish Basket and Mini Pearl Necklace 81; Nadia Zahran 85; Andrew White 86, 87; The Club Provincetown 90bl; Henrietta Hudson 93 all; Ryan Neeven 107; Marlie Regis and Sarah Laine @cloud_walks 113, 140tl, b, 162tl, 371, 375, 383; Ana Mello 150, 151; Amanda Bibiano 153t, bl, br; Santiago Barreiro (photographer), Juampy Ramirez & Daniel Arroyo Miranda (dancers) 156, 157; Isadora Secchi Silveira 159; David Hudson 169; Kristin Maria for Reykjavik Pride (2016) 173t; Grace Chu for Reykjavik Pride (2019) 173b; Marcin Sz and SHOUT! Festival 179t, b; Corinne Cumming 196, 197; Images courtesy of HUNGAMA & Ryan Lanji 200tl, bl, r; Yasmine Akim and Deen Atger 201 all; InXestuous Sisters (@ Disturbance 2020) 201tl; Team Ugly Duck 201tr; Deen Atger and artists 201mr; Helen Alix Mourier 2022 201b; Open Barbers photo credit Open Barbers 2016 203t; Open Barbers photo credit Greygory Vass 2018 203b; Iris Prize 214t, b; Shelf Life Books and Zines 215; La Reserve 218; Arenda de Hoop 223; IHLIA LGBTI Heritage 226t, m; Marilène Zeeman 229tr, mr, br; Queer Gym 231; © Disney 256, 257 all; Scott M Salt 260, 261; Alexander Schliephake @ Fox on the Run Photography 269; Velvet Ibiza 272, 273br; Jorge Pereira / Arosa Gay Ski Week 286; gaysalzburg.at 291; Lollipop Malta @lollipopmalta 303tl, bl, r; Shpagat 316t, b; GCircuit Songkran 349; Hanoi Social Club 356b; Chris Pavlich Photography 372, 373; Max Hayward 374t; Luke David 374bl, br; Copyright Coastal Twist LGBTIQ Arts & Culture Festival https://coastaltwist.org.au/ Photographer: Lisa Haymes 378; Winter Pride 365b, 393t, b;

Alamy: All Canada Photos 12m, 20; Jango / Stockimo 33t; Anchorage Daily News 33b; Barry King 52t, 53; Sipa US 52b; LHB Photo 61t; Cavan Images 61bl; Ken Howard 64; Norman Eggert 89; The Photo Works 97; Jeffrey Isaac Greenberg 20+ 98; REUTERS 103t; Newscom 114; Hemis 116, 117; 24BY36 120; Oliver Wintzen 121 tr; George Oze 121br; Oscar Dominguez 160; Renato Granieri 162tr; Y.Levy 164; Owain.B 180t; Andrew Smith 181t; Francesca Moore 184t, b; Zefrog 189bl, 204bl; WENN Rights Ltd 189br; ZUMA Press, Inc. 190bl, 191m; Everynight Images 204tl; tburrow / Stockimo 209bl; Oscar Elias 212, 213; Pjr Travel 219; Hemis 251; Luise Berg-Ehlers 290t; travelstock44 290b; FORRAY Didier 323br; Danita Delimont 353; KHernandez /Stockimo 387

Big Stock: Drew Lewis 118

Dreamstime: David Pillow 106; Julen Arabaolaza 253

Getty Images: powerofforever 6t, 15; Brook Mitchell / Stringer 7br, 385; Anchorage Daily News 33b; San Francisco Chronicle/Hearst Newspapers via Getty Images 37b, 42; JasonDoiy 40, 41; xavierarnau 41br; Tibrina Hobson 54; Miami Herald 70t, b; Raymond Boyd 78r; Danielle Del Valle / Stringer 84; Boston Globe 88, 90r, 91; Erik McGregor 104; Pacific Press 108t; JAG IMAGES 112m,145; MAURO PIMENTEL 113m, 152; YAMIL LAGE 119; EZEQUIEL BECERRA 135t; CARL DE SOUZA 147; PABLO PORCIUNCULA 154, 155; Agencia Makro 161b; Lorne Thomson 171t, 191t; Sam Mellish 182; Justin Lambert 183tl; Cristian Bortes / EyeEm 183bl; Tristan Fewings / Stringer 185t; Joseph Okpako 191b; Peter Dench / Stringer 194t, b; Darren Gerrish 195; Quintina Valero / Stringer 198t; Jo Hale 202t; Jamie Thistlethwaite / Stringer 204br; Jack Taylor / Stringer 205; Anthony Devlin / Stringer 209t; Shirlaine Forrest 209br; TORE MEEK 238, 239; VALERY HACHE 252t; Edward Berthelot 254; ullstein bild 264t; Carsten Koall / Stringer 267b; JAIME REINA / Stringer 271t, b; David Ramos / Stringer 279t; PATRICIA DE MELO MOREIRA 284; Amir Levy / Stringer 314r, 315; RODGER BOSCH 319t; Hindustan Times 311m, 324b; John Ye 334, 335; TPG 337t; fotoVoyager 337b; ED JONES 344; JEON HEON-KYUN/EPA-EFE 345t, b; The Asahi Shimbun 347; Suhaimi Abdullah / Stringer 358, 359; Ulet Ifansasti / Stringer 362; Brook Mitchell / Stringer 364br, 385; Michele Westmorland 366, 367; Nicolas Jupille 369; Don Arnold 384, 386; Fiona Goodall / Stringer 390, 391l

iStock: Tommy Wu 36; samuel howell 58b; senorcampesino 162bl; NoSystem images 168t; coldsnow storm 185b; bennymarty 370

Shutterstock: NDTeam (circle outline) 4, 5; sadclown20 (background artwork) 6, 7, 12, 13, 112, 113, 170, 171, 216, 217, 26, 287, 310, 311, 364, 365; iconaxey (world map) 6, 310, 311; Photocarioca 6b, 143b; Yusiki (map) 12, ~~13~~; Brent Eysler 13m, 103t; Jenari 14; LeonWang 16b; Canadian Press/Shutterstock 20b; Shawn Goldberg 21; Shawn Goldberg 22; Marc Bruxelle 23; Paul McKinnon 27t; BYUNGSUK KO 27b; NixZ 28; Matthew Zuech 29t, bl; mikecphoto 29br; Kobby Dagan 38b; SvetlanaSF 39t, m; JOHN G MABANGLO/EPA-EFE 39b; Jessica Ruscello 43t; 7maru 44; chrisdonaldsonphotography 45t; VidaHawaii 46t; Impassioned Images 46b; Diego G Diaz 47tr; Xiao Zhou 47bl; Lisa Bronitt 60; Charles Goudy 62r, 63; f11photo 68t; Fotoluminate LLC 68b; baileyc1 71t; Mia2you 71b; Chris_Harris 74t; Anthony Constantine 74b; Chicago Photographer 78bl; EQRoy 79; Tim Turner 80t, b; Heidi Besen 82; Brent Eysler 101t; lazyllama 101b; Robert R Condon 103b; John Penney 104b; EQRoy 108b; Anthony Ricci 109b; Nicole Glass Photography 111tl, br; Samuel Alia 111tr; DCStockPhotography 111bl; Luciano Marques 112t, 148tl, b; Bardocz Peter (map) 113; Bret Reyes 124t; Francisco J Ramos Gallego 124m; Loes Kieboom 124b, 125mr; kravka 125tl; Joanna Zaleska 125tr; Francisco J Ramos Gallego 125ml; ecstk22 125bl; photoshooter2015 125br; R.M. Nunes 126t; Anton_Ivanov 126b, 127; Chuy94 128t; Eduardo_Chavez 128b; Wandering views 129; eskystudio 130bl, 166tr, 166br; ooo.photography 130r, 131; Victor SG 134; Adrian Coto Rodriguez 135m, bl; Matthieu Cattin 136t, br; Jairo Paez 136bl; Gabriel Leonardo Guerrero 136mr; oscar garces 138; Roger.Rondon 139; StanislavBeloglazov 142tl; marchello74 142tr; ESB Professional 142ml; Mihai_Andritoiu 142mr; Salty View 142bl, 143t; Leonid Andronov 142br; Skreidzeleu 143m; lazyllama 144bl, 146; Nelson Antoine 149; Cristian fotografias 161t; Photo_Traveller 162br; Gaby Campo 165t; tatiav 165b; gary yim 166tl; L Jones 166ml; Rafael Tomazi 166mr; guillermo_celano 166bl; William Silver 167t; Daniel Korzeniewski 167m; Alexandr Vorobev 167b; singora vector 170; Andrew Mayovskyy 171tr, 309; trabantos 171ml, 233ml; Finn stock 171br, 241; Agnieszka Pas 176; Irene Fox 177; Stephen Maudsley 178bl; Mark N Dowell 180b; Lachlan1 181b; MagicBones 183br; BBA Photography 186; olesea vetrila 187m; cktravels.com 187b; Amer Ghazzal 188,189t; Pjp Photos 190tl; Karyn Louise 190tr; Inspired By Maps 190ml, mr, br; Laura De Meo 192l, r, 193l, r; Dosfotos 202b, 204tr; Debu55y 206, 207b; PhotoStock10 207tl; RootsShoots 207tr; ThirdFloorDraft 210; Skully 211t; Ludovic Farine 211m; Chedko 217t; Shutterstock 217b; Savvapanf Photo 220, 221l, br; kavalenkava 222t; Tania__Wild 222b; Ievgeniia Pavlenko 223t, b; Andrij Vatsyk 232m; Copenhagen Stock 232b; M E 233tl; Oliver Foerstner 233mr; ActionPix 233bl; Melanie Lemahieu 236t, b; SariMe 240; Iryna Dyba 242, 243; Tomas Lissaker 244l; BernadetteB 244r; michelmond 245; Stefan Holm 247 t; Guidemiu 247b; Kapi Ng 248, 249; Reuben Teo 252b; Elena Dijour 255tl; Action Press 262, 263; FELIPE TRUEBA/EPA-EFE 264b; turtix 265; Pani Garmyder 266; Lina Zavgorodnia 268t; Sriachai Y 268b; Marta Fernandez Jimenez 276t; bs_photo 276b; Bigflick 277t; 19bProduction 277b; ikumaru 278; Sonia Bonet 279b; Kevin Hellon 281t; Lianna Art 281b; MIGUEL A LOPES/EPA-EFE 282; iacomino FRiMAGES 283; MELANIE DUCHENE/EPA-EFE 287t; Olena Znak 287b; ENNIO LEANZA/ EPA-EFE 288t; Thomas Halvorsen 288b; Isa Fernandez Fernandez 292; BABAROGA 293; Sergiy Vovk 294, 295; Eduardo Manurae 296t; Raketir 296b; Tatiana Diuvbanova 297; Tinxi 298t; Dario Toledo 299t; Enrico Della Pietra 299b; Camelia Varsescu 304t; Giovanni Vale 304b; Iordanis 307b; KIM LUDBROOK/ EPA-EFE 317; Finn stock 310bl, 318bl; Lois GoBe 319bl, br; YESHIEL PANCHIA/EPA-EFE 322; JeanLuclchard 311b, 323t; INDIAviaMirror 324tl, tr; alexnika 326bl; Guzel Gashigullina 326r, 327; Jagadeesh Nv/EPA-EFE 310tl, 329tl, tr, b; Niranjan Shrestha/AP 330; Olga Gavrilova 331; Subash Shrestha/Pacific Press via ZUMA Wire 332t; HEMANTA SHRESTHA/ EPA-EFE 332b; e X p o s e 333; Richie Chan 336; RITCHIE B TONGO/EPA-EFE 338; Helen Rose Gabriel 339br; asiastock 342, 343; Guitar photographer 311t, 346; Alex Waltner Photography 348b; CyberEak 350t; Jade ThaiCatwalk 354, 355; LUONG THAI LINH/ EPA-EFE 356t; ROLEX DELA PENA/ EPA-EFE 357t; Marlou Bon-ao 357b; Gallery de Labux 363; Vladimir Molnar (map) 364; Viewtiful.Flower 364t, 379; Adam Calaitzis 364bl, 377; BIANCA DE MARCHI/EPA-EFE 365t, 381t; Mo Wu 376tl; Adam Calaitzis 376tr, bl; JOEL CARRETT/EPA-EFE 380, 381b; Stephen Bridger 382t, b; Seita 388, 389; Rudy Balasko 391br

Unsplash: Claudio Fonte 7m, 318r, 319; Juli Moreira 16tl; Leighann Blackwood 38tl; Patrick Perkins 38tr; Benjamin Rascoe 45b; Mercedes Mehling 47tl, br; David Everett Strickler 55; Vince Duque 61br; Lauren Chappell 66l; Lance Asper 66r, 67; Wesley Tingey 83; Josh Appel 99br; Brian Kyed 100t; Jessica Irani 100b; Gautam Krishnan 110; Alex Azabache 121tl; Ashly Araya 135br; Reiseuhu 140tr; Michael Barón 168b; ROBIN WORRALL 178t, br; Veerle Contant 183tr; Mark Hayward 187t; Glodi Miessi 198bl, br; Carlo Villarica 232t; Josè Maria Sava 233tr; Lisa Summerour 233br; Alexandra Mitache 234, 235; Tristan B. 250; Big Dodzy 255tr; Norbu GYACHUNG 258tl, tr, b; Hert Niks 270; Guille Sánchez 280; Karsten Winegeart 285t; Patrick Robert Doyle 285b; Mick De Paola 298b; Luis Cortés 300; Apostolos Vamvouras 305; Vlado Paunovic 306t; Stavrialena Gontzou 307t; Toa Heftiba 312; Alann Bobe 323bl; Waranont (Joe) 350b; Weyne Yew 376br